By Sword and Fire

The Destruction of Manila in World War II 3 February - 3 March 1945

ALFONSO J. ALUIT

Reprinted and Exclusively distributed by Bookmark, Inc.
264 Vito Cruz Ext., Makati
☎ 86•80•61 – 65

ISBN 971-569-162-5

Typeset by First Impressions Design House, Inc.

Pictorial layout by Raffy Guerrero

Cover design by Joanne de León

Printed by Studio Graphics

National Library Cataloging-in-Publication Data

Recommended entry:

Aluit, Alfonso J.
By sword and fire : the destruction of Manila in World War II, 3 February – 3 March 1945 / Alfonso J. Aluit. – Makati, Metro Manila : Bookmark, c1995.
1 v (various pagings)
Bibliography: p. 450–456. – Index: p. 457–468.

1. Manila – History – 1945. I. Title.

DS689.M2 1995 959.9212 P952000010
ISBN 971-569-162-5

They are dead now – they are all dead now –
a horrible death – by sword and fire. . .
They died with their house
and they died with their city –
and maybe it's just as well they did.
They could never have survived
the death of the old Manila.

And yet – listen! It is not dead;
it has not perished. Your city – my city –
the city of our fathers – still lives!
Something of it is left; something of it survives,
and will survive, as long as I live and remember –
I who have known and loved
and cherished these things!

NICK JOAQUIN
From *A Portrait of the Artist As Filipino*
(An Elegy in Three Scenes)

TO THE MEMORY OF THOSE WHO DIED

IN THE BATTLE FOR MANILA, FEBRUARY 1945,

THIS WORK IS DEDICATED

TABLE OF CONTENTS

PART TWO
THE PASSION AND DEATH OF THE DISTINGUISHED CITY

BY THE EXECUTIVE DIRECTOR/ COMMISSIONER NATIONAL COMMISSION FOR CULTURE AND THE ARTS (NCCA)

This book, *By Sword and Fire: The Destruction of Manila in World War II, 3 February - 3 March 1945*, by Alfonso J. Aluit, is a milestone in the great task of implementing the aims of the National Commission for Culture and the Arts (NCCA), and its mission of retrieving and conserving the record of the country's past.

By bringing together in a single volume knowledge and information scattered in obscure repositories or stored in the memories of individuals, the author renders yeoman service to our goal of eventually making a complete account of a critical period in the history of the Philippines.

This book manifests the readiness and the ability of NCCA to help writers, artists and scholars to realize works relevant to art and culture that are likely to remain unrealized without official support and encouragement.

The NCCA, therefore, takes great pride in having contributed to the ultimate materialization of this work. We are certain that it will help show the way for similar endeavors to come to fruition.

Carmen D. Padilla

12 January 1994
Manila, Philippines

CARMEN D. PADILLA

Foreword

BY THE AUTHOR

While this work is concerned with the destruction of Manila towards the end of World War II in the Pacific, it begins with a history of Manila and a reconstruction in words of its physical condition up to February 1945. It is our aim to show insofar as is practicable what actually was destroyed, not only the physical structures and material treasures of a city 400 years old, but also the way of life, the social organization of the people. Only if one understood and appreciated what it was that perished would the loss truly make sense.

There have been many attempts to make word-portraits of Manila. But none exists that is truly complete in every aspect. It is our earnest hope that someday some enterprising scholar will apply himself to that task, for which I am certain that a grateful legion will be in his debt. Meantime, this author contents himself with his own effort, inadequate as it may be.

At the trial of General Tomoyuki Yamashita, the defense counsel, Capt. A. Frank Reel, had occasion to declare, "We are trying to present here a picture of what went on during these days in Manila when these occurrences took place. It is not by way, sir, of condoning atrocities or crimes, but it is by way of explanation of what are otherwise inexplicable deeds."

In many ways, this is the function this author tried to make of the present work, to try to present a picture of what went on during those days in Manila, "by way of explanation of what are otherwise inexplicable deeds."

It was not an easy task. First, the author had to rely on material available in the Philippines. Except for all-too-brief periods at the United States National Archives and the Library of Congress in Washington, D.C., and the MacArthur Memorial in Norfolk, Virginia, during the early summer of 1983, I had recourse only to sources in my own city. To what extent that served the purpose, this work shows.

The experiences of the civilians came mainly from the records of the Yamashita trial. As I am made to understand, the only complete set of the records of the Yamashita trial in the Philippines is found at the Philippine Supreme Court Library.

The battle accounts related here owe much to Robert Ross Smith for his definitive work, *Triumph in the Philippines*. This work is basic to any understanding of American operations in the Philippines during the battle for liberation from the Japanese.

Also vital to the present work were the official histories of the American units that participated in the battle for Manila, including those of the 1st Cavalry Division by Bertram C. Wright, the 11th Airborne Division by Edward M. Flanagan, Jr., and that of the 37th Infantry Division by Stanley A. Frankel.

Significant testimonies and depositions of civilians that would later be used in the Yamashita trial were excerpted into a pamphlet titled *Report of the Resident Commissioner of the Philippines to the United States.* Material from the same source was included in another pamphlet titled *The Sack of Manila* and published by the United States Senate in 1945, with pictures.

A good deal of the experiences of civilians during the battle for Manila in 1945 is compiled in the Spanish language. There are *El Terror Amarillo en Filipinas* by Antonio Perez de Olaguer; *Terrorismo y Redención* by Jose G. Reyes; *Las Estrellas Vencen el Sol* by Madval (pseudonym); and Benigno del Rio's personal accounts, titled *Estampas de la Ocupación,* a diary of the war period, and *Siete Diás en El Infierno*, a relation of his incarceration by the Japanese. The diary of Maria Paz Zamora de Mascuñana appeared under the title *Nuestro Ultimo Cinco Diás Bajo el Yugo Nipon* in the *Bulletin* of the Philippine Historical Association, June 1958. I found a typescript of the diary of Sister Concepcion Gotera, DC, at the MacArthur Memorial Library in Norfolk, Virginia. I am responsible for the translations into English used in this work.

Interviews were conducted with Tomas S. Quirino, Mother Socorro Angela Reyes, SPC; Bro. Andrew Gonzalez, FSC; Mario X. Guerrero, M.D.; Fr. Leo English, CSsR; Estelita G. Juco, Virtudes Guinto-Gallegos, Geronima T. Pecson, Dolores Iturralde.

These interviews were valuable for an insight into the atmosphere of the period. In many cases interviews were used to confirm or corroborate certain points that are found in the written record.

The diaries were important too for the atmosphere they create, the feelings of individuals, their thoughts, the allusions to life as it was lived during those extraordinary times. Some valuable diaries were those of Lydia C. Gutierrez, Tressa Cates, Gladys Savary, Marcial Lichauco, Pedro M. Gimenez, Natalie Crouter, Faustino Aguilar (in Tagalog), Benigno del Rio, Sister Concepcion Gotera, Madval and Maria Paz Zamora de Mascuñana (the last four in Spanish). There was an unnamed person who wrote a day-to-day account of the holocaust as he experienced it and which was published in *Free Philippines* and is referred to in this work as the "Unknown Diarist."

The crucial 29 days of Manila from 3 February to 3 March 1945 are presented here in journal form, a day-to-day account pieced together from the sources I examined. Many of the testimonies and depositions of the participants and survivors of the events related here tended to be similar in the principal aspects. I chose the material that, aside from containing the principal features, are distinguished by certain detail, probably some extraordinary pathos, drama, or even humour, that the others did not contain. It was a difficult task for the vastness of the choice.

In this case I was guided by Tacitus who wrote, "My purpose is not to relate at length every motion, but only such as were conspicuous for excellence or notorious for infamy. This I regard as history's highest function, to let no worthy act be uncommemorated, and to hold out the reprobation of posterity as a terror to evil words and deeds."

An undertaking of this magnitude would hardly be faultless, and the faults of this work are many. They are all mine. There would have been more had it not been for the help I received from a legion among whom I have the pleasure of listing a succession of secretaries and research assistants of whom I remember best Leticia Ubaldo, Thelma Calucin and Susana Bisenio.

I am grateful for the kind and cheerful assistance extended me by the staff of the American Historical Collection of whom I remember Aurora P. Galvez and Arcadia C. Sabalones; the staff of the Lopez Memorial Library and Museum of whom I remember Alice M. Esteves, Celestina Boncan, Elvira C. Iremedio, Zenaida D. Cipriano, Epigenia B. San Pedro and Mercedita B. Servida; and the staff of the Supreme Court of the Philippines Library. I owe a particular debt of gratitude to Justice Gloria Y. Paras, then Clerk of Court, who intervened personally to permit me to do research in that library.

I am deeply indebted to the authors and publishers of sources from which material was drawn for this work, as much as I am indebted to those who made themselves available for interviews and otherwise assisted me in completing this book.

I am particularly grateful to Mr. Nick Joaquin for his permission to use the passage from his play, *A Portrait of the Artist As Filipino*, on the frontispiece.

The United States Army photographs used in this book are from the National Archives, Washington, D.C., and the MacArthur Memorial, Norfolk, Virginia, U.S.A. Other sources are indicated. I am grateful to the respective institutions for making these photos available to me.

I owe special thanks to Dr. Serafin D. Quiason whose professional commitment to historiography enabled him to find merit in this work, and whose personal concern led to its eventual publication.

ALFONSO J. ALUIT

18 April 1990
Manila, Philippines

PART ONE

THE DISTINGUISHED AND EVER LOYAL CITY

Charming city! Enchanted spot!
Within thee repose the cordiality,
the sweetness, the fresh and noble hospitality,
the friendly abandon, the sincere generosity
that arise from your surroundings as from
your very own hearth, to thee the distinctions
of rank and wealth disappear,
and cold protocol is unknown.
O Manila, of thee shall my last thoughts be!

JEAN MALLAT, *Les Iles Philippines, 1852*
(Translated from the French by the author)

PROLOGUE:

MACARTHUR OF THE PHILIPPINES

Touching earth in Darwin, Australia, 17 March 1942, Douglas MacArthur scribbled a few lines on the back of an old envelope and read it to waiting newspapermen.

Three words he wrote on that envelope were to become the MacArthurian hallmark: "I shall return!"[1]

MacArthur had been literally driven out of the Philippines by the Japanese. Humiliated in his own lofty estimate of himself, mortified in the eyes of the world, he had been smarting under the blow dealt by the despised "yellow race." In the safety of Darwin he had recovered enough of his old proud, pompous self, and with characteristic melodrama proclaimed: "I shall return!"

It took three long years, inestimable amounts of money and hundreds of thousands of human lives, but Douglas MacArthur did return to the Philippines. On 20 October 1944 the General waded ashore at Palo on the island of Leyte and announced to the world, his sense of melodrama not a bit tarnished: "I have returned!"[2]

Now MacArthur was to wreak a fearful vengeance on the enemy that humiliated him, except that the victim was to be the Philippines.

For these islands Douglas MacArthur desired so much to "redeem" from Japanese hands, his father General Arthur MacArthur, had coined a name. He called them a "tuitionate," which the elder MacArthur defined as a "territory the inhabitants of which are being tutored in the art of self-government."[3]

Arthur MacArthur hoped that by not encouraging assimilation which seems to be presumed in the word "territory," and by avoiding the odious implications of the word "colony," the Filipinos would yet develop a devotion to the United States so as to respond favorably when such devotion was needed for American profit.

The Philippines had been Douglas MacArthur's destiny. He had topped his class of 100 at West Point with scholastic records that would not be surpassed in a long time. Commissioned as a second lieutenant in the corps of engineers upon graduation in 1903, MacArthur was delighted no end when he drew the Philippines as his first assignment. His father, General Arthur MacArthur had been there earlier. The old man had served as military governor of the islands when William McKinley's administration decided to annex the Philippines.

As a young lieutenant Douglas MacArthur took part in laying roads across Bataan and Leyte, worked on harbor installations on Manila Bay. That these places would be the scene of his apotheosis within two score years, MacArthur probably had not the slightest notion.

He would return to the islands in 1922, now a Brigadier General, to command the 23rd Regiment of the Philippine Division, with headquarters at the military installation outside Manila now named after the President who annexed the islands for the United States. At Fort William McKinley, MacArthur, then 45, was promoted to Major General.

He would return anew to Fort McKinley in 1928, this time to serve as Commanding Officer of the Philippine Department. From this post he was recalled to the United States in 1930 to become Chief of Staff of the United States Army, at 50 the youngest ever to assume this post.

In 1935 he came back to Manila for another time yet, now as head of a military mission to plan the defense of the archipelago. On his staff was a young colonel named Dwight D. Eisenhower.

In Manila he was commissioned Field Marshal of the Philippine Army by the newly-established Commonwealth of the Philippines. He became the first and so far the only American ever to hold the title of Field Marshal.

In Manila MacArthur's mother died. He met the woman who became his mistress in Manila, and in Manila he courted the woman who became his wife. His only child was born in Manila.

On his last visit to the Philippines in 1961, MacArthur would declare, "It was here I lived my greatest moments and it is of here that I have my greatest memories."[4]

Now in October 1944, MacArthur stepped on Philippine earth again. Now was the moment to learn finally whether the devotion of the "tuitionate" of Arthur MacArthur's days was forthcoming as had been hoped for. The earth was red with human blood, it was churned and furrowed by bomb and shell, but on this earth Douglas MacArthur had a rendezvous with destiny. That the destiny of one country could be so entwined with the life of one man was a circumstance that would forever intrigue other men.

We take leave of the man at this point to take a closer look at this land that would become so inextricably linked with his great career, to a point that one admirer would call him, "MacArthur of the Philippines."

CHAPTER I

THE PRIZE OF THE CONQUISTADOR

The written history of the Philippines begins with the Portuguese adventurer named Hernao Magalhaes, hispanized into Fernando Magallanes and anglicized into Ferdinand Magellan.[1] While in the service of the King of Spain, Magellan wandered into the archipelago looking for spices. The date was 17 March 1521. Magellan did not find any spices but he did find death in the hands of a stubborn native chieftain named Lapu-lapu on the island of Mactan near Cebu, who refused to become a vassal of the intruders.

The survivors of the Magellan expedition led by Sebastian del Cano, were able to return to Spain. They brought home a cargo of spices they had found in other places enroute and the King decided that the route charted by Magellan was, after all, a profitable one. He sent several other expeditions to the archipelago in the succeeding years – the Loayza expedition in 1525, the Cabot expedition in 1527, that of Villalobos in 1535. It was Villalobos who gave the name Las Felipinas to the archipelago, in honor of Prince Philip of Asturias, who succeeded his father Charles I of Spain and reigned as Philip II.[2]

On 24 September 1559, King Philip II at Valladolid addressed a letter to his Viceroy in New Spain, Don Luis de Velasco, expressing his Royal wish: "... you dispatch two ships of such type and tonnage and with such crews and men as you deem appropriate, and send them out to the discovery of the Western islands towards the Moluccas, and then attempt to return to New Spain with a cargo of spices, in order to make essay of such trade and confirm the certainty of this return voyage."[3]

On the same day, Philip II wrote Fray Andres de Urdaneta, friar of the Order of St. Augustine, in the convent of San Agustin in Mexico City: "We have been informed that while still a layman, you went with the fleet of Loayza, passed the strait of Magellan and reached the Spice Islands, where you remained eight years in our service. As we have now charged Don Luis de Velasco, our Viceroy in that New Spain, with sending two ships for the discovery of the Western isles towards the Moluccas... we commission you to go with the said ships, and to do whatsoever might be ordered by the said Viceroy."[4]

Upon receiving the Royal Order, Fray Urdaneta drew up three alternative routes for the expedition being organized by Don Luis de Velasco. One route proposed to proceed to the Philippines; another route to Guinea, and the third to Japan. But he was opposed to the Philippine route. He wrote the King: "There could be some scruple or impropriety in making the voyage that Your Majesty has ordered to be made. . . for it is clear that the Philippine archipelago not only falls clearly within the term of the pledge (the Treaty of Zaragoza) but that the point which projects toward the East is on the meridian of the Moluccas Islands, and the provisions of this agreement are, in effect, that none of the fleets of Your Majesty or of your vassals can enter, or settle, or trade. . ."[5]

The Viceroy supported Urdaneta's views. He wished the fleet to proceed to the Moluccas to rescue the Spaniards who had been left on the islands, and then go on to New Guinea or Japan. Quite opposed to this view was the renowned pilot, Juan Pablo Carrion, who had been to the Orient in 1524 with Ruy Lopez de Villalobos. His opinion carried much weight, specially with regards to the futility of an expedition to New Guinea, for he had been there, and Urdaneta had not.

For five years, while the fleet was being assembled, the debate raged. In June 1564, the Viceroy died. The government of New Spain fell into the hands of the Royal Audiencia.

To avoid further delay, the Audiencia ordered the man who had been chosen as captain-general of the expedition, Don Miguel Lopez de Legazpi, to set sail immediately, and entrusted to him a sealed letter that carried his instructions, including his final destination. It was not to be opened until he was 300 leagues away from the American coast.

Born of a noble family in Zumarraga, Guipuzcoa, Spain, in 1505, Miguel Lopez de Legazpi was at this time well-past middle age.[6] A man of great probity and rectitude, he had served faithfully in New Spain for 30 years. In Mexico City he practiced law, served as a councilor, later as chief scrievener, still later as magistrate. The fleet over which he now took command consisted of two heavy galleons, one small galleon, a tender and a frigate. It carried 380 men, counting soldiers and seamen, and five Augustinian priests, among whom was the navigator Fray Andres de Urdaneta. The soldiers were commanded by Mateo de Saz as *maestro* de campo, and Martin de Goiti. The Royal treasurer was Guido de Lavezares. One of Legazpi's grandsons, Felipe de Salcedo, accompanied his grandfather.

The fleet sailed from Port Navidad on 21 November 1564. On the 25th, estimating that they were 300 leagues out at sea, Legazpi assembled his officers aboard his flagship and opened his sealed orders. His destination was the Philippines.

On 19 January 1565, the fleet sighted land and took possession of it in the name of the King of Spain. They were probably part of what are the Marshall Islands today. On 24 January they came to the Ladrones, now known as the Marianas, of which they took possession too. On the 20th February, they arrived at the island of Samar where Legazpi proclaimed sovereignty over the entire archipelago in the name of Philip II.

At the island of Leyte, the Spaniards were well-received by Rajah Malitik. But in Bohol, they found that the natives had fled to the hills when they heard of their approach. Legazpi sent a peace message to Rajah Sikatuna who, convinced of the Spaniard's sincerity, consented to a peace treaty, ratified by the blood compact, both men drinking from a cup of wine into which each had mixed some of his own blood.

From Bohol, the fleet sailed to Dapitan in Mindanao. On 27 April, they arrived in Cebu where Ferdinand Magellan had met death almost fifty years earlier, in the hands of Lapu-lapu. Thinking that the Spaniards had returned for revenge, Rajah Tupas met them at the beach in battle array. After a brief skirmish, Tupas surrendered and acknowledged himself a vassal of the King of Spain.

Properly established in Cebu, Legazpi now sent back one of his ships, the *San Pedro*, to find the return route to New Spain. The ship had Felipe de Salcedo as captain and Father Urdaneta as pilot. The ship sailed 1st June 1565.

On 20 August 1567, Felipe returned to Cebu with his brother Juan, with adequate men, arms and supplies. The route across the Pacific had been charted. Now, the conquest of the islands could begin in earnest. The task at hand was no longer trading for gold or spices, but extending Spanish sovereignty over the entire territory.

Finding difficulty in securing supplies in Cebu, Legazpi moved his capital to Panay, founding a new settlement where Roxas City (formerly Capiz) stands today.

Early in 1570, Juan de Salcedo sailed with a company of 30 Spanish soldiers and 500 native allies to wage war against pirates based on the island of Mindoro. He obtained quick victories and returned with rich booty.[7]

Upon his return, Salcedo joined Martin de Goiti, and with 120 Spaniards and 600 native allies, they sailed north to explore the island of Luzon. Goiti had heard reports of an extraordinary bay farther north, and upon arriving found two Muslim settlements situated on the opposite banks at the mouth of the river. The settlements were called May-nila and Tundok respectively, and the river was the Pasig.

May-nila was defended by a fort made of earthwork, with palisades made of coconut trunks. The fort was mounted with bronze cannon, and it was commanded by a dashing young man named Raha Solayman, also called the Raha Mura, or the young chieftain, as distinguished from his uncle, Lakandola, or the old chieftain, who ruled Tundok.

Goiti attempted to negotiate peace, but was repulsed. He laid siege on the palisaded fort and razed the settlement to the ground. Raha Solayman withdrew to the other side of the Pasig and regrouped his forces, readying for another struggle. After looting the abandoned village, Goiti thought it the better part of prudence to return to his ships and sail back south. Salcedo missed the action because he had left the fleet to explore Taal bay, and did not rejoin the party until later.

In Panay, Goiti made an enthusiastic report of his discoveries. He spoke in glowing terms of the safe and spacious harbor that is Manila bay, and the rich lands that spread out from the Pasig.

Legazpi liked what he heard, and the following year he himself led a force of 210 Spaniards and 1,000 native allies and sailed north. The Muslim chieftains at the mouth of the Pasig were not quite ready to succumb, but were quickly overpowered by the better-armed, better-organized invaders.

Legazpi negotiated for the site on which Solayman's razed settlement had stood, and on 19 May 1571, on the feastday of Santa Potenciana, the site was ceded to the Spaniards.

On 24 June 1571 the formal and solemn celebration of the foundation of the city of Manila was held. Santa Potenciana was proclaimed patroness of the new city and to this day, a street in Intramuros carries her name. In the great battles in defense of this city from rebellious Chinese and covetous Dutch, the faithful would swear that they saw her saintly figure etched against the clouds encouraging the defenders and confusing the enemy.

Legazpi, now called by his title *El Adelantado*, laid down a plan for the development of the city which he called *El Insigne y Siempre Leal Ciudad de Manila.* He decreed that housing lots be awarded according to the status of the recipient, and that space be reserved for a plaza and a church. As in Spanish America, the streets were laid out straight and parallel to one another, and the blocks were made nearly uniform in size, so that the city resembled a huge chessboard.

Having acquired the site where Solayman's fort stood, Legazpi began the work of strengthening the crude installations he found there. He ordered that the enclosure of the original Muslim settlement with a stockade begun by the natives be continued. This was the first step in fortifying Manila, and also staked out the perimeters of the city.

On 20 August 1572, *El Adelantado* died. Among his papers was found a sealed order he brought with him from the Royal Audiencia in Mexico, designating his treasurer Guido de Lavezares as governor and captain-general.

In 1574, Manila was confronted with its first test, when the Chinese corsair Limahong invaded the city from the north with 62 heavy ships and several thousand men.[8]

Limahong took the city by surprise. The *maestro de campo,* Martin de Goiti, fell among the first casualties. The pirate fleet had been sighted on its southward course on the China Sea by the young Juan de Salcedo from his *encomienda* in the Ilocos. He gathered a native army and sailed down along the coast, landing in Bataan and rushing to Manila by land. With the re-inforcements, the defenders of Manila drove the Chinese back to their ships. The day was 30 November 1574, the feast of St. Andrew the Apostle who thereupon was adopted the city's patron saint. The Chinese never returned.

Manila resumed its building activity. The buildings razed by Limahong were replaced with new ones made of wood, bamboo and nipa, materials readily available and with which the native workers were familiar.

In 1575, Dr. Francisco de Sande, president of the Audiencia of Mexico, was named governor and captain general of the Philippines. He arrived in Manila the same year.

Sande brought with him the military engineer Sancho Diaz de Ceballos, whom he commissioned to draw a map of the rising city and draft a plan of fortification. Ceballos recommended that the community be moved 500 paces away from the sea so that houses could be built on stronger foundation than the sand on which they stood. He pointed out that instead of constructing a castle to defend the city, the whole city itself be made a fort. Anyway, he explained, most of the residents were soldiers by occupation.[9]

In 1579 the monastery of the Augustinians burned down and a big section of the city burned with it. When the new governor Don Gonzalo Ronquillo de Peñaloza (1580-1583) arrived, he brought with him a big retinue composed of 600 men, some of whom brought their families. Manila suffered its first housing shortage, and new rules were issued on building construction.

During Ronquillo's term, the first bishop of the Philippines was appointed in the person of Fray Domingo de Salazar of the Dominican Order. He arrived in Manila with the first Jesuit priests assigned to this mission, Fathers Antonio Sedeño and Alonzo Sanchez. The former was a talented person who would play an important role in the construction of the city walls and the early stone and brick edifices in Manila.

In poor health since his arrival, Ronquillo died in 1583 and was buried in the monastery of San Agustin. He was succeeded by his son Diego Ronquillo. On the ninth day of memorial rites for the deceased governor-general, another huge conflagration broke out, starting from a candle that fell on combustible material on the dead governor's tomb. Fanned by a strong wind, the fire spread rapidly, reached the fort and ignited the ammunition stores. The new city was reduced to ashes.

At this time, orders came for the creation of the Royal Audiencia of Manila of which Don Santiago de Vera was named president, concurrent with his duties as governor-general. De Vera arrived in Manila in May 1584, with the *oidores* of the Audiencia, to assume his post.

Governor De Vera was responsible for the issuance of the requirement that buildings in Manila be made of stone and that the use of combustible materials be avoided. He encouraged the house owners to use brick and stone, and had the natives and the Chinese artisans learn to cut stone, manufacture bricks and tiles, and produce lime for mortar.

In 1585, Governor de Vera built a new fort south of the Augustinian convent fronting the sea and Bagumbayan. It was a small installation designed for a garrison of thirty to forty soldiers, and it was called Nuestra Señora de Guia.

When Governor Gomez Perez Dasmariñas arrived in May 1590, he noted that save for the Nuestra Señora de Guia, the young city was exposed on all sides. He launched a construction program to encircle the city with a stone wall. He started to rebuild the fort where Solayman's redoubt once stood, retaining the name Fort Santiago, after the patron saint of Spain, who was also his own patron saint, being a Knight of Santiago. Then he proceeded to connect Nuestra Señora de Guia and Fort Santiago with a wall. Thus started the conversion of the whole city into a fort as Sancho Diaz de Ceballos once advised Governor Sande. The wooden palisades Legazpi and Lavezares threw up around the city were torn down to give way to the stone walls. The new walls, however, followed more or less the lines of the old wooden palisades, and suffered but slight modification under the succeeding governors who took a hand in the development of the fortification.

By the end of Governor Dasmariñas' administration, he had raised two parallel stone walls from four to six feet apart, which remained to be filled with earth. Dasmariñas is remembered as having began the construction of the walls of Manila, although by no means did he complete them.

In the years 1580-1581, Governor Gonzalo Ronquillo concentrated the Chinese who were constantly growing in number to an area on the right bank of the Pasig called Parian. It was thought that by confining them into a narrow area, it would be easier to control them. for the Spaniards never really trusted them, although they carried on active commercial intercourse with them, and the city's life was in the hands of the Chinese for they held the major enterprises dealing with immediate necessities. Parian was close enough under the walls, so that the area was within range of musket fire.

At this time, there were about eight thousand Chinese residents of Parian, a veritable Chinese colony where the celestials had their homes and shops where they worked in iron, brass and silver, and bought and sold wares, serving as skilled carpenters, bakers and tailors to the city. Here they dwelt under military guard, surrounded by a high stockade. Only by special permission purchased by heavy bribes, were they allowed to live outside the stockade.

The spiritual care of the Parian was given to the Dominicans, many of whom became fluent in Chinese. The Dominicans built a church and a hospital in the area, and many Chinese were baptized Christians, very often with the Spanish godfather giving his Christian name. But rarely did the celestials abandon their original faith, except in name only.

During the administration of Governor Pedro Bravo de Acuña in 1603, a fleet of Chinese junks appeared in Manila Bay bearing three Mandarins who said they were sent by the Chinese Emperor to verify reports concerning a mountain of solid silver in Cavite. This rumor undoubtedly arose from curiosity as to the source of the vast amounts of silver that was paid for Chinese goods by the flourishing galleon trade.

Governor Acuna permitted the Chinese delegation to go about their business, certain that no such mountain existed, since the silver pesos paid for the silks and tea brought by the junks came from Mexico and Peru.

The arrival of the Chinese Mandarins disturbed the authorities, nonetheless, for they thought that a Chinese invasion was imminent. They prepared to arm. The preparations of the Spaniards alarmed the Chinese who in turn thought that they were in danger of being massacred. Their leader, Eng-Kang, known by his Christian name Juan Bautista de Vera, ordered every Chinaman to give him a needle so that he might know the numerical strength of his forces in the forthcoming insurrection. When the needles reached 22,150, he knew he had enough men to fight, and he fixed as the date of the uprising 30 November 1603, St. Andrew's Day.

Before the Chinese could strike, however, their plot was betrayed by a Filipino woman to Fr. Juan de Talavera, parish priest of Quiapo, who immediately relayed the information to the proper authorities. Both Filipinos and Spaniards were thus warned in time. Eng-Kang was quickly placed under arrest and put to death.

At about 11 o'clock on the night of Friday, 3 October 1603, the eve of the feast of St. Francis, the Chinese unfurled their dragon flags and attacked Tondo and Quiapo, setting the buildings on fire and slaugthering the population. A contingent of over 100 Spaniards led by Don Luis Perez Dasmariñas, son of Don Gomez Perez Dasmariñas and himself a former governor-general, and Captain Tomas Bravo de Acuña (Governor Acuña's nephew) marched against the Chinese rebels but they were ambushed and annihilated almost to a man. Inspired by their victory, the Chinese hordes assaulted the walls of Manila. But the city defenders Spaniards, including the civil and ecclesiastic officials, Filipinos and Japanese, repulsed the attackers.

At this critical hour, about 4,000 Pampanga warriors marched to the rescue of the city, and tipped the scales of battle in favor of Spain. The Chinese retreated to the mountains of San Pablo, Laguna and there made their last stand on 20 October 1603, against the government forces of 200 Spaniards, 300 Japanese and 1,500 Filipinos under the command of Don Cristobal de Axquesta Menchaca. On 14 November 1603, the victors returned to Manila triumphant.

Before the 16th century closed, Manila had its first archbishop, it had a printing press, a university, a hospital. As early as 1593 two books on Christian doctrine, one in Tagalog-Spanish and another in Chinese, were printed in Manila by means of the wood-block. The first book of America, the *Bay Psalm Book,* would not be printed until 29 years later. The first printing press in Manila using movable type was founded in 1602 by a Dominican friar. Thus printing came to Manila ahead of Philadelphia (1668), Calcutta (1780), Sydney (1795), and other cities of great importance.[10]

The first hospital in Manila was founded in 1578 by Brother Juan Clemente, a Franciscan friar. It was called the Hospitalito de Santa Ana. Out of this hospital there developed the Hospital de San Juan de Dios and the San Lazaro hospital.

The first university in Manila was the University of San Ignacio, started by the Jesuits as a college for boys in 1589. It became a university in 1621, and lasted until 1768 when the Jesuits were expelled from the islands.

The second university was the University of Santo Tomas, founded in 1611 as the College of the Holy Rosary. It became a university in 1645, and exists to this day. Harvard University was founded 25 years after

Santo Tomas. Before 1863, all colleges and schools whether for boys or girls, were exclusively for children of Spaniards. The schools were not opened to natives until 1863.

Succeeding governors contributed their part in completing the fortifications of Manila. Governor Francisco Tello in 1600, for instance, raised the height of the walls by at least a yard. Governor Juan Niño de Tabora, who arrived in 1633, noted inadequacies in the fortifications and forthwith proceeded with his own improvements, raising the walls higher and strengthening the fillings.

During the administration of Governor Sebastian Hurtado de Corcuera, who served for nine years from 1635 to 1644, a number of bastions were constructed which succeeding governors named after saints. Corcuera also dug the moats surrounding the walls.

Governor Corcuera is ranked among the most able Spanish governors of the islands. A distinguished record of service already behind him, he was sent to the Philippines for the specific purpose of suppressing moro piracies. He had served with distinction with the infantry in Flanders; had been general of cavalry in Peru and had served as governor of Panama. His campaigns against the moros were brilliantly executed and gained outstanding results. But Corcuera had the misfortune of wielding temporal leadership at the same time that Juan Guerrero, ranked among the worst archbishops to sit on the throne of the See of Manila, was wielding spiritual power over the city.

Guerrero had been promoted archbishop of Manila from the bishopric of Vigan (Nueva Segovia). His appointment papers were delayed and he blamed Governor Corcuera, apparently without reason. His antipathy towards the governor seems to have started here.

Corcuera had arrived in Manila with his nephew Pedro Corcuera, also a distinguished veteran who now served as *maestro de campo*. One day, Archbishop Guerrero sent a native girl to the protective custody of Pedro Corcuera's household. The girl had been purchased by an artilleryman named Francisco de Nava, who forced her to be his mistress.

Archbishop Guerrero broke up this relationship and now the girl came to live with Pedro Corcuera and his wife, Doña Maria de Francia. One afternoon, while the girl, with Doña Maria, was on a *paseo* and was passing by San Agustin church, the artilleryman espied her and forthwith halted the carriage. He tried to persuade the girl to return to him, and when the girl vehemently objected, he drew his dagger and stabbed her to death in front of the horrified Doña Maria. Then he ran to San Agustin church to seek sanctuary.

When Pedro Corcuera heard about this outrage, he gathered a group of pikemen and himself entered the church where he seized the miserable Francisco de Nava cowering before the altar of San Nicolas de Tolentino. The artilleryman was put on trial, and having been found guilty, was sentenced to death by hanging. The friars were up in arms in no time. They claimed that the seizure of Nava in church violated the right of sanctuary. Archbishop Guerrero attempted to have the culprit released to the custody of the church, failing which, he pronounced interdict on the governor-general, meaning he may not attend church nor receive the sacraments. When Nava was sentenced to hang, the Archbishop pronounced interdict on the entire city, closing all churches. In a gesture of irony, Governor Corcuera ordered that the gallows be erected right in front of San Agustin church, on the very spot where the poor girl was stabbed to death. This enraged the friars all the more.

Corcuera was succeeded as governor by Don Diego de Fajardo. Then sixty-three-years old, Don Diego would rather have avoided responsibility, delegating even weighty matters to his unscrupulous subordinates who took advantage of him. He solved conflicts with the clergy by yielding to them. Now to please the friars and the corrupt civil officials who had reason to hate the stern and upright Corcuera, Diego de Fajardo held his predecessor to his *residencia*, despite a letter from the King allowing his immediate return to Spain. For five long years, Corcuera languished in Fort Santiago. Finally, the court in Spain dismissed the charges brought up by his enemies, and as restitution, since all his property was confiscated in Manila, he was made governor of the Canary Islands, where he spent his last days.

During Fajardo's time, some remodelling was done on Corcuera's bastions, enlarging them and improving the connecting curtain between the bastions.

At about this time, Spain annexed Portugal and the Portuguese ports were closed to the Dutch, forcing the Dutch to seek trade in the Orient. A Dutch fleet of five vessels threatened Manila on 15 March 1646, at a time when there were but two galleons ready to defend the city. The two galleons sallied forth undaunted, nevertheless, trusting to win, as the ancient chronicler wrote, "more by spiritual weapons than by weapons of war," and while riding to confront the enemy, "the members of the said armada did with much devotion recite the Holy Rosary, on their knees and in two choirs, all trusting that by such means they might be found worthy to succeed against the foe."[11]

In the bay of Bolinao the two forces joined battle, beginning at two in the afternoon and ending at six in the evening, resulting in the Dutch fleeing in panic.

The following 29 July, this armada of two again sallied forth in defense of the city. The enemy had returned on seven large vessels "which carried such powerful artillery and some eight hundred men, not including the sailors -- and this battle (fought between Banton and Marinduque) was one of the fiercest and bloodiest in our day, lasting from seven in the evening till four at dawn -- at which time, seeing how grievously maltreated their ships were and one on fire, they did retreat and seek shelter, and would not give battle though we called them to it."

The enemy reappeared with six ships two days later and hostilities were resumed off the coast of Mindoro. This battle lasted from noon to dusk, when the Dutch fled a third time, having lost one ship and had another crippled. Before the initial battle, seeing the disparity between forces, the commanding-general "did make a vow to the Virgin of the Rosary, promising her a feast of thanksgiving should the victory fall on our side, and with every man in the armada to come on bare feet and offer thanks at her shrine in Manila; which vow and promise, when laid before the soldiery, they did accept and ratify."

Hardly had the two triumphant galleons reached Cavite when news came of a fresh Dutch fleet approaching Mariveles. Though badly battered and in need of repairs, the armada of two once again went and grappled with the superior force. This fourth encounter took place between the islands of Lubang and Ambil, and raged steadily for ten hours, "until seeing themselves hardpressed, the enemy did escape and take flight, our ships pursuing and giving fire still, though one, our *Capitana*, had been hit in the side and was much feared for and yet did not sink."

About a week later three of the Dutch ships, repaired and re-equipped, returned to the scene and found the disabled *Capitana* alone, her sister ship having sailed ahead, "and they did surround and fiercely set on her and did fire so close that there was long a danger of their boarding the ship; but our men, calling on God and Our Lady, did rise to the contest in such manner that they wrought a woeful destruction among the enemy, and did totally destroy one ship and scatter the others which, fleeing, were discovered and severely punished by the *Galera*, a ship dispatched to our assistance -- and though our *Capitana* had been engaged in such close quarters that for hours, it seemed to rain bullets, nevertheless we had but four men dead."

The Dutch menace prompted Governor Sabiniano Manrique de Lara, who served ten years from 1653 to 1663, to make further additions to the fortification of the city.

Manrique de Lara is ranked among the most outstanding Spanish governors of these islands. Yet when his administration closed, several charges were brought up against him, and he was fined the huge sum of P70,000. He appealed, and the decision was reversed and the fine remitted. But so disillusioned was he by the way the world used him, that he withdrew into a monastery in his native Malaga.

Up to that time, Manrique de Lara had had the longest tenure of a Spanish governor-general in the Philippines. With the advanced state of construction that he found upon arrival and with a longer term than any of his predecessors, he had greater opportunity to undertake significant constructions upon the city's fortifications. On the side fronting the bay, he built a bastion called San Francisco Javier, and four fortlets named San Eugenio, San Jose, San Pedro, and San Juan. On the side facing the river, he built a fortlet called Almacenes, and a small bastion called Santo Domingo. On the land side, he made extensive improvements on the bastions named San Gabriel, San Francisco de Dilao, and San Nicolas, or Carranza. He reconstructed the exit on this side which he named San Felipe.

Manrique de Lara was succeeded as governor by Don Diego de Salcedo, who arrived in Manila in 1663. A man with a high reputation for honesty, justice and integrity, he set out to conduct a just and impartial government for his King. Soon, however, he found himself at loggerheads with the meddlesome friars who fomented intrigue at every turn.

As firm as he was just, Salcedo intervened against the clergy's excesses, thereby incurring the ire of the friars and provoking Archbishop Poblete to complain directly to the King. In reprisal, Salcedo refused to pay salaries to the clergy from Royal funds.

When the post of dean in the Manila See became vacant, Archbishop Miguel de Poblete sought an interview with the governor-general, in whose hands lay the appointing power. Poblete wanted the post for his nephew, who was then Bishop of Nueva Segovia. Not only did the governor refuse the Archbishop's recommendation on the matter, but also rebuked him for complaining to the King.

The archbishop left the Governor's palace in high dander. Shortly after, he died. As it happened, the day after Poblete's death had been earlier set aside for ceremonies for swearing fealty to the new King, Charles II, old Philip IV having passed away. It was customary to refrain from ringing church bells until after the ceremonies when the acclamation became general, featured by gun salutes and the ringing of the bells. Despite this, Salcedo allowed the bells to be rung for Poblete. The body was embalmed and Salcedo acted as pallbearer at the funeral.

Now, while the Spanish Inquisition was established in the Philippines as early as 1583, it did not function here as it did in Spain and Mexico. Originally founded by St. Dominic Guzman, also founder of the Order of Preachers whose followers are better known as Dominicans, the Inquisition was intended to extirpate heresy, but very often it was the instrument for purposes other than what was intended. Some of the most heinous outrages in history arose out of the Spanish Inquisition. No *autos-da-fe were* conducted in the Philippines, although the instruments of torture, varied and sophisticated, were not wanting in this city. Santo Domingo convent was well stocked with them, as were the Audiencia and Fort Santiago.

The commissary of the Inquisition in Manila at this time was Fray Jose de Paternina. Now, this crafty monk who was not a Dominican but got the assignment by a lot of string-pulling, began to entertain charges against Governor Salcedo, most of which were trumped-up and baseless, in fact. Among these were that Salcedo forbade the tolling of the bells on Archbishop Poblete's death and he forbade the embalming of the body. It is said that Paternina held a grudge against the governor who had a mistress in Mexico City related to Paternina. On the night of 9 October 1668, the grand inquisitor moved on his prey and through deceit and subterfuge gained access to the governor's bed-chamber. He was dragged out of bed half-naked and put in chains and brought from one hiding place to another, so fearful was Paternina of having Salcedo's friends rally to rescue him. Finally, he was brought to the dungeons of San Agustin weighted down with chains. Then, Paternina arranged for his deportation to Mexico. After many delays, the ship finally set sail, but weakened by maltreatment and disease, Diego de Salcedo died in mid-journey and was buried at sea.[12]

The outrage reached the King himself, and when Don Juan de Vargas Hurtado arrived in Manila in 1678 as governor-general, he carried with him a decree from the King to the clergy of Manila, admonishing them for their complicity in the death of Salcedo. But almost from the start, de Vargas came in conflict with the archbishop of the time, Fray Felipe Pardo, a Dominican, a man of such irrational tendencies that he was known as the "Mad archbishop of Manila." With all his halberdiers, de Vargas could not serve the Royal Decree on the Dominicans; they seized the men he sent to deliver the decree, trussed them up and sent them back to the governor in a blatant act of contempt.

The split between bishop and governor progressed from bad to worse, and came to a head when Archbishop Pardo seized a cargo of goods newly arrived by galleon and consigned to the Jesuits, who were friendly to de Vargas. The Royal Audiencia decreed the archbishop's banishment to Lingayen, Pangasinan, and de Vargas signed the decree. Naturally, the archbishop resisted. But the soldiers were determined to carry through their orders and lifted the poor friar, throne and all, to the boat waiting on the Pasig to bring him to exile.

De Vargas was succeeded as governor-general by Don Gabriel Curuzalaegui Arriola. The new governor recalled Pardo from exile and held the outgoing de Vargas to his *residencia*, the administrative inquiry to which all retiring governors were subjected, when all parties with grievances came forward to make the governor make amends. Now, the archbishop lost no time in exacting penance from de Vargas. He decreed that de Vargas should stand at the gate of all principal churches of Manila and those in the districts of Tondo and Binondo, exposed to the church-going public, dressed in sackcloth, a lighted taper in his hands, and a rope around his neck.

Moved by the harshness of the punishment, the new governor mitigated it to imprisonment on the Isla de Convalescencia, an island on the Pasig, were the Hospicio de San Jose now stands. Here de Vargas lived for four years, with only his devoted wife Doña Isabela to keep him company, acting as secretary to her husband, taking down by hand long ponderous petitions in his defense.

In 1689, broken in body and spirit, the governor-general who tried to do his duty was released and allowed to return to Mexico. But he was so weakened by his ordeal in prison that he could not stand the arduous journey across the Pacific. He died in mid-ocean, and was buried at sea. Not long after, his persecutor, Archbishop Pardo died. He died so suddenly that he could not benefit from the comforts of his church.

For sixty years after the departure of Governor Manrique de Lara, no significant changes were made on Manila's defenses. The city grew and developed into a handsome medieval metropolis, elegant and gracious. The buildings were made of more substantial materials, and were decorated with the finest imports from China, Mexico and Spain, so lucrative was the galleon trade that the people could afford the best available. From 1662, when the Chinese pirate Koxinga threatened Manila, peace had reigned over the city, creating a complacent air and giving no cause to worry over the fortifications.

Don Fernando Manuel de Bustamante arrived in Manila in 1717 to serve as governor-general, having succeeded the Conde de Lizarraga under whose administration the Chinese were expelled from the country. Bustamante was a *mariscal de campo*, an unbending soldier of the old school whose valor had been tested in the battlefields of Flanders.

A no-nonsense administrator intent only in getting results, Bustamante immediately launched a program of reform in the management of the country's affairs, starting with putting to rights the city's finances. So successful was he that in one year the raids on the treasury, perpetrated by the corrupt civil and church officials, were halted and the city once again became solvent. From the money thus saved, he established the *praesidio* at Zamboanga as a stronghold against the moros. Zamboanga had been abandoned earlier, but Bustamante engaged Don Juan Sicarra, an eminent military engineer, who designed the fortifications of Zamboanga and named them after the Nuestra Señora del Pilar.

The friars were most affected by the reforms made by Bustamante, and now together with the civil officials among whom were members of the Audiencia who were similarly put to disadvantage, they began to plot ways and means to get even with the governor-general and regain the *status quo*. Bustamante got wind of the plot, however, and hit back by arresting the leaders many of whom sought sanctuary in the churches where they were welcomed by the friars. When Archbishop Geronimo de la Cuesta persistently refused to yield one of the most notorious of the corrupt officials, the governor ordered the archbishop's arrest and imprisonment at Fort Santiago.

In protest, the friars ordered the tolling of the bells in the churches of Intramuros. The governor on the other hand had ordered the army to assemble upon signal to uphold the authority of the King. On the night of 11 October 1719, the friars, seized by panic and fearful of reprisal, organized a mob whom they armed with weapons hidden in their monasteries. These were soon joined by others in the employ of the guilty officials and merchants. Soon Manila's streets were seething with an uncontrollable mass goaded to frenzy by the friars who gave them their church blessings and promised rich monetary rewards. Now the mob moved ominuously towards the governor's palace.

The palace guard had been dismissed by the officers in command who were secretly in league with the friars. The few who remained at their post offered no resistance. Bustamante was in his drawing room with a few friends, passing away a mild October evening. In another moment, they were fighting for their lives.

The governor's friends put up a determined defense and the stairs run red with the rabble's blood. But there was no containing a mob gone out of its mind. Though the days when he was the terror of the battlefields of Flanders were long past, Bustamante fought like the veteran of old. Twice he pushed back the attackers beyond the bloodied threshhold. Once more he ran his sword deep into an adversary's body, whereupon the others fell upon him with pikes and halberds. Then they dragged his torn body to a dungeon in the Audiencia where, bleeding from multiple wounds, he breathed out his last.[13]

The governor's son was *castellan* of Fort Santiago and when he heard the roar of the mob, he jumped on a horse and galloped to the palace, to rescue his father or share his fate. The mob recognized him and dragged him off his mount, and stabbed him until he was dead.

The mob next marched to Fort Santiago to liberate the imprisoned Archbishop Cuesta, who in accordance with the practice at the time, now became governor-general. In such manner did events in Manila transpire in those violent and confused days.

Among all the great maritime enterprises in history, the Manila Galleon had the longest existence. Started in 1565 it lasted until 1815, a period of 250 years during which unfailingly, one or two galleons sailed back and forth across the Pacific.[14]

As early as the 5th century, 1,000 years before the coming of the Spaniards, merchants from the southern coast of China were already trading with the islands that were to be known as the Philippines. After the arrival of the Spaniards, the Chinese renewed commercial activities in the islands and were delighted to find that the newcomers paid for their purchases with solid silver, a metal that was scarce and of great value in China.

The establishment of commercial relations was not an official act, but was the result of Chinese and Spanish private initiative. The first Chinese junks loaded with merchandise came to Manila in 1572. In 1573, the galleon trade brought to Acapulco 712 pieces of silk and 20,000 pieces of fine gilt porcelain. In 1574, six junks came to Manila, 15 in 1575, 21 in 1580 and 48 in 1588, in a continuously increasing pattern.

The trade between the Philippines and Mexico was governed by several laws. A law promulgated in 1593 fixed the exports of the Philippines to Mexico at not more than P250,000 worth of goods, while the sale of the cargo was fixed at P300,000. The amount of trade from the Philippines was increased to P300,000 in 1702, and to P500,000 in 1734.

By Royal Decree the departure of the galleon from Manila was set for June to take advantage of favorable winds. With all sorts of delays, though, departure often did not take place until July.

Once loaded, the galleon lay at anchor in front of the walls of Manila, while the procession in honor of the Virgin of Peace and Good Voyage was held. The statue of the Virgin accompanied many galleon trips. The image today is enshrined in the hill town of Antipolo east of Manila.

The archbishop then blessed the ship and her crew, the church bells rang and the governor-general read the order of departure. Four or five weeks later, the galleon sailed out into the Pacific through the San Bernardino strait.

From the strait to the coast of California, no land was sighted and the journey could last anywhere from four to six months.

The galleons used for the Manila-Acapulco trade were small ships ranging from 1,200 to 1,600 tons.

The cargo they carried from the Philippines consisted mostly of Chinese and Oriental goods – Chinese silks, Indian cotton, Persian rugs and carpets, Sumatran and Javan pepper, and various precious stones and jewelry. A small part of the cargo consisted of Philippine goods, like cordage, Ilocano blankets, hammocks and tablecloth.

To be able to load goods on the galleon, one had to have a *boleta*, or ticket. The number of *boletas* on a galleon corresponded to the number of compartments in the vessel, averaging 1,500 for each ship. *Boletas* were in effect, export licenses, each costing between P200 and P225.

The return trip from Acapulco to Manila was shorter and more pleasant. The eastern tradewinds kept the vessel in full sail continuously during the approximately two months crossing from Acapulco to Guam where the galleon usually made port when the native Chamorros were not in revolt. Guam to Manila took 20 to 30 days.

In 1766, a ship of the line *Buen Consejo* arrived in Manila from Cadiz, the first Spanish vessel to come to the Philippines since 1525, when the ill-fated expedition of Juan Garcia Jofre de Loayza set sail for the islands. The arrival of the *Buen Consejo* vessels presaged the end of the galleon trade.

The last galleon left Manila in 1811. In 1815 the galleon *Magallanes* left Acapulco for Manila, but she did not return. She was the last of the line.

In 1813, the use of the *boletas* was abolished by a law which authorized trading on private vessels. But only a sporadic traffic was carried on between San Blas and Manila, until 1825. After that, the American clipper ships and English and French merchant vessels took over the Philippine trade.

Although they were primarily cargo vessels, the great galleons at one time were virtually the exclusive means by which travelers from Europe could legally enter the Philippines via Mexico. Inbound traffic during this period consisted of civil and military officials assigned to duty in the islands, and their dependents, as well as ecclesiastics for the missions. Many of the missionaries transited in Manila en route to other destinations in the Orient.

The Mexico-bound galleons brought out the same civil and military functionaries and their dependents upon completion of their tours of duty. Many of them would by then have made their fortunes from exploitation of land and people and were going to enjoy their new wealth in Mexico or Spain.

On 25 August 1761, Charles III of Spain and his cousin Louis XV of France signed what is referred to as a "Pacto de Familia," a family pact, at Versailles. Locked in a bitter struggle for control of the maritime commerce of the time, France was waging war against England, the Seven Year's War that raged from 1756 to 1763, and Charles III had committed his country's aid to his Bourbon cousin, in return for which the French king was to restore Minorca to Spain.

On 2 January 1762, England declared war on Spain. King George III ordered his forces to attack Spanish possessions in America and in the Orient.

On 14 September 1762, a British ship appeared in Manila bay. It did not enter the harbor, however, for after taking soundings, it left. A week later, on the evening of 22 September, a squadron of thirteen British ships under the command of Admiral Samuel Cornish, anchored off the port of Cavite.

The next morning Cornish sent a delegation to the Acting Governor, Archbishop Manuel Antonio Rojo, with a letter demanding surrender of the islands. The demand was rejected. That evening British troops started landing and massed south of the Walled City.

On the afternoon of 28 September, the British ships started bombarding the sea walls. The next day they shifted the shelling to the city walls. By 2nd October the British had landed cannons which soon joined the ships in the bombardment of the walls. The next morning the walls were breached and through the openings British troops poured into the city.

When armed resistance ended, Archbishop-Governor Rojo signed the surrender papers. This did not mean that British rule over the islands became absolute, however, for the magistrate Simon de Anda y Salazar, with the approval of the Audiencia, had slipped out of the city with a considerable portion of the city's treasury. He reached Bacolor, Pampanga, where he set up a provisional government with himself as governor-general.

The administration of the government was taken over by the East India Company which sent Madras-born Dawsonne Drake to act as governor. Drake arrived in Manila, 2 December 1762, to assume his functions, together with a four-man council.[15]

The Seven Years' War ended with the signing of the Treaty of Paris, 10 February 1763. Official advice reached Manila, 23 July 1763, and the British started to evacuate the city. By the end of May 1764, they had all gone.

The effects of the British occupation were deep and far-reaching. The English brought with them their ideas of political and commercial liberalism, and for two years Manila was opened to world commerce. For the first time in the history of the colony, foreign merchants were allowed to do business in Manila. The British left in 1764, but their ideas remained.

At about this time a new economic concept was sweeping Europe, and the Philippines, too, was to fall under its sway. The protagonists of world trade during this period – England, France, Holland and Spain – sought to acquire power through foreign trading monopolies and government-imposed restrictions aimed at winning a favorable balance of trade.

This theory was challenged by a French physician named François Quesnay, who maintained that human government should leave certain things alone in the natural order. Out of this theory there arose the slogan which was finally corrupted into *"laissez faire."* It gained forceful articulation in the hands of a Scottish professor of moral philosophy named Adam Smith, whose *Wealth of Nations* gave rise to modern classic economics.

Charles III, who ruled Spain from 1759 to 1788 and who is held up in history as an excellent example of the enlightened despot, came under the influence of Quesnay and Smith. It was during his reign that the Economic Society of Friends of the Country would be founded in all Spanish colonies, the aim of which was to promote agriculture, commerce and industry.

Charles III named in succession three governors-general who clearly understood the Philippines and whose regimes would usher the country out of the medieval age into the modern world. They were a new breed of Spanish administrators, and they brought about revolutionary changes in the country. They were Simon de Anda y Salazar (1765-1776), Jose de Basco y Vargas (1778-1788) and Felix Berenguer de Marquina (1788-1793).

Anda's mission was to institute economic reforms. No man could have been better qualified, judging from the results of his work. In a famous memorial dated 12 April 1768, he denounced the evils of the theretofore sacrosanct galleon trade. He recommended the revision of commercial regulations, advised a new coinage of money, counselled extreme care in the selection of governors.

During Anda's time, direct trade between Spain and the Philippines began with the arrival of the vessels of the line *Buen Consejo.* It did not prosper, however, because Manila merchants still preferred the galleon trade. But the beginning was made, and a new age was in the offing.

Jose de Basco y Vargas arrived in Manila in July 1778. He served for ten years, one of the longest terms for a Spanish governor. Basco worked to improve agriculture, commerce and industry. He created a trading company called the Royal Company of the Philippines to exploit the Philippine-Spain trade and to encourage agricultural and industrial ventures in the country.

In 1789, during Governor Berenguer de Marquina's administration, foreign ships were allowed to carry Asian goods to Manila. Shortly Manila bay was filled with ships flying foreign flags.

When foreign ships were allowed to enter port, it was logical that foreign merchants should also be allowed ashore to transact business. In 1809, an English firm was allowed to set up shop in the city. Others followed in 1814.

With the Royal Company of the Philippines set up by Basco still holding a monopoly over foreign trade, however, unrestricted commercial intercourse with the rest of the world could not be established. On 28 May 1830, the company's constituted rights were revoked.

The dissolution of the Royal Company of the Philippines was a turning point in Philippine history. It paved the way for the declaration of Manila as an open port. This was accomplished with the issuance of the Royal Decree of 6 September 1834.

In 1842, the government in Spain sent the economist Don Sinibaldo de Mas to Manila to study economic conditions in the islands and submit recommendations. In his report submitted in 1843, de Mas recommended, among other things, the opening of more Philippine ports to world commerce. In conformity with this recommendation, the ports of Sual in Pangasinan, Iloilo on Panay island and Zamboanga in northern Mindanao were opened in 1855, that of Cebu in 1860, and those of Legazpi, Albay, and Tacloban, Leyte, in 1873.

The opening of the port of Manila to world trade meant that foreigners could now travel to this city for business, and presumably also for pleasure. This contrasted with the earlier period when the bulk of arrivals at the port of Manila were Spanish civil and military functionaries and their dependents.

There had been isolated exceptions to the general ban against foreign traders, however. Tomas de Comyn mentions an English merchant who left the city in 1798 after spending 20 years in Manila during which he accumulated a fortune. La Perouse also tells of a Frenchman who was doing business in Manila in the year 1787.

In 1826, Wise & Company were allowed to operate in Manila. It is still in business. The following year, Strachan Murray & Company followed suit. This latter company is the predecessor of the still-flourishing Ker & Company. It is clear, therefore, that even before 1834 when the decree opening the port of Manila was formally issued, certain merchants were already allowed to do business in this city.

The significance of having foreigners engage in business in Manila lies in the presumption that an awareness of this country was growing in the minds not only of the businessmen themselves but also their associates and principals abroad, their suppliers, their customers, their bankers and lawyers, and their governments, not to mention their families. In short, during this period, people in other countries were probably poring over their maps to locate the Philippines. The world was trying to get a fix on this country.

By 1837, a contemporary listing showed six British and two American trading houses established in Manila.

Another listing in 1859 showed 15 foreign firms operating in Manila, including seven British, three American, two French, two Swiss and one German.

While the opening of the port of Manila to commerce in effect signalled welcome to the world, the distance of the archipelago from Europe limited travel opportunities to few other than those under official compulsion (the government functionaries – civil and military), those compelled by lucre (the traders) or those who were truly determined, such as criminals trying to escape trial or the gallows.

On 17 March 1869, the Suez Canal was opened to world shipping. Suddenly the Philippines were very close to the centers of European trade and commerce. Whereas it took three months for a ship to negotiate the Barcelona-Manila route rounding the Cape of Good Hope, through the Suez Canal it took but one month.

Credit for the Suez Canal goes to the Frenchman Ferdinand de Lesseps, one of the dreamers and visionaries to whom are reserved the task of bringing to reality what others dismiss as impossible. He was neither engineer nor architect, neither financier nor manager. His was the idea of the Suez Canal and by sheer strength of will and dedication to purpose he translated his idea to reality.

Now in thirty days any Spaniard could make it to Manila. In 1810 there were but 4,000 Spaniards in the Philippines. By 1870 the number had increased to 13,500, and by 1898, there were 34,000.

Philippine trade expanded after the opening of the Philippines to foreigners and reached a wider market. This stimulated production in the Philippines and brought some prosperity, enabling Filipinos and mestizos (those who owned land and produced for export, and those who engaged in commercial exportation) to improve their economic status and form a higher social class. There emerged a political and social aristocracy called the *principalia.*

The prosperity brought about by increased agricultural production and expanded commerce elevated some farmers and merchants to a higher economic class. Their wealth enabled them to send their children to good schools in Manila and even to Spain and other European countries. There emerged a new middle class, the *ilustrados*, in whose ranks were priests, lawyers, doctors and teachers. From the *ilustrado* class arose the leaders who would shape the destiny of the Philippines.

The Spaniards encountered resistance from the Filipinos from their arrival in the Philippines in 1521 to the Philippine revolution in 1896. Lapu-lapu who slew Magellan on Mactan island was the first to refuse to bow to Spanish rule. His opposition was followed by revolts against Spanish sovereignty once established, at the rate of one every two years all throughout the 333 years of Spanish presence in these islands.

The revolts were brought about by one or a combination of two or more of the following causes: personal grievances; opposition to some practices or aspécts of Spanish rule; religious motives, and agrarian complaints.

But none of the revolts were movements for independence, nor were they motivated by any nationalistic ideal.

The independence of the South American countries from Spain was the work of the creoles, those born in those countries of Spanish parents. It was achieved by their rebellion, their growing nationalism and love for the land of their birth, a revolt against the Spaniards who saw the new nations as mere sources of wealth to be gained by the exploitation of land and men. Thus, Francisco Miranda, Jose de San Martin, Simon Bolivar, Cecilio del Valle, Miguel de Hidalgo, Agustin de Iturbide and all the others were creoles.

After the signing of the Treaty of Cordova secured Mexican independence, Agustin de Iturbide wrote to all the governments that had been dependent on the Viceroyship of Mexico and invited their allegiance. Guatemala and Yucatan accepted, but Cuba and the Philippines refused.

But the people of Manila learned of the developments in South America through various ways. Shortly, disturbances would erupt in the Philippines that had all signs of having been made in the South American pattern.

The first of these was a conspiracy uncovered on 17 April 1821, organized by Francisco Bayot, a creole. The uprising was put down quickly, but it jolted the authorities into an acute realization of the perilous position of Spanish rule in the islands. The government in Spain sent a new governor in the person of Don Juan Antonio Martinez de Alcovendas, who arrived with a new corps of Spanish officers. The new officers took over command of the armed forces, earlier held by creoles. This drew the resentment of the troops and led to the second insurrection, this one led by Andres de Novales and officers of the Fort Santiago garrison. Upon arrival of the new officers from Spain, Novales was relieved of his command and posted to the southern islands. On the eve of his departure, however, he led the 800 men of the garrison in a plot to capture Governor Martinez de Alcovendas and the former Governor

Mariano de Folgueras.

The latter was caught by surprise and killed, but the governor was away at his countryhome. Warned in time, Alcovendas called upon the loyal forces, beat down the uprising and had Novales seized. He was executed 2 July 1823.

Bayot's conspiracy and Novales' uprising were the first movements for liberty in the archipelago. They were the first stirrings against colonial rule in the Orient. They were actually a sequel to the Spanish-American struggles for independence. It would take seventy years more for a national conscience to develop that would promote national independence by force of arms.

A strong factor that served to fan Filipino nationalism was the religious controversies that plagued Spanish rule. In the beginning the controversies involved only the Spaniards themselves. But as Filipinos became priests and as the number of Filipino priests increased, they were ultimately drawn into the fight.[16]

At the Council of Trent (1545-1563), the Catholic church adopted a rule to have parishes handled only by secular priests, meaning those who were not members of religious orders. Regular priests, those who belonged to religious orders, could not be assigned to parishes except with the advice and consent of the bishop under whose jurisdiction the parish fell.

In 1567, King Philip II obtained from Pope Pius V the apostolic brief entitled *Exponi Nobis*, which authorized regulars to serve as parish priests without securing the permission of the bishop and without falling under his jurisdiction.

The assignment of regulars to serve as parish priests raised the question of whether they should be subject to the diocesan visitation, an administrative procedure whereby a church official visits or inspects a parish to see whether its affairs are being conducted properly.

In the beginning, the controversy was confined to the Spaniards themselves. In the 18th century, the Filipinos began to be involved when Archbishop Basilio Sancho de Santa Justa insisted on enforcing diocesan visitation on the friar curates. Rather than submit, the friars left their curacies.

On 9 November 1774, the King in Spain issued an order for the secularization of the parishes as fast as they became vacant. Archbishop Santa Justa quickly ordained Filipino seminarians and assigned them to the vacant parishes. But many of the Filipino priests were poorly and inadequately trained and turned out to be incompetent.

On 11 December 1776, the decree of 1774 was suspended and the friar curates were restored to their parishes.

After the decree of 1776, the church authorities took steps to prepare young Filipinos for eventual service as parish priests. But the Spanish administrators chose to follow a policy of despoliation, whereby parishes instead of being secularized, were given to regulars. This only embittered the Filipino priests and their adherents and sympathizers.

The controversies gave rise to the first Filipino leaders, foremost of whom were the two priests, Pedro Palaez and Jose Burgos. Both were sons of Spanish colonial officers. They wrote and preached against the iniquities of the system, exposed the abuses of the friars, and championed the cause of the native clergy. They incurred enemies in both the civil and ecclesiastical ranks of the Spaniards.

Padre Pelaez died among the ruins of the Manila Cathedral in the great earthquake of 1863. In his steps in the struggle for secularization, there came Padre Burgos, at one time his student at the University of Santo Tomas.[17]

The position of parish priest was the most important Filipinos could aspire to under Spanish rule. They were deeply resentful, therefore, when, not only were they prevented from becoming parish priests, but the parishes they held were also taken away from them.

On the night of 20 January 1872, Filipino soldiers at Fort San Felipe in Cavite rose in mutiny under the leadership of Sergeant Lamadrid. A reactionary governor, Rafael de Izquierdo, had succeeded a liberal one, Carlos Maria de la Torre, and the new governor had abolished certain privileges long-enjoyed by Filipino workers in the fort. The mutiny was quickly put down, but the authorities seized the occasion to take reprisals against suspected enemies, and several innocent persons were implicated in the uprising. Some were imprisoned, others were deported, and others still were executed.

Among those who were executed were the three priests, Jose Burgos, Mariano Gomez, Jacinto Zamora. After a trial best described as a farce, the three priests were executed at the garrote at Bagumbayan, 17 February 1872. To the last moment the archbishop of Manila, Don Gregorio Meliton Martinez, denied their guilt. He refused to unfrock them as the civil authorities demanded, and on their execution, he ordered the tolling of the church bells. The bells could as well have tolled the death knell of Spanish rule in the Philippines.

The unjust execution of the three priests was a turning point in Philippine history. It crystallized the nascent feelings of nationalism among the rising intelligentsia. Convinced that they could not advance their cause while on Philippine soil, the sons of wealthy families fled to Europe, there to wage a propaganda war for reform in the homeland.

The most distinguished in this group were Graciano Lopez Jaena, Marcelo H. del Pilar, Jose P. Rizal, Juan and Antonio Luna, Mariano

Ponce, Jose Ma. Panganiban, Eduardo de Lete, Isabelo de los Reyes, and several others. Inspired by a burning zeal for the betterment of their race, fired by love of country, these young men formed the vanguard for political and social reform in the islands.

They published a fortnightly newspaper called *La Solidaridad*, their propaganda vehicle. The first issue appeared on 16 February 1889 in Barcelona. It appeared regularly thereafter until its last number, issued in Madrid on 15 November 1895.

Probably the most gifted and the most eminent of those young men in the reform movement was Jose Protacio Rizal. Born in Calamba, Laguna, 19 June 1861, the son of prosperous farmers, Francisco Mercado and Teodora Alonzo, the young Rizal received his early schooling in Binyang, Laguna, later attended the Ateneo Municipal under the Jesuits. Later he studied at the University of Santo Tomas, but in 1882, at the age of 21, he left for Spain. He studied medicine, mastered several languages, expressed himself in prose and poetry. In 1886 he published his first novel, *Noli Me Tangere*, words from the New Testament which meant "touch me not." The following year he returned to Manila, but already he was identified as subversive, and feeling the pressure of the authorities on him, he returned to the safety of Europe. In 1891, his second novel, *El Filibusterismo*, appeared. The two novels are credited with having hardened the Filipino resolve against Spanish domination.

In 1892, Rizal returned to Manila and organized the *Liga Filipina* which sought the unification of Filipinos into a homogenous body, and the social and economic advancement of the people. On the night of 6 July 1892, Rizal was secretly arrested. The following day, Governor Eulogio Despujol ordered his banishment to Dapitan in Mindanao.

The news of Rizal's deportation shocked the people, for Rizal had come to personify their aspirations for freedom and betterment. That same night of 7 July 1892, a group of men led by Andres Bonifacio met in a house on Azcarraga street in Binondo. From this meeting there emerged the *Kataastaasan Kagalang-galang na Katipunan ng mga Anak ng Bayan*, or the Katipunan for short, a secret society pledged to the overthrow of Spanish rule by force of arms. Around a flickering oil lamp the men gathered and performed the ancient rite of the blood compact, and signed their names on the membership papers with their own blood.[18]

Andres Bonifacio was born in Tondo, the old kingdom of Lakandula, 30 November 1863. His parents were Santiago Bonifacio and Catalina de Castro. The death of his parents when he was still young forced him to leave school to become the provider for his family. In his teens he became a messenger-clerk in an English trading firm, later moved to another firm as a sales agent. But he continued to educate himself, read Dr. Rizal's novels, dwelt long on a book on the French revolution.

Compared to the European-educated scions of the *ilustrados*, Bonifacio was a rough, ignorant clod. But while the *ilustrados* never got far in their agitation for reform, Bonifacio, by the use of force, brought matters to a head. The middle-class intelligentsia held on to their belief that Spain would heed their cries for reform. Bonifacio had become convinced of the need to separate from Spain, and that this could be achieved only by the force of arms.

The Katipunan grew in membership, spread to the provinces of Bulacan, Cavite, Batangas, Nueva Ecija, Pampanga and Laguna. Soon it would spread to the Ilocos and the Visayas. They printed a newspaper on a press bought with money two Visayan Katipuneros won in a lottery, and kept running with type stolen by other Katipuneros from another printing press. The paper was called *Kalaya-an,* meaning Freedom. The first issue was edited by the young and brilliant Emilio Jacinto, a student at the University of Santo Tomas, on whom Bonifacio learned heavily for advice on legal matters.

Kalaya-an set the countryside aflame with patriotic zeal and the masses rallied to the Katipunan. But the authorities tracked the paper down to its headquarters and the first issue was also the last. It had done its work well. From the day the Katipunan was founded to the 1st January 1896, it had acquired no more than 300 members. After the appearance of *Kalaya-an*, membership rose to 30,000.

Slowly the Katipunan gained adherents and built strength, mainly from arms stolen from the Spanish arsenals. Attempts to secure help from other countries, like Japan, failed.

But the secret of the Katipunan was leaked out prematurely by a member who talked to a Spanish priest who happened to be an active agent in the government campaign against the subversives. The priest found evidence at the *Diario de Manila,* a printing press where Katipunan receipts were surreptitiously printed by Katipuneros working there. It was 19 August 1896, four years after the society's founding. Mass arrests followed and terror gripped Manila.

Andres Bonifacio and some close associates slipped through the roadblocks the Spaniards had set up around Manila. They fled to Balintawak, north of the city, and by the grapevine Bonifacio sent word for the leaders of the society to assemble. By 21st August about 500 of them had massed at Balintawak. That afternoon they moved to Kangkong, and on the 22nd moved farther to Pugadlawin. On the 23rd they gathered in the yard of Juan Ramos, whose mother, Melchora Aquino de Ramos, then 82-year-old, undertook the feeding of the men. The old woman later would nurse the wounded and the sick among the revolutionists and would be called "Mother of the Revolution."

Here Andres Bonifacio asked the men whether they were ready to fight and make the sacrifices the struggle demanded. Receiving a rousing affirmative reply, Bonifacio then asked the men to bring out their *cedulas,* the residence tax certificate which also served as an identity card, and tear them up to signify their rejection of Spanish sovereignty. The men did as they were asked, and shortly the ground was white with the bits of shredded paper. Up rose the cry, "Long live the Philippines." The incident is noted in Philippine history as the "Cry of Pugadlawin." The revolution had started.

On 29 August, Bonifacio issued a manifesto calling the people to arms. He led his men in attacks on enemy positions, but each time he was repulsed with heavy losses. But the spirit of revolt had caught the population and soon all the Tagalog provinces were in open rebellion, and the Ilocos, the Bicol and Visayas were soon in arms too.

Earlier, Andres Bonifacio had sent an emissary to Dr. Jose Rizal in his place of exile in Dapitan, seeking the patriot's support of the revolution. But Dr. Rizal declined to give support, saying that the country was not ready for armed revolution, that the rebels did not have the means to insure success, that the time was not ripe to separate from Spain, and that only the innocent masses would suffer.[19]

Later, Dr. Rizal petitioned the Spanish authorities for permission to leave the country and to serve as a volunteer physician in Cuba where the population was being decimated by yellow fever. Governor Ramon Blanco gave his permission and Rizal came to Manila to take the ship to Cuba. The ship had reached Singapore when the revolution broke out. Rizal's enemies saw their chance to do away with him once and for all, and orders were sent out for his arrest and his return to Manila.

After a trial which was but mere formality since justice did not seem to be its end, Rizal was condemned to die by musketry. Early in the morning of 30 December 1896 Jose Protacio Rizal walked the half-mile from his cell at Fort Santiago to meet martyrdom at the Luneta.

The execution of Rizal galvanized the rebels into renewed activity. Fighting broke out with new fury as the countryside arose.

In Cavite, south of Manila, the Katipuneros were led by a young schoolteacher named Emilio Aguinaldo. In the bloody fighting that followed, Aguinaldo dislodged the Spaniards from well-entrenched positions.

But the Katipunan in Cavite, even before fighting broke out, had split into two factions, known as the *Magdalo* and the *Magdiwang.* The split did not heal with the fighting, and in fact led to a series of reverses. The *Magdiwang* faction invited the Katipunan Supremo, Andres Bonifacio, to mediate the conflict. Bonifacio was hard-pressed in Morong, and begged off. They persisted, so toward the end of December 1896 he went to Cavite with his wife, Gregoria de Jesus, known as the *Lakambini*, or muse, and keeper of the Katipunan records, and his brothers, Procopio and Ciriaco.

At an assembly held at the estate-house, the country-home of the friars, in Tejeros, the *Magdiwang* insisted on the supremacy of the Katipunan over the revolution then raging. The *Magdalo* maintained otherwise. When the assembly adjourned, the conflict was still wide-open and in fact had caused new enmities.[20]

Now the friars had secured the relief of the moderate and conciliatory Governor Ramon Blanco. In his place came General Camilo de Polavieja, a reactionary after the friars' own hearts, who now undertook a massive military campaign to exterminate the rebels. One by one the rebel strongholds fell. Soon a third of Cavite was back in Spanish hands.

On 22 March 1897, the *Magdalo* and the *Magdiwang* met anew at the Tejeros estate-house, seeking to end animosities. The assembly agreed to phase out the Katipunan and now proceeded to organize the government of the Republic of the Philippines. In the election of officers, Aguinaldo became president, and Andres Bonifacio, secretary of the interior. Now, contrary to an earlier agreement to abide by decisions arrived at by majority vote, a Magdalo follower questioned the qualification of Bonifacio for the position to which he was elected. Humiliated, Bonifacio, still asserting his position as Katipunan Supremo, dissolved the assembly and declared void the assembly's actions.

The *Magdiwang* group returned to the Tejeros estate-house the following day, 23 March 1897, to explain why they could not accept the results of the previous day's assembly. Then Bonifacio left for Naik, smarting from the humiliation dealt him. At Naik, he and his group drew up a resolution to establish a government separate from that which the *Magdalo* had set up.

Aguinaldo had taken his oath of office as president. When he learned of the Naik resolution and its threat to a unified front against the enemy, he ordered the arrest of Bonifacio and his brothers. But the brothers resisted the arresters, and Ciriaco was slain and Andres and Procopio were wounded. A court martial was called, and on 4 May 1897, the brothers were sentenced to death after a trial notable for the insufficiency of evidence against the accused.

Aguinaldo commuted the sentence to banishment, but his aides convinced him of the continued danger to himself if Bonifacio lived. He withdrew his commutation. Early in the morning of the 10th of May 1897, the brothers Andres and Procopio Bonifacio were shot to death on the wooded slopes of Mount Buntis in Naik.

On 15 April 1897, the brutish Camilo de Polavieja, worn out by the battles he could not win, left the country. In his place Spain sent Fernando Primo de Rivera who had served an earlier term as governor-general of the Philippines. Primo de Rivera tried a policy of attraction. When this failed he launched a vigorous offensive that pursued and finally surrounded Aguinaldo in the hills of Batangas. The Filipino leader managed to slip through the tightening noose, crossed Morong into Bulacan where he holed up in the mountains of Biyak-na-Bato.

Here in the mountain fastnesses, Aguinaldo established a republican government 31 May 1897, and promulgated a constitution. On 1st November, the constitution was signed. The following day, the Supreme Council was created with Aguinaldo as president.

Sometime in August, a mestizo named Pedro Paterno offered his services to Governor Primo de Rivera, to act as mediator between the rebels and the government. During the period from August to December, Paterno plied between Biyak-na-Bato and Manila, threshing out details of a truce.

On 13 December 1897, the final document of the truce was signed, the principal terms of which were: 1) Emilio Aguinaldo and his companions would go into voluntary exile abroad; 2) the sum of P400,000 was to be paid to the rebels; 3) an additional sum of P800,000 was to be paid to the victims of the conflict as reparations.

On 27 December, Aguinaldo and his closest men left for Hongkong, a check for P400,000 in his hands.

Primo de Rivera may have thought he had the solutions to the problems of the Philippines, but a change of power in Spain brought a new governor-general to Manila in the person of General Basilio Augustin.

The sun of the conquistador had begun to set long before this. That it lingered over these eastern isles to this date was an aberration to explain which is not the function of this work. Suffice to say here that as the 20th century dawned, the last traces of Spain's days of empire faded.

But of all the great gems the conquistador amassed to lay at the feet of his Sovereign, none was more glamorous a prize than that which, through the ages, would be called "the Pearl of the Orient Seas."

CHAPTER II

THE CHRISTIAN CITY

The Spanish conquistador's sword, as the truism goes, brought to these shores the cross of Christ. Spain bequeathed a rich and varied legacy to the Filipinos, but it was Christianity that would endure.

The following is the story of the building of Manila into a Christian city – the only one in Asia, as Manilans like to point out. More particularly, this is the story of Manila's Christian institutions as they had become before that fateful month of February 1945.

The work of the Christian missionaries would describe the city of Manila, and the Philippine archipelago as a whole. By creating its principal institutions, the religious virtually governed the course of events and shaped the life of the country. They set the pace for its growth and development.

They not only evangelized; they civilized. Antonio de Morga would have occasion to write in the early 17th century: "At the same time the missionaries were preaching the tenets of religion to the natives, they labored to instruct them in matters of their own improvements."[1]

At the beginning of the 20th century, the first American Archbishop of Manila, Mons. Jeremiah J. Harty, would declare that the religious were men "who not only had the knowledge of physics, philosophy and theology, but were also architects and builders, advancers of civilizations."[2]

THE FIRST BISHOP. When the *Adelantado*, Don Miguel Lopez de Legazpi, in the year 1571 laid down the plans for the city of Manila, he reserved a choice lot fronting the proposed plaza for the city's cathedral.

The first church on the site where the cathedral stands today was constructed of bamboo and nipa under the direction of the secular priest Juan de Vivero, shortly after the Spaniards landed here in 1571. This building, like all other buildings in the area, burned down in the attack of the Chinese invader Limahong in 1574. A new building was erected, this one of wood, and was completed in 1581.[3]

Work on a proper cathedral, however, would not begin until March 1581 when Manila's first bishop, Fray Domingo de Salazar, arrived in the city. He was a Dominican friar (Order of Preachers), and for 20 years he had been a missionary in Mexico. He was promoted procurator-general of his province, in which position he would have opportunity to appear before the Court in Spain. On one occasion, he preached a sermon in defense of the natives of the New World, and so moved Philip II that the King gave due course to the recommendation that Fray Salazar be appointed to the newly-created Diocese of Manila.[4]

THE FIRST CATHEDRAL. Fray Domingo de Salazar arrived to take possession of his See in March 1581. On 21 December of the same year he laid the first stone for his church, by virtue of a Bull of Pope Gregory XIII. He gave his church the title Immaculate Conception, and a cathedral chapter was created. Before the year was over, there stood on the lot reserved for the cathedral a temporary building of wood, bamboo and nipa.

In 1583, fire swept the new city and the cathedral of wood, bamboo and nipa burned down. A Royal Decree dated 20 January 1587 addressed to the Governor Don Santiago de Vera, ordered work on a new church. That year a new building was started, but it would not be finished. It was roofed with straw and looked so ungainly that the Blessed Sacrament was not housed in it.

The city council of Manila in a letter dated 31 (sic) June 1588, advised King Philip II in Spain that with 3,000 pesos raised in three equal portions from among the natives, the Spanish residents and the Royal Treasury, the walls of the church were beginning to rise, this time in stone.

The same letter said that as a temporary measure taken after the fire of 1583, a church of wood roofed with straw was constructed. This makeshift cathedral was used until 15 June 1588, when it was torn down by a hurricane which destroyed a good part of the city.

Probably as a consequence of this letter, Gomez Perez Dasmariñas who had been appointed governor of the Philippines, was instructed to allocate 3,000 ducats for the construction of the church as soon as he arrived in Manila.

Perez Dasmariñas arrived in May 1590, and entered into his duties with such energy and enthusiasm that by the time Bishop Salazar returned to Spain in 1592, work on the nave of the new church had started.

When Father Alonso Sanchez, S. J., returned to Spain in 1586, the matter of the cathedral was among those he brought up before the King. He advised the sovereign that the cathedral should be built of more substantial material. He said that it was actually "built of wood and straw, so impoverished, and so poorly furnished."[5] Probably because of the Jesuit's representations a Royal Decree dated 11 June 1594 was issued, ordering the governor of the Philippines to release the sum of 12 thousand ducats for the completion of the church. In 1600, with the cathedral still unfinished, a strong earthquake hit Manila, and the unfinished edifice was badly damaged.

In the letter of instruction issued Don Francisco Tello who succeeded Dasmariñas as governor-general, he was ordered to visit the cathedral to see the actual status of the work, and to take steps to insure that everything was being done to hasten its completion.

On 6 July 1601, Tello wrote the King and reported that work was progressing on the cathedral but it still lacked a tower and sacristy. The King wrote back authorizing the use of 1,000 pesos to complete the cathedral. The money was never released, however. The explanation was that the Royal Treasury of the Philippines was in a perennial state of penury.

Nevertheless, although slowly, the edifice continued to rise. It received great impetus under Archbishop Miguel de Benavidez, who took over the See of Manila in August 1603, and who contributed much of his personal funds to the work. By 1607, the roof had fallen into such a state of disrepair that the church was actually unusable, and the sacred rites were transferred to the chapel of St. Andrew at the College of Sta. Potenciana. In a letter dated 10 July 1610, the cathedral chapter reported to the King that it was not only necessary to repair the woodwork, but to do the whole structure over again. Forthwith the chapter embarked upon the new project, this time designing a building "as would befit a cathedral church and as these islands would deserve."

The result was "a sumptuous work of stone, with three naves, seven chapels, including the main one, and 10 altars."[6]

This edifice was solemnly blessed by the Archbishop Don Diego Vasquez de Mercado, 6 December 1614. It was not to last long. On 1st August 1621, when the church was not yet seven years in existence, Manila suffered one of the most destructive earthquakes in its history. A note from the Audiencia dated 18 July 1622 stated that the cathedral was beyond repair. It had to be rebuilt entirely.

The cathedral was fully restored during the period between July 1641 and July 1645. The life of this edifice was very short, because it was totally destroyed by the earthquake on the feastday of St. Andrew, 30 November 1645. Because of the destruction, a shed of wood roofed with straw and bamboo was built in the middle of the public plaza, to enable the celebration of religious rites.

THE CATHEDRAL IN THE 17TH CENTURY. Work on the new cathedral did not begin until 1654, when the Archbishop Don Miguel de Poblete (1653-1667) laid the first stone. This church with three naves and in the doric-romanesque style lasted until 1863, although it underwent such extensive renovation in the middle of the 18th century, that the church that resulted may be considered a really new construction.

Earthquake and decay hastened by the intense tropical humidity plagued the great edifice, and repair work stopped. In 1725 the ecclesiastical council found itself once more harassed for funds with which to maintain the cathedral. In 1730 the council petitioned for an encomienda the proceeds from which would go to the upkeep of the cathedral. The petition was not acted upon, so it was renewed in 1735. Meantime, the cathedral progressively deteriorated.

It fell upon Archbishop Juan Angel Rodriguez, who took possession of his See 25 March 1736, to undertake necessary major repairs. The real construction, however, awaited Archbishop Pedro de la Santissima Trinidad Martinez y Arizala who took over the archdiocese 27 August 1747. The construction work was directed by a religious of the Order of St. Cayetano, a Florentine by birth, a great architect and engineer who came to Manila from the Malabar coast where he had served as engineer for the English. His name was Juan de Uguccioni.

Father Uguccioni arrived in Manila toward the end of 1750, and upon the request of Archbishop Martinez he designed plans for the reconstruction of the cathedral. The actual building proceeded very slowly, owing to paucity of funds and the difficulty of getting the necessary materials.

Archbishop Martinez died 28 May 1755, and the ecclesiastical council took over the reconstruction work. While the work proceeded, religious services were moved once more to the chapel St. Andrew at the College of Sta. Potenciana.

By 1756, the main body of the church was complete and the interiors, the ceilings, the artwork and the walls had been painted, while the retablos and altars had been fabricated and were ready for installation. Certain lesser parts still had to be completed, however.

On 22 July 1757, Don Manuel Antonio Rojo took possession of the

Archdiocese of Manila. The archbishop ordered that the work be accelerated. On the eve of the feast of the Immaculate Conception, the Blessed Sacrament and the image of the titular of the church were transferred from St. Andrew's chapel at the College of Sta. Potenciana. On the feastday itself, 8 December 1757, the archbishop said mass at the cathedral for the first time.

The edifice Fray Uguccioni had produced was an architectural and engineering masterwork. In the words of the bishop of Cebu, Fray Miguel Lino de Ezpeleta, it "evoked the admiration of all those who saw it, never tiring of pondering how there were brought to these remote islands with such precision the rigorous disciplines of architecture, and more marvelous is the fact that the work was able to patch together and united the new and the old so that on first sight the structure looks altogether new, up from its very foundations as though the result of an original masterplan."[7]

THE CATHEDRAL IN THE 18TH CENTURY. The cathedral was unscathed during the siege and bombardment of Manila by the British in 1762. Many parts, however, were still to be finished. When Don Basilio Sancho de Santa Justa y Rufina assumed office as archbishop, he took measures to have everything completed, specially the cupola which presented engineering problems. The cupola was finally installed, with the use of a curious composition which the engineer Miguel Antonio Gomez described as "made of lime, powdered brick, eggs of duck and molasses of sugar cane."[8]

The reconstruction work in the 18th century was of such magnitude that funds were a continuing problem. The archbishop, however, finally hit on a solution.

During the siege of Manila by the British in 1762, the church of Nuestra Señora de Guia (Our Lady of Guidance) in Ermita was destroyed. Fortunately, the image of the Virgin had been transferred to the cathedral earlier. After the British left in 1764, it was forbidden to construct any building of heavy materials in the vicinity of the city walls. The archbishop, therefore, ordered that the image of the Virgin be retained in the cathedral. The Virgin had 4,000 pesos in her coffers. It was one of the "richest" Madonnas of the time. It had a very popular cult and devotees by the thousands flocked to her shrine and left generous gifts. These the archbishop used for the construction work on the cathedral. In a way, therefore, it was Our Lady of Guidance (the image is now in the Ermita church) that completed the reconstruction of the Manila cathedral in the 18th century.

THE CATHEDRAL IN THE 19TH CENTURY. In June 1863, another earthquake made a mass of rubble of the Walled City. For several years no attempt was made to reconstruct the cathedral, until 1870, when work began while Don Gregorio Meliton Martinez was archbishop. The new cathedral was completed after nine years, and blessed on 8th December 1879 by the incumbent archbishop, Dr. Pedro Payo.

The following year, 1880, the newly completed cathedral suffered serious damages in still another earthquake. Undaunted, the people of Manila again restored their cathedral, led by the Archbishop Bernardino Nozaleda, who would be the last Spaniard to hold this See.

It was this building that was totally destroyed during the battle for Manila in February 1945.

The creation of the Diocese of Manila and the arrival of the first bishop are watersheds in the Christianization of the city and the country as a whole. The ecclesiastical government would serve as the understructure upon which the work of evangelization and civilization was built.

It was the religious orders, however, that served as the vanguard of this work. From the time the Augustinians arrived in 1565, the religious orders bore the brunt of the arduous work to bring the archipelago into the mainstream of the times. The history of Spain in the Philippines may well be read in the history of the religious orders in this country. The following is a brief narrative on the principal religious orders that were involved in this great task, with particular reference to institutions they created that would figure largely in the events of February 1945.

THE AUGUSTINIANS. Five members of the Order of St. Augustine (O.S.A.) were in the expedition of Miguel Lopez de Legazpi when he landed in Cebu in 1565.

Two Augustinians were in the voyage of conquest that reached Manila in May 1571.

From 1565 to 1898 when Spanish rule over the Philippines came to an end, 2,368 Augustinians came from Spain and Mexico to this country. They named their Philippine organization the Province of the Most Holy Name of Jesus. They founded 385 towns in Luzon and the Visayas.[9]

The first church and monastery of stone and mortar in Intramuros was built by the Augustinians. It would also be the last of the great houses of worship to be left more or less whole in the Walled City after 1945.[10]

Although more popularly known as the church of San Agustin (Saint Augustine), the titular is St. Paul. It is the motherhouse in this country of the order founded by Aurelius Agustinus, (A.D. 354-430), bishop of Hippo, son of St. Monica.

The first structure constructed on this site was made of bamboo and nipa, under the direction of Father Diego de Herrera, shortly after the landing of the Spaniards in Manila, 15 May 1571. On 19 May 1571, the first mass was held in this makeshift church.

Father Herrera was one of the five Augustinians who were with Miguel Lopez de Legazpi in the historic voyage of conquest that brought this archipelago under the Spanish crown. The other four were Fr. Andres de Urdaneta, the navigator of the expedition; Frs. Martin de Rada, Andres de Aguirre and Pedro Gamboa. Father Herrera accompanied Legazpi on the voyage to Manila, together with Father Francisco de Ortega.

The makeshift church Fr. Herrera built was destroyed by fire during the raid of the Chinese corsair Limahong, 2 December 1574. A second structure of lumber was built on the same spot. This was destroyed on 28 February 1583, in a fire that started from candles burning around the cenotaph of the newly-buried governor-general Don Gonzalo Ronquillo de Peñalosa.

Plans for the construction of the monastery were first laid out in 1586, evidently from designs drawn by Juan Macias. At the Augustinian chapter held in 1587, Fr. Juan de Valderama was elected provincial of the Order in the Philippines, and Fr. Diego de Alvarez was named prior of San Agustin. During their respective terms in these offices, construction work began. The latter has been described as an enthusiastic advocate and supporter of the monastery. The 1587 chapter appointed the Augustinian Fathers Francisco de Bustos and Pedro Ocampo to supervise the construction work. The work proceeded very slowly due to the paucity of funds and material and the scarcity of qualified artisans.

At the chapter of 1590, Fr. Idelfonso Perez was appointed as director of the construction work. He was succeeded by Fr. Diego de Avila in 1593. That year, Fr. Diego de Alvarez became provincial, and the work was pushed more vigorously, with funds for the construction raised from the various monasteries of the Augustinian province.

Slowly but steadily the work progressed. King Philip II in Spain authorized contributions from the Royal coffers. All Augustinian monasteries in the Philippines were assessed their share of the costs with the end in view of the swift and early completion of the monastery and church.

In 1599, Brother Alonzo Perea was re-appointed director of the construction. He must have been named to the post for the first time earlier.

The election of Fr. Pedro de Arce as provincial in 1602 gave new impetus to the work on the monastery and church. This friar and his counsellor, Fr. Diego de Cerrabe, undertook vigorous steps to raise money for the construction work, including petitioning the King anew to increase his financial support.

By 1604, Don Antonio de Morga could relate in his *Sucesos de las Islas Filipinas* that "inside the city of Manila, there is the monastery of San Agustin, very big and with many dormitories, refectory and offices; a temple, which is one the richest on these parts is being completed; this monastery houses usually 50 religious."

Finally, in a private chapter of the Augustinians held 19 January 1607, it was formally declared that the monastery and church of St. Paul in Manila was completed. The chapter also formally affirmed that the builder of the edifice was Juan Macias.

Fr. Isacio Rodriguez says that he had read somewhere that Juan Macias "originated from Pampanga." Was Juan Macias a native Filipino, or a Spaniard from Spain or Mexico who had come to the Philippines and had settled in Pampanga from where he was drawn to Manila? The documentation on Juan Macias is extremely sparse, as Fr. Rodriguez declares.

The authoritative source that Juan Macias is the builder of the church and monastery of San Agustin is the minutes of the special meeting of the Augustinians held at the monastery in Manila, 19 January 1607.[11]

Present at the meeting and signatories to the minutes were Fr. Pedro de Arce, provincial-rector; Fr. Juan de Montesdoca, ex-provincial, and Frs. Esteban Carillo, Pedro de Aguirre, Juan Bautista de Montoya and Bernabe de Villalobos, councilors.

The pertinent portion of the minutes declared: "The provincial council discussed whether Doña Olalia would be buried in the *new church* in order to transfer her remains as well as those of her heirs specially of her father, Juan Macias as we are recommended to do, *considering that the said Juan Macias is the builder of the church and that he served in the rest of his life.* It was left to our Father Rector-Provincial to give him the right of perpetual tomb for his remains and successors in the place he thinks best, and that this be implemented as we take it for granted." (Underscoring by Fr. Isacio Rodriguez).

Juan Macias must have been a Spaniard, whether he was born in Spain or Mexico is not ascertainable. It is quite certain that he was familiar with church architecture, and just as certain that he was familiar with the design of churches in Mexico. He was doubtless a master-builder.

THE FRANCISCANS. The Order of Friars Minor (O.F.M.) founded by St. Francis of Assisi in 1210, was the second religious order to arrive in the Philippines.

In 1576 a band of Franciscans had gathered in Seville intending to sail to a new mission in the Solomon Islands. King Philip II, however, obtained permission from the Pope to have the group diverted to the Philippines instead. Several in the group perished in the long voyage across the Atlántic, but other Franciscans joined the survivors in Mexico for the Philippine mission. Led by the Rev. Fr. Pedro Alfaro, the first group of 15 Franciscans landed in Manila, 24 June 1577. Since they had no provisions for themselves, they were taken in as guests by the Augustinians, while a convent was being constructed for them.[12]

The following 1st August, the Franciscans moved into a modest structure of wood and bamboo that was hastily built for them from gifts of Mariscal Don Gabriel de Rivera and Captain Don Martin de la Rea. They dedicated their church to Our Lady of the Angels.[13]

These buildings burned down in 1583, but the original benefactors rebuilt them, this time in wood and tile.

In 1602 the buildings were torn down and in their place new ones of stone began to rise, funded by Don Gabriel de Rivera who had entered the Franciscan Order.

The earthquake of 1645 damaged these edifices badly, but they were not demolished until 1739 when the cornerstone of the new buildings were laid by Governor General Gaspar de la Torre.

Across the Franciscan church and forming a right angle to it, the chapel of the *Venerable Orden Tercera* (VOT) was erected in 1678.

In 1863 when the Manila cathedral was destroyed by earthquake, the VOT church served as temporary cathedral. The remains of the governor-general Simon de Anda were temporarily buried here until they were transferred to the reconstructed cathedral.

The church of San Francisco of Intramuros, more properly the church of Our Lady of the Angels (*Nuestra Señora de los Angeles*), was a popular church, drawing great crowds of devotees of Saint Anthony of Padua.

The Franciscans named their Philippine organization the Province of St. Gregory the Great. They had a vocation as physicians and nurses, and they built several hospitals. Among these was the institution that was to be eminent in Manila history as the San Juan de Dios hospital.

THE SAN JUAN DE DIOS HOSPITAL. The history of this institution is among the most fascinating in Intramuros. The lay gatekeeper of the monastery of San Francisco, Brother Juan Clemente, who had arrived with the group of Father Alfaro, cared strongly for the poor who came to the gate to beg. Not content at doling alms to the beggars, he began to shelter and feed them, and care after them in sickness. He built a small hostel infront of the San Francisco gate towards the end of the year 1577. Brother Clemente named his hostel "Hospitalito de Santa Ana." The modest provisions continually underwent expansion and the *hospitalito* grew into such proportions that in 1596, the *Hermandad de la Santa Misericordia* was created to give it system and organization as it had grown beyond Brother Clemente's ability to handle by himself.[14]

The *Hermandad de la Santa Misericordia* was in the nature of a foundation supported by public funds that aided charitable work. The *Hermandad*, or Brotherhood, came about through the efforts of the Spanish Franciscan friar Don Juan de Hernandez, and another Franciscan, this one a Portuguese, Don Marcos de Lisboa. The *Hermandad* started operations 6 April 1594, with a board of directors called the Santa Mesa, composed of a chairman and twelve members who were mostly military officers.

Created initially to assist the Hospitalito de Santa Ana, the *Hermandad* later assumed other functions like supporting the work of the College of Santa Potenciana for orphanned daughters of Spanish soldiers.

Although the hospital was named "Santa Ana," it was commonly called "La Misericordia," probably because of the *Hermandad's* administration. Later it also became known as the "native hospital," to differentiate it from the "Royal hospital" which was exclusively for the Spanish. Still later, it became known as "San Lazaro," having taken in some Japanese lepers.

Subsequently the lepers were moved out of the Walled City to a spot between the walls and the Japanese village of Dilao. Much later a hospital for lepers was established in the Santa Cruz area, across the Pasig, where the San Lazaro hospital still exists.

By 1656, the institution that sprang out of Brother Juan Clemete's affinity for the poor had become a full-grown hospital, and it was given to the charge of the Hospitallers of St. John of God. From then on it became known as "Hospital de San Juan de Dios."

The story of the Order of Hospitallers of St. John of God in this country is just as fascinating as the institution they took over in 1656.

In 1611, the Reverend Fathers Juan de Gamboa and Lucas de los Angeles of the Order of Hospitallers of St. John of God arrived in Manila to establish a hospital for the less privileged classes.

They succeeded in establishing a convalescent hospital in Bagumbayan outside the walls. Unable to raise means to sustain the hospital, however, the two friars gave up this task and shortly returned to Mexico.

Years later, during the governorship of Don Sebastian Hurtado de Corcuera (1635-1644), an urgent request was sent to the Hospitallers of San Juan de Dios to send representatives anew to the Philippines. The Order's General Commissary in New Spain decided to send Fray Andres de San Jose to Manila to find out what properties the Order still held in Manila from the enterprise of the first mission, if any, and to ascertain whether they should establish a new mission or not.

In November 1641, Fray de San Jose and a lay brother, Antonio de Santiago, arrived in Cavite and with the permission of the authorities, established there a small hospital with 10 beds.

After two years in Cavite, Fray de San Jose, decided to restore the hospital which had been established in Bagumbayan by the first mission of his Order. On 14 April 1644 Governor Hurtado de Corcuera gave official permission to re-establish the hospital, on condition that the building be constructed or purchased not in Bagumbayan but anywhere on the right bank of the Pasig outside the walls.

Shortly after this Hurtado de Corcuera died and was succeeded by Don Diego Fajardo from whom Fray Andres de San Jose now asked permission to restore the hospital in Bagumbayan since no suitable place could be found as Corcuera specified. In his letter to the governor, Fray Andres advised that he had a new site near the hermitage of Nuestra Señora de Guia, almost at the same spot where the earlier hospital stood.

On 16 September 1644, Governor Fajardo gave his consent to Fray de San Jose's representations. In the meantime, however, Fray Francisco de Magallanes had arrived in Manila and had taken over from Fray de San Jose as superior of the Order's Philippine province. During Fray Magallanes' tenure the convalescent hospital was inaugurated, consisting of two wards, one for men and the other for women, with provisions for 20 persons. Not long after, however, this hospital was closed, because the San Juan de Dios hospitallers were given charge of the hospital that had been managed by the *Hermandad de Santa Misericordia.*

This was the old Hospitalito de Santa Ana which was started by Fray Juan Clemente in 1577 and which had been administered by the Brotherhood of the *Misericordia* since 1596.

By a deed executed on 15 March 1656, the Hospitallers of St. John of God took possession of the premises, the while agreeing to construct a chapel that would be open to the public. Archbishop Miguel de Poblete approved this agreement the following 11 May.

On 5 December 1659, the King issued a decree confirming the agreement that had been entered into. By this time the Hospitallers had been running the hospital for three years. It now had three wards with 12 beds each, with a small chapel and a residence for the religious.

On 19 July 1664, the chapel toppled in an earthquake, and Fray Francisco Cardoso, the incumbent superior, proceeded to build a bigger one. The new chapel in turn was destroyed in another earthquake in 1674. To reconstruct the San Juan de Dios chapel, the Hospitallers led by Fray Marcos de Mesa addressed a letter to the King in Spain, accompanied by a petition by the Procurator General of the Order, Fray Sebastian de Zea y Caicedo, for an encomienda to provide the money for the work. On 16 June the King issued a decree allocating to the Hospitallers rentals of 500 pesos earned annually by a certain property for the succeeding 20 years.

In 1703, the prior of the San Juan de Dios hospital requested the increase of the encomienda earlier granted. In a Royal Decree date 17 September 1705, this request was granted.

The chapel constructed by Fray Marcos de Mesa lasted until 1727 when a series of earthquakes caused such serious damage that the building was a virutal ruin.

The Reverend Fr. Pedro de Amaya took advantage of this situation to launch a campaign for funds from the city's faithful during the feast of St. John of God, 8 May that year. One by one many of those present came up to offer gifts. From one such gift of 300 pesos offered by Sargento Mayor Don Diego Monteverde work for the reconstruction was immediately started. On 28 November 1727, the Archbishop Don Carlos Bermudez de Castro laid the cornerstone for the new chapel assisted by the governor general, the Marques de Torre Campo.

When it was completed in 1732, the new church was a sumptuous masterwork. Now construction work started on the second phase to enlarge the hospital. On 10 July 1735, the Audiencia was informed that the new hall for ecclesiastics was completed, and work was starting on the new residence for the religious. In 1770, the hospital was declared finished in all aspects.

This building went the way of its predecessors in the great earthquake of 1863. Work started on a new building, but this succumbed to the earthquake of 1880. Successively, out of the ruins, the San Juan de Dios hospital would emerge bigger and sturdier yet.

The Royal Decree of 17 August 1865 ordered the Hospitallers of St. John of God to turn over the administration of the San Juan de Dios hospital to the government.

The Hospitallers moved to their convent in Cavite on 29 August 1866. The hospital and its properties were placed under the jurisdiction of the archbishop of Manila who created a board composed of the president of the Audiencia as chairman, and five others as members.

On 14 April 1868, the board turned over the care of the sick to the Daughters of Charity of St. Vincent de Paul.

By virtue of the Royal Decree of 1891, the management of San Juan de Dios hospital was turned over to the Provincial Superior of the Franciscans. Thus it remained until 1934, when the hospital passed into private ownership.

In 1917, while Dr. Benito Valdez served as director, the private wards were demolished and made into two large wards, one for men and another for women with 14 beds each.

In 1930, with Dr. Vicente Singian as director, the pharmacy was reconstructed, the kitchen and the central service area were improved.

The operating room was remodelled in 1932, to become the most modern in the Philippines. The X-ray laboratory was equipped with the most modern facilities. On 27 June 1936 a new annex was opened to provide more room for charity patients.

By the outbreak of World War II, the San Juan de Dios hospital of Intramuros had 271 beds, the second biggest hospital in the Philippines after the Philippine General hospital. This was the institution that disappeared from this spot in February 1945.

To accommodate the increasing number of seminarians, Archbishop Bernardino Nozaleda began the construction of a new seminary building behind the cathedral in Intramuros. The building was completed in 1897, but would be used as a seminary for only one year, because in 1898, following the American take-over of Manila, the building was leased to an American corporation which converted it into the St. Paul's hospital. The American Maryknoll Sisters were invited to run the hospital.

When Manila was occupied by the Japanese forces in January 1942, the American officials of St. Paul's hospital were interned at Los Baños. The American Maryknoll Sisters, however, were permitted to stay on as nurses.

The University of Santo Tomas medical students had been using the San Juan de Dios hospital as a clinic and training hospital. When the Japanese took over San Juan de Dios for use as a military hospital, the UST medical students were denied its use.

The UST authorities requested the Japanese officials permission to use the St. Paul's hospital as a clinic for their students. This was granted. The Maryknoll Sisters continued to serve as nurses at St. Paul's, until they were ordered into internment at Los Baños in July 1944.

In May 1942, the Japanese military took over the San Juan de Dios hospital for their own sick and wounded, although some members of the Daughters of Charity on the nursing staff were retained.

The civilian patients were moved to the YMCA building on Concepcion street, still under the care of the Daughters of Charity.

The following August, the Japanese authorities took over the Quezon Institute on España street in Quezon City for use as their military hospital. The tuberculosis patients at QI were transferred to the San Juan de Dios hospital in Intramuros, although a section remained open for non-tubercular patients.

In August 1944, St. Paul's hospital closed down, and the Daughters of Charity of St. Vincent de Paul who now served as nurses there moved to the San Juan de Dios which had resumed operations as a civilian hospital, with a section functioning as a tuberculosis sanitarium.

THE CONVENT OF SANTA CLARA. Another Franciscan institution that became part of the romantic story of old Manila was the Convent of Santa Clara, the exponent in the Philippines of the religious order founded by St. Clare of Assisi in 1215.

At the beginning of the 17th century there grew a feeling in Manila that there was a need for a convent of female religious, "where the daughters of residents of these islands would have recourse to the spiritual and temporal comfort they desire." With these words, the Ecclesiastical Council sought the establishment of such a convent, but 20 years passed before it would be realized. The governor-general had no objection to a convent, but he wanted to know which Order would be established, and how it would be maintained.[15]

Subsequently, the Audiencia set off inquiries as to whether the College of Santa Potenciana may be used for the proposed convent. On 11 July 1611, the Ecclesiastical Council replied that the college was not available because it served a purpose different from that of a convent. On the other hand, the Council pointed out that there was any number of buildings available for a convent since there were many Manila girls who wished the conventual life whose parents were willing to put up the money for rentals. This information was communicated to the King in Spain.

Years later, the procurator general of Manila in Spain, Don Hernando de los Rios Coronel, reviewing the petition for a convent, advised that the *Maestro de Campo* Pedro Chavez and his wife Doña Ana de Vera had donated a building for the convent and a *hacienda* the produce of which would sustain the community.

On 9 March 1620 a Royal Decree was issued permitting the establishment of the Clairist convent in Manila under Royal patronage.

On 5 July 1620 there left Cadiz for Mexico a group of seven Clairists led by Madre Jeronima de la Asuncion who had been abbess of the Clairist convent of Santa Isabel de los Reyes in Toledo. In Mexico three other nuns from the Clairist Convent of the Visitation in that city joined the group.

On 1st April 1621, the group left Acapulco and arrived in the Philippines 24 July that year. From Bolinao, then part of Zambales where the galleon had anchored, the nuns headed for Manila where they arrived on 5th August. One of them had died on the voyage across the Pacific and was buried at sea. The new arrivals were lodged at Doña Ana de Vera's countryhome in her Sampaloc *hacienda*. After four days here, they moved to the Franciscan convent of Our Lady of Loreto, also in Sampaloc.

On 1st November 1621, the Clairists took formal possession of their convent in Intramuros, formerly the mansion of the spouses Don Pedro de Chavez and Doña Ana de Vera. It adjoined the walls by the Pasig river, close to Fort Santiago, on a street which was subsequently named Santa Clara, infront of the Royal hospital for the Spaniards.

Years later, during the term of Governor Sebastian Hurtado de Corcuera, a new floor was added to the Royal hospital from whose windows patients could look down into the cells of the nuns. Moreover, the passage on the walls which led to the convent was sealed and in the area the headquarters of the cavalry was erected. The nuns protested the new arrangements and petitioned the King to restrain his governor from the new constructions.

The protest of the nuns was supported by the Franciscans, in which Order the Clairists belonged, and on 2 October 1638, a Royal Decree was issued prohibiting the governor from carrying out both projects.

The convent of Santa Clara was severely damaged in the earthquakes of 1645 and 1658, after which the nuns had to be temporarily sheltered in makeshift huts of nipa and bamboo in their own garden.

During the English invasion of 1762, the nuns were taken by armed escort to sanctuary at the Santa Ana convent. They stayed there throughout the British occupation of the city.

Madre Jeronima de la Asuncion died on 22 October 1630. The remains were incorrupt until 1670, when they were removed from the original niche and reinterred, as was the custom, covered with lime.

What became the nunnery of Santa Clara in Manila was originally the palace of the wealthy and pious Don Pedro Chavez, the conquistador of the Bicol region. He surrounded the building with walls 30 feet high, and here the nuns spent their lives: once the doors closed on them not even death could bring them out again, for they were buried inside the walls when they died.

THE DOMINICANS. The first members of the Order of Preachers to arrive in Manila were Fray Domingo de Salazar, the first bishop of Manila, and a companion, Brother Cristobal de Salvatierra. Otherwise known as Dominicans after their founder St. Dominic de Guzman, the two arrived in March 1581, together with the first Jesuit mission.

The first Dominican mission would not arrive in Manila until 2 July 1587. From that year until the end of Spanish rule over the Philippines in 1898, some 1,755 members of the Order of Preachers from Spain would serve in the Philippine province which they named after the Most Holy Rosary.[16]

The Dominicans were indefatigable builders and zealous educators. As missionaries they founded 90 towns in Bataan, Laguna, Pangasinan, Tarlac, Cagayan, and the Batanes. In each town they built great houses of worship many of which stand to this day. As educators they are responsible for two Manila institutions which have contributed richly to the life and character of this country and which have withstood the tests of time – the University of Santo Tomas and the College of San Juan de Letran.

The first Dominican mission was accommodated by Bishop Salazar at his palace. By 1587 alienable land in the Walled City was already scarce. Through the ministrations of the bishop who was himself a Dominican, however, a suitable lot was acquired from one Don Gaspar de la Isla. The lot overlooked the Pasig river and when the wall around the city was built it abutted the ramparts erected on this section. The land was swampy, and when Bishop Salazar officiated at the ceremonies to lay the corner-stone of theDominican church and monastery, 16 August 1588, he had to stand on a banca. It was a modest building of wood that arose on the spot.

On 1st July 1588, the Dominicans moved into their first house in Manila. It would not last long. After two years the main altar in the church collapsed over the image of Our Lady of the Rosary, although the image itself was unscathed. Padre Diego Aduarte described the incident thus, "The canopy over the image crumpled into the shape of a wing which served as a dust-guard or shade over Our Lady, an occurrence which aroused such intense devotion among the people. Later the convent acquired another image with a head of ivory for this altar. When the church was renovated, many devotees asked that the old image be placed where it could be venerated, so it stands today at the gate of the church."[17]

The new image of Our Lady of the Rosary was donated to the Dominicans by Don Luis Dasmariñas, acting governor-general at this time. It was sculpted by a Chinese convert under the direction of a prominent Manila resident, Captain Hernando de los Rios. In time this image would become the most beloved of the Manila Madonnas, becoming the focal point of much of the city's history, legend and tradition, in her role as Nuestra Señora del Rosario de la Naval de Manila.

Gaining lessons from the past, the Dominicans were determined to build their new church and monastery of stone, relying exclusively on voluntary contributions from Manila residents who responded with generous gifts.

Among the Fathers at the monastery was Fray Alonso Ximenez, son of a distinguished family from Salamanca, who arrived in Manila with the first Dominican mission. Assigned to Bataan as missionary, he contracted a grave illness and had to be brought to Manila for treatment. He was a fine architect, according to Padre Aduarte, and supervised the construction of the new church and monastery. He was elected prior of the convent in Manila and later provincial of the Order.

The old church was torn down at the end of 1589 and on 9 April 1592 the new church was inaugurated. Aside from the church, a sacristy was built, with a chapter hall, a refectory, a foyer, two large dormitories and other necessities, and the surroundings fenced with a stone wall.

Judging from the solidity of the construction of the church and monastery done by Father Ximenez, it would have lasted indefinitely, but it was destroyed in the great fire of 1603. The fire started at one end of the city and the Dominicans did not think that their compound was in danger, and they all rushed out to the fire scene. But the wind fanned the fire, which devoured the houses made of wood.

The fire eventually reached Santo Domingo and only the Blessed Sacrament and the image of Our Lady of the Rosary were saved. Part of the monastery stood, which, under extreme difficulty, sheltered the religious.

Under the direction of Fray Francisco Minayo, the church was reconstructed of heavier material, with a roof of stone. It look years to complete the new church, but it was a grand edifice that resulted, eventually costing 50,000 duros. This church lasted until 1645, when in the great earthquake on St. Andrew's feastday (30 November), its bell-tower which rivalled in height that of the cathedral, toppled down, while the roof crashed over the central nave.

On the feastday of St. Bernard in 1658 another earthquake brought down what still remained of the old church, and a completely new church had to be built.

Learning from experience that the soil on the lot could not support a stone roof, a church with three naves was planned, with a roof of tile, a ceiling of wood, well-wrought and moulded. The reconstruction was directed by Fray Juan de los Angeles, the prior. It cost 40,000 duros. This church had the longest life, lasting until the great earthquake of 1863.

The successor-church of Santo Domingo was described by George Miller as "one of the most impressive and interesting of all the Manila churches."[18]

"The exterior with its embattled towers and climbing buttresses is stately and massive," George Miller wrote of this edifice. "The view from the Ayuntamiento is striking, and the old Gothic windows of the semicircular apsis have a strong ecclesiastical flavor."

Following is George Miller's account of High Mass at Santo Domingo: "My first experience in a Manila church was at High Mass in Santo Domingo at the early hour. There were sixteen hundred candles shining in the gloom of the old sanctuary, and a thousand worshippers were kneeling on the polished floor. Among the high arches gathered smoke of the incense, and way up in the dome the morning sun streamed red and gold through the colored glass."

This was the church that became the first casualty of the Japanese bombing of Manila in December 1941, shortly after the outbreak of World War II.

THE UNIVERSITY OF SANTO TOMAS. Today, the Order of Preachers in the Philippines is best-known for the University of Santo Tomas, the oldest institution of higher learning in this country.[19] It is the oldest in Asia and antedates Harvard, the oldest university in the United States, by 25 years.

The foundation of the University of Santo Tomas is ascribed to the Most Reverend Miguel de Benavidez, Order of Preachers, the second archbishop of Manila.

Born in 1552 at Carrion de las Condes in the province of Valencia, Spain, Miguel de Benavidez entered the Dominican Order at Valladolid in 1567. He first came to Manila with the first group of Dominicans sent to this mission in 1587. He was transferred to China in 1590, but was subsequently expelled from that country and he returned to Manila where he helped build a hospital for the Chinese. Returning to Mexico, he was elected procurator-general of his Order, in which capacity he accompanied the Reverend Domingo de Salazar, bishop of Manila, to Spain.

In 1598, Fray Benavidez returned to the Philippines as bishop of Nueva Segovia, the seat of which was at Lal-lo, Cagayan. He occupied his bishopric at Lal-lo the following year, and there completed a Chinese dictionary which became very useful to the China missions.

Bishop Benavidez was promoted archbishop of Manila in 1601. It was not until 19 August 1603, however, that he was able to take possession of his See, becoming the second archbishop of this city. Bishop Salazar had been nominated the first archbishop of Manila, but he is not considered as such because he died before he could assume office. Father Benavidez succeeded the Reverend Ignacio de Santibañez.

On 26 July 1605, Archbishop Benavidez died. In his last will and testament he bequeathed his library and personal property worth 1,500 pesos to be used for the establishment of an institution of higher education.

The executor of the late archbishop's last will and testament was his close friend and associate, the Rev. Fr. Bernardo de Santa Catalina. Fray Bernardo was commissioned by his Dominican superiors to carry out Father Benavidez's wishes. He set in motion the necessary paperwork for organization, and succeeded in securing a building near the Dominican church and convent in Intramuros for the college.

In 1609, permission to open the college was requested from King Philip II, but the permit did not reach Manila until 1611. On 28 April

1611, the act of foundation was signed before the notary Juan Illan by the Dominican Fathers Baltazar Fort, Bernardo Navarro and Francisco Minado.

Later in the year of 1611, the college started operation using funds bequeathed by Archbishop Benavidez and the most Reverend Diego de Soria who had succeeded the former as bishop of Nueva Segovia. Other donors were Pablo Rodriguez de Aranjo who left 3,740 pesos, and Andres Hermoso who left 2,000 pesos for the purposes of the college.

The Rev. Fr. Baltazar Fort became the first rector of the college, which was originally called Colegio Seminario de Santo Tomas de Nuestra Señora del Rosario.

Baltazar Fort was a native of Mota in the province of Valencia, Spain. He entered the Dominican Order at Salamanca in 1586, and first came to Manila in 1602. He became provincial of his order in 1611.

On 15 August 1619, Father Fort was formally invested rector of the college, which had been renamed Colegio de Santo Tomas in 1616, after the great Dominican theologian St. Thomas Aquinas (1225-1274). Also in 1619, the college obtained official government recognition.

In 1624, King Philip IV authorized the conferment of academic degrees for a probational period. This period was extended for 10 years in 1627. At the end of the second period, in 1637, it was given "university" status by King Philip IV.

In 1785, King Charles III granted the university the title "Royal," in recognition of the gallantry of Santo Tomas students who fought the British when they invaded Manila in 1762. In 1902, Pope Leo XIII granted Santo Tomas the title "Pontifical."

The courses in the early curriculum were grammar, the arts, theology, logic, philosophy, canon law and civil law. Late in the 19th century, it offered courses in medicine, pharmacy, midwifery and dentistry. In the 20th century it established a college of fine arts and architecture, a college of philosophy, a conservatory of music and a college of education.

The university is the last of 24 universities the Order of Preachers founded in Spain and its possessions in both hemispheres during the 16th and 17th centuries. Santo Tomas was affiliated to the University of Mexico whose statutes it adopted bodily.

COLLEGE OF SAN JUAN DE LETRAN. A second great educational institution founded by the Dominicans is the College of San Juan de Letran.

This college originated from the concern of a Manila resident named Juan Jeronimo Guerrero, a retired military officer who took it upon himself to take care of the orphans of Spanish soldiers. In 1620, Captain

Guerrero started taking into his house destitute boys. His house was located infront of what later became the San Juan de Dios hospital, near the Parian gate. Here the captain fed and clothed the orphans and provided elementary instruction.

The work grew continually until Captain Guerrero who had become a Dominican lay brother had to appeal to the public for support. In 1623, the King gave formal approval to the institution and took it under the Royal patronage. No suitable building had been found for the institution, however, and it remained in Guerrero's house.

A Royal Decree of 1635 ordered Governor General Sebastian Hurtado de Corcuera to allocate to the new college a regular source of income.

Before his death, Juan Jeronimo Guerrero commended his work to the Dominican Order. In a council held in 1640, the Dominicans formally assumed charge of the college and named it College of St. Peter and St. Paul. The college was moved to the basement of the Dominican Convent of Santo Domingo, the Brother Porter, Fray Diego de Santa Maria, in-charge.

In 1643, the college was transferred to the unoccupied lodgings of the late Don Bartolome Tenorio which stood infront of the Santo Domingo church. Here it stayed for two years until the earthquake of 1645 destroyed the building. The city government provided a site outside the walls for the college, near the Parian, and a building was constructed here from donations. But this location was not considered healthful because it lay on marshlands. Also it was close to the Chinese quarters of Parian and distant from the University of Santo Tomas where the students attended classes.

In 1669 properties owned by Doña Maria Ramirez Brito were acquired, together with adjoining lots along the river banks close to the Santo Domingo convent, and here the college stayed permanently. In 1706, it was officially renamed College of San Juan de Letran.

Letran numbers among its distinguished alumni the national hero Jose P.Rizal and the president of the Philippine Commonwealth Manuel L.Quezon. Quezon had served as resident commissioner of the Philippines in the United States and had been instrumental in the passage of the Jones Law of 1916 which granted autonomy to the Filipinos over their local government. When Quezon returned to the Philippines that year, one of the highlights of the celebration of the passage of the Jones Law was the opening of the Quezon Gate on the northeastern corner of the citywalls, across from the entrance to the San Juan de Letran college.

THE AUGUSTINIAN RECOLLECTS. The Recollects are sometimes called Discalced (Barefoot) Augustinians. The Order was founded by Thomas de Jesus at Toledo in 1588. In 1622, Pope Gregory XV ratified the Order's separation from the Order of St. Augustine.

When the Recollects arrived in Manila in 1606, Intramuros was already crowded, so they had to look for a spot outside the walls for their church and monastery.[20]

In Bagumbayan outside the walls, Don Pedro Bravo de Acuña who was governor-general from 1602 to 1606, had built a stately summer house which was surrounded by beautiful gardens and reflecting pools. Before he could move in, however, Governor de Acuña died.

The Recollects raised the sum of P30,000 from friends and sympathizers and bought the late governor-general's summer house from his heirs. There was no church in Bagumbayan, so the Recollects built one dedicated to San Nicolas de Tolentino. The church became known as San Juan de Bagumbayan. It sheltered the image of Our Lady of Health (*Nuestra Señora de la Salud*) which soon had a regular cult.

The Recollect provincial was Fray Juan de San Jeronimo, who had himself negotiated in Rome the separation of the Recollects from the regular Augustinians.

Because of the threat of Dutch invasions and the unabating fears of uprisings by the Chinese in Parian and the Japanese in Dilao nearby, the Governor-General Don Sebastian Hurtado de Corcuera ordered all constructions of heavy material in the vicinity of the Walled City torn down. These buildings could be used as vantage points in a siege on the Walled City. Among those demolished was the Recollect property in Bagumbayan. In its place the governor-general ordered a fort erected. The governor-general would have cause to rue this action at his *residencia*, the administrative inquiry at the end of his term.The Recollects filed suit for indemnity for their demolished church and monastery. They won their suit. The outgoing governor was ordered to pay the sum of P25,000, and the plot of land was restored to the Recollects. The fort was torn down, and the Recollects built a new church and monastery on the spot.

In 1762 the British used the church of San Juan de Bagumbayan, together with the churches of Malate and Ermita, precisely as a staging point for their bombardment of the Walled City. When the British left in 1764, the authorities again had all heavy constructions within cannon shot of the walls torn down.

A sympathetic governor-general offered the Recollects a piece of land inside the walls, on Cabildo street, near the San Andres bastion.[21] Here the Recollect Fathers built a great edifice which turned out to be among the grandest in the area. Its belltower was considered an architectural masterwork. After the holocaust of World War II the belltower alone, along with some of the church walls, stood amidst the desolation.

During their heyday in Bagumbayan, the church of the Recollects was the center of a colorful celebration under the auspices of the religious brotherhood, *Transito de Nuestra Señora de la Salud.* Its procession on the third Friday of Lent was a grand event, marked by great display of religious fervor and much pageantry.

When it was re-established in Intramuros, the Recollect church remained the center of grand Lenten celebrations. On Palm Sunday evening, the procession of the Nazarene issued forth from the Recollect church. This is described by Quijano de Manila as a "classic procession, with *pasos* in violet robes and leafy crowns, the *Hermandad* in formal suits, the clergy carrying decorated palms, and antique lamps illuminating the stages of the Passion: the *Oración en el Huerto,* the *Señor de la Columna,* the *Paciencia* and the *Nazareno,* the last being the oldest image of Christ with the Cross in the Philippines, and to whose shrine the gentlefolk went on pilgrimage on Fridays."[22]

THE JESUITS. The first two Jesuit priests to arrive in Manila came with the city's first bishop, the Dominican Fray Domingo de Salazar, in March 1581. They were the Reverend Fathers Alonzo Sanchez and Antonio Sedeño.[23] They were accompanied by the Jesuit lay brother Nicolas Gallardo.

The two priests were distinguished men, but the second, Antonio Sedeño, was a very talented person who as a young man had been diplomat, soldier and engineer. As a Jesuit missionary he had served in Florida and in Mexico.

Father Sedeño introduced to the Philippines the cultivation of mulberry trees basic to the production of silk, taught Chinese artisans the rudiments of Christian iconography, and probably his most lasting monument, he introduced the manufacture of brick, tile and lime and taught the natives how to work stone. Father Sedeño would be instrumental in the construction of the walls of Intramuros. He was known as the "Tireless Jesuit" for the wide variety of his interests and the intensity of his dedication, and would devote the rest of his life to the Philippines.

At first, though, Padre Sedeño did not seem to see many prospects for the Jesuits in the Philippines and he wrote his superior suggesting that the Order withdraw from this country.

When Bishop Salazar heard this be pleaded with Padre Sedeño to stay and wrote the King suggesting that a college be opened in Manila to be operated by the Jesuits. The governor-general and Padre Sedeño himself endorsed the suggestion to the King.

By Royal Decree dated 8 June 1585, the King ordered that ways and means be found to sustain this college. The governor replied that while everyone agreed with the need for a college, the only way to sustain it would be from the Royal Treasury or directly from Mexico.

Meanwhile, Padre Prado arrived in Manila in 1584 and proceeded to conduct a course in theology without waiting for the establishment of a college.

But Captain Esteban Rodriguez de Figueroa seems to have started the ball rolling for the funding of a college because when Father Alonzo Sanchez, as procurator general, arrived in Rome in 1586, he reported this matter to the Father General of the Jesuits.

In 1589, Rome gave the title "Collegium" to the Manila venture, and Padre Sedeño was referred to as "Rector."

The previous year, in 1588, the Audiencia in Manila sent to the King an unfavorable report against starting a college in Manila. There followed a silence for the next seven years.

The matter was reopened in 1595 when the Jesuits presented to the Acting Governor General Don Luis Perez Dasmariñas the King's Decree of 1585. The governor agreed with the proposal to establish a college and allocated P1000 for this purpose with permission to the use of the title "Royal" and the Royal coat of arms. This permit was tentative, however, pending approval of the bishop and the King.

The school that started under this condition was for Spanish boys. In November 1595, the college received a gift from Capt. Esteban Rodriguez de Figueroa who allocated P1500 a year to the school and assumed a P6000 debt that the school Padre Prado started had incurred. Now the college was committed to have the government's funds pay for the education of native boys and Figueroa's gift pay for the education of the Spanish boys.[24]

In 1589 the King authorized the construction of a Jesuit house of studies, or formative college, in Manila, where in succeeding years theology, morals and the arts were taught. Subsequently, the Jesuits also started classes in Latin for boys.

In 1610, Capt. Esteban Rodriguez de Figueroa made a grant to found a college for boys, which was placed under the direction of the Jesuits. It would become the College of San Jose, built on the land assigned to the Society of Jesus between the Puerta Real and the Bastion San Diego along the walls.

In 1722, the King conferred the title "Royal" on the College of San Jose. Next to it was established the famed Beaterio de la Compañia, a community of native and half-breed women founded in 1694 by a Chinese-Filipino mestiza, Madre Ignacia del Espiritu Santo.

On 19 May 1767, the troops of Governor Jose Raon, complying with orders from Madrid, surrounded the Jesuit premises and, to the martial beating of drums, the religious marched out to the quays where a ship waited to bring them to Cadiz in Spain. The Jesuits had been expelled from every Spanish territory. Some 158 Jesuits had served in the Philippines by the time they were expelled. During this period they had founded 93 towns and ministered to 209,527 souls.

The Jesuit College of San Jose was turned over to the secular clergy. By the end of the 18th century it was in a state of decay. The Jesuit convent would have been taken over by the archbishop for use as a diocesan seminary, but the King found strong opposition to this, and the permit he had issued earlier was revoked.

This Jesuit corner of Intramuros would never recover. In what were once the gardens would be built the barracks for the Regiments of Asia and the Ligere. The church of San Ignacio fell into disuse and ruin. Modifications were made on the city fortifications at the end of the 18th century. The old building of San Jose was torn down when the Puerta Real was moved to align it with the Calle Real de Palacio.

In 1852, the government in Madrid permitted the return of the Jesuits to the archipelago, this time as missionaries in Mindanao. By 1893, towards the end of Spanish rule over the Philippines, there would be 132 Jesuits in the country. They were in charge of 33 towns and 223 missions and cared for 200,184 souls.

The Jesuits now relocated their convent to a lot across from the Santa Lucia gate. The series of earthquakes in 1880 brought the old San Ignacio church into final ruin. The sidewall fell on Calle Real de Palacio and the roof of the old seminary collapsed.

Next to the earlier edifice near the Santa Lucia gate the Jesuits built the new church of San Ignacio. George Miller, writing in 1912, would describe San Ignacio as "the bijou of Intramuros."[25]

"It is thoroughly modern in design and execution, and its exterior is destitute of comeliness," George Miller writes, "but the interior leaves nothing to ask in ravishing beauty and decoration."

The ornate interiors made good use of Philippine woods, "in carved molave and the design and finish of the work are of rich artistic merit," using Miller's words.

The ceiling was handcarved wooden filigree, the columns and arches richly adorned with exquisite tracery, and George Miller enthused about the natural and life-like figures.

He described the pulpit as a masterwork "worth going a long distance to see. Its bas-reliefs of gospel subjects are executed with a fineness of detail that is more remarkable when one is informed that the work was all done by native artists under the direction, of course, of the missionary architect."

Nick Joaquin described the church of San Ignacio as having "the most modern atmosphere (being managed by American Jesuits)."[26]

The Jesuit church was famous for the traditional Seven Last Words sermon on the afternoon of Good Friday, which was delivered in English. The feast of the Immaculate Conception on December 8 was a big celebration here. The first shrine of St. Therese of Lisieux whose cult is very popular in the Philippines was set up at San Ignacio.

ATENEO DE MANILA. In 1859, six Jesuit priests and four lay brothers arrived in Manila and while they prepared to go south to Mindanao, the governor general entrusted to them the direction of a small municipal school which had been established on Calle de Arzobispo. It was called *Escuela Pia*, a public school created by the municipal council of Manila.[27]

In 1865, the *Escuela Pia* was recognized by the government in Madrid as a college of two levels (elementary and high school). A new course of studies was approved that year and the school was renamed Ateneo Municipal de Manila.

The first group of graduates with the degree of bachelor of arts was turned out in March 1870, the first time this degree was conferred in the Philippines.

Under the American regime, the school was renamed Ateneo de Manila in 1901, and the subsidy from the municipal government ceased. In 1906, it was authorized to confer academic degrees by the American administration.

Radical changes took place in the Ateneo with the arrival of the Americans Jesuits on 12 July 1921. After 63 years, the Spanish Jesuits withdrew and the Americans from the Maryland-New York Jesuit Province took over. The Philippine organization became part of the Jesuit province of Maryland-New York. By that year, there were 46 Filipinos, 53 Americans and 77 Spaniards in the Philippine Jesuit organization.

The old Ateneo building in Intramuros burned down 13 August 1932. After one month the school reopened at the former site of the College of San Jose on almost six hectares of land on Padre Faura street in Ermita.

LA IGNACIANA. This property on Herran street in Santa Ana was acquired by the Jesuits in 1862 from Maximino M.A. Paterno, for the sum of P11,500. Because of its location on the Pasig, it was called "Jesus of the Riviera" *(El Jesus de la Ribera).* It was used as a retreat house for laymen and priests who came to take the spiritual exercises of the Jesuits.[28]

In time the old property fell into desrepair, and a new one was constructed on the same site. It was inaugurated on 17 October 1931, and named La Ignaciana.

THE CONGREGATION OF THE MISSION. Vincent de Paul (1530-1660) was ordained a priest at the age of twenty and for the rest of his life would labor for the poor. He organized lay people who shared his persuasions to assist him in his work, and in 1625 there emerged the Congregation of the Mission whose members would later become well-known as Vincentians. They were dedicated to missionary work and to the training of priests. From France, Vincentians would spread everywhere in the world.

The Congregation of the Mission of St. Vincent de Paul was authorized to serve in the Philippines by the Royal Decree of 1852 issued by Queen Isabela II.[29]

However the Vincentians would not arrive in Manila until 1862, when the Royal Decree of 1852 was implemented by the incumbent Governor General Don Rafael Echague y Berminhan.

The first Vincentians to arrive in Manila, 21 July 1862, were the Fathers Gregorio Velasco and Ildefonso Moral, with two lay assistants. With them were fifteen Daughters of Charity.

Shortly after their arrival, the archbishop of Manila Don Gregorio Meliton Martinez, turned over to the Vincentians the administration of the Manila seminary. From thereon the principal mission of the Vincentians in the Philippines was the operation of seminaries.

From their arrival in Manila in 1862, the Vincentian Fathers resided at the San Carlos seminary at the corner of Victoria and Palacio (General Luna) streets in Intramuros, which in earlier times had housed the San Ignacio college of the Jesuits.

In 1875, the Vincentians bought a six hectare lot in the barrio called San Marcelino outside the walls where they built a vacation house for professors and students of the seminary. A chapel was also built on the site which was opened to the faithful.

In 1880, a larger chapel was built, but when the San Carlos seminary building in Intramuros fell to ruin in the great earthquake that year, the seminarians were lodged in the newly-constructed chapel, so it was not used for religious services.

In 1884, Padre Pedro Payo, the archbishop of Manila, ordered the construction of a new building between the Jesuit church and the archbishop's palace in Intramuros, and the seminary was restored here. The seminarians lodged in the chapel of the Vincentians at San Marcelino moved to the new seminary building, and the chapel was opened to the public for religious services.

In 1890, the former vacation house of the Vincentians in San Marcelino was designated the Order's Central House and official residence of the provincial of the Order in the Philippines.

When armed hostilities broke out between the invading American forces and the Filipino revolutionary army in February 1899, the parish church of Paco was razed to the ground by the Americans. They had been misinformed that the church harbored enemy troops, and subjected it to bomb and shell. They killed a sacristan and the Franciscan parish priest fled.

For a while the Paco parish had no priest and no church, until Archbishop Bernardino Nozaleda who had succeeded Padre Payo requested the Vincentians to assign a parish priest and allow the use of their San Marcelino chapel as a temporary parish church for Paco.

The Vincentians acceded to this request and on 20 February 1899, Fr. Gregorio Tabar took over as interim parish priest. The St. Vincent chapel served as parish church, although Father Tabar said mass on Sundays at the Catholic chapel on Peñafrancia street in Paco district. This was the situation when the Paco parish was turned over to the Belgian missionaries of the Congregation of the Immaculate Heart of Mary.

On 6 December 1909, however, the American archbishop of Manila Jeremiah J. Harty decreed the creation of the new parish of St. Vincent de Paul, and the former chapel of the Vincentian Central House and seminary became the parish church.

Plans for a building worthy enough to be a parish church were laid out on the site of the old chapel, intended to be inaugurated during the celebration of the 50th anniversary of the arrival of the Vincentians in the Philippines in 1912.

The church was not finished on time for the event, however, and would not be consecrated until 16 July 1913. This was the church that would be destroyed in the events of February 1945, by then well-known as the sanctuary of Our Lady of the Miraculous Medal.

THE SEMINARY OF SAN CARLOS. The major seminary of Manila was opened on 15 June 1913 in Mandaluyong. Named after St. Charles Borromeo, the seminary also operated a college for boys called Santa Mesa college which offered courses on the elementary, high school and collegiate levels. The major seminary was established by the first American archbishop of Manila, Mons. Jeremiah J. Harty, as a source of priests for the archiocese.

In 1919, the new archbishop, Mons. Michael O'Doherty, decided to close the Santa Mesa college to concentrate resources on the seminary. In 1920 the seminary was moved to San Marcelino street in the main house of the Vincentian Fathers. It was named St. Vincent college, and functioned both as a major and minor seminary. In 1927 it was designated as the major seminary of Manila, with the minor seminary established separately.

The Paules church and the adjoining archdiocesan major seminary on San Marcelino street in Ermita were built on land which, in the early 17th century, was known as the Japanese village. Here Japanese Christians fleeing the persecutions of the Tokugawa shogun were provided sanctuary by the Spanish authorities. The community was headed by the Japanese Christian *daimyo* Takayama Ukon, known in Spanish records by his Christian name, Justo Ukondono.

The first chapel on this site was built in 1875. This chapel served as the parish church of Paco from 1898 to 1909. In 1909 the parish of St. Vincent de Paul was established, and this chapel became the first parish church. The concrete building here was completed in 1913 and consecrated that year to commemorate the 50th anniversary of the arrival of the Congregation of the Mission of St. Vincent de Paul in the Philippines. It was destroyed in the events of World War II.

The Paules church was the first shrine in the Philippines of Our Lady of the Miraculous Medal. The cult of the Miraculous Medal is of recent dâte, originating from the apparitions of the Virgin Mary before a postulant named Catherine Labouré, in a convent of the Daughters of Charity on Rue Le Bac in Paris, France. It became one of the most popular Marian cults in the Philippines.

From 3 March to 15 December 1942, the Japanese archbishop of Osaka, Monsignor Taguchi, lived in the Vincentian convent while on a goodwill mission to the Filipino Christian nation in behalf of the Japanese government. In September 1942, Archbishop Taguchi co-officiated the ceremonies honoring the Christian *daimyo*, Takayama Ukon.[30]

THE DAUGHTERS OF CHARITY OF ST. VINCENT DE PAUL. The Daughters of Charity of St. Vincent de Paul came to Manila mainly because Governor General Rafael de Echague y Berminhan, upon assuming office in 1862, recalled a Royal Decree issued by Queen Isabela II ten years earlier, authorizing the Order to serve in the Philippines. For various reasons, the Queen's Decree had not been implemented.

Governor Echague had served in the war in Africa and had seen there the beneficent work of the Daughters of Charity. Now with the support of the Archbishop Don Gregorio Meliton Martinez, the new governor proceeded to implement the Royal Order of 1852.

The first members of the Congregation of the Mission and the Daughters of Charity arrived in Manila, 21 July 1862, on board the frigate *Concepcion.* The Daughters of Charity who numbered fifteen were led by Sister Tiburcia Ayanz.

The Order had its beginning when St. Vincent de Paul organized a group of women, married and single, with the permission of their husbands and fathers, respectively, to assist in the care of the poor and the sick in their own parishes. St. Vincent was assisted in this activity by a noblewoman named Louise de Marillac. Later, the education of the underprivileged was added to the work of the Order.

A month after their arrival in Manila, the Daughters of Charity were dispersed to their respective tasks. Some were sent to hospitals as nurses and others to schools as teachers. From this date, 21 August 1862, began a great mission that touched on vital aspects of Philippine life and would color richly the fabric of the country's history.

As nurses and educators, the work of the Daughters of Charity in Manila and other parts of the Philippines would become milestones and the institutions they built great landmarks.

SANTA ISABEL COLLEGE. Among the schools where the Daughters of Charity were assigned was the Santa Isabel college.

The Santa Isabel college has its origin in the *Hermandad de la Santa Misericordia.* In the beginning the Hermandad's work was confined to supporting the Hospitalito de Santa Ana. The board of directors, composed mostly of military officers and commonly referred to as the Santa Mesa, had seen the laudable work of the College of Santa Potenciana for the orphanned daughters of Spanish soldiers. The board decided to open another college, much as the Santa Potenciana was, this one to serve the orphanned daughters of Spanish civilians.

By resolution of the Santa Mesa dated 24 October 1632, a college named Santa Isabel was established. The college honored Queen Isabel de Borbon, the first wife of King Philip II.

The Santa Isabel college was first housed on rented property. Between 1631 and 1634, a building and an adjoining church were built on property across from the San Agustin church, at the corner of Recogida and Calle Real de Palacio, largely from gifts of Captains Pedro Alvares, Francisco Roman and Gaspar Alvares. The first administrator was Doña Catalina de Aguirre. In 1733, Santa Isabel college was placed under Royal patronage.

The college prospered and by 1800, the modest facilities had grown into a grand edifice, spacious and richly furnished. This building was badly damaged in the earthquake of 1863. The following year, the college was placed under the administration of the Daughters of Charity who undertook the rehabilitation work. Under the Daughters of Charity, the college acquired new eminence as an educational institution for women.

In 1866, the Santa Isabel college absorbed the College of Santa Potenciana. This was the first school for girls in Manila, established in 1589 by authority of King Philip II, at the instance of Bishop de Salazar and the Franciscan Fathers.[31]

The college took into its care the orphanned daughters of Spanish soldiers and gave them the education of the time. The college was housed in a wooden building erected on a lot donated by Captain Luis de Vivanco at the corner of Calle Real de Palacio and Santa Potenciana street in Intramuros.

This building collapsed to the ground in the earthquake of 1645, and succeeding buildings, though built of stone, suffered the same fate in subsequent earthquakes. By the end of the 18th century, the college was in such condition that it had to be abandoned, and the inmates had to be housed in a private property.

The old premises were reconstructed, however, and expanded into grander dimensions. In 1863 the palace of the governor-general tumbled down in the great earthquake that year, and the incumbent had to find housing in Malacañang.

The succeeding governor, Don Manuel de Lara Irigoyen, apparently at the instigation of his wife, refused to live in Malacañang, on the ground that it was not sumptuous enough. Governor de Lara maneuvered the merger of the College of Santa Potenciana with the College of Santa Isabel, thus leaving the premises of the former vacant, and which the governor took over in 1866 as his new residence.

Succeeding governors chose to live in Malacañang, however, but the former Santa Potenciana premises stayed in government hands. Part of it became the residence of the military commander of the islands and other parts became the headquarters of the Infantry, Cavalry, Carbineers and the Civil Guard. This building was ruined in the earthquake of 1880, but was subsequently restored. Infront of this building the first demonstrations against Spanish rule were held by Filipino militants. In the final days of Spanish sovereignty over these islands, the governor-general took up residence here. Here General Fermin Jaudenes, the last man to hold the title, received the American delegation to whom he transferred authority over the city of Manila.

LA CONCORDIA COLLEGE. Among those who welcomed the Daughters of Charity upon their arrival in Manila in 1862, was the wealthy and civic-minded Doña Margarita Roxas de Ayala, daughter of the merchant Don Domingo Roxas, and wife of another merchant, Don Antonio de Ayala.[32]

Doña Margarita owned a big estate in Paco, named La Concordia where she maintained a countryhouse. She donated the estate, with her countryhouse, to the Daughters of Charity to be used as an orphanage and also as a school for poor girls. The college of La Concordia opened on 3 May 1868.

The original countryhome proved too small for the purposes of the college, so Doña Margarita undertook to raise the amount necessary to construct new buildings.

La Concordia grew into a very distinguished educational institution for women and became the motherhouse of the Daughters of Charity in the Philippines.

THE ASILO DE LOOBAN. The Asilo de Looban de San Vicente de Paul developed from the devotion of Sister Asuncion Ventura-Horcoma Bautista. Born in Bacolor, Pampanga, 30 July 1853, she studied as a young girl at La Concordia college. Influenced by the religious environment and encouraged by her family, she sought admission into the Order of the Daughters of Charity. She took the veil on 19 March 1875 and spent her novitiate at La Concordia college.[33]

Sister Asuncion's parents bequeathed her vast wealth. To provide for the work of the Asilo de Looban she acquired with her own funds the three-hectare site on what later became Isaac Peral street, in Looban. The board of the Daughters of Charity secured a loan on 13 June 1884 with which to start work on the site. When the construction was finished, the permit to operate was granted by Governor Terrero on 11 June 1885.

On 25 November 1885 Sister Asuncion joined the Asilo de Looban community and remained there until her death on 22 November 1923. She devoted her personal wealth to the asylum. She also sustained the Paco Catholic school and had the classes transferred to the Asilo premises.

THE COLLEGE OF SANTA ROSA. Madre Paula de la Santissima Trinidad of the Third Order of St. Dominic, was a native of Apluxucelba, Lerida, in the Catalan regions of Spain. She arrived in Manila in 1750. She was almost denied passage on the galleon in Mexico but a fortuitous hurricane caused the galleon to return to port, in turn causing the superstitious captain to change his mind and take the nun as a passenger. She carried with her a small statue of *The Child Jesus As A Pilgrim.*[34]

Madre Paula's mission in Manila was to establish a school for native girls. For this purpose she rented a house near Santo Domingo church, which she also turned into a *beaterio*. She named the institution the College of Santa Rosa, after the first saint of the Americas, who like her had been a member of the Third Order of St. Dominic in her native city of Lima, Peru. In her will Madre Paula placed the college under the patronage of the King, with the provincial of the Recollects as president of the board of management.

On 19 January 1866, upon the death of the incumbent director, the president of the board of management asked the Daughters of Charity to undertake the administration of the College of Santa Rosa.

Originally, the college occupied only a part of the property at the corner of Plaza Santo Tomas and Calle Solana in Intramuros. On the groundfloor of this building was the chapel in which the statue of *The Child Jesus As A Pilgrim* that had accompanied the founder on her voyage across the Pacific was enshrined. The earthquake of 1863 wrought severe damages on the building and for a long time repair work was not undertaken. When the Daughters of Charity, led by Sister Gervasia Sanchez, assumed control over the institution in 1866, they immediately undertook restoration work and acquired the entire property.

In 1876, Sister Josefa Nuñez was appointed supervisor of the College of Santa Rosa. A gifted administrator with great business acumen, Sister Nunez undertook extensive renovation work and succeeded in establishing a modern plant for the college. Her work was of such magnitude and of far-reaching significance that Sister Nuñez is referred to traditionally as the second founder of Santa Rosa. It was ranked among the most outstanding schools in the Philippines when World War II broke out in 1941.

It was the building that Sister Josefa Nuñez had labored on that went up in flames in the Japanese bombing of Manila towards the end of 1941. By February 1945, only the walls of the old Santa Rosa college stood, and these had been badly battered by the American bombardments.

THE CAPUCHIN FATHERS. The Order of Capuchin Friars was founded by Mateo Bassi and gained Papal approval in 1528. The Capuchins adopted the rules of St. Francis of Assisi and are sometimes referred to as a "branch" of the Franciscan Order.[35]

When Germany filed protests over the Carolinas, the Queen Regent in Spain had to reorganize the civil and ecclesiastic government of those islands on the Pacific.

On 15 March 1886, the Capuchins were officially named "Overseas Missionaries." To administer their Carolinas mission better, they established a procurement house in Manila, under Fr. Bernardo M. de Gieza.

In 1890 they opened a small chapel on Calle Real de Palacio in Intramuros. The chapel was subsequently enlarged into a church dedicated to Our Lady of Lourdes. It was consecrated in 1910.

The cult of Lourdes started in a town by this name in the south of France by the Pyrenees in 1858, when the Virgin Mary was reported to have appeared before a peasant girl, Bernadette Soubirous. The Capuchin church was the first Lourdes shrine in the Philippines.

"Capuchinos in Intramuros was very small, hardly more than a chapel," Nick Joaquin recalls, "without even a patio." But it had what Joaquin describes as a "modern look," and it became popular among Manilans for the Lourdes devotion.[36]

"By the late 30's," Nick Joaquin writes, "the Saturday crowds at Capuchinos had become phenomenal."[37]

Joaquin tells of the Lourdes fiesta: "On the evening of February 11, at Capuchinos in Intramuros, the tiples intoned the *Magnificat* and like a miracle, the image of the Virgin slowly emerged from the grotto high up on the altar and rung by rung, descended the silvery stairway down to the floor for the *ceremonia de besa-pies*."[38]

According to tradition, Manilans of Intramuros and places beyond had gathered at the Capuchinos that day in May 1898 when the commander of the American squadron on Manila bay, Commodore George Dewey, gave the order to fire on the Spanish fleet ranged in battle array before the old Fort San Felipe in Cavite. The Manilans prayed as one to the Virgin, begging that their city be spared by the guns of the new invader.

The city indeed was spared from the American guns. What happened in February 1945 was a different story. The Capuchin church went the way of the other edifices inside the Walled City. But the image of Our Lady of Lourdes had been moved to San Agustin church.[39] Providentially, this was the only structure left more or less whole after the holocaust.

CONGREGATION OF THE SISTERS OF THE ASSUMPTION. The Congregation of the Sisters of the Assumption was founded by a Frenchwoman named Ana Eugenia Milleret de Brou, who was born in Metz, 25 August 1817.[40]

Upon the death of her mother, Mlle. Milleret left for Paris at the age of 19 and came under the spiritual direction of Rev. Fr. Combalot. Mlle. Milleret became Mother Eugenia de Jesus when she entered the Convent of the Visitation. In Paris she organized a group of women to run schools for the children of the privileged classes. The first members of the new religious Order got together for the first time on 30 April 1839 in Paris and occupied rented quarters. The Order gained new adherents and spread to other countries, including Spain.

Acceding to a request of the Queen Regent of Spain, the first group of Spanish Assumption Sisters arrived in Manila in 1892. They opened the *Escuela Normal Superior de Maestras*, a training institution for women-teachers. They also opened a free school for the children of the poor. The first supervisor was R.M. Maria del Perpetuo Socorro.

The first Assumption school was located on Calle Anda in Intramuros. In 1895, the school was transferred to a new site at the corner of what later became known as Herran and Dakota streets in Ermita. This was formerly the site of Hospital de Santiago, as the old Royal hospital for the Spanish was called by this time. The Assumption school had three departments, a normal school, a school for girls, and a free school.

The outbreak of the revolution against Spain in 1898 caused the suspension of classes. The Spanish Assumption Sisters were taken aboard an English ship on the bay by the English consul. While awaiting the turn of events at the harbor, the ship was ordered to Hong Kong. The Sisters also had to go to Hong Kong where they were taken in by the Sisters of St. Paul de Chartres.

The Assumption Sisters did not return to Manila again until 1904, when under the new dispensation they were invited by the American Archbishop Jeremiah J. Harty to resume their work. The new group was led by a young Irishwoman, Mother Helen Margaret, who directed the Assumption Convent until her death in 1927.

CONGREGATION OF THE SISTERS OF ST. PAUL DE CHARTRES. This congregation was founded by the French priest M. l'Abbe Chouvet, curate of Levesvelle, Beouce, 25 kilometers from Chartres, in France. Organized to provide religious care and education to children of the poor, the members were first called Daughters of the School (*Filles de l'Ecole*).[41]

In 1703, the bishop of Chartres, Mons. Paul Godet des Marets, invited the members of the group to his diocese and gave them his patron's name. The Order's patron has since been St. Paul the Apostle of the Gentiles, and its members became known as Sisters of St. Paul de Chartres. Since 1727 the Order has spread to America and Asia.

The first Sisters of St. Paul de Chartres in the Philippines arrived in 1904, upon invitation of Bishop Rooker of Jaro (Iloilo). They took charge of a school in Dumaguete which Bishop Rooker founded.

In 1910 they established a novitiate in Manila. In 1933 they moved their novitiate to New Manila (Quezon City).

In 1912, the Order acquired the property on the Malate side of Herran street, bordered on the other three sides by L. Guerrero, Tennessee and Florida streets. This was still swampland and the nuns themselves undertook improvements on their property. The wooden buildings erected on the compound housed the novitiate.

That year of 1912, the nuns acceded to a request of residents in their Malate neighborhood to assume care of their pre-school children during day-hours. This was the beginning of St. Paul's Institution. From the kindergarten which had an enrollment of six, the Sisters of St. Paul added one grade in the elementary course every succeeding year. By 1915, enrollment had reached 300 and the original buildings had to be expanded. Intended for girls, the school admitted boys up to the second grade. In 1919, the school was granted government recognition. In 1924, the first year of the high school opened with three students. By 1928 when the first three high school students graduated, enrolment in both elementary and high school had reached almost 600.

In 1927, the St. Paul chapel was erected on the Herran campus, even as the school modernized its facilities following continuous expansion. The chapel was remarkable for the huge crucifix on its facade. It became a popular landmark, visible even from passing aircraft.

During the 1936-37 schoolyear, St. Paul opened its collegiate department, with offerings in the normal, secretarial and education courses.

In 1940, the school officially changed its name of St. Paul's Institution to St. Paul college of Manila. For the first time, it conferred baccalaureate degrees.

St. Paul had always had a high reputation for excellence. Under the dynamic leadership of Sister St. Xavier, a modernization program was launched. She adopted the policy of having the teaching nuns take graduate studies in education and for the nursing nuns to take formal nursing courses to better prepare them for their hospital work.

When World War II broke out in 1941, St. Paul de Chartres nurses were serving at the Clinica Singian, Lourdes hospital (Baguio), Hospital Espanol de Santiago in Makati, St. Joseph hospital, and the Quezon Institute. In 1942 the patients of the Quezon Institute were moved to the San Juan de Dios hospital in Intramuros, a section of which was designated Philippine Tuberculosis hospital.

THE BELGIAN SISTERS. Commonly known in Manila as the Belgian Sisters, the Congregation of the Missionary Cannonesses of St. Augustine was brought to the Philippines by the Rev. Mother Marie Louise de Meester, a native of Roulers, Belgium, where she was born, 8 April 1857.[42]

Mother Marie Louise joined the Cannonesses of St. Augustine in Ypres, Belgium, as a young girl. For several years she taught in a school for girls.

On 13 August 1894, she left Belgium with another nun for India where she founded an orphanage in Mulaganadou, in the south of Travancore. Her work prospered, and from India her mission expanded to the Philippines and the West Indies.

In May 1910, Mother de Meester left Colombo with four other nuns of her Order for Manila. She opened her first mission in Tagudin, Ilocos Sur, on 21 June 1910. From there her work spread to other parts of the Ilocos and to the Mountain Province.

The Cannonesses were later invited to Manila by Archbishop Jeremiah J. Harty. They opened a school for girls which was inaugurated on 1 June 1915, on the site on San Marcelino street earlier occupied by the school of the Benedictine Sisters. It was first known as the Dormitory of St. Theresa. Later it became known as the Academy of St. Theresa until it was renamed the College of St. Theresa.

At first it functioned as a dormitory, with an elementary school for boarders and non-boarders. In 1917 the high school department was opened. The college department opened in 1925. The campus expanded and the plant developed into a fine example of modern school-building design.

THE BENEDICTINE SISTERS. On 14 September 1906, there arrived from Genoa by way of Hong Kong, five Benedictine Sisters who had been invited by Mons. Ambrosio Agius, O.S.B., to serve in Manila. They opened their first school in the Tondo district.

In 1907 they moved their school to a bigger site across from the Paules church on San Marcelino street. Seven years later in 1914, the Benedictine Sisters moved to their permanent site on Pennsylvania street in Singalong. They named their school after St. Scholastica.

THE BROTHERS OF THE CHRISTIAN SCHOOLS. The Christian Brothers arrived in Manila in 1911 when the Catholic authorities stood in fear that Philippine education was falling into Protestant hands.[44] The Spanish clergy had withdrawn from the islands. Education had become a secular matter. Of 35 or 36 American school superintendents, only one was Catholic. Nearly all the American teachers who came over on the *U.S.S. Thomas* were Protestant. The country had been apportioned among the Protestant sects for purposes of evangelization. The Episcopalians had established an educational center in Baguio and the Presbyterians another in Dumaguete. There was need to re-establish Catholic education and locate a focal point.

The Christian Brothers came to the Philippines through the persistence of Mons. Jeremiah J. Harty, the first American archbishop of

Manila, who was a graduate of the Christian Brothers' college in St. Louis, Missouri.

Archbishop Harty had made repeated requests to the Christian Brothers to establish schools in the Philippines. A team of Christian Brothers had been to Manila in 1907 to conduct a survey and consult with the authorities, but nothing developed from that venture.

There were policy conditions that needed to be satisfied, failing which the Christian Brothers withheld positive action. The financing problem was foremost. The archdiocese of Manila could not underwrite the costs of a free school, and the Christian Brothers would not operate schools for the rich. The original vocation of St. John Baptist de la Salle who founded the Institute of Brothers of the Christian Schools in 1680 was the education of the children of the poor and the working classes.

During a visit to Rome in 1911, Archbishop Harty brought the matter of having the Christian Brothers in Manila directly to Pope St. Pius X. The Pope prodded the Christian Brothers forward through a letter to their Superior General at Lembecq, Belgium. On 19 March 1911, a three-man team led by Bro. Blimond Pierre arrived in Manila.

The three were joined shortly by Bro. Adolphe Alfred from Barcelona who was experienced in handling matters such as were required by the projected school. It was Bro. Alfred who negotiated the purchase of the lot at 417 Nozaleda street in Paco from Don Luis Perez Samanillo, for the school campus. The building on the lot had earlier been used by the American school. At a latter time, this address would become 1166 General Luna street. The Christian Brothers took possession of the property 27 April 1911.

DE LA SALLE COLLEGE. With the arrival of six other Christian Brothers on 13 May 1911, the school was now adequately staffed.

On 16 June 1911, the new school, named De la Salle college, after the founder of the Order, opened with an enrollment of 125 boys. Brother Blimond Pierre became the first director.

Since the archdiocese could not fund a free school, De la Salle college became a tuition school. It took in "upperclass children," whose rich parents could underwrite the costs, on the presumption that such children also needed "good moral and spiritual training." There were but few Filipino children in the early De la Salle college classes. Most students were Americans, Spaniards and Germans.

Illness caused Bro. Blimond Pierre to return to France in May 1912. He was succeeded by Bro. Goslin Camillus. That year, four other Christian Brothers arrived to augment the teaching staff, among whom was Bro. Egbert Xavier, an Irish national.

The Manila mission of the Christian Brothers prospered eminently and by 1915, it was evident that the General Luna property in Paco was inadequate. Bro. Aciselus Michael who had become director, negotiated the purchase of 30,300 sq.m. of land on Taft Avenue in the Singalong district. This area was the southern parameter of the city at this time. Vito Cruz street was only a proposal in city plans. The Rizal Stadium was not in anyone's mind and the site on which it would rise in another score of years was called Malate Park.

The Christian Brothers contemplated a modern educational plant on the site. The plans were drawn by Tomas Mapua, a graduate of Cornell University in Ithaca, New York. It would cost P200,000.On 11 November 1917, De la Salle college was authorized to confer academic degrees. It introduced a four-year high school course and withdrew the 3-year commercial high school curriculum. Three new Brothers arrived in 1919, among whom was Bro. Flavius Leo.

In 1920, the Paco property was sold to the businessman Vicente Madrigal. That year, Bro. Albinus Peter succeeded Bro. Michael as Director. Construction on the Taft Avenue campus began on April 1921. Japanese workers were engaged for the construction work and Chinese craftsmen were called in to make the doors and window sashes.

On 24 September 1921, although only the first floor and half of the second floor were finished, the Christian Brothers took possession of their new campus and the student body moved over. Construction work did not resume until the following year when Bro. Michael returned for a second term as director. It was Bro. Michael who acquired the adjoining 30,300 sq.m. lot to double the size of the De la Salle campus.

In 1937, Bro. Egbert Xavier became president-director of the De la Salle college. Bro. Xavier would make his mark on this institution by completing the north and south wings of the building on Taft Avenue.

Bro. Egbert Xavier was born William Kelly in Wicklow county, Ireland, in 1894. He first came to Manila at the age of 18, when De la Salle college had just started operations at the old Paco campus. He returned to the Order's Motherhouse in Belgium for his second novitiate in 1929, completing which he was posted to missionary work in Burma and Hong Kong. He returned to Manila from Hong Kong in 1935, and in 1937 succeeded to the premiere post at De la Salle college.

Bro. Xavier was destined to play a key role in future events at De la Salle. For the present he won compliments for the new chapel on the second floor of the south wing which was completed in August 1938. Dedicated to the Blessed Sacrament, it was blessed by the archbishop of Manila 8 December that year. It had a beautiful marble altar, the gift of former Director Bro. Albinus Peter, in memory of his parents.

In August 1939, the south wing was finally completed. What emerged on the 6.6 hectare lot was a three-storeyed, H-shaped building in the neo-classical style which became a very impressive landmark in this section of the city.

Following the outbreak of the war in Europe, the British expelled German nationals from their territories. On 8 July 1940, two German Brothers arrived in Manila from Hong Kong. Ten more came, 10 October 1940, from Singapore and Malaya.

De la Salle college was a flourishing institution when World War II broke out in the Philippines, 8 December 1941. It had a student body of 1,200 in all three levels, and a complement of 27 Christian Brothers in residence.

Classes were suspended when the Japanese started bombing objectives in Manila in December 1941. For a while, military personnel were quartered in the premises. Later, De la Salle was used as an emergency hospital to receive the overflow of war-injured at the Sternberg hospital at the corner of Arroceros and Concepcion streets.

When the Japanese occupied the city of Manila in January 1942, they established their Southern Manila Defense Headquarters at the De la Salle college building. Only the south wing was left to the Christian Brothers whose numbers were reduced following the internment of Allied nationals. Some of the American Brothers went to Baguio. Others were interned at Los Baños.

THE REDEMPTORISTS. The first members of the Congregation of the Most Holy Redeemer, popularly known as Redemptorists, to set foot on Philippine soil were Fr. Andrew Boylan, superior of the Irish Province, and Fr. Thomas O'Farrell, superior of the Australian mission. This was in 1905.[44-a]

Their arrival actually harkened to 1903 when the newly-appointed bishop of Cebu, Mons. Thomas Hendricks, visited Ireland and addressed the Irish hierarchy on the mission needs of the Philippines. Fr. Boylan would get to learn of Bishop Hendricks' representations, and although at this time the Irish province of the Redemptorists had been in existence for only five years, he strained at the leash for the opportunities offered by the Philippines as a missionfield.

That year of 1903, the superior general of the Redemptorists in Rome, Fr. Matthew Raus, had urged the Irish province to go to the West Indies to reinforce the Belgian Fathers in that mission. Fr. Boylan offered the counter-suggestion that a mission to the Philippines be considered instead.

Fr. Raus received this suggestion with much enthusiasm. The new

Apostolic Delegate to the Philippines, Bishop Ambrose Agius, OSB, had made a retreat at San Alfonso, the Redemptorist Motherhouse in Rome, and had intimated to Fr. Raus the dire conditions facing the Catholic church in the Philippines following the departure of the Spanish clergy from the islands.

Arriving in Manila in 1905 from a visitation in Australia, the Irishman Fr. Boylan seems to have overlooked the representations of the Englishman Bishop Agius to the Redemptorist superior general in Rome, and dealt directly with the American bishops.

Fr. Boylan focused on a Redemptorist foundation in Cebu, as suggested by Bishop Hendricks. The Apostolic Delegate had wanted to open the entire Philippines to the Redemptorists. Offered the parish of Opon on the historic island of Mactan in Cebu, Fr. Boylan accepted without much ado.

In 1906, a small group of Redemptorists led by Fr. Patrick Leo arrived in Opon to establish the first Redemptorist mission in the Philippines. With him were Fr. Denis Grogan and Fr. James Hegarty. The last was 65 at this time and he was back in Ireland before the year was out, owing to poor health.

The Redemptorists as a rule do not run parishes, but the Opon pioneers entered into their new occupation with patience and remarkable industry, although all the while, Fr. Leo had sought the aid of other missionary orders in Europe to take over the Opon parish so he and his group could be freed to their traditional evangelization work. To no avail. Fr. Leo sought a new mission in Luzon, probably in Lipa whose bishop had made attractive offers to the Redemptorists. The Apostolic Delegate advised them to stay put in Opon.

In 1911, a new superior for the Opon foundation arrived in the person of Fr. Patrick Maguire Lynch. He was a dynamic person who, before the year ended, had been on missions to Borneo and other places. He conducted missions in Manila, Corregidor among the Philippine Scouts, in Hong Kong and in Canton.

In 1912, the Archbishop of Manila Mons. Jeremiah J. Harty, applied to Fr. Patrick Murray, who had succeeded Fr. Raus as Redemptorist superior general in Rome, for a new mission in Manila. Archbishop Harty offered the Redemptorists charge of the Malate parish.

In 1913, Fr. Lynch left Opon to take over the Malate parish. Fr. Matthew O'Callaghan arrived from Ireland to head the Opon mission.

Archbishop Harty's contract with the Redemptorists was for them to run the Malate parish for seven years. His successor, Mons. Michael O'Doherty chose to overlook the seven-year provision and the Redemptorists, who were averse to running parishes, stayed in Malate for seventeen years.

Fr. Lynch was described as a "showman," and this talent was instrumental in bringing back the famous Malate church, shrine of Our Lady of Remedios, neglected for many years since the departure of the Spanish, into a position of pre-eminence.

Fr. Lynch made Malate widely-known as the English-speaking church, and American Catholics made it their church. When the new governor-general, Francis Burton Harrison, made it his church, Malate would flourish as it had not in the early years of the 20th century.

Fr. Lynch returned to Australia in 1915 and was succeeded by Fr. Terence Brown. It was Fr. Brown who acquired the land near the church and constructed the new building for the Malate parish school.

In 1923, the two Redemptorist Missions in the Philippines – Malate and Opon, were raised into a vice-province. The first superior was Fr. O'Callaghan who moved his residence from Opon to Malate. When Fr. O'Callaghan died in 1927, he was succeeded by Fr. V. R. W. Byrne who moved the residence back to Opon.

The Redemptorists remained in the Malate parish until May 1928 when they were replaced by the Columbans.

Freed of parish duties, the Redemptorists could concentrate on their traditional work. In April 1929, the archbishop of Manila awarded them a tract of land by the shoreline in Baclaran in what was then Pasay for their church and monastery. The property had been deeded to the Virgin Mary by a pious woman named Anastacia. After the Catholic church had established its rights to property deeded to the Virgin Mary, and after the area was cleared of squatters, the Redemptorists took possession.

On 13 September 1931, the cornerstone for the new church and monastery was laid. It was dedicated to St. Therese of the Child Jesus.

The first Redemptorist community in Baclaran arrived from Australia on 15 February 1932, composed of four Fathers and three Brothers, with Fr. E. Gallagher as superior. In this group was Fr. Francis J. Cosgrave.

Among the ardent supporters of the Redemptorists was the wealthy Ynchausti merchant family of Malate. Mrs. Ynchausti presented to the new church a copy of the picture of Our Lady of Perpetual Help, the original of which is venerated at the Redemptorist motherhouse of San Alfonso in Rome. She also provided funds for the construction of the main altar, and made it a condition that Our Lady's picture be mounted over the altar. Thus it was that the Redemptorist church in Baclaran became the shrine of Our Lady of Perpetual Help although it was dedicated to St. Therese.

In 1930, the Redemptorists established a second Luzon foundation in Lipa, Batangas, called Divino Amor. By this time, they had gained fame as preachers in the missions, fluent in Tagalog. This fame would be enhanced with the subsequent publication of the monumental English-Tagalog dictionary by Fr. Leo J. English, who arrived in the Philippines in 1936.

After the Philippines was occupied by the Japanese in 1942, the Redemptorists were permitted to continue their mission work, until mid-1944 when they were interned, together with other Allied nationals, in Los Baños. The exceptions were Fr. Francis J. Cosgrave, now the superior, and two Brothers, who were all Irish-born.

Fr. Cosgrave joined the Christian Brothers at De la Salle college as chaplain, while the two Brothers went to Lipa to maintain their Divino Amor property.

Many other religious orders from abroad would enter the Philippine mission. Many more, like the Religious of the Virgin Mary and the Augustinian Recollect Missionaries, arose from the local scene. Each would leave an indelible mark on the city of Manila, not only in the development of the spiritual life of the community and in the traditional mission fields of health, education and welfare, but also for the great edifices they built which, in time, would adorn their city like jewels on a dowager queen.

These edifices, each embodying the prevailing architectural concepts of its time adapted to the venue, would become in themselves living museums. They were repositories of works of art and inventions of science and technology. Here the religious assembled artifacts from all over the world and from the entire Philippine archipelago. Their libraries were in fact treasurehouses of the knowledge of their times. Their archives sheltered documents that collectively told the history of the country. Many of these were in the old Walled City and in the outlying *arrabales* of Ermita and Malate in south Manila.

In the prologue to his biography of Jose Rizal, the author and scholar Leon Maria Guerrero says, "The Spanish history of the Philippines begins and ends with the friar."[45]

By mid-19th century, however, the British observer Robert MacMicking would lament, "Alas, that priestly ambition and the desire of domination should in time usurp the place of those laborious, enthusiastic and pious missionaries who, so happily for the natives, had managed to revolutionize their minds . . ."[45]

Progressively to the end of Spanish rule over the Philippines, the quality of the men who took the priestly vows and undertook the voyage to these islands from the Peninsula, foreshortened and made easier now by the opening of the Suez Canal, deteriorated drastically. The purity of their purpose became diluted so that later historians would best remember their venalities, quite easily overlooking the great ministrations of the saintly pioneers.

Karl von Scherzer, an Austrian visitor in Manila in 1858, had occasion to remark, "Wheresoever the monks lift the finger, Spain has ceased to rule in the Philippines. The spiritual reins have ever bridled the secular authority and such a state of things is the severest impediment to the development of the country and its intellectual growth."[47]

In the end, the friar, as Guerrero would go on to say, "was the great antagonist of the first Filipino," and consequently of every Filipino who came after. But this could not obscure or alter the fact that, again using Guerrero's words, "the Spanish friar was the true explorer and conqueror of the archipelago."[48]

Physically, the Christian city of Manila was built around the church, as every Philippine community would be, henceforth. The Walled City's life devolved around the religious institutions more than on the secular. The events of the day were dictated by the church bells, from matins to compline. The passing of time was marked by the liturgy of the Christian church, from the ceremonies of Advent to those of Lent and back again.

The Americans introduced into the Philippines the Protestant denominations. These, too, worked in a large way in making Manila a Christian city. Filipinos in large numbers flocked to these new sects, probably responding to the appeal of the novel, but also probably out of disenchantment with the old Catholic order which came to be associated by many with the ancient woes of the land.

The Protestant churches established many institutions that would become landmarks on the Philippine scene. They built schools and hospitals where none existed before, and introduced new concepts and practices in social service.

The original city of Manila expanded into the surrounding marshlands and ricefields of the indigenous people, and the *arrabales* came into being. Still each *arrabal* would grow around the church, and life in each would be dictated by the Christian calendar.

Now the Christian city also evolved into a Marian city. It is intriguing to observe how every Manila township would create or adopt a madonna of its own, an image of the Virgin Mary, a portrait or a carving, the cult of which in time wove the social and cultural tapestries that gave richness and color to city life. [49]

Many of Manila's great customs and traditions sprang from the cult of the Mother of Christ, and the city's most lavish festivals were reserved in her honor as protectress, guide or inspiration.

In time there emerged the mystic devotions to Our Lady of La Naval at Santo Domingo, the Consuelo at San Agustin, the Lourdes at the

Capuchinos, the La Purisima at the cathedral. Outside the walls flourished fervid manifestations for the Guia of Ermita, the Biglang Awa and the Rosario of Binondo, the Remedios of Malate, the Peñafrancia of Paco, the Carmen of San Sebastian, the Loreto of Sampaloc, the Pilar of Santa Cruz, the Desamparados of Santa Ana, the Medalla Milagrosa of San Marcelino.

The following is an account of the origin and development of the *arrabales* of Manila, the Spanish townships which became the districts as they were known through the American occupation, and on to the events of February 1945.

INTRAMUROS. The conquistadores who laid its foundation stones called it *Real Fuerza de Santiago*. Today it is known simply as Fort Santiago, a redoubt built towards the end of the 16th century on a tongue of land which sticks out where the Pasig river flows into Manila bay. From this spot the city of Manila began.

Exactly on the same spot an earlier fort stood, when Manila was a Muslim village ruled by a scion of Borneo royalty named Solayman. Solayman's fort was no more than crude earthwork supported by a palisade made of coconut tree trunks, but it was defended by bronze cannon.[50]

When the Spaniards first appeared in Manila bay one day in May in the year 1570, Solayman was there to challenge them. The Spaniards put his resistance to naught, and Solayman withdrew his forces across the Pasig river to regroup and gain a second wind. The Spaniards did not pursue. After looting Solayman's village the invaders put it to the torch. They withdrew to their ships and out of Manila bay, southward to Iloilo where the main body of the Spanish colonizers had its headquarters.

The Spaniards would not appear in Manila bay again until the following May. This time they came to stay.

Solayman had rebuilt his village and had reconstructed his fort. Still he was not ready to yield to any invader, not without a fight, anyway. Once more his beloved Maynila came under the brutal cannons from the Spanish vessels. Once more the Muslim village went up in flames.

Solayman ceded the site of his fort to the newcomers and withdrew to await his time to fight anew. The time arose after two years. Again Solayman suffered defeat and in this final struggle he lost his life.

Upon the ruins of his palisaded fort Miguel Lopez de Legazpi, the *Adelantado* who led the newcomers, set up his own. And this fort was the focal point of the city that Legazpi named *Insigne y Siempre Leal Ciudad de Manila,* the Distinguished and Ever Loyal City of Manila.

Legazpi proceeded to lay down the blueprint of the city and shortly the principal edifices of this new outpost of Spanish civilization arose. The first thing he did was to reconstruct the ruined fort of palm trunks. A residence was erected for him, and also a church and convent for the priests. The residences for the ranking officials of the *Adelantado's* entourage then went up in heavy timber, cane and palm—the only building materials readily available at that time. On 20 August 1572, Legazpi died, and his treasurer, Guido de Lavezares, succeeded to his post.

Shortly after Lavezares became captain-general, the new city would come under siege from a Chinese adventurer named Limahong. The corsair appeared in Manila bay 29 November 1574, with a fleet of 62 ships and an army of 4,000 men. There were 1,500 women in the party, and they brought household utensils and farm implements with them, giving the impression that they had come to settle. Conscious that they were fighting for survival, the Spaniards and their native allies fought back desperately, driving Limahong and his fleet up the Luzon coast to Lingayen where he set up camp and from where he was finally dislodged, never to return. This was a decisive point in Philippine history. Had the Chinese prevailed, this country would today be a part of China.

Things went well for the newcomers and the King in Spain took measures to strengthen his position in the new colony. In 1584, he sent to Manila a new governor in the person of Dr. Santiago de Vera. De Vera found the wooden fort Legazpi built already falling to pieces. Learning that the vice-provincial of the Jesuits in Philippines, the Rev. Fr. Antonio Sedeño, was also an architect experienced in the construction of military fortifications, he commissioned the good priest to draw up plans for a new fort as well as defenses for the city of Manila.

Sedeño discovered adobe quarries to the east of Manila in the foothills of Montalban and from here the rock for the new fort was drawn. He taught the natives how to work the stone, trained them to make lime and bricks. Soon the city of palm and bamboo would disappear and in its place massive ramparts of brick, adobe and tile would rear their formidable facades.

Santiago de Vera gave the name of his patron saint, Santiago, James the Apostle, to the fort that Sedeño built. St. James was the patron saint of Spain and his name on the fort was considered auspicious.

Governor Gomez Perez Dasmariñas (1590-1593) who succeeded de Vera in 1590 thought that the name was well-considered, for he too, like de Vera, was a knight of the Order of Santiago. Perez Dasmariñas would complete the *Real Fuerza de Santiago* and begin the construction of the walls of Manila.[51]

Dasmariñas had been specially commissioned by Philip III to fortify Manila. Philip sent with the new governor an army of 400 to augment the forces then deployed in the islands.

Dasmariñas examined the work done by Governor de Vera and commissioned Leonardo Iturriano, an engineer in his retinue, to make new plans and supervise the construction of the fortified city. Dasmariñas was not to see the work completed. Concerned with the increasing influence of the Portuguese in the Moluccas, he organized an expedition to subdue them. On the way southward with his fleet, he put up on the island of Maricaban near Mindoro for repairs. His Chinese crew crept upon him treacherously, quartered his body and threw his remains to the sharks. His son Luis (1593-1595) served in his place as governor-general pending the arrival of the new governor from Mexico.

The defenses of the new city were to be put to a crucial test when the Chinese rose in arms in 1603. Panicked by rumors that the Spaniards were planning a pogrom, the Chinese massed in huge numbers in the areas north of the Pasig river, where the retired governor Luis Perez Dasmariñas then held his residence. He led a commando in pursuit of the Chinese but was ambushed and was killed. The rebellion was shortly put down, however, but it showed the weak points of the city's walls.

FORT SANTIAGO IN THE 17TH CENTURY. When Sebastian Hurtado de Corcuera (1635-1644) took office as governor-general in 1635, he declared the area surrounding the fortified city as a military zone and demolished all buildings then standing in the premises, including the convent of the Recollects.

His successor, Diego de Fajardo (1644-1653) increased the capacity of Fort Santiago to hold prisoners by ordering new tiers of dungeons and cells. Such foresight paid off when, at various times in the succeeding years, these dungeons and cells would spill-over with tenants.

Don Sebastian Manrique de Lara (1653-1663) who succeeded Governor Fajardo responded to a scare raised by the Chinese general Koxinga who had wrested Formosa from the Dutch, and hurried to strengthen further Fort Santiago's defenses. The height of the walls was raised and a platform 200 feet in circumference was constructed at the point facing the sea, big enough to hold twelve cannons. A cupola was erected with a neck 58 feet long and a radius of 32 feet, connected to the fort by an arched passageway.

Despite the continuing constructions on the Fort, Don Gabriel de Curuzaelegui (1685-1689) found it in a state of disrepair when he arrived to take over as governor. He ordered military engineers to inspect the fort and upon their recommendations, he ordered repairs and new constructions made. Two bastions were built, one overlooking the sea and another overlooking the river. A moat was dug to separate the fort from the city and a drawbridge was constructed over the moat. To protect the drawbridge, a revelin was built. Additional barracks were also built for the fort's enlarged garrison.

The new construction ordered by Curuzaelegui would not be completed until 1695, during the term of his successor Don Fausto Gongora Cruzat (1690-1701). Gongora himself would find occasion to make his own additions and revisions on the constructions he found, and each succeeding governor, each in his own fashion, would occupy himself with Fort Santiago, making repairs or adding new constructions.

FORT SANTIAGO IN THE 18TH CENTURY. When Don Jose de Torralba (1715-1717) became acting governor-general in 1715, he employed experts to study the city's fortifications. The experts recommended the creation of quarters inside Fort Santiago for the warden and the chaplain respectively. During Torralba's brief tenure of two years, he had the two houses constructed, demolished the existing barracks and in their place put up a two-storey building whose roof did not rise above the walls. The new building accommodated more soldiers and did not take too much space inside the fort.

Torralba's zealousness about Fort Santiago would get him into trouble. When Don Fernando Manuel de Bustamante (1717-1719) became governor-general, he appointed Ignacio Navamuel y Villegas as warden of Fort Santiago. Navamuel looked into the books of accounts of the construction and declared that the materials used by Torralba were overpriced. Charges were brought against Torralba, and the court found against him. He appealed his case to Madrid, and when the superior court sustained the decision against him which included heavy fines, he was reduced to penury and would die a pauper's death.

Bustamante would not fare so well either. In 1719 he was assassinated by a mob incited by the religious who disagreed with his ideas for reform. His son, the *castellan* of Fort Santiago, rushed to his side at the height of the tumult, and was also killed.

When Don Fernando Valdez Tamon (1729-1739) became governor-general, he had his engineers inspect Fort Santiago and report on their findings. Their recommendations were the basis for the repairs done in 1737 and 1738, and put the fort in such condition that Valdez Tamon could report to the King in Spain as follows:

"It has a circuit of 2,030 feet; its shape is almost triangular. Its fortification on the southern side which faces the city, included a curtain with *terreplein*, flanked by two demi-bastions; it has a *fause-braye* and a ditch which communicates with the river. On the northern side toward the entrance of the ditch in the place of the bastion is a raised cavalier with three faces or batteries; one of these fronts the sea (the anchorage included) another to the said entrance, and the third the river itself. This last side of the cavalier joins a large tower of the same height as the walls; and through the tower there is a descent to a semi-circular platform or battery, at the level of the water, with which the aforesaid triangular figure of this castle is completed. Through these sides the fort has the necessary communications with the city, through its principal gate, which faces that way; with the river, and with the shore or beach of the sea, by a postern gate which furnishes passages to it."

When Governor Pedro Manuel de Arandia (1754-1759) died in office in 1759, the archbishop of Manila, the Rev. Manuel Antonio Rojo, became acting governor-general. Archbishop-Governor Rojo saw how Fort Santiago had fallen into disrepair and proceeded to effect renovations. Repairs were made, new constructions were put up, but they would not keep the British invaders out when one day in September 1762 they would appear in Manila bay, put the city under siege and shortly would have Archbishop-Governor Rojo scurrying to the governor's palace, now occupied by the British General William Draper, there to surrender Manila adjectly. In Fort Santiago the Spanish colors were hauled down for the first time since Legazpi raised them in 1571. In their place the British flag went up and there it would fly until 23 July 1764, when news that the Seven Year's War had been ended under the Treaty of Paris of February that year, reached Manila. Rojo was not there to see the Spanish flag fly anew over Fort Santiago. He died a few days earlier. As the rumor went, he spent his last days insane.

Always wary of the envious eyes cast Manila-wards by other nations, the Spanish governors would make a fetish of keeping Fort Santiago in fighting form, so great was their stake in the fort's capability to defend the city.

Francisco de la Torre (1764-1765) despaired over its sorry state but did not seem to have done anything to improve it. But Jose Basco y Vargas (1778-1787) accomplished wonders during his term to strengthen the city walls and Fort Santiago. Rafael Maria Aguilar (1793-1806) increased the garrison and secured better ammunitions for the fort.

In 1817, Col. Ildefonso de Aragon, chief of the Corps of Engineers, submitted a plan which was approved, in which Intramuros was divided into four barrios, namely, San Antonio, San Gabriel, San Luis and San Carlos.

Then, as the modern age finally overtook the Philippines, as the last of the obscurantists in Madrid and in Manila faded away, the authorities found better things than fortifications to occupy them. No more mention of Fort Santiago is made in the records of the 19th century, except as a prison cell for political foes and as army headquarters.

By the end of the 19th century, the Walled City of Manila for all intents and purposes of the dawning age, was unhabitable. The ancient buildings were decrepit from age and neglect. The sanitary facilities were nonexistent. The wealthy and influential had moved out to the burgeoning suburbs of Binondo, Quiapo and Ermita. The governor-general lived in a modest villa by the Pasig river in San Miguel. Only those who had to remain in Intramuros did – the former aristocracy now impoverished, the students who now occupied the old stately mansions turned into dormitories, and the religious in their monasteries.

When the Americans arrived they wanted to tear the whole place down and build a modern city. There was a strong move to fill up the ancient moats, now lagoons of fetid water, and bring down the walls.The moats were indeed drained and turned into grassy lawns. The section of the walls fronting the river was torn down, and the rest was saved only by the unremitting protests of the academicians and antiaquarians among the Filipinos and Americans. Finding all official avenues to the governor-general blocked, they worked on the Honorable Henry C. Ide's two young daughters, Marjorie and Anne, and it is believed that it was the two teen-aged girls' behind-the-scenes representations that prevented the authorities from carrying out the decision to tear down the stone walls upon which generations and generations had toiled.

On 21 June 1920, Governor General Leonard Wood issued Proclamation No. 25, Series 1920, the first law governing the use of Intramuros. This law restricted itself to the Sunken Garden, as the filled-up moats were reffered to, reserving the Sunken Garden for a park, golf course and playground, withdrawing them from sale and disposition.

On 12 Novemvber 1936, Commonwealth Act No. 171 was passed, requiring that "all buildings to be constructed in said district shall adopt the Spanish-colonial type of architecture on its facade," and designating the consulting architect of the national government, through the city engineer of Manila, as the authority to approve all plans for such buildings.

When World War II broke out in December 1941, Intramuros was in an advanced state of decay. But it wore the patina of the centuries with dignity and grace, and it took a holocaust to grind its ancient face to earth.

BAGUMBAYAN. Bagumbayan, which means, "new town" in Tagalog, referred to the native settlement that grew outside the walled city of Intramuros. A memorial to the Spanish Supreme Court dated 1601 referred to the area as "nuevo barrio."

The name "Bagumbayan" appears in Spanish records as early as 1591.

At this time, Bagumbayan was reported to have 300 tributes, which meant that the new town had about 1,200 inhabitants.[52]

In 1622, Archbishop Miguel Garcia Serrano reported to the King in Spain that "150 Spaniards (120 of whom are men), besides another 100 mestizos and freemen, and 400 Indians and slaves are ministered to in Bagumbayan." This shows that in the slightly over 50 years since the coming of the Spanish, they had learned to live in harmony with the Filipinos. Moreover, many inter-marriages had taken place as shown by the number of half-breeds (mestizos) in the village.

Bagumbayan at this time offered sufficient allure to induce Governor General Pedro Bravo de Acuña (1602-1606) to build "a very fine summer house which had its green garden and its ponds in a site called Bagumbaian (sic), only 300 paces from the walls" (of Intramuros). Before the house could be finished, however, the governor died.

The Recollect Fathers who arrived in the Philippines in 1606, thought they could put the house to good use as a convent, and raised P3,000 with which to acquire it. What was intended as a secular house of relaxation thus became a house of religion. As there was no church nearby, the Recollects chose an adjoining site for a public church which was dedicated to San Nicolas de Tolentino. The convent became popularly known as San Juan de Bagumbayan. It sheltered the image of the *Nuestra Señora de la Salud* (Our Lady of Health) which was attributed with miraculous powers. It had a very popular cult during this period.

The Recollect mission in Bagumbayan was directed by Fray Juan de San Jeronimo, who negotiated in Rome the separation of the Recollects from the regular Augustinians, and became its first provincial in 1602. The convent expanded into a college where "the arts and theology were studied."[53]

Later, however, the Recollects had to move into a convent inside the Walled City because of threats posed by periodic Japanese and Chinese uprisings, and because of fears of Dutch invasions. The villages set aside for the Chinese (Parian) and the Japanese (Dilao) were close to Bagumbayan.

In the year 1642, the government had to intervene in the affairs of the Recollect convent in Bagumbayan. Because of the threat of a Dutch invasion, Governor Sebastian Hurtado de Corcuera had ordered all buildings constructed of permanent materials in Bagumbayan demolished. These buildings, it was believed, could serve as vantage points for a siege on the city. Despite the opposition of the friars, the Recollect convent was torn down and a new fort was started there. The Recollects refused the offer of the governor of P4,000 as compensation for their property, claiming that their destroyed properties were worth more than

P50,000. At Corcuera's *residencia,* the administrative inquiry held at the end of the term of an outgoing governor, the Recollects filed charges. The friars alleged that the steps taken by Corcuera were extremely unjust and unauthorized by the city council. Corcuera was sentenced to pay the Recollects P25,000 and the property was restored to them. The fort that Corcuera began was demolished, and a new church and convent were erected in its place.

Until the 18th century, nipa groves owned by the friars covered big sections of Bagumbayan and Ermita. But Governor General Pedro Manuel de Arandia (1754-1759) decreed that ownership of the swamplands be transferred to the state. The churchmen derived considerable income from the nipa groves owing to the demand for nipa among the natives as roofing for their houses. The friars appealed to the King in Spain, and Arandia was made to restore the property to them.

Bagumbayan provided the early Manilans a pleasant recreation spot. At the Paseo de Bagumbayan, as the early chroniclers called it, the aristocracy of the city would drive in their elegant carriages to enjoy the clean evening breeze and show-off their stylish attire. Dr. Antonio de Morga, a member of the Royal Audiencia of Manila towards the end of the 16th century, wrote in his monumental work on the Philippines:

"Manila has two drives (*paseos*) for recreation. One is by land along the point called *Nuestra Señora de Guia.* It extends for about a league along the shore, and it is very clean and level. Thence it passes through a native street and settlement called Bagumbayan, to a chapel frequented by the devout called *Nuestra Señora de Guia,* and continues for a goodly distance further to a monastery and missionhouse of the Augustinians called Mahalat (Malati)." This drive was actually a dike, called the Malecon, which separated the moat on the city wall from the sea.

Later the site began to be referred to as "Luneta," acquiring the name of the bastion that was raised to guard the Puerta Real, the Royal Gate, one of the entrances to the Walled City. The bastion was shaped like a halfmoon, or *medialuna,* hence the word "Luneta" which means "little moon." The area in which the bastion stood was called Paseo de Isabel II. The bastion was the headquarters of a native regiment, mostly Pampangos. It was demolished in 1910 by the American administration.

A description of the Luneta at the turn of the century was made by Dr. Dean C. Worcester, thus:

"Extending from the end of the fortification for some distance along the bay is Manila's great resort, the Luneta. It is a drive and promenade, the carriage road enclosing an oval piece of slightly raised ground, on which are a couple of bandstands, and numerous chairs and benches for the convenience of the public. The Luneta is deserted by day, but as evening draws near is thronged by constantly increasing crowds, representing every class from the highest to the lowest. Fine concerts are often given by excellent bands, composed of natives but drilled by Europeans. The carriages drive in endless circles around the promenade, all taking a direction contrary to that in which the hands of a watch move. Only the Governor General and the Archbishop may drive in the opposite direction, so that there is no excuse for failing to recognize and salute them as they pass. Fine music and the cool breezes from the bay combine to make the Luneta a delightful place on a pleasant evening."

In 1904, the American authorities engaged the eminent architect and urban planner Daniel H. Burnham to make a plan for the city of Manila. Burnham laid out his plan for the government center on the Luneta. He envisioned a U-shaped building, in the manner of the Louvre in Paris, with the base on what is now Taft Avenue, and with the ends closing on the site of the Rizal monument. He planned a set of five buildings on a grandiose scale at the base of the "U". Only two of the five materialized. Under the Commonwealth they became the Department of Agriculture and the Department of Finance buildings. At some point along the way, the plan was abandoned entirely.

A section of the Luneta was renamed Wallace Field where athletic tournaments were held. Another section was named Burnham Green. Every year a carnival-and-fair was held at the Luneta, providing opportunity for the people to see the social and economic progress of the country in the pavillions set up by each province and by the various government bureaus and private commercial and industrial establishments. Among the most memorable of these fairs was that held in 1921 to commemorate the 400th anniversary of the landing of Magellan in Cebu. Even then the Luneta was the locale of cultural happenings. The Sunday concert of the famous Philippine Constabulary band was enjoyed by Manilans who flocked to the Luneta for this regular event.

Luneta was also the scene of great religious celebrations. Among these were the First National Eucharistic Congress in 1930, the International Eucharistic Congress in 1937, and the canonical coronation of the Virgin of Antipolo (Our Lady of Peace and Good Voyage) in 1939.

ERMITA. South of Bagumbayan lay the *arrabal*, or township, of Ermita, so-called because of the hermitage which sheltered the image of Our Lady of Guidance.

This image of the Virgin Mary is known as the "Native Madonna" of the Philippines. Whereas most images of the Virgin Mary venerated in this country were brought here from abroad or were made here during the

Spanish period, the image in Ermita was found here, near the spot where the hermitage stands to this day.[54]

On 19 May 1571, one of the men in Miguel Lopez de Legazpi's company wandered into this area and found this image set among the branches of the pandanus tree which thrived on the shoreline. Apparently it was already the object of veneration among the natives. The soldier brought the image to two Augustinian priests in the company, Fray Diego de Herrera and Fray Francisco de Ortega. The pair declared the image to be that of the Virgin Mary.

The wooden image has a head carved out of *narra* and a body made of *kamagong*, woods prevalent in tropical Asia. It shows vestiges of monochromatic paint. Experts speculate that it may be an early Javanese carving. The image is in the stance and with the facial expression of a Balinese *legong* dancer. The painted garb is much like a Southeast Asian *sarong*. It might have been among the *anitos* venerated by the animist natives.

The Spaniards gave the image the name "*Nuestra Señora de Guia*," Our Lady of Guidance. Today it is also referred to as Our Lady of the Expectation, although the first name, Guia, is better known.

The first structure on this site that may have been called a "hermitage" was made of wood and palm, probably after the invasion of the Chinese corsair Limahong in 1575. The hermitage gave its name to the community that grew around it. It became known as Ermita.

In the first quarter of the 17th century a chapel of stone arose on this site but was razed in the great earthquake of 1645. A new one was built in the period between 1645 and 1662. This was torn down in 1662, in the scare raised by the Chinese pirate-king of Formosa named Koxinga. He did not make good his threatened invasion of Manila, but it sent the Spanish defenders into such a fit of apprehension so that they demolished all structures of stone within cannonshot of the Walled City to prevent their use as vantage points in a siege.

A new church came up on the same site, even as the cult of the Native Madonna prospered. With the advent of the 18th century, however, it had moldered into disrepair and had to be torn down in favor of a new one. Inaugurated in 1712, this was the church that the English used, in fact as the defenders of 1662 had feared, as the vantage point for shelling Intramuros when they invaded the city in 1762. The image of Our Lady had been brought to safety in the cathedral inside the walls. In Ermita a wooden shed was built on the same site in 1771, which served as a parish church.

The modest chapel was probably refurbished continually through the years as fire and hurricane visited the land, until finally the fears of an invasion were completely laid down. A new church, the seventh in the line, came up in 1880, but was seriously damaged in the earthquake of 1885. A sumptuous building, the eighth on the same site, took its place. This was the hermitage that modern Manilans would remember. It disappeared in the holocaust of 1945.

In 1591, Pope Gregory XIV granted a perpetual jubilee to devotees at Our Lady's Ermita shrine. In 1711 Archbishop Francisco de la Cuesta granted special indulgences for devotions in honor of the patroness of Ermita. In 1758, the King in Spain issued a decree designating Our Lady of Guidance of Ermita as patroness of Manila. A special devotion to her grew among seamen, as she was declared "Capitana" of the galleons. Always the image was portrayed atop a pandanus tree, and in later times a lighthouse would become its symbol. A vast cult developed around her and devotees flocked to her shrine. The *arrabal* of Ermita prospered.

In the siege of the Walled City by the British in 1762 the hermitage was destroyed. The image had been brought earlier to the cathedral in Intramuros for safekeeping. The devotees followed the image there. They came by the hundreds everyday, by the thousands on Wednesdays. The devotees left generous gifts. Because the image generated so much income, and since the cathedral needed funds, mostly for the repair and maintenance of the huge edifice, successive archbishops of Manila kept it there and ignored or refused representations of Ermita-folk for the return of their Madonna, even when her shrine had been restored. So for over 150 years Our Lady of Guidance of the *arrabal* of Ermita remained at the cathedral, a prisoner, as the Ermita-folk claimed. Until 1918, when the incumbent archbishop agreed to return her to her shrine.

Ermita lay along a narrow strip of swampy land that extended from the borders of the new town outside the walls to an arbitrary point around Herran street on the south where the *arrabal* of Malate began. The sea lapped on its western parameters which reached up to what is now the narrow alley called Alhambra street. On the east, along what is now A. Mabini street, was the Camino Real, the coastal highway that stretched from the Puerta Real, the Royal Gate to Intramuros, up to Cavite where the galleons hove to. Along the Camino Real the gold of the galleons was hauled under armed escort. Along this highway viceroy and prelate newly-arrived to assume their posts rode with much pomp and pageantry to the city gates. When this area was populated and the old trail became an urban street, it was named Calle Nueva. It was renamed after Apolinario Mabini in 1913.

Many streets in Ermita and Malate were named after American states, thus Dakota, Florida, Nebraska, Arkansas, Colorado, Pennsylvania, Oregon, California, Tennessee, Indiana, Vermont, Georgia, etc., parallel to or crossing each other, without regard to the geography of the United

States.

Other streets in Ermita as in Intramuros were named after saints -- San Luis, San Marcelino, Santa Monica.

The old *arrabal* of Ermita became the university district during the American regime, centered on the University of the Philippines campus on the block surrounded by Taft Avenue on the east, Padre Faura on the south, Florida on the west and Isaac Peral on the north.

The University of the Philippines received its charter, 18 June 1908, from the Philippine Commission, the body established by the United States to govern the Philippines.

The university acquired its 10-hectare campus in Ermita in 1910 when the government paid P206,000 for the 100,000-square meter property.

The sale was negotiated by a real estate agent named George C. Sellner, who himself disposed of 35,000 square meters of land for which he received P86,256. Some P56,000 more went to Jose Enriques and his wife Lucia Peñabella. A total of P43,000 was paid to the heirs of Enrique Peñabella. The Recollect Order received P22,000 for part of the Peñabella property which they had acquired earlier.

On Padre Faura street beyond UP was the Jesuit-run Ateneo de Manila college for boys.

The Ateneo de Manila campus on Padre Faura covered 50,000 sq. m. of choice real estate. It abutted the grounds of the Philippine General hospital on the east. In the campus were the main academic building, the famous Manila Observatory, the auditorium, the gymnasium, the laboratories, the library, and the chapel.

The new college buildings on Padre Faura street were built of concrete, some of wood, others of mixed materials with the lower floor of volcanic rock and the upper floors of wood.

The street outside was named after the famous Jesuit Father Federico Faura. Born in Spain in 1840, Padre Faura was teaching at the Ateneo de Manila in 1865 when he was led into meteorology. In 1869 he founded the Manila Observatory which became the Philippine Weather Bureau under the American administration. He is credited with many discoveries in weather forecasting and invented the Faura Barometer.

By 1945, the work Padre Faura started had been taken over by another distinguished Spanish Jesuit scientist, Father Miguel Selga. The Manila Observatory with its large dome was the area's most notable landmark.

Diagonally on the same block, on Dakota and Herran streets, was the Assumption Convent for girls ran by the Assumption Sisters.

Across Herran street was St. Paul college for girls ran by the Sisters of St. Paul de Chartres.

The UP college of medicine and college of pharmacy were across the street from St. Paul college on the same compound as the Bureau of Science.

On streets all over this area comprising Ermita were residences of managerial types, successful professionals and executives of government and private business.

This was the area favored by the early American residents. The Protestant Americans built the Methodist Central church on San Luis street. The Episcopalian Cathedral of St. Mary and St. John was on Florida street a block away, the Presbyterian Union church was at the corner of A. Mabini and Padre Faura, and a Baptist church was on Padre Faura and Pennsylvania street.

Dormitories for students abounded in the area. So were small shops catering to student needs.

Old acacia trees grew proud and stately on Taft Avenue from Isaac Peral to Vito Cruz. Trees lined Isaac Peral, Padre Faura and Herran, giving a cool, quiet elegance to the neat, clean-lined structures that had come up in this district from the early days of the American occupation.

When the seaside boulevard, later named after the hero of the battle of Manila Bay, was constructed, the area alongside reclaimed from the sea became prime real estate.

Quick to seize opportunities, the American groups early gained possession of choice spots in this area close by the baywaters. As early as 1910, the Army and Navy Club established itself on the reclaimed land where it still stands.

The Elks club acquired property, as did the University Club. On this piece of land overlooking the bay later arose the American High Commissioner's residence. High-rise apartment houses came up here. So did the early hotels.

MALATE. South of Ermita is the *arrabal* of Malate. This word is believed to be a corruption of the Tagalog *ma-alat*, which means "salty." The tidewaters flowed into the foreshores, and of course made the well-waters salty. At the time the Spanish arrived in 1571, this was a small village of fisherfolk who traded their catch with the farmers who lived inland.

At a later time, the dividing line between Ermita and Malate was set along Herran street. The boundaries on the south lay along Vito Cruz street, so-named after the wealthy donor of the land which was converted into the roadway. Beyond was the township of Pasay, the former domains of the bastard son of the fabled Lakan Tagkan of old. To the east, setting off Malate from the township of Singalong, is Taft Avenue.

In 1578 the area was awarded as a mission to the Augustinians. The Augustinians built their church of stone. In 1624 the image of Our Lady of Remedios was brought to Manila by the Augustinian friar Juan Guevara and was enshrined here. It was designated the patroness of women in childbirth, and at all times the shrine attracted pregnant women come to pray for a safe delivery, and other women with their newborn babies come to give thanks.

The Augustinians expanded their church and raised it higher. In 1762, during the siege of Intramuros by the British, the Malate church was used as a vantage point for the invaders' artillery. When the British had gone, the Spanish authorities had the church torn down. It had proven to be dangerous to the security of the city.

Towards the latter half of the 18th century, a new church was constructed on the same site. It is basically the same church today, except for reconstructions and modifications that were necessitated by earthquake and the ravages of time.

This is how Fathers Buzeta and Bravo saw Malate in their 1850 work: "In this town is the headquarters of the Infantry with handsome pavilions for the officers. To the south overlooking the bay is the Fort San Antonio Abad, with barrio Maitubig to the east. Cutting through the town is the highway leading to Parañaque, Las Piñas, Bacoor and Cavite. On the side of the church is another highway which leads to Santa Ana, San Fernando de Dilao or Paco. etc.[55]

"The principal industry is the weaving of fabrics from pineapple fiber, which are exquisitely embroidered . . . this and salt-making are the town's principal commercial activities."

The Augustinian Father Manuel Buzeta had special affection for Malate, having once served as parish priest here.

For a long time, the Malate parish was administered by the Augustinians. Later it came under the secular clergy. In the American period the Malate parish was awarded to the Redemptorists, who were succeeded by the Sacred Heart Fathers, from whom the Columbans took over. It was under the Columbans, mostly Irishmen, when World War II broke out.

In front of the church there was erected in 1896 the monument to the Spanish Queen Isabel II. This statue has a curious history.[56]

Daughter of King Fernando VII, granddaughter of the King Carlos IV who introduced vaccination to Manila, Isabel II was born in 1830. Upon the death of her father in 1833, she was proclaimed Queen of Spain, although her mother Maria Cristina ruled as Queen Regent until 1843. Under the Salic laws only males could ascend the Spanish throne, but Fernando VII had decreed otherwise in his daughter's behalf. Fernando's brother Carlos did not like that, so when his niece Isabel became queen, fighting broke out. Carlos had a lot of friends who did not like that sort of thing either. This was the Carlist War which raged until 1839, the effects of which are still re-echoing in Spain today.

In 1844 Isabel married her cousin, Francisco de Asis, who seems to have been something of a pansy.

In 1854 a campaign was launched in Manila for funds for a fitting monument to honor the reigning monarch. As it materialized, the statue is the work of the Spanish sculptor Ponciano Ponzano and was cast in Spain in 1857. It arrived in Manila in 1860 and was unveiled on 28 June that year, at the approximate spot that became known as Plaza Lawton in the American regime.

The conflict that raged around Isabel culminated in the battle of Alcolea where her supporters lost to the revolutionists. She was forced to abdicate in favor of her son who became King Alfonso XII. Her farewell message was poignant, having delivered which she fled to Paris. She died there in 1904.

The liberal regime that took over Spain after Isabel's departure sent Don Carlos Maria de La Torre to Manila as governor-general. He took one look at the queen in bronze and said, "Take it away!".

A functionary by the name of Bartolome Barretto was commissioned to do the job of dismantling the poor queen. The new governor-general was a popular one. But the governor's action to bring down the statue of the erstwhile queen was not popular at all. Filipino laborers refused to undertake the job, so Barretto had to hire Chinese workmen to do it. Barretto did not have the heart to destroy the statue. He was right. It is a fine piece of sculpture. So he had it stored under his house. The Economic Society of Friends of the Country wanted it for their museum, but old Don Carlos Maria chose to be caddish about it, and consigned the poor queen to a bodega at the Ayuntamiento, and there it gathered cobwebs, bothering no liberal and exciting no monarchist either, until 1896, when it was unveiled anew infront of the Malate church.

To the southwest of the church overlooking the sea, the Spanish constructed the Fort San Antonio Abad. Started in 1584, the fort, mounted with cannon and garrisoned by a small force, guarded the southern approaches to the Walled City.

From the fort eastward was open land, wilderness when the Fort San Antonio Abad was started. To the north nearby flowed a small stream and to the west was the shoreline.

During the American regime this area was opened with the construction of what are now Taft Avenue and Marcelo H. del Pilar streets.

In 1921 the Christian Brothers erected their school along Taft Avenue, to the east of Fort San Antonio Abad. The Brothers of the Christian Schools are a congregation founded by St. John Baptist de la Salle in 1680. Its vocation is the education of youth. The order is officially known as Fratres Scholarum Christianum.

At the invitation of the first American archbishop of Manila, the Christian Brothers opened their first school in the city on 16 June 1911. The school was located on General Luna street in Paco. It was transferred to Taft Avenue in 1921.

In 1934 the Philippines was host to the 3rd Far Eastern Olympics. To accommodate the athletic events the Rizal Memorial Stadium was constructed in the area between Fort San Antonio Abad and De la Salle college. The sports complex, fronting Vito Cruz street, consisted of a baseball stadium, a basketball stadium, a football field, swimming pools and a track and field oval.

The open space intervening between Fort San Antonio Abad and the stadium became public playgrounds and was named Harrison Park after the American Governor-General Francis Burton Harrison (1911-1921).

The district of Malate, like Ermita, developed as a fashionable residential area for merchants and managers of the American era. The old Spanish mestizo families stayed on, and the American expatriates populated the early highrise apartment buildings that sprouted in the district.

The university district spilled beyond Ermita into Malate. On Taft avenue southward beyond Herran on the Malate side was the Philippine Women's university bounded by Tennessee, Vermont and Pennsylvania on three sides.

SINGALONG. This is a small district on the southeastern perimeters of Manila, bounded by Paco to the north, Malate to the west and Makati to the south and east. From the earliest times this was a residential district, bringing together the developing middle class who were out of place both in the plebeian precincts of Tondo and the newly-chic bounds of Ermita and Malate. The name of the district is believed to derive from the old Tagalog word for a kitchen utensil – a cup made of bamboo.

This was Capuchin territory, and the Order administered the church dedicated to St. Gregory the Great.

In 1914, the Benedictine Sisters established a school for girls, called St. Scholastica college, on Pennsylvania street off Vito Cruz street. It became a fashionable school, drawing the daughters of the comers in the nearby districts of Malate and Ermita.

PANDACAN. The native pandan tree thrived lushly along the riverbanks at this point by the Pasig at the time the Spanish arrived.

"Pandanan," the people called the place. Inept in the nuances of the native tongue, the Spanish mispronounced the word as "Pandacan." By this name the place became known thenceforth.

The first mission in Pandacan was established by the Augustinians in 1574. It was part of the parish of Sampaloc. Pandacan would not become a separate parish until 1712.

The town's economic activity during the early 19th century is recorded by Buzeta and Bravo thus: "Pandacan produces rice, sugar cane in small quantities, vegetables and fruits. Aside from agriculture, it produces brick and tile, cotton lace of various colors in limited amounts, and is engaged in rice-milling. It is populated by shoemakers, boatmen and artists."[57]

Late in the Spanish period and early in the American regime, Pandacan would become the first industrial estate in Manila. The cigar factories of the Compañia General de Tabacos de Filipinas were established along Marques de Commillas street in 1882. The street was named after Antonio Lopez, the founder of Tabacalera, who became the first Marques de Comillas, after his native town. In 1903 the Manila Electric Light & Power Company established its plant on Isla de Provisor, an island off the Pasig. The oil companies later set up their depots along the riverbank off the Nagtahan bridge. Early during the American occupation, the gas works would rise on this site. A coconut oil processing firm and a rope factory also set up factories here.

Pandacan would become reknown as an artists' colony. In this district at various periods lived and worked many distinguished personages in Philippine arts and letters, starting with Francisco Baltazar who, as Balagtas, set some of his best-known works in Pandacan. The musician Ladislao Bonus, the playwrights Pantaleon Lopez and Miguel Masilungan, the Tagalog language theorist Lope K. Santos all were from Pandacan.

The first stone church of Pandacan on the site where the present one stands was started in 1732 when Fr. Francisco del Rosario was the parish priest. It would not be finished until 1760 under Fr. Florencio de San Jose.

In this stone church was enshrined the image of the Holy Child Jesus. According to tradition, the image was recovered from a well in the vicinity of the church. The water from the well was acclaimed for its curative qualities, and attracted believers seeking cure. The civil authorities were not as disposed as the believers were, however, and the use of the polluted waters of the well has long since been disallowed and the well covered. The cult of the Santo Niño de Pandacan, however, is still popular, and its feastday on the third week of January has become even more festive.

The old church, like most churches in Manila, would succumb to the periodic earthquakes to which the city was prone. The earthquake of 1852 toppled the old edifice. The successor became unusable after the earthquake of 1880. Each time, the people of Pandacan, led by their devoted curates, would rally to restore their church.

When Malacañang Palace across the river from this point underwent renovation and expansion in the 1920's and 1930's, it was believed opportune to use the land opposite for government purposes. So this section of Pandacan was acquired from the original owners. Named Malacañang Park, it became the headquarters of the palace guard and playground for the official palace residents.

Pandacan developed as a residential district for working people. It gathered within its confines early immigrants from the provinces who came to work in the factories in the area. For old residents, however, it never lost its aura as "Little Italy," the source of the city's musical fare in the earlier days.[58]

PACO. In 1592, the Spanish established a district called Dilao, which means yellow in Tagalog, to which the early Japanese residents of the city were restricted. The original Dilao was in the area close by the walls of Intramuros, today bounded by Padre Burgos Drive, San Marcelino and Concepcion streets. Here the Japanese lived and plied their trades. During the day they were allowed out to other parts of the city, but they had to return here by nightfall, even as the Chinese did in the district called Parian a bit to the north of Dilao.

In 1762, the district of Dilao was moved to the site now dominated by the Paco Railroad Station. After 1762, the Japanese population of Dilao steadily declined as Japan closed its ports and Japanese emigration stopped. The old site of Dilao grew and developed into the district of Paco.

This area had been awarded as a mission to the Franciscans who built the first church here in 1580. The church was dedicated to the Purification of Our Lady. It was built of nipa and cane. In 1599 the Franciscan friar Juan Garrovillos started a modest church of brick and stone. It was completed in 1601. During the Chinese uprising of 1603, Fray Garrovillos' church was destroyed. It was restored three years later, mainly from gifts of the Rev. Francisco Gomez Arellano, one-time archdeacon of the Manila cathedral.

In 1791, while Don Felix Berenguer y Marquina was governor, the name San Fernando was added to Dilao. Thus, the district became known as San Fernando de Dilao. By the 19th century, however, the place was already referred to as Paco. Whether this is the diminutive of Francisco (accent on the first syllable), or a corruption of the name of the edible fern paco (accent on the second syllable) that grew on the riverbanks, it cannot be ascertained.

In the early 18th century work started on the church that would become the focal point of the township of Paco. Under the direction of Fray Bernardo de la Concepcion an imposing edifice of brick and stone arose on the same site of the earlier churches, with an impressive facade and an imposing belfry. In 1842, Fray Miguel Richar, then parish priest, ordered a great bell cast as befitted such a grand belfry.

In 1852 the church built by Fray de la Concepcion was seriously damaged by earthquake. Another earthquake in 1880 finished what the earthquake of 1852 started, and for a long time the Paco parishioners made do with a church of nipa and cane as in the earlier times. Under the direction of the new parish priest, Don Gilber Martin, a new church of brick and stone began to rise. But a typhoon in 1892 made short work of the almost completed edifice, so Father Martin and his flock had to start all over again.

Finally the great church dedicated to Our Lady of Candlemas (La Candelaria) was opened to the faithful. The Spanish era was coming to an end, and shortly the parish was turned over to the Belgian Fathers as the members of the Congregation of the Immaculate Heart of Mary are popularly known.

By the outbreak of World War II, Paco had become a workingman's district, harboring salaried people from the small factories that had sprang up in the area, small tradesmen and the masses of employees from the government center to the west and the industrial estates of Pandacan to the north.[59]

SANTA ANA. Fron Paco eastward at a rather amorphous point, but no farther than the old Jesuit property on Herran street known as La Ignaciana, a retreat house for priests and laymen, is the district of Santa Ana. Santa Ana (St. Anne) is traditionally referred to as the mother of the Virgin Mary.

This area on marshy land close by the banks of the Pasig was the seat of a pre-Spanish settlement called Namayan. The natives called the marshes *sapa.* When the area was awarded to the Franciscans they called their new mission Santa Ana de Sapa.

According to tradition Namayan was ruled by the chieftain Lakan Tagkan and his wife Buwan. Lakan Tagkan's domain stretched from here eastward and southward to include territories of present-day San Juan, Mandaluyong, Makati, Paco, and Pandacan. The couple had five sons. Lakan Tagkan also had a bastard son named Pasay to whom he bequeathed lands that lay to the southeast by the bay. It is that area now known as Pasay.

The Franciscans built their church on a low promontory overlooking the river, a site that had been the burial grounds of the Lakan's community. In 1719 the Franciscan friar Vicente Ingles brought to this church an image of Our Lady of the Abandoned, a copy of the original venerated at the metropolitan cathedral of Valencia in Spain. In time this Madonna, advocate of the forsaken, of orphans, the aged, the insane, would develop a popular cult. In 1720, the archbishop of Manila, Don Francisco de la Cuesta, presented her the golden sceptre she still holds in her hands. In an urn under the altar is the gift of another archbishop of Manila, Don Pedro de la Santissima Trinidad y Arizala, who presented her his heart.

Santa Ana is remembered in Buzeta and Bravo thus: "This town counts with about 1,505 houses, mostly of light material, although there is a big number made of stone, done in the pleasant English style, which serve as countryhomes of the Spanish and Europeans in Manila and adjoining areas. These houses extend down to the riverbanks of the Pasig, each one with a garden. Altogether they present a picturesque and pleasant sight."[60]

Way into the American era, Santa Ana was vacation land for Manilans, as the wealthy of the city built resthouses by the Pasig river banks. La Ignaciana for instance, was originally a vacation house for the Jesuits.

In time a street led out to this area from the bayfront, making it easily accessible from Ermita and Malate. It was called Calle Real de Paco. Later this street was named after Jose de la Herran, a captain in the Spanish Navy.

TONDO. Tondo (Tundok) on the north bank of the Pasig at the point where the river debouches into the bay was the ancient kingdom of Lakandola, the uncle of Solayman who ruled May-nila on the south bank. Lakandola's domain may have stretched eastward from here to the foothills of the Sierra Madre. This area eventually became the politico-military district of Tondo under the Spanish. It would later become the province of Morong, which the Americans renamed after Jose Rizal.

Tondo developed into a residential district that sheltered Indios from the time of Lakandola. Early during the Spanish period it remained agricultural land which supplied grain and vegetables to the districts on the south bank.

Buzeta and Bravo describe the Tondo of their time, thus, "The streets are wide, adorned with fine buildings of stone and wood, done in the European style . . . The most important industry is fishing. Tondo provides the capital and adjoining areas with fresh fish. It also provisions the ships with dried and preserved fish."[461]

The Augustinians built in Tondo the church which enshrined the image of the Holy Child. The church became the focal point of life in this district which continued to receive the effluence of the wealthier areas. The working class lived here, the dockworkers, the drivers of the horsedrawn rigs, the laborers in the foundries and factories of Binondo.

During the American regime a Protestant missionary group established a hospital here amidst the shanties of the burgeoning city's poorest, by the mudflats of Manila bay. In a latter time, the Mary Johnston hospital would wrest from the Tondo church the qualification of being the focal point of life in this district, an index to the points of emphasis between the old regime – religion and the spirit, and the new – the body and temporal well-being.

During the American era, the bayfront was assigned to local shipping and became known as the North Harbor. Here piers were constructed to accommodate interisland ships and coastwise vessels. This left the Port Area, newly reclaimed from the sea, to foreign shipping.

BINONDO. "Minundok," the natives called this island surrounded by the Pasig river and its tributaries. It was a small village inhabited by farmers and fisherfolk when the Spanish arrived in 1571. Across a narrow stream on the northwest lay a smaller village called Baybay. It is believed that Baybay on the foreshore of the bay was the place where the Chinese junks anchored during the trading season in pre-Spanish times. Many of the Chinese would stay when the junks sailed away. Some intermarried with native women. When the Spanish arrived they found a thriving Chinese community in Baybay. This area was turned over to the Dominicans who established a convent and a hospital for the natives named San Gabriel.

The island called Minundok across the river from the Walled City was awarded as an encomienda to the spouses Don Antonio Velada and Doña Sebastiana del Valle. On 24 March 1594, the spouses Velada sold their holdings to Don Luis Perez Dasmariñas. Son of the late-lamented Don Gomez Perez Dasmariñas, governor from 1590-92, Don Luis distinguished himself as the leader of the expedition that surveyed the eastern coast of Luzon from Nueva Ecija up to the Cagayan Valley. When his father the governor was killed by his Chinese crew while himself leading an expedition to subdue Portuguese marauders in Mindanao in 1592, Don Luis succeeded as acting governor-general.

When Luis Perez Dasmarinas acquired the island of Minundok, the adjoining village of Baybay was merged with it. Thus was created the *arrabal* of Binondo. Baybay became the sub-district of San Nicolas.

Don Luis would suffer an infamous end. In the Chinese uprising of 1603, he unwittingly walked into an ambush by the rebels while leading a commando of loyal natives. The commando unit was annihilated to a man.

Binondo developed into the commercial center of the Spanish era. Buzeta and Bravo have this to say of Binondo: "In this district, center of the wealth and commerce of the country, there are about 900 dry goods shops, big and small. There is a fine foundry of small-calibre artillery, the products of which are those found mounted on small ships and those that are fired by natives during the great festivals or in special celebrations. There is a factory that produces various types of bells, *peroles,* kettles, *batidores,* candleholders, frying pans called *carajais* by the natives, and various other articles and instruments of cast iron."[62]

Also from the Fathers Buzeta and Bravo: "From here originates extensive commercial traffic with the provinces which forms the major portion of the business done by the Chinese, the mestizos and the Europeans, thereby making the district the principal and the most important marketplace in the archipelago. The bigger share of the business, second only to that of the Europeans, is held by the mestizos."

Charles Wilkes, an American who visited Manila in 1842, wrote: "The suburbs, or Binondo quarter, contains more inhabitants than the city itself, and is the commercial town. They have all the stir and life incident to a large population actively engaged in trade, and in this respect the contrast with the city proper is great."

Wilkes found the Binondo commercial center picturesque and colorful: " . . . in each quarter of the Binondo suburb the privilege of occupancy is claimed by some particular kinds of shops. In passing up the Escolta (which is longest and main street in this district) the cabinet-makers, men busily at work in their shops, are first met with; next to these come the tinkers and blacksmiths, etc. These are flanked by outdoor occupations; and in each quarter are numerous cooks, frying cakes, stewing, etc., in movable kitchens, while here and there are to be seen betel-nut sellers, either moving about to obtain customers, or taking a stand in some great thoroughfare. The moving throng, composed of carriers, waiters, messengers, etc., pass quietly and without noise. They are generally seen with the Chinese umbrella, painted of many colours, screening themselves from the sun. The whole population wears slippers, and move along with a slipshod gait."

From the Plaza de San Gabriel where the Dominicans built their hospital the district grew, expanding through Calle Rosario at the end of which stood the grand neo-Renaissance shrine of Our Lady of the Rosary.

Parallel to Rosario street was Calle Anloague, so called from the carpentry shops that lined the street. It would become Calle Juan Luna during the American regime. The Escolta ran from Plaza San Gabriel southward to the courtyard of Santa Cruz church.

In time the area sprouted the handsome mansions where the wealthy merchants resided, lining the *esteros* and the avenues that criscrossed the district.

The export-import houses set up shop here, so did the banks and the insurance companies when these came into being. Smart department stores lined Rosario and the Escolta.

SANTA CRUZ. This area on the left bank of the Pasig between Binondo and Quiapo districts was awarded as a mission to the Jesuits who first arrived in Manila in 1581. The first church on the site where the Santa Cruz church stands today was constructed by the Jesuits to serve their Chinese parishioners.

In 1643 the image of Our Lady of the Pillar was enshrined in the church. The image drew devotees and a popular cult grew around it.

In the year 1632, the Shogun of Japan allowed a group of 134 Japanese Christians to go into exile in the Philippines. It turned out that 130 in the group were lepers. The lepers were welcomed by the Franciscan Fathers who brought them to their Hospitalito de Santa Ana in Intramuros.

Because a stigma was developing over the hospital as one for lepers, a hospital name "San Lazaro" was established for the Japanese lepers in Dilao, the Japanese quarter outside the walls. In 1662, the San Lazaro hospital was moved temporarily to Quiapo. It was later restored to the southside of the Pasig along Arroceros street. This hospital was used as a vantage point by the British when they invaded Manila in 1762. After the British left, the hospital was demolished.

On 24 June 1784, the King deeded to the San Lazaro hospital about 200 hectares of land in the Santa Cruz district, then owned by the Hacienda de Mayhaligue. Here the hospital for lepers finally was established.

This is how Buzeta and Bravo record Santa Cruz: "On the south side of the headquarters of the cavalry which stands on the site of the College of San Ildefonso, once ran by the Jesuit Fathers, there is a small plaza called Santa Cruz. From here begins the barrio named San Estanislao, the main street of which leads northwards to Dulong-bayan where the slaughterhouse and meat-market are located. About 24 minutes away from the cavalry headquarters is the sitio called Mayhaligue which has many orchards and cultivated fields beyond which is the hospital of San Lazaro, for lepers. Farther beyond Mayhaligue is the cemetery for Chinese, or non-Christian *sangeleyes.*"[63]

In 1859, the Franciscan Fr. Felix Huertas was given charge of the San Lazaro hospital. It was Father Huertas who developed San Lazaro into a famous refuge for the afflicted. By the time he died in 1894, his hospital had become a famous recourse for all the ailing in the north side of the Pasig.

Under the American regime, San Lazaro was turned into a hospital for communicable diseases, including cholera, smallpox, bubonic plague, diptheria, venereal diseases, etc. A new hospital for lepers was established outside Manila.

When the Department of Health was created, its offices were set up at the old San Lazaro compound, where it has stayed to this day.

Santa Cruz developed into a residential section harboring the huge masses of workers from adjoining industrial and commercial districts. Certain areas along the main thoroughfare which grew into present day Rizal Avenue became the business center for this side of the Pasig. In later times it would become the "downtown" section, referring to the concentration of department and specialty stores that spread into this area from the Escolta, and the entertainment section where the big moviehouses sprang up.

QUIAPO. Quiapo today is bounded by the Pasig river on the west and Claro M. Recto (Azcarraga) on the east and extends from Rizal Avenue on the north to P. Casal and Legarda on the South. It is the hub of what Manilans used to call "downtown," bisected as it were by Quezon Boulevard from the bridge to the underpass-overpass complex on Recto Avenue.

Established as a township in 1582 when Don Santiago de Vera was governor-general, Quiapo derives its name from the water-weed called *kiyapo* that floated down the river Pasig.

In 1582 when it was established as a new township with its own *gobernadorcillo*, it was but a small community of fisherfolk working the still-productive Pasig. Much of the land was truck-farms growing fruits and vegetables, much of it tilled by expatriate Chinese.

Under the ministrations of Don Gaspar de Azabo the first church on the site where the present one stands today arose in the year 1592, made of bamboo and palm. Succeeding edifices were made of more substantial material but successively they succumbed to fire and earthquake. The last one toppled in the great earthquake of 1863, and it would take 26 years before the people of Quiapo would arouse themselves enough, led by their parish priests, Don Eusebio de Leon and Don Manuel Roxas, to construct a new one.

"The inhabitants are engaged in various trades," Buzeta and Bravo wrote about Quiapo in the 1800s, "and here exist a considerable number of stores and commercial exchanges (*lonjas*). Also, the natives are carpenters, blacksmiths and carriage-makers."

In 1852 the first bridge on approximately the same site as the present Quezon bridge was constructed. It was called the Claveria (or Arroceros) bridge. It led from the Puerta Isabel II on the northeast section of the walls into the site where Quinta market is today.

By the end of the 19th century, *Ilustración Filipina*, the chronicler of the day, would describe Quiapo thus: "It is bounded in the north by Curtidor, a barrio of Santa Cruz; the east by the barrio of San Sebastian, with Sampaloc and San Miguel, in the southwest with the Pasig river by the barrio of San Anton and Buenavista; and in the west by Santa Cruz. All these towns are connected by good bridges . . .

"Quiapo has beautiful and symmetrical streets almost totally lined with factories. It has a beautiful plaza with a good municipal building, a grandiose church and rectory and a school."

Even then the focal point of the district was the church which is the shrine of the Black Nazarene. This image was brought to the country by a Recollect priest, when it is not certain, but it could not have been later than the second half of the 18th century because it is known to have been blessed by Archbishop Basilio Sancho de Santa Justa y Rufina (1766-1787) during one of his annual visitations.

This is a statue of Christ falling under His cross. Its Mexican provenance seems to be underscored by the Indian features of the image and the dark color with which it was painted.

"Nuestro Padre Jesus Nazareno," the image is called, and from the earliest days inspired a deep and intense devotion among believers. Its fiesta on 9 January each year is occasion for fervid displays of near-hysterical faith. Every Friday huge throngs jam the church and its surroundings. The location of the shrine at the cross-roads of the metropolis makes it convenient to the faithful who take it in the ordinary course of the day's business.

In 1929 fire destroyed the church once more. The present neo-Rennaisance edifice is the work of the Filipino architect Juan Nakpil and was completed in 1935.

Quiapo gathered the mestizo aristocracy of the late Spanish and the early American periods. What is now Calle Resurreccion Hidalgo was lined by the elegant mansions of the rich and powerful. The Legardas, Paternos, Aranetas, Hidalgos lived here.

The area along the river developed into a commercial center. Silversmiths and goldsmiths plied their trade in a street still called Platerias. Craftsmen and artisans worked wood and stone in small shops on what is now Evangelista and in ateliers along Arlegui.

Along the street later named Tanduay a small chapel was erected to shelter the image of Our Lady of Carmel which was brought to Manila in 1617 by the provincial of the Augustinian Recollects. The reverend worthy had visited the convent of the Carmelite Fathers in Mexico City and received the image as a gift.

The image of Our Lady of Carmel developed a popular cult and on its feastday it had to be brought to the Recollect church in Intramuros to accommodate the huge crowd of devotees.

The southeast section of Quiapo was a barrio called San Sebastian. Late in the 16th century the area was awarded as an *encomienda* to the spouses Don Bernardino del Castillo and Doña Maria Enriques. A church was erected here in 1621 by the Augustinian Recollects.

Adjoining the church was a convent of Augustinian nuns founded by Filipino women, which became formally known as the Augustinian Recollect Missionaries.

The Augustinian Recollect Missionaries had their beginning on 16 July 1725 when two native women, the sisters Dionisia and Cecilia Talampas, were formally invested by Fray Diego de San Jose as Recollect Tertiaries.

Fray de San Jose authorized the construction of a house for the two sisters in the garden of the Recollect convent of San Sebastian in Quiapo.

Other women joined the Talampas sisters and a bigger house had to be constructed. In 1731, the convent of the Augustinian Recollect Missionaries was formally inaugurated by Fray Andres de San Fulgencio, the prior of San Sebastian. The co-founders were the Sisters Maria de Santa Monica, Maria de Sta. Teresa, T. Gatdula del Espiritu Santo and Maria de los Sagrados Corazones.

In 1907, the community opened an elementary school on their old site, now called San Rafael street, off Plaza del Carmen. Their school was named after St. Rita of Casia. A high school was opened in 1924.

Like all constructions of brick and stone in the Manila area during the Spanish period, the churches built by the Recollects in San Sebastian succumbed successively to earthquake. This prompted the Recollect Fathers to consider other material and other construction techniques. They came up with the idea of an all-steel church.

In 1891 work started on the new church, designed in the neo-gothic style. The steel was prefabricated in Belgium and brought across the seas by ship, piece by piece.

The French architect Gustave Eiffel who built the all-steel tower bearing his name in Paris served as consultant in the construction. The church was completed in 1899 and consecrated in the same year. The image of Our Lady of Carmel was transferred here from its chapel on Tanduay street. The plaza by the church became known as Plaza del Carmen.

Even in the Spanish period Quiapo was known as the city's entertainment center. During the latter half of the 19th century zarzuela companies, vaudeville and visiting theatre groups performed in one or the other of the three theatres in Quiapo. These were the Teatro Filipino, the Teatro

Principal, and the Teatro de Tondo.

During the American period, moviehouses came up in the vicinity of the church. When Quezon Boulevard was constructed during the Commonwealth period, Quiapo's reputation as the entertainment district of Manila was well-established.

Focal point of the district is Plaza Miranda at the foot of Quezon bridge infront of the church. It was named after Jose Miranda who was the Spanish secretary of the treasury in 1860.

Quezon bridge and the boulevard into which it extends was named after the Filipino nationalist who is often referred to as "The Father of His Country". A half-breed, he looked more Spanish than Filipino. As a young man he served with the Spanish militia against the Filipino revolutionists, then with the Filipinos against the American invaders. A student at the University of Santo Tomas school of law at the turn of the century when the Americans occupied the country, he joined the Filipino army and rose to the rank of major. He was captured in a skirmish in Bayambang, Pangasinan, and was brought to Manila to serve as orderly of an American officer. After the war he returned to his law studies at Santo Tomas. Upon graduation he served as the fiscal in his native province of Tayabas, served in the same capacity in other provinces in Southern Luzon, before becoming governor of Tayabas.

Quezon was elected to the first Philippine legislature in 1907. In 1910 he became Resident Commissioner in Washington D.C. (Resident Commissioners sat in the House of Representatives in the American capital and participated in debate but could not vote.) He came home to run for the Philippine Senate when this body was created with the passage of the Jones Law in 1916, became president of the Senate and thereafter dominated Philippine politics under the American regime. With the establishment of the Philippine Commonwealth in 1935, he became the first president.

SAN MIGUEL. The first district in Manila named San Miguel was located in the area along San Marcelino street where St. Theresa's college and the church and seminary of St. Vincent de Paul were later established. The district of San Miguel was created in 1615 specially for the Christian Japanese exiles led by the *daimyos* (noblemen) Takayama Ukon and Naito Yukiyasu.

In 1783, the district was re-established on the area along the north bank of the Pasig river bearing the name San Miguel today. By that time, however, there were but few Japanese residents in San Miguel.

This district borders the Pasig river and late in the Spanish period became a fashionable residential area where the wealthy built their resthouses. Among these resthouses was that called Malacañang which would become the residence of the Spanish governor-general.

One source claims that the word Malacañang evolved from the Tagalog word "*mamalakaya*," meaning "village of fishermen." Fishing villages were strung along the Pasig in earlier times. Another source says that Malacañang is a corruption of the Spanish phrase "mala caña," referring to the wild reed that thrived lushly in the area. According to tradition, however, Malacañang originated from the Tagalog words "*may lakan diyan*", meaning "a chief (or a nobleman) lives there." This last is the more widely accepted version of the origin of the word Malacañang.[64]

Entrance into the palace grounds was through Gate 4. Approximately where Gate 4 is, Numero 4 Malacañang stood, the opulently-appointed country home of Don Luis Rocha, scion of a Spanish nobleman who had migrated to this country and who prospered here, partly by marrying into the wealthy and influential Tuason family. Rocha's countryhome was the setting of lavish parties to which the city's aristocracy flocked. Visiting dignitaries were feted here. Viceroy and prelate were frequent guests. Probably because he spent so much for his elegant levees, Rocha soon found he had to dispose of some properties, and the 16-hectare estate by the Pasig was placed on the block. It went to Colonel Jose Miguel Formento, an officer in the Spanish army, for P1,100, a princely sum in the year 1802.

Colonel Formento did not have the predilection for social life Don Luis had, and he allowed the property to go to waste. When he died, his heirs put up the estate for sale again.

In 1824, Mariscal Don Juan Antonio Marquez negotiated the purchase of the property for the Spanish government. In January 1825, the government paid P5,100 for it. The property was refurbished and used as temporary residence for army and navy officers awaiting reassignment or return to Spain. The governor-general availed of the place occasionally to entertain friends and distinguished visitors.

On 7 December 1847, Governor-General Narciso Claveria (1844-1849) secured a Royal Decree designating the estate the summer residence of the governor-general. For the first time the term Poseción de Malacanang was used in official papers.

Buzeta and Bravo in 1850 wrote of Malacañang, thus: "The houses of the town are lined along the riverbanks following a curve that starts from the Quinta bridge and ends in the country house called Malacañang. This was purchased a few years ago as a recreation place for the governors-general of these islands, where they spend the hot season. This property lies on a spacious territory, with an orchard and a garden and a bathhouse on the riverbank. The house is not very large, but is elegant and offers good views, particularly on the riverside where it has an observatory and a colonnaded gallery."[65]

On 3 June 1863, an earthquake of extraordinary intensity rocked Manila. Virtually every edifice in the Walled City toppled down, save the San Agustin church and monastery and the walls themselves.

The incumbent governor, Don Rafael Echague y Berminhan (1862-1865), set up housekeeping at Malacañang. Here his wife delivered a baby girl, probably the only baby born in Malacañang to an official resident. The wife later died, probably the first official resident to die in Malacañang.

The Palacio Real in Intramuros was never restored, and all Spanish governors after Echague took up residence at Malacañang. Throughout the final quarter of the 19th century Malacañang underwent constant reconstruction and remodelling. Earthquake, fire, typhoon and flood took their toll, and each time workmen were called in.

As the seat of Spanish sovereignty over the Philippines, Malacañang was of particular interest to the American invaders. Shortly after the fall of Manila to the Americans, on the afternoon of 13 August 1898, Major General Wesley E. Meritt occupied Malacañang. He served as the first American military governor of the Philippines, followed by General Elwell S. Otis (1898-1900) and General Arthur MacArthur (1900-1901), whose son Douglas would make history in these same islands. All American governors lived in Malacañang.

On 4 July 1901, the civil government was inaugurated by the Americans, with William Howard Taft as civil governor. He had come to Manila on 3 June 1900 as chairman of a commission to lay out the governmental organization in the country. He served as civil governor until 23 December 1903, when he was summoned back to the United States to serve as secretary of war in Theodore Roosevelt's cabinet. He would become president of the United States, and later chief justice of the U.S. Supreme Court.

Taft was succeeded by Luke E. Wright, who became the first American to assume the title of governor-general of the Philippines. When Woodrow Wilson was elected president of the United States in 1912, he sent a Democratic governor-general to these islands in the person of Francis Burton Harrison. He effected many reforms and worked for greater participation of Filipinos in their own government. He also started remodelling Malacañang to make it more livable according to American standards. He served the longest term among the American governors, from 1912 to 1921. He found commuting to his office in the old Walled City everyday inconvenient and time-consuming. In 1920 he ordered work started on the building adjoining the Palace which would house the executive offices. He would not use it as governor, though, for a Republican administration would send its own man to Manila.

In 1929, the millionaire-sportsman Dwight F. Davis, after whom the tennis Davis Cup is named, was appointed governor-general. He effected extensive renovations on the palace, acquired adjoining property to expand the palace grounds, and by the time he left the country in 1932, a good part of the reconstruction work was completed.

Each Malacañang occupant would introduce new decorating schemes in the palace interiors to meet his taste, but the palace remained very much what it was by 1939 when all principal constructions were completed.

SAMPALOC. The early Spanish religious spelled the name of this area as San Paloc, giving the impression that it is the name of a saint. It is not so. The name of this district is derived from the Tagalog word for the tamarind tree – sampaloc.[66]

This area was awarded as an encomienda to the spouses Don Pedro de Chavez and Doña Ana de Vera. At this time, Sampaloc was wilderness remote from the developing urban center in Intramuros and the populated area along the north side of the Pasig river. It was distant enough from the new city so that the early Manilans built their countryhomes here. When the first Poor Clares of St. Francis arrived on 5 August 1621, they were lodged at the countryhome of the spouses de Chavez.

Sampaloc from the earliest days was a mission of the Franciscans. They built a church here dedicated to Our Lady of Loreto.

The pious Don Pedro and Doña Ana de Chavez deeded their encomienda to the Poor Clares, aside from turning over to them their Intramuros mansion for use as a convent. This was swampy land, and the Poor Clares derived income only from the grass used as horse-fodder.

Buzeta and Bravo described Sampaloc as, "located on flat swampy ground, surrounded by streams and canals, which overflow their banks during the rainy season and flood the territory such that the town becomes entirely isolated, without means of communication with its neighbors."[67]

In 1905 the businessmen Don Antonio de la Riva and Don Alfredo Chicote negotiated to take the unproductive land off the hands of the Poor Clares. The purchase price was P300,000 which the businessmen borrowed from the Dominican Fathers. In return for this loan, the two entrepreneurs donated to the Dominicans a portion of the vast estate. This portion, about 22 hectares, is now the University of Santo Tomas campus.

The enterprising land developers organized the Sulucan Estates Subdivision and proceeded to transform the former swamplands into a residential community. They drained the land, laid out streets, and the new Sampaloc was born.

From the beginning Sampaloc was a residential quarter. During the American regime it would develop into the educational center of the left bank following the establishment of the National University in 1901, the Centro Escolar de Señoritas in 1907, and the University of Manila in 1914. In 1927, the University of Santo Tomas opened its new campus here. The Far Eastern University established its plant in the same area in 1933.

The Benedictines arrived in Manila at the turn of the century. They set up their priory and school here in 1925, moving from their first site on Arlegui and Tanduay in Quiapo. In their chapel was enshrined the image of Our Lady of Montserrat, a copy of the image venerated at Montserrat in Barcelona from where the Benedictine mission came.

Interestingly, the first red light district in Manila, the notorious Gardenia district, developed in Sampaloc.[68]

The Gardenia district was part of the vast estate owned by the eminent and illustrious Tuason and Legarda families. The Gardenia occupied a whole block just off the Loreto church of the Franciscans, bounded by what then were known as G. Tuazon, Lavanderos, Manrique, Lardizabal, Castaños, and Lipa streets.

The district got its name from the flower gardenia, sometimes known as rosal, much-prized for its delicate fragrance. Here in sprawling ramshackle wooden buildings, and in a few better-constructed houses, several hundred women of various nationalities plied their trade in regular brothels that flourished in the period from 1905 to 1917.

There were three types of houses -- first, second and third. The girls in the first class were white -- Americans, French, Spanish, Russians, who were available at five pesos per seance, a munificent sum in 1905. The girls in the second class houses were mestizas (half-breed) and new recruits from the provinces, at three pesos per. At the third class houses, it was caveat emptor, for a peso or two. There were houses which specialized on Japanese and Chinese women, for two or three pesos.

In 1917, a crusading city mayor named Justo Lukban who was a physician mercilessly put an end to this idyll. One night, Mayor Lukban had the police round up all the women they could find in the area, hustle them into police wagons right off to the piers where they were put aboard a ship. When Manila awoke the next morning, the better part of the Gardenia population was well on its way on the high seas to Davao.

Of course, this raised a high uproar. Not all the women were prostitutes. In their zeal, the policemen managed to get hold of some truly respectable women who had the misfortune of being in the neighborhood at the time of the raids. The mayor faced a number of suits for damages. And, of course, the advocates of civil liberties had their dander up in no time.

Mayor Lukban's action was ruled illegal by the courts and most of the women returned to Manila and presumably to the profession, although many were known to have turned a new leaf, got married and raised families. But Gardenia was never the same again. To deodorize the area, the names of streets which became associated with vice were changed into the names of virtues – Lealtad (Loyalty), Economia (Economy), Trabajo (Industry), Sobriedad (Sobriety).

On the occasion of the third centenary of the University of Santo Tomas in December 1911, the cornerstone for a projected new university building was laid on the site fronting España Avenue which the entrepreneurs Antonio de la Riva and Alfredo Chicote had deeded to the Dominicans.[69]

The UST had outgrown its Intramuros campus and much pressure was on the university authorities to ease the congestion. Owing to the paucity of funds, however, the Dominicans could not start construction on their Sampaloc site immediately.

In January 1923, construction work began on what would become the UST Main building. The design was the work of the Rev. Fr. Roque Ruano, O.P., one of the first graduates of the UST college of engineering, class of 1912. He also supervised the construction. The Dominicans were wary of earthquakes, conscious of the history of Intramuros. So Fr. Ruano was sent to Japan to study the development of earthquake-proof buildings and purchase steel bars.

By the time they were ready to build, the cornerstone which was laid on 11 December 1911 could no longer be located. No one could seem to remember where it lay. Despite an arduous search, it was never found again. But work started, nevertheless.

Modifications were continually made on Father Ruano's plans, and the costs increased continually. At times work stopped, while funds were gathered. Finally, on 13 November 1927, the new building was inaugurated and various university units moved here from Intramuros. By the outbreak of World War II in December 1941, only the college of law remained in Intramuros.

As the year 1940 ended, war began to look inevitable. Americans in Manila began serious plans to protect their interests in the event of hostilities. In January 1941, their leaders met to form the American Coordinating Committee, which later affiliated with the Red Cross under the name American Emergency Committee.

When the war broke out in the Philippines, 8 December 1941, classes at UST were suspended and the United States Army took over the campus for use as a motor pool.

By 20 December 1941, it became clear that Manila would be occupied by the Japanese forces. The American Emergency Committee started to plan for the time when Americans would be interned. The officers of the committee were authorized to make representations with the Dominican Fathers of UST for the use of their premises as concentration camp. The Dominicans agreed. The choice was presented to the Japanese when they occupied Manila on New Year's Day 1942.[70]

On 3 January 1942, Americans were rounded up by the Japanese wherever they were found – in their homes, in their clubs, in their offices, on the streets, in their hotels. They were temporarily concentrated at the Bay View Hotel and at the Rizal Stadium. Starting 4 January 1942, they were brought in directly to the University of Santo Tomas. With the internment accomplished, the American Emergency Committee ceased to function.

The camp population increased rapidly. The Japanese combed all sections of the city, rounding up all Americans, British and other "enemy aliens" and transporting them to Santo Tomas. The initial number of 300 internees brought on 4 January shot up to 2,000 on the 6th, and by the middle of the month there were 3,300 men, women and children quartered in the Main building, annex and gymnasium of the university.

The Santo Tomas Internment Camp existed for 37 months, from 4 January 1942 to 3 February 1945. A total of 3,787 persons were interned, grouped by nationality as follows: 2,792 Americans; 733 British; 100 Australians; 61 Canadians; 51 Dutch; eight Frenchmen; one Swiss; two Egyptians; two Spaniards; one German and one Slovak.

During the period that the camp existed, 75 babies were born; 45 in 1942; 14 in 1943; 14 in 1944, and two in 1945.

A total of 466 internees died in camp. No internee escaped from the camp. Three men were shot to death for trying to escape on 15 February 1942. One internee did escape towards the end of the war, when the Japanese were already preparing to leave the camp in January 1945.

The outbreak of World War II in the Philippines would not notably upset the physical order of things in Manila. In December 1941, after Pearl Harbor, the Japanese conducted air raids on various points of the city. The first victims were the offices and plant of the D-M-H-M Publications and San Juan de Letran college, all in Intramuros. The Japanese eventually learned Manila geography, or their bombers developed more accuracy, and started dropping bombs on shipping on the bay instead.

Douglas MacArthur declared Manila an "open city." Forthwith, all military personnel and supplies were withdrawn from the city. By the end of December 1941, the withdrawal would be accomplished. And none-too-soon, because on New Year's Day 1942, a Japanese courier appeared in Manila to announce that the Japanese forces, encamped in Parañaque to the south, would enter the city the next day.

The Japanese occupation of Manila would not alter the old city's face in any remarkable way. They did not have the means to undertake heavy constructions and for three years were content with using the city's old facilities to support Manila's role as the entrepot of their East Asia traffic in troops, supplies and equipment.

Thus, beyond giving streets, bridges, plazas and other landmarks Japanese names, there would be no notable change on Manila's physical appearance under the flag with the red sun.

CHAPTER III

THE PREY OF THE INTERLOPER

While the Filipinos were struggling for freedom from Spain, the Cubans on the other side of the globe were also engaged in a similar struggle. In the United States, there was popular sympathy for the Cubans, for even then there was much American money invested in Cuba.

As early as 3rd August 1897, Theodore Roosevelt, Assistant Secretary of the Navy, remarked that it would be to the advantage of the United States if firm action could be taken "in behalf of the wretched Cubans."[1]

The following 18th November, Roosevelt reiterated a desire "to send the Asiatic squadron to the Philippines as soon as war had been declared."[2]

Roosevelt was the spokesman of the expansionists and the imperialists, the forces that demanded a show of arms on the part of the United States. He ardently advocated the expansion of the U.S. Navy on one hand and the expansion of the United States towards the Pacific on the other. He was strongly supported by the Pulitzer and the Hearst newspaper chains, which capitalized on the Cuban situation to boost circulation.

American public opinion, fanned by the press, was agitating for intervention in Cuba, prompted by the imprisonment of American nationals following anti-Spanish rioting in Havana. The situation was playing right into the hands of Theodore Roosevelt, and now he found opportunity to intervene as well in Asia. Already he had decided on Commodore George Dewey, then president of the board of inspection, to command the Asiatic Squadron. Roosevelt pulled political strings to secure the appointment of Dewey, who left for his new post 7 December 1897.

On 15 February 1898, the American battleship *Maine* sunk in the harbor in Havana, killing two American officers and 264 men. Roosevelt seized the occasion to foment antagonisms and goad his country to war, saying: "I would give anything if President McKinley would order the fleet to Havana tomorrow. The *Maine* was sunk by an act of dirty treachery on the part of the Spaniards."[3] He had no evidence for that wild charge, of course, but already he may have been having visions of another wild charge up San Juan hill.

On 25 February, Secretary of the Navy John D. Long, exhausted by the frenetic activity, took the afternoon off. Roosevelt took over as Acting Secretary. In that brief afternoon he seized opportunity to cable Dewey: "Order the squadron . . . to Hong Kong. Keep full of coal. In the event of declaration of war with Spain, your duty will be to see that Spanish squadron does not leave the Asiatic coast, and then offensive operations in Philippine islands . . ."[4]

Sensing that war was imminent, Dewey asked for the plans of Manila's fortifications from the American consul in Hong Kong. He also received information from the American consul in Manila concerning the Spanish fleet, movement of troops and plans for defense.

On 23 April, the American consul in Manila, having been ordered by the home office to evacuate, advised Dewey that he would be arriving in Hong Kong with more information on the Spanish defense organization. The American fleet moved out of Hong Kong harbor and readied for action. The ammunition was passed out to the rest of the flotilla.

Shortly before noon on 25th April, Dewey received the cable from Secretary Long with the instruction: "War has commenced between the United States and Spain. Proceed at once to Philippine islands. Commence operations particularly against Spanish fleet. And you must capture vessels or destroy. Use utmost endeavor."[5] On the 27th, the American consul from Manila arrived in Hong Kong. Dewey heard him, then gave orders to head for Manila bay.

The Spanish fleet in Manila was commanded by Admiral Patricio Montojo, a distinguished and able naval officer. The Spaniards had more ships, but they were lighter and had fewer guns. The American fleet had more tonnage, was better-armed, and the men were better-trained and better-organized.

On 30 April, Admiral Montojo maneuvered his fleet into battle formation. Dewey, meanwhile, was rushing southward on the China sea. At five o'clock in the morning of 1st May, he reached the outer limit of the Manila anchorage. The Spanish batteries at the Luneta and at Fort San

Antonio Abad opened fire. But the Americans were beyond range, and no damage resulted. At break of day, Dewey sighted the Spanish fleet in crescent formation off Cavite.

At 6:40 a.m., Dewey calmly told the captain of his flagship: "Fire when you are ready, Gridley."[6] At 12:30 p.m. that day a white flag was hoisted atop the government building in Cavite. Theodore Roosevelt's days of empire were at hand.

In Hong Kong, General Aguinaldo was being dunned by a group of his fellow revolutionists in exile, who wanted a share of the P400,000 the Spaniards paid. Aguinaldo was waiting for an opportunity to return to Manila to continue the struggle, and the sum was intended for the purchase of arms. To avoid appearing in court, Aguinaldo, accompanied by two trusted aides, left for Saigon where he took another boat for Singapore, arriving there 23 April 1898. Upon arrival he was contacted by the American consul in Singapore, E. Spencer Pratt, who talked to him about joining forces with the Americans against the Spaniards. Aguinaldo was persuaded. This was the opportunity to renew the fight against Spain he was waiting for. Pratt advised Dewey in Hong Kong accordingly, and Dewey replied: "Tell Aguinaldo come as soon as possible."[7] Aguinaldo left for Hong Kong 26 April, but Dewey had left for his fateful rendezvous with the Spanish fleet in Manila bay.

Following Dewey's victory over the Spanish fleet, the Filipino revolutionary junta in Hong Kong decided that Aguinaldo should return to Manila and lead the Filipinos against Spain anew, taking advantage of the arrival of the Americans to advance their own revolutionary goals.

On 19 May Aguinaldo arrived in Cavite, and shortly was in conference with Dewey to map joint action against a common enemy.

The news of Aguinaldo's return swept Luzon. The arms he had procured in Hong Kong were landed. Together with arms from the Americans, these were distributed to the revolutionary forces now massing.

One by one the pueblos fell into rebel hands. Soon vast areas in the Tagalog provinces, in the Bicol and the Ilocos were freed from Spanish control. By June 1898, virtually all of Luzon, except Manila and the Cavite port, were in rebel hands.

The Spaniards tried to turn Filipino sentiment against the Americans, and both ecclesiastic and civil authorities issued ringing manifestoes rallying the Filipinos to the Spanish flag. A case of "too little, too late," all efforts failed.

Blockaded at sea by Dewey's navy, besieged on land by Aguinaldo's army, the hours were counted before Manila would surrender. Manila, of course, meant the old Walled City of Intramuros. The area around it was occupied by the Filipino army. Aguinaldo cut off the food and water supply to the city, and on the 16th and again on the 17th of June, offered honorable surrender terms to Governor Basilio Augustin. The Spaniard refused. Aguinaldo tightened the siege, and waited for hunger and thirst to complete the job.[8]

Meanwhile, Dewey asked for reinforcement, and on 30 June the first troops arrived under General Thomas Anderson. The second batch arrived 17 July under General Francis Greene, and the third arrived 31 July under General Arthur MacArthur.

Dewey now felt he could take on Manila. He arranged for the Belgian consul, Edward André, to negotiate with the Spaniards for the surrender of the city. Governor-General Augustin found his position no longer tenable, and was disposed to capitulate. When Madrid learned of his plans to surrender, he was relieved of his post and General Fermin Jaudenes was appointed in his stead.

Jaudenes, too, was convinced that the Spanish position was helpless, but like Augustin, he placed a high premium on the Spanish code of honor. So he entered into a bizarre compact with the Americans, calculated to save the precious Spanish face, whereby a mock battle would be staged after which the Spaniards were to surrender. Jaudenes also made it a condition that the Filipinos be kept out of the city walls and not to be made parties to the surrender. The Americans agreed, offering to fire on the Filipinos should they attack.

At 9:30 in the morning, 13 August 1898, the American flotilla on the bay started firing at the Spanish positions. At 11:00 o'clock, American troops under General MacArthur advanced on the walls. General Aguinaldo refused to stand by and watch so he deployed his men close to Intramuros. For their part, the Spaniards put up a gallant display of fireworks from the ramparts. Then at 11:20 in the morning, they raised the white flag of surrender. The mock battle was over and Manila had fallen.

Upon his arrival from Hong Kong, 19 May 1898, Aguinaldo issued a decree setting up a dictatorial form of government. This decree voided the republican government he had established at Biyak-na-bato.

With a government functioning, Aguinaldo decided to declare the independence of the Philippines. On 12 June 1898, in the town of Kawit, Cavite province, between 4 and 5 o'clock in the afternoon, the independence ceremonies were held. For the first time, the Philippine national flag was unfurled. Aguinaldo had asked Mrs. Marcela Mariño Agoncillo to make the flag in Hong Kong. For the first time, the Philippine national anthem was played. Aguinaldo had asked Julian Felipe of Cavite to compose the anthem.

At about this time Emilio Aguinaldo was introduced to a young man gifted with a brilliant mind but whose legs were paralyzed. His name was Apolinario Mabini, a young lawyer recently graduated from the University of Santo Tomas, the son of lowly farmers from a small barrio in Batangas. He had hurdled extreme hardships to gain what at that time was just about the highest rungs of education available to Filipinos. His parents had wanted him to be a priest; the priesthood was the highest ambition parents had for their children. But he had wanted to defend the poor he saw oppressed around him, and shortly he was launched on his law career. He had joined Dr. Rizal's *Liga Filipina*. But then he was taken ill, and his legs were paralyzed as a consequence.

Mabini was recuperating in Los Baños, Laguna, when Aguinaldo sent for him. Felipe Agoncillo had told Aguinaldo in Hong Kong about this gifted young man. Now they made a special hammock for him, and through 12 municipalities in insurgent hands, hundreds of men took turns to carry him.

Now face-to-face with Mabini, Aguinaldo was appalled. What could this pale, sickly man with the paralyzed legs do for the revolution? Then Mabini spoke, and Aguinaldo saw a man whose brilliant mind was matched only by his selfless zeal and the purity of his purpose. In later times, he would be called "the sublime paralytic," although he is just as well remembered as "the brains of the revolution."[9]

On 23 June 1898, Aguinaldo, at the instance of Mabini, changed the dictatorial government into a revolutionary government. Aguinaldo named a cabinet, called a constitutional convention which opened at Malolos, Bulacan, 15 September that year. The leaders of the emerging nation gathered at the church of Barasoain in Malolos, north of Manila, to forge the organic laws of the land. On 21 January 1899, the new constitution was promulgated. On the 23rd of January, the Republic of the Philippines was inaugurated in solemn ceremonies.[10]

In consonance with the Protocol of Peace of 12 August 1898, five American and five Spanish commissioners were appointed to meet in Paris to discuss the peace terms between Spain and the United States. The Peace Commission met in Paris from October to December 1898. On 10 December the Treaty of Paris was signed. It provided that Spain would cede the Philippines to the United States for the sum of $20 million.

The treaty went to the United States Senate for ratification. Here it met stern opposition, for many senators thought the treaty was unfair to the Filipinos. But on 4th February 1899, the Filipino-American war broke out, leading the erstwhile oppositionists to the treaty to vote for ratification.

William McKinley professed not to know what to do with the Philippines.[11] Vested interests were at work, however, pressuring American annexation of the islands. With the Treaty of Paris ratified, this was achieved. On 21 October 1998, McKinley issued what he called his "Benevolent Manifesto" in which he declared that the United States would assume control over the archipelago. He instructed his military commanders to extend American conquest over the country by force.

At about eight in the evening of 4th February 1899, an American patrol advanced towards San Juan east of Manila to ascertain the presence of Filipino troops in an area declared off-limits to them. Suddenly four armed men loomed before the patrol. "Halt!", the American private Willie Grayson yelled. One of the men ahead moved. "Halt!", Grayson yelled again. "Alto!", the man yelled back. Grayson fired. The man at the other end dropped. Grayson had fired the first shot in the Filipino-American war.[12]

Forthwith, the Americans turned on their erstwhile allies. Swiftly, they cut through Pasig and other towns south of Manila. In late February and early March, more American troops arrived. They launched an offensive to the north and the south, and by 30 March, they were at the gates of Malolos, the capital of the Republic. Aguinaldo moved his capital to San Isidro, Nueva Ecija.

Mabini, as premier and secretary of foreign affairs urged a determined stand to the bitter end. But a faction in Congress favored the American offer of autonomy. Mabini's government fell.

The chief of staff of Aguinaldo's forces, General Antonio Luna, was educated in Europe and had studied military science and tactics. He was best-prepared among the revolutionary generals to lead the fight against the Americans. Early in June 1899, while Luna was at Bayambang, Pangasinan, preparing the defense for an expected enemy attack, he received a telegram summoning him to Cabanatuan, Nueva Ecija, to see Aguinaldo. Accompanied by an aide and a few men, he arrived in Cabanatuan in the afternoon of 5 June. He headed for the town convento which was Aguinaldo's headquarters, but the President was not there. Instead, he found Felipe Buencamino, the secretary of foreign affairs, with whom he had had earlier brushes, and on whom he now vented his irritation. At the stairs, a group of soldiers fell upon him with guns and knives. Bleeding from 40 wounds Luna staggered to the street and fell, shouting, "Cowards! Assassins!"

The assassination of General Luna severely demoralized the Filipino troops, for he was highly respected. Aguinaldo now began his retreat north. On 6 September 1900, he reached Palanan, Isabela, a place on the Pacific coast virtually inaccessible by land and open only on the sea.

Through an elaborate subterfuge, using Filipino troops masquerading as reinforcements, the Americans crashed through Aguinaldo's security and on 23 March 1901, he fell into American hands.

On 1st April 1901, Aguinaldo was brought to Manila where he took his oath of allegiance to the United States. On 19 April, he issued a proclamation appealing to the Filipinos to accept American sovereignty.

"By acknowledging and accepting the sovereignty of the United States throughout the entire archipelago," he declared, "I believe that I am serving thee, my beloved country. May happiness be thine."[13]

Contemporary Filipinos like to engage themselves in the intellectual exercise that revolves on the theme, "What would have happened had the United States, as it did in Cuba, withdrawn, and left the Philippines to the Filipinos?"

It is a futile exercise and this is not the place where one should go into it. One adverts to it here only because the Philippines, throughout its history, has been prey to interlopers, and now, as it redeemed itself from Spanish bondage by the blood and tears of its people, another yoke was placed on its shoulders.

On 4th March 1899, a commission headed by Jacob Gould Schurman arrived in Manila to investigate conditions in the islands and make recommendations to President McKinley. On 31 January 1900, the Schurman commission submitted its report, recommending the withdrawal of military rule and the establishment of civil government with a bicameral legislature, and the establishment of a system of free public education.[14]

A second commission was dispatched, 9 April 1900, headed by William Howard Taft. This commission was vested with legislative powers in the Philippines starting 1st September 1900. Taft was made chief executive officer in the pacified provinces starting 4 July 1901, becoming the first civil governor of the islands under the American regime. In 1905, during the term of Luke E. Wright, the title was changed to governor-general.[15]

Before 1907, the central government established by the Americans was purely authoritarian. The first elective positions in the national government were provided for by the Philippine Bill of 1902, through the establishment of the Philippine Assembly, the first law-making body in the country. Eighty members of the first Philippine Assembly were elected in 1907. The inaugural session was held 16 October that year at the Manila Grand Opera House, with Sergio Osmeña as speaker and Manuel Quezon as majority floor leader.

The highest office in government, that of governor-general, was held by the Americans. The executive departments were headed by American members of the commission. The victory of the Democratic party with Woodrow Wilson as president in 1912 and again in 1916 resulted in increased participation of Filipinos in the government. It led to the enactment of the Jones Law in 1916 which provided for Filipino control over domestic affairs.

On 2nd December 1920, four years after the passage of the Jones Law, President Wilson sent a message to the United States Congress, recommending the grant of independence to the Philippines.

"The people of the Philippines have succeeded in maintaining stable government," Wilson declared. "It is now our liberty and our duty to keep our promise to the people of those islands by granting them the independence which they so honorably covet."[16]

It was an empty gesture. In the elections the previous November, the Republicans had captured both the White House and the two houses of Congress.

In 1921, President Warren G. Harding sent a two-man investigation mission to the Philippines to report on the state of affairs in the islands. The mission was composed of General Leonard Wood as head and William Cameron Forbes as the other member. Both had served in the Philippines earlier.

The Wood-Forbes mission arrived in Manila 4th May 1921 and stayed four months, visiting almost every part of the Philippines. General Wood returned to Manila to become governor-general. Forbes went to Washington to submit the mission's report to Harding. The mission recommended the continuation of American rule over the islands, "until the people have had time to absorb and master thoroughly the powers already in their hands."[17]

Leonard Wood had been colonel in the Rough Riders in the Spanish-American War and had served as military governor of Cuba. He was a leading contender for the Republican presidential nomination in 1920, but lost to Harding.

Wood soon found himself at odds with the Filipino leaders because his idea of control by the governor-general extended to matters of a purely domestic nature. The Filipino leaders believed that this violated the spirit of the Jones Law. On 7 July 1923, all the Filipino members of the Cabinet resigned. Wood accepted all resignations. Government virtually ground to a halt. The controversy ended only when Wood returned to the United States for medical treatment. On 20 August 1927, while undergoing surgery in Boston for a brain tumor, Leonard Wood died.

Wood's successors were able to work in harmony with the Filipinos. They were Henry Stimson (1928-1929), Dwight F. Davis (1929-1932), Theodore Roosevelt, Jr. (1932-1933), and Frank Murphy (1933-1935).

The last was a Democrat appointed by President Franklin D. Roosevelt. He became the first American High Commissioner when the Philippine Commonwealth was inaugurated in 1935.

The American occupation launched the land into the 20th century. The United States introduced the concepts of democracy. For the first time the people participated in making their own laws. Government was freed from the strictures of religion. The administration of justice was modernized, a civil service was created, and windows were opened on the arts and sciences.

"The American occupation broke the continuity of Philippine history, introduced the Filipinos to new principles and ideals of life, and different conceptions of the essential legal and political rights of individuals," an American observer noted.[18]

Three of the new appurtenances of civilization the Americans brought over, however, were more vital in bringing the Philippines into modern times than the others. These were the public school system, infrastructure and public transport, and mass media.

On 13 August 1898, less than three weeks after the American occupation of Manila, seven schools were reopened, and a teacher of English was installed in each under the informal supervision of Rev. Fr William D. McKinnon, chaplain of the First California Regiment.[19] The teachers were soldiers chosen for certain special qualifications. Their work was the beginning of the public school system in the Philippines under American rule.[20]

On 1st June 1899, Lt. George P. Anderson was detailed as city superintendent of schools for Manila. There was an enrollment of 4,500 in the public schools during the schoolyear. In 1900, Capt. Albert Todd was detailed as superintendent of schools for the entire Philippine islands.

By 1900, over 100,000 Filipino children were attending school. To get the children to classes they were given free books, notebooks, slates and pencils, and even candies.

Where the Spanish sent missionaries who established churches, the Americans sent teachers who opened schools. The schools were no less effective in imposing the social and political modes of the new regime, than the churches in the former.

In June 1901, the U.S. Army transport *Sheridan* brought 48 American schoolteachers to Manila. They were the first civilian teachers and began to take over from the soldiers who were the first teachers in English.

On 29 August 1901, another U.S. Army transport, this one the famous *Thomas*, brought another batch of 600 teachers to Manila. The teachers thereupon became known as the "Thomasites."

"Never before in the history of the world has any country sent out an army like this," Dr. Gilbert S. Perez, himself a schoolteacher who came out to Manila in 1909, would write.[21] They came every year after that, until 1933.

One of the early Acts passed by the Philippine Commission was Act 74 creating the Department of Public Instruction, "to ensure to the people of the Philippines a system of free public schools."

On 4 July 1901, when the civil government was established, the department passed into civilian authority.

Act 74 partitioned the archipelago into school divisions. A school was opened in every municipality, with English as the medium of instruction. Optional religious instruction was allowed. Act 74 also provided for 1,000 American schoolteachers.

By December 1901, there were 765 American teachers in the Philippines. To provide for the training of Filipino schoolteachers, the Philippine Normal School was established in 1901.

By 1902 a four-year primary course and a three-year intermediate course had been established. A four-year program of secondary instruction was introduced in 1903. Eventually, a provincial high school was established in the capital of each province.

In 1908, the University of the Philippines came into being, completing the state system of education in the American regime.

In 1910, there would be 800 American teachers in 4,531 schools with 610,493 students. By the end of the American administration of the islands in 1935, there would be but 100 American teachers in about 10,000 schools with over 1.2 million students.

The work of education, while under American administration, was financed by Filipino money.

Charles Burke Elliot writing in 1916 said, "There are in the Philippines, approximately one million two hundred thousand children of school age, of which less than one half are receiving instruction at any time. The frequent appeals to Congress for financial assistance for the educational work have fallen upon deaf ears and the Filipinos have been left to pay all the bills for the education of their children."[22]

Also, "In fact, the government at Washington had done nothing for education in the Philippines other than permit certain Americans to labor there in the service of the insular government and spend there money which the Filipinos and residents are able to furnish." Elliot served in the Philippine Commission from 1910 to 1912.

After the educational system which opened windows for the Filipino intellect on the world as it had become by then, the second truly vital development the Americans introduced was in the field of transportation and communication.

The nation that built America now lent its technology to this archipelago. The first act of the Philippine Commission, the body created by the American government to administer civil affairs in these islands in 1900, concerned infrastructure. On 21 September that year, the Philippine Commission passed Act No. 1, appropriating P2 million for the construction of roads and bridges.

From the passage of Act No. 1 of the Philippine Commission on 21 September 1900, to the cessation of American authority over civil affairs in this country with the inauguration of the Philippine Commonwealth, 15 November 1935, the United States regime constructed 20,826 kilometers of roads and 8,100 bridges, and extended the railroads to 1,395 kilometers.[23]

The true magnitude of these figures may be better appreciated if one learned that through the 330 years of Spanish presence in these islands, they constructed but 2,475 kilometers of roads, 2,600 bridges and 195 kilometers of railroad.[24]

No matter that the Spanish roads, as the Americans found out, were barely passable. Lt. Col. James Parker of the American expeditionary force described some of these roads: "The roads, both in the rice plains and on higher ground, are usually abominable; from a ditch alongside, the soft dirt is thrown into the middle, the road rarely containing any stone or gravel . . . All of the country roads, and many roads designated as high roads, are mere mud tracks in the wet season and little more than trails in the dry season."[25]

General Arthur MacArthur testifying before the U.S. Senate, nevertheless commented with apparent admiration on the many roads the Spanish had built on Luzon and expressed surprise that only a few of them appeared on maps. "Some of them are not passable at all seasons of the year, but they are still roads," he said. In short, the Americans did not start from scratch on their infrastructure program. [26]

In March 1903, the municipal board of Manila awarded to the entrepreneur Charles M. Swift of Detroit the franchise to operate an electric street railway service and furnish electric light and power to the city for a 50-year period. Swift raised the capital and started to organize the Manila Electric Railroad and Light Company. The firm's acronym, MERALCO, would become a byword in the life of Manila.[27]

The horsedrawn *tranvia* of the *Compania de los Tranvias de Filipinas* established in 1878 by Zobel and Bayo had by this time deteriorated so that in 1902 it was operating but 10 tramcars daily.

Meralco had no use for the old rolling stock of the *Compañia de Tranvias*, but it bought out the company nevertheless to establish a clear monopoly. Probably for the same reason, Meralco also bought out the existing power firm, *La Electricista*, which first started operation in 1895 and was partly owned by Tabacalera.

In September 1903, Meralco began work on a new powerhouse on Isla de Provisor on the Pasig, and started to lay the track and raise the overhead system for the electric streetcar. On 10 April 1905, the new service was inaugurated.

Before the end of 1905, the Manila *tranvia* had about 40 miles of track, with five lines radiating from Plaza Goiti. The trucks carried five times more than the 12 passenger capacity of the horse-drawn *tranvia*. The trucks were of wood and steel with open sides. They were called La Jardinera. Fares were 12 centavos for the first class (front seats) and 10 centavos for second (back seats). The streetcar covered all the areas served by the horse-drawn tranvia, and beyond that to what were then the limits of the city, like San Lazaro to the north, Santa Mesa and Santa Ana to the east and to the approaches of Pasay, then wilderness, in the south, and on to Malabon which was served by the Spanish-period company with a steam tramway.

Aside from providing Manilans with a convenient and comfortable transport system that outpaced the cheaper calesa, the streetcar forced two things which metamorphosed Manila into the beginnings of the future megalopolis.

First, it pushed the parameters of the city; second, it nudged the authorities to expand and develop the road system.

Regarding the first point, people began to build homes wherever the streetcar went. The city grew beyond its original confines, surging into riceland and woodland and cogonal. The wilderness gave way.

As to the second point, Manila had to modernize its streets. With a modern public conveyance system, the few cobbled streets were improved, the dirt roads were paved. The road network expanded in every direction, wherever the *tranvia* led.

The *tranvia* grew through the years and by 1925, the network consisted of 52 miles of track, with 50 single-truck and 123 double-truck cars. In that year of 1925, the system ferried 35.1 million passengers, about 95 times the Manila population of 365,700.

In 1903, the first automobile appeared on Manila streets. Doubtless it was a sensation in this city where the *tranvia* was still horse-drawn. Shortly, the wealthy and those fascinated with the new and stylish were bringing in other cars.

The Americans, of course, took the lead in bringing in motor vehicles. Used to the modern conveniences of America, the young colonials, civil and military, and their families, probably considered this a benighted city with but a few streets with electric lights and hardly any electric appliances. Going about in horse-drawn *carruajes* was definitely not in their style, since the Ford Model T by then was commonplace where they came from.

By 1912, some form of regulation and control over motor vehicles became necessary, and that year the motor vehicle law was passed. In that year of 1912, there were registered 947 automobiles, 180 trucks and 450 motorcycles.

By the end of the American civil administration in the Philippines in 1935, there would be registered 26,507 automobiles, 15,868 trucks and 534 motorcycles.

The motor vehicle would revolutionize internal travel in the Philippines. Now people found many reasons to travel aside from the traditional ones of trade and commerce, the practice of crafts and professions, family movements and religious pilgrimages. Now people could travel for the pleasure of it. The development of the resort sites like Baguio during this period became a happy corollary to the development of land travel.

Realizing that the electric trolley was not the best way of meeting the continually growing public need for transportation, the Meralco decided to launch an autobus service.

In 1927, Meralco fielded 20 autobuses. The bodies were constructed in Meralco's own shops and the engines and chassises were imported. That year, the University of Santo Tomas opened its new campus on España street in the Sampaloc district of Manila, and the responsive public utility company deemed this sufficient enough reason to open a new route serviced by bus.

New lines opened periodically and new buses were commissioned into duty, but as the autobus complement grew, the streetcars declined. By 1941 when the Pacific War broke out, there were 190 autobus units in the service, while the streetcar fleet stagnated at 109. By then, 28 million persons were using the streetcars and 31 million the buses.

The United States Armed Forces in the Far East (USAFFE) commandeered the autobuses to ferry men and supplies from Manila to Bataan when war broke out in December 1941. Manila was declared an open city and had to be cleared of army personnel and material.

When the Japanese occupied Manila in January 1942, they took over the operations of the trolley system. The network went into inevitable decline, lacking maintenance and spare parts. But it remained for the battle for the liberation of Manila in February 1945 to reduce the colorful system's streetcars and tracks to complete ruin.

A Philippine institution in the pre-World War II period was the Manila Carnival held each year in January or February. The carnival was in the nature of a trade and agricultural fair where the cities and provinces, government agencies and private firms exhibited their products and publicized their services. It was also occasion for much merrymaking, highlighted by the selection of a carnival queen who reigned over the festivities.

The carnival was first held at the Bagumbayan Field, or Luneta, in 1905, and was held more or less regularly thereafter up to the eve of World War II.

In 1911, the Manila Carnival had a particularly spectacular attraction – the airplane. Two airplanes, in fact, brought here by a travelling troupe of air-stuntmen led by Capt. Thomas "Lucky" Baldwin.[28]

At 5 o'clock in the afternoon, 21 February 1911, a biplane christened "Skylark" piloted by James "Bud" Mars, 34, took off from the Luneta and rose to 1,000 feet before it came down again. The aircraft had a skeleton frame with cloth-covered wings, powered by a Breguet F11 engine, constructed by Todd Schriver. Mars flew daily exhibition flights until 28 February 1911, at one time attaining a maximum altitude of 3,500 feet.

On February 27, Lucky Baldwin also flew his plane named "Red Devil." Now the air age had overtaken the Philippines.

The next year, 1912, the United States Army brought into the Philippines the first army planes in this country. The Air Corps during this period was part of the U.S. Army.

In 1918, a section of Fort Stotsenberg in Angeles, Pampanga, was named Clark Field, in honor of a pioneer American aviator, Harold Clark. It became the headquarters of the Air Corps.

In 1919, an army plane flew from Manila to Cebu and on to Bacolod and Iloilo, and back to Manila. The pilots were Maj. J.E.H. Stevenot and A.J. Croft. This was the first inter-island flight in the Philippines. The skies over the islands were opening up.

In May 1926, the first transcontinental flight to Manila was successfully negotiated from Madrid by the two pioneering Spanish aviators, Captain Eduardo Gonzalez Gallarza and Captain Joaquin Loriga.

The historic 17,000-kilometer air voyage on a single-engine Breguet XIV named *Legazpi*, after the *Adelantado* who founded the city of Manila, began in Madrid on 5 April 1926, and ended at Nichols Field outside Manila on 13 May 1926. It was an epic voyage comparable in its significance to Philippine travel to the sea voyage of Miguel Lopez de Legazpi from Mexico to Cebu in 1565. It charted new routes in the way Legazpi's voyage did, this time by air.

The Gallarza-Loriga Madrid-Manila flight of 1926 showed the possibilities of commercial air travel to the Orient. It opened a new channel to these islands from outside. The Spanish aviators, however, did not return to Madrid by air. They went home by steamship after celebrations in Manila that lasted for two weeks.

In 1930, the Philippine Aerial Taxi Company (PATCO) was organized with Major J.E.H. Stevenot as president.

Starting 16 February 1931, PATCO operated a fleet of two-seaters and four-seaters on interisland routes, flying mail and businessmen and government officials and others who could afford the costs. Now there was an alternative to sea travel to reach the far-flung outposts of the archipelago.

Aside from roads, bridges, piers, the scope of infrastructure now included airports. To oversee the construction and management of airports, and to regulate the new transportation service, the government established the Civil Aeronautics Administration in 1931.

In 1933, the Iloilo-Negros Air Express Company (INAEC) was established. This may be taken as a measure of the success of domestic air travel, its acceptance by the travelling public and its usefulness to human activity.

A milestone in Philippine travel was marked on 29 November 1935, with the arrival at Sangley Point in Cavite of the Pan-American Airways *China Clipper* on its first voyage across the Pacific. This was an event of such great significance to Philippine travel that it may be compared in its effects to the epic voyage of Ferdinand Magellan across the Pacific in 1521. Magellan made the trip in three-and-a-half months. The modern American ocean liners negotiated the same distance in 17 days. The Pan Am *China Clipper* made it in five days.

In 1936, two pioneer Filipino aviators, Antonio Arnaiz and Juan Calvo undertook the air voyage from Manila to Madrid, taking the return route of the Gallarza-Loriga flight in 1926. The reverse voyage charted the route of the Europe-Philippine flight and paved the way for commercial air trips from that continent to the Pacific.

From, hereon, Manila became the focal point of air lanes in the Asia-Pacific region. Soon flights originating from Spain, Holland, Germany, Italy, China, Japan, Australia and various points in the region were calling at Manila.

Philippine Air Lines was incorporated on 26 February 1941, by a group of businessmen led by Andres Soriano, a scion of the old creole Ayala-Roxas family, long-distinguished in Philippine industry.

On 15 March 1941, PAL made its first flight, Manila-Baguio-Manila, on a twin-engine Beech Model 18 owned by Andres Soriano y Cia., Soriano's management company which served as managers for PAL. The plane was piloted by Paul I. Gunn and Emil S. Scott. Ticket No. 1 was issued to William Smith.

By December 1941, when World War II in the Pacific broke out, PAL had two Beech Model 18s and was flying regularly to Zamboanga and

Davao. With the outbreak of the war 8 December 1941, PAL ceased all activity. Its planes were used to evacuate allied officers and pilots to Australia and were destroyed in action.

The early American administrators believed that an informed public opinion was essential in a democratic society. Consequently there emerged a press patterned after the wheeling and dealing American system. It required sometime before it simmered down into a sober constructive institution.

The first American publication in Manila started on 10 September 1898 and was called *The American Soldier*. The following 11 October, the *Manila Times*, the first daily newspaper under the American regime, made its appearance. On its heels, on 15 October, came *The American*. These publications were aimed at the American army and navy personnel and were edited by the armed forces people themselves.[29]

The Freedom appeared in early 1899, this one owned and edited by American civilians. In early 1900, the *Manila Daily Bulletin* first appeared as a shipping journal.

In August 1902, the *Cablenews* was founded as a serious attempt at journalism in support of economic growth.

For the most part, these newspapers were characterized as "disgraceful examples of the worst kind of journalism." But they represented the beginning of the free flow of information not known in these islands before.

Other publications came up, like the *The Philippine Teacher*, (1904), *The Philippine Education* (1906) and the *Philippines Free Press* (1907). In 1908 the *Cablenews* merged with *The American*.

Publications in the Spanish language also sprang up during this period, mostly to serve the political aims of the Filipinos themselves. The first was *La Democracia* which first appeared on 16 May 1899. That same year *El Grito del Pueblo* (The Cry of the People) and *El Filipino Libre* (The Free Filipino) followed.

In Cebu, Sergio Osmeña founded *Nuevo Dia* (New Day) in 1900. The following year, *El Renacimiento* (The Reawakening) appeared in Manila. On 1st April 1902, *El Mercantil* (The Mercantile) began publication.

Others followed in the succeeding decades. *El Ideal* started in 1910, and *La Vanguardia* in 1916.

As Filipinos mastered English, publications in this language made their appearance. The first Filipino-owned and staffed weekly in English, *The Independent,* began publication in 1915.

On 8 August 1920, *The Philippines Herald* was launched by a group of Filipino business and political leaders headed by Manuel L. Quezon. It became the first Filipino daily in English.

On 1st April 1925, *The Tribune*, also a daily in English, made the newspaper stands. It became part of the chain owned by Don Alejandro Roces, Sr., that eventually included *La Vanguardia* and *Taliba*.

Vernacular publications also made their appearance. Aside from the *Tagalog Taliba*, there was *Mabuhay*.

Other vernacular periodicals that emerged during the period were weekly magazines, like *Liwayway* and *Bulaklak* in Tagalog, *Bisaya* in Cebuano, *Hiligaynon* in Ilonggo, and *Bannawag* in Ilocano.

By 1924, there were 26 periodicals in the English language, 26 in Spanish, 13 in Visayan, 10 in Tagalog, five in Ilocano, four in Chinese, three in Pampango and one in Pangasinan.

By 1930, ninety publications in English or in English and one other language were running a total of 505,440 copies. Sixty periodicals in Spanish had a total circulation of 182,318 and 22 Tagalog periodicals had a circulation of 237,494.

When American control over domestic affairs phased out in 1935, there were 270 publications officially registered, published in various languages with a combined circulation of two million. Sixty per cent of this number were published in the English language.

There also developed in this country the profession of the journalist. By channelling the free flow of information the journalist shaped public opinion and became among the prime movers of the nation that was emerging.

The development of a free press is an index, first, to the growth of literacy among the people, and second, to the growth of social consciousness. Now the people wanted to know.

The twenties brought a new medium – the movies. Now Hollywood would impose its will on a populace quite literally mesmerized.

Probably no other medium would succeed in moulding taste and opinion in this country, for better and for worse, than American movies. From Theda Bara to Judy Garland, from the silent classics of Charles Chaplin to the grand spectaculars of Cecil B. De Mille, American movies offered a pattern after which the hapless Filipino audience cut its manners, viewpoints, fashions, lifestyles.

Some wag would thereafter characterize the Filipino of the time as the product of 300 years in a convent and 40 years in Hollywood.

During the 1930s radio was introduced into the Philippines. It opened new areas not only in communications but also in entertainment. Now the dissemination of news entered the electronic age and the formation of popular tastes became faster and easier under the techniques of the radio era.

By the time World War II broke out in the Philippines in 1941, American culture lay over the land like a thick sleazy veneer.

The triumph of American culture and the near-extirpation of the native Malay civilization with its Spanish overlay was started by the schools, but it was completed by the mass media.

In the words of an American observer, "American culture had triumphed almost to the point of embarrassment to its own citizens. Originally promoted by the government through the schools, by the end of the First World War, it was American technology, primarily the automobile, and the media industry -- first the newspapers and next films -- which it seemed had almost liquidated Spanish-Malay culture."[30]

As can be gathered, the Republican party consistently opposed the grant of independence to the Philippines. The Republicans wanted a defensive buffer to the U.S. Pacific coast, a ready source of cheap raw material for American industry, and a dumping ground for the surplus produce of American agriculture and manufacture.[31]

In the U.S. congressional elections of 1930, the Democrats won a majority in the Lower House. Although the Senate was still in Republican hands, the chances for the passage of an independence bill suddenly brightened. An independence mission was sent to Washington, D.C., headed by Sergio Osmeña and Manuel Roxas.

Several bills providing for Philippine independence had been filed in the American congress. One of these, authored by Senators Harry B. Hawes and Bronson Cutting, became the basis for discussions in the Senate. A similar bill was introduced in the Lower House by Congressman Butler B. Hare. From the two bills emerged the Hare-Hawes-Cutting Bill which was approved by both Houses in December 1932.

The bill provided for a 10-year transition period with a government to be called the Commonwealth of the Philippine Islands. A convention was to be called to adopt a constitution for the Commonwealth, subject to approval by the President of the United States. At the end of the 10-year period, the independence of the Philippines was to be granted and recognized by the United States.

On 13 January 1933, President Herbert Hoover vetoed the bill. Congress overrode the veto, and the Hare-Hawes-Cutting bill became law.

The law had to be accepted by the Philippine legislature, however, before it could go into effect. But even while it was being deliberated upon in the U.S. Congress, Manuel L. Quezon had opined that it would bring hardships on the Philippines. He wanted economic concessions, and many members of the assembly agreed with him.

Philippine officialdom split into the pros, who accepted the Hare-

Hawes-Cutting Act, headed by Sergio Osmeña, and the antis, who opposed the Act, led by Quezon. In the general referendum, Quezon's faction prevailed. In October 1933, the Philippine legislature approved a resolution informing the U.S. Congress that the Hare-Hawes-Cutting Act was not acceptable to the Filipinos. A new independence mission headed by Manuel L. Quezon left for the United States in November 1933.

The Quezon mission negotiated the independence bill which was filed in the U.S. Senate by Senator Millard Tydings, and by Rep. John McDuffie in the Lower House. The bill was passed by both Houses, and subsequently signed into law by President Roosevelt.

On 1st May 1934, the Tydings-McDuffie Act was unanimously accepted by the Philippine legislature. As called for by the law, elections were held for 202 delegates to a constitutional convention which opened 30 July 1934.

It took over six months to draft the constitution which was approved 8 February 1935. The following 23rd March, it was signed by President Roosevelt. On 14 May, it was accepted by the Filipinos in a plebiscite.

With the adoption of a constitution, the Filipinos took steps to establish the Commonwealth. The constitution was to serve as the fundamental law not only of the Commonwealth but also of the Republic to be inaugurated in 1946. Elections were held the following September 1935, in which Quezon was elected president and Osmeña vice-president. They were sworn into office during the ceremonies to inaugurate the new Commonwealth held 15 November 1935.

Militarism began to rear its gory head in the totalitarian states of Asia and Europe in the early 1930s. In 1931-32, Japan annexed Manchuria. Encouraged by its success, Japan conducted a military campaign which sought to bring China under its control. The Sino-Japanese war broke out on a total scale in 1937.

On 25 November 1936, Japan and Germany signed the Anti-Comintern Pact, and on 6 November 1937, they were joined by Italy.

On 16 September 1940, President Roosevelt signed the Selective Service Act, and on 29 October the same year, for the first time in its history, the United States instituted compulsory military service while it was not at war.

On 19 June 1941, President Quezon pledged the loyalty of the Philippines to the United States, if the United States entered the war. The Philippines thus was aligned with the world's democracies.

In August 1941, Roosevelt and Winston Churchill met at sea and drew up the Atlantic Charter, which outlined the allied peace aims under eight points. The following 8th October, General Hideki Tojo became premier of Japan.

In November, President Roosevelt and Secretary Cordell Hull received in Washington the special envoys of Japan, Ambassador Saburo Karuso and Admiral Kichisaburo Nomura, to confer on the Far Eastern situation. On 6 December 1941, President Roosevelt sent a last appeal to Emperor Hirohito to avoid conflict in the Pacific.

On 7 December, Japan declared war on the United States, Great Britain, Australia, Canada, New Zealand, and the Union of South Africa. Before this declaration could reach Washington by air or cable, the Japanese made the infamous attack on Pearl Harbor where the Pacific Fleet lay awaiting its orders. Almost simultaneously, similar attacks were made on Philippine soil. On 27 December they bombed Manila. On 2 January 1942, they occupied the city.

A new interloper cast its shadow upon the ancient land!

Before assuming the presidency of the Philippine Commonwealth, Manuel L. Quezon had worked out a system of national defense. He was aware of his responsibility to safeguard the future independence of the Philippines as pledged by the United States. On a visit to Washington in 1935, he had bluntly asked the U.S. Army Chief of Staff: "Is the Philippines defensible?"

The man to whom that question was posed at that time was completing an extended term in this office, to which he had been appointed at the age of 50, the youngest ever to become Chief of Staff in the history of the U.S. Army. His name was Douglas MacArthur.[32]

MacArthur now gave Quezon some pointers on military science and concluded that the Philippines may, indeed, "achieve a respectable defense and enjoy a reasonable safety if it is prepared and determined to repel attacks."

President Quezon brought the matter of Philippine defense direct to President Roosevelt, and sought the services of the U.S. Army Chief of Staff as military adviser to the Philippine government. Immediately Roosevelt sent MacArthur to the islands, assisted by Col. Dwight D. Eisenhower and Col. James B. Ord.

General MacArthur and his staff immediately buckled down to the task of preparing a national defense program for the Philippines. When he appeared for the first time before the Philippine legislature, President Quezon submitted as the first measure of his administration, the national defense program which, among other things, made military service compulsory to all male Filipinos.

On 25 November 1935, the National Defense Act was passed by the legislative body. Retired from the U.S. Army, General MacArthur was commissioned Field Marshal of the Philippine Armed Forces.

As America's relations with theAxis powers deteriorated, all U.S. military forces in the Philippines were incorporated into the U.S. Armed Forces in the Far East. MacArthur was recalled to active service and made commanding general of the new armed force. By this time, 100,000 reserves had been trained for the Philippine Army under the National Defense Act. War plans were rushed up and military installations were built.

Before the outbreak of hostilities, the U.S. Army had been setting up fortifications in Bataan. These efforts were intensified. Opposite Bataan, across a narrow inlet, Corregidor lay with its big guns aimed westward to the China Sea. High cliffs towered on the west, north and east side of Bataan. Approach from the east was possible only through well-guarded highways sweeping in from the Central Plains of Luzon. The south and left flank was accessible only by water across Manila Bay, or by land through Hagonoy in Bulacan. The mountains of Morong, Bagac and Mariveles formed a triangular base of operations against approaches from all sides. Such were the defense lines of Bataan to which MacArthur now withdrew his command as the enemy cut down the opposition of the skeleton forces that gallantly though futilely sought to stem the tide. By 30 December 1941, MacArthur had all his forces within the confines of Bataan.

Manila was declared an open city, and all military installations were removed and armed forces withdrawn. This did not protect the city from enemy bombs, however. The Japanese continued their daily raids, and Manilans wept as they watched treasured landmarks, some as old as the city itself, go up in smoke and flames.[33]

Two Japanese columns moved upon Manila from points north and south. On the evening of New Year's Day 1942, a Japanese courier brought notice to Manila that the invasion forces were bivouacked at Parañaque to the south and would enter the city the next day.

Between 9 and 10 o'clock on the morning of 2nd January 1942, the Japanese swept into the ancient city of the Solaymans and the Lakandolas.

The decision to declare Manila an open city was made to spare the city from the death and destruction brought about by military operations. To enlarge the safe zone, the outlying areas were brought into a new administrative jurisdiction called Greater Manila. The post of mayor of the city of Greater Manila was given to Jorge B. Vargas, formerly executive secretary to President Quezon. It was now Vargases duty to hand over the city to the conquerors.

When Mayor Vargas called on the Japanese commanding general to deliver the city, he was asked to present the ranking Filipino leaders. When the leaders, with Vargas, appeared the following day, they were confronted with a choice of three ways by which the country may be governed under the new regime: first, by a purely military administration under the Japanese; second, by a dictatorial form of government under General Artemio Ricarte, a hero of the Revolution and a contemporary of General Aguinaldo, who exiled himself to Japan when American rule became invincible, and who vowed never to return to his homeland while it was under American domination; third, government by a commission selected by Filipino leaders. The Filipino leaders consented to a government by a commission the members of which were to be selected from among themselves.

The Philippine Executive Commission was thus established with Jorge B. Vargas as Chairman. The authority of the Commission was extended beyond Manila to include the entire country.

When Vargas assumed the position of chairman of the Philippine Executive Commission, he had to yield the position of mayor of Greater Manila to which he had been named by President Quezon at the outbreak of the war in 1941. Now Vargas nominated Leon G. Guinto, Sr., to the post of mayor of Greater Manila, a position Guinto held to the end of the war.

When he was appointed mayor of Greater Manila in 1942, Leon G. Guinto, Sr. had had a long and distinguished career in government.

Born 28 June 1896 in barrio San Nicolas, Bacoor, Cavite, south of Manila, to the spouses Juan P. Guinto and Pia Gawaran, Leon G. Guinto had his early schooling in his hometown and at San Juan de Letran college in Manila.

In 1906 he found employment as weather observer at the Weather Bureau on Padre Faura street in Manila. In 1908, he married Marta Montes of Atimonan, Tayabas. They had three sons and two daughters.

In 1916, Guinto enrolled in the old Escuela de Derechos, leaving his employment at the Weather Bureau. Guinto completed his law studies in 1920 and the same year qualified for the practice of law. He was employed shortly after as a private secretary to then Senate President Manuel L. Quezon.

Using, Atimonan, Tayabas, the hometown of his wife, Doña Marta Montes, as his base, Guinto ran for the provincial board of Tayabas in 1922 and won. In 1925 he ran for representative of the second district of

Tayabas in the Lower House of the Philippine legislature and won. He served in this capacity until 1931, during which he gained some distinction among his peers as a legislator.

In 1931, Leon G. Guinto won election as governor of the province of Tayabas and served in this position until his appointment as Commissioner of Public Safety in 1933 while Theodore Roosevelt, Jr. was governor-general. Later in that year of 1933, he was named Undersecretary of the Interior in the administration of Governor-General Frank Murphy. When the Departments of the Interior and Labor were merged in 1934, Guinto continued as Undersecretary. He became Secretary of Labor in 1940 in the Commonwealth government of President Manuel L. Quezon.

By this time, Guinto had developed strong ties to the labor movement of the Philippines. As wartime mayor of Greater Manila, Leon G. Guinto drew from his contacts in labor for the yeoman workers he needed for his administration. This explains why many labor leaders served in various capacities in the wartime government of Manila.

In 1936, Doña Marta Montes died. In 1938, Leon G. Guinto married Doña Remedios Lizares of the *hacendado* family of Talisay, Negros Occidental. They were childless.

This was the Leon G. Guinto, Sr. who was catapulted to the extremely crucial position of mayor of Greater Manila during World War II in the Philippines.

Realizing the hopeless situation of the U.S. Armed Forces in the Far East, President Roosevelt ordered General MacArthur to Australia to assume command over U.S. forces in the Southwest Pacific area. With his family, MacArthur slipped off Corregidor 11 March 1942. He landed in Mindanao from where he was flown to Australia. Upon landing in Australia, he made the famous pledge: "I shall return."

Lt. Gen. Jonathan M. Wainwright succeeded to the post of commander of the Philippine-American forces in the Philippines. The defenders of Bataan and Corregidor held their ground and repulsed all attacks. "Bataan still stands," the Voice of Freedom on Corregidor radioed to the world.

The 3rd of April 1942 came. It was Good Friday for Christian Philippines and *Jimmu Tenno* Day for the Japanese, commemorating the birth anniversary of the legendary first emperor of Japan. General Masaharu Homma, commander of the Japanese forces, chose this day to unleash the total strength of Japan in the Philippines on Bataan. Japanese infantry swept against the Filipino-American lines, supported by heavy artillery and motorized cavalry. The Japanese had complete control of the air and strafed and bombed the defense positions with deadly accuracy.

Hunger and disease combined with fatigue to erode the strength of the defenders. The moment came, and surrender was inevitable. On 9 April 1942, the Voice of Freedom would announce to the world, "Bataan has fallen."[34]

The task of yielding Bataan to the enemy fell to General Edward P. King, commander of the Bataan forces. Some 76,000 officers and men, Filipino and American, and 11 generals, six of them Filipinos, laid down their arms.

The Japanese later explained that they miscalculated the strength of the Bataan defense forces, and their preparations for the transportation of the prisoners to concentration camps fell very much below the requirement. Instead of calling for more vehicles the Japanese ordered what is now known in history as the infamous "Death March." The exact number of those who perished in the Death March was never ascertained. They run into thousands.

All through the years 1942 and 1943 and the better part of 1944, the Philippines suffered the lot of the vanquished.

Under the Japanese occupation all political parties were proscribed. On 8 December 1942, Jorge B. Vargas as chairman of the Philippine Executive Commission issued Executive Order No. 109 creating the *Kapisanan sa Paglilingkod sa Bagong Pilipinas* (Association for Service to the New Philippines), that became better-known as Kalibapi.

Vargas described the functions of the Kalibapi as follows:

"It will aim at the mental education, moral regeneration, physical invigoration, and economic rehabilitation of the Philippines under the guidance of the Japanese Military Administration. It will develop even greater cooperation with the Japanese Empire, in its historic task of lifting the kindred Oriental races to their proper places in the Order of Greater East Asia, thus promoting and assuring our stability and prosperity as a people. In a word, the Association will be the strong right arm of the administration in the pursuit of our common welfare."[35]

On 19 June 1943, the Kalibapi held a convention in Manila and elected twenty of their number to form the Preparatory Commission for Philippine Independence. The commission was headed by Jose P. Laurel. The commission was charged with drafting a constitution for the Republic of the Philippines which had been promised by the Japanese Premier Hideki Tojo on his visit to Manila, 6 May 1943.

On 4 September 1943, the Preparatory Commission presented its draft of the proposed constitution and on the following 7 September, this draft was ratified by the general assembly of the Kalibapi.

On 20 September 1943, representative groups of the Kalibapi in the provinces and cities elected 54 members of the National Assembly, the legislative body prescribed by the new constitution. The provincial governors and city mayors served as ex-officio members of the National Assembly, completing its membership of 108.

The National Assembly held its inaugural session on 23 September at the pre-war Legislative Building in Manila and elected Benigno Aquino as Speaker. At this session the National Assembly elected Jose P. Laurel as President of the new Republic of the Philippines.

On Thursday, 14 October 1943, the Republic of the Philippines, the Japanese-sponsored version, was inaugurated, and Jose P. Laurel was sworn in as President.

On 16 October 1943, Laurel called the National Assembly to a six-day special session that would open the following 18th, to ratify the Pact of Alliance between the new Republic and Japan that had been signed on the 14th.

Now Japan and its friends came up one by one to recognize the Republic of the Philippines. After Japan gave recognition on 14 October, Manchukuo and Thailand followed the next day, Germany and Burma on the 16th, Croatia on the 18th, and Italy on the 21st. Spain sent "greetings."

On 25 November 1943, the National Assembly opened its regular 60-day session. The first bill the Assembly passed was one creating the Food Administration Office which grouped together all the food control agencies then existing. The bill was signed into law by Laurel on 3 December, and Jose Sanvictores was appointed as Food Administrator.

The food shortage plagued the people and the problem engaged the Laurel government which grappled with it as best it could.

On 1st January 1944, the Bigasang Bayan, or BIBA was established supplanting the rice-purchasing agencies then existing. The BIBA procured rice from the Central Luzon provinces for resale in Manila. Another organization called the Beikokubu, the Rice Procurement Bureau of the Japanese Army, assumed the responsibility for the rest of the country. BIBA bought rice in Nueva Ecija, Tarlac, Pangasinan, and Pampanga, at P8 for a sack of 44 kilos. The rice was rationed to the people at 120 grams a day each person, for P.40 a kilo. But this was but half the normal per capita requirement for the average Filipino.

Other foodstuffs were scarce and prices in the open market rocketed. Beef sold for P17 a kilo, pork for P9, carabao meat for P8.50, chicken for P18 each. Fish when available sold from P2 to P8 a kilo. Bangus which was grown in fishponds was under strict control.

It was during this time that free kitchens appeared in Manila. About 75 such kitchens which dispensed free meals to "dependents," were opened. The city government operated 25 of these kitchens, the Bureau of Public Weifare 11, the Philippine Red Cross eight, and the National Federation of Women's Clubs three.

Although the most serious by far, food was but one of the city's problems. Clothing became a premium commodity. So were medicines. Fuel was a critical item. Sanitation became a grave problem as public services broke down.

This was at a time when the minimum salary of government employees was P70 a month and government laborers were paid P2.40 a day. The value of the war notes plunged unabatedly so that in May 1944, P100 bills had to be issued, followed shortly by P500 notes.

In April 1944, Laurel created the Economic Planning Board of which Manuel Roxas became chairman. Later, Roxas became chairman of the board of directors of BIBA.

The following May, the Food Administrator, Jose Sanvictores fixed the price of rice in Manila at P200 a cavan, or at P20 a ganta. The BIBA ration, however, remained at P1.20 a kilo. In the provinces, rice was available for P135 to P250 a sack.

By the end of May, the Ministry of Health, Labor and Public Welfare had taken over the operation of the free kitchens. Community kitchens sprung up in various districts in the city, funded by contributions of better-off individuals.

Under Mayor Guinto, the territory of Manila proper was apportioned into four districts, as follows:

Bagumbayan (South Manila), with Eustaquio Balagtas as District Chief; Bagumpanahon (Sampaloc, Quiapo, San Miguel and Santa Cruz), with Ruperto Cristobal as District Chief; Bagumbuhay (Tondo), with Bartolome Gatmaitan as District Chief, and Bagong Diwa (Binondo and San Nicolas), with Roberto Teodoro as District Chief. The District Chiefs served as Deputy Mayors.

Quezon City was divided into two districts. All the other municipalities in the Greater Manila jurisdiction which included Pasay, Makati, Las Piñas, Parañaque, Mandaluyong, San Juan, Malabon, Navotas and Caloocan became individual districts, each with a District Chief.

In turn the various districts were organized into Neighborhood Associations, each association identified by a number and headed by a president. This was a new use for the ancient barangay organization of pre-Spanish times, although this time it was a system of socio-political control.

The names of residents in every neighborhood were listed in the association book. Each household head was responsible for reporting deaths and births to the district office, and was supposed to report as well every visit by friends or relatives, so that a constant watch was kept over the comings and goings of householders, as well as the presence of non-residents in the community.

Aside from being useful in galvanizing mass participation in government-sponsored rallies and demonstrations, the Neighborhood Associations were also convenient channels through which food rations and basic commodities supplied by the government reached the householders.

In May 1944, President Jose P. Laurel issued an executive order granting the Kalibapi a new charter which converted it from a "non-political service organization," into the "sole political organization to back the government."

To strengthen the Kalibapi and extend its reach, an attempt to organize a women's section was made. Mrs. Geronima T. Pecson was present at the occasion and gave testimony to this incident. The women leaders of the time were gathered at Malacañang and after President Jose P. Laurel gave a presentation of the matter, Mrs. Francisca Tirona Benitez, president of the Philippine Women's University, acting as spokeswoman for the group, stood up and said, "Mr. President, *sa kabila po kami.*" (Mr. President, we are on the other side.)[36]

Laurel burst into a loud and hearty laughter and the entire assembly joined him. The Kalibapi never had a women's section.

On 10 November 1944, a group of pro-Japanese Filipinos led by veteran generals of the revolution against Spain who also fought the Americans at the beginning of the century met in Quezon City to organize an armed force that was called *Makabayang Pilipino*, or *Makapili,* for short. In the group were Generals Artemio Ricarte, Leon Villafuerte and Andres Villanueva, and civilians including Pio Duran, Benigno Ramos and his son Marcos P. Ramos.

Benigno Ramos was head of the Ganap Party, a pre-war radical group that advocated liberation from American rule by violent means and had a large following among the peasants of Central Luzon.

Now the *Makapilis* were boosted with the Ganap membership, on paper, at least. It is believed that about 5,000 men were armed in the Manila area and in the neighboring provinces of Rizal, Laguna, Bulacan and Nueva Ecija.

But the *Makapili*s who actually served the Japanese were believed to be outcasts, mostly from the criminal elements, who now became spies or orderlies for the Japanese military.

All throughout the Japanese occupation of the Philippines guerrilla warfare raged. From the moment that Japanese authority became patent over the islands, Filipinos banded into guerrilla groups, led by Filipino and American members of the United States Armed Forces in the Philippines who were not captured and did not surrender.[37]

In Manila, the anti-Japanese resistance movement assumed bizarre proportions. Personnel of City Hall were known to be active guerrillas and the movement's network extended into various areas of the city government.

In his monograph on Leon G. Guinto, Sr., the author Ruperto S. Cristobal, himself District Chief of Bagumpanahon, mentions secret meetings the mayor held in his City Hall office with city government officials who were active guerrillas. Cristobal names among these, Pedro D. Fernandez, market master of Arranque market on Azcarraga, and Hugo Ritaga, market master of Quinta market in Quiapo.

Cristobal says that Mayor Guinto had appropriated one million pesos monthly for the purchase of food stuffs ostensibly for distribution to neighborhood association members but which were actually channelled to guerrilla organizations.

During this period, the Japanese conducted purge systems among the civilian population, calculated to ferret out and liquidate guerrillas and their supporters in the city. These were known as the dreaded "zona". In the "zona," a neighborhood suspected of harboring resistance elements would be cordoned off at certain hours and sentries placed at all possible entrances and exits. All residents would be compelled to come down their homes and made to file past the "secret eye," a person whose identity was concealed by a hood, improvised by a burlap sack or straw bag with slits for the eyes. As the people filed by, the "secret eye" would indicate to the Japanese officers present by a nod or a gesture the alleged guerrilla, who would be pulled out of line and detained. People thus held and taken away were rarely known to return to their homes.

PART TWO

THE PASSION AND DEATH OF THE DISTINGUISHED CITY

*Once more the nameless tragedy of the Philippines
is here unveiled before the world,
so that the whole world will know and,
to honor its victims, will not forget!*

ANTONIO PEREZ DE OLAGUER
El Terror Amarillo en Filipinas, 1947
(Translated from the Spanish by the author.)

CHAPTER IV

MANILA WAITS

"I shall return," Douglas MacArthur told newspapermen upon arriving at Batchelor Field south of Darwin, 17 March 1942.

The Philippines waited. For three long years they waited.

On 9 August 1944, the first American air attack on Japanese military installations in the Philippines took place in Davao. On 21 September, the first air attack on Manila was made, and all through the first three weeks of October 1944 the Americans intensified bombings on military objectives in the country.

On 20 October 1944, an American force of four army divisions aboard a fleet of 650 warships landed at Leyte. After the first wave of assault troops had established a beachhead, General Douglas MacArthur waded ashore with the words, "I have returned."[1]

The landing in Leyte caught the Japanese off-balance; they had expected the landings to be made in southern Mindanao. The Japanese commander-in-chief, Lt. Gen. Tomoyuki Yamashita, rushed reinforcements by air and sea.

While the land battles raged, the Japanese sailed in three columns to Leyte Gulf, intent on trapping MacArthur on the island. In a series of sea engagements fought from 23 to 26 October 1944, known as The Second Battle of the Philippine Sea or The Battle of Leyte Gulf, the Japanese forces were obliterated. These sea battles proved decisive to the liberation of the Philippines and to eventual Allied victory over Japan.

On 15 December 1944, American forces landed on Mindoro. On 9 January 1945, MacArthur made a full-scale landing on Lingayen. The liberation forces levelled all opposition as it headed for Manila.

In the earlier part of the war, the Philippines served as the entrepot for Japanese troops and equipment in Southeast Asia.

Starting March 1944, the islands became a rear operational base for the campaign in the Marianas and New Guinea. At this time, Japanese Imperial Headquarters developed new plans which included the Philippines among areas designated as "the principal areas of decisive battle."[2]

The following May, Marshal Count Hisaichi Terauchi moved the Southern Army Headquarters to Manila, in order to supervise more closely the implementation of the new plans.

On 4 August 1944, the Army command in the Philippines was reorganized with the creation of the 14th Area Army out of the former 14th Army and the formation of the 35th Army to take over operations in the Visayas and Mindanao.

The following day, Terauchi designated Luzon "as the main area for the decisive ground battles."[3]

Lt. Gen. Sosaku Suzuki was named commander of the 35th Army with headquarters in Cebu. Up to this time, Lt. Gen. Shigenori Kuroda commanded the 14th Area Army.

On 21 September 1944, the Japanese Imperial General Headquarters designated the Philippines as "the area of decisive battle and estimates that the time of this battle will be sometime during or before the last ten days of October."[4]

On 25 September 1944, General Tomoyuki Yamashita's Manchukuo headquarters received notice of his appointment to command the 14th Area Army in the Philippines. He arrived in Manila the following 6 October.

On 17 November 1944, Marshal Count Terauchi moved his headquarters from Manila to Saigon. When the Americans landed in Mindoro, Terauchi ordered Yamashita to launch a counter-attack. Yamashita did not move, so Terauchi sent his chief of staff, General Jo Iimura, to prod him. Yamashita consented only to launch harassing attacks on the Americans.

On 7 December 1944, Ormoc in the north of Leyte fell to the Americans. Yamashita decided to concentrate on the defense of Luzon.

Apparently contrary to the view of others in his command, Yamashita decided not to defend Manila. Yamashita reported this decision to Marshal Terauchi at the headquarters of the Southern Army in Saigon. This is variously dated 6 or 7 December 1944. On 7 or 8 December 1944, Yamashita received a reply from Terauchi that his plans were satisfactory. Whether this had reference to Yamashita's defense plans for Luzon as a whole or his plans for Manila is not clear. The reply did not make specific mention of Manila.

On 26 December 1944, Yamashita moved his headquarters from Fort McKinley to Ipo, forty kilometers in the foothills of the Sierra Madre northeast of Manila. At Ipo, Yamashita was finally able to draw up a battle plan. He had under his command about 275,000 men. However, "his divisions had been hurriedly formed from garrison units; and his artillery was manned by a motley collection of regulars, convalescents, survivors from ships sunk off the islands, and even civilians who had come out to work in the commissariat offices."[5]

Now Yamashita deployed his army into three groups. The Kembu Group consisted of 30,000 men under the command of Maj. Gen. Rikichi Tsukada, assigned to the mountainous region on the west, from Bataan to the Clark Field area. The Shimbu Group consisted of 80,000 men, disposed on the broad southern end of Luzon from Manila Bay to the Bicol Peninsula, with Lt. Gen. Shizuo Yokoyama commanding.[6]

Yamashita retained command of the Shobu Group, with 150,000 men deployed over the northern half of Luzon from Lingayen Gulf upwards and across the hill regions to the Cagayan Valley.

The Japanese 14th Area Army's plan for the defense of Luzon vested responsibility for the protection of Manila on the Manila Defense Force under the command of Maj. Gen. Takahashi Kobayashi.

The Shimbu Group under Lt. Gen. Shizou Yokoyama stood on the line along the foothills of the Sierra Madre east and northeast of Manila.

Yamashita placed Kobayashi's Manila Defense Force under the Shimbu Group. The decision not to defend Manila having been made, Yokoyama's principal mission was to oversee the evacuation of troops and supplies from the city. This had been going on through December 1944. Now Yokoyama ordered General Kobayashi to speed-up the process.

The plan was to retain a small Army force in Manila to carry out the evacuation, maintain order, protect supply movements, and finally, to blow up bridges over the Pasig and the Marikina rivers.

This Army force consisted of two units. The first was the Noguchi Detachment commanded by Col. Katzuo Noguchi, composed of two provisional infantry detachments. The second was the Abe Battalion commanded by Capt. Saburo Abe, composed of a reinforced provisional infantry battalion.

The Noguchi Detachment was assigned to the north Manila area and the suburbs north of the Pasig. It was under orders to withdraw eastward once it had blown the bridges.

The Abe Battalion was assigned to south Manila with responsibility for blocking the southern approaches along the Hagonoy Isthmus separating Manila bay from Laguna de Bay.

Japanese units accordingly started to pull out of Manila and environs into the Sierra Madre foothills east and northeast of the city. By 25 January 1945, only about 1,500 of the Kobayashi troops remained in Manila.

However, while the Army was pulling out of Manila, Japanese Navy units were moving in.

The ranking Japanese Naval officer in the Philippines at this time was Vice Admiral Denshichi Okoochi, commander of the Southwestern Area Fleet.

When the Americans landed on Mindoro, Okoochi, like Yamashita, had to make quick changes on plans that had earlier been drawn up. Now Okoochi decided to bolster the naval defense of Manila. For this purpose a new organization was created, called the Manila Naval Defense Force, in the command of Rear Admiral Sanji Iwabuchi, the commander of the 31st Naval Special Force.

There were at this time, about 16,000 Japanese Naval troops in Manila. Having assigned 4,000 men to the Manila Naval Defense Force, Okoochi intended to send the balance of 12,000 men to the Kembu Group in the Clark Field area. By this time, however, supply and transportation problems had become acute and Okoochi's plans in this respect were never carried out.

On 2nd January 1945, General Yamashita and Admiral Okoochi transferred their respective headquarters to Baguio.[7]

Okoochi had left Iwabuchi orders which included, 1) to hold Nichols Field and the Cavite Naval Base; 2) complete the mining of Manila bay; 3) direct Navy suicide boat operations on Manila bay; 4) arrange for the evacuation of ships and small craft of the 31st Naval Special Base Force; 5) destroy all Japanese naval installations and supplies in the Manila and Cavite areas.

Upon his departure for Baguio, Admiral Okoochi transferred "operational control" of the Manila Naval Defense Force to the Shimbu Group under General Yokoyama.

At dawn on the 6th January 1945, American naval units sailed into Lingayen gulf and laid down a bombardment on the Japanese installations on the shore.

On the night of the 9th January 1945, the Sixth Army under General Walter Krueger started to land on the Lingayen gulf shoreline. The Sixth Army consisted of four divisions – the 6th and 43rd in I Corps, Maj. Gen. Innis P. Swift, commanding, and the 37th and 40th in XIV Corps, in the command of Lt. Gen. Oscar M. Griswold. The Allied Naval Force in the command of Admiral Kinkaid transported the force, while the Third

Fleet provided strategic support. The U.S. 5th and 13th Air Force under General George Kenney provided air cover.

By 11th January, the Americans had linked up from Rabon in San Fabian to the mouth of the Agno river.

On 26 January 1945, General Walter Krueger commanding the Sixth Army, directed the XIV Corps to send troops southward to the Pampanga river, with the strategic railroad crossings at Calumpit as objective.

The next day, the 37th Infantry Division sent down its 37th Reconnaissance Troop and the 148th Infantry Regiment towards Calumpit.

By the afternoon of 30th January, patrols of the 37th were within sight of Calumpit and the Pampanga river. The same afternoon, General MacArthur made a personal tour of Route 3 from San Fernando, the capital of Pampanga province. He came back from this tour to make the observation to General Krueger that the 37th had shown "a noticeable lack of drive and aggressive initiative" on its southward thrust.[8]

Robert Ross Smith notes that this was "by design" on the part of Griswold and Beightler, commanding the XIV Corps and the 37th Infantry Division respectively. "They had little information on the Japanese deployment south of the Pampanga."[9]

By design or not, probably stung by MacArthur's observation, Krueger now directed the XIV Corps to speed up its drive towards Manila. The next day, 31st January, the 148th Infantry Regiment crossed the Pampanga river. General Beightler withdrew the 145th Infantry from Clark Field and sent it down Route 3. Meantime, the 148th rushed down Route 3 and on 1st February, secured Malolos, the capital town of Bulacan province.

On 2nd February, patrols reached Marilao farther south, while another force hit eastward to Plaridel where a unit from the Shimbu Group, 500-man strong, put up a stern opposition. Crashing through the Japanese defenses, the 148th established contact with elements of the 1st Cavalry Division near midnight.

Landing in the Mabilao area of Lingayen gulf, 27 January 1945, the 1st Cavalry Division in the command of Maj. Gen. Vernon D. Mudge, unloaded quickly and concentrated in the vicinity of Urdaneta in Pangasinan. The next day, 28 January, it began moving to its assembly area in Guimba, Nueva Ecija, 35 miles inland.

Heretofore the 1st Cavalry Division had been part of I Corps under General Swift. On 30 January it passed to XIV Corps, in the command of General Griswold.

On 31 January, General MacArthur visited the Division command Post at Guimba and handed down to General Mudge, commanding the

1st Cavalry, the order: "Go to Manila. Go around the Nips, bounce off the Nips, but go to Manila. Free the internees at Santo Tomas.Take Mala-cañang and the Legislative building."[10]

The 1st Cavalry Division was composed of "shock troops." They won a reputation in the bloody fighting in the Admiralty Islands and were chosen to spearhead the landing in Leyte.

Now mobile units to spearhead the 100-mile drive to Manila were organized as follows:

1st Serial: Lt. Col. William E. Lobit, commanding -- 2nd Squadron, Reconnaissance Platoon, Anti-tank Platoon, and Medical Detachment, all from the 5th Cavalry; Battery "A", 82nd Field Artillery Batallion; Company "A", 44th Tank Battalion; 3rd Platoon, Troop "A", 8th Engineers; and 1st Platoon, Troop "A", 1st Medical Squadron.

2nd Serial: Lt. Col. Haskett L. Conner, Jr., commanding – 2nd Squadron, Reconnaissance Platoon; Anti-tank Platoon, one section of .50 caliber machine-guns, and Maintenance Section, all from the 8th Cavalry; Company "B", 44th Tank Battalion; Battery "B", 61st Field Artillery Battalion; 1st Platoon, Troop "C", 8th Engineers; and 1st Platoon, Troop "B", Medical Squadron.

3rd Serial: Lt. Col. Tom Ross, commanding – 44th Tank Battalion, less Companies "A" and "B", and the 302nd Reconnaissance Troop.

Early in the morning of 1st February, the lead troops rolled out of Guimba in three columns. At dawn, Cabanatuan came in sight. The Japanese put up a stiff resistance and the fighting was fierce. Later this day, General Mudge designated the mobile units as a "Flying Column" in the command of Brig. Gen. William C. Chase.

The 12th and 7th Cavalry Regiments arrived in Cabanatuan to carry on the battle, allowing the Flying Column to proceed. Lt. Col. Tom Ross led his tanks across the Pampanga river and cleared the highway leading to Gapan, but he was killed in the fighting.

By daylight on 2 February, the Flying Column was on its way again. The column got excellent air cover, flank protection and reconnaissance provided by the Marine Air Groups 24 and 32. To the south, all bridges across the river were down.

It was at this point, in the vicinity of Plaridel town, that the 1st Cavalry linked up with the 37th Infantry Division.

Virtually unopposed on the southward drive, with the 37th encountering opposition only near Plaridel, the two divisions closed their pincers and made contact at midnight, 2 February 1945, about 120 kilometers north of Manila.

General Richard Eichelberger commanding the Eighth Army seems to have entertained ambitions of beating Krueger's Sixth Army to Manila. For this task, Eichelberger chose the 11th Airborne Division, Maj. Gen. Joseph M. Swing, commanding.

Robert Ross Smith reports that General Eichelberger declared to him (Smith) that MacArthur, through General Sutherland, had given oral instructions at the Eighth Army headquarters in Leyte for Eichelberger to capture Manila.[11]

Smith never found documentation to support Eichelberger's statement. Nevertheless, Smith has been led to conclude that "there can be no doubt that General Eichelberger would have liked a share in the honor of seizing Manila and that he would dearly have loved to beat Sixth Army into the capital city."[12]

Eichelberger had laid out careful plans to land the 11th Airborne at Nasugbu in the province of Batangas on the southwestern edge of Luzon fronting the China Sea.[13]

The division's two glider-infantry regiments would have been sent in an amphibian assault on the beaches, from where they would push inland along Route 17 to Tagaytay Ridge.

At Tagaytay Ridge, the 11th Airborne's 511th Parachute Infantry would drop to secure an assembly point for the units to stage their northward drive to Manila.

On 20 January 1945, General MacArthur approved the idea of landing at Nasugbu but ordered approaches other than those planned by Eichelberger.

Now MacArthur ordered the Eighth Army to land one, not two of the glider-infantry regiments at Nasugbu, to push up to Tagaytay Ridge. Should the ridge be weakly defended by the Japanese, Eichelberger then could use it as an assembly point from where to control Japanese forces all over the southwestern Luzon area. Eichelberger's visions of a swift drive to Manila faded.

The 11th Airborne Division commanded by General Swing had gained considerable experience in the Leyte campaign. It numbered 8,200 men. The two glider-infantry regiments, the 187th and 188th, had 1,500 men each. Each regiment consisted of two battalions, each battalion composed of three rifle companies.

The 511th Parachute Infantry consisted of three battalions, each battalion with three rifle companies, totalling 2,000 men.

The artillery support included two battalions of 75-mm pack howitzers, one 105-mm howitzer battalion, and an airborne anti-aircraft artillery battalion, armed with 40-mm and .50 caliber guns.

For reinforcements the 11th Airborne counted on the Cannon Company, 21st Infantry, 24th Division; Company C, 532 Engineer Boat and Shore Regiment, Engineer Special Brigade; two anti-aircraft batteries and various service units. The 19th Infantry, 24th Division, based in Mindoro, was available on call.

On the Japanese side, the Southern Luzon area was in the jurisdiction of the Shimbu Group and had assigned the defense of the territory to the Fuji Force in the command of Col. Masatoshi Fujishige, who also commanded the 17th Infantry Regiment under the Japanese 8th Division.

The Fuji Force numbered 8,500 men from the 17th Infantry, less the 3rd Battalion; the 3rd Battalion, 31st Infantry; one battalion of mixed artillery, combat engineers and service troops from the 8th Division.

Attached to the Fuji Force was the 2nd Surface Raiaing Base Force, composed of 5,000 men. These consisted of suicide boat units called Surface Raiding Squadrons and their base supports called Surface Raiding Base Battalions. Normally, each Raiding Squadron would consist of 100 suicide boats and an equal number of men. Each Base Battalion consisted of 900 men, mostly service troops.

Col. Fujishige had deployed the West Sector Unit to the area facing the American 11th Airborne Division. The unit had 2,250 men, mostly from the 3rd Battalion, 31st Infantry. Of these, 100 were in Nasugbu area. Some 600 men with artillery support stood west of Tagaytay Ridge, while 400 men defended the southwestern approach to the ridge. The rest of the West Sector Unit was scattered all over southwestern Luzon.

On the afternoon of 27 January 1945, Task Force 78.2 left Leyte gulf for Nasugbu bay. In the convoy was the 11th Airborne Division less the 511th Parachute Infantry.

At 8:15 in the morning of 28 January, the 1st Battalion, 188th Glider Infantry hit shore. There was slight opposition, mostly with rifle and machinegun-fire and light mortar fire.

The 188th drove through the town of Nasugbu for the Palico river to the highway that led to Tagaytay Ridge. At 11:15, General Eichelberger ordered the balance of the troops to land.

By 12:30 in the afternoon, the 187th Glider Infantry had caught up with the 188th's rear.

The battle came out well for the 11th Airborne and now Eichelberger planned to assemble the entire division, including the 511th Parachute, on Tagaytay Ridge by 2nd February.

The parachutists were scheduled to drop on 3rd February, but Eichelberger now set the date ahead by one day. He also asked that his reinforcement, the 19th Infantry, 24th Division, based in Mindoro, be released to his command.

General MacArthur, however, approved the release of but one battalion from the 19th, while another, already under Eichelberger, was loading for Luzon.

Shortly after midnight on 1st February, the 188th pushed up Route 17, heading for Tagaytay Ridge. At the defile west of the ridge they ran into stiff opposition. This delayed the 11th Airborne's advance and caused Eichelberger to set the parachute drop back to 3rd February. He was under orders not to call the 511th Parachute unless there was assurance that the parachutists would make contact with the rest of the 11th Airborne when they hit the ground.

After noon on 2nd February, the 188th broke through the Japanese opposition at Barrio Aga and by six o'clock in the evening, was two miles to the west end of Tagaytay Ridge.

General Yokoyama's Shimbu Shudan was composed of the Kawashima, Kobayashi and Noguchi Heidans (or groups) and the Kawagoshi Force.[14]

The city proper had been designated by the Japanese as the Manila Defense Area, under the responsibility of the Manila Defense Force, headed by Maj. Gen. Takahashi Kobayashi.

The Manila Defense Area was apportioned into ten sections, defended by 23,300 Japanese troops.

The northwestern section, centered on the Polo-Obando-Dampalit area, together with a small portion of the northern part along the bay, was assigned to the Kawagoshi Force in the command of Lt. Col. Masanori Kawagoshi. The Kawagoshi defense line extended to the west side of Highway 3, northwards to Marilao. The Kawagoshi Force was composed of five Japanese battalions with roughly 3,900 men.

In the beginning of the battle for Manila, the Kobayashi Group was responsible for the central section of the Manila Defense Area. On 10 January 1945, however, the Kobayashi troops started leaving for the Sierra Madre foothills. By 25 January 1945, only two detachments of the original Kobayashi Group were left in the Manila area.

The rest of the ten sections of the Manila Defense Area was under the Manila Naval Defense Force commanded by Rear Admiral Sanji Iwabuchi. This is not to be confused with the Manila Defense Force.

Although Iwabuchi's Manila Naval Defense Force was under the "operational control" of General Yokoyama, it functioned quite independently, technically under Navy authority.

Admiral Iwabuchi's area of responsibility covered about 250 square miles, from Manila bay northwards extending two-and-a-half miles inland; northeast to Novaliches and east to the Marikina river, then south to the western limits of Laguna de Bay and westward from this point across the

Hagonoy Isthmus to the base of the Cavite peninsula.

Under Iwabuchi's command were 17,000 troops of which 12,500 were Navy and 4,500 Army. Some 3,500 troops from Iwabuchi's original 16,000 naval personnel were on the islands on Manila bay or had joined the main body of the Shimbu Group in the hills east of Manila.

Iwabuchi organized the 17,000 troops in his command into three combat forces, namely, the Northern Force under Col. Katzuo Noguchi, the Central Force under Iwabuchi himself, and the Southern Force under Navy Captain Takasue Furuse.

There was a Fourth Command that was intended to be naval but was actually deployed on land, either along the bayfront or on islands on the bay. A Fifth Command was composed of "attached units," which included engineers, supply troops, medical units, etc.

The Northern Force under Col. Noguchi was responsible for the area north of the Pasig River, the suburbs to the north and northeast, and the eastern sector of Manila up to the boundaries under Iwabuchi's responsibility, and the area immediately south of the river, including Intramuros.

Under Noguchi were the 2nd and 3rd Provisional Infantry Battalions which composed the original Noguchi Detachment, plus the 1st Independent Naval Battalion. In all he had about 4,500 men.

Iwabuchi's Central Force included the 1st and 2nd Naval Battalions, the Headquarters Sector Unit and the 5th Naval Battalion. In consisted of about 5,000 men.

The Central force was responsible for South Manila, including Makati, where Nielson airfield was located.

The Southern Force under Capt. Furuse was responsible for Nichols field, Fort McKinley to the northeast, and the Hagonoy Isthmus. His command included the 3rd and 4th Naval Battalions and the Army's Abe Battalion.

Noguchi assigned small detachments to the northern approaches to the city and deployed the 1st Independent Naval Battalion to the eastern suburbs, with the bulk in San Juan del Monte.

He assigned one army battalion to the bridges spanning the Pasig. Miscellaneous service units manned defenses in Intramuros. When various Army shipping units from the 3rd Maritime Transport Command were transferred to him, Noguchi stationed them in the port areas on both sides of the river mouth.

Iwabuchi assigned the 1st and 2nd Naval Battalions to defend the southern part of Manila. The Headquarters Sector Unit was concentrated in the strategic Ermita area east and south of Intramuros, manning the crucial government center and bayfront sectors, where it was joined by the 5th Naval Battalion after it withdrew from Cavite on 2nd February 1945.

Furuse's 3rd and 4th Naval Battalions were stationed at Nichols Field and Fort McKinley. Captain Abe's Battalion defended the Hagonoy Isthmus. His mission was to hold Route 1 and Route 59 along the western shore of Laguna de Bay. Small detachments were stationed at Parañaque, with the bulk of the Abe Battalion entrenched on the Laguna de Bay shore across the isthmus from Parañaque.

This was how the contending forces stood on the eve of that fateful day of Saturday, 3 February 1945.

The city seethed in uncertainty. After the first bombing raid conducted by the Americans on 21st September 1944, the semblance of order that the civil government had managed to impose on the city started to come apart.

Food was the critical problem. On 3 October 1944, The Japanese had suggested the merger of the Bigasang Bayan (BIBA), the rice procurement agency established by the civilian government, and the Beikokubu, the Japanese organization with the same functions in the provinces. On 11 October 1944, a joint committee composed of representatives of the two bodies met to consider the merger. The following 8 November, a new procurement agency called the Rice and Corn Administration (RICOA) was announced. By placing Japanese officials in key positions in the New RICOA, a good portion of the rice procured was now channelled to the Japanese.

In May 1944, rice was still available to Manilans for P500 a sack. Before the first American bombing in September 1944, rice was being sold for P3000 a sack. After the bombings, the price jumped to P5000 a sack.

In October 1944, posters were seen on walls in various parts of the city encouraging the people to move out to the provinces. The posters pointed out that food was abundant in the provinces. But there was no organized program to evacuate the city. Two things precluded this, first, the lack of vehicles and fuel, and second, the unpredictable guerrilla situation.

Apparently, however, people who could do so moved out to points in Bulacan in the north, and Laguna and Batangas in the south. Nevertheless, authorities placed the city population at this time at about one million.

Now in this city of one million, over 200,000 persons were on relief rolls. The government provided for about half of this number; private charity provided for the rest as best it could. All Manila scrounged for itself.

When he was appointed mayor of Greater Manila in 1942, Leon G. Guinto, Sr. was provided with an official residence on Concepcion street near the corner on San Marcelino in the Ermita area, not far from the Manila City Hall.[15]

The Guinto family lived here through all the war years. In January 1945, the Japanese aide of Mayor Guinto by the name of Lieutenant Ueda advised him to transfer to another residence, preferably to the northern side of the city. The mayor instead moved south, to a property owned by relatives of Mrs. Guinto on Paris street, a *cul-de-sac* that opened on Pennsylvania street in Singalong. The short street was lined on both sides by middle-class homes, in one of which resided Judge Jose Carlos. At No. 4 Paris street, lived Col. Alejo Valdes.

With the Mayor and Mrs. Guinto were three of his children, Virtudes, Noli and Piedad. The mayor was incommunicado in his home on Paris street in Singalong. Japanese sentries stood at his gate.

It is not clear whether Mayor Guinto was under official detention by the Japanese at this time. Insofar as surviving members of his family recall, no orders were issued him to that effect. It is possible that the guards were posted to provide security for himself and his family. The fact was that, he could not leave his residence and he could not receive callers.

On 4 February 1945, at about ten o'clock in the morning, the phone went dead at the Paris street home of Mayor Guinto. From thereon, the mayor was cut off from his constituency.

In mid-1944, a "Northside City Hall" was established in the Oriente building at the corner of Azcarraga and Evangelista street in Quiapo, where the Bigasang Bayan (BIBA) had its offices.

This second City Hall served the districts north of the Pasig river. It was administered by Jose Figueras, who had the title of Assistant to the Mayor. The Northside City Hall functioned until the arrival of the Americans, 3 February 1945.

By this date, the political structure of the city of Manila had totally collapsed. The civil government no longer exercised the functions expected of it.

In the words of Frankel, "No one was able to fathom either the social or political situation in Manila on the eve of the battle for the metropolis The only effective control in the city was that of Japanese force . . ."[16]

CHAPTER V

THE ORDEAL BY SWORD AND FIRE

The events of the 30-day battle for Manila from 3 February to 3 March 1945 included in this work are presented as vignettes in journal form. The events are related as they happened to individuals or to groups, civilians and military, ranged round the clock, where possible.

SATURDAY, 3 FEBRUARY 1945

At daybreak, a serial of the Flying Column under Col. Haskett L. Conner, Jr., ran into the Japanese positions north of Novaliches, 17 kilometers northeast of Manila, which had been dubbed "the Hot Corner" by the Americans for the exceptionally fiery welcome the Japanese defenders accorded intruders.[1]

In Imus, Cavite, 23 kilometers south of Manila, the 11th Airborne stood poised on its onward drive.[2]

In Tondo on the northwest section of Manila, the Noguchi Detachment was torching military stores in warehouses at the North Harbor.[3]

Unknown to each other, all three parties had unleashed the chain of events that altogether would constitute the passion of the Distinguished and Ever Loyal City.

A tremendous blast roused the internees at the Santo Tomas internment camp at dawn today. A.V.H. Hartendorp, an internee, remarks that it was an ammunition dump that had been detonated at Fort McKinley, 18 kilometers to the southeast.[4]

It had been a restless night. From their vantage point at the top floor of the Santo Tomas University Main building, the internees had a good view of fires raging in every direction, close to the Santo Tomas area. In the vicinity of the Manila North Cemetery, the conflagration raged unchecked. Grace Park farther to the northeast, Pasig to the southeast, Tondo to the north were in flames.

The fire in Tondo had been raging since early yesterday morning when the Japanese blew up depots and set fire to warehouses on the waterfront at the North Harbor.[5] They worked gradually inland towards the core of the district on Plaza Moriones by the Tondo church, systematically torching factories and industrial plants. The people at first tried to fight the fire when it threatened their homes, but the Japanese machine-gunned them. The fire reached the crowded residential section and the conflagration raged without let-up. All day deep into the night the blasting and burning would go on in Tondo.

At 8:15 this morning, forty-six C-47 planes loaded with men from the 11th Parachute Regiment disgorged their passengers over Tagaytay Ridge, about sixty kilometers south of Manila. A second lift of fifty-one C-47s followed.[6]

The paratroopers encountered no opposition and successfully assembled at the designated zones. By one o'clock this afternoon, having cleared Tagaytay Ridge, they joined up with elements from the 18th Infantry which had landed at Nasugbu to the south earlier, and which now came up Highway 17. From Tagaytay, the road to Manila was clear.

Today the Japanese ordered the Vincentian Fathers at their convent on San Marcelino street in Ermita to assemble, together with their staff, in the refectory.[7]

Despite the disruptions caused by wartime incidents, the Vincentian Fathers had kept their Manila Seminary open. In June 1944, the seminary started the schoolyear as usual. There were 43 major seminary students and 70 minor seminary students. Fr. Zacarias Subiñas was the rector.

The following 19 August, the Father Provincial, the Rev. Fr. Jose Tejada, 53, received notice that the Japanese would occupy the seminary building. On 12 September, classes were summarily suspended and the students dispersed to their own homes. The Japanese moved in, converting the premises into a food and munitions depot.

The Father Provincial advised the resident priests, most of whom were members of the seminary faculty, to seek shelter where they could, although he wanted a few to stay on as caretakers.

Several of the priests proceeded to other Vincentian properties, such as those in the towns of Malolos and Hagonoy in Bulacan, or went to serve as chaplains to religious houses and charitable institutions in the Manila suburbs.

A number of Jesuit Scholastics had been residents here since the Ateneo de Manila compound was commandeered for military use by the Japanese in the early days of 1943. Now the Jesuits had to relocate to other housing.

The Vincentian Fathers had hoped that the Manila Seminary premises would be respected by the Japanese.

The Catholic bishop of Osaka, the Rev. Mons. Taguchi, had resided here as the Vincentian community's special guest from 3 March to 15 December 1942, while he served as special emissary of the Japanese government and liaison between the Philippine church authorities and the Japanese occupation forces.

At the Paules church on San Marcelino, ceremonies had been held with Bishop Taguchi officiating in connection with the filing of the petition to the Vatican for the beatification of the Japanese Christian samurai, Lord Takayama Ukon. He was a powerful *daimyo* in the time of the overlord Hideyoshi, who had chosen to flee his country rather than apostasize during the anti-Christian persecutions waged by the Tokugawa shogun in the early 17th century. Takayama Ukon whose Christian name was Justo Ukondono died in Manila, in the Japanese village the Spanish had set up for him and his companions, on the very site where the Paules church and the Vincentian Central House and Manila Seminary now stood.

But now the Vincentian Fathers found that this historical affinity would not guarantee their security.

Except for a small suite of rooms on the East Wing, the Japanese took over the entire building. Rev. Fr. Tejada had lived here since he first arrived in the Philippines in 1932. While he advised his confreres to seek shelter where they could, he himself decided to stay, the munitions stockpiles a few steps from his quarters notwithstanding.

The parish priest, the Rev. Fr. Jose Fernandez, 54, much-loved by parishioners and widely-acclaimed as a poet in the Spanish language, and his assistant, the Rev. Fr. Jose Aguirreche, also decided to stay with their flock.

The religious were kept under strict surveillance. A sentry was on duty at all hours at their door. No one was allowed to go out except for the two young Filipinos who served as acolytes, Eusebio Quintana and N. Magno. There was a truck garden behind the seminary complex which the Vincentians had leased to a group of Chinese where they raised vegetables and chickens. Every morning, the two acolytes would be allowed out to fetch vegetables and whatever food supplies were available from the Chinese.

Aside from Frs. Tejada, Fernandez and Aguirreche, there were ten other priests, all Spanish, and one Filipino seminarian, with the two Filipino acolytes in residence at San Marcelino at this time.

Now the community of St. Vincent de Paul was under detention in their own refectory and in an adjoining hallway.

This morning Tatsunori Uewaki, a Japanese civilian expatriate whose family had lived in Manila for a long time, walked from his home on Taft Avenue across to the Philippine General hospital.[8]

Like all Japanese civilians in Manila, Uewaki had been drafted into military service. Uewaki had been given the designation "non-regular navy liaison officer." He did not relish the idea, however. Now he sought Dr. Antonio G. Sison, the director of the PGH, to seek asylum in the hospital premises. Uewaki had an elder brother who was a physician, a graduate of the University of the Philippines college of medicine, a former student of Dr. Sison. After Uewaki had identified himself, Dr. Sison sat back thoughtfully and then said, "We have some problem. Please come this way."

Dr. Antonio G. Sison led Tatsunori Uewaki, a Japanese civilian, down the corridor to a wing in which a patient lay on a bed curtained-off from the others. Referring to the patient, Dr. Sison asked Uewaki, "Does his face pass for a Chinese?"

The man who lay in a deep coma on the bed was the Japanese expatriate Kiyoshi Osawa, 39, managing director of the wartime Liquid Fuel Distribution Union. This was a powerful agency that controlled the supply of petrol, alcohol, coconut oil, heavy oil and all other fuel products for military and civilian use.

Osawa had first come to the Philippines in 1925 as a 19-year-old free immigrant. He had worked in Mindanao and finally came to Manila, achieving modest success in business and some eminence in the local Japanese community. He had occupied his position in the fuel agency since the outbreak of the war.

On 7 January 1945, Kiyoshi Osawa had been ordered to bring stocks of fuel oil in Manila to Baguio where the Japanese Military Headquarters had moved. At dawn the next day, Osawa had led a convoy of 16 vehicles carrying oil and other supplies in an attempt to deliver them to Baguio. The convoy could only go as far as Malolos, Bulacan, however, the highways having been rendered impassable by Filipino guerrilla activities and the American bombing and strafing. Forced to turn back to Manila the same night of 8 January, a truck in the convoy driving in the pitch-dark highway fell into a ditch. While helping to get the truck on the road again,

Kiyoshi Osawa slipped and the rear wheel of the truck passed over his thighs above the knees. Conscious though in extreme pain Osawa asked an associate to drive another truck while his own driver propped him up on his lap. Osawa asked to be taken to the Philippine General hospital and placed in the care of Dr. Antonio G. Sison, the hospital director, himself. By midnight he was at the PGH, but Dr. Sison was not available. Instead, he came under the care of Dr. Ambrosio Tangco whom Osawa described as "a sturdy, broad-shouldered young man."

Next morning, when he was off anaesthesia, Dr. Tangco told the Japanese patient, "The flesh of both thighs was crushed to the bones. It took us 4 1/2 hours just to clean the affected parts and connect the severed nerve fibers."

On 10 January, the day following, Dr. Antonio G. Sison came to see Osawa. "Don't worry," Dr. Sison assured the patient, "I'll take care of you." A nurse named Miss Aytona was assigned to Osawa. His driver brought in his wife to do chores for his ailing employer.

Osawa was in extreme pain and his condition worsened. He could not eat. On 26 January 1945 he fell into convulsions and lapsed into a coma. He had all the symptoms of tetanus. He has been in a coma since.

Dr. Sison was concerned that Filipinos would do his patient violence once they discovered he was Japanese. Now he wanted the brother of his former student, Dr. Uewaki, to tell him whether Kiyoshi Osawa could pass for Chinese. Uewaki looked but he was himself uncertain. But Dr. Sison allowed Uewaki to stay in the PGH premises. Uewaki set himself up on another bed beside Kiyoshi Osawa.

This afternoon a flight of six or eight planes swooped low over the Santo Tomas camp grounds, so low that the internees could see the goggled pilots grinning. One of the planes dropped what turned out to be a pair of goggles. When located on the ground, the goggles contained a written message: "Roll out the barrel. Christmas will be either today or tomorrow." The camp writhed in almost unbearable expectation.[9]

Since noon, General Oscar Griswold, commanding the XIV Corps, had known that the Flying Column would reach Manila today. Now he gave permission for the 1st Cavalry Division to enter the city.

Meeting strong resistance at Norzagaray, the 1st Cavalry swung around and struck through Santa Maria and Novaliches. Falling under heavy attack from both sides of the road at Novaliches, the 1st Cavalry smashed through the opposition and by 6:30 this evening, 3rd February, it stood at the gate to the city by the Bonifacio monument at Grace Park. It had made a 62-kilometer run all the way from San Fernando, Pampanga.[10]

The 37th Infantry Division was twelve hours behind. To prevent the two divisions from inadvertently confronting each other, Griswold moved the limits of the 1st Cavalry territory westward.

At around 7 o'clock this evening a Japanese unit in the vicinity of the Chinese cemetery at La Loma opened fire. A pitched-battle ensued until the opposition was overcome.

Now the main body of the Flying Column plunged down Rizal Avenue from the Bonifacio monument, meeting but slight opposition.

Narciso G. Reyes gives this account: "Across the street from a Japanese sentry post on Tayuman, a group of little children started to sing, *God Bless America*. A gang of laborers passing by took up the tune and soon the whole neighborhood was ringing with the song."[11]

When the American contingent reached the intersection of Rizal Avenue and Doroteo Jose, it split into two. One group turned left, and proceeded to Oroquieta street where it turned right. It turned left on Azcarraga street and left again on Quezon Boulevard.

The other group turned right on Doroteo Jose, proceeded left on Misericordia street where it turned left again on Azcarraga. The Central Hotel at the corner of Rizal Avenue and Azcarraga street was the headquarters of the Japanese Kempeitai (military police). The building had been fortified and the Japanese defenders fought to the last man. There were in the building several Filipino male and female *makapilis* (quislings). Several of these were captured alive.

Heavy artillery was called for to blast the pillboxes at the entrance to the Central Hotel. Crowds of street urchins trailed after the American soldiers, ignoring admonitions of the latter for them to go away for cover. The children attached themselves to the machine-gun and artillery crews and pointed out where the Japanese were hiding.

In this area the Japanese began their house-to-house defense of territory they held. Many of the buildings had been mined and these exploded before the Japanese abandoned them. As the Americans approached, the Mapua Institute of Technology on Misericordia street burst into flames and the neighborhood caught fire, spreading up the street until Azcarraga, where the conflagration spread farther to the right and to the left.

At her home on Park Avenue in Pasay south of Manila Gladys Savary crouched over her clandestine radio, listening to the Voice of Freedom.[12] From the radio she learned that the American troops had passed Calumpit town in Bulacan province, north of Manila. The phone rang. It was a friend who told her, "Don't buy any more beans." Madame Savary understood that to mean that redemption was close.

The family of 14-year-old Lydia Gutierrez on Remedios street in Malate, in south Manila, did not get any such coded message.[13] Lydia writes in her diary: "Early in the afternoon Papa, Frank and Nong came home with three *bayongs* full of money (Papa had mortgaged the farm). We knew that the Americans were near, so we decided to spend the money quickly." This afternoon the Gutierrez family bought beans at P400 a kilo.

Sunset over Manila Bay had been particularly resplendent in the afternoon. "The sky dazzled our eyes with the colors of a Master's brush," diarist Tressa R. Cates writes, and she was not referring to the glow cast by the raging fires.[14]

". . . a mass of red, the end of a splendid day," Frederick H. Stevens recalls of that memorable sunset.[15]

Young Benigno del Rio, too, would remark on the dazzling sunset this day. "Red, the setting sun was red," he writes in his diary. He wondered whether the redness presaged bloodshed.[16]

Day had dawned on Benigno del Rio at the family mansion in the Pasay section of Taft Avenue not far from the Vito Cruz street boundary with Manila. All that was in his young mind was that he had promised his fiancee the previous afternoon that on this day he would help her all-female family move from their residence on A. Mabini street in Malate to another house. Benigno went to his sister's house also on Taft Avenue, to use her phone since that in his own home was not working. He could not get through to his fiancee. Already the streets were dangerous. A dense gray haze hang over the city and explosions shook the earth intermittently. Benigno spent the day agonizing over his incapacity to be with his fiancee when she needed him.

Before retiring for the night Benigno del Rio went into the garden. The skies glowed fiercely as distant fires raged, though none seemed to be alit in the direction of his fiancee's residence. Through the picket fence he saw moving stealthily on both sides of the otherwise deserted avenue fronting the house a squad of Japanese soldiers, heavily armed, elaborately camouflaged with foliage. Benigno del Rio withdrew into the house and to bed, but he could not sleep.

Benigno del Rio's fiancee was the beautiful Teresa Palanca, daughter of a Spanish mother and a wealthy Chinese father.

Benigno had left her chic Mitchell apartments residence on A. Mabini street in Malate the previous afternoon, after promising to help the family transfer to another residence in the morning. Shortly after Benigno left, the man the Palancas contracted to help them move appeared with his two trucks. But the family was not ready to move and Teresa wanted her fiance to be with them when they did. She frantically called him through his sister Lolita's phone, but was unable to talk to him.

This morning early the Palanca ladies were prepared to move out. Shortly the man who would move them appeared and said now it was impossible to go as all the streets were barricaded and the Japanese forbade any kind of vehicular traffic. Teresa Palanca was incredulous so she went with the man into the streets, and Teresa saw the truth for herself.

Natalie Stark Crouter did not miss today's spectacular sunset from her internee quarters at the Bilibid Prisons. She writes in her diary, "At sunset, the sun was a copper disk in the sky as it is during forest-fire at home."[17]

Natalie and her husband Jerry Crouter today marked their 18th wedding anniversay. On this day in 1927, the couple was married in Tientsin, China.

The Crouters were in a batch of almost 500 civilian internees from Allied nations who had been moved to Bilibid on 29 December 1944 from Baguio. The Crouters had two children, June, 15, and Frederick (Bodie), 13.

At their prison quarters this evening, the couple and their children opened a tin of Spam to celebrate. It was the next to their last tin. They were saving the last for Bodie's birthday the following week.

As the family finished its slender anniversary dinner, three close internee friends came in with a big pot of steaming tea, complete with syrup, a great treat these days. Another friend came in and the occasion became truly festive, a surprise for the celebrants. The party was in for another surprise before the night would end.

There were at this time close to 1,500 American prisoners-of-war and Allied civilian internees in the confines of the Bilibid prisons.

Bilibid was the former national penitentiary on the large block bounded by Quezon Boulevard, Azcarraga, Oroquieta and Zurbaran streets in the Sampaloc district where it abuts Santa Cruz on the north and Quiapo on the west.

Earlier, there had been about 800 American prisoners-of-war, members of United States armed forces who had been captured or had surrendered when the Japanese overrun the country, in Bilibid.

On 22 December 1944, 170 men originally from the prisoner-of-war camp at Cabanatuan, Nueva Ecija, were transferred to Fort McKinley, ostensibly to be moved out to Japan. When the Americans intensified bombings on Fort McKinley, this group was moved to Bilibid.

On 29 and 30 December 1944, about 467 civilian internees, mostly Americans but including other Allied nationals, were moved to Bilibid from Baguio. Natalie Crouter and her family were in this group.

The prisoners-of-war were quartered in one section of the Bilibid compound, over which a Captain Nogi was commandant.

The civilians were quartered in another section, with a Major Ebiko as commandant.

Now the sound of gunfire reached Natalie Crouter in the civilian section of Bilibid. Her son Bodie came running, excited and out of breath, to tell her, "There's a heavy humming noise getting nearer from the north and people think it is tanks coming in."

Mother and son rushed with others to openings that looked out on the streets, but they could only see people running down the pavement or peering from their doorways or windows. Now the din of battle surged in from outside the Bilibid walls.

"Rifles, machine guns and bigger guns began ripping all around us and we could hear the grind of more than one tank," Natalie Crouter writes in her diary. "The Committee ordered everyone inside and people poured into the building."

Now everyone on the second floor was ordered downstairs for the night. Shortly the internees saw their Japanese guards come into the big hall and go up to the rooftop, lugging assorted weapons.

Just outside the walls, a large building broke into flames. "It made me sick to see how quickly it happened and to wonder if any people might be inside," Natalie Crouter writes.

Looking up from their compound, the internees at Bilibid could see the sky aglow from raging fires.

"The sky was ablaze all night," Natalie Crouter says. "The oily gray pall has hung over us since, some of it a greasy brown color."

The excited internees could not retire to bed. Now a group keeping vigil heard a tank stop just outside the wall. They heard a southern voice drawl, "Okay, Harvey, let's turn around and go back down this street again."

"There was no mistake about his language – it was distinctly American soldiers," Natalie Crouter exults. "The Marines and Army were here."

Curfew at Santo Tomas was set for 6:30 this evening. Because of the continuing air-raids, the Japanese had turned off the central switch. The camp was in near-total darkness, as the Japanese prohibited any kind of light which could be used as signals.

At 7 o'clock this evening the sound of heavy machine gun-fire came from the direction of Balintawak, some five kilometers to the northeast. New fires appeared to have been lit in other areas. From all over the city the sound of shooting came up sporadically. Suddenly the shooting seemed to come closer. A.V.H. Hartendorp reckoned that they came from the front and the back gates of Santo Tomas. The internees braced for a sleepless night ahead.

At about 8 o'clock tonight, an automobile and four trucks were observed driving up to the Japanese quarters at the Education building. Some Japanese were seen getting into the vehicles and driving away. Shortly, however, the small convoy was back in camp.

The rumbling of heavy tanks was heard in the distance and appeared to come closer. In their blacked-out quarters, tension among the internees rose to a pitch. There was a stampede to the windows.

In Frederic H. Stevens' quarters a man raced down the hallway shouting, "American tanks are coming." A mad rush down the unlighted stairways ensued as people scrambled for the ground-floor gates.[18]

The internees had feared Japanese plans for reprisals should things turn out against them. The hour had come and deliverance was at hand. But what did the Japanese have in store at the other end? Anxiety mingled with anticipation in the internees' collective thoughts.

The Assumption Sisters at the Madrigal compound on General Luna street in Paco were reciting the Litany of the Saints a bit after 8 o'clock this evening when the phone rang. It was a friend from across the Pasig river telling the nuns that the Americans had arrived in the north of Manila.[19]

On 7 August 1944, the Japanese commandeered for military use the premises of the Assumption Convent, a school for girls, at the corner of Herran and Dakota streets in Ermita, leaving but a limited space to the 38 members of the Assumption community. With the inadequate space, the community decided to disperse. One group of 23 went to the Order's house in Baguio and another group of 10 went to a house in a large compound owned by the millionaire-businessman Vicente Madrigal. The rest of the sisters remained at the Assumption Convent as caretakers.

The Assumption community in Paco was headed by Sister Mary Philomene Kelly, an Irishwoman, as Superior. Chaplain for the community was the Franciscan Father Antonio Saravia.

At the Main building of the University of Santo Tomas, the ground floor lobby jammed with agitated internees. The internee-guards refused to open the gates. A fast exchange of machinegun-fire was heard at the front gate. Then grenade explosions. A huge blast tore open the inner gate of *sawali* (bamboo-matting).

From where they watched at the lobby of the Main building, the internees could see a tank lumbering up, followed by four more at close intervals.

"Honey, they are here," Tressa R. Cates' fiance shouted into her ear.[20]

"As in a dream," Tressa R. Cates notes in her diary, "we watched the armored monsters, the lead tank with powerful searchlights, coming up the familiar road towards the Big House."

A.V.H. Hartendorp marked the time at 8:40.[21]

The section of the Flying Column that reached Santo Tomas at this hour was composed of less than 200 men from the 8th Regiment, 1st Brigade, 1st Cavalry Division, backed by five tanks from the 44th Tank Battalion.

The Flying Column was part of a contingent of about 1,000 men, including a squadron of about 650 men, with 17 medium-sized tanks from the 44th Tank Battalion, several artillery units of 105s, field guns, howitzers, mortars and rocket-guns.

A group of Filipino guerrillas among whom was one named Manuel Colayco served as scouts and led the 1st Brigade to the Santo Tomas compound on España Avenue. Approaching the gate, Colayco who was on the lead jeep, fell to sniper fire.

About 100 men from the Flying Column clambered over the wall along the southwest corner of the Santo Tomas campus and attacked the Japanese guarding the gate at the same time the tanks led by one marked "Battling Basic," came roaring in.

Now the first four tanks ground to a halt before the Main building in the Santo Tomas campus, while the fifth pulled out and clanked its way to the rear gate.

Two men in combat gear walked infront of the tanks. They were later identified as Major James C. Gerhert and Captain J.L. Walters. Gerhert strode up to the crowd bottled up in the lobby and said, casually, "Hello, folks."[22]

The dam holding back the crowd gave way and the internees swung out as a body, pell-mell towards the men emerging from the tanks. Screaming and stunned silent, laughing and weeping, ecstatic and hysterical they engulfed their liberators in hugs and kisses.

Now the internees calmed down enough to sing "God Bless America," followed by "America" and ended up with "The Star-Spangled Banner."

One tank had the legend "Georgia Peach" painted on its turret. "Where are the Japs," one of the men from the Georgia Peach shouted. "In the Education building," the crowd shouted back, pointing to the large building to their left.[23]

At around 8 o'clock earlier this evening, the Japanese reinforced the sentries at the Education building. Internees were allowed to enter, but no one was allowed to leave. Now, the internees inside were leaning out of their windows screaming, "Let us out, let us out!"

The Japanese used all of the ground floor of the Education building as offices and quarters for the Commandant and his staff. Half of the second floor was occupied by Japanese civilians. The Japanese used the central stairways to the second floor. The internees used the stairs at either end of the building. The Japanese sections were sealed off from the internees by bamboo-matting (*sawali*) partitions.

The internees in the Education building first learned of the arrival of the American soldiers when a little boy looked out the window and shouted, "They are here! The Americans are here! Look at the tanks!"[24]

As the internees rushed down the corridors and stairways to the ground floor, the Japanese broke down the *sawali* walls and took positions on the landings. With chairs and tables they barricaded the stairways, halting the internees in their tracks.

At this time, W.A. Weidman, an internee, was living in the third floor.[25] He writes: "The Japanese stood ready with their rifles, one or two machine guns, and hand-grenades."

"In due course, three tanks moved forward to reconnoiter the building," Weidman recalls. "The internees on the third floor shouted out warnings, describing positions of the Japanese and the preparations they had made to defend the entrances. There was a parley as the commanding officer of the American forces, with the camp interpreters, demanded the surrender of the Japanese. The Nipponese definitely refused to give up."

Shooting broke out, apparently machine guns aimed at the second floor of the building. The Japanese ran up to the third floor, taking positions among the internees. The internees were ordered by the American force out of the central corridor, to get under the beds and keep quiet. Shortly, machine gun-fire broke out anew, raking the corridors. They came from the Main building. Several Japanese were hit. Machine guns kept sweeping the corridors, but the Japanese were safe amidst the internees, and all demands from the outside to surrender were met with silence.

While the American column moved up Azcarraga, Troop F, 8th Cavalry Regiment, a contingent of about 100 men under the command of Capt. Emery M. Hickman, had detached itself from the main body and proceeded to Malacañang. The palace was undefended.

The Presidential Guard Battalion in the command of the young Capt. Jesus Vargas, composed of Filipinos, had remained at its post. Recognizing the newcomers as Americans, the Filipinos had hesitated to open the gates, afraid that they would be mistaken for Japanese. The lead tank nosed into the old wrought-iron gate and brought it down.

Inside Malacañang, Mrs. Geronima T. Pecson, the unofficial housekeeper, was having a shower in a palace bathroom. She stepped out of the bathroom in her robe, her head wrapped in a towel.

She called out to a Malacañang household servant and asked, "What's all that noise outside about?"[26]

The boy answered, "Ma'am, they are here!" From behind the boy stepped an American soldier.

And that was how an astounded Mrs. Pecson welcomed the liberation army to Malacañang, dressed in her bathrobe, fresh off the shower.

After the departure of President Laurel for Baguio, Mrs. Pecson remained in Malacañang. When the American forces crashed into the palace at this time, there were only Mrs. Geronima T. Pecson; Mrs. Remedios Laurel, the wife of Jose B. Laurel, Jr., son of President Laurel; and Malacañang assistants Arsenio Bonifacio and Nicanor Roxas, in residence together with a few of the palace servants and employees.

Mrs. Jose B. Laurel, Jr. had refused to leave Manila for what had been considered safer places. She did not leave with the rest of the family of President Laurel for Baguio. At Malacañang, through all these days, she had baked bread and cookies, assisted by the daughters of Arsenio Bonifacio. She brewed coffee to serve the remaining palace residents.

This afternoon, Mrs. Remedios Laurel had baked a new batch of cookies. This evening a big pot of coffee was brewing on the stove. Thus Malacañang welcomed the American forces with freshly-baked cookies and great mugs of hot coffee.

A few blocks to the west of the Santo Tomas campus the Far Eastern University stood across from the Bilibid Prison where American prisoners-of-war were interned. The Japanese had fortified the FEU campus.

A part of Troop C, 8th Cavalry, now set out from Santo Tomas for the Legislative building across the Pasig river.

Racing along Quezon boulevard, the contingent ran smack into the Japanese positions at FEU. As the troops approached, the Japanese poured out withering fire, letting loose with anti-tank guns, heavy machine guns and mortars. The cavalry men dismounted and a fierce battle raged. The neighborhood caught fire.

The American soldiers wounded in the encounters on Quezon boulevard in the vicinity of the Far Eastern University were brought into Malacañang. Now Geronima T. Pecson organized the Malacañang staff to set up thirty beds in the east wing of the Executive building.[27]

Earlier, at the instance of Mrs. Francisca T. Benitez, president of the Philippine Women's University, Mrs. Pecson had secured a complete set of surgical instruments and had amassed quantities of bed linen and surgical dressings. Now she brought out her supplies and presented them to the incredulous American medical officer who could not believe his good fortune. It was thus that the Presidential Palace became an emergency military hospital.

General Chase's command post was twenty minutes behind the main column. Now, joined by the 5th Cavalry which had been detained by a firefight in Norzagaray, the new convoy moved down the same route the main column had taken and into Quezon Boulevard where the pitched battle raged.

General Chase ordered the column to turn into a narrow street and head for Santo Tomas. At 11:30 tonight the column was inside the Santo Tomas compound.

Across the FEU compound on Lerma street stood the Harris Memorial building which had been converted into Red Cross Children's Home No. 3. Dr. J. Horacio Yanzon was in-charge of the home which sheltered at this time 27 children, aged two to ten, all of whom were orphans, or had been rescued, destitute and abandoned, from the streets.[28]

The neighborhood was in flames, and in the crossfire was Red Cross Children's Home No. 3. Now J. Horacio Yanzon decided to flee the Home and seek safety in the Manila Hospital building across the street, which he believed was built of stronger material. Dr. Yanzon calmed down his wards and led them across the street. As the line of children came out into the battleground, the Red Cross emblem on the ambulance which preceded them stood out in the light of burning buildings. Firing from the American sector ceased.

Now Dr. Yanzon had his wards in the relative safety of the ground floor of the Manila Hospital building. Later in the night as the battle raged, a shell from the American side tore off the roof of the building, followed by another right into the top floor. Realizing the mortal danger they were in, Yanzon bundled up his small charges anew, packed them into the ambulance and another Red Cross vehicle, and taking the lead vehicle he guided the small convoy through streets turned into battlegrounds on to safety a distance away from the firing line. Not one of the 27 children suffered a scratch.

Meanwhile, the situation at the Education building in Santo Tomas ground into an impasse. Weidman testifies:

"During the night the internees lay on the floor under their beds. The tanks stood guard outside, their searchlights on the building. Now and then a Japanese soldier would creep forward, rest his rifle on the window ledge and shoot. Whenever this occurred, a burst of machine gun-fire would be directed to the point but the Japanese would already have drawn back. Some of the bullets passed through the cement wall of the building, endangering the cowering occupants. A number of our men outside tanks were wounded by these pot-shots and the tank lights were turned off. The night passed slowly without change in the deadlock."[29]

SUNDAY, 4 FEBRUARY 1945

Shortly after midnight, Fukuchi Fukomoto turned on the press at the printing plant of the *Manila Tribune*, the city newspaper during the Japanese occupation, located on Florentino Torres street in Santa Cruz district. Fukomoto was the senior officer left in-charge. He did not know that the Americans were in Manila, nor of the events at Santo Tomas. Also, he did not know how to turn off the press, once turned on. He ran off 100,000 copies of the *Manila Tribune* for 4 February 1945. This was the biggest number of copies the paper ever had, it was the last issue, and the one that did not get distributed.[1]

At 3 o'clock this morning, Jose Mendoza, a lawyer who lived on Urdaneta street in Intramuros, was awakened by an insistent pounding on his door. It was a squad of Japanese who ordered everyone in the house to the street. Resident in this house at this time, aside from Jose Mendoza, were his wife, the former Trinidad Gardiner, their 15-year-old daughter, Remy, and Mrs. Mendoza's father.[2]

The family joined neighbors in the street, many of them in their nightclothes and underwear. The men were herded into Fort Santiago and the women to the church and monastery of San Agustin.

At San Agustin church, Mrs. Trinidad Gardiner-Mendoza and her daughter Remy were reunited with Mrs. Mendoza's sister Mercedes and other relatives. She would not see her husband again.

Mrs. Isabel Benitez de Santa Isabel, too, found herself in the San Agustin church this morning, not to worship, but as a hostage. Her family lived on Muralla near Victoria street in Intramuros. Called out into the street in the early hours, she saw her husband Numeriano Sta. Isabel, the organist of the Paules church on San Marcelino street outside the walls, and their three sons, led away to Fort Santiago. She never saw them again. She herself joined the other women at San Agustin.

In Tondo, the fire continued to eat up what remained of the district. During the night the Japanese garrison at Plaza Moriones moved out. However, machine gun emplacements had been set-up in the big concrete buildings that still stood. Field guns appeared in the plaza and one was set-up right on the frontsteps of the Tondo church.

Early this morning, Father Paul de Guzman, S.J., with two other priests, opened the church for Sunday mass.[3] A few persons slipped in, apparently more for shelter than for prayer, as the Japanese were shooting people moving about in the streets. It was this tiny congregation that brought Father de Guzman the news that the Americans had liberated Santo Tomas.

The Santo Tomas camp was now bristling with war material. More tanks, heavy guns, trucks and that new creature, the jeep, had arrived during the night. Soldiers were raising tents and setting-up kitchens while others dug trenches and foxholes.[4]

Brig. Gen. William C. Chase, commanding the Flying Column, had arrived in camp the previous night and was directing the siege of the Education building.

The Japanese commandant, Lt. Col. Toshio Hayashi, demanded safe conduct for himself and his troops to leave the camp and rejoin the main body of the Japanese forces.

General Chase's strategy was to gain time. He did not want the Japanese to leave camp knowing that but a small force occupied Santo Tomas. The interpreters Stanley and Cary returned to the Education building to inform the Japanese commandant that if no harm came to the internees, his demands might be accepted upon approval by higher authorities. In the meantime, both sides agreed that there would be no more firing.

This morning, elements of the 37th Infantry Division entered Manila and the Santo Tomas occupation force was greatly augmented.

From Tagaytay, the airborne units began to advance against Manila. Japanese detachments deployed at strategic points along the highway gave slight opposition in the nature of delaying tactics. These were quickly overwhelmed. All along the route of the northward advance the paratroopers received a triumphal welcome from crowds of Filipinos who lined the highways wherever it was safe.[5]

In Malate, Lydia Gutierrez and her family went to Sunday Mass. She noted that the Japanese had turned more bellicose on the streets and were slapping people. Word of the arrival of the Americans in the northside had reached the people of Malate. It had reached the Japanese, too.[6]

At 8 o'clock this morning, Angel Dionzon, 75, stood in the lobby of the China Banking Corporation on Dasmariñas street in Binondo and watched, sorely puzzled, as a Japanese team lugged a five-gallon can of gasoline and armloads of gunny sacks into the groundfloor of the bank.[7]

Late in 1944, the Japanese had commandeered the China Bank building for their own use. They evacuated the building in early 1945. Dionzon served as caretaker of the building and stayed on after the Japanese left.

Now Angel Dionzon stood away from the bunch of Japanese and quietly watched as they soaked the gunny sacks in gasoline and scattered them around the lobby. As the group withdrew, one of them exploded a hand grenade into a pile of sacks, setting it on fire. The flames rapidly spread all over the ground floor of the China Bank building and Angel Dionzon fled into the street. The adjoining buildings were on fire, and shortly the upper floors of the China Bank building were ablaze.

Not far from here, at the corner of Dasmarinas and Marquina streets, Yu Cheng Kho, 34, a Chinese businessman, looked out of the mezzanine of the Yucuanseh Drug at the sound of a truck stopping at the rear of the building, along San Vicente street.

The truck was driven by a Japanese with seven other Japanese aboard. On the truck Yu saw about a dozen bombs, each approximately four feet-long and six or eight inches in diameter. As Yu watched from his mezzanine window unobserved from below, two of the Japanese on the truck passed a bomb to one of their fellows who carried it into the back of the Crystal Arcade building.

The Japanese came and went, four or five times, each time lugging one bomb inside the Crystal Arcade building through the rear entrance.

Now the truck turned into Marquina street and moved on to the corner of Nueva and Dasmariñas streets infront of the Yutivo Sons Hardware building, where Yu worked. There were Japanese sentries infront of the Yutivo building. Now Yu Cheng Kho watched as the Japanese carried one of the bombs inside the Yutivo Sons Hardware building.

Later this evening, the fire spread to the Dasmariñas area. Yu Cheng Kho dashed into the street as the fire unabatingly came closer to the Yucuanseh Drug building. Scurrying along, Yu felt the ground shake under his feet as a huge explosion rocked the Crystal Arcade building. Yu rushed on to safety. Shortly, the area came under heavy shelling from the American side.

This morning, Modesto Farolan, 45, arrived at the Red Cross headquarters on Isaac Peral street in Ermita on the south side.[8] Farolan was editor of the *Philippines Herald*, a leading Manila daily, when World War II broke out in the Philippines in December 1941.

On 22 December 1944, Don Jose Paez, manager of the Philippine Red Cross society at this time, who was also minister of public works and communications in the cabinet of wartime President Jose P. Laurel, was advised to join other ranking cabinet officials who were being evacuated to Baguio. At 5 o'clock in the afternoon of that day, Paez had asked Don Vicente Madrigal, chairman of the board of directors of the Philippine Red Cross society, to an emergency conference.

Madrigal was the owner of the *Philippines Herald* which had ceased publication, although he still retained Modesto Farolan as his administrative assistant. Farolan also served as Madrigal's liaison man with the Red Cross. Farolan was with Madrigal at the emergency conference on the afternoon of 22 December 1944.

Paez had to turn over the managership of the Philippine Red Cross society and he and Madrigal agreed on the designation of Modesto Farolan to the post of acting manager. The following day, 23 December, Farolan received his formal appointment to this post.

Modesto Farolan now undertook the difficult task of preparing the Red Cross to handle emergency situations under actual combat. Red Cross headquarters on Isaac Peral street was a modest two-storey building of stucco done in the California-mission style, completed in 1932. Now the building was converted into an emergency hospital.

All through this morning civilian refugees streamed into Red Cross headquarters on Isaac Peral street as homes in the Ermita district came under American shelling, or were put to the torch by the Japanese.

"We became a refugee center from this day on," Farolan testified.

In May 1944, the Japanese commandeered the four-hectare property of the Congregation of St. Paul de Chartres in Quezon City, where the Order had its novitiate.[9] The resident community numbering 105 moved to the St. Paul college complex on Herran street in Malate, where 85 other religious were already in residence.

In July 1944, the nuns learned that their Herran property was also to be requisitioned by the Japanese. They bargained to retain at least a part of the college premises, and for a while the Japanese seemed to agree. They assigned certain buildings to the nuns. With the prospect of severely-reduced living space, the nuns decided to disperse. The bulk of 50 went to their novitiate in Baguio where the Order served at the Lourdes hospital in that city, and others braved by then hazardous journeys to St. Paul houses in Cagayan and the Ilocos.

There remained 40 nuns at St. Paul college in Manila, led by the Superior, Mother Bernard du Sacre Coeur, SPC, a Belgian national. On 11 September 1944, the Sisters of St. Paul de Chartres were ordered to vacate their Herran street property entirely for the exclusive use of the Japanese. They were given three days to pack. With an exquisite sense of irony, the nuns were offered the use of the Temple of the Freemasons on Taft Avenue. They refused. But they agreed to go to St. Theresa's college on San Marcelino street on condition that the Augustinian Cannonesses (Belgian Sisters) of St. Theresa who were still in residence remained with them.

St. Theresa's college itself was partly occupied by Japanese marines. A few of the Belgian Sisters remained with some students as caretakers.

This morning the St. Paul Sisters at St. Theresa's college noted that the

Japanese guards at the gate were particularly bellicose. The nuns had no way of knowing about the events on the north side.

Today, St. Theresa's college was turned into a fortress. Teams of Japanese marines came in and mounted machine-guns at the windows and on the roof, installed heavy guns in the gardens while bunkers were dug all over the grounds

"They tried to reassure us by saying they were doing all these for 'our protection'," Sister Charles, SPC, writes.

This afternoon, General Verne D. Mudge, commanding the 1st Cavalry Division, directed General Chase to seize Quezon bridge which American intelligence indicated to be the only remaining bridge over the Pasig at this time.[10]

The 2nd Squadron, 5th Cavalry, was assigned to this task. Setting out from the Santo Tomas camp where the Americans had assembled, the 5th Cavalry ran into the strongly-garrisonned Japanese positions at the Far Eastern University campus on Quezon Boulevard. The Japanese had mined the whole length of Quezon Boulevard westward from Azcarraga street and had set up formidable roadblocks which were heavily fortified. The 5th Cavalry could not proceed. At this point, the Japanese Northern Force under Colonel Noguchi blew up Quezon bridge.

Over at the civilian internees section at Bilibid Prisons, eight Japanese soldiers who had kept watch on the rooftop came down to the ground at daylight.[11]

At about 10 o'clock this morning, the chairman of the internee committee was called to the quarters of the Japanese commandant. The internee chairman was soon back, a sheaf of papers in his hands. They were orders formally releasing the prisoners. Major Ebiko's letter had been dated 7 January 1945. The internee chairman insisted that the original date be crossed out in favor of today's date. The letter read:

"(From) Commandant Major Ebiko:

"1. The Japanese Army is now going to release all the prisoners-of-war and internees here on its own accord.

"2. We are assigned to another duty and shall be here no more.

"3. You are at liberty to act and live as free persons, but you must be aware of probable dangers if you go out.

"4. We shall leave here foodstuffs, medicines and other necessities of which you may avail yourselves for the time being.

"5. We have arranged to put up signboard at the front gate, bearing following contex (sic): - Lawfully released Prisoners of War and Internees are quartered here. Please do not molest them unless they make positive resistance."

Now the internee chairman brought a hand-sewn American flag they had brought with them from Baguio out of a table drawer in the narrow space he used as an office and held it up before the gathered internees. Now the assembly broke out into the *Star-Spangled Banner* and followed that with *God Bless America.*

Natalie Crouter extricated herself from the crowd and went to her family quarters where she found her daughter June, 15, comforting her father Jerry who sat bowed, his face in his hands.

"I put my arms around his shoulders," Natalie Crouter writes in her diary, "and the three of us sat there with tears running down our cheeks for quite a long while, not saying anything."

At about this time, over at the prisoner-of-war section of Bilibid, the Japanese staff too was moving out. Before he marched his men out of the gates, the Japanese commandant, Captain Nogi, handed a letter to a member of the internee committee, who now assembled the internees to read the letter.[12]

"Japanese have received new assignment we are leaving Bilibid from now on you are free but we warn Manila very dangerous and advise remain in the walls of Bilibid. We are leaving you plenty supply of food medicine (sic)."

This afternoon a detachment of about 150 Japanese troops and *Makapilis* came up Estrada street in Singalong and halted along Taft Avenue infront of the De la Salle college. After an hour, the detachment moved on. The area was tranquil and only the sight of armed men indicated that there was a war going on.[13]

In residence at De la Salle college at this time was a community of seventeen Christian Brothers led by the college director, Brother Egbert Xavier, 51, an Irish national. The Brothers came from countries with which Japan was not at war. They included two Irishmen, one Hungarian, one Czech and thirteen Germans.

Chaplain to the De la Salle community was the Rev. Fr. Francis J. Cosgrave, 48, an Irish-born Australian citizen, the superior of the Congregation of the Most Holy Redeemer in Manila, whose members are popularly known as Redemptorists.

When the church and convent of the Redemptorists in Baclaran were requisitioned by the Japanese for military use in mid-1944, Fr. Cosgrave was invited by Brother Xavier to serve as chaplain to the Christian Brothers at De la Salle. Fr. Cosgrave consented.

Also at De la Salle college at this time was a number of refugee families from the neighborhood.

When his home on Paris street in Singalong, right across from that of Mayor Leon G. Guinto, Sr., was commandeered by the Japanese early in January 1945, Judge Jose Carlos, 47, brought his family over to the nearby De la Salle college as refugees. The Carlos family included Mrs. Juanita Uychuico Carlos, 43, and the children -- Rosario, 21; Asela, 20; Gloria, 17; Dionisia, 16; Cecilia, 12; Antonio, 6, and Jose, Jr., 3. With them were their household staff -- Mateo, Francisco and Isabel.

With the Carlos family went the family of Dr. Antonio Cojuangco, 45, whose wife Victoria, 37, was the sister of Mrs. Carlos. They had four children -- Ramon, 20, married to the former Natividad de las Alas, also 20; Trinidad, 18, married to Servillano Aquino, 25; Antonio,17, and Lourdes, 15. The Cojuangcos had an adopted son, Ricardo, 3, and a household staff that included the male nurse Filomeno Inolin, the coachman Apolinario and the maidservants Juanita Tamayo, Felisa and Rita. The young Aquino couple had a maidservant, Fortunata Salonga, 14.

Towards the end of January 1945, the home of the Spanish expatriate-businessman Enrique Vazquez-Prada on Taft Avenue across from De la Salle college was also commandeered by the Japanese. Now Vazquez-Prada, 59, brought his family over to De la Salle college as refugees.

Highly-rated in his community and much-admired by his peers, Enrique Vazquez-Prada was the founder and general manager of La Urbana Mutual Building and Loan Association and president of Casino Español. His wife, the elegant and sophisticated Helen Leowinsohn, 46, was Austrian, a tall and stately blonde who was much-appreciated in Manila society in earlier days. They had four sons -- Enrique, Jr., 24; Herman, 20; Alfonso, 13, and Fernando, 5, all of whom had been students at De la Salle. With them were their househelp, Antonio and Armenia. Don Enrique had suffered a cerebral stroke and at this time was slowly recuperating. He was sorely handicapped.

At the start of February 1945, Dr. Clemente Uychuico, 32, the younger brother of Mrs. Carlos and Mrs. Cojuangco, joined his sisters and their families at De la Salle. Dr. Uychuico's own family included his wife, the former Felicidad Conui, 33, and their three small children -- Soledad, 6; Ramon, 4; and Paz, 3. With them were their househelp -- Clarita Roldan, 17, and Regina.

These families with the Christian Brothers and their chaplain, composed the De la Salle college civilian population at this time, Also resident were members of the college staff which included Vicente Serillo, Anselmo Sudlan, Teofilo Candari, Julian Cinco, Pamfilo Almodan, Ceferino Villamor and the college secretary, Martin Hain.

The civilians were quartered in the south wing of the De la Salle college main building. The rest of the building was garrisonned by Japanese marines.

On 1st February, the captain of the garrison had called on Brother Egbert Xavier, the college director, to advise that the civilians move out in 48 hours. The area was strategic and was certain to become battleground.

"After 48 hours, I have no more responsibility for the lives of the inhabitants of this house," the Japanese captain told Brother Xavier. But the latter refused to move and replied that he would assume responsibility for the situation.

The same afternoon, Brother Mutwald, 38, disagreeing with the director's decision to stay put, went to see the archbishop of Manila, Mons. Michael O'Doherty, to seek advice. The archbishop advised that the community and the civilian refugees leave the premises. When apprised of this, Brother Xavier stood firm on his decision, although he agreed to bring the matter up for discussion at the community's meeting the following Monday.

Yesterday, 2nd February, conscious of the undercurrents of discontent among his associates over his decision to remain in the premises, Brother Xavier called an unscheduled meeting of the community. Here he demanded obedience to his decision.

Still unhappy about the matter, several of the Brothers went to consult with the Apostolic Delegate, Mons. William Piani. He advised the community to comply with the director's decision. This settled the matter.

The main building of De la Salle college on Taft Avenue at this time was H-shaped, three-storeyed, with a neo-classic facade painted stark white, a very impressive landmark in this section of the city.

At ground level, the south wing of the building, the right-hand section of the H facing Taft Avenue was the assembly hall, accessible from a southside entrance that led to a spacious foyer. The staircase led to the second floor. Under the staircase was the wine cellar which became a bomb shelter under battle conditions.

At the second floor was the chapel, designed in the romanesque style, large enough to accommodate the pre-war college population of 1,200. Over the entrance to the chapel was the choirloft and organ gallery. Flanked by balconies that looked out on views of south Manila, the large hall ended in the elevated altar, set off by carved wooden railings. On either side of the altar screened by wrought-iron gratings were twin spiral staircases that led to the sacristy, right over the altar area. The rest of the second floor was given to dormitories and offices of the Christian Brothers community.

At 6 o'clock this evening, the Japanese set fire to three large structures on Herran street in Paco that had once been garment factories where hundreds of Filipino girls hand-embroidered dresses. The Japanese had converted the buildings into warehouses and considerable equipment had been transferred here since the Americans started bombing the Port Area.[14]

There had been gasoline drums in the buildings, and these exploded when the flames reached them and further fed the fires.

"All three warehouses were soon enveloped in flames," Marcial F. Lichauco writes in his diary. "The heat was so intense that we could not look out of our windows . . ."

The fire raged for hours and consumed everything within reach. There was no breeze and the fire did not spread.

Later this evening, at the Santo Tomas camp, Col. C.E. Brady told the American interpreter Stanley and his Japanese counterpart Luki that the Japanese at the Education building would be escorted to a point they desired in the city at 7 o'clock the following morning. The Japanese would be allowed to take their sidearms but no machine guns and no hand grenades.[15]

Ultimately, Brady and the Japanese commandant, Lt. Col. Toshio Hayashi, agreed that the Japanese may take their swords, pistols and rifles.

Tonight the Japanese started torching buildings in Ermita. This is what Rodolfo G. Tupas remembers of this night: "Two Japanese marines were crawling like snakes in the grass in the backyard of another neighbor on Pennsylvania street. They were dragging along a drum of gasoline. I wondered what they were up to until they spilled the gasoline on the house and set it on fire."[16]

By midnight, the neighborhood was in chaos. Rod Tupas recalls: "The panicked male boarders at the YMCA at the corner of Pennsylvania and Oregon were scaling the wall of the Lichauco home trying to flee the guns of the Japanese marines . . ."

Rod turned to his own frontyard. "A stout Japanese marine with a gauze mask was aiming his pistol by bringing it down slowly from a high position." Rod dashed inside the house.

About 8 o'clock this evening, the 2nd Battalion, 148th Infantry, reached the intersection of Rizal Avenue and Azcarraga street, a block from Oroquieta street which fronted the north gate of Old Bilibid. The 2nd Battalion, 148th Infantry, formed the rear of elements from the 37th Infantry Division which entered Manila today.[17]

The 2nd Battalion, 148th Infantry, was actually two blocks away from the 2nd Squadron, 5th Cavalry, and the 2nd Squadron, 8th Cavalry, which were engaged in a furious battle with the Japanese garrison at the

Far Eastern University compound.

In the barracks where the group of Dr. W.H. Waterous was confined in the prisoners-of-war section at Bilibid, the sound of the raging battle was "music." Suddenly, this group heard urgent pounding on the boards that covered one of the windows on their side of the compound. The battering continued until the boards gave way.

"A 37th Infantry man, some Wop from New York . . . stuck his head through the bars," Dr. Waterous writes," and yelled, 'Any goddamn Nips here . . .'"

One of the inmates yelled back, "Christ, this is an American prison camp!"

A soldier outside shouted a name. It was the name of his brother who had been in the 31st Infantry and was a prisoner at Bilibid. In a few minutes the two brothers were hugging each other in a happy embrace.

MONDAY, 5 FEBRUARY 1945

Before dawn the 511th Parachute Infantry crossed the Parañaque river and drove north along Route 1. This route is squeezed tightly between the river on the east and the sea on the west, and the Japanese defended the area house-to-house, pillbox-to-pillbox. The 511th was supported only lightly by artillery, but fought back with flame-throwers and 60-mm. mortars.[1]

Today the main body of the 37th Infantry Division entered Manila. General Oscar Griswold apportioned the northern part of Manila between the two American divisions now inside city limits. The western half was allocated to the Infantry and the Cavalry got the eastern half.[2]

This morning, the 145th Infantry Regiment began clearing operations in Tondo district. Passing through Tondo, elements of the 145th swept westward to San Nicolas and Binondo districts.

On the east, troops from the 148th Infantry Regiment cleared out machine gun-emplacements and snipers in buildings, working towards Santa Cruz district.

On the eastern sector of north Manila assigned to the 1st Cavalry Division, clearing operations proceeded smoothly and quickly as the area was but lightly defended. By today, the Flying Column organization of the 1st Cavalry Division had been dissolved.

Nemesio Francisco, a teacher at the Manila high school in Intramuros, was awakened early this morning by angry pounding on his door. From his second-storey window he looked out on a big crowd of his neighbors on the street in front of his apartment house, guarded by Japanese troops.

Under the menacing threats of the Japanese, Francisco came down and joined the crowd. From here, the company was marched under guard to the Manila cathedral.[3]

At 6:45 this morning, at the Santo Tomas camp, Col. Brady and the interpreter Stanley proceeded to the Education building to hurry up the Japanese. Shortly, 47 Japanese officers and men led by Lt. Col. Toshio Hayashi filed out of the building.[4]

With an escort of about 100 American soldiers led by Col. Brady himself, the Japanese marched out of Santo Tomas at 7 o'clock this morning. Carl Mydans, the *Life Magazine* photographer, ran ahead taking pictures.

The Japanese indicated they wanted to proceed to the Sampaloc Rotonda where Santa Mesa boulevard, Legarda and Nagtahan streets converge and where Aviles street comes to an end. Malacañang Palace stands on Aviles. The Japanese seemed to have made a wrong turn enroute, and arrived at the Rotonda by a roundabout way.

At the Rotonda, the Americans and the Japanese exchanged salutes. The American escort made an "about face," and the Japanese, in fact, were on their own.

The Japanese Lt. Col. Hayashi did not know that Malacañang was now in American hands. Marching along Aviles, they came within gunsight of the Americans mounting guard at the Palace gate. Several Japanese were killed here, among them Lt. Col. Hayashi.

Apparently some escaped. Later this afternoon, six of the 47 who left the Santo Tomas camp in the morning were brought back alive to Santo Tomas. This time they were already in civilian clothes. Also this time, they came in as prisoners.

By 12:30 this afternoon, Company I, 148th Infantry Regiment, was inside Binondo district, two hundred yards from the Pasig river. The buildings along the Escolta were on fire, however, and the heat was intense, forcing Company I to withdraw two hundred yards inland.

The spearhead of the 148th was formed by Company K, which was ordered to seize Jones bridge which spanned the Pasig at this point.

The attack on the Jones bridge was launched from Azcarraga street at the intersection with Magdalena street and proceeded westward to the Escolta.

By noon today, Company K, 148th Infantry, had crossed the Estero de la Reina. The conflagration raging on the Escolta made movement difficult for the Americans. The approaches to the small bridge crossing the Estero de la Reina were mined and Japanese mortar and rifle fire fell without let-up. At 12:30 this afternoon, Company K, too, was forced to withdraw from the area.

The point platoon of the 3rd Battalion, 148th Infantry was commanded by Lt. Bob Viale.[5] Single-handedly Viale had demolished two Japanese pillboxes during the advance towards Jones bridge. Now he directed a rocket-launcher against a third pillbox as his platoon came up the small bridge spanning the Estero de la Reina.

When the orders came to withdraw, Lt. Viale found that all withdrawal routes were dominated by Japanese machine gun-positions in a series of pillboxes. Now Viale led his platoon into a ruined building which overlooked several of these pillboxes. He climbed up a ladder and prepared to throw a grenade down a window to the enemy below. He had been wounded in the arm earlier. Now as he was about to cast his armed grenade, he slipped on the ladder and the grenade clattered to the floor.

Viale jumped after the grenade. The platoon crowded the small room. Now Viale calmly lay on his stomach over the live grenade in a corner. The explosion killed him but none of his comrades suffered a scratch.

Father Paul de Guzman and the other priests went into the Tondo church before noon today and shortly, a Japanese squad appeared and mounted guard at the church door. The guards allowed people to enter the church but forbade them from leaving.[6]

At 2 o'clock this afternoon, the Japanese started firing the field-gun on the steps of the church, aiming in the direction of Gagalangin. Overhead a reconnaissance plane appeared. Fr. de Guzman was certain it was American. Shortly after, the shots of the Japanese artillery were being returned. The first shot was wide. The second came closer. The next fifteen shots slammed into the church, wreaking terror among the civilians inside. Then one came w-h-a-a-m right on the Japanese field-gun. It was silent from thereon.

At 3:30 this afternoon, Michael Goldenberg, 56, a French national and long-time resident of Manila, was at the office building he owned at 419 Dasmariñas street in the business district of Binondo.[7]

From his office window at the mezzanine floor, he saw a Japanese squad, one of whose members lugged a five-gallon gasoline can into the Chun Sing building adjacent to his own, at the corner of Nueva and Dasmariñas streets. Presently the building blew up in a huge explosion and a blaze shot up the various floors of the concrete edifice.

Michael Goldenberg and a male servant threw folders of official papers into a bag and together ran out into the street. A Japanese soldier espied the two as they ran and fired. Both sustained slight injuries in the legs. They kept running towards safety.

At 4 o'clock this afternoon, Ramsingh Mayasingh, 66, an Indian national employed as watchman in a store which was owned by another Indian at 82 Escolta, stood in the lobby of the Capitol theatre on the same street.

Ramsingh watched unobserved from the theatre lobby as a group of Japanese set up a bomb at 27 Escolta. Shortly the bomb was detonated and the building went up in a huge blaze.

Another detonation blew up the Cu Unjieng building at 103 Escolta and from these two buildings, the fire spread to T. Pinpin and Nueva streets.

This afternoon, Sancho Enriquez, 49, Manila schools supervisor, and his family were routed out of their home at 188 Cabildo street in Intramuros and with their neighbors, were led to the Manila cathedral. In this group was Juan Palada, 36, who lived at 100 Anda street.[8]

Rosalinda Andoy, 11, lived with her parents and two aunts at 53 Magallanes street in Intramuros. Today, the members of the Andoy household found themselves in the august precincts of the Manila Cathedral, now used as a detention center for civilian residents of Intramuros.[9]

This afternoon, Japanese marines barged into the home of Luis Gallent, a Spanish national, at 88 Postigo street, Intramuros. The Japanese found nothing that interested them but they took Luis Gallent's yunger brother with them to Fort Santiago.[10]

All through this day men, women and children from homes in Intramuros were brought into the cathedral. By nightfall, there were almost 2,000 in the nave of the great house of worship. There were no arrangements for food or water, nor for toilet facilities.

The La Concordia college on Herran street in Paco had been officially designated by the city government as a refugee reception center.[11]

Founded in 1868 as a school for girls, La Concordia college was run by the Daughters of Charity of St. Vincent de Paul. The mayor of Greater Manila had ordered that a Red Cross flag be raised over the premises to signify that the site is neutral for humanitarian reasons.

Towards the first week of January 1945, the Hospicio de San Jose on Isla de Convalescencia on the Pasig river off the Ayala bridge was ordered vacated by the Japanese. The site was a strategic point on the river and they wanted it for military use. The Hospicio de San Jose is an orphanage and home for the aged run by the Daughters of Charity and the Vincentian Fathers.

One morning in January the children in the orphanage and the elderly folk supervised by the Daughters of Charity were brought by barge to the landing on the riverbank in the backyard of La Ignaciana, the Jesuit retreat-house on Herran street in Paco. The Hospicio residents were being brought over to La Concordia college, a few blocks westward on Herran. Another group composed of invalids and disabled were brought to La Concordia by land transportation.

Today, La Concordia college became a refugee center as the Japanese started withdrawing from the Santa Ana and Paco areas. They mined streets and set fire to their former depots. The fires spread to private residences and the people ran out to the streets. They were met with machine gunfire by the Japanese. Hundreds of civilians from the neighborhood now jammed into La Concordia.

In Tondo, the area surrounding the church was a sea of flames.[12] Plaza Moriones was crowded with refugees. Dense smoke swirled into the open space. The three priests urged people to get into the church. Very few did. The others feared that the building may have been mined by the Japanese. They had seen the Japanese wiring large buildings before blasting them into bits. Groups of refugees raced down the streets leading away from the smoke-shrouded Plaza Moriones. At the other end of the streets Japanese lay waiting, firing at anything that moved. The exits from Plaza Moriones were blocked.

At 7 o'clock this evening word was passed on to the internees at Bilibid to get ready to move out. Battle raged in the vicinity as the Japanese in the heavily fortified Far Eastern University campus sternly opposed the American advance. The internees had to be moved out of the battle zone.

At the civilian internees section, Natalie Crouter and her husband Jerry who hobbled on crutches, packed their large baggage pieces. They stowed away in their portion of the internee lodgings family treasures they had managed to keep through all these years of internment. With their two children they joined other internees to the street outside and waited for trucks that were to ferry them, where, they did not know.[13]

It had been a hectic day for the Crouters as it was for all the internees at Bilibid, spent mostly getting used to freedom and catching up on news brought in by the American soldiers.

Now the Crouters and their fellow internees boarded trucks that wound up at the Ang Tibay shoe factory compound in Caloocan to the north of Manila, which turned out to be Division Headquarters. Here they spent the night.

Deep into the night Col. Noguchi's Northern Force continued its demolition operation in Tondo.[14] The U.S. 37th Infantry observed the firing and blowing up of military stores, concluding which the Japanese now began to withdraw across the Pasig.

"There was no wanton destruction," Robert Ross Smith writes, "and in all probability the fires resulting from the demolitions would have been confined to the North Port Area."[15] At about 8:30 this evening, however, the wind changed and drove the flames north and west inland.

Now the 37th Infantry Division started its own demolitions in an attempt to block the spread of the fire.

"The extent of the demolition cannot be ascertained," Robert Ross Smith writes," although it is known that the work of destruction continued nearly 24 hours and it is an academic point at best since the demolition proved largely ineffective in controlling the flames."[16]

The fire spread northwards from the river banks to Azcarragá, leaping across the street into the North Harbor area and the congested residential section where the houses were built of highly imflammable material.

Earlier, as night fell and as the flames began to subside, the 2nd Battalion, 148th Infantry Regiment, had surged once more towards the Pasig along the Binondo and Santa Cruz side. The opposition was firm, and the Japanese fell where they stood fighting. All through the night the battle raged.

Tonight the big guns mounted on the lawns of St. Theresa's college on San Marcelino street started returning the barrages from the American sector on the north side of the Pasig. The nuns at St. Theresa's swept through the corridors in near-hysteria. A huge explosion hit close by.[17]

"We took shelter in a room we thought safest," Sister Charles writes. "We did not realize we were in the battle zone until a shower of falling steel shattered our last doubt . . . we ran under the cement stairs and there awaited our doom."

Here the nuns were joined by their chaplain, the Vincentian Father Elias Gonzalez who gave them general absolution and Holy Communion.

"Jesus came to calm our overwrought nerves and a soothing stillness downed our panic," Sister Charles says of tonight's aggravation which, however, waned towards morning.

TUESDAY, 6 FEBRUARY 1945

In Parañaque, the 511th Parachute Infantry had paused to wait for the 188th to which the 1st Battalion, 187th Infantry, was attached. It was due down Tagaytay Ridge.[1]

The 11th Airborne intended to field the 188th against Nichols airdrome, while the 511th drove west across the Paranaque river.

Reaching Parañaque, the 188th now moved up about four kilometers southeast of Nichols.

Nichols served the Japanese naval service and was garrisoned by the 3rd Naval Battalion. The Japanese had expected the main attack against Manila to come from the south rather than from the north, and Nichols Field was heavily defended, largely with anti-aircraft guns. The carefully-camouflaged gun positions were protected by a network of bunkers and pillboxes.

In Tondo, the fire continued to spread and intensify. At one o'clock this morning the Japanese themselves decided to withdraw. Only then were the thousands bottled up in Plaza Moriones and adjoining streets able to flee.[2]

Father Paul de Guzman, S.J., and the two other priests led a huge throng out of the area, but were driven back by Japanese stragglers who threw handgrenades from second-storey windows.[2-a]

A rear-guard crew was working on the fuse of a bomb set between the Tondo church and a nearby school. The fuse would not light and the Japanese crew gave up to join their retreating main group.

When the conflagration reached the churchyard, the parish priest, Monsignor Jose Jovellanos, took the image of the Santo Niño in his arms and led the exodus out of the burning heart of Tondo.[2-b]

Monsignor Jovellanos had on a steel helmet, a bag of medical supplies and first aid equipment slung on one shoulder. Behind him followed his assistants, one of them carrying the Blessed Sacrament, and the refugees, weeping and whining in terror.

As the group passed the Tondo public school which the Japanese used as barracks, a hand grenade was hurled at them. No one was hurt, though the Monsignor would later recall that he felt something strike his steel helmet.

The refugee group made its way through the roaring fires on Juan Luna street, reached the Pritil *estero,* but the bridge had been blown up. The men in the group scrounged for wooden planks which they laid across the ruined bridge. On the other side, the Americans waited. The group reached the Santa Monica chapel on Dagupan street where the image of the Santo Niño found refuge, and where the people huddled together, with their parish priest, for the rest of the night.

Francisco Lopez, Filipino executive of a film distribution company, lived at 239 San Marcelino street, near the corner of San Luis, less than 100 yards from the German Club.[3]

At 2 o'clock this morning, the family of Francisco Lopez which included his mother, two brothers, a sister and a cousin who had been adopted by the family, fled their home on San Marcelino street for the German Club of Manila. Also with them were an elderly uncle and an aunt, their children and five male servants.

The German Club was the fellowship center of the German community of Manila. The clubhouse was a low-slung building fronting San Luis street in Ermita. On adjoining property to the west was the Casino Español, the Spanish fellowship club, which faced Taft Avenue. The German Club was separated from the grounds of the church and seminary of St. Vincent de Paul to the north by an adobe wall.

The German Club, throughout the Japanese occupation of Manila, enjoyed certain privileges befitting a wartime ally. Many Germans in Manila at this time openly displayed their affinity with the Japanese. Many flew the swastika on their vehicles and in their homes, as the German Club did. Because of the privileges that it obviously enjoyed from the Japanese, and because of its massive construction, the German Club, to many refugees these days, was a haven.

Today, this section of Ermita came under heavy American artillery fire. Many residents of the area sought shelter in the German Club premises. The building was constructed of substantial material and underneath shelters had been dug.

This morning General Douglas MacArthur announced to the world, "At 6:30 this morning, Manila had fallen."[4]

MacArthur also said:

"The fall of Manila was the end of one great phase of the Pacific struggle and set the stage for another.

"We shall not rest until our enemy is completely overthrown.

"We do not consider anything done as long as anything remains to be done.

"We are well on the way, but Japan itself is our final goal.

"With Australia saved, the Philippines liberated and the ultimate redemption of the East Indies and Malaya made a certainty, our motto becomes: "On to Tokyo." . . ."

While MacArthur was making this announcement, Gladys Savary in Pasay south of Manila was writing in her diary: "There is no water, except our little well . . . no food to be bought, no lights, no phone, no gas to cook by . . ."[5]

Few people in Manila, indeed, knew as General MacArthur had announced to the world, that the city had fallen back to American hands. But President Franklin Delano Roosevelt had been told. He was in Teheran conferring with Russian Marshal Josef Stalin and British Prime Minister Winston Churchill. From Teheran Roosevelt sent a congratulatory message to President Sergio Osmeña who was in makeshift headquarters at Hacienda Luisita in Tarlac north of Manila.

President Roosevelt said: "The American people rejoice with me in the liberation of your capital."

This morning the nuns at St. Theresa's college saw what narrowly missed them last night. An American shell had made a direct hit on the house next door, making a total wreck out of it and killing one inhabitant.

The nuns were forbidden to lock doors, even those to their private quarters, so the Japanese would be free to move around on their defensive measures. The commanding officer was sympathetic, but some of his men seemed to be drunk, and he had little control.

"He promised to notify us in case we should have to leave the place," Sister Charles writes.[6]

Colonel Jose Guido lived with his family at 1185 Singalong street. Jose Guido had had a distinguished military career. When World War II broke out in the Philippines in December 1941, he was chief of intelligence of the Philippine Constabulary. With him at his residence today were his wife, Doña Justa, their four sons and two daughters, and several servants.[7]

At 8 o'clock this morning, a Japanese naval officer led four of his men into the Guido residence. They got hold of the two older Guido sons, Justo and Jose Jr., and led them away.

At 11 o'clock this morning, the same Japanese naval officer, now with 13 men, returned to the Guido home with the two Guido boys. The soldiers deployed around the yard while the officer led a group inside the house. They ordered Mrs. Guido to open cabinets, trunks and closets. In one cabinet they found Col. Guido's military uniforms. They ordered Mrs. Guido to open a safe in an upstairs bedroom. From the safe they took away jewelry and P5,000 in pre-war Philippine bills.

Now the Japanese bound Col. Jose Guido by the wrists and tied him to his son Justo. They tied Jose, Jr. to the younger son Raymond.

"How old are you?", the Japanese had asked the boy Raymond. His mother spoke for him and said, "Twelve!" But the boy corrected his mother and said, "Mama, I am fourteen," whereupon the 14-year-old Raymond was tied to his older brother Jose, Jr., 17.

The Japanese opened the wine cabinet and helped themselves to its contents. Lunch was cooking in the kitchen. When it was ready, the servants laid it out on the dining table and the Japanese ate the food. Done with lunch, the band left the house, Colonel Jose Guido and his three eldest sons in tow.

About 500 persons from various parts of Intramuros had sought shelter in the church of San Francisco in the Walled City. At 9 o'clock this morning the Japanese ordered the Franciscan Fathers to evacuate their church and monastery. Now the priests, the lay brothers and their staff, led by the

Provincial Superior, Rev. Fr. Salvador Rodriguez, and the civilian refugees in the church came out into the patio and into the adjoining streets. The monastic cells and the cloisters were emptied, the windows and doors barred from the inside. The last person to exit was the gatekeeper, Brother Jose Maria Manjabacas, 71, who crawled out of a ground-floor window. Having accomplished the sealing of the Franciscan church and monastery, Brother Jose Maria now handed the keys to the Father Commissary.[8]

For five hours under the hot sun the Franciscan community and their erstwhile refugees stayed on the open patio of the church, under the watchful eyes of Japanese guards, awaiting orders. At 3:30 this afternoon, the group was ordered to form ranks of four abreast and was marched to the San Agustin church and monastery. The men walked on one side of the street and the women on the other.

At San Agustin the Franciscans sought out the Japanese officer-in-charge and inquired what was needed of them. They were told that they were being concentrated. They begged to be allowed to pick up essential needs from their monastery. They were given a half-hour to do so. Now the Franciscans hastened to their monastery to pick up provisions.

Back at San Agustin, the Franciscans joined other religious from other Orders in a small room. There were 36 of them in the room.

The San Agustin church and monastery by this time was full of hostages, men, women and children. The church sheltered the women and children. The men overflowed into the cloisters and patios.

Among the civilians held hostage at San Agustin today is the Spanish expatriate Epifanio Gutierrez Muñoz who operated the *Manila Bar* at the Hotel Cantabria at the corner of Victoria and General Luna streets in Intramuros.[9]

Under Japanese orders for Intramuros residents to assemble at the San Agustin church and monastery, Epifanio Gutierrez Muñoz at three o'clock this afternoon closed up the *Manila Bar*, his lifework, and together with other Spanish civilians who had gathered at the Hotel Cantabria which was owned by the Spanish Ocejo family, hied over to the ancient church.

Sister Caridad Ocampo, 45, was a Daughter of Charity on the staff of Santa Isabel college in Intramuros. Earlier this month, Sister Caridad accompanied the Mother Superior of the Daughters of Charity at Santa Isabel college to seek shelter for her community of ten in the church and monastery of San Agustin which was right across the street from the college itself. The community was, therefore, quartered in a section of the San Agustin complex when, today, 6 February, the civilians of Intramuros were ordered to assemble here.[10]

Tonight, Sister Caridad found herself a new role as girls rushed up to her and the other nuns, seeking protection. Japanese personnel, singly and in groups, were going about the San Agustin church where the women and children were confined, shining flashlights or lamps into the faces of the women. Anyone they fancied would be forcibly taken to secluded corners, or upstairs to the vacated quarters of the Augustinian Fathers, and subjected to sexual abuse. Many young women were thus molested tonight. The others would break away and run to the Daughters of Charity who, by the moral authority of their religious habiliments, could hold the Japanese at bay.

They were not always successful. In one incident, Sister Pilar was slapped across the face, and an elderly nun, Sister Carmen, had her veil torn away, when they stood in the way of a Japanese who was forcibly hauling away a girl he desired.

This morning the family of Luis Gallent moved out of their own house at 88 Postigo street in Intramuros to the house next door. It was constructed of heavier material and offered better protection from the American shelling.[11]

While the Gallents were having supper this evening, a Japanese squad barged into their refuge and ordered everyone to move to the Manila cathedral. The Gallents joined the exodus to the great house of worship. Luis Gallent estimated the crowd in the cathedral when they arrived at three to five thousand.

This afternoon, the family of Rosalinda Andoy with many others was ordered out of the cathedral to the Santa Rosa college compound. Her father was not with them. He had joined other male hostages in the cathedral who were brought to Fort Santiago.[12]

Sancho Enriquez, the school supervisor, also left the female members of his family and joined the other men who were marched off to the Fort. So did Juan Palada. Juan estimated the men who were led from the cathedral to Fort Santiago to number 2,000.[13]

At Fort Santiago, Juan Palada, with around 100 others, was led to a room about 20 feet square, with but one small window way up high. The men could not sit or lie down, so tightly packed were they in the small room. They were given no food or water.

At sunset today the men in Juan Palada's cell at Fort Santiago were led out into a courtyard. One-by-one they were made to stand on a box before a wall made of galvanized iron sheets in the middle of which, at eye level, was a tiny hole. The man who stood on the box before the wall would then hear a voice, in the accent of a Japanese who knew English, and the voice would call out either of two English words, "Room," and "Back."

When the voice said "Room," the man would be dragged down from the box, kicked and knocked in the head and generally roughed up, and led away.

When the voice said "Back," the man would be allowed to step down the box and returned to his cell.

When it was Juan Palada's turn to stand on the box the voice behind the mysterious wall of galvanized iron sheets shouted, "Room." Palada was hustled from his stand by a Japanese and hauled to a cell which gradually filled with other men who received the same judgment the word "Room" imposed. When the cell was full, a Japanese came in and started rapping the men over the head with the flat of an unsheathed bayonet. The men were brought out two at a time and tied behind their backs. When Palada's turn came, his hands were tied but he was returned to his cell. Shortly he was taken out again, this time paired with a man whom he identified as Raymundo Victorio. The pair was led past a table before which the Japanese divested them of valuables.

Now the pair of Juan Palada and Raymundo Victorio was led out to the edge of a large pit dug in the Fort grounds. Before the pit they were made to kneel. Now Juan Palada saw Raymundo Victorio bayonetted in the back and heard him cry in pain as he hurtled head-long into the pit. Suddenly Juan Palada felt a violent thrust into his own back. He felt himself falling and his face hit bodies already down in the pit. Writhing in pain, his hands tied behind him, Juan Palada managed to twist around and watched a Japanese soldier circling above him who stuck his bayonet into anyone in the pit who moved or cried out. Juan Palada slipped into oblivion.

When he regained consciousness, Juan Palada realized it was late into the night. In the light of fires raging, he crawled out of the pit, managed to loosen his bonds, and edged towards a stone wall. He clambered over the wall and found himself on the river bank. He waited until dawn and in the half-light swam across the Pasig to the opposite bank.

Carolina Coruna, 22, a nurse at the St. Paul's hospital in Intramuros, lived with the Velez family at 96 Anda street, in the Walled City.[14] Aside from Miss Coruna, there were on this day at this address, Mrs. Velez and her two-month-old baby, and Mrs. Velez's sister. Mr. Velez, the husband, had been called out to the street one morning by the Japanese and never returned.

The baby had been crying, ostensibly from hunger, and now a Japanese marine banged at the door. Miss Coruna responded.

"Are there any men in there?", the Japanese asked.

"There are only the baby and three women," Miss Coruna, who knew a little Japanese replied.

"Keep the baby quiet," the Japanese ordered.

Carolina Coruna turned away to go back into the house and as she did so the Japanese fired. Hit in the legs, Miss Coruna collapsed to the ground.

From where she lay Carolina Coruna saw the Japanese enter the apartment and seek out the other occupants. Mrs. Velez appeared, her hand clapped on the baby's mouth to quiet it. The Japanese thrust his bayonet into the baby's head. Mrs. Velez screamed in terror and the Japanese fired at her point-blank. She probably died instantly. The Japanese turned to Mrs. Velez's sister and fired once more. The woman dropped dead. Only then did the Japanese marine leave the house.

In severe trauma from her wounds and in shock from terror, Carolina Coruna lay where she fell on the ground. When darkness set in she dragged herself to the street. TwoFilipinos came upon her and carried her along. They were spotted by Japanese soldiers at one intersection and bullets flew fast. The men fell. Miss Coruna was not hit.

From here Carolina Coruna managed to reach Calle Real which led to one of the gates of Intramuros, where she found shelter among the ruins.

Towards the end of January 1945, the Japanese commandeered the out-patient department of the Philippine General hospital and about 50 troops moved in.[15] This building which was also known as the dispensary faced Taft Avenue. In front of this building the Japanese dug trenches which extended to the south gate of the hospital, and piled sandbags and strung barbed wire before the entrances.

When Dr. Antonio G. Sison, the hospital director, discovered this, he confronted the Japanese commander, pointing out that the hospital was protected by the Red Cross emblem and that the premises ought not to be used for military purposes. The Japanese claimed they had permission to occupy the building from the military governor of Manila.

Later Japanese troops also moved into the Nurses' Home on Taft Avenue and Padre Faura.

The Japanese ordered Dr. Sison not to accept refugees into the hospital. But the Japanese themselves brought in refugees in groups at all times. The front doors of the PGH were closed, but refugees knocked at all hours and were let in, whether they were by themselves or accompanied by Japanese troops.

Dr. Antonio G. Sison, who at this time also served as president of the University of the Philippines, estimated that a total of 9,000 patients and refugees were sheltered at the PGH at the peak of the battle for liberation.

On this date, the family of Rodolfo G. Tupas was ensconced in the relative safety of Ward II, the Pediatrics Ward at the Philippine General hospital on Taft Avenue in Ermita, of which Rod's father, Dr. Alberto Tupas, the distinguished pediatrician, was chief.[16]

Rod Tupas recalls, "When the Americans started to bombard the PGH within 155-mm. and 240. howitzers,16,000 refugees from Ermita and Malate (my father's estimate) were crammed into the PGH."

In Paco, Marcial P. Lichauco was confiding to his diary: "The fires and explosions from various parts of the city continue unabated . . . There is no electricity, of course, so that even those who had been clandestinely operating their short-wave radios are unable to tune in . . . The water supply was cut yesterday. There had been no garbage collections for sometime. There is not a scrap of food available in the public markets . . . we shall be lucky if we pull through . . ."[17]

Luck was what many people in Manila needed on this day. And courage. There is no doubt that Gladys Savary's courage never flagged. "I alternate between cooking on the charcoal stove and mixing rum and water to keep our courage up", she writes in her diary.[18]

That's how her courage stayed up. Rum and water. Her curiosity never waned either. "My curiosity got the better of me," she writes in her diary. "A hectic war going on and I shut in behind walls."

With big guns booming, planes swooping low, Japanese in the streets and the neighborhood on fire, Gladys Savary climbed over the back wall, against dire warnings from her household. The Spanish girl Felie, a neighbor who had found shelter in Mrs. Savary's home, went with her.

They went on to the Pasay market, which was, of course, deserted. They walked up Libertad street, which she says was deserted. Still, she was able to buy an earthen jar, or olla, she writes, for what purpose she does not say nor from whom. A fine time for shopping, but that was Gladys Savary. Now she was going sightseeing. With Felie she walked over to the Manila Polo Club on Dewey Boulevard. She found the clubhouse still standing. The Baldwin house at the edge of the polo grounds was burning. Suddenly a big crowd rushed down the street pursued by Japanese. Looters! Madame and Felie jumped into a ditch, olla and all.

"We both wished we had taken good advise and stayed behind our own walls," she would later write in her diary. But wishing so did not send her and Felie hurrying to the safety of their walls.

Through with shopping and having had enough of sightseeing, Madame went visiting. "We went on to see some friends who were living near the bay and farther out to Parañaque."

Her friends, Gladys found, had had a bad time. The house had received a direct hit and was partly in shambles. The air-raid shelter was far from the house, so the friends constructed a sort of shelter in the living room out of the chairs and tables. When planes came strafing the friends would duck under this shelter, just as they did now as Gladys was visiting.

"I chose to stay outside," Madame writes. A little strafing was beyond scaring her now, but Felie did dive under with the rest.

Felie emerged cracking jokes. Another salvo came up. Felie screamed and doubled-over. "A piece of shrapnel struck her in the fleshy part of her back, below the waist," Madame writes.

"Nothing ever happens to me," Gladys Savary fusses. "I dash around sticking my neck out constantly, but poor Felie! Shot in the filet!"

It was in that delicate part, too, that the lady-neighbor of Rodolfo G. Tupas got hers. Rod lived on Pennsylvania street in Ermita.

"I remember most the sound of a Japanese bullet whizzing past by me," Rod writes. "The bullet was fired by a Japanese sniper from our neighbor's dormitory at the back of our house . . . It passed between me and my cousing Jimmy as we descended the back steps... It missed both of us, but found another target: the comely middle-aged lady who rented our first floor."[19] The comely lady was bent over a basin of water, washing her face, it seems. Suddenly she unbent and let out a long, drawn-out scream.

"She was a coloratura soprano," Rod recalls.

At this time, Remedios Rodriguez lived with her five children, a daughter and four sons, at 278 Zobel street in Ermita not far from San Marcelino street. Today, residents of this area were ordered by the Japanese to vacate their homes and move southward. The area was to be torched, they were told.[20]

The Rodriguez family gathered a few belongings and went up San Marcelino street to the home of their friends, the Bereciarde family. Here they found the eldest Rodriguez boy. He had been caught on this side by the interdiction to cross the bridge over the *estero* on San Marcelino street the previous day, and had sought shelter at the family friend's home.

The San Juan de Dios hospital in Intramuros had also become a tuberculosis sanatorium.[21] A section of the hospital had been designated Philippine tuberculosis hospital when, in January 1942, the Japanese ordered the transfer of the tubercular patients from the Quezon Institute on España Avenue in Quezon City to San Juan de Dios so they could use Quezon Institute as a hospital for their own sick and wounded.

Mass was offered as usual this morning at the San Juan de Dios hospital chapel in Intramuros. Sister Concepcion Gotera, 33, Daughter of Charity, a Spanish national, a member of the hospital nursing staff, writes in her diary: "We heard Mass while flitting in and out of the chapel door. With every artillery barrage we fall to the floor. At the solemn moment of the elevation of the Host a particularly violent explosion crashed directly overhead so that we expected the priest to be buried under the rubble. But his faith and devotion were stronger and through the perilous moments he brought the Holy Mass to conclusion."[22]

This morning, a group of 20 to 30 Japanese led by a medical officer with the rank of colonel entered the San Juan de Dios hospital in Intramuros. Accompanied by the senior physician still on duty, Dr. Manuel Lahoz, who now assumed the functions of acting director, the Japanese inspected the hospital and searched the wards, the rooms and the private quarters of the staff. The hospital was suspected as a source of communications to the Americans in north Manila. The American artillery had been making extremely accurate hits on Japanese gun emplacements in the vicinity of the Walled City. The Japanese took a census of the hospital population -- patients, refugees and staff, and enjoined everyone against leaving the premises.

The staff of Dr. Manuel Lahoz at this time included the resident physician Dr. Cecilio Noriega, and the hospital dentist Dr. Leandro Corrales, with a nursing staff composed largely of Daughters of Charity of St. Vincent de Paul. There were also about 50 hospital attendants, male and female. There were 90 patients in the hospital at this time, several of whom were in the tuberculosis ward. There were six foreigners among the patients, most of them from the Santo Tomas internment camp. There were four bed-ridden tuberculars, three females and one male.

This afternoon, the same Japanese officer who had been there earlier in the morning, returned to the San Juan de Dios hospital with his group and ordered the staff to vacate the premises, together with their patients. The staff remonstrated, pleading that several patients could not be moved out of their beds. The Japanese retorted that anyone who could not be moved be abandoned, and left to perish in the fire. The building was to be burned. They ordered the nuns of the nursing staff to remove their religious habits. The nuns pretended not to understand, and none removed her habit.

Sister Concepcion Gotera recalls of that afternoon:

"We went out to the street. But horrors! Fire here, fire there and fire everywhere! The situation was just beyond description! There was nowhere to go!"[23]

With two other nuns, Sister Concepcion pushed a handcart loaded with bundles and cartons of supplies. Along the streets they found many wounded civilians bathed in their own blood or asprawl in grotesque postures. "But we could not do anything for them," Sister Concepcion writes, "beyond giving them a compassionate look."

The San Juan de Dios group formed a ragged procession in the streets turned battlegrounds and tried to make it to the ruins of the Santo Domingo church. The Japanese shooed them away. They headed for the ruins of the Santa Rosa college instead.

"We were cast up, as it were, on the sidewalk in front of the ruined Santa Rosa college," Sister Concepcion Gotera writes in her diary. "We sat on the ground awaiting God's will, with nothing overhead but the thick smoke. Then we were ordered inside the ruined walls which offered a bit more shelter. Everyone entered the ruins except our group of three and the boys with us who remained to guard our bundles which lay scattered all over the street."

Sister Donatienne de Marie, 48, a French national and member of the Congregation of St. Paul de Chartres, was on the nursing staff of the tuberculosis section at the San Juan de Dios hospital.

When the San Juan de Dios group arrived at the ruins of the Santa Rosa college, Sister Donatienne saw that there was already a huge crowd of women and children assembled there. The men had been hauled over to Fort Santiago. Santa Rosa college had been destroyed by Japanese bombs during air raids in the early days of World War II, in December 1941. Only the walls of the college buildings stood. These had been further battered since the American shellings began.

By seven this evening, the San Juan de Dios hospital group was installed in the ruins of the Santa Rosa college. The staff gathered the burnt galvanized iron sheets and formed them into "tents," under which the patients and everyone else tried to be comfortable.

There were now several hundred refugees in the Santa Rosa college ruins. There was little food, no water, no toilet facilities. The San Juan de Dios stocks of food and medicine soon ran out. The hospital staff dug a hole in one corner of the yard deep enough for water to spring up. The water was really mud, but there was hardly any recourse. There was an artesian well in the Plaza Santo Tomas outside, but it was hazardous to get there owing to the incessant shelling from the American side and the trigger-happy Japanese who shot at everything that moved in the streets.

"From where I crouched I watched the top of the belltower of the cathedral come apart, feeling as though my own heart were indeed coming apart," Sister Concepcion Gotera writes.

The fire raged towards the San Juan de Dios refugees huddling in the ruins of the Santa Rosa college. When the heat became unbearable, Sister Gotera's group swept over to the other side of the compound, joining the rest of the nuns and their patients.

"We were no safer here," says Sister Gotera, "but at least we were all together again." But in the process they had abandoned their supplies to the fire.

"What horrors," Sister Gotera writes. ". . . mothers transfixed with grief with dead infants in their arms; human bodies roasted alive in the fire; toddlers bathed in their own blood; uncomprehending children watching over their mothers' bodies stretched lifeless on the hard earth, and so many wounded, so many wounded . . ."

"By the wall where I huddled," Sister Concepcion writes, "was a young mother, a very young mother who cradled a cherub-like infant in her arms. With us was another mother with three very young sons. How I wept for them . . . I did not see them anymore afterwards and later I was told that they fell victims of the shelling."

Early this evening, a Japanese patrol entered the Madrigal compound on General Luna street in Paco and tramped into the provisional convent of the Assumption Sisters. They inquired after the nationalities of the religious, walked into rooms and inspected cabinets.[24]

One of the Sisters kept saying, "Kyokai, Kyokai," which is the Japanese word for church. Just then, the chaplain, the Spanish Franciscan Father Antonio Saravia, came in the door. Seeing him in his priestly habit, a Japanese soldier aimed his bayonetted rifle at the priest whereupon Padre Saravia raised his hands and cried, "Christus, Christus!" The assembled Sisters chorused after him, "Christus, Christus!" The commanding officer barked an order and the Japanese tramped out of the compound without further incident.

Today, two Japanese soldiers appeared before the De la Salle college Brothers and asked for the names and nationalities of the community members and the refugees.[25]

Brother Anthony heard the Japanese inquire from the Director, Brother Xavier, how many persons were in the premises, and the latter replied, "One hundred and one."

One of the Brothers, Brother Maximin, had studied Nippon-go and could deal with the Japanese in their own language. Now Brother Maximin typed the census of residents in the south wing of the De la Salle main building, which totalled only 68 persons.

WEDNESDAY, 7 FEBRUARY 1945

This morning Douglas MacArthur made his triumphal entry into Manila. Waiting for him at the city gates were Lt. Gen. Oscar W. Griswold, commanding the XIV Corps; General Vernon D. Mudge, commanding the 1st Cavalry Division; Brig. Gen. William C. Chase, who had commanded the Flying column, and their respective staffs.[1]

Profuse with his congratulations for the successful achievement of objectives he had laid down, General MacArthur here announced the promotion of Brig. Gen. Chase to major general and his assignment as commander of the 38th Infantry Division which was then fighting for the recovery of the Bataan peninsula.

Now MacArthur rode down the streets of the city that deified him. The people were ragged and hungry, but before him they laid with great fervor their gratitude for the reality of his return.

Today, the 1st Cavalry Division was relieved from north Manila by the 37th Infantry Division.

By evening, the 8th Cavalry Regiment had cleared out the suburbs up to San Juan. The 5th Cavalry Regiment was heading towards Pasig.[2]

Except for pockets of resistance in Tondo and the continuing operations in the eastern suburbs, north Manila had been cleared as of today.

Yesterday General Walter Krueger, commanding the Sixth Army, issued orders for the seizure of the power plant on Isla de Provisor on the south bank of the Pasig.

At 10:15 this morning, Maj. Gen. Oscar W. Griswold, commander of the XIV Corps, issued the directive for the 37th Infantry Division and the 1st Cavalry Division to cross the Pasig river.[3]

General Robert S. Beightler, commanding the 37th Infantry Division, assigned the 148th Infantry Regiment to make the initial assault, to be followed by the 129th Infantry, in turn to be followed by the 1st Battalion, 145th Infantry.

The objective was to establish a bridgehead on the south bank of the Pasig. The 3rd Battalion, 148th Infantry Regiment, under Lt. Col. Howard Schultz, would spearhead the mission.

Now the reconnaissance parties under the 117th Engineer Battalion, commanded by Lt. Col. Tom Simpson, launched a search for a possible staging area for the amphibious attack against the south bank. By noon today Simpson's men had settled on a spot close to the San Miguel Brewery compound to the westside of Malacañang as the launching area. The landing area on the opposite bank was the Malacañang Park directly across from the palace.

At 2 o'clock this afternoon, 30 assault boats assembled from various points by the 117th Engineers gathered at the staging point.

The Japanese had fortified strongpoints on the south bank, mainly in the area of the oil storage tanks in Pandacan and the Manila Gas Company. Otherwise, this section of south Manila was lightly defended.

The 148th was instructed to clear Pandacan and Paco and make a flanking movement on Manila bay westward.

The 129th would secure the Isla de Provisor power plants.

Now the 672nd Amphibian Tractor Battalion which had accompanied the 37th Infantry Division all the way from Lingayen gulf assembled its LVT's on the take-off point.

At 3 o'clock, under cover of the 140th Field Artillery Battalion, elements from the 3rd Battalion, 148th Infantry Regiment, were aboard their assault crafts in four concealed points in the staging area.

At 3:15 this afternoon, under cover of a 105 mm. artillery barrage, the 3rd Battalion, 148th Infantry Regiment, shoved off on the first assault wave.

This went unnoticed from the opposite bank and invited no response, but the second wave was greeted by intense artillery, machine-gun and mortar-fire. At the landing area in Malacañang Park, however, the welcoming committee was thin. The bridgehead was easily established.

When the Japanese finally got the point of the assault, the staging area came under heavy machine-gun and mortar fire. The 2nd Battalion, 148th Infantry Regiment, fell on the heels of the 3rd at the embarkation point and got the hotter part of the heated reception from the Japanese.

By 8 o'clock this evening, two battalions had crossed the Pasig river. The Americans now held an area that reached 300 yards south along Calle Cristobal to a bridge over the Estero de Concordia northeast about 1,000 yards, and back to the river along the west bank of a tributary stream.

During this day, the 188th Parachute Infantry moved on Nichols Field but was greeted by intense artillery, mortar and machine-gun fire. The attack stalled.

The 511th Parachute Infantry crossed the Parañaque river to approach Nichols from the southwest. Here, too, it stalled.

Before 9 o'clock this morning, A.V.H. Hartendorp noted an honor guard drawn up across the entrance to the Main building at Santo Tomas. General MacArthur was expected, he was told.

Starting early this morning Japanese shells had been raining all over the camp. One shell hit the Seminary building, another the Education building, wrecking the clinic on the third floor. This far there had been no casualties.

A crowd now gathered before the Main building, expectantly awaiting the appearance of MacArthur. A shell exploded a hundred yards away. Was there a connection between the intense shelling and MacArthur's visit, the Americans wondered.

Now the great man appeared with an entourage of high ranking officers and newspapermen. Upon seeing the General, the inmates broke out into excited yells. Thousands of emotionally-charged people pressed MacArthur to the wall. They fought to touch him, clasp his hands. Men wept unashamedly, women screamed for attention and held up their children for him to touch.

"I cannot recall, even in a life filled with emotional scenes, a more moving spectacle than my first visit to Santo Tomas camp," MacArthur would reminisce.[4]

From the Santo Tomas internment camp, MacArthur visited the Old Bilibid Prisons. In his *Reminiscences*, he would write of the time he walked down the line as the American prisoners-of-war stood at attention.

"They remained silent as though at inspection. I looked down the lines of men bearded and soiled . . . with ripped and soiled shirts and trousers, with toes sticking out of such shoes as remained, with suffering and torture written on their gaunt faces. Here was all that was left of my men of Bataan and Corregidor . . . As I passed slowly down the scrawny, suffering column, a murmur accompanied me as each man barely speaking above a whisper, said, 'You're back,' or 'You made it,' I could only reply, 'I'm a little late, but we finally came.'"

At the civilian internees section of Bilibid, Natalie Crouter heard loud cheering in the hall and she heard someone say that General MacArthur and his staff were visiting.[5]

Natalie Crouter was standing by her family's bunk when she saw MacArthur come in the door at the end of the hall. In her mind just recovering from three years of regimentation from Japanese internment camp officials, she thought, "Here comes another Commandant . . . I wonder if I should bow from the waist down."

MacArthur strode up to her bunk.

"When the General passed the bunk he turned and looked into my face directly. He grabbed my hand and shook it, over and over, up and down. I could not say a word and just looked back at him speechless as we pumped our arms up and down, up and down. All of the last three years were in my mind and face, and at this actual moment of release, the biggest moment of my life, I felt no joy or relief, only deep sadness which could not come into words...

"I was the only one he stopped to speak to in this long room, and there was no reason for it – it wasn't recognition of anyone he knew or thought was familiar . . .

"He was sincerely comprehending of my strained face which showed what all of us had suffered . . . He was deeply shocked and sorry for all of us, and looked it without trying to say so. For this I was grateful."

Through the day and deep into the night, the Japanese lobbed shell-after-shell into Santo Tomas. During this Wednesday memorable to many inmates as the day MacArthur visited the camp, 22 persons were killed of whom 12 were internees, two American soldiers, and eight Filipino and Chinese workers. Thirty-nine others were wounded, 27 of whom were internees, one American soldier and 11 workers.[6]

American intelligence had identified La Concordia college on Herran street in Paco as a Japanese stronghold.[7] This morning, American artillery started shelling La Concordia college which sheltered former residents of the Hospicio de San Jose, an orphanage and home for the aged on Isla de Convalescencia on the Pasig river. Hundreds of refugees from the surrounding neighborhood were also at La Concordia. The shelling continued without let-up the whole day and through the night. Scores perished and hundreds fell wounded.

From her rented apartment on M.H. del Pilar street in Ermita, Sophie Natalie Morgin and her landlord, a Frenchman, listened apprehensively as explosions came closer, and watched the flashes reflected on the nearby Valdez apartment building.[8]

At the streetgate a man in civilian clothes approached. When he came closer, Miss Morgin saw that he was a Japanese. She stared, fear-stricken, and the Japanese growled, "What are you looking at?"

Miss Morgin was rendered speechless, and her French landlord answered for her, "Nothing."

The Japanese tried to push the gate open but it was securely chained. Beyond the gate was the house, now darkened, as the power had been cut off.

Between 10 and 11 o'clock this morning, a well-dressed Filipino, obviously a *makapili*, his identity concealed by a cloth hood over his head, was seen by members of the De la Salle community talking to the Japanese sentry infront of the building on Taft Avenue.[9]

The sentry was seen to gesture in the direction of the South Wing. The *makapili* left, but was back shortly, this time with a band of 20 Japanese soldiers led by two or three officers.

The *makapili* and the Japanese tramped up and down corridors, went up the grand staircase to the second floor where they assembled the Christian Brothers. Here they announced that the premises were to be searched for guerrillas and for arms. The residents lined up the hallway and were made to empty their pockets and bags. The rooms were searched.

The search over and finding nothing they wanted, the Japanese got together the Brothers and the heads of the refugee families. The *makapili* with the hood over his head stood beside the Japanese commander and probably by pre-arrangement, motioned towards the director, Brother Egbert Xavier, and Judge Jose Carlos. The two were tied behind their backs and led away. They were never seen again.

This morning, the religious from the various Orders who were detained in the refectory and ante-refectory of San Agustin monastery in Intramuros requested permission from the Japanese to enter the church and celebrate Mass. The request was denied.[10]

The religious were under strict guard. When anyone had to leave the hall for the toilet he was accompanied by one of the eight Japanese guards at the gate. The religious asked that a makeshift altar be set-up in the refectory and that they be allowed to celebrate Mass there. This too was denied.

Today the premises of San Agustin were bursting with civilians being held as hostages. The women and children were restricted to the church. In the cloister and in the inner patios, the men hunkered. Father Belarmino de Celis, OSA, a Spanish national, the procurator, or supply officer, of San Agustin, estimated the assembly at 6,000 persons.

Later in the day, the male civilians, numbering about 1,600, were ordered to form ranks and, marching four abreast, were led to Fort Santiago.

In this crowd of 1,600 men was the host of *Manila Bar,* Epifanio Gutierrez Muñoz.[11] Short, fat, with a crown of silver hair, he was the easy-going, wide-open stereotype of the successful barkeeper, Naturally friendly and warm, Gutierrez was always smiling. In recent times, he had been smiling to himself at the prospect of soon having the young and thirsty American soldiers line up for the liquid delicacies he served at his bar. He had smiled to himself at the pleasure of serving them. Today, the keeper of the *Manila Bar* did not have much to smile about.

At Fort Santiago the men were made to empty their pockets and forced to surrender wallets, pens, watches – above all watches – and even eyeglasses.

The Spanish and other Caucasians were separated from the Filipinos and Chinese. The Spanish were led to a narrow cell without sanitary facilities and with hardly any ventilation.

"In Fort Santiago, we were herded into this building," Dr. Antonio O. Gisbert recalls, "so crowded with thousands of men no one was able to sit down."[11]

This afternoon, the *convento* or residence of the priests of San Agustin in Intramuros, caught fire. The male detainees had been marched off to Fort Santiago and only women and children and ailing males were in the premises.[12]

The Daughters of Charity of St. Vincent de Paul, themselves refugees at San Agustin, organized the women to save some of the properties of the friars in their quarters. When the fire became too intense, the women had to abandon the *convento.*

Now the Daughters of Charity saw their Santa Isabel college across the street threatened by the flames. They rushed out of San Agustin to try to save some of their belongings. A section of Santa Isabel college had been occupied for the past several months by the Japanese Navy. Now the nuns saw the Japanese marines throwing buckets of water into the ground floor windows. When they got close, they smelled gasoline. The Japanese marines were throwing gasoline, not water, into the building which now was in flames!

True to his promise, the captain commanding the Japanese marine contingent at St. Theresa's college on San Marcelino street today advised the St. Paul and Belgian nuns quartered in the premises to leave for a safer place. Isla de Provisor was a short distance from this point, and the captain thought the area was certain to become battleground. The captain suggested Santa Ana as the safest possibility. But under the conditions then availing, the nuns realized that it would hardly be possible to negotiate the distance on foot. They opted for the Assumption Convent at the corner of Dakota and Herran in Ermita, across from St. Paul college. The Japanese captain issued the nuns a safeconduct to get them past the checkpoints.[13]

Now the St. Paul and Belgian nuns and their students altogether numbering 83 hastily piled the few items they could get together into two pushcarts. They divided themselves into small groups for easier passage through streets strung with barbed wire, cratered by bombs, studded with landmines and barricaded at strategic points. The shelling from the American sector was peaking and explosions tore up the earth and kicked up clouds of dust as the nuns moved in relays. Around them the Japanese dashed everywhere with bayonetted rifles and elaborate camouflage, menacing the nuns with bellicose gestures.

"In ordinary times we would have arrived at our destination in half-an-hour," Sister Charles says, "but with all these obstacles and formalities with angry sentries, the last group arrived at nightfall."

This was Sister Charles' group. They had passed all sentry points but one on the way to the Assumption Convent on Herran and Dakota, and the last proved to be the toughest. "We were subjected to a rigorous search," Sister Charles writes, their safeconduct notwithstanding.

Then their pushcart lost a wheel. Sister Charles' group consisting of three other nuns and a boy-helper took hours to get it back again. The party reached the Assumption Convent as darkness set in. Their tardiness had caused the others much agitation and already they had sent out a search party.

At the Convent school, the Assumption caretaker group that had remained, led by Mother Esperanza Cu-Unjieng, welcomed the refugee party. The premises were already crowded with civilian refugees.

All through this night the nuns cowered in mortal fear in their makeshift quarters as the shelling intensified. "The planes did not stop flying over our heads," Sister Charles writes.

This afternoon at about 5:30, a Japanese squad led by a captain knocked at the door of Don Bartolome Pons, a wealthy Spaniard, at 503 Figueroa Street in Paco.[14] It was the Señora de Pons who responded. The Japanese captain demanded chickens from Señor Ponses flock. Doña Rosario

Garcia de Pons was a haughty, imperious woman who held herself high above crowds, and now she screamed at this impudent Japanese who wanted her chickens, "For you, nothing," or something to that effect in her elaborate Castilian.

For more innocuous behavior during these perilous days people had been known to drop dead, but the Japanese captain only wanted a chicken or two and a loud argument followed. Now the doña grabbed the Japanese closest to her by the hair and jerked his head back and forth, the while screaming Spanish imprecations in high C. The soldier did not use his gun, but his captain vowed vengeance.

At 7 o'clock this evening the Japanese captain and his men were back at the door of Don Bartolome Pons.

Basilio Umagap, 18, was the houseboy of the Ponses. With others in the household, Umagap was hustled by the Japanese to the ground floor of the house. In the group was the Pons couple, two men aside from Basilio Umagap, and three women, the third of whom, named Pacita, was pregnant and carried an 11-month-old baby in her arms. On the ground floor everyone had his or her wrists tied behind and made to line up against the wall. The Japanese officer, probably the one who wanted chickens, stepped up and started shooting with his pistol. First in the line was Don Bartolome Pons, then a man Basilio Umagap remembers as Isaac, after whom came Doña Rosario Garcia de Pons. Basilio came next. They were all tied together, and when the persons ahead of him fell, Basilio Umagap was pulled down to the floor by the sheer weight of the others. The officer passed on to the next person still standing and missed Basilio completely.

When everyone was down on the floor, bloodied, dead or dying, the Japanese started to leave. Just then the 11-month old baby of Pacita started to cry.One Japanese soldier turned back and fired twice.The baby was silent from thereon. Unhurt, Basilio Umagap, 18, loosened his bonds and fled.

In the backyard of the del Rio home on Taft Avenue in Pasay, the family raised two dozen chickens, four ducks and one pig. A Japanese captain was billeted in a neighboring house. He spoke fluent English and the del Rios were on quite cordial terms with him and his two orderlies who seemed to be outside the stereotype – they were cheerful and friendly. In the first few days of February 1945 the captain would send his orderlies over to the del Rio home to "requisition" a chicken for his pot.[15]

The two dozen chickens in the backyard were owned by Benigno del Rio and his elder sister Lolita in equal share. Invariably, however, Benigno would hand over to the Japanese a pullet tagged as his sister's.

"Why don't you give them one of your chickens?", Lolita demanded.

"They prefer yours, they are nicer," Benigno countered.

"Next time you give your chicken," Lolita insisted.

"Next time you deal with them yourself," Benigno retorted.

In two days the Japanese orderlies were back with a new requisition, but Lolita was afraid to face any Japanese. So Benigno gave them another of her chickens.

Now the streets of Pasay had become extremely dangerous. But the young Benigno del Rio would not be cooped-up in the family manse on Taft. A block away on Sandejas street the family rented a house where they had stored some family belongings. Sneaking down back alleys Benigno reached Sandejas and was greeted by a spectacle that "delighted" him in a morbid way. For almost an hour Benigno watched an interminable procession of the Japanese forces evacuating their sick and wounded. On nearly every kind of wheeled vehicles – cars, trucks, personnel carriers, ambulances, horse-drawn and man-pushed carts, on bicycles and on foot, thousands of Japanese casualties were being moved, men swathed in bandages, draped with sheets, men crippled and bleeding, lying in rows on make-shift caissons.

"A sad and sorrowful spectable," a subdued Benigno del Rio writes in his diary.

Antonio J.Beltran, a Filipino business executive, lived at 1328-D Pennsylvania street in Singalong. The rear windows of his residence looked out into a vacant lot adjoining a paper factory which had been operated by Japanese civilians.[16]

At 2 o'clock this afternoon, Antonio J. Beltran stood by a closed window at the rear of his residence and through a crack watched as Col. Jose Guido and his three sons, still bound together, were led by a group of Japanese into the vacant lot. From where he stood he heard the sounds of rifle-shots. Shortly the Japanese left the vacant lot. The Guidos were no longer with them.

Col. Alejo Valdes and his family lived at 4 Paris street, a blind alley that led off Pennsylvania street in the Singalong district of south Manila.[17]

Alejo Valdes had retired from the Philippine Army as a colonel. With the outbreak of World War II in December 1941, Col.Valdes was recalled to active duty as commanding officer of the Manila Harbor Police. Upon cessation of hostilities and the advent of the Japanese occupation, he reverted to civilian status. His elder brother, General Basilio Valdes, was chief of staff of the Philippine Army when war broke out. Now General Valdes was in Washington, D.C. as Secretary of Defense of the PhilippineCommonwealth-in-exile.

At 4 o'clock this afternoon, a squad of Japanese soldiers entered the Valdes home and began a search of the house. In one cabinet they came upon the military uniforms of Colonel Valdes. They piled the uniforms in the yard and set fire to the pile.

Another Japanese found Valdeses saber and brought it to his officer. As a conciliatory gesture, Valdcs offered the saber to the officer as a gift. This gesture enraged the officer. He snapped the saber into two and threw the pieces into the fire in the yard, the while shouting obscenities in Japanese. Then he led his group away without further incident.

Alberto P. Delfino was consul of Venezuela in Manila. At this time, Consul Delfino lived at 1298 Interior I, Pennsylvania street, in Singalong, with his wife Lolita, and a son, Francis, 17. With them was a Filipino housemaid, Beatriz Teodora Amigo, 30, who had served the Delfinos for six years.[18]

Living with the Delfinos on Pennsylvania street at this time as refugees were Raoul Kahn, his wife Gitina and their small son, and Mrs. Leopoldo Kahn and her three sons. Raoul had two Chinese houseboys, Ah Fat and Ah Kam. Mrs. Leopoldo Kahn had a housemaid, Segundina Butin, who had a son, Miguel, 6, and a daughter, Rafaela, 8. There was also another housemaid named Gloria.

Today the Japanese commandeered the house of Alberto P. Delfino for their own use. The Delfinos and their houseguests moved out. Delfino and his small family with their househelp Beatriz Amigo sought shelter in a house at the corner of Pennsylvania and Dagonoy. Mrs. Leopoldo Kahn and her sons, with their servants, went with the Delfinos. Raoul Kahn and his small family, with the Chinese houseboys, moved to another house on Aragon street, not far away.

In their respective refugee-lodgings these groups tried to make the best of the situation. The American shelling was murderous. The Japanese were getting more vicious. The refugees stayed indoors.

Sharing with other Manilans premonitions of impending doom, Don Alfredo Chicote Beltran, a distinguished lawyer and patriarch of an expatriate Spanish family, decided to bring together around him at his home, dubbed "La Casona," in Ermita, the far-flung members of his large clan. He was suffering from a chronic blood ailment, and his wife at this time was bedridden from a kidney disease.[19]

From their own residences in various Manila districts the Chicote sons and daughters and their respective broods gathered, except for two daughters and their respective spouses and children.

Today, at *La Casona* on San Carlos street between Isaac Peral and San Luis streets in Ermita, there were reunited 24 men, women and children, scions of Alfredo Chicote Beltran.

At 3 o'clock this afternoon, an American shell crashed into the roof of the Chicote home. The only victim was Don Alfredo's youngest daughter, Maria Paz, who was hit in the leg by shrapnel.

Maria Paz had to be brought to a hospital for treatment. There was a clinic around the block on A. Mabini street, a minute's stroll in ordinary times. But today, conditions on the streets had become perilous. Still, the girl needed professional attention.

Now the eldest Chicote son, Prudencio Chicote Lalana placed his wounded sister in a pushcart, and with her his mother whose condition had worsened, and his own son Prudencio, Jr., who was running a high fever.

Shells shrieked overhead and exploded with a deafening roar. Machine gun-fire crackled in hair-raising bursts. And everywhere there were Japanese marines with fixed bayonets whose intentions no one could divine. Through all these Prudencio Chicote and his two younger brothers maneuvered their pushcart-turned-ambulance and reached the clinic on A. Mabini street without incident.

The clinic was located in a multi-storey building. Here it was decided that Mrs. Chicote and Maria Paz needed to be confined. After treatment, Prudencio Chicote brought back home his infant son.

Dr. Alfredo Guerrero lived at 117 A. Mabini street, noteworthy as one of two residences in this neighborhood that are three-storeyed, the other being that of engineer Moreta at the corner of Isaac Peral and Florida streets.[20]

Scion of the eminent Guerrero family of Ermita, Dr. Guerrero was a founder of the Manila Central University and the first dean of this institution's college of medicine. His wife, the former Filomena Francisco, was the first Filipino woman-pharmacist.

At this time, Dr. Guerrero maintained a small consulting office in his residence, a *consultorio* as it was commonly termed. Under battle conditions, the consulting office inevitably became an emergency clinic. It was into this clinic that the Chicote mother-and-daughter were brought.

Dr. Alfredo Guerrero had three children. The eldest, the lawyer Leon Maria, was on the staff of the wartime Republic of the Philippines embassy in Tokyo; the second, the physician Mario Xavier, lived with his small family in the home of his father-in-law, Don Ramon Roces, in Pasay, and the youngest, Carmen, married to Ismael Arguelles Cruz, lived with her own family in the Cruz home on California street in Paco.

Now Dr. Guerrero consented to take under his care the wife and daughter of Don Alfredo Chicote Beltran of San Carlos street, Ermita. But the patients had to provide their own food and medicine, the clinic, under the circumstances, being unable to provide any.

From this day, it became the chore of another Chicote daughter,

Adelina, to bring to the clinic the food and medicine for her mother and sister.

Adelina Chicote was a tall, well-proportioned young woman, intelligent and alert. "She could handle anything," her brother Prudencio described her. Moreover, she had learned to speak Japanese, and this gave her much confidence. From today, she would leave home in the morning with her bundles in a *bayong*, and come back in the afternoon. She would return to the clinic later in the afternoon, spend the night in the clinic, and come back home in the morning.

When he saw what happened to Maria Paz Chicote, Jose Goicochea, husband of another Chicote daughter, Pilar, decided that the building was not safe enough, that there must be a safer place.

He wanted to get out of *La Casona* with his wife, their seven-year old son Jose Angel, and the boy's Filipina nursemaid. Don Alfredo Chicote Beltran and the rest of the family agreed to this decision, and this afternoon, Jose Goicochea and his small family left San Carlos street, crossed Ermita district and safely arrived at Wright street in Malate. On Calle Wright he knocked at the door of a friend, Don Gonzalo Yrezabal. Here the refugee-family was made welcome, and here they decided to stay.

After the Goicocheas had left *La Casona*, two other men married to Chicote women decided that it might indeed be wiser to disperse. "If we stuck together, it was evident that no one would be left to tell the story," Prudencio Chicote relates.

Now Carlos Garcia Buch, married to Paquita Chicote, with their small son and daughter, and Luis Zabaljauregui, married to Carolina Chicote, with their small daughter, bundled off to the San Carlos apartments on adjoining property on the same street.

This part of Ermita during this period harbored a small Spanish expatriate community. Close to the Chicote's *La Casona*, for instance, was a modest two-storey chalet which was the residence of Don Tirso Lizarraga, a wealthy sugar exporter, and his family.[21]

On Christmas Eve 1944, the Lizarraga family who lived in another section of the city suddenly found themselves thrown out on the sidewalks. Their home was commandeered by the Japanese for military use. The Lizarragas found shelter here, in this small chalet on San Carlos street in Ermita.

With Tirso Lizarraga at this time were his two unmarried teenaged daughters, Maria Rosa and Maria Victoria, and the eldest daughter, Maria Elena, with her husband Jose Maldonado, and their small son, Tirso, named after his grandfather.

At Fort Santiago, the process of getting the civilian detainees to stand one-by-one on a box before the galvanized-iron wall set up in a courtyard continued today.[22]

When the turn of Sancho Enriquez, the school supervisor, came to stand on the box, it was night. Now a Japanese held a candle to the face of the man on the box, and the implacable voice behind the wall would cry out, "Room," or "Back." The word pronounced on Sancho Enriquez was "Back." He was led back to his cell.

The cell Sancho Enriquez shared with 30 or 40 other men and boys looked out into a courtyard where another team of Japanese was engaged in another form of execution. Groups of civilians would be led from their cells in the Fort and made to stand before a Japanese officer who roared, "You guerrilla!" The group would roar back, "No!" Guns would belch nonetheless and the men would drop to the ground.

This evening, two Japanese came into the corridor outside the cell of Sancho Enriquez, each bearing a kerosene lamp which they left on the floor. When they returned, one held a wooden bench and the other an empty bucket. Now the men were brought out of the cells along the corridor by threes. Singly each was blindfolded and made to kneel before the bench, and a Japanese would swing a saber at his neck. The head would fall into the bucket and the body would slump behind the bench.

Sancho Enriquez and his cellmates watched this ritual through cracks on the wall of their cell for three hours, during which Sancho estimates that 130 men were beheaded.

Suddenly a boy in the cell who was also watching the proceedings in the corridor through a crack in the wall jumped up and screamed in Tagalog, "Father, Father! That's my father! They're killing my father!"

The others tried to hold the boy and calm him down, but he kept jumping up wildly, raising sorrowful outcries. Now the Japanese came in and gruffly led the boy out, still yelling his lamentations. The others never saw him again.

THURSDAY, 8 FEBRUARY 1945

At 9 o'clock this morning, the Americans on the south bank held the line they had established last night. It starts from the Pasig riverbank and extends along the Estero de la Concordia up to Calle Otis, and down to Calle Jesus on the Estero de Pandacan, circling back to the Pasig.[1]

Except for intermittent rifle and mortar fire from the Japanese the night had passed uneventfully. Now, the 2nd and 3rd Battallions, 148th Infantry, moved southward as a body. The Japanese efficiently checked the movement from heavy installations at the Paco Railroad station on Plaza Dilao. The Americans stalled.

Late this afternoon, the 1st and 2nd Battalions, 129th Infantry, crossed over to the south bank. Their mission was to seize Isla de Provisor. This evening one company attempted to cross the narrow Estero de Tanque at one end of the island but was repulsed.

Provisor is an island about 125 yards long and 400 yards wide. On one side is the Pasig river. It is separated from the mainland on the other sides by esteros, the drainage canals that crisscross Manila and which at one time gained for the city the nomenclature, "Venice of the East."

On Isla de Provisor are five large buildings which house one of the principal power-generating plants of the Manila Electric company. These are surrounded by lesser constructions. The island had been fortified, mainly with heavy machineguns. The garrison consisted of men from the Japanese 1st Naval Battalion. The island was connected to the mainland on the westside by a footbridge. It was protected by support fire from surrounding positions.

This morning the Japanese installed a heavy gun in the frontyard of the Asilo de Looban de San Vicente de Paul, an orphanage and training school run by the Vincentian Fathers and the Daughters of Charity.[2]

Part of the Asilo de Looban on Isaac Peral street in Paco had been used by the Japanese since August 1944. During November and December 1944, they constructed a network of underground shelters in the compound, using heavy material and elaborate camouflage. The Japanese, however, had withdrawn from the compound. Now the shelters they had constructed were occupied mostly by Spanish officials of the Compañia General de Tabacos de Filipinas (Tabacalera) and their families, and their Filipino employees. The Spanish protested the installation of the Japanese howitzer in the grounds, to no avail.

Shortly the Japanese howitzer was lobbing shell-after-shell at the American landing point on Nagtahan. Not long after, the spotter planes overhead communicated the location of the adversary gun to American artillery. Now the American shells rained on the Asilo de Looban premises. Hundreds of the refugees were injured.

Then the Japanese officer commanding the gun crew fell wounded. This threw the crew into confusion. The wounded Japanese officer was evacuated and shortly the cannon was pushed out of the compound into the street.

At around 9 o'clock this morning, the Japanese entered the Santa Rosa college ruins in Intramuros and over the protests of the erstwhile San Juan de Dios hospital staff, took away the six foreigners who were among the patients. One of the six was a woman. They were never seen again.[3]

Also this morning, at the Manila Cathedral, Luis Gallent with his father and younger brother, found themselves in a group which Luis estimated at 2,000, the new batch of males culled from the mass of civilians assembled there. The group was told that they were to fetch water for the cathedral detainees, but they were marched to Fort Santiago instead.[4]

At the Fort, Luis Gallent's party was systematically divested of valuables. Now Luis found himself in a cell packed with 80 other men. The cell was jammed such that the men could only stand. So they leaned on each other or propped each other up, and slept on their feet.

Late this afternoon, the cell in the building at Fort Santiago where Sancho Enriquez, the school supervisor, was confined with about 40 others, was doused with gasoline and ignited. Almost simultaneously other cells were set afire and the entire building was soon ablaze. In Sancho's cell there was a stampede to the exit, but it was barred. The men clambered up the wall and broke through the ceiling. They pushed each other up the walls, pulled each other through the ceiling and out through the roof. They edged down the eaves and dropped to the ground below.[5]

Sancho Enriquez landed safely on his feet on the ground. Now he and the others who made it out of the burning building clambered over a stone wall before them and dropped to the other side. It turned out to be open parade grounds with Japanese milling around. Some of the men had their clothes on fire. They were easily shot down by the Japanese. The others dashed irrationally across the open space and were gunned down. Sancho Enriquez hugged the earth and made himself inconspicuous, inching his way on the ground towards the stone wall across the open space.

In the darkness relieved only by the raging fires, Sancho Enriquez succeeded in scaling the wall to the top, along which was a barbed-wire entanglement. He crawled under the wires and worked his way to a spot on the walls facing the Pasig river. He jumped to the ground below. Now he realized that he was stark naked. When his cell started to burn, he had stripped himself of every piece of clothing.

Sancho Enriquez, quondam school supervisor, cowered in the shadows at the foot of the walls of Fort Santiago overlooking the Pasig. He waited for the flames to subside and in the dark he swam across the river to the opposite shore.

The family of Ricardo Mascuñana had passed the night in the bomb shelter in their backyard on Padre Faura street in Ermita, between Colorado and Pennsylvania streets. His wife is the noted writer in the Spanish language, Maria Paz Zamora de Mascuñana. The artillery barrages today had been most discomfitting, prompting the Señora de Mascuñana to ask sardonically, "Are these the Americans who are coming to liberate us?"[6]

There was a Japanese garrison at the fire station on San Marcelino street near the corner with Padre Faura, and Japanese personnel passed by the Mascuñana property frequently. The family had boarded up the streetside windows. Now from their shelter they saw people from the northern section of Ermita in the upper reaches of San Marcelino, going down the streets. They gathered that that area was to be torched.

Suddenly huge explosions shook the Mascuñana shelter. "Bang! Whiiiz . . . bang!" is how Doña Paz put it in her diary. From a window of her home Doña Paz saw the Japanese rushing away from their headquarters at the corner. The building was on fire. Mrs. Mascuñana heard people rushing down the street and crying, "The Japanese have set fire to their headquarters!" Presently the building was a roaring blaze and the Mascuñana home was in the way of the spreading flames.

"For a moment I lost my head," Mrs. Mascuñana writes. "What should I save from the fire? My books, my paintings, my sculptures . . ."

"But I had to run down . . . goodbye, house . . . goodbye my priceless treasures . . . how I wished to gaze on them just a bit longer, touch them, enjoy them a minute more! Give me a brief moment, Lord! But I had to run down . . ."

Away from the fire, thinking everyone was accounted for including her pet dog, Lady, Mrs. Mascunana suddenly missed her Chinese houseboy, Lee Tong. Presently the boy came rushing up, tearful and distressed, crying, "Señora, we have lost everything! Señora, we are homeless!" Doña Paz slapped the boy's hand and said, herself dry-eyed, "But we are alive, don't you see, and the Americans are nearby!"

The Mascuñanas dashed to another house they owned on nearby Colorado street which had been recently vacated by a detachment of Japanese. The house was empty of furniture, but the lower floor had thick concrete walls. The neighbors who had been turned out of their homes by the fire joined them. The ground floor soon filled up and overflowed with people, into the garage and the patio, but none dared go up the second floor for fear of bullets and shrapnel flying.

The men broke down the stone walls separating the properties and created openings leading to Oregon street. The fire had razed ten grand residences on both sides of Padre Faura street from San Marcelino west to the corner of Pennsylvania street and had turned inward to General Luna street on the north. Land mines had been laid by the Japanese at the entrance to Padre Faura street from General Luna, and fearful of the explosions should these land mines go off, the Mascuñana group left their streetside shelter and moved farther inside, into the garden of Judge Manuel V. del Rosario. Now the rain began to fall, and the party had to move back inside the house.

The shelling of La Concordia college continued all through this morning, wreaking havoc among the refugees in the compound on Herran street in

Paco. At 2 o'clock this afternoon, the shelling from the American sector ceased.

An American patrol had reached La Concordia and members were stunned to find only civilians in the compound. One soldier remarked to a Daughter of Charity attending to the victims of the shelling, "It is a miracle that not everyone was killed. This spot was marked for liquidation as our information said it was full of Japanese."[7]

Shortly after, at about 2:30 in the afternoon, La Concordia came under fire again, this time from Japanese artillery based at the Paco parish church a few blocks to the west. The Japanese had ascertained the presence of Americans on the site.

There were two Filipino physicians among the refugees at La Concordia. They ministered to the casualties, assisted by the Daughters of Charity. There were also three Spanish chaplains who gave spiritual comfort to the dying.

This evening, the roof of La Concordia college main building was blown off by the bombardment from the Japanese sector. Inside the compound, hundreds lay dead, hit by shrapnel, or buried under falling debris. Hundreds more were injured. Individuals and groups tried to flee the premises, but Japanese patrols in the neighborhood fired at them.

This afternoon, a shell landed in the living room of the Bereciarde home on San Marcelino street where Remedios Rodriguez and her children were refugees. The Rodriguezes and their hosts moved out to the safety offered by the German Club on San Luis street.

Under the German Club building, several hundreds from the neighborhood had found shelter, including the family of Francisco Lopez.

The premises in fact teemed with refugees – men, women and children, with the barest comfort, very little food and water and no toilet facilities.[8]

The Japanese who had been at Sophy Natalie Morgin's gate on M.H. del Pilar street in Ermita the previous evening showed up this afternoon, this time in uniform. There were three other soldiers with him. The French landlord was ordered out of the house and the Japanese soldiers searched every room. They found nothing they wanted except the French landlord's fieldglasses. To Miss Morgin's surprise, one of the men who spoke perfect English apologized. He explained that sniper fire had been noted increasingly in the past several nights and every house in the area was suspected as a vantage point.[9]

In the refectory of the Augustinian monastery in Intramuros, 42 religious are being detained by the Japanese. In the group are Franciscans,

Recollects, Capuchins and Augustinians, both Spaniards and Filipinos.

Also in the premises are over 1,000 male Filipinos, most of whom had been brought here from their homes in Intramuros. Segregated from the males and confined inside the church are close to 1,000 women and children.[10]

Today the men were marched to Fort Santiago, the religious included. At Fort Santiago, the Spaniards were separated from the Filipinos. The Filipino religious were made to join the civilians.

The Spanish religious were led into a small room in one section of the Fort.

"We could not all lie down at the same time," Father Belarmino de Celis, OSA, writes, "so that not everyone was able to sleep and some had to remain standing. The floor was earth, and as we were not allowed to leave the room for any reason whatever, we were forced to make use of the floor as a toilet."

At 4 o'clock this afternoon, another band of Japanese entered the home of Colonel Alejo Valdes on Paris street in Singalong.

Again the Japanese opened cabinets and closets. In one cabinet they found the remains of two old broken-down radio sets with which the Valdes children tinkered but which did not work. Enraged with their find, apparently convinced that the owners were in radio communication with others outside, the Japanese hurled the radio sets in Colonel Valdeses face.[11]

Now they bound Alejo Valdeses wrists behind him. They did the same to his son Ramon, 24, and his brother-in-law, Ernesto Murillo, and led the three away.

From behind the windows in their house across the street, Mayor Leon C. Guinto, Sr. and his family watched helplessly.[12]

At 6 o'clock this afternoon, Antonio J. Beltran resumed his watch at the rear of his residence on Pennsylvania street and saw Alejo Valdes with seven other men led to the vacant lot in front of the Japanese paper factory. Beltran saw Valdes, blindfolded, kneel down and bow as in prayer, then rise to his feet again. Beltran saw the Japanese soldiers fire and watched in horror as the men fell. Then another Japanese with a machine-gun walked up and fired at the fallen bodies till no one moved or uttered a sound.[13]

At 10 o'clock this evening, a band of about 35 Japanese marines knocked on Eulogio Malibiran's door at 1343 Leveriza street in Pasay. Malibiran, 33, worked as assistant cook for the Japanese garrison at the Rizal Stadium on Vito Cruz street not far from this point.[14]

Tonight he opened his door and the Japanese inquired if there were Americans or white people in the neighborhood. Eulogio Malibiran said no and the band moved on to the next house which belonged to Felipe Canillas.

From a crack in his window in an upstairs room, Eulogio Malibiran watched the Japanese surround the Canillas home. Three of them went up the house and from his observation post Malibiran heard the sounds of general mayhem in his neighbor's house. Furniture being smashed, slamming doors, women screaming. Then everything was quiet.

Shortly Eulogio Malibiran observed a crowd of about 30 civilians, men and women, most of them he knew from the neighborhood, being lined up by the Japanese on the street in the front of the house.

FRIDAY, 9 FEBRUARY 1945

This morning, Admiral Iwabuchi moved his headquarters to Fort McKinley. His position has deteriorated so rapidly and so completely that the need to evacuate his forces may have by now become apparent to him.[1]

At about this time, however, General Yokoyama issued an order for the Manila Naval Defense Force to stand in place. He was planning a counterattack with the aim, first, to isolate the Americans in the city, and second, to get the Manila Naval Defense Force out of Manila. Now he told Iwabuchi that he must stand firm in Manila until after the counter-attack, which he scheduled for the night of 16-17 February.

At 6 o'clock this morning, Eulogio Malibiran opened his door at Leveriza street in Pasay to his neighbor Felipe Canillas, who was severely distressed. Felipe told Malibiran that his two sons, Robert and Charles, and two daughters, Africa and Amparo, were taken away, probably to the Rizal Stadium garrison, by the Japanese in the previous night's round-up.[2]

Now Felipe Canillas begged Eulogio Malibiran to please look for his children at the Rizal Stadium and to see what could be done for them. Eulogio had planned not to report for work at the Japanese garrison's kitchen today. His neighborhood was under heavy shelling from the American sector and prudence seemed to dictate that he stay in with his family.

From Eulogio's house, the very much-agitated Felipe Canillas went to his eldest son, Fred, 38, who lived a short distance away also on Leveriza street and related to him what happened at his home the past night. He told his son of the uncertain fate of the other two sons and two daughters who had been taken away.

Now Fred Canillas shared his father's distress. He accompanied his father back to his house and there comforted his mother. Mrs. Trinidad

Canillas told Fred that the Japanese took away the family jewelry and the watches of the other children. Fred recalled that Charles who had been an ROTC cadet kept a .45 pistol. He searched for the firearm and found it. He also found the shortwave radio receiver set his father had operated throughout the Japanese occupation. He took the gun and the radio back to his own house.

At 10 o'clock this morning, the Filipino chief cook for the Japanese at the Rizal Stadium garrison on Vito Cruz street appeared at Eulogio Malibiran's door to fetch him to work, the heavy shelling notwithstanding. Together the two proceeded to the Rizal Stadium. At the stadium gate Eulogio recognized the sentry on duty as one of the Japanese who had been at Leveriza street the previous night. The sentry told Eulogio that all the 30 persons hauled away from the Leveriza street area last night had been killed.

Today, the 2nd Battalion, 148th Infantry, held a line along the Estero de Paco from the Pasig River to Isaac Peral street. The 3rd Battalion assembled on the east bank of the Estero de Paco. The 1st Battalion stood to the right of the 3rd near the Manila Gas Company plant. The Japanese now subjected the area to heavy mortar and artillery fire, and the American casualty list mounted rapidly. Thirty-one enlisted men and two officers were ordered out of front line duties to help the Medical Detachment evacuate the wounded.

In the group of 31 was Pfc. Joseph J. Cichetti, platoon messenger of Company A. Now Cichetti led a litter team and in four hours under heavy bombardment, successfully retrieved fourteen wounded men and brought them back to safety.[3]

While returning from one recovery trip, the team's path was raked by machine gun-fire. Cichetti deliberately exposed himself to the enemy to pinpoint the source. He fired back and silenced the opposition.

Now Cichetti turned to a group of wounded about fifty yards away. The enemy bombardment did not let-up and before he could reach his objective, Cichetti was hit in the head by a shell fragment. Although badly wounded, he managed to haul one man over his shoulder and made for the 50-yard return dash. As he laid down his burden, Cichetti collapsed from his injuries. In minutes he was dead.

The American assault on the Isla de Provisor was launched at 8 o'clock this morning by Company G, 129th Infantry, following an intense softening-up artillery barrage.[4]

By 8:30 Company G had 15 men inside the boiler plant. Shortly, however, they were thrown out by the defenders. Unable to withdraw and unable to get reinforcements, the fifteen held on behind a coalpile throughout the day.

After dark, Company G commander Capt. George West swam across the *estero* dragging an assault boat behind him to the opposite bank, and ferried his men back to safety. At midnight, noses were counted and it was found that Company G had six killed, five wounded and six missing.

This evening, one troop of the 8th Cavalry Regiment crossed the Pasig river and landed at the Philippine Racing Club grounds in Santa Ana on the eastern limits of the city. The crossing was unopposed.

Now Company B, 2nd Battalion, 148th Infantry, commanded by Captain Buster Ferris, was directed to seize the Paco Railroad station. The station was on a strategic line that overlooked the entry points to several streets in the Paco district. It had been heavily fortified by the Japanese who surrounded the station with interlocking gun-emplacements which in turn were protected by a network of pillboxes and foxholes. Each corner of the station was sandbagged and defended by 20 mm. guns. A central concrete pillbox was defended by a 37 mm. gun. The garrison was estimated to be 300-strong.

Now the 2nd Platoon, Company B, 148th Infantry, was ordered to make a frontal asault on the Paco Railroad station. The platoon dashed across rubble-strewn open fields but was pinned down a hundred yards short of the building. Now Pfc. Elbert E. Jones, the bazooka man, crawled within fifty yards of the station and managed to fire twenty rounds before he fell mortally wounded by machine gun-fire. But he had succeeded in driving the Japanese to one wing of the building and had enabled his comrades to bring away their wounded.

At this point, first class privates John N. Reese and Cleto Rodriguez, both BAR men of Company B, inched their way to within sixty yards of the station. In two-and-a-half hours during which the two fired almost 100 rounds, they killed 82 Japanese and wounded many more. They put out of combat one 20 mm. gun and one heavy machine gun. However, while withdrawing when their ammunition ran out, John N. Reese was killed.[5]

Today, 9 February, the first issue (Vol. I, No. 1) of *Free Philippines* published by the General Headquarters, Office of War Information, was released.[6]

This issue consisted of one page measuring 10 inches by 14 inches printed on both sides. The paper was handed out on streets north of the Pasig, passed out at the mess line at the Santo Tomas camp, and later dropped from spotter cubs over South Manila.

On this day the Unknown Diarist of the *Free Philippines* made this entry: "Leaflets dropped on the Ateneo compound, copies of the *Free Philippines* of Feb. 5 (sic) where an account was given of the sudden thrust of American forces into the city and the taking of Santo Tomas and Malacañang brought us our first official information regarding the liberation of the north side."

The *Free Philippines* issue of today contains an account of the destruction in the north side following a survey conducted by the American military authorities. According to this account, in the Sampaloc district, half of the block bounded by Lepanto, Azcarraga, Tortousa and Gastambide was completely razed. All the houses along Morayta street were burned down. The whole block bounded by Isabelo de los Reyes, P. Noval, P. Campa and España streets was a total loss.

In the Quiapo district, all buildings along Azcarraga from Quezon boulevard up to Benavidez street were burned. All buildings on the block bounded by Echague, Carriedo and Rizal avenue were razed. The Quiapo church stood, although severely pockmarked, but the parish house on Evangelista street was a total loss. All the buildings within the block enclosed by Raon, Evangelista, P. Paterno and Quezon boulevard were totally destroyed.

In the Santa Cruz district all houses bounded by Azcarraga, O'Donnell, Doroteo Jose and Oroquieta streets were destroyed.

This was but a partial report of the destruction.

Sophy Natalie Morgin also saw leaflets fluttering in the air. One dropped in the garden infront of her apartment house on M.H. del Pilar street and she ran to pick it up. It was the first issue of *Free Philippines*.[7]

This afternoon, the polite Japanese soldier who spoke English in the previous day's search party appeared at Miss Morgin's gate. He brought the residents of the apartment house an unopened bottle of genuine Black and White whiskey. He stayed to chat with Miss Morgin and the French landlord and others in the house.

"He made himself at home," Miss Morgin writes, "and talked about the foolishness of war."

At eight o'clock in the evening the English-speaking Japanese came back to the apartment house. This time he brought a sack of rice and a can of Klim.

"In three days," he said, "the Americans would be in Malate."

The man described himself as a poet and that he began to wear a military uniform but a few days before. He may have been a civilian employee in the Imperial Navy.

"Why can't people live in harmony," he sighed. "I'd rather go fishing than be doing this thing."

"He made me forget that he was a Japanese soldier," Sophy Natalie Morgin writes. "He had tears in his eyes as he sympathized with our plight, and with advice to be careful, he left never to return."

A squad of Japanese marines entered Red Cross headquarters on Isaac Peral street this morning and inquired why the place was packed full of people. The Red Cross staff explained that the people had come in from the neighborhood seeking shelter from the shelling and the bombing. Thousands of shells had rained over south Manila since 4 February, and the Red Cross building had been hit but three times. A Red Cross flag flew over the building. The Japanese seemed satisfied and left, admonishing the Red Cross staff to take in only Filipinos and Germans.[8]

Mass was in progress in the makeshift chapel of the Assumption Sisters in their temporary convent in the Madrigal compound on General Luna street in Paco. Hundreds of civilians had joined them as refugees in the compound.[9]

The chaplain, Padre Antonio Saravia, was officiating at Mass and was about to raise the Host when a dozen shells crashed in rapid succession into the compound. A nervous, high-strung person, Padre Saravia collapsed on his knees and sank into a catalepsy-like fit. For long minutes the priest froze in this position, immobile and unblinking, with the terrified nuns forming a wall close around him.

The priest finally came to and Mass continued. He had given communion to two nuns when a shell exploded particularly close by. The priest skipped out of the chapel leaving the chalice on the altar but carrying the paten with the Hosts. The nuns followed on his heels.

In another room the priest resumed giving communion to the nuns. At this moment a shell slammed into the building and the priest ran out again, the nuns chasing after him, this time straight to the bomb-shelter.

Only Mother Ma. Philomene Kelly, the Superior, remained. She scurried from room-to-room seeking out other refugees and directing them to the shelter. Suddenly a shell burst right in front of the nun and she fell, seriously injured.

In the German Club on San Luis street in Ermita, about 1500 persons from the neighborhood huddled in shelters under the clubhouse and in rooms upstairs.

This morning the retired American General Charles E. Nathorst and his family moved out of their suite at the Lopez apartments on San Marcelino street near the Paules church and went to the German Club.[10]

General Nathorst had been an officer in the Philippine Department of the United States Army and had served in the Philippine Constabulary since the early days of the American occupation. At this time he was 80 years-old and enfeebled. Because of his condition, he was not interned. He lived with his wife and daughter, and was cared for by a Filipino nurse, Miss Asuncion R. Marbas.

Before noon, Nurse Marbas led the 80-year-old retired General Charles E. Nathorst to the underground shelters at the German Club, while Mrs. Nathorst and her daughter made ready quarters in the first floor of the building. At 6 o'clock this evening, they brought the general to his new lodgings.

In the section where the family of Remedios Rodriguez sheltered under the German Club building, it was found that there were now about 50 persons.

Towards noon today, the beautiful Adelina Chicote left her La Casona home on San Carlos street in Ermita on her chore of bringing food and medicine to her mother and sister who were confined in a private clinic some blocks away along A. Mabini street.

At the corner of Isaac Peral and Mabini streets, Adelina Chicote, tall and svelte, black-eyed and raven – tressed, was accosted by the Japanese sentry. She explained her mission, gestured in the direction of her destination, the multi-storey building whose top-floor could be seen from this point. The sentry looked into her *bayong*, seemed to satisfy himself and, smiling, allowed the Spanish girl to pass.[11]

Adelina Chicote turned her back and took one, two steps, to cross the street. Suddenly the smiling Japanese lunged at her with his flashing bayonet, hitting the girl between the shoulder blades. Adelina fell to the ground, her *bayong* scattering its contents all around. Without a whimper, without a cry, Adelina Chicote struggled to rise. Again the Japanese sentry struck with his bayonet, and again, until his victim moved no more.

Now it started to rain. Now it was pouring a deluge in Manila where bomb and shell also rained down. On the corner of Isaac Peral and Mabini streets one block from her own door, the body of Adelina Chicote Lalana lay, tiny and forsaken, her blood running into rivulets with the rainwater into the drain.

The family of Lydia Gutierrez on Remedios street in Malate awoke to the rumbling of tanks which they thought to be American, at last. They were Japanese. The family was in for another frightful day in the dugout in the yard, with shells bursting all around them.[12]

"An American shell hit our roof this morning," Marcial P. Lichauco in Santa Ana records in his diary. The shell ploughed through the ceiling, embedded itself on the kitchen table, but did not explode. The percussion cap had become disengaged and dropped harmlessly to the floor where it rolled around until the cook, who was standing a few feet away, picked it up.[13]

Another such shell made a direct hit on the facade of Red Cross

Children's Home No. 1 at 1132 California street at the corner of San Marcelino in Ermita. This was one of the three such homes operated by the Philippine Red Cross as a shelter for orphans, children of destitute parents and abandoned children picked up by Red Cross workers on the streets. These homes had been in operation since the final months of 1944.

Red Cross Children's Home No. 1 sheltered 39 children with seven attendants under the direction of Miss Teresa S. Nava, at this time in her early twenties. The building across the street was on fire.[14]

The Japanese were on the streets shooting people who ventured out. The bombing and the shelling continued without let up. Now Miss Nava decided to abandon the home and led her helpers and their wards to what she believed would be safety. Breaking down fences, cutting through backyards, crawling under houses, the party found shelter in another house on Herran street. When they looked back, they saw the home they had abandoned enveloped in flames.

There was but scanty food for the Red Cross children, only the clothing on their backs, no medicine for the many who were ill, but little water, and this for only the smallest and sickliest of the lot.

Mrs. Francisca Guinto-Juco, 37, recently widowed, lived with her five children in an apartment house at the corner of San Marcelino and Herran streets, at the other end of the block from the Red Cross Children's Home No. 1.[15]

With the food stores in the house down, Mrs. Juco stepped out early this morning to see what could be bought at the Paco market a few blocks up Herran. Shortly she was back, pale and shaking. The streets were hardly passable. Japanese were shooting people, the American artillery barrage was rising in tempo.

She got her children, Estelita, 14; Corazon, 12; Teddy, 8; Victoria, 7; and Antonia, 3, to bundle up necessities, and prepare to flee the house. She started to cook a big stock of ready food.

At about 10 o'clock this morning 14-year-old Estelita Juco looked up from doing her bundles to harken more closely to an unusual sound in the street outside. Fronting her apartment building on San Marcelino street was a Chinese grade school. A Japanese pillbox was on the northeast corner of San Marcelino and Herran, matched by another on the southeast corner, in front of what was known to be a whorehouse for the Japanese military.

Estelita Juco looked out of her window and saw the Chinese grade school enveloped in flames. This produced the strange crackling and whistling sound she heard. Now the Juco family picked up what they could of their bundles and through an upstairs window went down the backside of the building. Their neighbors did the same as the San Marcelino street front was impassable.

The Jucos and their neighbors now found themselves inside a compound that belonged to the Soliven family. The Solivens had left Manila earlier, and only caretakers were around.

The fire did not cross San Marcelino street at this point, and the shelling spared the compound. Through the night the Jucos and their neighbors huddled in makeshift shelters inside the Soliven property.

Fire raged unchecked farther up San Marcelino street between General Luna and Oregon streets. The family of Ricardo Mascuñana had sought shelter in a property they owned on Colorado street when their home on Padre Faura nearby burned yesterday.[16]

As the fire along San Marcelino street raged, the Mascuñana shelter filled with more refugees, "loaded with bundles, children, dogs and chickens and even two piglets," Dona Paz de Mascuñana writes.

Japanese troops were heard tramping up and down the streets outside and silence was enjoined upon everyone in the shelter, "but how to silence babes-in-arms and over-excited animals," Doña Paz despairs.

The day waned and would pass somewhat uneventfully for the group, "not because the shelling was less frequent or hit farther away," Doña Paz writes, "but because now we are more accustomed to everything."

It was not an uneventful day for Don Elpidio Quirino and his family, a few paces away from the Mascuñana shelter.[17]

Elpidio Quirino lived at 506 Colorado street, close to the intersection with Oregon. At this time, Mr.Quirino was senator-elect, since the Senate to which he had been elected in November 1941 had not convened.

Risen to great eminence in Philippine affairs, Elpidio Quirino had graduated from the college of law of the University of the Philippines in 1914 and went on to become secretary to then Senate President Manuel L. Quezon. He launched himself into a political career and successively became Senator for the First District (Ilocos), Assemblyman for Ilocos Sur, delegate to the Constitutional Convention of 1935, and Secretary of Finance and later Secretary of the Interior in the cabinet of President Quezon in the Commonwealth government.

The Quirino home was half of a duplex owned by the Syquia family, a comfortable two-storey building in this affluent neighborhood. With Quirino and his wife, the elegant and aristocratic Alicia Syquia, were their children -- Tomas (Tommy), 21; Armando (Dody), 20; Norma, 18; Victoria (Vicky), 13; and the baby Fe Angela, two-years-old, and their household staff. The other half of the duplex was occupied by Mrs. Quirino's brother, Cesar Syquia, and his family.

This section of Ermita was in chaos. The neighborhood was on fire.

Smoke hang thickly over the area and shells fell unrelentingly in the carpet-pattern the Americans now employed. Grenades exploded on all sides and the sound of machine gun-fire came from everywhere.

At mid-morning, an American shell crashed into the Quirino home, making it untenable. Elpidio Quirino organized his family to flee.

Doña Alicia, the infant Fe Angela in her arms, led Tommy, Norma and Vicky out the gate and up the sidewalk on Colorado towards the intersection with California street.

Elpidio Quirino and the second son, Armando, 20, were in the house, frenziedly getting together foodstuffs and valuables.

At the southwest corner of Colorado and California streets stood the home of the Syquia matriarch, Doña Concepcion Jimenez de Syquia. With her were her unmarried children, Hector and Margarita; her daughter Petronila, who was married to the lawyer Vicente Mendoza. The couple had six children – Gregorio, 18; Luis, 16; Raul, 13; Milagros, 11; Enrique, 8, and Renato, 5.

Now Mrs. Quirino and her children raced towards her mother's home, braving the relentless shelling and the Japanese squad that stood at the corner of Colorado and Oregon streets.

Doña Alicia Syquia de Quirino's family group did reach the northeast corner of Colorado and California streets. The intersection was mined and partly barricaded. At the end of the block, at the corner of California and Pennsylvania, was a Japanese machine gun-nest. Now it opened fire on the small group.

After the first burst, Tommy and Vicky sprang across the street and sprinted to the safety of their grandmother's driveway. Here Don Vicente Mendoza and his eldest, Gregorio, 18, waited. Tommy and Vicky got to them safely but all had to fall to the ground on their bellies as American shells showered all around them.

From where he crouched Tommy Quirino, 21, heard his mother's hysterical pleas in Spanish. Then her screams stopped. When he looked, Tommy saw the group asprawl on the ground. Neither Don Elpidio nor Armando were in sight.

No one in the Syquia driveway dared raise his head as the shelling never paused. The machine gun at the west end of the block chattered away in heart-stopping bursts. Dense smoke billowed over the neighborhood.

Elpidio Quirino had fled his home but could not get out to the street. He tore down fences with his bare hands, clambered over walls and crawled under houses trying to get to California street. When night fell he found shelter as best he could. He did not know the fate that had befallen his family. Armando he did not get to see again.[18]

Tommy and Vicky awaited their father at their grandmother's home.

Through the night they waited. He did not come.

The YMCA of Manila maintained a dormitory at the northeast corner of Oregon and Pennsylvania streets. Resident at the YMCA dormitory at this time was a small group of five, among whom were James Papa, Jr., who had worked for the Manila Electric company before the war, and the janitor, Nicetas Vera.[19]

Priscilo Mendiola, 33, a chauffeur, lived at 1448 General Luna street, with his wife Feliciana and their three children – Rosalinda, 7; Priscilo, Jr., 5, and Emmanuel, two-and-a-half.

At about 7 o'clock this morning, the Mendiolas joined a group of neighbors and set out for the Philippine General hospital four short blocks away from General Luna street. The shelling was murderous. The neighborhood was in an uproar. People milled in groups big and small in the streets trying to avoid the exploding shells and the Japanese at the same time.

Priscilo Mendiola estimated his group to number forty, many of them children. At the corner of Oregon and Pennsylvania, one block short of the Philippine General hospital, the band was stopped by the Japanese. The women and children were sorted out of the group and allowed to proceed to the hospital. The men, except for one old man who was allowed to proceed, were ordered into the YMCA building at the corner. Inside, Priscilo Mendiola and his party came upon 20 others, mostly from the same neighborhood.

At 1029 Oregon street, next door to the YMCA, Aquiles Laguda lived with his family of ten. They employed a young man, Antonio de Mayo, 18, as cook.

At 5 o'clock this afternoon when his home was threatened by flames, Aquiles Laguda moved his household to the YMCA next door. Several other families from the neighborhood which swirled in chaos had sought refuge here earlier.

This evening a Japanese squad entered the YMCA premises and ordered the women and children to proceed to the Philippine General hospital, one block from this point across Taft Avenue. When the women and children had gone, the Japanese questioned the men of whom there were about 16, trying to ferret out guerrillas among them. No one admitted being a guerrilla. The men were ordered to stay inside and a sentry was posted infront of the building.

James Woo, Sr., 49, a Chinese stockbroker, lived at 407 Colorado street, not far from the YMCA dormitory. With James Woo, Sr., were his wife whose Chinese name was Chua So Ping, 47, his son James, Jr., and four unmarried younger brothers – Pedro, Edward, William and Henry. A nephew, Chua Kok Hun, lived with them.[20]

The Woo home on Colorado was razed in this afternoon's fire. The Woos now sought refuge in the home of Delfin de la Paz, a professor at the University of the Philippines, which still stood, also on Colorado street.

Franz Rosenzwaig, 61, was a Russian emigre who lived with his wife Maria, 41, and their daughter Vera, 12, at 421 San Marcelino street, in Ermita. Franz had been in the circus. Now he operated the Manila Universal Store in Quiapo.[21]

This afternoon, the Rosenzwaigs watched helplessly as their home on San Marcelino street was devoured by flames. They moved to a small house painted green behind their own home. With them was an elderly Russian emigré couple, Mr. and Mrs. Nicolai Afaneseff; a friend, Vassiliy Ignatoff, who had been a clown named KoKo in Rosenzwaig's circus, and a Filipina maidservant, Ana de la Cruz.

Now Franz dashed back to their frontyard to recover a suitcase from the pushcart. He came back to the green house behind their burning home very much shaken. He got his wife and daughter to their knees with him and led them in a prayer. He told them KoKo the former clown and old man Afaneseff were dead, hit by shrapnel as they were crossing the street. Mrs. Afaneseff was in the green house, one leg shattered.

For three nights the nurse Carolina Coruna had lain in her shelter among the debris near Calle Real outside one of the entrances into Intramuros. Today when darkness fell she dragged herself through the rubble and the ruins, and assisted by two Filipino men who came upon her, she reached a compound on Pennsylvania street in Ermita which was still untouched by fire. It turned out to be the residence of Dr. Jose Celeste.[22]

Celeste had been a ranking official in the Budget Commission of the Philippine Commonwealth government. Now in the wartime government, Celeste was vice minister of economic affairs.

Many people had sought shelter in his compound as the Japanese seem to have identified Dr. Celeste as an important official. For a time, Japanese sentries stood at his gates. The building had not been squarely hit by shelling and had not been reached by fire.

A large crowd has been gathering at St. Paul college on Herran street in Malate since this morning, but the nuns of the Congregation of St. Paul de Chartres who are refugees at Assumption Convent across the street are not aware of it.[23]

Japanese teams were rounding up people in the neighborhood and odering them to the St. Paul college grounds. At 11 o'clock this morning, one such team knocked at the door of Luisa Barahona, 30, on Vermont street. Luisa lived with her parents, her sister, Angeles, 28, and their family cook. The Barahonas are Spanish expatriates. Now they trudged over to St. Paul college on Herran and joined the assembly which Luisa estimated to be over 800.

A Japanese team also knocked at 714 Georgia street where Rosario Fernandez, 25, lived with 12 other members of her family, including her father, her son, her sisters and their children. Now the family joined neighbors streaming down the streets in the direction of St. Paul college. Rosario estimated the crowd to number 800 men, women and children – Filipinos, Chinese, Spanish, Indian and other nationalities.

The distinguished physician Antonio Vasquez lived at 815 Wright street. His elder son Luis was also a doctor, and the second son, Daniel, was a medical student. The family of doctors had turned their Wright street home into an emergency hospital, and they accepted the wounded from the streets for treatment. The two sons also volunteered as doctors at the Philippine General hospital.

After lunch today, Dr. Luis Vasquez and his brother Daniel left their house for duty at the hospital. The brothers were in white physicians' suits, with Red Cross armbands. Luis Vasquez carried his stethoscope.

At the gate to the University of the Philippines college of medicine on Herran street the brothers were accosted by a Japanese sentry and hauled over to the St. Paul college compound across the street from this point. Here the two joined the crowd already assembled from the neighborhood.

Concepcion Colma, 32, a widow, lived with her five children at 416 Herran street. Her children were Iluminada, 15; Camilo, 14; Winifred, 13; Violeta, 10, and the youngest, Orlando. This afternoon the family joined their neighbors, under Japanese orders, at the St. Paul college compound.

At about 2 o'clock this afternoon it started to rain. The Japanese ordered the people, scattered in groups big and small all over the premises, to move indoors. The family of Rosario Fernandez entered a small room, probably one of the classrooms. The Barahonas went into a small room which Luisa understood to be the kitchen in the Home Economics building.

Later this afternoon at around 5 o'clock, the family groups were brought together in a large hall which turned out to be the dining room for student boarders in a building along Florida street. Rosario Fernandez estimated the assembly at 1,000, of both sexes, of all ages.

Now some Japanese carried into the center of the hall two cases of rice wine (sake) and two cartons of candies. To show that the wine was safe to drink, two soldiers opened a couple of bottles and took a few swigs each. Children and adults, many actually starving, surged forward.

With the others, Concepcion Colma and her five children had entered the "big room," as Winifred, 13, remembers the St. Paul college dining room. Winifred recalls partaking of the wine, and candies, and drinking water passed around by the Japanese.

The Barahonas huddled on the floor, tightly wedged in among the other detainees. Now Luisa Barahona felt her cook beside her nudging her, saying, "Miss, the lamps are moving," indicating the chandelier in the ceiling. Luisa looked up at the chandelier in time to see it crash down and explode on the floor.

Rosario Fernandez was in the back of the crowd against the wall. Suddenly she heard a loud explosion followed by terrified screams. Other witnesses had noted that the chandelier over the middle of the hall was wrapped in black cloth. A rope led from the chandelier to an adjoining vacant room. When a big crowd had gathered around the cases of sake and candies, someone tugged on the rope, the chandelier crashed to the floor and at least three huge explosions followed. Several fell dead. several others were wounded, and a general stampede towards the exits ensued as the hall burst into flames.

As Winifred Colma recalls it, suddenly "grenades came out of the lights." Actually, the chandelier was wrapped in black cloth, part of the blackout precautions current at the time. The explosives seem to have been attached to the chandelier which crashed to the floor when the rope which held it was released.

In the explosion, Concepcion Colma, 32, was struck dead, along with her two daughters, Iluminada, 15, and Violeta, 10, and a son, Camilo, 14. Winifred, 13, was dazed, but otherwise unhurt. So was her brother, Orlando.

Over at the Assumption Convent across Herran street, Sister Charles, SPC, and another nun had dared step out of their shelter into the garden. A tree was burning, its huge trunk split open and aflame. A young man, hobbling on an injured foot, came up to splash pails of water on the burning tree.[24]

Feeling brave, Sister Charles and her companion ventured farther into the yard to a spot where they could see the belltower of the St. Paul college chapel. The tower had two small bells which the St. Paul community had affectionately nicknamed "Pierrette" and "Paulette."

"Look how they dominate the whole situation," Sister Charles proudly said of the bells as explosions sounded in all directions and smoke swirled densely over the burning neighborhood. At this precise moment the roof over the chapel of St. Paul college was lifted and blown away, "like a mat of straw," Sister Charles says.

Among the Sisters of St. Paul de Chartres who were refugees at Assumption Convent was Sister Anna de Jesus, a Belgian national, who had been teaching at St. Paul college for 21 years. From their shelter in the Assumption compound the Sisters heard a huge explosion from across the street, and peering through a porthole Sister Anna saw a section of the roof over the dining hall of St. Paul college detach itself and sail in the air to land approximately three blocks away. Now Sister Anna watched fearfully as this section of the St. Paul college started to burn.

The St. Paul nuns at Assumption Convent rushed madly up to the third floor of their quarters for a better view of the destruction of their property.

"The labor of so many years," Sister Charles writes, "gone in twenty minutes."

The others couldn't watch. They went down on their knees in the Assumption chapel, "to borrow strength from the Tabernacled Christ," in the words of Sister Charles.

In the dining hall at St. Paul college, several more explosions followed as the Japanese threw hand grenades into the panicked crowd. Some of the men caught the grenades as they fell and hurled them towards the windows. The exploding grenades tore open the wrought-iron grills. The people now rushed out of the openings thus created. The doorways had been barred from outside and bodies piled up before them as the people fought to get out.

Rosario Fernandez, separated from her family, started to lift herself up one window blown open by a grenade, but a stout woman held tightly onto her dress.

"Save me," the fat woman cried, "take me with you!"

"I can't carry you," Rosario protested. "You are too big!"

Each time Rosario Fernandez attempted to lift herself up the window the fat woman held on to her. The hall was burning, people were pressing on her. Rosario tore away her skirt, leaving it in the fat woman's hands, and jumped out the window into Florida street.

At this point Angeles Barahona, 28, Luisa's sister, saw a Japanese grab a baby from its mother's arms and toss it into the air. Angeles watched horror-stricken, as another Japanese sprang up and at the point of his bayonetted rifle caught the falling baby, impaling it to death. Angeles Barahona went into shock and dropped to the floor.

Luisa Barahona held her unconscious sister on her left. On her right, her mother too collapsed in a dead faint. Luisa propped both women on either arm and dragged them to a window that had been blasted open. With the help of her father and the family cook, Luisa pushed the two out of the window. Together the family managed to cross Florida street into the compound of Dr. Gloria where they joined several others in the garage.

At the sound of the explosions, Dr. Luis Vasquez dropped to the floor. When he raised his head he saw the window ahead of him suddenly wide open. He could not see his brother Daniel, so he jumped out of the open window as quickly as he could.

Racing along Florida street with a horde of others, Luis Vasquez came upon his brother Daniel. The two skipped over what they believed to be land mines, crawled under barbed wire barricades at the intersections, until they reached the safety of their compound on Calle Wright.

On Tennessee street around the corner from Florida street was the residence of the prominent physician, Dr. Herminio Velarde, Sr. In his yard was a big air-raid shelter. Here Rosario Fernandez joined about 100 persons who had escaped from the St. Paul college compound. Outside, the Japanese fired at people moving around. In Dr. Velarde's yard, Rosario Fernandez came upon her father and her sisters with their children. In a corner of the yard behind a clump of banana trees they huddled the night through.

Back at the St. Paul compound, Winifred Colma sat dazed on the floor of the dining room, her family scattered dead and dying around her. She watched as her brother Orlando picked himself up and jumped out an open window. She followed. Together the two children raced with the others to the Velarde compound.

But there was no sanctuary here. "I saw Japanese killing the small children and the ladies," Winifred says.

"I am afraid to see," she says. "I run out."

Winifred was separated from her brother Orlando. Running down the street a Japanese fired at her and grazed her back. But she found her way to her own home on Herran street. Later she learned that her brother had been killed by shelling on the street. Of Concepcion Colma's brood, only 13-year-old Winifred survived.

In the evening, a band of Japanese found the refugees in the Gloria garage on Florida street among whom was the Barahona family. With guns menacingly aimed at their chests, the refugees lined up against the back wall. At this moment a grenade blast shook the garage door. The Japanese rushed out to investigate. The people lined against the wall turned in the other direction and fled pell-mell.

The nuns at the Assumption Convent at this time had no notion of the dreadful events taking place in their neighborhood. The Sisters had been quartered in a building along Dakota street. Believing that this section was not safe, they had moved into another building in the compound.[25]

At about 7 o'clock this evening, through the explosions and the conflagration outside, as the nuns were seated before a lean supper, a squad of Japanese appeared at the gate and ordered everyone to come down to the lawn. Fearful of the intentions of the Japanese, the nuns now knelt one-by-one before the chaplain to receive Holy Communion. Now the nuns from all three orders – the Augustinian Cannonesses (Belgian Sisters), the Sisters of St. Paul de Chartres and the Assumption Sisters, and the civilians, men, women and children, altogether 256 persons, lined up by twos, hands in the air, and filed between a phalanx of Japanese soldiers, "some with bayonets dripping blood," Sister Charles, SPC, writes.

During the early part of the Japanese occupation, several Japanese Catholic nuns had come from Japan to St. Paul college in Manila to teach Nippon-go. The Japanese nuns had returned to Japan before the American landing in October 1944. Several St. Paul Sisters, therefore, were competent in Japanese. Now one of them, Sister Marie Paul, approached the leader of the Japanese band to find out what was wanted of the refugees.

She was told that the Japanese only wanted the building in which the civilians were quartered for their own use. The nuns and the civilians must transfer to another building in the compound.

Now the group moved across the Assumption campus, the figures silhouetted against the fierce glow of the fire consuming the Ateneo de Manila buildings on the north and St. Paul college on the south. They were led to the home economics building on the Dakota street side. Here the refugee party settled, packed tightly in the available space.Having abandoned their bundles in the other building, including those in the pushcart that had remained parked in the yard ready for an emergency flight, the nuns now found they had nothing but the clothes on their backs.

At 10 o'clock this evening, Eulogio Malibiran again had a band of Japanese marines at his door. He did not open up. He had barricaded the door and though the Japanese pushed and hammered on it, it stayed closed. Again the Japanese moved on to Felipe Canillas' home next door.[26]

At his observation post in an upstairs room, Eulogio Malibiran saw four Japanese go up the Canillas home. Again he heard the sounds of mayhem and one of the Canillas girls scream, "Mother, oh my God!"

"They were all running around the house," Eulogio would recall. "Seems as though those soldiers were chasing the girls. They were screaming. And finally it was quiet. At the same time I saw the house infront of mine already burning and we took shelter. We went out of the house."

Eduardo de los Reyes, 19, lived in a house behind that of Felipe Canillas. Alarmed by the sounds of violence in the house to the front, Eduardo hid himself behind a shutter where he could look into his neighbor's house.[26]

Eduardo saw Felipe Canillas open the door to the street at the Japanese's pounding. He watched Felipe and the Japanese exchange a few words which he could not hear from where he watched. Suddenly the Japanese marine lunged with his bayonetted rifle and Canillas staggered backwards, clutching his abdomen.

Eduardo de los Reyes looked from his hiding place into the Canillas house through an open window and he saw Japanese marines breaking into the bedroom upstairs, casting out the contents of cabinets and trunks. He saw two of the Canillas girls being held by the Japanese and watched horrified as they were dragged away.

"The bombing has been terrific all afternoon and many more fires are burning," Gladys Savary in Pasay writes in her diary. "Ermita and Malate are burning. We can see the flames sky high."[28]

But Madame has other problems. "Confidentially shot and shell aren't so bad to take as the plumbing problem. Eight people, four children among them, make a lot of bathroom traffic at any time, and with no water in the pipes, it's hellish. We carry water from the well to the bathroom, but it isn't a very satisfactory method. I call it the hot-and-cold-running-boy system, only some times the boy is me."

Tressa Cates and other residents at the Santo Tomas camp had another sort of problem. "After each meal I would be seized by cramps and diarrhea. No matter how hard I tried to chew my food slowly and tried to remain calm, nothing seemed to help. I wished desperately that I could have sat down to one meal without starting to bawl. I was beginning to dread mealtime . . . Our death rate was still mounting. Those who died after shelling and those who died from starvation. The good and plentiful army chow came too late for them. In many instances, the good food hastened their death."[29]

A.V.H. Hartendorp kept track of deaths at Santo tomas after the arrival of the liberation forces. Two died on the 3rd of February, aged 57 and 58; two more on the 4th, aged 56 and 68; three on the 5th, aged 62, 64 and 66. "All of them dying of malnutrition as a contributing factor if not the chief cause of death," Hartendorp writes. "The better meals did not save them."[30]

Late this afternoon, a squad of Japanese soldiers entered Red Cross headquarters on Isaac Peral street. They wanted to set up in the backyard one of those machines which simulated artillery fire, intended to confuse the adversary about the number and location of their own artillery pieces. These machines were used extensively all over south Manila and very effectively duplicated the nerve-wracking sound of an artillery barrage. Unable to object but unwilling to have the premises so used, Red Cross Acting Manager Modesto Farolan stood guard over the backyard. The Japanese did not mount their noise-making machines, blocked the doors leading to the backyard and there went to sleep.[31]

Between the Paules church and seminary fronting San Marcelino street and the jai-alai fronton on Taft Avenue was a tract of land which was leased to a Chinese named Jun Pac who cultivated it as a truck garden.[32]

Jun Pac employed eight fellow-Chinese and two Filipino helpers. They had a shack in the garden, close to which they had constructed a bomb shelter. Among the Chinese gardeners was Co Ching, 34.

At about 6 o'clock this evening a passerby told the Chinese that Japanese were shooting people in the streets. The group got into the shelter and stayed there.

At 11 o'clock tonight, the Japanese brusquely ordered the Vincentian community on San Marcelino street in Ermita out of the convent refectory where they had been held prisoner since the 3rd February. Upon orders of the commanding officer the Japanese soldiers hauled out the priests led by the Father Provincial, the Most Reverend Jose Tejada, and tied their wrists behind their backs with twine. The group was marched out to the banks of the *estero* (drainage canal) behind the Paules church and seminary building. Here with their backs to the narrow, smelly stream, the Vincentian community with the Filipino seminarian and the two young acolytes, faced the Japanese machineguns. No one was spared.[33]

Later a group of ten Chinese was brought into the outer patio of the Paules church and seminary and lined-up before a machinegun. One of them, named Sing Koh, was hit in the neck and fell. Feigning death, Sing Koh allowed himself to be dragged behind the seminary buildings and thrown with the dead into the *estero*. When the Japanese had gone he climbed over the banks of the *estero* and hid among the rubble of ruined houses in the neighborhood.

At the south wing of the De la Salle college on Taft Avenue, the Christian Brothers and the refugee families passed the hours in deep anxiety. The family of Judge Jose Carlos was distraught. The judge and the De la Salle director, Brother Egbert Xavier, had been hauled away by the Japanese on 7th February, and had not returned. They were believed to have been brought over to the Nippon Club which adjoined the De la Salle property to the south on Taft Avenue. There was no way of ascertaining the two men's fate. The area was under heavy bombardment from the north side.[34]

Today, Brother Paternus Paul, the De la Salle procurator, urged the Filipino college secretary, Martin Hain, to leave the premises and head for the safe zones.

Hain had worked with the Christian Brothers for three years and lived at De La Salle all this time. This evening Hain slipped out the back way unobserved by anyone, crossed the *estero* between De La Salle and the Rizal Stadium, and eventually reached the safety zone in Santa Ana.

At this time, Eugene Adreevitch Kremleff lived with his wife, the former Helen Bruzinsky, and their children, Alexander, 5, and Olga, 3 1/2, at 34 Del Pan street in Pasay.[35] He was a Russian expatriate who had been executive of a mining firm before the war. This afternoon this area in Pasay came under American artillery fire. Mrs. Helen Kremleff took the children into the air-raid shelter in the backyard. Just then three Japanese soldiers entered the yard. They demanded to see Kremleff's papers. They said the entire family must go with them for investigation. Kremleff said he was willing to go but his wife and children must be left in the house. The Japanese consented. One of the soldiers stayed in the air-raid shelter while the other two took Kremleff away. In a half-hour the two were back, without Kremleff. He will be back in five minutes, they told Mrs. Kremleff, and the three Japanese left.

When at 8 o'clock this evening her husband did not show up, Helen Kremleff decided to go out to look for him. She stepped out of her yard and ran into a Japanese sentry at the corner. The sentry dragged her back into the air-raid shelter and Helen Kremleff found herself in a violent struggle as the Japanese tried to force himself on her. The two small children screamed wildly in terror. Their screams distracted the Japanese. Momentarily freed, Helen Kremleff grabbed the two children and ran into a neighbor's house. The Japanese did not pursue.

Early this evening, groups of Japanese banged on doors of residences in the area surrounding Plaza Fergusson in Ermita. They ordered residents to assemble at Plaza Fergusson.[36]

The plaza was named after the American colonial officer Arthur Fergusson who served as executive secretary to William Howard Taft and subsequently to every succeeding American governor of the Philippines until his death in 1908. The plaza extended from Dewey Boulevard on the west, fronting the residence of the U.S. High Commissioner, eastward to M.H. del Pilar right before the Ermita church. Alhambra and L. Guerrero streets cut through the plaza over which the handsome bronze bust of Arthur Fergusson presided, set upon an ornate marble pedestal.

On this spot on 4 May 1571, a Spanish soldier in the command of the *Adelantado*, Don Miguel Lopez de-Legazpi, found a wooden carving which was taken to be an image of the Virgin Mary, set among the branches of the native pandan tree. Already the image was the object of veneration among the people who lived on the site. The Spanish named the image after Our Lady of Expectation, although it became more popularly known as Our Lady of Guidance (Guia). Near the spot a hermitage was built, where the image was enshrined. It would become the focal point of a popular cult around which elaborate traditions grew. Devotees of the Virgin thronged her shrine, and the parish of Ermita, so-named after the hermitage, prospered.

By the year 1941 when World War II broke out, this section of Ermita had become a prestigious residential area which attracted Manila's cosmopolitan community. Ermita was populated by old mestizo families, prosperous merchants and successful professionals.

Fancy boutiques, elegant restaurants and chic cafes and the first high-rise hotels and apartment houses in the city sprouted in this section.

Tonight, residents of the area filed out of their doors into Plaza Fergusson. A witness estimated the crowd at 1,500 – men, women and children.

The young women and young girls were culled from the assembly, and about 400 of them were herded into the Bay View Hotel nearby, fronting the boulevard. The rest of the crowd, mostly males and elderly females and children, were dispersed to large buildings in the area, many of them to the Peralta apartments at the corner of L. Guerrero and Isaac Peral streets.

The group of young women and girls brought to the Bay View Hotel was composed of many nationalities. Aside from the brown-skinned Filipinas and sloe-eyed Chinese, there were fair-skinned Caucasians. Many were mestizas of Spanish, American, Russian, French, Portuguese parentage. Some were blonde.

The ladies were assigned to rooms in the Bay View, in groups big and small. The big mass of them was confined in the main dining room on the second floor. Many were family groups – mothers and daughters, sisters and aunts, cousins and in-laws. Some had nursing babies-in-arms. Others had very young children, among whom were little boys. In the group were ladies from old distinguished families, wealthy and socially elite. Some had their cooks and servants with them. Others were entertainers from the clubs and cocktail lounges in the area.

One family group consisted of the mother and three daughters, the eldest of whom was 24 and had been married for six years, the second 15 and the third 14.

The three were separated from their mother upon reaching the Bay View Hotel. They found themselves in a room with about 25 other women aged 15 to 25, on the second floor of the hotel, the fourth room in the left wing facing the boulevard.

This is the testimony of the eldest girl, 24.

". . . there were three Japanese who came inside the room and they dragged me out of the room. I tried to resist but I couldn't do anything ... They were just dragging me out. And they took me out to a room and all three of them were there. They started slapping me when I tried to resist. I couldn't do anything. They tore my pants off and they pushed me down to the floor and I laid there while one of them stood guard. One of them had a bayonet fixed in his rifle and the other two had just a bayonet here (indicating). When the first one was doing things to me the other two of them were just looking and laughing all the time. It took him about ten minutes to have his intercourse with me, and after he finished the other one just jumped on top of me, and when the other finished the other one just jumped on top of me. I was so exhausted. I didn't know just what to do. They had slapped me so much I was in a daze. And then they sent me back to the room and all the whole night they kept coming back and forth, coming back and forth.

". . . my friends told me they got me out from 12 to 15 times...

". . . we stayed until six o'clock in the morning.

"I fought all I could, but . . . After they beat me the first time, I lost all my strength . . . I don't know. I was dizzy. I couldn't even think anymore. They just came to the room and lighted me with candles and they just dragged me out of the room. They kept doing that the whole night. I couldn't even resist. I would stay in the room for two minutes and here they come again and drag me out the whole night that way."

This is the testimony of the woman's younger sister, aged 15.

"He took me by the arm and pulled me and told me to come to him. At first I didn't want to go, he started pulling me and slapping me. And what else could I do . . . He had a gun . . .

"He took me to a room facing Alhambra street. And when we got to the room he took me to the window and pointed me to the other side of the river and told me that there were Americans on the other side of the river, but me and him wouldn't see them; we would all be dead.

"After that he told me to take off my clothes. Of course I didn't want to take them off. And he grabbed me by the arm and told me to take them off and not be silly. I didn't take my clothes off, so he took hold of my blouse and tore it open and took it off. Then he shook me by the skirt and told me to take it off. And then I had my slip and my panties on and I still didn't want to take them off. And he took them off. After that I was in my panties and I didn't want to take them off.

"He told me to lie down on the floor, and when we got there he took off all his clothes and he laid the bayonet on one side and the gun on the other side of me. And he wanted to – oh my God. He – then he started to do something to me but he couldn't do anything. So he took his knife and cut me open and then he finally succeeded. He had – he had sexual intercourse.

"I was bleeding very badly and I was feeling, oh, I was feeling bad. He took me by the arm and pushed me to the floor and I fell down. And after that, I don't know. I guess I fainted. Or – I don't know.

"About 30 minutes later another Jap came. He was very, very young. And he took me by the arm and told me to get up and go with him. And I shouted and screamed and told him that I had finished already. He slapped me and kicked me and he dragged me out of the room. He took me into a room on the same floor facing Alhambra street. In that room there was a bed. He didn't tell me to take off my clothes. He just took my panties off and threw me on the bed. He was drunk – completely drunk. He was so drunk that he tried to, but he couldn't do anything to me . . . he gave me some water and took me back.

"About 30 minutes afterwards another Jap came and took hold of me... I started shouting and screaming and I said I didn't want anymore. He took his gun, pointed at my back and told me to come. There was nothing to do . . . he took me to a room on the same floor facing the boulevard, and there was nothing in that room except hay . . . He took off my pants and he unbuttoned the front part and he started having sexual intercourse with me . . . He took me back to a room thinking that it was our room, but when he opened the door there was a girl and another Japanese there . . . my room was the next room. You see we got mixed up. He was drunk too.

"The second one came in again and took me and I started shouting but he took me just the same. He took me to the same room and this time I guess he was sober . . . He pulled me to the bed and he – he had sexual emission this time, and after that he let me go to the room by myself.

"On the morning of the 10th I met my mother and we were with her all the time.

"They tried to every night but they couldn't do anything because my mother covered me with blankets . . ."

This is the testimony of the third sister, 14.

"He tried to pull me in. I tried to tell him not to take me, but he just pulled me by the arm and brought me to a room on the fifth floor . . .

"We were taken to the same room (with her second sister) but they separated us.

"He tried to pull my dress off and I told him not to because I was sick. So he just lifted my skirt and when he saw I was in menstruation he just kicked me . . .

"He brought me back. I had hardly time to sit down when another came and grabbed me. He took me to a room on the fifth floor.

"He did the same as the first one, but he didn't believe. So he took a piece of cotton and stuck his finger in, and when he saw it was that, he just let me go by myself.

"The Jap let me go by myself and I went to my mother."

From this night Bay View Hotel became a *joro* house, a brothel for the Japanese military. Singly or in groups, Japanese soldiers and marines, sometimes sotted, would come into the rooms where the women were held. They would shine flashlights, lighted candles or kerosene lamps at the faces of the women, and by force and violence take away the one they would fancy into any of the rooms in the hotel.

SATURDAY, 10 FEBRUARY 1945

Now it is after midnight and south Manila is under massive artillery and mortar bombardment from the American sector. Houses of imflammable material easily succumb to the white phosphorous shells. Reinforced concrete, cement and brick resist the projectiles, but are not impervious.

Entire blocks of houses disappear in flames, are reduced to debris. The wider streets and occasional stands of trees block the conflagration in some instances. Many houses, singly or in clumps are thus spared. Hardly any edifice stands undamaged.

A series of direct hits found the top floors of the San Carlos apartment building in Ermita where Carlos Garcia Buch and Luis Zabaljauregui had taken their respective families from *La Casona* next door. Now the men scooped up their respective broods and braved the open to get back to the ancestral home of the Chicote family.[1]

At *La Casona* on San Carlos street between Isaac Peral and San Luis the patriarch Alfredo Chicote Beltran decreed that everyone run. Now the party of about twenty persons, the wives carrying children and the men and unmarried women lugging bundles and crates, moved out into the blazing streets, half-crazed with terror. The Chicotes were joined by other groups to form a large crowd of hysterical human beings, driven here now by deafening explosions, and again there by machine gun-fire.

The Chicotes pressed forward where they could, scaled the barricades the Japanese had set up at strategic points. Where the fire has not reached, the houses are tightly boarded-up. Familiar doorways stare, sullen and forbidding. The people inside are dead-set against all intrusions. For those outside, there is no haven.

Towards dawn the Chicote family found itself by the ruins of a wooden building. It had not burned, but it was a total wreck. In the shadows of the wooden walls the family collapsed like one body, exhausted and benumbed.

In broad daylight, through the crackling of the fires just beginning to subside, through the shelling that never stopped, the Chicotes realized that they had been racing in circles in their own neighborhood. Now they saw that *La Casona* still stood in a row of three or four houses on San Carlos street before which the flames had unaccountably halted. The rest of the elegant homes and fashionable multi-storey apartment houses in this aristocratic residential section had been reduced to smouldering heaps of ash and charcoal. Now the Chicotes distributed themselves among the houses still habitable.

Don Alfredo Chicote Beltran, very ill but alert and still patriarchal, took into *La Casona* his sister, two unmarried daughters, and one unmarried son. Into an adjoining house, Antonio Chicote brought his wife, Camilla, and their six-month-old baby-girl.

The San Carlos apartment building was still tenable although in shambles. Prudencio Chicote Lalana took his small family into a suite of rooms. His two brothers-in-law with their respective families, and other families in similar straits, took abandoned suites. There was little food, hardly any water. The shelling continued pitilessly. The Japanese roamed the streets. Now the Chicote family finding itself beyond its physical capabilities organized itself into round-the-clock prayer vigil groups.

Without food or water, in mortal fear of the incessant American shelling, many south Manilans may have considered the Japanese guns and bayonets the least of the evils they faced.

This morning a resident of San Carlos street in Ermita emerged from his gate to negotiate from a Japanese patrol permission to relocate his family. Infront of his own gate the man was summarily shot dead.

On the street for all who remained on San Carlos to see from their windows, the body lay, the wide-open eyes staring blankly at the sky. In the sun the body began to putrefy. Before the day was over the stench became unbearable, but the neighbors could do nothing about it.

A squad of Japanese rattled the knocker at the gate of Tirso Lizarraga on San Carlos street. The dog barked and snarled menacingly. A Japanese soldier clambered up the wrought-iron gate so he could look down into the compound, aimed at the dog and silenced it foreover.[2]

The Lizarragas opened their gate. All the Japanese wanted were watches and fountain pens, having been handed some fine specimens of which, they went away quite contented.

Just past midnight, the Leveriza neighborhood in Pasay is in chaos. The area is aflame and residents dash here and there trying to salvage belongings from their homes, trying to evade the American shelling on one hand and the Japanese marines on the other, all at the same time.[3]

There is ominous silence in the house of Felipe Canillas in the midst of the general uproar. Now a neighbor, Zoilo Llave, approached another neighbor, Fortunato Baredo, 26, a onetime sailor who now lived at 1359 Leveriza street, to join him and find out what had happened to the Canillas family. Now the two went up the silent Canillas home. In a bloody pool by the kitchen the two found Felipe Canillas lying with a gaping wound on his abdomen and two more stab wounds on his chest. In a bedroom upstairs they found the headless body of his wife, Trinidad Canillas. They could not find the head. There was no trace of the three Canillas girls.

Zoilo Llave and his friend Fortunato Baredo gathered up the headless body of Mrs. Trinidad Canillas and brought it to an adjoining vacant lot where some neighbors had gathered away from the flames. They placed the dying Felipe Canillas on a chair in which he was carried out to the vacant lot.

Eduardo de los Reyes was helping other members of his family save belongings from their home now threatened by fire. From the vacant lot Eduardo saw Zoilo Llave at the door to the house of Felipe Canillas. Eduardo heard a gun shot and saw Zoilo Llave slump to the ground. A Japanese marine approached the fallen Llave and struck with his bayonet until the man lay still.

At 5 o'clock this morning, the neighbors found Felipe Canillas dead on the chair in which they had carried him out of his home. Now they scooped out a shallow grave in the vacant lot and buried the bodies of Felipe Canillas and his friend, Zoilo Llave, together.

In the wee hours the tiny Provisor islet on the right bank of the Pasig was subjected to carpet-shelling from the 37th Infantry Division's big guns and mortars while Company E prepared to launch six engineer assault boats with 90 men over the Estero de Tanque.[4]

At 2:30 this morning, the bombardment was lifted. Two assault boats crossed the *estero* safely. At this point the moon came out and in its full light the other boats were sitting ducks. The Japanese loosed their own bombardment and three of the American boats disappeared into the murky waters. A fuel tank exploded and its light revealed the men who had made it across cowering on the shore. Not until the moon set and the fuel fire burned itself out could they lift their heads.

In the half-light of dawn the American infantrymen dashed into the boiler plant. The Japanese were waiting inside, and the men now chased each other among the great machinery in an otherwise merry game of hide-and-seek, except that death was the penalty for getting tagged.

By daybreak, Company E occupied the eastern half of the boiler plant. The Japanese held the opposite half.

By 9:50 this morning, all of the 8th Cavalry Regiment had made it across the Pasig to Santa Ana. By nightfall, the 8th had secured a bridgehead extending 1,000 yards inland.

At 3 o'clock this afternoon, one squadron of the 5th Cavalry Regiment crossed the Pasig at Makati. Quickly it secured what they believed to be an electric power sub-station. It was in fact a bill-collecting sub-office. The 5th Cavalry's crossing was unopposed, but shortly after it landed, mortar and machine gun-fire from the direction of Fort McKinley to the southeast started to rain down on the landing area.[5]

Today, the 8th linked-up with elements of the 37th Infantry on Plaza Dilao near the Paco Railroad station. On the east, it linked-up with troops from the 5th Cavalry.[6]

The 11th Airborne Division established a solid line on the western side of Nichols Field today. Japanese resistance on this side ceased.

The 511th Parachute Infantry pressed hard on Route I and today stood three kilometers beyond Nichols on the northwest.

The Japanese position on Nichols Field remained formidable, however. Resistance from the naval guns was so strong that the American infantry could not advance.

At 2 o'clock this afternoon, the 11th Airborne Division passed into the jurisdiction of the Sixth Army and Nichols Field came into the Sixth's area of responsibility.

Now, the Sixth Army had two bridgeheads on South Manila, with the 37th Infantry Division on the Estero de Paco and the 1st Cavalry Division to its left. With the 11th Airborne to the south, all withdrawal routes for the Japanese in south Manila were closed.

The Japanese soldiers who had spent the night in the backyard of Red Cross headquarters on Isaac Peral in Ermita upon waking this morning toured the building. They inspected rooms, looked into storage bins, watched the Red Cross staff attend to the wounded among the refugees.[7]

Two Red Cross flags which hang infront of the building had fallen during the night. A Red Cross worker was going to run them up again. The Japanese prevented him. Now the building was not identifiable from outside.

At dawn, the Gutierrez family of 613 Remedios street in Malate is up. Fourteen-year-old Lydia Gutierrez writes in her diary: "We are preparing to run away. For my knapsack I got a nepa bag and put one change of clothing, my veil, rosary and some clean strips of cloth in case anyone got wounded. Mama gave each of us rice, red beans and some money. We also were given a tag with our name and address written in india ink. We pinned it with our blessed miraculous medals. We were never to remove it."[8]

Not far from the Gutierrez house, on Alonso street, Jose C. Villanueva, a distinguished writer and member of the staff of the House of Representatives in the pre-war government, lived with his family.[9]

The neighborhood was in flames. Many of their neighbors had fled their homes. Now their own home was in danger and flight seemed the only way out. Mrs. Villanueva remembered a family named Santos who lived on Vermont street adjacent to the Doctors' Hospital, and which they deemed safe. With the family of their neighbor, Major Alfonso Fresnido, bandmaster of the Philippine Constabulary before the war, the Villanuevas bundled up and dashed through the streets to the Santos home. Many people were already there, but the Santoses welcomed them just as well.

Several male refugees were out in the Santos yard when a Japanese patrol came by. The Japanese called the men out into the street, lined them up against the wall and shot each one down. Inside the house the other refugees cowered terror-stricken, but the Japanese did not enter the yard.

In the Soliven compound at the corner of San Marcelino and Herran, Mrs. Francisca Guinto-Juco and her five children and several other families now found the place untenable. The flames were closing in, the American artillery barrage fell in a carpet-pattern. The refugee party decided to flee.[10]

Now Mrs. Juco led her children out of the Soliven compound down Herran, intending to seek shelter at the Spanish consulate at the corner of Herran and Pennsylvania streets a block away. The Spanish consulate was believed neutral ground and the building provided considerable shelter. The Juco family, evading exploding shells on the street, was instead led to the opposite corner on Herran and Pennsylvania streets.

Estelita Juco, 14, recalls that the building may have been the Union Theological seminary. She recalls spending the night under the stairs, unable to find shelter elsewhere.

All around the Asilo de Looban on Isaac Peral street shells rained. Now the orphanage looked more like a hospital as wounded from within the compound and from without were brought into the corridors.[11]

At 7:30 this morning a shell from the American sector landed in the dining hall which at this hour was packed full of people. Several perished; several more were injured. The compound roiled in hysteria. A heavy pall of smoke enveloped the premises and now the roof of the chapel burst into flames. The fire spread rapidly and shortly, the famous Asilo de Looban over which the religious had labored for decades was reduced to ashes.

No one was hurt in the fire. The Daughters of Charity calmly herded their wards to safety and the officials and staff of the Tabacalera who were sheltered there were all safely evacuated.

This afternoon the Spanish religious detained at Fort Santiago were ordered back to San Agustin church and monastery. The Spanish civilians at Fort Santiago were also ordered out of their cells and marched back to San Agustin.

"In San Agustin we were well-treated," Father Belarmino de Celis, O.S.A., writes, "even though we suffered many inconveniences -- but in comparison with the past, we were well-treated."

Father de Celis notes that there were some Filipinos with the group, "but they were spies -- that is what they told us themselves."[12]

Of the 1,600 men of various nationalities who were ordered out of San Agustin on 7 February, 150 Spanish nationals returned to the church and monastery today. The Filipinos and Chinese remained at the Fort.

San Agustin was filled with a great mass of humanity. The church itself was jammed to capacity. So were the crypt, the refectory and the cloisters of the monastery, and the patios. The religious were confined in the sacristy. All over the church and monastery dead bodies lay, victims of the incessant shelling from the American sector.

But the shelling did not come from the American sector alone on this day.

The Japanese were able to lob in a few into the Santo Tomas camp, killing four American internees and two Filipino workers, wounding seven internees, three American soldiers and six Filipino workers.

In Santa Ana, a new sound came up to the windows: scurrying feet on the erstwhile deserted streets, and for once, happy, excited voices.

"They are here, at last," Marcial P. Lichauco exults in his diary.[13]

Now there were repeated on the Santa Ana streets the scenes that had met American soldiers everywhere they first appeared in the Philippines in this year of 1945. People laughing hysterically, weeping unashamedly, reaching out to touch, to hug, to kiss.

The distinguished Manila lawyer Marcial Lichauco brought his little daughter Cornelia out of the house for the first time in a long time, "to enable her to have her first look at a Yankee." Lichauco seemed inexplicably disappointed, though, because "the first dozen soldiers we met proved to be Texans." However, the Texans gave his little girl chewing gum. It was something completely new to the girl. "I have been having quite a time since then explaining to her how to enjoy it," Lichauco says.

Now the Franciscan parish priest of Santa Ana ordered the church bells to be rang. They had been silent these past several months. "People on the streets cheered when they heard the familiar chimes once more," Lichauco writes.

This morning the German Club on San Luis street in Ermita caught fire. Hundreds of refugees in the dugouts under the clubhouse roiled in pandemonium. They were choking from the thick smoke that swept into their shelters, but the Japanese shot down those who ran out.[14]

From his hideout Francisco Lopez saw the manager of the German Club whom he identified as Mr. Ohauss approach the Japanese to intercede in behalf of the refugees. He was repulsed.

A delegation of women cradling suckling babies with small children in tow, approached the Japanese to beg to be let out. They knelt before the troopers to plead in behalf of their families and the other refugees in the compound. Those in the shelters watched in horror as the Japanese bayonetted the children, flung away the babies, and started ripping off the women's clothes in attempts to abuse them.

Inside the dugout where the family of Francisco Lopez cowered, the men made a decision – to dash into the open, brave the Japanese menace, and try to seek safety, instead of being burned to death inside the shelter.

Francisco Lopez and his younger brother, over the remonstrations of their mother who pointed to them what was happening to those who dared go out into the yard, jumped over the burning debris. The two were greeted by a burst of gunfire. The younger brother fell dead, shot in the chest. They missed Francisco with the first burst, but his clothes were ablaze. He was slapping down the flames over his body when a bullet pierced his left foot. The pain was unbearable and Francisco Lopez lost consciousness.

In another dugout under the German Club building, the family of Remedios Rodriguez huddled closely together, listening to the explosions followed by screams coming from outside. The shelter was filling with smoke and people were gasping and choking by turns.

Now they saw grenades rolling to the mouth of their shelter, exploding with deafening impact. Over their terror, or probably indulging themselves in a self-delusion born of despair, the refugees came to a consensus, recalling a Japanese fondness for small children.

"Send out the children," they cried, "let them plead for us to go."

A delegation of five small boys, among them Remedios Rodriguez's 11-year-old son Augusto, went out the door. Remedios watched from the opening as the Japanese gunned down the innocent delegation, her son among them. Young Helena Rodriguez did not see this happen but she heard her mother cry out. Helena rushed to her side just as Remedios ran out, probably to retrieve her son's body. At this moment a hand-grenade landed before her, and Helena watched her mother's body come apart in a deafening explosion. The girl dashed inside the shelter and withdrew to a dark corner.

In shock from witnessing her mother's death by hand-grenade, Helena Rodriguez, in her remote corner in the shelter under the German Club, now heard a new sound, like newspapers crackling, she thought. It was the building on fire crumbling over her head.

Helena Rodriguez watched a man jump out the burning exit. She followed. The fire seared her arms and legs, scorched her face and singed her hair. A few steps from the door she fell into a foxhole. As it happened, the man had preceded her in the hole. Within minutes, one woman who turned out to be a family friend, and another man fell on her in the foxhole.

Helena Rodriguez hurt painfully from her burns and the others pressed on her in the narrow foxhole which was intended for one person. But she kept still. The others too feigned death. They could hear Japanese calling to each other, sometimes laughing in glee. They could hear gunfire and explosions and screams of pain and terror.

In another part of the German Club compound on San Luis street, Francisco Lopez lay on the ground, slowly regaining consciousness. His left foot was torn by a bullet and his burns hurt. He could not move. But he thought he could identify the voices of his mother, his brother, his sister and his cousins in the shelter he had escaped from, their screams piercing his ears over the terrifying sound of the holocaust.

From where he lay Francisco Lopez saw one of the family servants, Bernardino Callo, 20, skip out of the burning shelter with a two-year-old-boy in his arms. A Japanese with a bamboo spear ran after him and stuck the baby boy. Bernardino Callo let go the dying baby and fought the Japanese for possession of the bamboo spear. Other Japanese joined the struggle and Bernardino was overpowered. Now they tore off the man's trousers. While some Japanese pinned him to the ground, the others cut off his genitals and stuck it into his mouth. Around the agonizing

Bernardino Callo, twenty-years-old, members of the party stomped their feet and laughed and roared in glee as the terrified Francisco Lopez watched on the ground.

Under heavy shelling from the American sector, the Nathorst group had moved into one of the shelters under the German Club building. When the building caught fire, Nurse Asuncion Marbas found herself cowering behind a wall of mattresses. Six times hand-grenades were exploded in the shelter but Asuncion Marbas was safe behind the mattresses.

When the heat in the dugout became unbearable, the nurse of the retired General Nathorst dashed through the flaming exit, suffering burns in the process. She ran in the direction of the wall which separated the German Club compound from the Paules church and seminary complex. In a shallow crater caused by a exploding shell, she crouched on all fours. She saw the Japanese firing at people who stood or moved in the compound. Now a band of three Japanese soldiers discovered her, still prostrate on the ground. One of them poked his bayonet at her buttocks.

Three times the Japanese stuck the nurse's behind with the bayonet, not a violent, murderous thrust, but a playful mischievous poke. More angry than hurt, Asuncion Marbas held her temper. The Japanese knew she was faking. Now they arranged combustible material around her head and tried to light the pile. Their matches would not light. In disgust they flung the matchbox at her head and left. Shortly they were back with a bottle of rum and a choice piece of roast chicken which they set within her reach. They waited, chuckling speculatively, chattering in Japanese among themselves. The nurse kept still and held her breath. The Japanese left her, taking with them the rum and the roast chicken.

Asuncion Marbas waited for darkness to make her escape from the German Club. She never saw nor heard from the Nathorst family again.

Francisco Lopez, hurting from serious burns and a shattered foot, crawled from the German Club premises to an air-raid shelter in an adjoining property on San Luis street. When night fell he was joined here by nine others, men and women. The hole in the ground over which the building had collapsed could hold only five bodies. Now there were ten. Each one was wounded. When one of the ten moved, the others groaned painfully. They had neither food nor water. One of them found a length of iron bar. He started digging in the earth. Soon he hit water. The water was more like mud, but it sustained the group for the three days they stayed in the dugout.

This morning the distress of the refugee community at De la Salle college on Taft Avenue heightened as the area seems to have become the focus of the bombardment from the American sector. The refectory received a direct hit. Dr. Antonio Cojuangco, Sr., sustained a slight wound from stray bit of shrapnel and was attended to by his brother-in-law, Dr. Clemente Uychuico.[15]

Now the residents congregated in the foyer on the ground floor which appeared to be the safest area in the south wing. The foot of the staircase by the wine cellar's door was a favored spot. Led by Brother Romuald and Brother Friedbert by turns, the residents recited the rosary in continuous relays.

Each time the locale came into the focus of the shelling-Father Cosgrave would give general absolution as everyone lapsed into morbid silence broken only by frightened gasps and exclamations.

The priest conducted his daily Mass at the chapel door on the second floor instead of at the altar. The interior of the chapel, with balconies open on both sides, was not considered safe. Here at the entrance to the chapel, the three-year-old adopted son of the Cojuangcos, Ricardo Bartolome, was baptized this morning.

This morning, Elpidio Quirino finally reached his mother-in-law's home at the corner of Colorado and California streets, and was reunited with his children, Tommy and Vicky. He learned of the fate that had befallen his wife and two daughters. He agonized over the fate of Armando.[16]

This morning, the Quirinos and Mendozas attempted to recover the bodies that lay at the streetcorner. The shelling never let up and they could only retrieve the body of the baby. Now they buried little Fe Angela, two-years-old, in the open space by her grandmother's garage.

The Syquia home stood in the path of the flames. There was no lull in the shelling from the American sector. Now the Quirinos, the Mendozas and the Syquias bundled a few necessities and trooped in terror-stricken relays up the block where they found shelter in the home of the Rodriguez family along Herran street, between Colorado and Pennsylvania.

But there was no sanctuary here, either, and the clan again picked up kit-and-caboodle and dashed down Herran and around the block up Pennsylvania, where it crashed as a body into a building just before the corner on Tennessee street.

This afternoon fire reached the area on Pennsylvania street in Ermita where the residence of Dr. Jose Celeste stood. A squad of Japanese soldiers entered the compound and called Dr. Celeste out of the house.

Confronted with bayonets to his chest, Dr. Celeste cried, "I am a vice minister," while waving his identification papers. The Japanese fired and Celeste crumpled to the ground.

Now the Japanese sprayed the interior of the house with machine gun-fire. Those inside who were not hit ran out and were met with bullets by the Japanese waiting outside.

The nurse, Carolina Coruna, wounded in the legs and unable to stand, lay inside the air-raid shelter in the yard.[17]

Among those who rushed out of the house when the shooting started was Mrs. Jose Celeste. She was injured only slightly but she fell under several bodies.

For several hours Mrs. Celeste lay where she fell, dead bodies atop and beside her. She dared not move from where she lay, as a Japanese soldier stood guard over the compound. After a while, unable to contain herself, she spoke in a whisper and said, "I am Mama, if any of my children is alive please speak to me."

Another whisper, not far from where she lay, reached her: "Mama, I am alive too."[18]

The two lay quiet and still among the mass of dead bodies which, as the day passed began to stink. Japanese soldiers still moved outside the gate. Hours passed and all the two heard was the sound of exploding shell and machine gun-fire.

Then the child said, "Mama, I am hungry. Father is dead and already smells." The mother, a few yards away, advised the child to urinate into a piece of cloth without standing up, and squeeze the piece of cloth over her mouth.

Jose Carcereny Barta, a Spanish national, lived with his family at 552-A Pennsylvania street, between California and Oregon streets in Ermita, close to the Celeste compound. The family included Carcereny's two sons, the elder of whom was married, with a two-year-old boy of his own.

At one o'clock this afternoon the fire which had been raging in their neighborhood came dangerously close to the rented apartment of the Carcerenys. With their landlords, Dr. and Mrs. Joaquin Marañon, and residents of adjoining houses, they decided to flee. Out of their gate they dashed around the corner from Pennsylvania to California street into the Price compound.[19]

The Price mansion was built of stone and brick and was surrounded by a high concrete wall. The building was large, set in a spacious garden. It offered considerable shelter from the incessant shelling. Actually the property abutted the Marañon's but the main entrance was on California, with a sidegate on Colorado street.

The Carcereny party huddled on the driveway leading to California street. Presently a group of Japanese came up the gate and set-up a machine gun facing the Carcereny group which numbered 25 men, women and children. The men in the group remonstrated with the Japanese. There are mostly women and children here, they said. The Japanese withdrew with their machine gun.

At about 4 o'clock this afternoon another squad of Japanese entered the Price compound. They ordered those inside the house to get out, and motioned those outside towards the garage at the back. Before the Carcerenys could reach the garage, the Japanese opened fire. The people dropped like flies before the machine gun and rifle fire. Before his eyes the critically wounded Jose Carcereny Barta saw his two sons die together with his daughter-in-law and his two-year-old grandson. Those who did not die instantly were bayonetted where they lay until they were still.

At about 7 o'clock this evening another band of Japanese entered the Price compound through the Colorado sidegate. The survivors of the earlier assault had moved along the front wall on the California street side. Now they were discovered here by the Japanese. It was their turn to face the machine guns.

Over the cries of the wounded and the dying in the garden outside, the Japanese entered the house and found stocks of whiskey. Now they broke open the bottles and launched into a drinking spree. Shortly they were singing, in disorganized choruses, Japanese schoolboy and army marching songs, accompanied by rhythmic hand-clapping.

Outside, Dr. Joaquin Marañon, a distinguished scientist in the Bureau of Science, felt one side of his face growing numb. Blood was flowing into his shirtfront from a headwound. He saw his wife nearby with a shattered leg, trying to get to him. Dr. Marañon signalled her to keep still. Inside the house, the Japanese sang boisterously and made merry, the sound of glass breaking on the floor rising sharply above the cries of the dying and the unending staccato of the American shells.

Not far from this point, on Colorado street, a big group cowered at the gound floor of the Mascuñana property. Several family groups left the shelter today. The place had become so congested that everyone sat haunched up, without space to extend ones legs. Incessantly children cried, and the pet dogs whimpered and howled.[20]

"If a shell hit the house," Doña Paz de Mascuñana pondered wearily, "would an orderly exit be possible?"

A sudden shift of the wind had spared some buildings on this side of the street from the fires and Mrs. Mascuñana's brothers with their families had left for nearby houses still standing. But even while others left the shelter, many others came in, driven away from San Marcelino and General

Luna streets.

Now Judge Manuel V. del Rosario came into the Mascuñana shelter and invited the couple to his house nearby "to straighten out our backs," according to Mrs. Mascuñana who had spent the past two nights sitting up, so tight was the space. She found the judge's invitation irresistible.

A casualty of the previous day's shelling was being buried in Judge del Rosario's garden. The widow and her son were in Mrs. Mascuñana's house-turned-shelter, and requested her to bring back the man's watch and ring. Mrs. Mascuñana obliged and proceeded to Judge del Rosario's, accompanied by husband Ricardo. But Ricardo Mascuñana did not stay to enjoy the beds laid out in the judge's living room. He hurried back to his own shelter.

Mrs. Mascuñana stayed to enjoy the luxurious armchairs. Presently she jumped and dove under the dining table at the sound of shells exploding all around. She was joined by Mr. and Mrs. Ramon Zaragoza, their daughter and son-in-law, and a niece. Mrs. Zaragoza was Doña Paz's sister.

"How difficult it is to have to contort this way at our age," Ramon Zaragoza remarked to Doña Paz, keeping his head down.

"Patience, Ramon," she replied, her head down also. "This is the last time we have to bow to Hirohito."

Just then the sound of screams and gun-fire came from the adjoining property. Mrs. Mascuñana rushed to the window and saw a band of Japanese going up the house of Col. Telesforo Martinez next door. She skipped down the stairs to her own house.

To her surprise she found her group quite happy, smiling with balls of boiled rice in their hands. "The Japanese have been here and gave us rice," she was told.

Now Mrs. Mascuñana would exclaim, "Who can decipher what goes on in the minds of these Japanese?"

In the next lot the Japanese gunned down several persons, and here they gave out gifts of boiled rice. They had ordered the men out of the Martinez property to the garden, turning away the women and children. The men were lined against a wall and the Japanese let go with the machine guns. Not all were killed. Two in the group, Ernesto Lagdameo and Juan La O, though badly wounded, crawled to the Mascuñana shelter where they were given first aid.

Now Mrs. Mascuñana went with the other women to see what happened in the Martinez compound. They found Ramon Zaragoza dead, Joaquin and Luis Rojo and their father apparently dead, Col. Telesforo Martinez and his son dead. They found Paco Marin, his intestines on his lap, dying. Several male servants of the respective families in the neighborhood were dead.

At *La Casona*, the home of the Chicote family on San Carlos street, the rest of the Chicotes awaited Adelina's return from the clinic on A. Mabini street. When by this afternoon, she did not come home, they decided she had stayed at the clinic probably owing to restrictions imposed by the Japanese.

When Adelina Chicote did not arrive at the clinic on A. Mabini in Ermita all through yesterday, her mother and sister who were confined there thought that conditions on the streets had made it impossible for her to undertake her chore.

Malate today seemed to be the target of American shelling. A good part of Wright street was on fire. The home of Gonzalo Yrezabal where the family of Jose Goicochea had found refuge was surrounded on four sides by burning houses. The Yrezabals decided to flee, and with them their houseguests.[20]

Shouldering their few bundles, the Goicocheas raced up the street, their seven-year-old son and his nursemaid scurrying behind them. Suddenly Pilar Chicote de Goicochea collapsed, hit by shrapnel. Leaving his son and his nursemaid with the Yrezabals, Jose Goicochea took his wife in his arms and through the flaming streets and amidst the exploding shells carried her towards the Philippine General hospital, three blocks away.

At one intersection Goicochea came upon a building still untouched by fire and miraculously spared by shell, over which a Red Cross flag fluttered. It might have been the residence of Dr. Antonio Vasquez on Wright and Vermont streets which had been converted into an emergency hospital. Here the doctor in attendance, probably Dr. Vasquez himself, told Jose Goicochea that his wife's injuries required more assistance than he could provide. He advised that she be brought to the Philippine General hospital.

Again Jose Goicochea gathered the torn body of his wife into his arms and himself half-dead from anguish and fright sought salvation in the hospital. It was so close from this point he knew, yet under battle-conditions, so incredibly distant.

Jose Goicochea did reach the gates of the PGH. Here, he too, fell, this Spaniard whom fate had stranded on Philippine earth, whether from a Japanese bullet or a piece of American shrapnel, no one could tell. Pilar Chicote may have already been dead in her husband's arms when he fell.

Dolores Iturralde, 17, lived with her parents, two brothers and three sisters, in rented quarters in a building on San Marcelino street in the Singalong district of Manila.[22]

At 10 o'clock this morning during the heavy artillery barrage a shell tore away the roof of the house. Dolores reeled from the impact but managed to skip downstairs, in an effort to find cover under the house.

As she ran she did not feel the shrapnel tear into her right leg, just above the knee, but she saw the white bone protruding out of the hideous wound. The explosion had temporarily deafened her. The neighborhood was in chaos and everyone dashed in every direction as shells peppered the area. Dolores felt herself soaking in blood. Another bit of shrapnel had nicked her nape and it was bleeding profusely.

Under the same barrage, Dolores recalls that the 3-month-old baby girl of Police Lt. Bernardino Versoza, a neighbor, was killed by shrapnel. Another neighbor, Pablo Cañizares, principal of the Singalong elementary school where Dolores had studied, fell seriously wounded.

Dolores Iturralde's family got the neighborhood first aider to apply a tourniquet on the shattered leg. They improvised a stretcher from a wooden plank on which the 17-year-old girl was brought through the blazing streets to the Philippine General hospital. The first aid party braved exploding shells, landmines and trigger-happy Japanese, but eventually reached PGH.

One look at the girl's injuries and the doctor said the leg could not be saved under the emergency conditions then availing. When she regained consciousness, Dolores Iturralde, 17, was without her right leg.

From behind the shutters of his home on Nebraska street in Ermita the Unknown Diarist of the *Free Philippines* looked down the street below. He saw a boy with a pushcart containing four cans of water. A Japanese sentry stood about 20 meters behind the boy. Now the sentry aimed coolly and fired. The boy crashed to earth. The soldier strode to the side of the fallen youth. When the boy, not yet dead, lifted his face, the Japanese thrust his bayonet into the victim's back. He kicked the boy on the head.[23]

"There were more shots in the distance," our Unknown Diarist writes of his experience on this day. "Later I saw the bodies of the dead."

This afternoon a terrific explosion tore up the Union Church at the corner of Padre Faura and A. Mabini streets in Ermita. A big blaze sprang up and soon the entire neighborhood was on fire.

"I did not know what to do," our Unknown Diarist writes. He went upstairs and looked out the window. He saw Japanese enter the nearby Nebraska Hall, a dormitory for men, with gasoline cans. Then they came out and went into the Ateneo de Manila college compound. Fifteen minutes later, the Nebraska Hall was ablaze.

Almost at the same time as the Union Church, the Ermita parish church on M.H. del Pilar street went up in flames. In the same compound were the parish house and the Ermita Catholic school. From the church the fire spread to these edifices, and from here on up along Mabini street towards Isaac Peral northward, and to Padre Faura to the south. The parish was in the care of the Capuchin Fathers who now, with their staff, sought refuge in a nearby concrete building.

In the same area was the St. Joseph's Academy run by the Religious of the Virgin Mary. When the fire endangered their quarters in the premises, the nuns dashed for shelter to the Ateneo de Manila compound.

Also at this time, a huge explosion blew up the University of the Philippines boys' high school building on Florida street. The building had recently been vacated by Japanese soldiers who were billeted here.

The Ateneo de Manila campus across Padre Faura street from the University of the Philippines, covered about 50,000 sq.m. of choice real estate in Manila's primary district outside the Walled City. It abutted the Philippine General hospital compound on the east. In the campus were the main academic building, the famous Manila Observatory, the auditorium, the gymnasium, the laboratories, the library and the chapel. The Ateneo buildings were of concrete, some were of wood, others of mixed materials, with the lower floors of volcanic rock and the upper floors of wood.

"When the house right across from ours caught fire," our Unknown Diarist writes, "I decided to risk it and run. With my wife and children I made as fast as I could for the Ateneo. The Japanese fired at us but we got across safely."

Others were not so fortunate. One was a nun, probably from the St. Joseph's Academy. She had reached the Ateneo compound safely. Then she went to a Japanese sentry at the gate and asked if she could get her bundle which was lying on the sidewalk across the street. The Japanese said "No", so the nun turned to go back into the building. When she turned, the Japanese shot her in the back and she dropped dead.

When the Union Church was blown up and the fire spread down Padre Faura and towards M.H. del Pilar, Sophy Natalie Morgin and the other residents in her apartment house bundled up what they could and fled the building.[24]

The entire area was in flames and salvation seemed to lie in the direction of Dewey boulevard. "But a Japanese with a revolver ordered us not to go near the boulevard," Sophy writes, "or he would shoot."

The only alternative for the group was to seek shelter in the garage of the adjoining Valdez apartments which was itself burning. Many in the party would not stay in the premises of the burning building. "But I stayed," Sophy writes, "as I knew the stone building would not collapse."

Soon there were about 150 people in the garage of the Valdez apartments. The building finally burned down and from the garage many moved into the still-smoking ruins.

The whole night shells exploded all over the grounds. Miss Morgin lay under a mattress. She heard the cries of fellow refugees who were hit by shrapnel. She saw people rush out in panic and drop dead in their tracks, hit by American shrapnel or Japanese sniper fire.

At 7 o'clock this morning a band of Japanese discovered the bomb-shelter in the truck garden between the Paules church and the jai-alai fronton on Taft Avenue.

Through air vents on the roof of the shelter, the Japanese poked their rifles and fired at the people inside. Then they hurled grenades into the shelter.

When the smoke cleared, six of the eight Chinese and one of the two Filipinos inside were dead. One of the two Chinese survivors was Co Ching. He gave testimony to the fate of his group.[25]

When the Japanese had gone, the survivors dragged out the dead and piled them by the entrance to the shelter.

At around 10 o'clock this evening, the men inside the shelter heard a faint rapping on their door. Peering out they saw a civilian whose shirt front was bloodied all over. It was the Chinese Sing Koh who had escaped from the *estero* behind the Paules church near this point the previous night. He was badly wounded in the neck. He told the others what he saw happened to the Vincentian Fathers last night. In about 30 minutes, Sing Koh was dead.

Benjamin Urrutia at this time lived at 1151 Singalong street in Paco.[26] At about 3 o'clock this afternoon, he was ordered out of his home by the Japanese to another house at 1186 up the same street. Here Urrutia joined about 200 other men whose hands were already tied behind their backs. Now the men were blindfolded and one at a time were led inside the house. A hole had been knocked out of one wall in the house. As it turned out, a large hole had been dug in the ground below the wall. As a man was led towards the hole in the wall, a Japanese officer would put an arm around him and tell him gently, "The Japanese and Filipinos are good friends." Another Japanese would slash at the man's neck with a saber, and the man would hurtle through the hole in the wall into the hole waiting in the ground below.

Now Benjamin Urrutia, blindfolded, his hands tied behind him, heard the Japanese officer say sympathetically, "The Japanese and Filipinos are good friends." Then Urrutia felt a stunning blow across the face. He felt blood spurt out of his nose and mouth and found himself falling. He landed on top of other bodies in the hole in the ground.

Benjamin Urrutia lay where he fell choking in his own blood. Although in extreme pain, he stayed conscious. Now he felt loose earth falling on him. The hole into which he had fallen was being filled in. The earth piled over him. Now Banjamin Urrutia could not breathe. A great heavy load sat on his chest. The blood in his throat throttled him. He lost consciousness.

For how long Urrutia lay half-buried with a mass of other bodies in the hole, he could not tell. When he came to, the blindfold was loose under his chin, but he could not see anything. He thought he had gone blind. Actually it was late into the night, and it was pitch-dark.

Benjamin Urrutia lay half-buried. His head was lightly covered, but his torso and lower limbs were under heavy layers of loose earth. With great difficulty he raised his body and pulled his limbs from under the earth-pile, inch-by-inch, one leg at a time. His hands were still tied behind him. Now he was free. He stood up on wobbly legs and ran, the while shaking off his bonds.

Federico Davantes lived at 1170 F. Muñoz street in Paco.[27] At 3 o'clock this afternoon, he was taken from his home by Japanese soldiers to nearby Remy street, and with about 200 others already assembled there, was marched to the bank of the Estero de Tripa Gallina which cut through this section of the city. The men had their hands tied behind their backs. One-by-one they were brought to a spot by the waterline where a Japanese swung with his sword at their necks and pushed them into the water. Those who thrashed about in the water or cried out were shot by another Japanese who stood by with a rifle.

When it was the turn of Federico Davantes to stand at the spot by the *estero,* he cried piteously, "Tomodachi! Kodomo takusan!" His Japanese pidgin was supposed to mean, "I am a friend. Have pity, I have many children."

Terror-stricken and hardly coherent, Federico Davantes circled around the Japanese with the sword. Each time the Japanese took a step towards him, Federico took two steps backward. Inexorably the Japanese came closer. Davantes edged away warily, growing hoarse shouting, "Tomodachi! Kodomo takusan!" The Japanese kept coming. Again Davantes stepped back, this time right over the clay bank into the water. He tumbled over the dead and the dying and found himself sinking. When he bobbed up, his head was covered with water lily which camouflaged him effectively. The Japanese looked but could not see him.

When any of wounded in the water cried out, the Japanese on the *estero* bank shot him until he was quiet. Davantes kept quiet. Now he lost his footing in the shallow water and the water lily over his head floated away. The Japanese saw him and fired. Davantes dove into the muddy water now tinged with red. Everytime Davantes came up for air, he was fired at. Federico Davantes found himself moving slowly towards the opposite bank. His hands were still tied behind him and he could not raise himself over the water's edge.

At about midnight, when he was certain the Japanese had gone, Federico Davantes lifted himself out of the water to the other side of the *estero*. In the darkness he could discern the mass of dead bodies in the shallow waterway.

Jose Cabañero also lived on F. Muñoz street in Paco.[28] At 3 o'clock this afternoon, Jose and his brother Felicisimo and their cousin Jose Dicini were digging a bomb-shelter in their backyard when a band of Japanese marines came upon them. The three were made to abandon what they were doing and were led to a large building on Remy street where they joined about 200 other men. The men were lined up along F. Muñoz and San Isidro streets and then were marched to a point by the *estero* farther along Muñoz street. Here Cabanero's group found about 150 others, their hands tied behind their back. Now the Japanese proceeded to bind the hands of the new arrivals. Presently the area came under heavy shelling from the American sector and the group, now almost 400 strong, was marched back to the area on Remy street near Muñoz and Dart. One at a time the men were ordered to step forward and made to walk around a corner. Each time a man disappeared around the corner Jose Cabañero heard one rifle shot. The man would not return and the next man in the line would be called forward.

Jose Cabañero managed to loosen the twine that bound his wrists behind him. When he was ordered to step forward he slipped off his bonds and launched into a wild gallop. The Japanese on guard fired at him but missed. Another Japanese fired at him and missed too. Now Jose was gaining distance. Suddenly a Japanese officer appeared on his path. Jose detoured and did not slacken his mad dash. The Japanese officer gave chase, swinging his saber all the while. Jose was exhausted. The Japanese closed on him until, still swinging his saber, he gashed Jose on the nape.

Jose Cabañero stumbled headlong, his face hitting the dirt. The Japanese officer came at him with a two-handed grip on the saber and swung at his neck. Jose thrashed about, his head suddenly loose at its base. The Japanese officer kicked him over on his back. He slashed at the fallen man again, slicing off his nose. Twice he slashed at Jose, each time flicking off bits of his right ear. Jose rolled on the ground. Now the Japanese pinned him down with his saber. Twice the Japanese stuck his saber into the man on the ground, one thrust piercing through the chest to the back. Now the Japanese officer, spent, stalked away, leaving Jose Cabañero for dead.

Jose writhed in agony and pressed one hand to the wound at the back of his neck which hurt most. He lost consciousness.

Jose Cabañero was not disturbed where he lay. When he came to, he could not open his eyes. Blood had dried over his eyelids, holding them down tightly. He scraped off the dried blood, little by little, until he could see. He estimated that it was almost midnight. Now Jose Cabañero pulled himself up and realizing that he was not too far from his own home, he crawled away. He never saw his brother and his cousin again.

At about 5 o'clock this afternoon, the brown Filipino women in the Bayview hotel were separated from the Caucasians and mestizas. About 150 Filipinas were taken to the Alhambra apartment hotel on the street at the back of Bayview, and about 30 were brought to the Miramar apartment nearby on Roxas Boulevard.

At the Alhambra apartments the women were brought to a large hall on the second storey where they huddled on the bare floor. The Japanese marines and soldiers would come in at all hours, day and night, and force their choice of the assembled women to go with them to any of the rooms in the hotel. The women would return to the big hall, dishevelled, weeping and often, bleeding.

One woman sat on the floor nursing her baby. A Japanese seemed to take a fancy on her. "I give you beer," he told her. "No, go away," she said. "I give your baby milk," he said. "We'd rather die," she answered. The Japanese pinched the baby until it screamed in pain. Then he went away.[29]

Back at the Mascuñana shelter a few houses from the Martinez home on Colorado street, a band of Japanese entered the premises and splashed gasoline on the wooden doors and window shutters.[30] Others stood by with rifles on the ready. The gasoline was ignited and when the people tried to beat down the flames, the Japanese gunned them down. Many fell wounded, including Mrs. Mascuñana's brother-in-law Agustin Moreno and his son Ernesto. The flames spread rapidly and soon the house was enveloped by the fire. The refugees had to flee, abandoning the fallen to the flames.

The Japanese fired at the fleeing crowd, milling on the lawn. Now people ran for the breaches on the walls that lead to Oregon street, intending to make it to the Philippine General hospital two blocks away. However, groups of Japanese stood outside on Oregon. The only way to reach Oregon street was to cut through the Martinez grounds where dead bodies lay asprawl in the backyard. Rushing on the others' heels, Mrs. Mascuñana was stunned to come upon the two Rojo sons, Joaquin and Luis, still alive, but their legs shattered. She had passed them up for dead. Helpless in the circumstances, Mrs. Mascuñana started for the exit when hobnailed steps approached, apparently attracted by the cries of the two boys pleading for help. She hurried back to the boys on the ground, but she could not do anything for them. Now the Japanese came through the breach on the wall on Oregon street. The refugees were made to raise their arms over their heads and ordered to go up the staircase of the Martinez house which was already burning.

"They are going to burn us alive," Mrs. Mascuñana realized. Any thought of resistance collapsed. "Not even a dull knife . . . not even a stick within reach . . ."

A woman who spoke Japanese headed for the officer who seemed to be in-charge. The Japanese officer turned to his companions who ordered the refugees to come down the burning house. Now the group was conducted across the lawn and out the exits to Oregon street.

The group asked to go to the PGH, but was told it was dangerous to move in the streets. They were instead taken to two small adjoining houses along Oregon. Here the families of Judge Felix Bautista and Luis Castillo were taken to the upper floor as hostages, and the rest now crowded into the lower floors. "We were packed like sardines," Mrs. Mascuñana writes in her diary.

Nearby, what Mrs. Mascuñana thought to be a Japanese artillery unit kept up incessant replies to the shelling from the American side. The Mascuñana group spent the night tightly wedged in their designated quarters, half-deaf from the shelling that went on outside.

Mrs. Mascuñana noted a Japanese in an acacia tree nearby who aimed potshots at them. "Happily," she writes, "he was such a poor shot that he hit no one . . ." He caused such an agitation among the refugees, however, that another Japanese soldier poked his head inside the door to command silence. He was told that the children were thirsty and the Japanese disappeared. Shortly he was back with a steel drum full of water.

"Like a dream," Doña Paz writes, ". . . so unbelievable, but there he was!"

All throughout this day the 16 men in the YMCA dormitory at the corner of Oregon and Pennsylvania streets in Ermita huddled in fear as the neighborhood burned. At 7 o'clock this evening the YMCA building caught fire. The Japanese sentry at the gate had gone and the men rushed into the street. There was a burnt-out area on Padre Faura street between Pennsylvania and Colorado where a crowd from the neighborhood had assembled. The men from the YMCA joined the crowd.[31]

While rushing out from the YMCA building a Japanese soldier accosted James Papa, Jr., 28, an American national. James stood out for being fair. The Japanese fired and James Papa, Jr. fell, hit point-black in the chest. A companion from the YMCA group, Manuel Sotto, and Antonio de Mayo, the young cook of Aquiles Laguda, picked James Papa, Jr. up from where he fell and carried him to the sidewalk. Papa advised the two to leave him and save themselves. Sotto and de Mayo joined the group scurrying to the vacant lot on Padre Faura street.

The Rosenzwaigs had remained at the house painted green behind their burned-out home on San Marcelino street. At 7 o'clock this evening the green house too caught fire. Franz Rosenzwaig, Russian expatriate, gathered his small family composed of his wife Maria and daughter Vera, and joined the crowd at the burnt-out area on Padre Faura street. Mrs. Sofia Afanaseff, crippled by a wound in the leg, was abandoned in the burning house.

When the de la Paz home on Colorado street where they were refugees burned down, the family of James Woo, Sr. sought shelter in the ruins of their own home which had burned down earlier on the same street. Prof. Delfin de la Paz himself with his family moved over to the vacant lot on Padre Faura street.

At 7 o'clock this evening the Woos were called out of their shelter by the Japanese who were rounding up people in the neighborhood. The Woos and several others joined the crowd gathered in the burnt-out area on Padre Faura street, now numbering 400 men, women and children, in Mrs. Woo's estimate. There were Filipinos, Chinese, Spanish and Indian nationals in the group.

Under the Japanese guard the crowd moved out of the vacant lot and marched up Padre Faura. At the corner of Padre Faura and Taft Avenue, the crowd was halted and the Japanese separated the men and boys over 12 from the women and small children.

In the confusion, Maria Rosenzwaig and her daughter Vera were separated from her husband Franz. Now Maria saw her husband on the opposite corner on Taft Avenue and Padre Faura. She ran to him intending to get from him a suitcase containing money and jewelry. The Japanese prevented her.

The women and children, among them Mrs. James Woo, Sr. and Mrs. Franz Rosenzwaig, were led to the Philippine General hospital. They would not see their men again.

Now about 300 men and boys stood in two lines that stretched along Taft Avenue southward from Padre Faura street. In the group were former Supreme Court Justice Anacleto Diaz, 65, who was in a wheelchair, and his two sons, Teodoro, 35, and Carlos, 30.

When the women and children had gone, two Japanese soldiers with machine guns went down the line firing at the men. Before the machine guns the men fell like the proverbial stalks before the scythe. The Japanese came back up the line firing methodically at the men thrashing and moaning on the ground.

Priscilo Mendiola, 33, stood in line with the other men. At the first machine gun-burst, he was knocked to the ground, although he was not wounded himself. Someone who lay wounded behind him cried out in agony. A Japanese came over and bayonetted the man into silence. Priscilo Mendiola desperately tried to get back to his feet.

At this moment a Japanese aimed a .45 calibre pistol and hit him in the back. Another came at him with a bayonet. Numbed by fear, Priscilo Mendiola did not seem to feel his wounds. He stayed conscious all the time and lay immobile on the ground.

Antonio de Mayo, 18, the cook of Aquiles Laguda, stood in the second line, at the back. When those in front were hit by the first burst of machine gun-fire, they crashed on the second line. Antonio de Mayo was not hit, but now he found himself asprawl on the ground. He raised his head and saw his employer Aquiles Laguda dead beside him. Antonio lay still.

Alfredo V. Lagmay was a student. When their home went up in flames, Lagmay and his family got caught up with the crowd in the vacant lot on Padre Faura street off Colorado.

Lagmay recalls being lined up with the other males, one hundred in his estimate, in front of Corona restaurant on Padre Faura street. Then the onslaught began.

Lagmay testified: "They struck with their sabers, sir, and the soldiers joined in with bayonets and with their iron-pointed poles, sir. Kept on thrusting up and down the line."

Lagmay stood at the end of the line. He was not hit by the machine gun-fire, but an officer came up to him where he remained on his feet and slashed at him with his saber. Alfredo agilely jumped beyond reach. He did not see the Japanese soldier approach from another side and fire with his rifle three feet away. Lagmay was hit in the arm and fell. As he fell, the officer swung at him again. Slashed in the thigh, Lagmay lost consciousness.

Chua Kok Hun, 20, a Chinese student, was also way back in the line. When the Japanese started firing and those in front collapsed upon those behind, Chua fell under a mass of bodies. A Japanese soldier came up and bayonetted those who moved or cried out. A rifle butt hit Chua in the head, but he kept still.

Chua Kok Hun lay where he fell, weighted down by the dead. When he sensed that the Japanese had gone, he extricated himself from under the pile of bodies and crawled away. When he could, he got up and started running.

Antonio de Mayo, 18, was unhurt. He rolled on the ground away from the dead bodies, along the pavement on Padre Faura street. When he got his bearings he realized that he was behind the Bordner school. Nearby was a bomb shelter. Antonio jumped into the shelter.

When Alfredo Lagmay regained consciousness, he heard Japanese calling from the direction of thePhilippine General hospital. The Japanese who stood at the intersection of Padre Faura and Taft Avenue responded. Now this group walked away to join their fellows infront of the PGH.

Alfredo Lagmay, Priscilo Mendiola and the others who could make it to their feet got up and started running. Justice Anacleto Diaz and his two sons, Teodoro and Carlos, remained on the ground, dead. Professor Delfin de la Paz too, lay dead. His son Delfin, Jr., was wounded in the ankle. He crawled away to the bomb shelter behind the Bordner school where he found Antonio de Mayo. James Woo, Sr., his son and his four brothers, all lay still on the ground, dead.

Since early this morning vast crowds jammed the Red Cross headquarters building now turned into an emergency hospital on Isaac Peral street a block away from Padre Faura in Ermita. It was about the only building of strong construction left standing in the area. Refugees from all over the neighborhood sought shelter here.

Since Sunday, 4 February, the staff led by Modesto Farolan had been on round-the-clock duty. The wounded came in or were brought in from the streets.[32]

Physician and surgeon for the Red Cross emergency hospital was Dr. German de Venecia, a volunteer. Shortly before the outbreak of the war in 1941, Dr. de Venecia entered the service of the Philippine Red Cross as physician and surgeon and was appointed director of Red Cross Emergency Hospital No. 1 on Marques de Comillas street in Paco, where he served until the hospital was closed.

When news of American landings in Leyte reached Manila in October 1944, Dr. de Venecia again enlisted for Red Cross duty, this time as a volunteer. In the subsequent bombings of Manila by the Americans, Dr. de Venecia was attached to an ambulance unit which picked up the wounded on the streets who were given emergency first aid treatment while being rushed to hospitals.

At 10 o'clock this morning, Patrocinio Abad, 26, arrived at Red Cross headquarters on Isaac Peral street in Ermita from her Makati residence. She was a beautiful film star whose screen name was Corazon Noble. She had with her, her 10-month-old-baby girl Maria Lourdes Vera, her two brothers and several cousins.

Juan P. Juan, 47, a businessman, and his large family lived on General Luna street not far from Red Cross headquarters. When the house received a direct hit from an American shell this morning, Juan moved his family to another property he owned adjacent to the Red Cross compound from which it was separated only by an adobe wall.

With Juan P. Juan were his wife, the former Lucia Santos; his eldest daughter Juanita Juan-Marcelo and her four children; another daughter Paulina Juan-Zabala who had just given birth to a baby girl; a niece of Mrs. Juan, Nenita Recio de Santos and her two children, and several Juan sons-in-law. Because of the condition of Paulina and trusting to the moral authority of the Red Cross flag which flew over the building, Juan P. Juan this morning moved his entire brood over to the Red Cross headquarters.

A group of expatriate German Jews had rented the Juan property adjacent to the Red Cross compound. When the area came under heavy shelling this morning, the group, numbering ten, mostly elderly couples, gathered their bundles and went out to the street intending to go on to Pasay where one of them had a friend.

At the intersection on Taft Avenue and Isaac Peral the Japanese sentry intercepted the German Jews and prevented them from proceeding. The sentry gestured in the direction of Red Cross headquarters and the group entered the building.

There were at this time close to 100 men, women and children in the building which, although it had two storeys, was not very large. The German Jews pre-empted the women's toilet by the stairs on the ground floor and tried to make themselves comfortable there. Among them was the Kohnke family which included the husband-and-wife and their daughter Irene who was engaged to the bachelor in the group, John K. Lewy, 28.

In the afternoon the Juan men clambered over the wall in the backyard into their own property to prepare supper for their large party. The Juan women and children were left in the Red Cross building. Mrs. Lucia Santos-Juan was with the recuperating Paulina and her baby in the dispensary downstairs. In all, four women and seven children in the family of Juan P. Juan were in the Red Cross building.

At about 5 o'clock this afternoon a band of four Japanese marines approached the main entrance to the building fronting Isaac Peral street. Finding it locked, one of them fired through the wooden panel. A small girl who happened to be right behind the door inside fell, mortally wounded. The Japanese outside continued firing until the lock gave way.

When the Japanese crashed through the door, Patrocinio Abad was in the foyer by the main entrance, her 10-month-old baby in her arms. She saw the little girl at the door fall at the first sound of firing and heard the girl's mother scream as she rushed to pick the girl up. Patrocinio Abad a.k.a. Corazon Noble, popular film star, stood rooted to the floor and watched in horror as a Japanese marine came in and aim his rifle at her. Miss Abad sidled behind a nearby medicine cabinet, clutching her baby to her bosom. The medicine cabinet hid her body, but her right elbow stuck out. The Japanese fired, shattering Miss Abad's elbow. Leaning against the cabinet, she slid slowly to the floor.

The Japanese marine walked over to Patrocinio Abad a.k.a. Corazon Noble, popular film star in pre-war Manila. He stabbed the woman fallen on the floor. Nine times he thrust his bayonet into the woman on the floor. Patrocinio Abad was hit in the chest, in the abdomen, in the back, a rib was shattered, her legs were slashed, her arms were pierced. She tried to parry the thrusts, twisting here and there, screaming fearfully. She did not notice that her 10-month-old baby, stabbed three times, was dead in her arms.

When she heard the firing at the door, Red Cross nurse Gliceria Andaya, 32, turned into the corridor to investigate and there met the mother of the girl who had been shot, holding the body in her arms. Miss Andaya assisted the mother into the dispensary and left the two with Dr. de Venecia and Red Cross nurse Florita Loberiza, 32.

"Give her oxygen," Dr. de Venecia ordered Nurse Loberiza and she proceeded to do that. The doctor turned away to prepare for surgery.

Nurse Andaya went out with a girl who knew Japanese in an effort to find out what the marines wanted. In the corridor the Red Cross nurse confronted the Japanese marines. "This is a Red Cross hospital, we are Red Cross workers, these people are sick or are refugees," she remonstrated.

Hearing Miss Andaya's brave protestations the bloodied Patrocinio Abad, a.k.a. Corazon Noble, beautiful film star, looked up from where she lay in time to see the Red Cross nurse fall backwards, a bayonet stuck into her chest. The nurse was so stunned she did not utter a sound.

When the screaming and firing in the corridor did not stop, Dr. de Venecia motioned Nurse Loberiza to stop readying the dying little girl for surgery and both stepped out of the make-shift operating room.

This was the erstwhile conference room of the Philippine Red Cross. Half of it was now used as the office of the officer-in-charge, Modesto Farolan. The other half was equipped for emergency surgery.

Also in the room at this time were Modesto Farolan and Miss Marina de Paz, a refugee who served as a volunteer nursing assistant. A Japanese marine appeared at the door, bayonetted rifle on the ready. He aimed at Dr. de Venecia and fired twice in quick succession. The doctor fell dead. Farolan ducked under his desk. The Japanese fired at Miss de Paz and missed. Miss de Paz scampered to join Miss Loberiza who had moved quickly to cover herself with a mattress on the floor. The Japanese fired at Miss de Paz again and hit her in the back. He turned to two patients who had slipped off their cots to the floor. Each got a bayonet thrust. Both may have died instantly. The Japanese peered under the desk where Modesto Farolan crouched and fired twice. The bullets passed between Farolan's feet. The Japanese turned to the others in the dispensary, one of them the young Paulina Juan-Zabala with her 10-day-old baby, and the baby's grandmother, Mrs. Juan P. Juan. Successively he fired point blank at each, done with which he left the room.

Under his office desk Modesto Farolan froze. He could hear shooting from all over the building. He could hear screams of terror and pain, the agonized cries of women and children and the sound of feet scurrying in panic every which way.

From where she lay on the floor in the corridor, gasping for breath, Red Cross nurse Gliceria Andaya had heard Dr. de Venecia cry out the Tagalog expression of pain, "A-r-r-u-y!" Now she heard the Japanese shouting, "Americans, Americans!" They had discovered the German Jews in the women's toilet.

John K. Lewy was upstairs with others when the sound of shooting broke out in the ground floor. He ran down to warn his fellows in the women's toilet. A Japanese marine spotted him and followed him inside the toilet. Once discovered, the shooting and bayonetting of the Jews in the women's toilet began. Lewy lay on the floor beside Mr. Kohnke who was already dead from a bullet wound. Lewy got up. The Japanese shot him but missed. Now Lewy slipped into the second toilet stall and straddled the toilet seat, his back to the door, his hands over the back of his head. The Japanese entered the stall and Lewy felt the sharp bayonet rip into his hip. The Japanese struck again and thrust his bayonet through Lewy's thigh, pinning it to the wooden seat-cover where the bayonet got stuck. Now the Japanese wiggled the blade this way and that, trying to get it loose. Lewy fainted from pain. The Japanese left him for dead.[32]

A small Filipino girl had crept into the toilet with the German Jews. In a corner she cowered in terror. The Japanese ignored her. Only the little girl and Lewy survived the attack in the toilet.

The Juan men on the other side of the adobe wall separating the property from the Red Cross compound heard the shooting and screaming. Juan P. Juan's conclusion was, "Now they've discovered the Jews."

The husband of Paulina Zabala wanted to cross over the wall to be with his wife and new-born baby. He was stopped from doing so and Juan P. Juan ordered all the younger men into the house.

Romano Abad, brother of Patrocinio Abad, was in the backyard of the Red Cross building when the shooting started. He clambered over the wall into the Juan property.

Now Patrocinio Abad roused herself and assessed her injuries. Her wounds were grievous, her right arm was useless, her baby was dead. She scooped up the pitiful remains and crawled out as best she could into the backyard. Her brother Romano saw her over the wall and came down to pick her up. Patrocinio Abad handed over the bloody little bundle that was her 10-month-old baby and passed out.

The Japanese ransacked the Red Cross stores. Some helped themselves to a meager supper laid out on a table but which had not been touched.

At 10 p.m., hearing only moans and sobbing, Modesto Farolan dared to whisper and inquire whether anyone within hearing was alive. Miss Loberiza was unhurt but Miss de Paz was bleeding from the wound on her back. Farolan crept out of his shelter and cautiously looked around.

All through this day, deep into the night, the Japanese conducted a pogrom, as it were, in the districts of Paco and Ermita on the right bank of the Pasig in Manila.

Japanese teams would barge into homes and haul away males, variously from 12 or 14 up, bring them to assembly areas, and quite literally put them to the sword.

At the Paco home of Don Ismael Cruz, nephew of the national hero Jose Rizal, at the corner of California and General Luna streets, a Japanese band broke in and took away the houseowner and his two sons, the younger being Ismael Cruz, Jr., married to Carmen Guerrero.

Carmen Guerrero Cruz, mother of one and expecting another, never saw her husband or her in-laws again.

SUNDAY, 11 FEBRUARY 1945

At dawn today, Modesto Farolan climbed over the back wall in the Red Cross compound on Isaac Peral street in Ermita into the adjoining property. He scaled fences and crawled under houses, seeking cover where he could. He had seen a boy and a girl try to cross General Luna street and watched in horror as the Japanese sentry at the streetcorner felled them in succession with rifle shots.

All through this day Modesto Marolan cowered behind crates, lay down beside logs and watched as surrounding buildings caught fire and disappeared in smoke.[1]

So Ting, a Chinese, and his wife Ang Be, 38, lived with their children in an apartment in the Dee Cho lumber yard at 990 Isaac Peral street. The couple had four children aged three to seventeen. Living with the family at this time were So Ting's mother, his sisters and a brother.[2]

The So family had joined the other residents of the compound, mostly employees of Dee Cho, Chinese and Filipinos, in a large bomb shelter that had been dug in the premises. There were at this time about 50 persons in the shelter. The shelling from the American sector was heavy. The area was close to Isla de Provisor. The group spent the night in the shelter.

Between three and four o'clock this morning, a band of about 15 Japanese entered the Dee Cho compound at 990 Isaac Peral street and discovered the refugees in the bomb shelter.

Driven out of their shelter by the Japanese, the company was lined up and the people made to raise their hands. Then they were made to kneel on the ground. While they were in this position the Japanese came around and tied their hands behind their backs. Only the women who carried babies and the very small children were not tied.

Out of the Dee Cho lumber yard, the group was marched along Isaac Peral westward toward Marques de Comillas street. At the intersection the group was halted and the men were separated from the women and children. There resulted two small groups, one of about 20 men and another of about 30 women and children.

So Peng, 41, was in the group of about 20 men, Chinese and Filipinos.[3] The men were herded into a building in the Compañia Tabacalera compound on Marques de Comillas street. From the building, the men were led out in twos and threes. Outside, a group of Japanese waited with bayonets on the ready.

As his group of three stepped out of the gate, So Peng, his hands behind his back, was bayonetted in the chest and fell. The Japanese stabbed him twice more as he lay on the ground. He lost consciousness. When he came to, there was silence in the compound.

Another survivor, Yu Tsu, also Chinese, lay nearby and noted that So Peng still moved. The two wounded men propped each other up and together they sought shelter in a banana grove.

Separated from her husband So Ting, Ang Be was in the company of women and children that was taken to the back of a house behind a gasoline station at the corner of Isaac Peral and Marques de Comillas. Now the Japanese came at the women and children with their bayonets.

Ang Be carried her youngest, So Shao Pi, 3, a boy, in her arms. When the Japanese thrust at her she offered her back and sheltered her son. Three times Ang Be was stabbed. She fell in a dead faint. When she regained consciousness the boy in her arms was dead. Everyone in the group was dead, except Ang Be and her daughter So Shao Ching, a.k.a., Aurora, 13, who was seriously wounded.

So Luan, 29, Chinese, also lived in the Dee Cho Lumber yard. A bachelor, he did not join the group in the large bomb shelter in the compound and had slept in a small foxhole about 100 yards away.[4]

When So Luan awoke this morning, he was greeted by American soldiers who had occupied the Dee Cho compound in the hours before sunrise. The Americans told him to leave the area and cross Estero de Tanque to the liberated sections of Paco. Exultant, So Luan ran to the large bomb shelter to rouse his companions. He found the place deserted. Puzzled, deeply agitated, So Luan crossed the Estero de Tanque to safety, alone.

At daybreak a constant murmur hang over the refugees in the house where the group of Doña Paz Zamora de Mascuñana was confined on Oregon street in Ermita.[5]

"Like in a church," she writes. "Death stood close by and these were not ordinary prayers but the pleas of the dying and the prayers for a good death . . ."

Suddenly a blinding flash lit the premises and a deafening explosion tore up the earth, tumbling objects to the floor. Smoke issued from the eaves of the house and fearing that it was on fire, the people rushed outside, dragging their wounded along. Access to the street was barred and the crowd jammed-up in the backyard. Now the group noted that the Japanese patrol that had conducted them to this place the previous night was at the street corner, heavily camouflaged with leaves, lying in wait. Now the patrol made the people to open their bundles and to kneel with their arms up in the air. The chief of the Japanese band, machine gun on the ready, strode before the kneeling line, as though scrutinizing faces.

"Whom are they looking for?", Doña Paz de Mascuñana wondered. "What do they want?" Now they started pulling out men from the lines, among them Ernesto Lagdameo who had escaped the massacre yesterday but was badly wounded. Now seven men stood separated from the group.

The others stayed on their knees, their arms upraised. Now from the sky came the roar of motors. Looking up they discerned planes in smart group formation sweeping low.

"Ours!", Mrs. Mascuñana exulted. "Parachutists will drop and save us!"

For over a half-hour the Mascuñana partly knelt on the ground as the sun rose higher and higher. The shelling did not stop. Now shrapnel showered over the group and several fell wounded. The Japanese did nothing. Presently they allowed the group to stand but the men were hustled away, Ricardo Mascuñana among them.

Tottering to her feet, Paz de Mascuñana said in her mind, "God, is this real . . . I must have seen it in a movie or read it in a book, it must be a bad dream . . ."

"But it is real," Doña Paz concluded, as the harsh screams of women and children crying for their husbands or fathers who were being led away assaulted her ears. In the distance, the American planes soared away.

The women and children were ordered to one of the houses that had not caught fire. Some women started after their men but bayonets were held to their chests and they desisted.

Now under the house where the refugees cowered, the news was passed on that the men who had been taken away were detained in an adjoining house. But the seven in Ernesto Lagdameo's group were tied to a tree in the yard, and told, "You will stay here until the Americans kill you with their shrapnel."

Among the wounded from American shrapnel that fell early this morning two boys died. The dead body of a woman lay across the entrance to the shelter under the house, but no one moved it out of the way. The women found a gasoline drum that contained water but which smelled of gasoline. But so thirsty were they that it tasted good.

The afternoon was spent trying to exchange signals with the men in the house next door who could peep through the windows.

"We were like convent girls trying to communicate with their gallants under the strict surveillance of the nuns," Paz de Mascuñana muses in her diary.

At 8:15 this morning, elements of the148th Infantry Regiment advanced from the Estero de Paco three hundred yards inland. At 11:30, however, progress halted when they were pinned down by Japanese positions at the Paco market. American artillery and mortar fire were directed to the area and by 2 o'clock this afternoon, the Americans occupied the marketplace.[6]

Now the Americans inched their way westward against the intermittent enemy fire, until they were stalled on Perez street by a 25-man Japanese contingent with rifles and one heavy machine gun.

Now Lt. Donald C. Zimmer, Company B, 148th Infantry, ordered his squad to cease firing as he sprinted thirty yards to the building where the Japanese held out. From the base of the building Zimmer threw five hand grenades in quick succession through an open window. Twenty-four of the Japanese in the building were annihilated and the 25th surrendered.[7]

Beyond this point lies the old Paco Cemetery which had been heavily fortified by the Japanese. This is a Spanish-era cemetery completed in

1820 and first used in the cholera epidemic that swept the city that year. It is composed of two concentric walls of adobe into which the niches were hollowed. The tops of the walls are promenades. The chapel in the cemetery is consecrated to St. Pancratius. The cemetery has not been used since 1920.

The .Japanese used the former cemetery as a supply depot and inside the walls were concentrated huge stocks of ammunition and food supplies. It was defended by a network of trenches and pillboxes manned by machine-gunners and riflemen.

Now the 1st Battalion, 148th Infantry Regiment, also found that the Paco cemetery area was the nest of at least three 75 mm. guns. The 1st Battalion backed off from a confrontation. All through the day and into the night the area was subjected by the Americans to high-angle artillery bombardment.

This morning the Assumption community at the Madrigal compound on General Luna street in Paco heard Mass in an air-raid shelter to celebrate the feast of Our Lady of Lourdes.[8]

Mother Superior Mary Philomene Kelly, wounded on the 9th, lay dying. The shelling from the American sector continued relentlessly. Flames surrounded the shelter of the nuns. Hundreds from the neighborhood had sought shelter in the compound. Screams of pain and terror rang in the dying Mother Superior's ears. A new series of explosions rocked the shelter. The Sister attending the Mother Superior hugged the earth. When she raised her head again Mother Mary Philomene Kelly was dead.

Outside, at this moment, an American soldier dashed into the Madrigal compound. This section of Paco was in American hands.

On Park Avenue in Pasay City, Gladys Savary was ready to drop from exhaustion.[9] The neighborhood was on fire and Madame's household had spent the previous night fending off sparks on their roof. They formed a bucket brigade from the well, passed the pails of water down the line to Helge Janson up on the roof who splashed water on burning debris landing on the boards.

"Providence switched the wind," Madame Savary writes. "The wind turned at the exact moment when it seemed as though the roof was doomed."

Morning came and Madame and her household were all in. Now she heard a big crowd rushing down her street, shouting in cheerful voices. Looters, she thought. Then a neighbor hollered at her from the gate: "The Americans are here, just in the next street."

This was the moment she had waited for so eagerly the last three years.

Gladys Savary jumped and with her housemate Dorothy Janson tore down the street. At the other end a small man with yellow complexion in green uniform appeared. Japanese! Madame and Mrs. Janson raced backward!

"Hey you," the strange man shouted, "Are youse Americans?"

Madame peered closely at him.

"It isn't Japs, Dorothy," she screamed. "It's Brooklyn!" The yellow complexion was caused by atabrine and the uniform was the 11th Airborne. Gladys Savary had not seen either before.

Not far from here, Constantine Strashnikow who lived at 80-A Del Pan street in Pasay, was told by men of the 511th Parachute Infantry that the body of a white man was discovered in a neighboring compound.[10] Strashnikow, a Russian emigre, went with the group. They found the man's body, with the hands tied behind. The head had a bullet wound, and the body was severely burned. Strashnikow tore away a piece of the dead man's shirt and brought it to Helen Kremleff. She recognized the shirt her husband was wearing when the Japanese took him away on the 9th.

The family of Mrs. Francisca Guinto-Juco had spent the night at the Union Theological seminary at the corner of Herran and Pennsylvania. Today the family Juco decided to return to their shelter in the Soliven compound, behind their wrecked apartment building at the corner of San Marcelino and Herran.[11]

As fire closed on their shelter in the Soliven property, Mrs. Juco and her five small children were left no choice except to flee. Small groups came up the perilous streets and they joined one such group to the Philippine General hospital.

Here the Jucos found neighbors and acquaintances. The place was jammed full and the family had to move from corridor-to-corridor, from one pavillion to the other, as shells crashed into the building and fire broke out at various points.

On the ground floor of a ruined building on Herran street near the intersection with Colorado street in Ermita, the erstwhile inmates of Red Cross Children's Home No. 1 in the care of the young Teresa S. Nava cowered in terror, faint from hunger and thirst. Some were actually dying from untreated illnesses.[12]

Now the adjoining buildings were on fire and the half-wrecked house where the 39 children and eight adults sheltered was in grave danger. Teresa S. Nava saw no way to salvation except to move out and attempt to reach shelter at the Philippine General hospital a few short blocks away.

First, Teresa Nava improvised a Red Cross flag out of a white handtowel to which she pinned two strips of red cloth she tore out of a pillowcase. She found a bamboo stick and hang her makeshift Red Cross flag at the other end.

Then Teresa lined up the children who could walk. The bigger children carried smaller ones. The seven women helpers carried boxes of their remaining supplies on their heads or strapped to their backs, with as many children as each could hold in her arms.

Now holding aloft the improvised Red Cross flag with one hand and cradling a child on the other, Teresa Nava gave the order to march. The ragged procession wended its way out of the shelter which was now ablaze and stepped into the cratered, rubble-strewn street where fallen timber burned and dead bodies lay in grotesque postures. Other refugees came out of hiding and joined the procession.

In normal times, PGH would be but a short stroll away from this point. Today this was a long and perilous journey. The area was battleground. Buildings burned where they had not crumbled to rubble. Dead bodies littered the streets and it took Miss Nava's procession time and effort to step around or over them. Shells from the American sector rained incessantly and every few steps the party would drop to the ground and wait long and dangerous minutes for the barrage to lighten. At every intersection groups of Japanese stood. They fired at everything that moved. One such group stood at the intersection of Herran and Taft Avenue. The refugee group under the Red Cross flag hove into view. The Japanese held their fire and watched.

By midafternoon the refugee-party reached the Philippine General hospital. Teresa Nava counted noses and found that four of her charges were missing.

The behaviour of some Japanese soldiers in the vicinity of the PGH at this time stands out as unique. In a day characterized by madness, when death and destruction reigned, a few of these men retained their basic humanity and acted with decency and grace.

Aside from the experience of Teresa Nava and her wards, Rodolfo G. Tupas records these instances: "The families in our neighborhood were inching their way towards the Philippine General hospital . . . At that precise moment in that particular neighborhood other Japanese marines were slaughtering all males within sight . . . Thus it was short of a miracle that the soldier escorted us across Taft Avenue."[13]

"I remember somebody in the group had asked for water for the children from the Japanese soldiers. One brushed her aside but another poured water in her cup and then gave the others as well."

This morning, Admiral Iwabuchi returned to Manila from Fort McKinley. When he left for McKinley on the 9th, Iwabuchi had placed the commander of the Northern Force, Col. Noguchi, in command of troops within city limits. Noguchi complained of difficulty in controlling the naval forces in his command and asked Iwabuchi to assign a senior naval officer for this purpose.[14]

Today, fearing that Fort McKinley might fall to American hands, Iwabuchi decided to return to Manila and himself assume command once more.

This morning the del Rios of Taft Avenue in Pasay butchered the pig in the backyard, mainly because they could not feed it anymore. They salted the major portion because "we do not know how long this wave of barbarism will last," as Benigno del Rio put it in his diary.[15]

This afternoon the Japanese put the torch to Pasay. A huge explosion wrecked the Manila Sanitarium hospital on Donada street and it started to burn. From here the fire spread in every direction. The Manila Sanitarium was operated by the Seventh-Day Adventists. Since early 1944 it had been used as the Japanese Navy hospital.

In Malate, the Gutierrez family of Remedios street also butchered their pig, their last resource.[16] At least there was food – fried pork chops, pork adobo, salted pork.

But the family spent most of the day in the dugout behind the house as shells burst all around without letup. A big fire was raging. It had started at the Masonic Temple on Taft Avenue and Vermont street. The wind blew and adjoining buildings caught, and now the Gutierrez house was in the path of the fire. The Gutierrezes thought that a neighboring house owned by the Gonzales family might be safer as it was made of concrete. They broke down a section of the stone fence and dashed under the Gonzalez house.

They could hear the sound of Japanese hobnailed boots trampling up and down the streets. A Japanese team was observed infront of the house setting-up mines.

Now a crowd of civilians rushed up to the Gutierrez shelter. Many in the crowd were wounded. Many were in hysterics. They were survivors of new massacres.

"They said the Japs threw hand-grenades at their shelter," Lydia Gutierrez writes in her diary. "They got separated from their families. We gave them water and they ran out again."

The fire was now close to the Gonzalez house. Smoke got into the eyes of those in the Gutierrez shelter. The Gutierrezes decided to run.

On Florida street they came upon a corner of a ruined house. Three walls still stood. Now they pulled pieces of iron roofing from the smoking ruins and set them up on the open side. Behind this shelter the Gutierrez family crouched. The heat from the fire was intense. There were explosions in every direction. But the crisis waned and seeing their own house still standing, the Gutierrez family crept back.

It was not a good day for pigs![17]

Over at the De la Salle college on Taft Avenue, a pig in the compound that had been sharing the lot of the refugees fell casualty to the shelling. The untimely demise of the animal provided the refugees an unscheduled feast. From hereon, to save on fuel and for convenience's sake, the refugees and the Brothers agreed to pool their resources and cook but once a day for the meal they would all share.

The residents of De la Salle heard the chaplain, Rev. Fr. Francis J. Cosgrave, say Mass, even as the area came under particularly heavy shelling.

Later this morning, some Japanese from among those quartered in another section of the building came around and distributed biscuits, soap and cigarettes.

After Mass this morning, there remained but one Host which Father Cosgrave kept in the tabernacle at the altar. This afternoon the shelling intensified and the priest no longer thought the tabernacle safe enough. He decided to give communion to Brother Leo, the eldest member of the community and deemed the most deserving of the last Host.

As night fell, the shelling reached a new peak. The De la Salle refugees jammed the wine cellar under the staircase in the south wing.

Today, Japanese resistance on Isla de Provisor ceased.[18] By midafternoon, the island was cleared. Also, the power plant had lost whatever usefulness it would have had as a source of electricity, the ostensible reason General Walter Krueger had for its early seizure.

The 511th Parachute Infantry pushed north along the bayfront, reaching Libertad street in Pasay about three kilometers from the Manila boundary. In this northward attack, the 511th commander, Col. Hauges was killed. At Libertad, General Griswold, commanding the XIV Corps, halted the 511th.

From the northeast, the 5th and 8th Cavalry Regiments were rushing headlong to the bayfront.

Tonight, the 18th Parachute Infantry gained control of the southeast section of Nichols Field. Griswold ordered a concerted attack for the next day.

The garage of the Valdez apartments on M.H. del Pilar street in Ermita was jammed with refugees of various nationalities – Swiss, Spanish, Jewish, American, but mostly Filipinos.[19]

"We are crowded like sardines," Sophy Natalie Morgin writes. "We have only one thing in common – hope!"

In the afternoon a squad of Japanese soldiers barged into the garage. One soldier singled out a Filipino youth who cowered beside Miss Morgin and menacingly poised his bayonet, shouting, "You guerrilla!"

Stoutly Miss Morgin interposed. She spoke fluent Japanese and her intervention stupefied the Japanese who could only stare at her. The group withdrew, threatening, "If there is one guerrilla among you, all of you will be killed!"

Later in the evening the same group was back looking for the white woman who spoke Japanese. Miss Morgin had feared this. Now she lay apparently in *extremis,* with a group of fellow refugees solicitously hovering over her, applying cold towels to her forehead.

"Where is that woman," the Japanese demanded.

Very feebly Miss Morgin spoke up. "I am extremely ill," she said.

"We will take care of you," the Japanese said. But Miss Morgin pretended unable to move so convincingly that the Japanese departed without further incident.

At the ruined German Club compound on San Luis street in Ermita, Helena Rodriguez, 21, her burns tormenting her, dared to peer out of the tight foxhole which she had shared the night through with three others.[20]

The clubhouse had burned down. The premises were littered with dead bodies. Now two Japanese soldiers discovered Helena's foxhole. The two lifted one of the men out of the hole and bayonetted him. Down in the foxhole Helena Rodriguez recited all the prayers she knew. The Japanese went away but were back shortly. Now Helena smelled gasoline. She looked up to see that the mattress which covered the foxhole was burning. Helena Rodriguez lost consciousness. When she came to she found that the fire had not caught. Helena and her two companions, one of them a woman-friend, kept still in the foxhole.

At Fort Santiago, Luis Gallent stood with about 40 others in a narrow cell.[21] They were so tightly wedged in that they could hardly move. They have had no food or water since they were brought in here on the 8th February.

Today, a Spanish boy collapsed. The other detainees in the cell asked the Japanese guard for water to give to the boy. The Japanese guard brought in a coconut-shell cupful, but it did not reach the boy as everyone else pounced on it.

This afternoon, the Spaniards in the cell, Luis Gallent, his father and brother among them, were separated from the rest and brought to ano-ther cell. There were nine in the Spanish group. Here at least the Spaniards could stretch out on the floor.

Now the fire which had raged in the Ermita area finally reached the residence of Dr. Alfredo Guerrero at 117 A. Mabini street, where several sick and injured were being cared for. The patients were bundled up and in the company of relatives and other residents of the area, were brought to points of safety.[22] Among those taken to the Ateneo de Manila compound on Padre Faura street were Mrs. Alfredo Chicote and her daughter Maria Paz.

When the Japanese hauled away her husband, Ismael Cruz, Jr., her father-in-law and her brother-in-law from their home at the corner of General Luna and California streets in Paco, Carmen Guerrero-Cruz decided to join her own parents at their A. Mabini home in Ermita. Against all odds, Mrs. Cruz, her small daughter in her arms and pregnant with another child, crossed the strategic Taft Avenue which divided the south Manila area into eastside and westside, and against all odds she was able to reach her family home.

Now Carmen Guerrero-Cruz, her parents, Dr. and Mrs. Alfredo Guerrero and several relatives, their home now ravaged by flames, hustled off to the premises of the Ermita church where there was a large bomb shelter. The buildings in the compound were wrecked or on fire and there was scant protection here. Scrambling out of one shelter, the group looked back in time to see the same shelter they had just vacated blow up from a direct hit.

Dr. Guerrero's party raced up A. Mabini street towards the Malate area and arrived at the Realistic Beauty Salon compound beyond Herran street where they joined the Garcia family, the caretakers, in a bomb shelter.

Raymond Joseph Toomey was the son of an American father and a Filipino mother.[23] He had been registered as a United States citizen but was not interned by the Japanese because he represented himself as German. He lived with his grandmother Doña Maria Sequera at 221 Progreso street in Pasay.

This morning Raymond started walking south and reached the American lines. At three o'clock this afternoon, elated by finding that the liberation forces were that close, he started home to his grandmother, against the advise of his new-found American friends.

As he approached his neighborhood on Harrison Boulevard he came upon people rushing southwards, many of them bloodied. As he neared his home, he saw the houseboy of a neighbor, Dr. Luis Reyes, chained by both hands to a fence. As Raymond watched two Japanese soldiers splashed gasoline on the legs of the boy whom Raymond knew only as Pedro, and set the gasoline on fire. Pedro screamed in pain and terror and twisted against the fence. Fearfully Raymond Toomey edged away from the scene.

Now Toomey took the path to his home to look for his grandmother, Doña Maria Sequera. On the street he saw Dr. Luis Reyes and his wife and daughter pushing a handcart. Suddenly a Japanese soldier jumped out of the doorway of a partly-ruined house. The Japanese lunged at the doctor with his bayonet and the latter crumpled to the ground, clutching his abdomen. The Japanese strode away leaving the women alone.

Now Raymond Joseph Toomey was in his own frontyard. He found his grandmother lying on the ground with another woman from the neighborhood whose name he did not know. The woman now told Raymond that the Japanese had set their home on Progreso street on fire, shutting up Doña Maria Sequera inside. The two women escaped by the backdoor. On the street the two women were espied by a Japanese who fired at them, hitting the elder woman in the back of the head. She may have died instantly. Although wounded herself, the other woman pulled Doña Maria's body from the street into the yard, where Raymond Toomey found them.

Insecure in their refugee-quarters on Pennsylvania street, the Quirino-Mendoza-Syquia clan this morning decided to return to the Rodriguez home, which still stood, on Herran street.[24]

Night fell again and the shelling from the American sector only seemed to intensify. In a particularly mean barrage, a shell crashed through a wall of the Rodriguez home and showered hot steel all over the place. Margarita Syquia fell, slashed by shrapnel just below the waist, almost cutting her body in half.

During the barrage, the grand matriarch Doña Concepcion Jimenez de Syquia had crawled under the bed with her small grandchildren. She emerged from under the bed to crumple into a motionless heap, dead from heart failure.

Now the clan gathered itself again, abandoning the dead body of their matriarch and carrying the agonizing Margarita Syquia, and dashed around the block to Pennsylvania street once more, back to the building they had fled earlier in the day.

From her foxhole at the German Club compound on San Luis street in

Ermita, Helena Rodriguez could hear the voices of children calling to each other in the dark. The Japanese had-gone.[25]

Helena crept out of her foxhole followed by her two companions. They found a group of boys who were searching for family members among the dead. The boys led the three to a large dugout where many more children still cowered fearfully. One of them wept inconsolably over his mother's dead body. Near the dugout, Helena's woman-friend stumbled over a corpse. It was her husband's body riddled with bayonet wounds.

Now Helena Rodriguez found she was all alone in the world. Among the dead were her mother and all four of her brothers.

At 10 o'clock tonight a huge blaze lit up the house on Oregon street where the refugee-party of Mrs. Paz de Mascuñana sheltered.[26] The refugees rushed out helter-skelter. But they were met by one of the male hostages in the next house who was allowed out to tell the women, "The Japanese will shoot anyone who leaves a house that's not actually burning." Their shelter not being on fire although sorely menaced by adjoining houses in flames, the women and children went back.

Near midnight, the Japanese set fire to one wall of the Mascuñana party's shelter. The refugees burst out of the exits. One of the neighbors had a garage which had been turned into a poultryhouse, and had remained undiscovered. Now the refugees ran through the poultryhouse, upsetting the chicken-coops and turning the occupants loose. Attracted by the clamor of excited chickens flying and scuttling about, the Japanese came running leaving unguarded the doors of the house where the men were detained. The men ran out after the Japanese.

"The Japanese decided on a change of menu," Doña Paz de Mascuñana observed as the Japanese chased the chickens and turned their guns on the flock.

The refugees, joined by their men, dashed every which way, each family to itself. For the moment they were left to their own devices by the Japanese who were now out on a bizarre chicken-hunt, this strange midnight aglow from the flames of a burning city.

The Mascuñana family was soon reunited. Where to go? Several groups headed for the PGH, among them the family of Ernesto Lagdameo who had freed himself with the others. But the better-part of the refugee-group headed for Padre Faura where the Alzona lot was still surrounded by a concrete wall. The Mascuñana garage and the servants' quarters had been spared by the fire, and here the family found a refuge. Looking back to Oregon street, they saw the last houses still standing now hidden behind a curtain of fire.

At 11 o'clock tonight, the right wing of La Concordia college building, already in ruins, caught fire.[27] The dead bodies and the wounded inside were incinerated. Many survivors rushed out of the building to the street to be met by machine gun-fire from Japanese positions outside. Other survivors tore down the stone walls in the rear of the compound, and escaped to the open fields along the railway tracks to the safe zone now in American hands in Pandacan.

The Rev. Fr. Elias H. Gonzalez was a Spanish member of the Congregation of the Mission of St. Vincent de Paul who first arrived in Manila in 1937. Now he served as chaplain of the Canoness Sisters of St. Augustine, popularly known in Manila as the Belgian Sisters(Madres Belgas) since the original group came from Belgium.

When the Belgian Sisters were ordered to vacate their St. Theresa's college which stood on San Marcelino street across from the Vincentian Central House and Seminary, Fr. Gonzalez had remained with the Sisters who stayed on as caretakers.

The chaplain of the Sisters of the Congregation of St. Paul de Chartres at their St. Paul college campus on Herran street in Malate was the Rev. Fr. Pedro Martinez, also a Spanish member of the Congregation of the Mission of St. Vincent de Paul.

Fr. Martinez was an elderly priest who first arrived in Manila in 1906. When the St. Paul Sisters were ordered out of their property on Herran street, and had to seek refuge at St. Theresa's college on San Marcelino street, their chaplain went with them.

When the Sisters from both Orders were ordered out of St. Theresa's college to the Assumption Convent at the corner of Herran street and Dakota in Ermita, on 7 February 1945, their respective chaplains, of course, accompanied them.

Fr. Gonzalez had learned the Japanese language during the war period. He knew enough Japanese to be able to preach to Japanese Catholics who were civilian employees in the Japanese Imperial forces.

Tonight a Japanese band came around to the Assumption Convent grounds and barged into the building where the refugees were crowded in, apparently with lewd designs on the women. They were repulsed, and the Sisters reported the incident to Fr. Gonzalez. When the Japanese came around again later that night, the chaplain confronted them at the gate and gave them a severe scolding, in their own language.

At 11 o'clock tonight Benigno del Rio stood at the window of his room at his family's Taft Avenue home in Pasay, watching neighboring houses one-by-one become engulfed in flames. Benigno stared fascinatedly as familiar landmarks to the west across from his own house disappeared behind fire and smoke. These buildings had been occupied by the

Japanese Navy since March the previous year and used as hospitals. The fire spread to the south, then to the north.[28]

MONDAY, 12 FEBRUARY 1945

Now the clock in the del Rio home on Taft Avenue struck one. Still keeping vigil by his window Benigno del Rio espied on the street below a squad of Japanese soldiers engrossed with their work. They were pushing carts containing drums, apparently of gasoline. Now Benigno saw the squad leader gesture in the direction of his home. Immediately two of the soldiers poured gasoline into tin cans, and together with one who carried a rifle with fixed bayonet approached the house. When they reached the del Rio gate young Benigno skipped down the stairs.

"I looked for the last time around me," Benigno del Rio writes in his diary. "I stopped for a few seconds in the library to bid goodbye to my books. It has been but seven years since I became serious with books, and here I still kept the first complete book I had read, *Los Mineros de Alaska* (The Miners of Alaska) by Emilio Salgar . . . goodbye!"

He dashed out the back door to the adjoining property, the hobnailed steps of the torch team ringing in his ears. On the way he met his father and his younger brother Joaquin. Then he heard a neighbor scream, "The house of Don Tomas del Rio is burning."[1]

The del Rios joined a crowd heading in the direction of Dominga street in the next block. Bullets whistled overhead. Turning a corner, Benigno saw the girl ahead of him fall, gravely wounded. Dominga street was jammed with agitated refugees. The del Rios sought shelter in the compound of a friend, Don Rosendo Guzman, who suggested that the group move on to the open field beyond the abandoned tracks. The rumor that the Japanese were now firing houses adjacent to their shelter triggered a mass exodus to the open fields. Here the del Rios found that "thousands and thousands" had preceded them.

Then it began to rain. Now the rain fell in sheets, aggravating the misery of the vast crowd of refugees out in the open. The del Rios huddled under a huge mango tree.

In the dawn hours today the family of Ricardo Mascuñana was back in the ruins of their home on Padre Faura street. A phosphorus shell landed on the Mascuñana lot and many of the refugees sustained serious burns.[2] Mrs. Mascuñana discovered the burned body of the hysterical woman who had endangered them at their Colorado shelter, lying on the street.

There was nothing to eat. The group found green fruits of the banana trees in the backyard, half-cooked from the previous day's fire. The burnt bananas calmed down their hunger, somehow.

Now a new crisis struck the Mascuñana shelter. "Is there a nurse around?" "Is there a doctor?" This time it was not for the wounded as presently a new-born baby's cries rang over the place, loud and clear, rising over the fury of the cannonade and the rattle of machine gun-fire.

Having completed operations on Isla de Provisor, the 2nd Battalion, 129th Infantry, early this morning crossed the *estero* to the mainland. Opposition from the Japanese was heavy and strong and despite intense artillery support, the Americans could progress only very slowly. Moving westward between Isla de Provisor and Isaac Peral street, the 129th this morning established a line on Marques de Comillas street.[3]

At 9 o'clock this morning the 5th Calvary Regiment swept across Nielson Field in Makati, reaching Culi-Culi and Route 57. This route extends westward to Pasay where it is called Calle Libertad. Here the 511th Parachute Infantry stood.

Now the 5th Cavalry drove up Libertad into Pasay and at 10:40 this morning linked-up with the 511th Parachute Infantry. From here the 5th pushed farther to the bayfront, turning north to the junction of Dewey Boulevard and Villaruel street.

This afternoon, General Verne D. Mudge, commander of the 1st Cavalry Division, sent the 12th Cavalry Regiment south to join the 5th. At 2:30 this afternoon, the 2nd Squadron, 12th Cavalry, reached Dewey Boulevard. Now the encirclement of Manila was complete.

This morning, the Marine Corps SBD's from Lingayen Gulf launched a series of air strikes on Nichols Field. Together with concentrated artillery and mortar barrages, this was part of the preparation for the ground assaults.

When the softening process lifted, the 2nd Battalion, 187th Infantry, struck eastward from its position on the northwest corner of Nichols Field. The 188th Infantry and the 1st Battalion, 187th Infantry, drove in from the south and the southeast respectively.

By nightfall, Nichols Field only needed to be mopped-up.

Now the 1st Squadron, 5th Cavalry Regiment, turned east and began the assault on Fort McKinley. The area was considered strategic as it commanded approaches to the advanced lines of the Shimbu Army. Fort McKinley was heavily fortified by the Japanese who were determined to defend it.

Sanji Iwabuchi's command had dwindled rapidly. The Central Force under his command now consisted only of the Headquarters Sector Unit, the 5th Naval Battalion, the Northern Force's 3rd Provisional Infantry Battalion, and service units, remnants of Colonel Noguchi's 2nd Provisional Infantry Battalion. These comprised about 6,000 troops.[4]

By today, nearly all of Iwabuchi's artillery had been silenced. Rapidly, one-by-one, his mortars were being knocked out. Machine gun-emplacements, except those in fortified buildings, were going fast.

Today the 148 Infantry discovered that there were armed Japanese in the premises of the Philippine General hospital. The XIV Corps had restricted operations against the hospital, which was identified by red crosses on the roofs. Today, in the belief that PGH was defended, the XIV Corps lifted the restriction.[5]

At 4:30 this afternoon element from the 3rd Battalion, 148th Infantry, reached Pennsylvania street in Ermita, one block from Taft Avenue fronting the vital Philippine General hospital compound and the University of the Philippines campus. Now Japanese 20 m.m. and 40 m.m. shells rained on the 3rd Battalion. Without their own artillery support, the casualty list shot up and the 3rd Battalion withdrew, while American batteries countered the Japanese in the area.[6]

In a remote corner of a ward at the PGH, Kiyoshi Osawa, 39, the Japanese expatriate who heads the Liquid Fuel Distribution Union in wartime Manila, is in impenetrable coma. He has been in this state since the 26th of January.[7]

Today, one of the nurses assigned to attend to him, Miss Aytona by name, left the ward. She did not return. This left a young nursing assistant, Miss Almania, to tend to Osawa.

"Many other people who left the hospital like her (Miss Aytona) were never seen again," Miss Almania relates. "We all wondered what happened to them."

Miss Almania recalled life for some of those inside PGH at this time, thus: "At night Japanese soldiers came into the ward looking for women, and violently stabbed their bayonets into a bed or on the walls, just to scare the people. We used to hear a woman or several of them screaming almost every night. There were about 50 of us, all scared to death, who used to sleep in the narrow corner under the stairway huddled against one another. The doctors were on guard outside to protect us."

This morning the Pedro Campos compound at 1462 Taft Avenue was packed full of refugees from the neighborhood as more people came in seeking shelter from the American-shelling. Among the refugees were Judge Arsenio Locsin and his family, who lived at No. 1452 next door.[8]

This afternoon at about 4 o'clock the Locsin home adjoining the Pedro Campos compound was torched by the Japanese.

The Locsins watched from their refuge next door. The fire spread to other houses, but not to the Campos residence.

At about 4 o'clock this afternoon, the Bayview Hotel caught fire. Some 150 Caucasian and mestiza women and girls were being held in the hotel which the Japanese used as a brothel.[9]

Now the women dashed out the exits into the streets around the building. Many would perish while rushing down into the open and others still met death in the ruins of the Ermita neighborhood because of the constant shelling.

For the Elpidio Quirino group, it has been catch-as - catch can since that fateful morning of the 9th. This morning, the clan moved still farther up Pennsylvania street to another building behind the Philippine Women's University, close to Vermont street. There was little food, hardly any water. The refugees huddled in a narrow passageway in the building. The area was in the focus of the bombardment, the ostensible objective of which, or so it seemed to the refugees, was the obliteration of the Philippine Women's University plant.[10]

Through the night Margarita Syquia had been in shock from the trauma of the injuries she sustained in last night's shelling. This morning she died.

Elpidio Quirino left the refugee quarters to reconnoiter the area for a safer sanctuary for his large group.

Shortly after he stepped out, a shell exploded into the building. In the narrow passage hall, the cousins Tommy Quirino, 21, and Gregorio Mendoza, 18, sat facing each other on the floor, backs to the wall. So narrow was the space that the young men could not stretch out their legs in front of them. Gregorio sat with his right leg flexed up, with Tommy's left leg propped on his lap. When the shell crashed into their quarters, a piece of shrapnel pierced Gregorio's upraised thigh and went through Tommy's left leg. An artery may have been severed in Gregorio's thigh for he bled, literally to death.

Nearby Gregorio's younger brother Raul, 13, sat, his arms crossed over his chest. A bit of shrapnel pierced his right arm above the elbow and exited though the lower arm shattering the bone at both points.

Their father, Don Vicente Mendoza, got the shrapnel into his abdomen. Painfully he endured, slowly dying from the trauma and loss of blood.

Hector Syquia took the shrapnel in his lungs. He succumbed in minutes.

The Mendoza family *mayordoma* leaned against the wall, cradling Vicky Quirino's head on her lap as the girl curled up on the floor. The shrapnel tore through the *mayordoma's* head, blowing half her face away. She slumped forward to the floor as Vicky, 13, bolted upright, brushing away from her dressfront blobs of blood, bits of brain and shards of skull.

Now Elpidio Quirino returned from reconnoitering the area for a more secure shelter. He had located a bomb shelter along Vermont street close to San Marcelino street. He had not reckoned with the blood he now found splattered all over the place.

Now Elpidio Quirino picked up his wounded son Tommy, as the distraught Doña Petronila Syquia de Mendoza organized the terrified survivors to flee once again. They made a sorry spectacle in their flight up Vermont street, the 13-year-old Raul Mendoza woebegone with a shattered arm and the smaller children terror-stricken. The dead and wounded were left behind.

Having settled down the survivors of his clan in the bomb-shelter on Vermont street, Elpidio Quirino again hazarded the American shells and the Japanese sharpshooters and made the perilous journey two long blocks back to their erstwhile sanctuary on Pennsylvania street.

Here Quirino pulled away a burnt-out sheet of galvanized iron roofing from a ruined heap, laid the agonizing lawyer Vicente Mendoza, his brother-in-law, upon it, lifted one end and dragged it behind him like a primitive sled, up the cratered and rubble-strewn street on both sides of which smouldered dangerous fires. Shells whistled overhead, shook the earth and kicked up clouds when they hit. In streetcorners Japanese riflemen stood watchfully, and they shot at everything for every reason, and for none.

Elpidio Quirino pulled his burden resolutely to the clan's newfound refuge where he deposited the torn body of Vicente Mendoza.

Now Quirino returned to Pennsylvania street, this time for Gregorio Mendoza, 18, who was hemorrhaging from a shattered thigh. Quirino lifted the young Gregorio into his ingenious ambulance, but now a particularly vicious barrage fell on the area. Quirino ran for cover.

For an hour or so Elpidio Quirino crouched in his shelter. When the barrage eased up he returned to his galvanized iron sheet turned into an ambulance, but the wounded Gregorio Mendoza was not on it. Quirino returned alone to his anxious clan on Vermont street. Here he found that Vicente Mendoza had died.[10-a]

Again Elpidio Quirino left the survivors in his clan. Beyond a certain line somewhere, he knew, permanent peace had come. He must get there. His son was dying. The others must be saved. He must find relief.

In the bomb-shelter, the wounded Tommy Quirino was faint with thirst and pain. The small children wailed for water. Luis Mendoza, 16, dazed from witnessing so much bloodshed and death, would not budge.

Victoria Quirino, 13, scrounged around for containers and found two empty cans that would serve as buckets. Now Victoria Quirino, 13, convent-bred heiress, stepped out into the unremitting gunfire. The minutes ticked away slowly in the bomb-shelter and she did not return. But finally she did, with the water everyone needed.

Elpidio Quirino, statesman, walked the hazardous streets eastward to Paco. This was now liberated territory. Here Quirino found people who recognized him and gave him food and water, and the new, highly-prized commodity, symbol of new times – American cigarettes!

Elpidio Quirino returned to the shelter on Vermont street and found his son Tommy sinking into a stupor. The wounded leg was festering, the young man was listless from hunger and pain.

"Tommy, perk up," Quirino ordered his son and gave him a sharp slap across the face. "Here," he said, triumphantly pulling out a cigarette out of his shirt pocket and lighting it for Tommy.

Again Elpidio Quirino gathered his son into his arms and the bedraggled procession, much reduced in numbers, followed him. The body of the dead Vicente Mendoza was left behind.

The group stopped on the west bank of the Estero de Paco. The bridge across the *estero* had been blown. Quirino went from one group to another among the refugees on the *estero* bank, seeking food He gathered enough rice over which salt was sprinkled to bring back to the remnants of his clan. Tonight they bedded down beside the *estero*.

The daily Mass at the De la Salle college on Taft Avenue was not celebrated this morning. The shelling was so intense that the chaplain, Rev. Fr. Francis J. Cosgrave, CSsR, would not risk gathering so many people in one spot.[11]

Shortly before noon the residents gathered at the foyer for lunch. In the circumstances, no amenities for a decent meal were at hand. The food was laid out in pots and pans on the floor and each person reached out as one could for what was available.

Done with lunch, the group started to disperse. Most of them sought favored corners in the foyer, stood around in small groups, withdrew to the cellar, or went up to the second floor to stretch their legs and take in the clearer air.

Now a band of Japanese led by an officer appeared at the gate where Brother Maximin confronted them. It seems that they suspected the building was being used as a sniper's nest. They tramped up and down the corridors and looked into the rooms. Finding nothing that interested them, they left.

Shortly the same officer was back with two men. Now they grabbed the Carlos family manservant Mateo and two members of the college staff,

Anselmo Sudlan and Panfilo Almodan, and hustled them away, ignoring Brother Maximin's loud protests.

One of the soldiers stayed. He had a tin of sardines, probably his lunch ration, but had nothing with which to open it. Brother Mutwald opened the can for him and fetched him some rice to go with the sardines. The Japanese soldier was just starting to eat when the gate abruptly swung open again and the three men who had been taken away hurtled through, two of them seriously wounded. Seeing the soldier eating, the officer dashed to him and gave him a resounding slap across the face. Both marched out of the hall. The community gathered around the wounded men, deeply agitated. Panfilo's intestines were spilling out.

Now a large band of about 20 Japanese stormed through the gate. The officer yelled a harsh command and a rifle shot reverberated across the hall.

At this moment, Brother Leo, the senior Brother in residence, and the chaplain, Father Cosgrave, were sitting quietly on a bench outside the wine cellar door.

Mrs. Victoria Cojuangco, coddling her adopted son Ricardo, and her daughter Lourdes, 15, had entered the wine cellar. With them were Mrs. Felicidad Uychuico, her daughters Soledad, 6, and Paz, 3, and two Carlos sisters, Gloria, 17, and Dionisia, 16.

Dr. Antonio Cojuangco had gone up the second floor to his son, Antonio, Jr., 17, who was recuperating from typhoid in a small room to the right of the entrance to the chapel. With him were Mr. and Mrs. Servillano Aquino and the male nurse, Filomeno Inolin.

The Carlos sisters, Rosario, 21, and Asela, 20, hang around the chapel door. Along the corridors were Fortunata Salonga, 14, the young Aquino servantmaid, and Regina, the Uychuico househelp. Inside the chapel, 6-year-old Antonio Carlos had pre-empted the confessional box and now lounged in it quite unconcernedly.

Along the corridors, too, at this time, were Brothers Mutwald, Anthony and Victor, taking a respite.

On the staircase, Mrs. Juanita Carlos, with her youngest, Jose, Jr., 3, was coming up.

Don Enrique Vazquez-Prada was in a stall in the toilet on the second floor. The young cook of the De la Salle Brothers, Teofilo Candari, 23, was in his small room on the same floor.

Brother Leo, 69, formerly dean of studies at De la Salle college, was knowledgable in Oriental languages and understood Japanese. When he heard the Japanese officer's command, Brother Leo slipped to his knees from the bench by the cellar door where he had been sitting with Father Cosgrave and cried, "On your knees, everyone! Father Cosgrave, please grant us absolution!"

The shooting and bayonetting began!

Ramon Cojuangco, 20, stood with his recent bride, the former Natividad de las Alas, also 20, near the cellar door. Now he dashed into the cellar to warn his mother and the others inside. His wife screamed and dashed after him but was overtaken by a Japanese who lunged with his bayonet. She fell, mortally wounded.

When Ramon Cojuangco popped into the cellar to shout a warning, many of those inside rushed out panic-stricken, among them his mother, Mrs. Victoria Cojuangco who was toting her adopted son, Ricardo, 3; Mrs. Felicidad Uychuico and Dionisia Carlos. They met with bayonets outside the cellar door. Mortally stricken, Mrs. Cojuangco crawled back into the cellar and would perish in minutes. She had lost hold of her son, Ricardo, who was critically wounded and now lay bloodied by the door. Mrs. Uychuico and Dionisia Carlos were wounded but slightly and stumbled back into the cellar. The others had stayed put inside and were unscathed.

The Uychuico maidservant Clarita Roldan, 17, was sitting on the bottom steps of the staircase when she heard the first shot. She dove under a mattress which lay at her feet on the floor and stayed there.

The Japanese split into two groups. One pursued those who ran up the staircase while the other busied itself in the foyer.

Brother Leo was on his knees before Father Cosgrave, seeking absolution. Father Cosgrave raised his right arm to make the sign of the cross over the kneeling Brother and at this precise moment, the Japanese struck with his bayonet. It passed under Father Cosgrave's arm into Brother Leo's chest. The Brother slumped against the priest's legs and the latter could not move. Now the Japanese turned his bayonet on Father Cosgrave. The priest was hit in the right side of the chest and found himself sprawling on the floor.

In the initial onslaught, the three older Vazquez-Prada boys, tall husky young men, were among the first to fall. The 5-year-old Fernando Vazquez-Prada was thrown to the floor and a Japanese went after him. Three times the Japanese swung at the boy with his bayonet, each time but nicking him slightly as he squirmed fearfully on the floor. At this point Helen Vazquez-Prada sprang up and scooped the boy off the floor. Like an enraged tigress she fought back. She kicked, she bit, she swung her free fist, the boy Fernando under one arm.

When the Japanese officer with the saber lunged at the boy the mother offered her body. She was slashed across the shoulders, a big piece of flesh was hacked out of one thigh. She parried the blows with her hands and the fingers on both were neatly sliced away. Stabbed in the abdomen, Helen Vazquez-Prada fell to the floor, but the boy Fernando, 5, was not hurt further.

One-by-one and in bunches the Christian Brothers fell, big husky men in the prime of life. The Japanese-speaking Brother Maximin shouted, "I am German," in a bid to calm down the attackers, to no avail. He turned and dashed to the stairs. Some Brothers had reached the cellar but rushed out again. Now they grappled with their adversaries, struggling for possession of arms. All were overcome. Some died instantly, others fell with severe injuries and would die slowly, painfully. Brothers Lucian, Gebhard, Paul and Hubert managed to scramble up the stairs.

Mrs. Juanita Carlos, with her youngest, Jose, Jr., 3, was going up the stairs when the shooting started. She scooped up the boy but was overtaken by a Japanese marine at the second landing. She fell from a rifle shot but she sheltered her son with her body. Brother Baptist de la Salle was dashing up behind the two and grabbed the boy when the mother fell. With his own body the Brother shielded the 3-year-old Jose Carlos, Jr.

Cecilia Carlos, 12, was tagging after her mother, with the servantmaids Juanita and Felisa, when they were caught up in the mad scramble to the second floor. Cecilia was shot but managed to reach the chapel door where she fell dead. Felisa was slightly wounded and picked up the 3-year-old Jose Carlos, Jr. where Brother Baptist had concealed him under a mattress before he collapsed. Juanita had a finger shot away from her left hand, but suffered no further injury.

The first Japanese to reach the second floor now came upon the girls who stood rooted to the floor by the chapel door, terror-stricken. Rosario Carlos, 21, stuck close to her sister Asela, 20. They were joined by the servantmaids Fortunata, who served the Aquino couple, and Regina, who served the Uychuico family.

Now Rosario stood face-to-face with this Japanese marine with the rifle poised not three feet away. Rosario remembers seeing a flash accompanied by a deafening shot. She felt herself falling helplessly. The bullet had entered the left side of her chest and exited in the back. But she remained conscious. She heard others scream in terror and the crash of gunfire was horrible to her ears, but Rosario Carlos picked herself up and made it to the chapel threshhold where she fell again.

Asela Carlos, 20, and Fortunata Salonga, 14, were subjected to saber blows and bayonet stabs. Asela's arms were almost severed at the elbows. Fortunata lay prostrate with lethal wounds. Regina had slipped inside the chapel with but a scratch near the mouth.

When Servillano Aquino, 25, first heard the screaming and shooting in the foyer, he stepped out of the room beside the chapel door where he and his wife were visiting with Antonio Cojuangco, Jr., 17, who was recovering from illness. Also in the room were Dr. Antonio Cojuangco, Sr., and the male nurse, Filomeno Inolin.

Aquino started down the staircase to find out what was happening when one of the Brothers below, already fighting for his life motioned him away. Aquino returned to the sick boy's room. The group locked itself in. From outside came the sound of a stampede. A gunshot was heard followed by many more accompanied by fearful screams. Aquino distinctly recognized Asela's terrified screams.

Shortly there was loud banging on the door and the group inside had no choice but to open up. The male nurse Filomeno Inolin was the first to step out of the room. He was followed by Dr. Cojuangco. Servillano Aquino came next. The first thing Aquino saw was Asela Carlos sitting on the floor near the chapel door, her back against the wall, her left arm dangling precariously. The Japanese ordered Inolin to turn around and when the male nurse did so, the Japanese stabbed him in the back repeatedly with his bayonet. Aquino watched the nurse fall sprawling on the floor and his eyes were led to the bloodied body of the family help Fortunata Salonga, 14, on the floor.

Terror-stricken Dr. Cojuangco dashed towards the chapel. A Japanese sprang after him and Aquino only heard his father-in-law cry out in pain, "A-a-a-g-h."

Now another Japanese ordered Aquino to turn around. But Aquino had seen what happened to Filomeno Inolin. Instead, he lunged at the Japanese in a determined bid to get hold of the rifle. But the Japanese was quicker and Aquino got the bayonet into his chest, just below the left nipple. He staggered backwards. The Japanese stabbed him again, this time on the right side of the chest. Again the Japanese lunged at Servillano Aquino who got the bayonet in the neck. He fell to the floor.

From where he lay Servillano saw a Japanese drag the recuperating Antonio Cojuangco, Jr., 17, out of his sick room. The boy was so weak he could hardly stand. The Japanese stabbed him twice with his bayonetted rifle and the boy collapsed in a dead heap on the floor.

Now the Japanese pushed Aquino along the floor forward, "like he was cleaning the floor with my body," Aquino testified.

Aquino's month-long bride, the former Trinidad Cojuangco, 18, stood petrified. Suddenly she darted towards her husband. One Japanese shot her in the back. She collapsed to the floor. Now the Japanese tormenting Aquino walked over to the woman on the floor and struck with his bayonet again and again until she was quiet and still. He returned to Aquino and bayonetted him twice more. Aquino passed out.

Wounded in the foyer, Brother Maximin ran up the stairs to the chapel door where Brother Anthony stood trembling and breathless. "They are going to kill us all," Maximin shouted and stumbled inside the chapel, Anthony close on his heels.

Now Brothers Lucian, Gebhard, Lambert, Paul, Hubert, Victor and Mutwald joined Anthony who was trying to stem Maximin's bleeding where the latter lay below the communion railing.

Gebhard and Paul sank to the floor between the middle pews. Mutwald and Victor crouched between the pews farther up. Behind them, the Uychuico servantmaid Regina, but slightly hurt, whimpered in terror. Inside the confessional box, 6-year-old Antonio Carlos lolled about, apparently oblivious to peril. At the door, still on their feet, Brothers Lucian, Lambert and Hubert made as though to bar entry.

A band of five Japanese led by an officer with a saber menacingly confronted the three Brothers at the chapel door. Brother Lucian grappled with the nearest man but the officer with the saber slashed at him with savage blows. Lambert and Hubert too, fell, cruelly mutilated by blades.

Now the band entered the chapel and one after the other the Brothers cowering between the pews came under the sword. Those who did not perish instantly would bleed to death or never come out of shock. Now the 6-year-old Antonio Carlos, now fully conscious of danger, scrambled out of the confessional box. One Japanese chased the terrified child and stuck him in the back, then lifted the 6-year-old's body still stuck on the blade and dashed it to the floor. Antonio had little chance.

Brother Anthony now abandoned Maximin by the communion rail and ran for the exit. He was cornered near the door. One Japanese swung his bayonetted rifle at the Christian Brother. The first blow stuck so deeply that to extricate the blade the Japanese had to place a foot on the Brother's chest. Two successive blows from another assailant sank deep into the abdomen. Five times more the Japanese thrust at Anthony but he was able to parry them and his arms were badly slashed. Bleeding profusely and hurting from his wounds, Anthony reeled into the chapel and fell between the pews. His tormentors left him for dead.

Enrique Vazquez-Prada, 59, half-paralyzed from a stroke, was in the bathroom on the second floor when the Japanese struck in the foyer below. He heard the fearful screams and the shouting, the crash of gunfire and the scurrying of feet down the corridors. Mindful of his condition, Señor Vazquez-Prada stayed in the bathroom.

Also in the bathroom at this time was Teofilo Candari, 23, the cook and baker of the De la Salle community. Teofilo had a small room to himself on the second floor and was up there when he heard the sound of mayhem in the foyer. Teofilo went to the bathroom and locked himself inside a stall.

Now a Japanese marine walked into the toilet and discovered Teofilo Candari in his hiding place. "Are there others here?", the Japanese asked.

"No one," Teofilo replied, whereupon the Japanese struck at him with his fixed-bayonet. Teofilo agilely jumped aside and grappled for the bayonetted rifle. He swung wildly with his fist and sent his adversary on his back to the floor. At this moment, another Japanese marine appeared and slashed at Candari with his bayonet. Candari's right thigh was ripped open. Candari went for this Japanese too, but bleeding and in pain, he took the worst part. His arms were slashed, he was stabbed in the neck and in the back. The bayonet opened his abdomen and Teofilo Candari saw his intestines pop out. He fell, bloodied and gasping, his intestines in his hands. The Japanese left him to die. But Teofilo Candari, bleeding from 33 wounds, did not die. He rolled on the floor till he came where the other wounded lay at the entrance to the chapel.

Sated, the Japanese surveyed their handiwork. In the foyer, the torn bodies, bloodsoaked and with gaping wounds, sprawled everywhere. Some lay quiet and still, dead. Some quivered or moaned in their final throes and were given quick coups-de-grace. The rest lay unconscious from the terrible trauma or in shock from loss of blood. The floor ran with blood. The walls were spangled with red where the wounded had been thrown against them.

Up the staircase, the bodies lay tiny and forsaken. All along the corridors and into the chapel, the dead and dying were scattered.

Inside the chapel, the bodies of the Christian Brothers, clad in their religious habits, sprawled on the tile floor. Blood flowed on the floor, was splashed on the walls and was congealing on the pews.

Now the Japanese started to leave. Behind them there settled a deep, eerie silence, broken only by a sharp gasp or a pained cry from some crushed body that was dying hard. Outside, the shelling did not bate.

Inside the wine cellar, Mrs. Antonio Cojuangco, 37, lay dead. Also inside the cellar, Mrs. Clemente Uychuico and her niece Dionisia Carlos were wounded but alive. Her small daughters Soledad and Paz, and another niece Gloria Carlos, cringed in unmitigated terror, but were unhurt. So was Ramon Cojuangco. Just outside the cellar door,Cojuangco's recent bride, neé Natividad de las Alas, lay dying. Close to her was the lifeless body of the newly-baptized adopted son of the Cojuangcos, Ricardo, 3.

Father Cosgrave lay where he fell, unconscious, blood oozing from stab wounds in the chest. The bodies of two Vazquez-Prada boys sprawled across the priest's legs, dead. Lourdes Cojuangco, 15, sprawled across his head, unconscious. Close to the priest sprawled the dead body of Brother Leo. Brother Arkadius lay within arm's-length, with grievous head injuries, brain matter leaking from his skull.

At the foot of the staircase, Helen Vazquez-Prada, bleeding from multiple wounds, leaned against the wall, her legs extended on the floor. Beside her, Fernando, 5, kept quiet and still, as his mother admonished him. Under a mattress nearby, Clarita Roldan, 17, lay scarcely breathing, but unscathed.

When Rosario Carlos, 21, got her bearings, she found herself under a chair in the corridor to the chapel. The shells from the American sector crashed terrifyingly outside and fearful of getting hit, Rosario slid along the floor towards the chapel door. She reached the door but she was too weak to raise herself over the threshhold into the chapel. She lay there, on the doorstep, aching and confused.

Inside the chapel, the servantmaid Regina had suffered a scratch on the face, but was in near-hysteria. Seeing Brother Anthony alive, she sidled up to him probably seeking comfort in the face of so much death. The wounded Brother asked the convulsively sobbing girl to help him up, but she moved away confused and speechless and sought shelter behind a pew.

Bleeding profusely, Brother Anthony dragged himself to the corridor. He could go no farther and lapsed into unconsciousness again.

Just beyond the gate downstairs, the Japanese made merry. They sang boisterously and shouted, gadding drunkenly about the enclosure as though celebrating something grand. Occasionally some of them would walk into the hall that now reeked with blood, apparently to check whether anyone still moved.

Night fell. In the foyer Father Cosgrave regained consciousness but he was too weak to pull himself from under the bodies that had fallen on him. Lourdes Cojuangco, 15, lay across his head. Now Lourdes stirred and came to, and slid away to nurse her injuries.

Father Cosgrave struggled to his feet and went from one body to another giving absolution to those still alive. Stumbling upon dead bodies, literally slushing through pools of blood, the priest dragged himself up the staircase to the chapel on the second floor. He crawled to the narrow space behind the altar where he collapsed and lost consciousness again.

On the second floor, Enrique Vazquez-Prada, 59 and half-paralyzed, shuffled out of his bathroom stall and through the deathly corridors he crept down the stairway now slippery with blood, searching for his family.

He found the three older boys dead. He was too feeble to do anything for his wife who lay with her legs extended on the floor and her back against the wall by the staircase. Now he took the 5-year-old Fernando back upstairs, seeking food. They found a tin of adobo and Don Enrique fed his son. It was while doing this that a team of Japanese came upon them. Now Enrique Vazquez-Prada fell to bayonet stabs, right before his son's eyes. The boy, himself wounded, was spared. Now he crept back to his hiding place beside his mother by the wall near the staircase in the foyer.

Helen Vazquez-Prada suffered from intense thirst and cried out for water. Lourdes Cojuangco, 15, herself asprawl near the cellar door, advised little Fernando to give his mother the rice washings in a container nearby:

Fernando refused. The water was dirty. Lourdes insisted it was all right. Fernando stoutly refused. Now the Japanese were back, their hob-nailed steps like sentences of death. The two kept still.

When all was quiet again, Ramon Cojuangco crept out of the cellar to pull Lourdes inside. He found his bride barely alive and took her inside too.

At various times the Japanese would tramp into the hall. Once they looked into the cellar, but everyone kept still and they were left unmolested.

Again Ramon Cojuangco ventured out of the cellar and found two of the De la Salle college staff and a male househelp still alive and able to move. He got the three together and his sister Lourdes up the staircase to the chapel where they found Father Cosgrave behind the altar. Ramon's wife could not move and was left in the cellar.

Lourdes came upon Brother Maximin lying by the communion rail, his eyes wide open. Lourdes said something to him only to recoil in horror to find she was talking to a corpse. One of the college staff had a key to the sacristy over the altar. The small group went up the spiral staircase and locked itself in. Here they stayed the night through.

Brother Anthony had regained consciousness and from the corridor where he had collapsed, he struggled down the staircase, hoping that someone in the foyer might be able to help him.

At the foot of the stairs he shouted for help. But none was forthcoming.The Brother made the arduous trip back upstairs and crawled, staggered and slid on the floor, to his own room on the second floor.

In the dark Helen Vazquez-Prada was beset by chills. She cried out for blankets. In the cellar, Dionisia Carlos, 16, recovered from shock, heard the woman's pitiful cries. She rummaged among the boxes in the cellar and found a scarf which she now brought out and wrapped around Mrs. Vazquez-Prada's shoulders.

In the dark, Servillano Aquino lay on the cold tiles in the corridor on the second floor where he had fallen. He could hear Asela Carlos crying for water. Someone came up to her with water. Shortly Asela lay quiet and still. Servillano knew she was dead.

Again in the dark Servillano Aquino heard the voice of his family's maidservant Fortunata Salonga, crying for water. Someone came up with water for her. Shortly, little Fortunata too lay dead.

From other parts of the corridor Servillano could hear the low moans and labored breathing of the wounded. He knew that somewhere near him in the dark his father-in-law Dr. Antonio Cojuangco, Sr., the male nurse Filomeno Inolin, and Rosario Carlos, lay wounded, but were alive.

The distinguished businessman Don Carlos Perez-Rubio lived with his family in an ornate mansion at 150 Vito Cruz street in Malate.[12]

Gatekeeper at the Perez-Rubio mansion was Jose Balboa, who had quarters at the back of the house. This morning at about 10 o'clock the Japanese entered the compound. They hauled Jose Balboa from his quarters and ordered him into the main house. With eight others, Balboa was bundled off to an upstairs room where they were machine-gunned. The Japanese left those who fell for dead. Jose Balboa was not hit, but fell with the rest. Now he forced open a window and dropped to the ground. A Japanese was on the spot as he landed on the ground and slashed at him with a bayonetted rifle. Balboa was hit in the right leg but was able to flee.

Florencio Homol was a houseboy at the Hubert Fox family residence at 151 Balagtas street at the back of the mansion of Carlos Perez-Rubio Mrs. Natti Perez-Rubio Fox was a sister of Don Carlos.

Towards noon today, three Japanese soldiers forced themselves into the Fox premises and searched the house. The three left but were back in fifteen minutes with five other Japanese.

Now the group rounded up the houseboy Florencio Homol, two other Filipino males and a Chinese woman. From here the four were brought around the corner to the residence of Carlos Perez-Rubio on Vito Cruz street.

In the Perez-Rubio garden, the group of Florencio Homol joined about 40 persons, among whom were Don Carlos himself, his wife and children, their servants and people from the neighborhood. The Japanese lined up everybody and divested them of watches, rings, necklaces and other valuables.

Now the Japanese ordered everyone inside the house and got a group to gather the furniture, the rugs and the drapes and pile them in the main hall. The Japanese ordered everyone into the hall, doused the piled combustibles with gasoline, and presently the hall was up in a roaring blaze.

The door was barred from outside but those inside broke it down. Florencio Homol dashed out followed by a young Perez-Rubio daughter. Several people were at a window in an upstairs room screaming for help. Homol looked over his shoulder and saw Miss Perez-Rubio turn back to the burning house, probably to try to unlock the upstairs room, Homol would later declare.

Now the people streamed out of the exits pell-mell, straight into the waiting machine guns of the Japanese in the garden outside. Florencio Homol looked back in time to see Don Carlos Perez-Rubio and his wife fall from the machine gun fire. Homol dashed away to safety and survived to give witness to this incident.

At this time, the noted surgeon Walter K. Frankel, 56, a professor at the University of the Philippines, lived with his wife and sister at Pax Court, a housing compound consisting of four duplexes at 176 Balagtas street in Pasay not far from the Perez-Rubio premises.[12]

Pax Court was owned by Associate Justice of the Philippine Supreme Court Antonio Villareal who lived with his family in a big house in the compound.

The Frankels were passing the afternoon away quietly at four o'clock, when there was heavy knocking at the door. It was a Japanese sergeant. Dr. Frankel showed his papers which identified him as a German-Jew. The Japanese took one look and ordered the three out into the courtyard. Here Dr. Frankel saw his neighbors already assembled, under the bayonets of about 16 Japanese marines. There were 19 persons in the group of whom 13 were Filipino and six Europeans. Eight were small children. The occupants of the other houses in the compound had earlier fled to what they deemed safer places, many to the Perez-Rubio mansion on Vito Cruz street nearby.

Now the Japanese proceeded to tie the hands of everyone behind their backs, finished with which they herded the group into the living room of the duplex apartment rented by Dr. H.A. Luerse, 45, a refugee German chemist. Here they were made to kneel, facing the wall. Now the Japanese proceeded to heap around the kneeling group pieces of furniture, cushions, pillows and strawbags. Upon these they splashed gasoline out of a bottle and set the pile ablaze. Then the sergeant hurled a hand-grenade. Justice Villareal might have been killed instantly. Mrs. Villareal jumped up screaming and was shot dead. Mrs. Frankel raised her head towards her husband and was shot dead, too. Mrs. Luerse moved and she got a fatal bullet. Now the room was all smoke and flames. The Japanese withdrew elsewhere in the compound.

Because Dr. Frankel had a bad leg and could not kneel, he lay on his side on the floor. One of the housemaids in the group had loosened her bonds and now was untying Dr. Frankel.

"Run upstairs," Frankel told the maid who grabbed a small girl and dashed away. The two were presently back down the stairs screaming, their clothes on fire.

Dr. Frankel helped his sister Mrs. Alice Stahl up and together with Dr. Luerse and his nine-year-old daughter Jutta, they skipped through the flames to the door and out into the garage. The other houses in the compound were now burning. Dr. Frankel found a knife and cut the three others from their bonds. Behind the big house occupied by Justice Villareal and his family was a bomb shelter. Unobserved by the Japanese, the four darted inside the shelter.

Refugees at the Santos home on Vermont street in Malate since the 10th, Jose G. Villanueva and his family lived in terror with each passing hour.[14] Japanese patrols roamed the streets. Bomb and shell exploded relentlessly and now the fires raged close to their refuge.

This afternoon, Jose G. Villanueva got his family together once more and raced through streets turned into battlegrounds to the ruins of the house of Dr. de la Paz on nearby Florida street. Major Alfonso Fresnido and his family ran with them. Other refugees had the same inspiration, it seems, for the Villanuevas and the Fresnidos found about 400 persons already in the place. The house was gutted but the concrete walls provided shelter.

A refugee from the Japanese and the carpet-shelling from the American sector since Saturday, 10 February, Modesto Farolan today cowered behind every kind of shelter in the compound on Gonzalez street, off San Marcelino.[15] The shelling never ceased and by daylight today the building in the compound where he had found cover started to burn. Farolan sprinted across General Luna street to the ruins of another compound. All day the area was the target of American artillery.

This afternoon, seeing no way of escaping from the area, with Japanese sentries positioned at all possible exit points, Farolan dashed back to the Gonzalez street compound where the buildings smouldered. Leaping from shelter to shelter, he chanced upon the foxhole where the Red Cross nurses Florita Loberiza and Marina de Paz huddled, having fled the Red Cross building. The other nurse, Gliceria Andaya, badly wounded, was still in the Red Cross building.

In a bomb shelter off Pennsylvania street in Singalong, Alberto Delfino, Venezuelan consul in Manila, and his group huddled in fear.[16] They had been here since 9 February, when a shell crashed into their lodgings at the corner of Pennsylvania and Dagonoy streets. With them were eight women who were known to be friendly, in sexual terms, with the Japanese.

At 6 o'clock this evening, Mrs. Leopold Kahn decided to leave the bomb shelter for what she considered to be the safer confines of the Pedro Campos compound nearby. With her went her three sons -- Gilbert, Dennis and Pierre, and their servantmaid Gloria. That left the Delfinos, their househelp Beatriz Amigo, and the eight women of doubtful virtue in the bomb shelter. There was also a husband-and-wife team who used to serve the Francisco Pellicer family. The man, Igmidio Ramos, was the cook. The Pellicers had occupied an apartment unit adjacent to the Delfinos. Mrs. Kahn's househelp, Segundina Butin, and her two small children, also remained.

At 9 o'clock this evening, a band of four Japanese came into the bomb-shelter and called the refugees outside. A group of 12 emerged from the shelter, led by the Venezuelan consul Alberto P. Delfino and his wife. One of the eight prostitutes came out with them. The other seven, with their huge stock of food and clothing, stayed inside. The Japanese did not mind.

The group of four Japanese tied the men behind their backs and then tied them to each other. They did not tie-up the women and children. The Japanese then led the group of 12 up Taft Avenue to the corner at Vito Cruz, and brought them into a cafe named *The White Dove*. The Japanese told the group that they would be brought to St. Scholastica college where there were spacious bomb-shelters. They stayed at *The White Dove* overnight.

At 9 o'clock this evening two armed Filipinos came up to the refugees in the ruins of the de la Paz home on Florida street. They were *makapilis.* Presently the refugee-group was being fired upon, whether by the *makapilis,* Jose G. Villanueva could not tell. Grenade explosions tore up the area and in the dark Villanueva could hear people screaming in pain. Later Villanueva found that his friend Major Alfonso Fresnido was killed during the explosions, together with a daughter and a nephew.[17]

Now shells literally rained down as though the spot itself was on target. One deafening explosion hit particularly close by. People screamed in pain and terror. Jose G. Villanueva felt a tingling sensation on his head. He looked down to see himself bathed in his own blood. Blinded temporarily by the blood flowing down his face, choking from the dust kicked up by the explosions, Villanueva called out the names of his children one-by-one. The eldest did not respond. Only then did he realize that his son Ernesto, 21, who lay alongside him, was dead.

Ensconced in the bomb shelter in the ruins of the family mansion on Padre Faura street, Paz Zamora de Mascuñana managed to drop off to sleep.[18] Shortly she was awake again. A band of Japanese had entered the premises, firing indiscriminately and tossing hand grenades, "right and left," Mrs. Mascuñana writes. From her dugout Mrs. Mascuñana could hear terrorized cries of young people pleading, "Please don't shoot, we are non-combatants."

Inside the dugout Mrs. Mascuñana began to recite the prayers to the Virgin of the Miraculous Medal she had learned for the moments near death. The young househelp cried out to their absent parents. The houseboy Lee Tong muzzled the dog Lady with his hands to prevent if from barking. The prayer had been composed by the Vincentian Father Jose Fernandez, parish priest of San Marcelino, for those in crisis, but now Mrs. Mascuñana could not remember a word beyond exclaiming, "Little Virgin, abandon not those about to die . . ."

The Japanese left. Mrs. Mascuñana suffered a slight scratch from flying grenade fragments. But now the shelling from the American side had become more violent. The group curled up tightly in the dugout, scarcely breathing.

TUESDAY, 13 FEBRUARY 1945

Convinced that the situation in Manila had become irreversible, General Yokoyama today ordered Iwabuchi to return to Fort McKinley and start the withdrawal of troops from the city without waiting for the counterattack scheduled for the night of 16-17 February.[1]

Between Taft Avenue and Marques de Comillas street a set of heavily fortified buildings constituted a formidable strongpoint. These included the Hike Shoe factory at the corner formed by Marques de Comillas and Isaac Peral, with the Manila club, the headquarters of the association of British nationals, adjoining to the north, beyond which was the Santa Teresa college for girls ran by the Belgian Sisters.

Across San Marcelino street from Santa Teresa college was the Paules church and seminary, to the south of which was the German club near the corner of San Luis and San Marcelino streets. Beyond this point on San Marcelino extending to the corner at Isaac Peral, was the new Manila Police headquarters. All these buildings were constructed of substantial material and were strongly defended.

This morning the Manila club and the new Manila Police headquarters came under heavy artillery bombardment. Fire-power from 155-mm. howitzers, 105-mm. high explosive shells from self-propelled mounts, and the high-velocity 76-mm. guns of a tank destroyer were concentrated on the two buildings with but little noticeable effect on the defenders.

As dawn broke, apprehension gripped the refugees in the ruins of the Mascuñana property on Padre Faura street in Ermita. The survivors of the previous night's grenade attack feared that the Japanese might return.[2]

In her shelter Doña Paz Zamora de Mascuñana passed out confidential instructions to members of her family in the event the unwanted occurred and the others survived. Where she carried the money, where to find the keys to the bank vaults, where to find the family jewelry . . .

In such despair did the day begin that Doña Paz was unprepared for the smile-wreathed face of a youth that appeared over the wall separating her property from the next, nor for the jubilant tone of his voice as he announced, "The Americans are here. . ."

"Like a marvelous vision in the morning twilight," Mrs. Mascuñana writes, "there bobbed up from behind the wall the heads of American soldiers, bronzed by the tropical sun, laughing and smiling . . ."

At 7 o'clock this morning, Modesto Farolan peered out of his hiding place on Isaac Peral street and saw a Filipino guerrilla on the prowl.[3] He was a scout for the American forces who had reached the Paco Cemetery off General Luna street nearby. The scout urged the refugees to clear the area. People now came out of shelter and a stampede in the direction of the Paco Cemetery ensued. Farolan followed the crowd. As he ran he saw the Red Cross nurses, Florita Loberiza and Marina de Paz, dash in the direction of the Red Cross building. He presumed they were going for the other Red Cross nurse, Gliceria Andaya.

At the Paco Cemetery the American soldiers told the refugees to follow the telephone wires on the ground to the liberated sector. The crowds ran through streets newly-cleared of mines and across backyards and through the charred ruins of their own neighborhoods, on towards Pandacan. Modesto Farolan had made it to safety.

At Red Cross headquarters, Nurse Florita Loberiza did her best to comfort the wounded and the dying. Nurse Gliceria Andaya was seriously wounded, but she was alive. Marina de Paz, though herself suffering from a wound in the back, managed to help Miss Loberiza take care of the others.

Towards noon, a new sound came up from the streets. American soldiers were in the area and were directing the refugees towards the safe zones. The Red Cross nurses joined the exodus.[4]

Morning found Jose G. Villanueva and his family still cowering among the ruins on Florida street in Malate. The dead from the previous night's shelling lay among the living. Mrs. Villanueva, grief-stricken, was determined that her family leave the place immediately.[5]

Abandoning the dead body of their son and the few bundles they had salvaged of their belongings, the Villanuevas again took to the open space, except now the family could not find its bearings. This was their own neighborhood, but all familiar landmarks had disappeared. Now amidst the debris, the Villanueva family was lost while shells exploded all around them.

In the distance they saw some elderly people picking their way among the rubble. The Villanuevas followed. In this way Jose G. Villanueva and the surviving members of his family reached Remedios street and Taft Avenue, and on to the liberated territories in Paco.

Battling every step of the way from the Estero de Paco, the 148th Regiment reached Taft Avenue today.[6]

The 148th's left flank extended from Herran street southward to Harrison Boulevard where it touched the 12th Cavalry Regiment.

The 148th's right flank was held up between Marques de Comillas and General Luna street to the east, blocked by the new Manila Police headquarters strongpoint on Isaac Peral and San Marcelino.

Today the 2nd Battalion, 148th Infantry, took its turn to confront the Japanese on the Taft Avenue line, fronting the PGH and the University of the Philippines. Now the Japanese opened up with mortar and rifle fire on the 2nd which stood on Pennsylvania street a block from Taft. The American artillery had been restrained from firing on PGH targets as it was known that the hospital harbored civilian refugees.

Since the streets approaching Taft Avenue from the east were covered by gun-emplacements in the PGH and UP premises, the 148th Infantry now prepared to assault from the westside.

In the light of day, the young Uychuico househelp, Clarita Roldan, 17, her sense of responsibility and her presence of mind intact through all her harrowing experience, now had better opportunity to assess the aftermath of yesterday's incidents at the south wing of the De la Salle college on Taft Avenue in Malate. She looked over the foyer area and ascertained who were still alive and who were beyond help.[7]

Brother Arkadius, with grievous head injuries, lay dying, but none knew how to assuage his suffering.

By the staircase, Mrs. Helen Vazquez-Prada agonized unmitigatedly. Her injuries were lethal. Beside her clung her son. Fernando, 5.

In the cellar, Mrs. Ramon Cojuangco, nee Natividad de las Alas, succumbed this morning.

Now Clarita Roldan ventured up to the second floor. On the staircase, she came upon the dead body of her employer, Dr. Clemente Uychuico, with his son, Ramon, 4, also dead, in his arms.

On the corridor, Clarita came upon Dr. Antonio Cojuangco, extremely faint but alive, and still able to direct the girl to fetch calcium pills for him from his little black bag in the sick room adjoining the chapel. Dr.

Cojuangco asked Clarita to get Dr. Uychuico, if still alive, to come over and attend to him. When told that Dr. Uychuico was dead, the doctor lapsed into impenetrable depression. He may have died not long after.

Servillano Aquino, 25, lay where he fell in the corridor, too weak to pick himself up.

Rosario Carlos, 21, lay across the threshhold to the chapel. But she was too weak to move herself up the single step to get inside.

On one of the pews Brother Hubert lay, critically wounded.

Sometime this morning, unknown to the others, Mrs. Felicidad Uychuico, wounded superficially in the leg, carefully concealed her two small daughters, Soledad, 6, and Paz, 3, behind the dead body of Mrs. Antonio Cojuangco in the cellar. Now Mrs. Uychuico shuffled out of the De la Salle gate into the open, oblivious of the shelling from the American sector and the menace from the Japanese. Her clothes were stiff with dried blood. She was worn and dishevelled. Anyone who saw her may have thought her lost and demented. Alone and uncaring, she crossed the crucial Taft Avenue battleline and ambled on, eyes staring blankly, until she reached her parent's home on Tramo street.

Back on the second floor of the south wing at De la Salle, a band of Japanese came up. One of them divested Servillano Aquino of his ring, watch and shoes. Close by was the dead body of Fortunata Salonga. As Aquino watched, a pair of Japanese attempted to molest the dead girl. They tore off the girl's underwear. But rigor mortis had set in and they could not part the girl's legs. The two abandoned their enterprise. They left the dead girl's body, the genitals exposed, within Aquino's view, an arm's length away. But he was too badly hurt to move himself.

When the Japanese had gone, Clarita Roldan got together the other servant girls who had been but slightly hurt, including Felisa with the 3-year-old Jose Carlos, Jr., in her arms, Juanita and Regina, who had regained her composure. To make themselves inconspicuous to the Japanese outside, they donned the black robes of the Christian Brothers.

The girls discovered the group of five up in the sacristy over the altar area. Now Clarita organized those in the cellar to get up to the relative safety of the sacristy. These included the Carlos sisters Gloria and Dionisia and their little brother, Jose, Jr., the little Uychuico girls, Soledad and Paz. The boy Fernando Vazquez-Prada, 5, would not leave his mother's side.

The group assisted Rosario Carlos and Servillano Aquino into the chapel where they lay down on the pews. The college helper, Anselmo Sudlan who was seriously wounded when the Japanese took him away Monday afternoon with two others, was also helped into the chapel.

When her own home at 4035 Pennsylvania street burned down on the 10th February, Mrs. Maria Campos-Lopez, 43, and her two children, fled to the home of her sister-in-law, Mrs. Concepcion Campos, widow of the late Don Pedro Campos, at 1462 Taft Avenue not far from De la Salle college.[8] The Campos residence was constructed of heavy material and was surrounded by a high concrete wall.

At about 8 o'clock this morning, a band of Japanese knocked at the door of the home of Concepcion Campos. Mrs. Campos herself and her daughter Pilar opened the door and were immediately shot down. There were about 120 persons who had sought refuge in the Campos compound at this time. Now the Japanese called out the people inside the house to the garden. The people walked out of the house, singly and in groups, clinging together in fear. The Japanese started firing.

The family of Judge Arsenio Locsin, refugees in the Campos compound, was together and almost together they fell in the first machine gun-burst. The daughter, Carmen, 20, was hit four times in different parts of the body. She fell and got up again and staggered to a corner of the garden where she collapsed.[9]

Mrs. Maria Campos-Lopez was cooking breakfast when the firing began. She rushed to the living room where she found about 40 terrified persons clinging to each other in bunches. A Japanese soldier came in and without a word started splashing alcohol from a bottle all over the room, on the pieces of furniture and on the drapes. He lit the alcohol and leaped away as the room burst into flames. The people in the burning room dashed for the exits. As they ran out they were greeted with machine gun-fire by the Japanese waiting outside.

Mrs. Lopez ran out too but was not seriously hurt. She clambered over the wall to the adjoining property and watched as her late brother's home was consumed by flames.

Carmen Locsin lay in a corner of the garden until 5o'clock this afternoon. The others lay where they fell. When the Japanese had gone, someone she did not know pulled Carmen to her feet and helped her up a ladder propped on the back fence of the Campos garden and over to an adjoining property. Here she was joined by Pilar Campos, who was grievously wounded.[10]

This morning, a Japanese squad came into Luis Gallent's cell at Fort Santiago and picked four of the men to go with them.[11] The four, among them Gallent, were led to the fire station near the entrance to the Fort to collect food that had been brought there by families of the detainees.

As it turned out, women and children had managed to put together bits of food and had brought them to Fort Santiago for their relatives. The

Japanese ordered them to leave their small bundles at the fire station. The Japanese would then help themselves to the contents of the bundles and leave the rest lying around.

Still, there had accumulated over the past several days a small stock of leftover food. Now the Japanese wanted this to be distributed to the civilian detainees in the Fort.

Luis Gallent and his party gathered as much of the food as they could, but they could not find containers for distribution. But they found a book which they tore apart page-by-page. They deposited bits of food on each page which they handed to each detainee in their cell. It all amounted to about a handful of food on one page for each detainee in that cell.

Umberto de Poli, 60, at this time lived at 478 Luis Francisco street in Pasay.[12] He was an Italian expatriate who had lived in the Philippines for 35 years. At 9 o'clock this morning he went out to bring a basket of provisions to his wife who was staying with relatives in Malate, farther north from this point. At the corner of Vito Cruz and Dominga, the Japanese sentry hailed de Poli and waved him over to his side of the street. When de Poli came within reach the Japanese sentry slapped him in the face, w-h-a-p to the right and w-h-a-p to the left. The sentry took away his basket of provisions, snatched his eyeglasses off his nose. De Poli showed his passport which stated his nationality. It did not do him any good. His papers were confiscated.

From this point Umberto de Poli was hauled over to *The White Dove* café at the corner of Vito Cruz and Taft Avenue. Here he found six men tied by the wrists behind their backs and strung together. One of the men was the consul of Venezuela in Manila, Albert O. Delfino.

From *The White Dove* café the group now consisting of 13 persons was marched to a compound at 1609 Taft Avenue. In the yard the party found another group of about 30, among whom were many women and children. From the yard the whole group was brought to one of the houses in the compound and lined up in two rows in an upstairs room. They were made to stand facing the windows away from the door, whereupon de Poli heard the sound of machine gun-fire from behind. The first row closer to the door fell upon the second row by the windows, and de Poli found himself under several bodies. Killed in the first burst of machine gun-fire were the Venezuelan consul Albert O. Delfino and his wife, and their son Francis, 17.

The people were tied together by the wrist and Umberto de Poli struggled in a tight bind as the others strung with him thrashed about in their death throes. A Japanese splashed a bucket of gasoline into the room and a blaze sprang up. The cries of the children drowned the groans of the dying.

From the floor de Poli looked up and saw against the wall a statuette of the Virgin Mary with the Child Jesus in her arms. In his mind Umberto de Poli now saw himself as a child with his own mother in Italy and the lessons of his Catholic childhood rushed back to him.

Now with all the fervor he could muster he said in his heart, addressing the image of the Virgin, "If you can do something, at least for these children, please do it."

From where he lay prostrate on the floor of the burning room, Umberto de Poli saw a little girl rise from the heap of writhing bodies, loosen her bonds and start to untie everyone else who was still alive. Ten persons were freed by the little girl, among them Umberto de Poli, 60.

The door was barred from behind. The survivors battered the door down and dashed into the yard. The Japanese were outside the gate. Now de Poli threw his weight on a papaya tree in the yard and knocked it to the ground. Then he leaned the papaya tree trunk against the garden wall, and all eleven survivors by turns clambered up the trunk over the wall into the adjoining property, and on to safety.

Cringing inside their shelter on Remedios street in Malate, 14-year-old Lydia Gutierrez was able to identify a new kind of shell.[13] "It buries itself in the earth and the earth shakes," she recalls in her diary. A neighbor was hit by a fragment of this new kind of shell. He screamed in pain and probably more in terror, and his body "was full of straight black lines and he was smoking, even his hair."

The shelling did not let-up. Towards noon a new terror arrived: planes started dropping bombs. "There were shells again and no more lulls," Lydia writes. "Just shells and bombs and shrapnel. We were just waiting to die."

In the afternoon a lull did come. Peering out of their shelter the Gutierrez refugee group saw people walking on the street with their hands up, like they were in the act of surrendering. When they dared to inquire, the Gutierrezes were told that the Americans were on Taft Avenue and guerrilla scouts had told people to head in that direction. The Gutierrezes hesitated. A neighbor arrived and confirmed the information that the area from Taft Avenue eastward to Paco had been liberated. Now the family got together what they had saved of their belongings, piled them on pushcarts with the children, and joined the trek eastwards. Guerrillas were in the streets giving directions.

How did a guerrilla look like? "We recognized many of them," Lydia writes. "Also the man selling bananas in the market."

At the corner of Taft Avenue and Remedios street, Lydia's group saw what they feared to be Japanese in darkgreen uniform and helmets and guns. But they were big men. As the group approached closer they saw that these were not Japanese. They were Americans. With the simplicity of the overwhelmed and the relieved, Lydia Gutierrez closes her narrative of a fearful period in her fourteen years with four words: "We were so happy!"

Today elements of the 1st Cavalry reached Pasay from Santa Ana. Hearing from neighbor Don Rosendo Guzman that American troops were on Buendia street, Benigno del Rio raced with other young men all the way from Dominga street. Just at this moment Japanese artillery started firing on the area from Fort McKinley. Unable to get nearer the Americans, Benigno and his eager fellow-welcomers raced back to Dominga street.[14]

Later in the day, the Americans reached Dominga street. But Benigno del Rio found difficulty savoring the moment. Each American, or so it seemed to him, was surrounded by at least twenty Filipinos, and he had to jostle his way close to one.

"The people of Pasay were so happy to see the liberators that they hardly allowed them breathing-space," Del Rio writes in his diary.

Through the night the survivors of the Pax Court massacre on Balagtas street in Pasay huddled in the air-raid shelter behind their late landlord's house.[15] At 3 o'clock this morning little Jutta Luerse became restless. In a few minutes she was dead.

"I think by the effect of the smoke and heart weakness," Dr. Walter F. Frankel declares.

Now in Pasay elements of the 11th Airborne were about the streets. At 4:30 this afternoon a patrol wandered into the burntout Pax Court and found the survivors sheltered there.

In his house on Remedios street in Malate, Dr. Aristeo Ubaldo Rizal cowered terror-stricken.[16] He was a distinguished opthalmologist and nephew of the national hero Jose Rizal (his mother Olympia was Rizal's sister). Dr.Ubaldo had seen his wife and children hauled away by the Japanese. Now an American shell made a direct hit on the adjoining house. Dr. Ubaldo rushed out of his own house. Panicky crowds swirled on the streets and the doctor was drawn into the vortex.

Rushing madly down the street without direction, the crowd met two Filipinos who solicitously pointed to the relative safety offered by a nearby stone-fenced compound. The agitated group entered the compound and indeed felt grateful for the suggestion. The two men left and shortly were back, this time with two Japanese marines who were laughing in apparent glee but with fixed bayonets in their hands. The Filipinos were *makapilis.*

The Japanese ordered all men in the compound to stand. When the men stood up, Dr. Ubaldo among them, they were ordered to file out in batches of ten. The batches of ten were tied together with twine and herded into an apartment house that belonged to Dr. Paz Mendoza-Guazon, where they were detained. The door to the apartment house was barred from outside. Now the Japanese threw hand-grenades into the hall.

Inside, Dr. Ubaldo lost consciousness. He came to when he felt the man next to him kicking him. He opened his eyes to see that the building they were in was on fire. Now Dr. Ubaldo and the others still alive battered the door down and fled the burning apartment house.

Dr. Ubaldo returned to his house which was still untouched by fire. He hid in the kitchen from where he could see the neighborhood in flames. Then his son-in-law arrived and together the two left the house and ran from shelter-to-shelter until they reached the liberated area across Taft Avenue.

Elpidio Quirino stood among other refugees on the west bank of the Estero de Paco. Across the *estero* was liberated territory.

Now Quirino retrieved a door that had been blown off its hinges from a building nearby and using the door as a raft, he ferried the surviving members of his clan across the *estero*. First Tommy Quirino, whose wounded leg had become gangrenous, then Raul Mendoza with his shattered arm. Then followed Doña Nila Syquia-Mendoza and her daughter Millie, 11, and the small boys, Enrique, 8, and Renato, 5. Five times Elpidio Quirino, distinguished statesman, swam across the *estero* in Paco, ferrying the surviving members of his family on board the raft that had been once a door.[17]

Vicky Quirino, 13, and her cousin, Luis Mendoza, 16, swam across the murky waters to the opposite bank.

It was at this point, on this day, that Felipe Buencamino III saw Senator Quirino. He wrote: "The first I saw amid the fire-levelled district of Paco was former Senator Elpidio Quirino. Senator Quirino had aged in ten days and his face had a lost expression. He was not the same man I had seen so often in the past . . . His wife and two daughters had been killed by the Japanese. His son Tommy was injured . . ."

Felipe Buencamino III was a journalist who had joined advance parties of the 1st Cavalry into Malate. He wrote of what he saw this day in *Free Philippines.*[18]

"I saw Mrs. Pura Villanueva-Kalaw, widow of the late Don Teodoro

Kalaw, sitting on the ground beside a cart containing all that was left of her belongings," Buencamino wrote. Don Teodoro Kalaw was the eminent Filipino journalist and scholar, who spent his last years as director of the National Library. His widow was equally eminent as writer and feminist leader. She was the custodian of great cultural treasures collected by her husband. Now Mrs. Kalaw told Felipe Buencamino III that the historic papers of the Katipunan and the original papers of Philippine masonry were lost in her burning home. It relieved her that she was able to save the diploma of Jose Rizal and the originals of writings of Apolinario Mabini.

"I met Mrs. Alejandro Roces, Sr., and her daughter Bebeng looking for the other members of their family," Buencamino wrote. Mrs. Roces was the widow of the publisher Alejandro Roces, Sr, who died earlier during the Japanese occupation.

"I saw Dr. Antonio Vasquez and his son Dr. Luis Vasquez helping the wounded," Buencamino wrote, "giving first aid treatment to the injured amid intermittent fire." The Vasquezes had turned their home on Vermont and Wright streets in Malate into an emergency hospital. Hundreds of wounded were brought in here for emergency treatment.

Elpidio Quirino had collected the surviving members of his family on the east bank of the Estero de Paco. Now he took off again in the direction of Pandacan.

"I ventured to look for a first aid station which I had failed to see the night before," Quirino would recall, "in order to dress the wounds of two dying members of my family, and at last I saw a Red Cross flag flying over the devastated and bloody area in Pandacan. My soul was simply lifted up to heaven."[19]

Through the chaos, Quirino was able to locate a motor vehicle and was driven back to the *estero* to pick up his family. Tommy's toes were turning black. Raul with his shattered arm was in no better straits. The group was first brought across the bailey bridge at Nagtahan to Malacañang but the emergency hospital at the palace had no room for the civilian injured. They went to San Beda college but the situation was the same. So they were brought to San Lazaro hospital where they were taken in.

Having secured the hospitalization of his wounded, Elpidio Quirino returned to Malacañang. Geronima T. Pecson walked into a hall as Elpidio Quirino, bedraggled and bloodstained, his daughter Victoria in tow, hove into view. Through his ordeal, Quirino had remained his portly self. Mrs. Pecson rummaged hard and long among her supplies to find the rightsize clothing for the statesman, now but one more refugee.[20]

In a ward at the San Lazaro hospital, Tomas Quirino lay helter-skelter with hundreds of others, bloodied and mutilated, torn and mangled, dead and dying. Tommy's untreated leg had festered and gangrene had set in.

"That (the leg) will have to go," the American medical officer decided.

"But no," Tomas Quirino insisted. "I want to see my cousin, Dr. May Quirino."

Dr. May Quirino was on the staff of the San Lazaro hospital. She was the daughter of the lawyer Ernesto Quirino, Elpidio Quirino's elder brother. Dr. Quirino had been on duty continuously at the San Lazaro hospital all through this period and presently she was beside her cousin. Tomas Quirino's leg was saved.

When World War II broke out in the Philippines in December 1941, the Malate Catholic school at the corner of A. Mabini and San Andres streets in Malate was converted into an emergency hospital and designated Red Cross hospital No. 4.[21]

In May 1942, the Red Cross closed its emergency operations and the Catholic Women's League took over the administration of the hospital, now named Remedios hospital.

A section of the former school building housed the small community of five Irish Columban priests who administered the Malate parish. Father Henaghan was superior of the community, Father Patrick Kelly was parish priest and Father John Lallor was superintendent of buildings. The other two were Fathers Peter Fallon and Joseph Monaghan.[22]

Today the Remedios hospital sheltered not only the wounded brought in from the streets but also refugees from the Malate area.

At the Bureau of Plant Industry compound on San Andres street in Malate, several employees cringed in their bomb-shelter in the premises. Many of them had been here for several days, unable to return to their own homes. Among them was the eminent food scientist Maria Y. Orosa, 52.[23]

As chief of the food utilization division of the Bureau of Plant Industry, Miss Orosa has had a distinguished career in a field of expertise which came into full use during the crises of World War II in the Philippines.

Today Miss Orosa shared a dugout in the BPI compound on San Andres with several members of her staff. The shelling was particularly heavy and the area seemed to be in the focus of the bombardment. With Miss Orosa were close associates Antonia Claraval, Gloria Blanco and Felicidad Geronimo. Now the bomb-shelter received a direct-hit. Two persons in the shelter were killed instantly. Miss Claraval was seriously injured and Miss Orosa sustained a minor wound on the foot. The survivors managed to bring the two to the Remedios hospital not far from this point. While awaiting treatment, Antonia Claraval expired. Miss Orosa lay awaiting attention when a shell fell close by. A piece of shrapnel found its way straight into Maria Orosa's heart, killing her outright.

This afternoon the Alhambra apartments in the vicinity of the Bayview hotel caught fire. About 150 Filipino women and girls and a few Spanish women are being held in the apartment building. They had earlier been moved to this place from the Bayview hotel.

Now the women rushed out into the streets nearby. The neighborhood was a total ruin and the gutted buildings offered scant protection.

In the group of women many of whom carried babies and small children was Erlinda Querubin, 25.[24] She had escaped being ravished by dabbing her face with dirt and otherwise looking unattractive. Whenever a Japanese showed interest in her she pretended to nurse a friend's baby.

Now Erlinda Querubin and her group moved out to the Luneta. The area was crisscrossed by trenches and bunkers which the Japanese had dug as part of their defense lines.

The party of women, many of them ill, crouched in the trenches. Now and then the Japanese would come out and take pot-shots at them.

"They would aim their rifles at us and say, the Americans are coming but you won't see them," Erlinda Querubin testified.

This evening a drunken Japanese officer barged into the Santa Rosa college ruins where the staff of the erstwhile San Juan de Dios hospital and their surviving patients were refugees.[25]

Sister Teresa Vilatela, 58, a Spanish national and Superior of the Daughters of Charity on the nursing staff, relates: ". . . a woman shouted that a drunken Japanese had entered. He was half-naked with a freesword swinging in the air . . . all of us ran – stumbling over weak patients and stones."

Sister Concepcion Gotera recalls the incident, thus: "He caught one of our aged, rheumatic Sisters, and holding her in a corner, he swung high his sword to cut off her head. If the brutal act was not carried out it was just really a miracle."

Two Japanese soldiers arrived but did not intervene. They claimed no one may divest a Japanese officer of his sword. They watched the drunken officer prance about menacing the refugees and laughed. Finally, exhausted and bleeding from cuts made by his own sword, the Japanese officer allowed himself to be led out of the Santa Rosa college ruins by the soldiers.

Early this evening at Fort Santiago, Luis Gallent saw Japanese bring in gasoline drums into the building where his group was confined.[26] The Japanese pierced the drums with bayonets and let the gasoline flow down the corridors. They ignited the gasoline and it shot up in a huge blaze.

The door on Gallent's cell was barred from outside. One of the men climbed up to the window and destroyed the transoms. Seven of the nine men made it out of the cell, the other two being so enfeebled they could not climb up to the tiny window. Luis Gallent estimates that there were 3,000 persons milling around the burning premises at this time.

The building was crumbling down. Burning timber was falling on the floor. Now Luis Gallent watched horror-stricken as his father fell while dashing for the stairway. The stampede passed over the elderly man's body and Luis Gallent never saw his father again.

At one end of the corridor the Japanese had mounted a machine gun. Now, as the men milled around for the exits, they opened fire.Luis jumped out the window into what turned out to be a garage. His younger brother was behind him. From the ground Luis watched his brother struggle to lift himself up the window. Other men were pressing on the young man. Now Luis saw his brother fall backwards. He did not appear at the window again.

Luis Gallent ran towards the stone walls and clambered to the top. His hand was pierced by barbed-wire. For a moment he stood on top of the wall nursing his pierced palm. At this moment, other fleeing men brushed past him and he was nudged down the wall into the riverbank below. Luis Gallent lost consciousness. When he came to, he found that he could not move. He lay where he fell, his back broken.

This evening a band of Japanese marines from among those quartered in the Zobel mansion, an ornate confection in the manner of a mediterranean villa, at the corner of Padre Faura street and Dewey Boulevard, entered the garage of the g utted Valdez apartment where an international group of refugees huddled.[27]

The shelling from the American sector was intense and the entire area was now virtually rubble. The Zobel home and the servants' quarters at the back had escaped a direct hit. Now the Japanese urged the refugees to move out to the Zobel compound which they said was safer. Afraid not to heed this advice, the refugees moved out as a group. Except Sophy Natalie Morgin. She saw that the other place was as much in peril, with shrapnel flying all around and shells bursting on nearly every square yard of ground.

"I thought I would be just as safe where I was, if not safer," she writes, "away from those marines."

Now Sophy Natalie Morgin was alone in the half-dark. Shells whistled overhead and the earth trembled when they hit. Machine gun-fire rattled close by. Now by the glow of the raging fire Miss Morgin saw in the shadows of the derelict garage a sheeted figure rise and float about. Confronted by what she thought was a ghost on one hand, and on the other by a wicked combination of exploding American shells and murderous Japanese marines, Sophy Natalie Morgin came to a momentous decision. She ran out of the garage, screaming!

WEDNESDAY, 14 FEBRUARY 1945

Company A, 754th Tank Battalion, was called in to support the 129th Infantry in the renewed siege on the Japanese strongpoints at the Marques de Comillas-Isaac Peral area this morning.[1] The tank guns laid down a pre-dawn barrage that shook the Manila Police headquarters to its foundations.

At dawn today, Company A, 129th Infantry, broke into the building, surprising the Japanese who had withdrawn from positions during the pre-assault artillery and tank bombardment. Crashing through windows on the first floor, the Americans took the initial advantage.

Meanwhile, a platoon of Company C, 129th Infantry, burst into the basement. Capitalizing on the surprise element, they easily gained the upperhand.

To the north along San Marcelino street, Company B, 129th Infantry, tackled the Manila Club.

The Americans in the basement and the first floor of the Manila Police headquarters faced a grim task. Each square foot of space was bitterly contested. Still, the Americans gained ground.Driven upwards, the Japanese now resorted to a new trick: they started dropping explosives through holes chopped on the second floor.

By nightfall, Company A and Company C had been turned out of the Manila Police headquarters building. Company B held tightly onto the precious ground it had won at the Manila Club.

At the residence of the Chicote family fancifully dubbed by its owners *La Casona*, on San Carlos street in Ermita, the aging Don Alfredo Chicote Beltran passed anxious hours with his sister Encarnacion; two daughters, Eloisa and Conchita; and a son, Jose Maria. In the next house was another son, Antonio, with his wife Camilla and their six-month-old baby girl. The eldest son Prudencio and his family were in the adjacent San Carlos apartments. So were two Chicote daughters, their respective spouses and their children.[2]

Early this morning a squad of Japanese marines burst into *La Casona* and the neighboring houses on San Carlos street in Ermita. They did not go up the San Carlos apartment building. Under flashing bayonets the occupants of these houses were led out to the street and from there, to the Luneta.

At the Luneta, the San Carlos street party joined a throng of several hundred civilians. The Japanese ordered each person to empty his or her pockets. Everyone was divested of valuables he or she carried on his or her person.

The men were separated from the women. The men were herded to the Peralta apartment building on Isaac Peral street, and the women to the Manila Hotel.

Later this morning, Prudencio Chicote scaled the wall that separated San Carlos apartments from the *La Casona* compound and entered the house through the backdoor. In the past few days he had been doing this several times a day. This morning he was greeted by ominous silence. He called out names. He ran from room-to-room. The house was deserted. Pale and shaken, he hurried back to his wife and son.

When the Bayview Hotel burned down on the 12th February, Nadia Nestrenko, a white Russian expatriate and owner of the *Butterfly Cafe* on Plaza Fergusson, was among the women who escaped. With others she hid out in the ruins of another building in the neighborhood.[3]

This morning a band of Japanese discovered their hiding place and the women were hauled to the Manila Hotel.

On Taft Avenue in Malate, Carmen Locsin, 20, lay in the ruins of a house adjoining the burntout Campos residence. She has had no food nor water since the massacres in the Campos compound the previous day.[4]

With Carmen was Miss Pilar Campos, daughter of the late Don Pedro Campos, who was critically wounded. Carmen fell asleep and when she awoke this afternoon, she discovered that Pilar Campos had died beside her.

Now Carmen Locsin also found she was all alone. She lost both her parents, both her brother and her sister in the massacre in the Campos compound.

Today the 11th Airborne completely cleared Nichols Field and occupied the Cavite Naval Base. The fighting at Nichols had been extraordinarily fierce.[5]

Some 111 enemy pillboxes have been destroyed, and large quantities of equipment captured, including 75 pieces of artillery of various calibers, 112 machine guns and 300 tons of ammunition.

Other elements of the 129th Infantry launched a frontal assault on the German Club on San Luis street around the block from the Manila Police headquarters building. The compound was defended by interlocking machine gun emplacements and shortly nine of the attackers were down, many of them lying in exposed areas. Under a heavy screen of American mortar fire, the wounded were retrieved, but the German Club compound remained in Japanese hands.

Ten survivors of the German Club massacres, among them the executive of a film distribution company, Francisco Lopez, lay in a narrow dugout off San Luis street. This morning a shell exploded near their shelter, uncovering their dugout. The group decided to flee.[6]

Francisco Lopez's shattered left foot had ballooned. An elderly man, Don Joaquin Navarro, 80, and his daughter-in-law, propped Francisco Lopez between themselves, although both were themselves suffering from foot injuries and hobbled painfully.

The Paules church on San Marcelino street was the logical sanctuary front this point, but the group saw Japanese soldiers in the belltower, sniping away northwards. They decided to cross San Marcelino street to the Santa Teresa college compound. As they approached the college premises, Japanese soldiers raised their heads over a barricade and fired at the group of three. They dropped as one and kept still. Consulting each other, they decided to throw themselves at the mercy of the Japanese, trusting to a mercy that had not shown itself in the last few days. Now the Navarro daughter-in-law untied the white handkerchief that bound her injured left hand and waved it aloft from where she lay. The Japanese held their fire.

"At the count of three and they don't fire," the girl said, "we all stand up."

Slowly she counted to three. Now she and her father-in-law stood up, then bent down to pick up Francisco Lopez who could not make it to his feet by himself. At this moment the Japanese fired. The two dropped, mortally wounded. They died in minutes.

His injuries notwithstanding, Francisco Lopez crawled away to safety and survived to give testimony to his ordeal. He lost everyone in his family.

The 2nd Battalion, 148th, was stalled on Pennsylvania street unable to approach Taft Avenue. A heavy machine gun-nest pinned down the 2nd. Now Pfc. Stanley F. Perkins intending to locate the nest, dashed forward to draw enemy gunfire. On the third lap of a mad dash forward, the machine gun-nest showed itself. Perkins opened up with his BAR and destroyed the four-man crew.

In another encounter this afternoon, Pfc. Stanley F. Perkinses luck ran out. Enemy fire got to him and he died of his injuries.[7]

Today elements of the 148th came upon the Jose Celeste compound on Pennsylvania street where they found Carolina Coruna, badly wounded and faint from hunger and thirst, but still alive. Also here were Mrs. Celeste and one of her daughters, bedraggled and weak from hunger and terror, but alive to tell their story.

Today, the 140th Field Artillery fired 2,091 rounds of high explosive 105-mm. ammunition into the PGH-UP premises on Taft Avenue. At the same time, the 4.2 inch mortars of the 82nd Chemical Mortar Battalion poured 1,101 rounds of high explosives and 264 rounds of white phosphorus into the same area.[8]

With several hundred others, Dr. Alberto Tupas and his family cowered in Ward II, the Pediatrics Ward of PGH. This is what his son Rodolfo G. Tupas remembers of today: "I can hear it now – the crushing, grinding, tearing sound of artillery shells exploding into a mass of concrete or on the hospital grounds.[9]

"The shells were preceded by eerie whistling sounds. Everytime there was a barrage, the whole ward went into fervent prayer. I can still hear it now – the long murmur of fright."

Behind the barrage the 2nd Battalion, 148th Infantry, tried to cross Taft Avenue, but the Japanese defenses barred all approaches with crossfires.With mortar, machine gun and rifle-fire from positions in the Bureau of Science building at the northwestern corner of Taft and Herran, from the frontyard of the main hospital building on Taft and from the Nurses' Home at the southwestern corner of Taft and Padre Faura, the Japanese interdiction was impassable.

Shell-after-shell slammed into the Ateneo de Manila college chapel on Padre Faura street in Ermita, its share of the whole lot being spewed by the 140th Field Artillery and the 82nd Chemical Mortar Battalion. The dead piled up. The Unknown Diarist and his family crawled out of the chapel for the relative safety of the Ateneo main building.[10]

Today, unable to bear the stench of the dead, the Ateneo de Manila refugees braved all risks and organized a burial detail. While the detail worked in the grounds outside, Japanese snipers at the nearby Assumption Convent fired potshots at them.

In the afternoon the artillery barrage intensified. "The most terrific in our experience," the Unknown Diarist describes it. At five o'clock the Ateneo de Manila main building caught fire. With the survivors who remained in the Ateneo compound our Unknown Diarist and his family fled to the adjoining Philippine General hospital.

"The place was packed full," the Unknown Diarist described the PGH at this point. "No food, little water, less facilities."

Among the refugees in the Ateneo de Manila main building were Mrs. Alfredo Chicote, seriously ill from a kidney disease, and her daughter

Maria Paz, with a crippled leg.

They had been brought here by other refugees who rescued them when the clinic on A. Mabini street in which they were undergoing treatment burned down.

When the other refugees fled the Ateneo de Manila compound today, the Chicote mother-and-daughter were caught up in another exodus, this time westward. In the company of kindly souls that never abandoned them, the two reached the Elena apartments across from the Ateneo compound on Dakota street. Here a Filipino family in one suite took in the elderly lady and her hobbling daughter.[11]

Over at the half-ruined De la Salle college on Taft Avenue in Malate, the survivors of the Monday afternoon incidents huddled hungry and thirsty in the chapel on the second floor of the South Wing.[12]

A group was in the narrow space between the altar and the wall and another was in the sacristy over the altar area. Stretched out on pews in the chapel were Rosario Carlos, Servillano Aquino, the college helper Anselmo Sudlan, and Brother Hubert who was critically injured.

On the third floor, Brother Anthony lay in a room that had been occupied by the Vazquez-Prada family.

Only Helen Vazquez-Prada and her son, Fernando, 5, were left on the first floor. This morning, Helen Vazquez-Prada succumbed. Fernando would not leave her side.[113]

Father Francis J. Cosgrave, CSsR, was kept busy ministering to the spiritual needs of the survivors.

The Uychuico servantmaid Clarita Roldan, 17, and the other house-help foraged all over the south wing for food and water.

This evening, a band of Japanese came to the chapel and ignited a can of gasoline near the door.

Despite his injuries, Brother Hubert dragged himself up from where he lay and brought out two bottles of carbon tetrachloride which he had salvaged from the laboratories and stored in a nearby cabinet. Now Brother Hubert cast the bottles into the flames and succeeded in extinguishing them.

The Japanese were back shortly after and found that the fire they started had not caught. They started another fire, lighting rags soaked in gasoline and left again. Brother Hubert got up once more and began beating down the flames. At this moment, the Japanese returned. Servillano Aquino who lay wounded on a pew in the chapel heard Brother Hubert cry out, "A-a-a-g-h, a-a-a-g-h," as the Japanese struck at him with bayonets. In the darkness Aquino heard nothing more, but the flames died down and the Japanese left.

Now Clarita Roldan and her fellows decided to bring the wounded on the pews up to the sacristy seeing how the Japanese kept returning. They succeeded in bringing up Rosario Carlos and Anselmo Sudlan, but the latter would succumb before morning.

Servillano Aquino was too heavy and too weak to be moved up the sacristy. They brought him behind the altar with Father Cosgrave.

Today, His Grace, Mons. Michael J. O'Doherty, archbishop of Manila, instructed the faithful to dispense with fasting and abstinence during the Lenten Season.[14]

In a pastoral letter to all parish priests and rectors of churches in the Manila archdiocese, the archbishop said that the food shortage and emergency conditions made it prudent to adopt this policy. The priests were asked "to enjoin all our faithful who participate in this privilege to pray . . for our people."

Near midnight, the Jesuit scholastic Ricardo Pimentel, 29, lay quietly under the second of two wooden tables he had stood one on top of the other near the gate to the Ateneo gymnasium in the Padre Faura compound.

As he lay under his shelter, a piece of shrapnel crashed through the gym's galvanized iron roofing, came through the ceiling and penetrated the tops of the two wooden tables, straight into Pimentel's head, killing him outright.[15]

THURSDAY, 15 FEBRUARY 1945

At 4 o'clock this morning the family of Don Tirso Lizarraga was forced into the street. Their home on San Carlos street in Ermita was on fire.[1]

The Chicotes at the San Carlos apartments nearby decided that the building was no longer tenable. It had taken too many direct hits and now was also in flames.

San Carlos street seethed in chaos as the remaining inhabitants spilled out of their gates.

Altogether there materialized a group of 67 – men, women and children, of various nationalities.

The Lizarragas included Don Tirso and his eldest daughter, Maria Elena, 22, with her husband, Don Jose Maldonado, 38, an executive of Tabacalera and an authentic Spanish grandee, with their 6-month-old son, and Señor Lizarraga's two teenaged daughters, Maria Victoria and Maria Rosa.

The Chicotes included the families of Prudencio Chicote, Luis Zabaljauregui and Carlos Garcia Buch. There were in all 42 Filipinos, 14 Spanish,

10 Chinese who were all males, and one Portuguese woman.

Bunched in family groups, big and small, the refugees dashed from shelter-to-shelter, moving away from the open spaces of the Luneta. At this time, there was only one building of strong construction left more or less whole in the entire area bounded by San Luis on the north, Taft Avenue on the east, M.H. del Pilar on the west and Padre Faura southwards. This was the residence of Dr. Rafael Moreta at 417 Isaac Peral at the corner of Nebraska street.

The ground floor of Dr. Moreta's home was reinforced concrete and formed a considerable bulwark against the shelling. The upper floors were half-wrecked. On the ground floor the refugees from San Carlos street crouched, numb from terror.

This morning a shell crashed into Dr. Moreta's dining room, killing one of the refugees from San Carlos street, Mrs. Vicente Julian. Further demoralized by this incident, the survivors decided to seek refuge at the Philippine General hospital, two blocks away. A Japanese marine stood guard at the corner. Now, one of the refugees, Don Emilio de la Paz, a former member of the Philippine National Assembly, summoned whatever authority still reposed in his person and demanded that the guard escort the party to the PGH. The Japanese consented.

Along Florida street, a few steps short of Padre Faura, however, the Japanese escort turned back. The road is safe and clear, he said, and he must resume his guard duty. The party of 66, with the body of Mrs. Vicente Julian, proceeded. Just before reaching the intersection of Padre Faura and Florida streets a Japanese machine gun-position behind them opened fire. Maria Elena Maldonado's foot was pierced through by a bullet, and her sister Maria Victoria Lizarraga suffered a shattered leg. The refugee-party rushed back to Dr. Moreta's half-ruined house.

Except for Jose Maldonado, who scooped up his wounded wife and their 6-month-old baby-boy, and with the wounded Maria Victoria in the charge of Maria Rosa Lizarraga, scurried to a nearby air-raid shelter off Nebraska street. Now they noted that their father Don Tirso Lizarraga was not with them.

There was neither food nor water in the air-raid shelter on Nebraska street. Their boxes which contained meager supplies were lost enroute. Baby Tirso Maldonado began to sink into stupor. There was nothing except a bottle of cologne in the tiny bundle his parents had saved. They applied drops of cologne on the baby's lips. He perked up.

At his headquarters in Baguio City, General Yamashita was stunned by the news that Imperial Navy men were still in Manila. Immediately he contacted Lt. Gen. Yokoyama at the headquarters of the Shimbu army in Ipo

Dam in the hills northeast of Manila.[2]

Yamashita issued a stern censure to Yokoyama for surrendering command over Manila to the commanding officer of the Japanese navy forces, Admiral Iwabuchi. Now Yamashita ordered Yokoyama to launch a counterattack, create a line between the hills and the city, and attempt to get the Navy forces out of Manila.

This morning, a battalion of 105-mm. howitzers and one of 155-mm. howitzers laid down an hour-long barrage on the De la Salle college premises and the Japanese Club on adjoining property on Taft Avenue. When the barrage lifted elements of the 12th Cavalry Regiment burst into the college ruins.[3]

The Redemptorist Superior Fr. Francis J. Cosgrave huddled with other survivors in the narrow space behind the main altar in the chapel.[4]

Now Fr. Cosgrave heard voices speaking in English with a strange accent. Fr. Cosgrave's heart literally leaped in his chest. "Americans," he said in his mind.

Peering around the altar he saw three husky young Americans up in the choirloft. Fr. Cosgrave shouted to them, but his voice was so faint that it would not carry. He staggered to his feet, waving his arms and shouting. Three times the Redemptorist Superior pulled out all the air off his chest, to no avail. Despairing, he tried again. The Americans noticed him.

The chapel was the only part of the De la Salle building relatively whole. The survivors had been in hiding since Monday, the 12th, after the massacres and through the shelling and bombing, with no food and only the water, stale and putrid, they found in the flower vases on the altar.

Now the 12th Cavalry laid siege on the Rizal Memorial Stadium behind the De la Salle college across a narrow *estero*.[5]

Completed in 1934 for the Far Eastern Olympics, the complex included a baseball park, a track and field oval with a two-storey covered grandstand, an indoor coliseum, tennis courts and swimming pools. Here the Japanese had stored huge quantities of food and ammunition and it was heavily fortified. Attempts of the American cavalry to crash into the premises were sternly repulsed.

The 2nd Squadron, 5th Cavalry, pressed hard from the Pasay sector, down Dewey boulevard on the bayfront, forcing Japanese entrenched on Harrison Park into the Rizal Stadium. Late this afternoon, the 5th Cavalry pushed its way into the stadium but was pushed out before nightfall.

Today the 3rd Battalion, 148th Infantry, rushed down Herran street towards Dewey boulevard by the bay. Then it turned around and approached PGH from behind.[6]

The 2nd Battalion, meantime, was stalled on the east side of Taft

Avenue, unable to cross.

Now a platoon of medium tanks, one tank destroyer and the self-propelled 105-mm. howitzers from Cannon Company were called in to support the 2nd battalion, 148th Infantry. Early this morning, the 3rd Battalion, 129th Infantry relieved the 2nd, 148th Infantry.

The tanks and the howitzers crashed into the line of pillboxes and concrete gun emplacements along Taft Avenue. In the process, hundreds of rounds also slammed into the PGH buildings, wreaking havoc among the refugees inside. Only now was the 3rd Battalion, 129th Infantry, able to cross.

Evidently, neither attackers nor defenders knew or cared about the ordeal of the patients and refugees inside the hospital.

"While the artillery barrage continued without let-up, food and water became scarce," the young Rodolfo G. Tupas would write. "One meal for each member in our family consisted of three spoonfuls of *lugao*. Later, I remember, I had one glorious calcium pill for dinner."[7]

The toll on the civilians was heavy. Rod Tupas writes: "I remember young surgeons like Dr. Victor Reyes operating on the casualties 20-hours a day. I remember Dr. Reyes because I held the plasma for a young boy I picked up in the corridor and brought to the operating room. I remember this because after staring at the pool of blood for hours, I felt faint and asked a nurse to hold the plasma."

Throughout this day, the Japanese strongpoints at the Marques de Comillas-Isaac Peral area in Ermita were subjected to pitiless bombardment from tanks, TD's, M7 SPM's, and 105-mm. guns. The Japanese stood their ground.[8]

Elsewhere, the 129th had its hands full on Plaza Lawton off the Central Post Office building where the Quezon and Santa Cruz bridges opened up.

At 4:30 this morning, a band of 40 Japanese crept up on Company B, 129th Infantry Regiment, but was turned back with heavy losses.

At 11 o'clock, the 2nd Battalion was relieved by the 3rd, and a new assault was launched against the Agriculture building. The defenders fought back stoutly, and the attackers backed off.

Among the hundreds of men of various nationalities detained at the Peralta apartments on Isaac Peral street, were Don Alfredo Chicote Beltran and his sons, Jose Maria and Antonio.[9]

Terminally ill from leukemia, bleeding from a wound in the head caused by a stray bit of shrapnel, sorely tried by hunger, thirst and fatigue, Alfredo Chicote Beltran today succumbed.

Inexplicably, the Peralta apartments building was loosely guarded.

Now the men who could make it on their feet dashed out the door to the street outside. Among them were the brothers Chicote, Antonio and Jose Maria.

The entire neighborhood was in ruins. Their *La Casona* home was razed. The brothers huddled in the rubble of the Ermita church.

Two young Japanese soldiers were among the tuberculosis patients who had been confined at the San Juan de Dios hospital in Intramuros.[10] One had been a seminarian who had joined the Roman Catholic Salesian Order in Japan and who had been pressed into military service and assigned to duty in the Philippines. Here his health deteriorated. He had hoped to continue his religious studies in Manila, but this was frustrated. While in confinement at San Juan de Dios he was visited by Monsignor Guillermo Piani, a Salesian himself, who was at this time Apostolic Delegate to the Philippines. Monsignor Piani had particularly commended the young Japanese patient to the care of the Sisters who nursed in the hospital.

Today the young Japanese Salesian for whom fate ordained only the bitter ironies of war and tuberculosis died, victim not only of the bacilli but the exhaustion, deprivation, the loneliness of exile and the terror of battle. In a shallow hole scooped out of the earth at the foot of the monument to Archbishop Miguel de Benavidez, the founder of the University of Santo Tomas, the Daughters of Charity and their surviving assistants gave the young Salesian a temporary resting place.

At about 5:30 this afternoon, the nuns on the San Juan de Dios hospital staff gathered, as they have unfailingly done through these hazardous days, for the Angelus prayers in their shelter at the ruined Santa Rosa college compound.[11] Suddenly the area was torn up by deafening explosions. A shower of rubble fell over the praying nuns and dense smoke enveloped the place.

On regaining her wits, Sister Concepcion Gotera asked herself, "Where do I run to?" She closed her eyes and sat on her heels, waiting for death to descend on her. When she found courage to look, Sister Concepcion realized she was soaking in blood. It was the blood of another nun who had been praying close to her, who now lay lifeless on the ground.

"And who is this . . . My God, my God, Sister Solisitas de St. Paul . . . but just a moment ago she was cheerfully comforting her patients!"[12]

Close by lay the body of a hospital attendant whose shoulders had been neatly slashed away. The dead surrounded Sister Concepcion.

Night fell over the nuns of San Juan de Dios hospital while they buried their dead in a shallow grave they scooped out in the premises. "If we could we would shed tears of blood . . ."[13]

FRIDAY, 16 FEBRUARY 1945

This morning General Yokoyama launched a two-pronged counter-attack from north and south.[1]

The northern prong consisting of troops from the Japanese 5th and 105th Divisions would sally forth from the Shimbu Army's center, strike across the Marikina river and head for the Novaliches Dam and Route 3 north of Manila.

The southern prong consisting of elements from the Kobayashi Force would drive across the Marikina river towards the Balara Water Filters and link up with the northern force in the vicinity of Grace Park.

The counterattack from the north was met by the United States 112th Cavalry RCT and in a series of skirmishes starting today turned back the Japanese without allowing them near their objective.

The southern force ran into the 7th and 8th Cavalry Regiments operating east and northeast of Manila. This morning, American artillery caught the Japanese attempting to cross the Marikina river and threw them back.

The Japanese who were now defending but the narrow ground on the perimeters of Intramuros also launched a counter-attack this morning. The remaining Japanese batteries in Intramuros and adjoining areas in the piers laid a barrage on the attackers' territory, from Dewey Boulevard and the Luneta to the south and the City Hall complex to the east.

Also this morning, three tanks set to work blasting their way through the concrete wall on the east side of the Rizal Stadium on Vito Cruz street which barred the way to the baseball park. The 5th Cavalry finally was able to clear the area. The Japanese had constructed heavy bunkers on the basefall diamond and under the grandstand and resistance was fierce. By 4:30 this afternoon, the 5th Cavalry had silenced all opposition.[2]

Harrison Park lay across Dakota street from the Rizal Stadium. The park was the community playground for this section of the city and it had soccer and baseball fields. Now "E" Troop, 5th Cavalry, swept across the baseball field. At this moment, the Japanese in concrete bunkers under the bleachers let loose with heavy gunfire. One "E" trooper was hit and lay exposed to enemy fire on the ground when Pvt. Ernest E. Pittman of Morrisville, Missouri, saw him. Pittman dashed to the fallen trooper and administered first aid, but in the process was himself hit. General Vernon D. Mudge had witnessed Pittman's gallant act. Braving enemy fire, Mudge led rescuers to Pittman's side, drew a Silver Star from his pocket, and pinned it on Pittman. Grabbing Pittman's rifle, Mudge now led the assault on the Japanese bunkers.[3]

Beyond Harrison Park, in other sections of the Rizal Stadium and in the ruins of the old Fort San Antonio Abad fronting Dewey Boulevard on the shoreline, the 12th Cavalry met with similar success.

Today, the 1st Cavalry Brigade, less the 2nd Squadron, 12th Cavalry, passed to the control of the 37th Infantry Division.

The brigade's mission was to secure all ground between Harrison Park and Isaac Peral street northward, and between the baywaters and Taft Avenue eastward.

The 12th Cavalry less the 2nd Squadron, now laid siege on the United States High Commissioner's residence on the water's edge fronting Dewey Boulevard, between Padre Faura street on the south and Isaac Peral on the north.

Today, General Griswold asked General Krueger, commanding the Sixth Army, for dive-bombing and napalm strikes against the Japanese in Intramuros. Krueger referred the matter to General MacArthur.

MacArthur replied: "The use of air attacks on a part of a city occupied by friendly and allied population is unthinkable. The inaccuracy of this type of bombardment would result beyond question in the death of thousands of innocent civilians. It is not believed, moreover, that this would appreciably lower our own casualty rate although it would unquestionably hasten the conclusion of the operations. For these reasons I do not approve the use of air bombardment on the Intramuros district."[4]

In the bomb shelter off Nebraska street in Ermita, Jose Maldonado and his wife and infant-son, with two sisters-in-law, cowered in mortal fear, half-mad from hunger and thirst.[5] With them were several women from their San Carlos street neighborhood. They have been here since the 13th. All supplies had ran out, even the bottle of cologne which they had passed from mouth-to-mouth. Confronted by a choice between being killed by Japanese machine guns or American shrapnel outside their shelter, or perishing from hunger and thirst inside, Jose Maldonado made a decision. He picked up his infant-son and half-dragged his wounded wife and fled the air-raid shelter. Behind them hurried Maria Rosa Lizarraga. Maria Victoria's leg was almost severed. It was festering. She was left behind.

The Maldonado group headed for the Moreta residence on Isaac Peral street which was still tenable. In fact they found the San Carlos crowd here, including Don Tirso Lizarraga who became agitated over the absence of Maria Victoria.

"She could not be moved," Jose Madonado explained. "We have to bring water to her."

At 2:30 this afternoon, the XIV Corps Headquarters broadcast a message on a radio circuit to the Japanese in Intramuros. The transmission was on the frequency of the Japanese radio circuit and before transmission the XIV Corps radio operator exchanged radio operators' procedures with the Japanese station. Through this interchange of transmission and the fact that the message was sent in clear text there is reasonable assurance that the message was received. The text of the message follows:[6]

To the Commander of the Japanese Forces in Intramuros:

Your situation is hopeless – your defeat inevitable. I offer you an honorable surrender. If you decide to accept, raise a large Filipino flag over the Red Cross flag now flying and send an unarmed emissary with a white flag to our lines. This must be done in four hours or I am coming in. In the event you do not accept my offer I exhort you that, true to the spirit of the BUSHIDO and the code of the SAMURAI, you permit all civilians to evacuate the INTRAMUROS by the VICTORIA gate without delay, in order that no innocent blood be shed.

COMMANDING GENERAL
UNITED STATES ARMY FORCES
Signed/GORDON W . . . (illegible)
FOR WILLIAM H. FISHER
Capt., Cav.
Executive Officer

The siege of the Japanese-held Marques de Comillas-Isaac Peral strongpoints entered its fourth day today. Probing attacks by 129th Infantry elements got nowhere. The siege was proving costly. Its attrition effect on American personnel was telling heavily.[7]

This afternoon the 148th Infantry learned of the presence of civilians inside PGH. The 2nd Battalion, 148th Infantry was responsible for directing the fire of the tanks, tank-destroyers and self-propelled mounts against the hospital buildings. Now the 2nd Battalion tried to protect the civilians by directing its support fire to the foundations of the buildings, in the belief that the Japanese were entrenched there.[8]

Ironically, only Filipino refugees were down there.

Rodolfo G. Tupas writes: ". . . as the bombardment reached its greatest intensity, many people moved into the basement (under the first floor)."[9]

"There were only a handful of Japanese at the PGH," Rod Tupas writes. "The only Japanese I remember were the few who dressed as doctors and ordered the men (refugees) to put out the fire wherever it started. The rest were outside the PGH along Taft Avenue."

Under cover of intense support fire, the 2nd Battalion crashed into the

Nurses' Home at the corner of Taft and Padre Faura. Actually, this was the territory of the 129th Infantry Regiment, which at this time was locked in a bitter struggle for the Manila Police headquarters on Isaac Peral. Inside the Nurses' Home the adversaries clashed in hand-to-hand combat, from room-to-room. By nightfall the Americans had settled in.[10]

Other troops, meanwhile, had entered the Bureau of Science building on Herran street. By nightfall, however, they were forced to withdraw.

SATURDAY, 17 FEBRUARY 1945

About 2 o'clock this morning, Mrs. Benita Lahoz, 31, wife of the acting director of the San Juan de Dios hospital, was roused from sleep in their makeshift shelter in the ruins of the Santa Rosa college in Intramuros. From other parts of the compound Mrs. Lahoz heard screams of women in distress.[1]

A hospital attendant came to where Dr. Manuel Lahoz lay and said that the Japanese were looking for him. Dr. Lahoz dressed and put on his shoes. He got his senior staff together composed of the physician Cecilio Noriega and the dentist Leandro Corrales, and with three male medical attendants, went out to meet the Japanese. Sister Nelly de Jesus Virata, a member of the nursing staff, identified the three male attendants as Luis Urrutia, Lazaro Cordero and Conrado Pili.

From the Santa Rosa college ruins the six men were brought across a small plaza to the ruins of the Santo Domingo church. Here the men lined up before the waiting Japanese and were bayonetted one after the other.

In the Santo Domingo church ruins at this time were other hostages who were fated to a similar end. Among them was Rosa Calalang, 32. She watched in horror as the men fell from bayonet thrusts, one-by-one. At her feet the body of Dr. Leandro Corrales sprawled. Now she heard the dentist plead, "Please help me. Raise my head. I could hardly breathe." Rosa Calalang raised the man's head. Even as she did so he gasped loudly and was dead. Rosa Calalang herself was wounded but survived to give testimony to this incident.[2]

Communications between the Shimbu Army's headquarters at Ipo and Iwabuchi's in Manila had become so bad that the latter received General Yokoyama's orders of the 13th only today. Also today he received General Yamashita's orders of the 15th.[3]

Today, the American forces had effectively cut off all possible withdrawal routes from Manila. Iwabuchi did not attempt to move any of his troops from the city.

This morning Iwabuchi informed Yokoyama that withdrawal from Manila was no longer possible. He also affirmed his decision to keep his headquarters in Manila in order for him to personally direct the city's defense.[4]

At Fort McKinley, the 2nd Squadron, 5th Cavalry, was relieved by the 2nd Squadron, 12th Cavalry. The Fort came under sustained attack from artillery and mortar. The Japanese stood pat.

Up McKinley Road, A Company, 511th RCT, moved steadily. Japanese gun emplacements on both sides of the road made progress slow. Out of twelve gun emplacements, A Company had demolished eleven. Now only the twelfth stood on the way to Fort McKinley.

Pfc. Manuel Perez, Jr. had destroyed one pillbox single-handedly.[5] On the slow march forward, Perez had killed five of the enemy and had accounted for four others in their dugouts which he blasted with grenades. Now Perez went around the remaining twelfth gun emplacement and approached within 20 yards. The emplacement was mounted with two twin-mount .50 caliber dual-purpose machine guns and they chattered away unremittingly. On the way up Perez had disposed of four Japanese. Now Perez cast a grenade at the gun emplacement. The blast set the crew scampering through a tunnel to the rear. Perez fired away and knocked off four of the fleeing Japanese crew. Reloading, Perez hit four others of the enemy, but was caught off-guard by one who turned on him, throwing a bayonetted rifle like a spear. Perez agilely jumped away but lost hold of his own rifle. He seized the Japanese rifle and knocked off two more of his enemies who were not quick enough to get away. Now Perez rushed the gun-emplacement where three Japanese got in the way of his rifle butt, and disposed of the lone enemy inside. In all, Perez killed 18 Japanese in securing the final 12th enemy position. Now the 511th RCT could move up again.

This morning, the 1st Battalion, 129th Infantry, seized the Hike shoe factory on Isaac Peral street, now but a sorry pile of rubble. Other troops crashed into the Santa Teresa college compound on San Marcelino street, but were ultimately driven back.[6]

Today, the 1st Battalion, 145th Infantry, moved in to relieve the 129th. The new Manila Police headquarters remained in Japanese hands.

At 8:30 this morning, men from the 2nd Battalion, 148th Infantry, under Lt. Col. Radcliffe, boldly jumped Taft Avenue and crashed into the Science building at the corner on Herran street. The battle was hand-to-hand and resulted in the Americans being thrown back.

At this point T/4 Eugene J. Callaghan, flame-thrower in hand, launched on a mad dash across Taft. Halfway across he was hit in both legs and collapsed. Callaghan regained his footing and got within flame-thrower's reach of the Science building.[7]

The Science building had been fortified. All windows and doors had been cemented leaving only narrow shooting slits.

Now T/4 Eugene J. Callaghan unleashed his flame-thrower at the narrow slits on the windows and doors. Shortly all resistance ceased. The body count disclosed 28 dead Japanese scorched black by the flames.

From behind the PGH the 1st Battalion, 148th Infantry, under Lt. Col. Jim Gall, dashed up Herran street halting at the corner of Wright street, where it touched the 2nd Battalion.

Now the 2nd Battalion, having secured the Science building, moved on the University of the Philippines Medical college building in the same compound. The 1st Battalion spread out from Herran along Dakota, barring the way of Japanese fleeing the Medical college. At this point refugees in the PGH compound started to pour out, restricting the American movements.

At noon today, elements of the 2nd Battalion occupied the Nurses Home at the corner of Taft and Padre Faura, and small groups had infiltrated the main PGH building along Taft.

Now, the last vestiges of resistance at the Nurses' Home and at the Bureau of Science building within the PGH block were overcome.

The 1st Battalion, 148th Infantry, took over the support fires against the PGH while the 2nd Battalion battered its way into the hospital pavillions fronting Taft Avenue.

Early this morning, 8-year-old Teddy Juco had been out to the pump-well in a PGH courtyard to draw water for his family. This chore had grown into a hazardous enterprise. Shrapnel flew thick and fast, combat raged in the area. At the well, young Juco espied a stray chicken and gave chase until he landed his quarry. Triumphant, he came back to the family shelter in a PGH ward with water and a wildly squawking chicken.[8]

What luck, his elder sister Estelita, 14, thought, as she dressed the chicken for lunch. At about 11 o'clock the Jucos at the Philippine General hospital got ready for a chicken dinner. The family members took time gathering, however, and the impatient Teddy Juco, 8, pre-empted a choice cut of his chicken. "I caught it, didn't I?", he reminded sister Estelita. "Wait for the others," Estelita sternly advised, slapping the piece of chicken out of Teddy's hand.

Outside, the bombardment intensified. Shells rained over the compound, crashing into the hospital wards. Now the people rushed madly down corridors and crowded into halls, as the remaining glass panels shattered and the walls collapsed. The PGH wards swirled in confusion. Shrill screams punctuated the unending crescendo of deafening explosions.

The Juco family, together now, forgot the chicken dinner. Now only survival was on their collective mind. Estelita, the eldest at 14, helped her mother calm her brood. The girl stooped to pick up her small bundle and as she did so, a burst of shrapnel neatly sliced off her right arm, gashed her left arm, cracked her left kneecap and cut through her bundle of clothes. But Estelita did not know this. She only heard a deafening explosion and felt a hot blast sweep by her and wondered why now she could hardly keep herself upright. She was in a terrible daze and somehow she felt her view of things was not correct. A tiny particle of steel had embedded itself in her right eye, and now the eye was blind. But Estelita Juco, 14, did not know this.

Now she heard her brother, Teddy, 8, whom she had denied that piece of chicken, tell her, "Your right arm is gone!" Estelita looked down with her good eye and saw herself soaking in her own blood.

Mrs. Juco was hysterical and screamed madly. Estelita looked dead on the floor. Teddy was asprawl too, his abdomen slashed open. The mother implored for help. but in the general confusion none was forthcoming.

Now the first echelon of Americans rushed in through the front gate.

Estelita Juco, pulled off the corridor into a small room, looked up into the face of an American soldier, sunburned, sweaty, but still the face she had been expecting all this time. Now the second-year high school student, one eye blind, one arm torn away and the other useless, now Estelita Juco, 14, would exclaim in precise English, "America, you came too late!" Near her, 8-year old Teddy, his intestines in his hands, lay silent.

"There was hysterical shouting in the next ward, Ward 9," Rodolfo G. Tupas relates.[9]

Ward 9, where American civilians and prisoners were confined, was the first ward to be liberated.

"The battle, at least for us, was over," Rod Tupas writes. He looked at his father, the distinguished pediatrician, and his mother, the former Anastacia Giron, a pioneer Filipino nurse and herself formerly chief nurse at PGH. "They had aged," Rod notes.

For 21 days Kiyoshi Osawa, Japanese expatriate, had lain in a coma in his corner in a ward at the Philippine General hospital.[12] At this precise moment, by some unverifiable force, Osawa snapped into full consciousness and opened his eyes. For 21 days he had been in lockjaw as a consequence of tetanus, acquired when he was hurt in a truck accident.

Now Osawa was "no more than a heap of skin and bones," in the words of his young nurse, Miss Almania.

Lying on his bed, Kiyoshi Osawa felt intense heat, his face was flushed. Now he felt himself being lifted out of bed and being laid down again. He felt the bed being wheeled out of the room and into the open corridors. He saw that the building was on fire and the mango trees outside were also in flames. He wondered where he was, what was going on. The sound of bullets whistling past and ricocheting against the wall shocked him into recalling that there was a war going on.

He felt someone bend over him and heard a female voice whisper in his ear, "Oh dear, you almost had it, didn't you?" Now Osawa became aware that his bed was in a dark corner and the nurse was changing his pajamas. He felt better.

Now Osawa heard cries of "Americano, Americano!" From his bed he saw American soldiers swarming all over the place. He would recall, "The American soldiers came rushing in, sweat pouring down their sunburned faces. The patients were hysterically crying and screaming."

Now Osawa's nurse wheeled the bed forward towards the Americans. The nurse leaned over him again to say, "I must go now." It all seemed strange to Osawa, just emerging from a deep stupor.

All through the period from the 3rd February until its liberation today, the 17th, the Philippine General hospital functioned as best it could.

The hospital director, the eminent and highly-respected Dr. Antonio G. Sison, never left the hospital during this period. Dr. Sison would relate while recuperating at the St. Joseph hospital where he was brought after PGH fell to the Americans: "Operations were made, cases treated, despite the almost insurmountable difficulties."[11]

"Life in the hospital was bedlam," Dr. Sison relates. "Every Japanese soldier or sergeant, or anyone with a sword, was giving orders and counterorders. They would speak to me with a bayonet pointed at my chest."

Among the American patients at Ward 9 was the business manager of the *Philippines Free Press*, F. Theo Rogers.[12] Suddenly there were heavy steps scurrying on the corridor outside his ward and the first man to appear at the door to the ward was Capt. Donald Digby, Rogers' old friend.

Rogers would praise the heroism of the hospital staff and denounce the cowardice of the others. He had high praise for Dr. Antonio G. Sison, the director, and his son, Dr. Antonio Sison Jr., an intern.

He recalled the ironic sacrifice of the young intern Honorato Quisumbing who, a bare one hour before the Americans burst in, was hit by sniper fire while dashing across the hospital grounds to bring bandages needed elsewhere in the compound.

Rogers would also recall the work of a Javanese intern named Donald, and a girl intern, Cherry Stanislaw, who did their job "with admirable constancy and calmness under fire." He recalled the heroic work of Dr. Stransky and had high praise for an attendant, Alipio Camba, "who took water from the well during shelling so that the disabled may drink."

Water, of course, had become a premium commodity at the PGH during this period. Rod Tupas has this story to tell as waterboy for his refugee-family:[13] "Water had to be fetched at the artesian well at the hospital grounds at the south wing. My cousin Jimmy and I fetched water in demijohns. But this chore become perilous when the barrage started. I remember one afternoon the barrage caught us while we were still on our way back. Shrapnel hit the demijohn my cousin Jimmy had firmly over his head. The demijohn burst and the water bathed my cousin while his hands were still over his shoulders as if he was surrendering. Good thing for my cousin Jimmy -- he hadn't taken a bath in weeks."

After this experience, the water-fetching pair of Rod and Jimmy would be offered a *bayong*-full of Japanese money if they fetched a jar of water for another refugee-family. "We just smiled politely," Rod Tupas writes.

Probably no one felt more relieved at PGH than the young Teresa Nava.[14] Since the 10th February when her refugee group from the erstwhile Red Cross Children's Home No. 1 reached the PGH, they had had hardly any food to eat, no water to drink.

Of the 39 children in Miss Nava's care, four had been lost while moving out to PGH from their temporary shelter on Herran street. Now there were 26, together with her seven adult helpers. Some of the children died of illness, aggravated by hunger, thirst, exposure, exhaustion and terror. One was killed and two more were wounded when the Japanese hurled a hand grenade through the open window of the hospital ward where they huddled together.

Dr. Alberto Tupas estimated that there were at one time up to 16,000 refugees at the PGH. The figure may have been closer to 7,000.[15] Of this number, 500 were patients who were brought in from the surrounding areas or who were injured while in the hospital premises. Some 50 of these were Americans. A.V.H. Hartendorp estimates that no more than 150 refugees were killed during the shelling to which the PGH compound was subjected by the American batteries. About 1,000 others were wounded.

An order had been given for everyone on their feet to clear the premises and move out into the safe zones across Taft Avenue. Mrs. Juco was distraught. Abandon her two wounded children? But she was given no choice. She got together her three other children, said goodbye to the two who lay bloodied on the floor, bestowed her blessings and rushed out with the crowd.

Seventeen-year-old Dolores Iturralde, her right leg amputated above the knee, had been in extreme pain and had been under the care of PGH Nurse Fe Isaac, one of thc few who remained at their posts throughout this period.

Now Dolores found herself with others being rushed through still-smoking neighborhoods to the National Psychopathic hospital in Mandaluyong outside Manila. Some of the pavillions of this hospital had been converted into emergency reception centers for the wounded.

Now the Japanese expatriate Kiyoshi Osawa felt himself being lifted again, this time into a stretcher and finally into an ambulance. Through the streets turned battlegrounds the patients from the Philippine General hospital, this Japanese among them, were brought to the San Lazaro hospital in the Santa Cruz district of north Manila.

The brother-and-sister Teddy and Estelita Juco shared one stretcher, and together were brought with other wounded to the San Lazaro hospital.

Over the fence from the PGH compound, in the premises of the Assumption Convent, the wooden buildings had been reduced to ashes, those of stone were mounds of rubble. Miraculously, the building along Dakota street, in the narrow hall of which 253 persons cowered in fear, remained more or less whole although pockmarked. The hall shared by the nuns from St. Paul and the other Orders was tightly packed.

"It was impossible to circulate without elbowing one another," Sister Charles, SPC, writes. "We had to take turns sleeping on the bare cement floor . . ."[16]

Through all this time, the Vincentian Fr. Elias Gonzalez, the St. Paul Sisters' chaplain, had heard confessions, instructed children in the cathecism, otherwise prepared the faithful for death. He even solemnized some marriages between couples who had lived to this time outside Catholic wedlock. The priest's continuous private sessions with individuals and groups seem to have been construed by the Japanese to be preparations for an uprising. Now Fr. Elias Gonzales, C.M., was seized by the Japanese guards and taken away. He was never seen alive again.

Tonight a Japanese soldier entered the jampacked hall, grenade in hand. Sister Marie Paul who spoke Japanese stepped up to him. The rest of the room watched.

"He was demonstrating how a hand-grenade worked," Sister Charles, SPC, writes. "And when he was about to throw it, silently we made the Act of Contrition."

Poised with the grenade in one hand, the Japanese suddenly pressed his forehead with the other. "You have a headache," Sister Marie Paul said. "I'll get medicine for you." Whereupon she turned and presently was back counting pills into the soldier's palm. The Japanese took the pills, turned around and hurled his grenade into the street outside where it exploded with a huge bang, and walked away.

In a corridor at the San Lazaro hospital in Santa Cruz district on the north side, Estelita Juco, 14, bloody from several wounds, and her brother Teddy, 8, probably this time actually dying from his slashed stomach, lay on the floor with row-on-row of similarly distressed victims.

Estelita looked up and saw a priest administering extreme unction to those who lay on the blood-stained floor. She recalls asking for the final rites for herself. But the priest did not seem to think she was *in extremis,* and passed on to others in graver need.

Now Kiyoshi Osawa again found himself on a bed, a living skeleton, weak and half-conscious, but alive.[17]

"Where am I now?", he cried out faintly. He was in a corridor at San Lazaro hospital. On hearing Osawa cry out, a group of men slowly gathered around him, suspicion in their eyes, and Osawa heard someone say, "If he is Japanese, let's kill him." A new sense of panic struck Kiyoshi Osawa through the haze in his mind.

"I have been receiving treatment at the PGH," he cried, as strongly as his faint voice would carry. The men looked him over closely and seemed to be satisfied that he was not a Japanese soldier.

Now an American officer strode into the room and sizing up the situation, said sternly, "Is he Japanese? Don't kill him! I shall take care of him!" Whereupon he left the hall again.

Again the Filipinos closed around the bed, ominously silent, menace in their eyes. Breathing came to Osawa in rapid shallow gasps. At this moment, the American officer came in again. "I cannot let you kill him," he announced. Shortly, Osawa found himself being loaded into an ambulance again, this time to the Bilibid Prison on Azcarraga street.

In the garage of the Zobel mansion fronting Dewey Boulevard, Sophy Natalie Morgin hunkered desparingly. It has been eight days since she fled her burning apartment house. During those eight days there had been hardly any food or water, and for Miss Morgin no sleep.[18]

"I remember having read in some magazine that no one could go without sleep for one whole week and still be alive," she writes. "If this is true, I proved to be the exception."

The fighting now reached into the garden of the Zobel mansion. The refugees watched as a Japanese marine fell from the guerrilla's rifle shot. They had seen Japanese marines step out of the grounds never to return. Now but 40 Japanese remained in the premises.

At nine o'clock this morning, Sophy Natalie Morgin dared to step out of her shelter to walk in the garden infront of the mansion, now a pock-marked wreck.

She noticed a man wearing a uniform in the same olive-drab color as that the Japanese marines wore. But this man was tall and his eyes were blue. Now he walked up to Sophy Natalie Morgin smiling and said, "Good morning!"

"Although during the seven hectic days and nights I had kept my mind intact," Miss Morgin writes, "I temporarily lost it when the tall soldier greeted me."

Trucks were waiting on M.H. del Pilar street, the refugees were told. They were told to leave everything behind and run for the trucks.

"Althought it was unpleasant to see nothing but skeletons of once-beautiful buildings and dead Japanese lying on the streets, the ride in the truck was a real joy-ride," Miss Morgin writes.

Today, the Americans began the bombardment of Intramuros in preparation for the actual assault. The objective was to create an opening in the east wall, which at this point was 40 feet thick at the base, 16 feet high and 20 feet across at the top.[19]

Pinpointed targets, mainly Japanese battery positions, had earlier been attacked from land and air. These batteries have long since been silenced.

Now Battery C, 465th Field Artillery, set its 8-inch howitzers to work on the section of the wall between the Parian and the Victoria Gates. When they were finished, they had put 150 rounds of high explosives into the great ramparts of volcanic rock filled with earth and stone.

Now it was the turn of the 765th Field Artillery to show its stuff. With one 155-mm. howitzer at a range of 800 yards, it started blasting away to create a breach south of the Quezon Gate. After it had sent in 150 rounds of high explosives, there was an opening at this point, 10 feet down from the top of the wall and about 50 feet long.

This section of the walls was now a pile of rubble, over which hung a cloud of white smoke and dust, visible for miles around. The work of a long succession of Spanish governors, starting from the tireless Gomez Perez Dasmariñas in 1590, had at last met its nemesis.

To smooth out the rubble, an 8-inch howitzer sent in 29 carefully placed rounds, in the nature of finishing touches, to create a ramp and thus make it easier for the assault, details of which were still being contemplated at the headquarters of the 37th Infantry Division.

Fired upon from behind, the San Carlos refugee-group had failed to clear Padre Faura street in their effort to get to the Philippine General hospital compound. The PGH was liberated today, and the group was still at the Moreta house at 417 Isaac Peral street.

The party had with them the body of Mrs. Vicente Julian who was killed on the 15th, rolled in a straw mat. The Japanese would not let them out into the open to bury it. This morning after much pleading, the Japanese allowed a group of four to inter the body in an adjoining vacant lot.

At about 12:30 this afternoon, a platoon of Japanese soldiers under the command of a captain burst into the ruins of the Moreta house. The refugees were herded into what once was the living room. The women were ordered into the kitchen and the men were forced into the bathroom. Packed tightly in the bathroom were about 15 or 16 males of various nationalities.[20]

First, Don Vicente Julian was taken away by the Japanese from the bathroom. The men left inside heard one shot and a dull thud on the floor. Then they took away Don Tirso Lizarraga. The same sounds, one rifle shot and a body crashing to the floor. Now the Japanese came into the bathroom and blindfolded the Chicote son-in-law Carlos Garcia Buch, but they changed their mind and did not bring him out. Then they brought out Prudencio Chicote Lalana, but the captain ordered him back into the bathroom. At this point, Carlos Garcia Buch fell to his knees and started reciting the Act of Contrition.

Stealthily the door to the bathroom opened and a hand grenade was hurled in. It fell in the back of the room. Jose Maldonado kicked the grenade away from him at the moment it exploded and it tore away half of his foot. He fell into the bathtub and lay there. The grenade burst caught Carlos Garcia Buch, who was on his knees reciting the Act of Contrition, in the chest. He died in minutes. Several others were wounded.

Four more grenades were thrown into the bathroom at short intervals. Several died, among them the other Chicote son-in-law Luis Zabaljauregui. Everyone in the bathroom sustained injuries.

When the men were locked up in the bathroom, the Japanese ordered the women in the kitchen back into the living room, with the children.

Four of the Japanese each picked one woman and brought them to the kitchen. Here the women were ravaged and subsequently mutilated and killed with bayonet thrusts.

In the living room the other women, with the children, were called by a Japanese team one at a time to stand at a spot infront of the bathroom door. At this point the women and children were subjected to bayonet stabs.

Maria Elena Lizarraga de Maldonado, 22, gave an eyewitness account of what happened. "We were all ordered into the kitchen and we stayed there. Some of the women got a bit nervous, so they shot two shots. One hit me here on the neck. Then one person next to me was a bit nervous and she asked for medicine, and a Jap called me out and said he would give me medicine. He took me to the hall and as I was walking, down he bayonetted me in the back and I fell and from there I saw everything that happened. I saw all the women and children come out one-by-one and the same thing done to them."

When the Japanese had gone, Ma. Elena Maldonado, herself badly wounded, deposited her infant son in the arms of her sister Maria Rosa, who was near death, and dragging her foot which had been pierced by a bullet staggered to the bathroom.

Now the bathroom door opened a sixth time, and the survivors inside braced themselves for a new explosion. But instead of a grenade, it was Ma. Elena Maldonado in hysterics screaming for her husband, Jose Maldonado.

The survivors inside who could get to their feet fell out of the bathroom door. Prudencio Chicote Lalana was wounded in the legs but he rushed to the living room in search of his wife and infant son. There on the living room floor which literally ran with blood, lay dozens of bodies of women and children dying and dead.

Chicote instantly recognized his wife Maria Luisa Carbo, lying on the floor. She was dead from bayonet wounds. Under her body as though she tried to protect him to the very end lay the dead body of the 20-month-old Prudencio Chicote Carbo.

Near the two was the body of Paquita Chicote, the wife of Carlos Garcia Buch, also dead. Close to her sprawled the lifeless body of her daughter, Carmina, six-year-old. Her 3-year-old son Carlos was severely wounded, but he survived. Carolina Chicote Zabaljauregui was dead, so was her three-year-old daughter Ana Marie.

Of the 61 persons in Dr. Rafael Moreta's ruined house this afternoon, 13 men were killed and 11 were wounded but survived; 13 women were killed and 10 were wounded and lived; nine children were killed and five were wounded but survived.

Jose Maldonado, with only half his right foot, clung to his wife. They dragged themselves to where Ma. Rosa Lizarraga lay dying to recover the 6-month-old Tirsito Maldonado. Now the girl whispered to her sister Ma. Elena.

"I am sorry I lost your ring. They took away everything." Then Maria Rosa Lizarraga, 18, sank into oblivion.

Forgetting that the danger to their own lives had not passed, their grief weighing terribly upon them, the survivors of the Moreta house-massacre gathered their wounded and prepared to bury the dead.

But the Japanese came back in the afternoon and fired into the ruined house from outside. The survivors cowered in the kitchen. Again in the evening the Japanese returned and stealthily cast hand-grenades inside. No one was hurt.

Later in the night, fearful that the Japanese were determined to finish them, the survivors collected the wounded and abandoned the Moreta house. Some of them returned to San Carlos street, among them the disconsolate Prudencio Chicote Lalana and the Maldonados. Between the husband and wife they had only two good feet, but they had their infant son, and they were alive.

At San Carlos the group found a section of the old Chicote home, *La Casona,* with cement walls still standing. Clearing the debris they took shelter here to nurse their own wounds and the wounded members of their families, as best they could.

SUNDAY, 18 FEBRUARY 1945

At 7 o'clock this morning, one of the three male San Juan de Dios hospital attendants who were taken out of the Santa Rosa college ruins with Dr. Manuel Lahoz last night crept back into their makeshift shelter. His name was Luis Urrutia. His wife was a patient, and he had himself joined the hospital staff. Luis Urrutia sustained three serious bayonet wounds in the back.[1]

Urrutia related to Mrs. Benita Lahoz what happened at the ruins of the Santo Domingo church. When he was bayonetted he fell and lost consciousness. The Japanese left him for dead. He recovered consciousness and waited for daylight and returned to the Santa Rosa college compound.

Now Mrs. Lahoz asked another hospital attendant to ascertain the presence of the five bodies, including that of her husband, in the ruins of the Santo Domingo church. Shortly the attendant was back with a positive report.

At about 10:30 this morning, the Japanese herded away the male patients of the erstwhile San Juan de Dios hospital who were refugees in the ruins of the Santa Rosa college in Intramuros.

"What a pitiful spectacle," Sister Donatienne de Marie testified. "Over a hundred sick men, each trying to sustain the other as they struggled to keep pace . . ."[2]

Conrado Tauro had been a seaman before he contracted tuberculosis. He was in Manila when the war broke out in 1941 and had been transferred to the Philippine Tuberculosis hospital in Intramuros from the Quezon Institute.[3]

Now Conrado Tauro and 57 other male patients from the San Juan de Dios hospital were led by the Japanese guards to the ruins of the University of Manila. In the erstwhile ROTC armory in the university compound, the sick men were confined. Then the Japanese left. There were no guards.

The stronger patients forced open the door and singly and in small groups the patients started leaving their confinement. Conrado Tauro stayed.

Among the women detained at the Manila Hotel were the four Chicotes - Don Alfredo's spinster sister Encarnacion; his two unmarried daughters, Eloisa and Conchita; and his daughter-in-law, Camilla, wife of Antonio Chicote, with her six-month-old baby girl.

There were thousands of civilians detained by the Japanese as hostages at the Manila Hotel at this time. One estimate placed the number at 5,000.[4] There were men, women and children, of various nationalities and various races. They were distributed in the guest rooms on all floors, both in the main building and in the annex, in the vast ballroom and in the many function rooms. Throughout this period, the Japanese served the detainees a few handfuls of boiled rice, once a day.

A big number of women was housed in rooms in the annex building. This building was used as a brothel by the Japanese troops. During this period, Japanese singly and in groups would come into these rooms to help themselves.

At about five o'clock this afternoon, the four Chicote women, formerly of San Carlos street in Ermita, managing somehow to stick together always, were brought with many other women to a room at the top floor of the Manila Hotel annex. Now the building was crammed full of women. Groups of Japanese were assiduously at work in the rooms and the corridors, picking up chairs and tables, tearing down the wooden wall panels, and throwing them out the windows. On the ground, other teams of Japanese gathered these pieces of wood and in turn hurled them into the basement.

In the basement other Japanese were building a huge bonfire which shortly was ignited. A huge explosion rocked the building and it swayed and shuddered as though it were in the focus of a great earthquake. Now smoke and flames shot out of the basement and began to spread upwards.

"We heard a crash," Eloisa Chicote, 36, would recall, "and we felt the building all trembling like an earthquake, a great earthquake, and then a green smoke blew in the door, and the roof came over us, and . . . I don't know anymore . . . I was hurt. I had four wounds in the back. I don't know . . . I fainted."

At this moment, Eloisa's younger sister, Conchita Chicote, was in the bathroom. She did not come out again. Their sister-in-law, Camilla de Chicote, cradling her baby in her arms, was sitting on the floor, her back to the wall and her legs extended forward. There was no furniture in the room as the Japanese had cast everything out the windows. In the huge explosion, a section of the cement wall collapsed, pinning down Camilla's extended legs, severing both below the knees. Her baby was catapulted violently out of her arms, hurtling across the room almost to the opposite wall. Doña Encarnacion Chicote jumped to pick it up. The baby yelled in fright, but it was otherwise unhurt. Within minutes, Camilla de Chicote succumbed to the terrific trauma and from severe loss of blood.

At this point, Encarnacion Chicote, the baby in her arms, dragged the bloodied and half-conscious Eloisa Chicote and together they rushed out of the room, down the corridor and into a staircase. On the ground floor, the gates were barred. They turned into a hallway and jumped out of a ground-floor window into the gardens outside. The Japanese did not stop them. The two women, with other survivors, dashed across the open space to the Luneta. Denuded, there was no shelter in the vast park except the monument of Jose Rizal. Here at the foot of this monument which was designed by a Swiss architect and built by an Italian to honor a Filipino, the women fleeing the Japanese huddled, half-dead from fright and exhaustion. There were Filipinas and Chinese in the group, Spanish and other Europeans.

o In the ruins of *La Casona* on San Carlos street not far from the Luneta, Prudencio Chicote Lalana nursed his 3-year-old nephew Carlos Garcia Chicote, who sustained bayonet wounds from the Moreta residence massacre.[5]

Jose Maldonado's foot was festering and he was near despair. His wife Maria Elena Lizarraga limped about on her shattered foot and would not despair. She rummaged in the ruins of the kitchen and found six tins of corned beef, half-cooked in the fire. A teenaged boy in the group braved all dangers and managed to secure water from the neighborhood well. Life went on.

At the hall in the Assumption Convent compound where 253 refugees huddled, the nuns recited the prayers for the dying amidst the hungry and thirsty children's noisy clamor. The Assumptionist Mother Esperanza Cu-Unjieng had managed to salvage some of the convent's food store, including a little milk, jam and rice. The milk Mother Esperanza devoted exclusively to the children. The past few days, the rations from Mother Esperanza's store had been reduced to "two spoonfuls of raw unwashed rice mixed with a few grains of sugar," for each adult during mealtime. By pleading with the Japanese guard and pointing to the unceasing cries of the children, the group had managed to bring in water from the well outside. Now it was impossible to go out for water. The refugees dug a hole outside their door until it was deep enough to yield muddy water.[6]

This morning even the raw rice was gone. The children had lapsed into an unnatural stupor.

"We had a presentiment of something decisive, either death or deliverance," the chronicler Sister Charles, SPC, writes. "No place seemed to be safe, every corner was liable to crumble down or burn."

Suddenly the brick wall of the garage fronting the refugee's shelter did crumble down, "like a house of cards," according to Sister Charles, and a tank nosed towards the refugees. Another tank came through the brick fence, its gun aimed at the building which alone still stood in the compound.

The Japanese guards were at the door and the refugees had been under strict orders to keep quiet. The refugees sensed that the tanks meant salvation, but how to warn them not to fire? "Make the babies cry," they said. But the babies who earlier had yelled unheeding of the Japanese's stern commands had fallen into a strange quiet and would not utter a sound. Somebody shouted, "Filipinos, civilians!" Some nuns easily recognizable by their habits ran out into the open. The tanks stopped in their tracks. The Japanese guards had gone.

An American soldier appeared and pointed to the opening on the wall made by the tank. "Leave at once," he said, "Follow our soldiers to the first Red Cross station."

The chronicler Sister Charles, SPC, writes: "You can imagine the bustle when 253 persons forced their way through a narrow opening and ran helter-skelter over all kinds of debris, seeking in vain for the familiar streets and houses . . . Not a living creature was to be seen except now and then an American soldier who smiled sympathetically as he indicated the way to the next sentry."

This afternoon, the Spanish religious at San Agustin were again ordered out and again marched to Fort Santiago.

At the Fort, the group was corralled in a warehouse fronting the Convent of Santa Clara. Here the religious huddled together in cramped space, without food or water.

Only two of the religious did not leave San Agustin. One was the Superior of the Augustinian Fathers in the Philippines, the Most Reverend Manuel Diez Canseco, O.S.A.

"I remained in the convent because I was wounded in the foot," Father Diez writes, "caused by one of those grenades which the Japanese were continuously throwing from above."[7]

On the march back to Fort Santiago, the Japanese would not be burdened with a man who could not walk.

The other was the Franciscan friar Joaquin Garcia Sanchez. He was ill from dysentery and had become very weak. He simply refused to budge when ordered to move. The Japanese consulted among themselves and finally left him alone.[8]

Sharing the warehouse at Fort Santiago with the Spanish religious but lodged in another section were about 150 Spanish civilians, among them the barkeeper Epifanio Gutierrez Muñoz and his son, Junior. Old man Gutierrez was despondent. He had been told that Hotel Cantabria had been reduced to a hillock of rubble, and with it, the achievement of his life, the *Manila Bar*.[9]

Now American tanks and M7's poured hundreds of rounds into the Marquez de Comillas-Isaac Peral strongpoints. When the bombardment lifted, the 1st Battalion, 145th Infantry launched a new assault. The Santa Teresa college compound fell.[10]

Once again the Americans crashed into the new Manila Police headquarters at the corner of San Marcelino and Isaac Peral. Once again before the day was over they were thrown back.

The Japanese had constructed an extremely tight defense system inside the building. Each room held two or more pillboxes. The corridors were defended from various points with crossfire. The outside walls were now heavily pockmarked. Through the holes the Japanese directed supporting firepower from the Paules church and seminary on the north. Again today, the attackers had no alternative but to withdraw.[11]

Who were these men that composed this force holding south Manila with such unyielding ferocity? What kind of men were these who fought with such fanatical tenacity?

Admiral Sanji Iwabuchi's troops were basically naval, with some 16,000 Imperial Navy men out of the 20,000 that composed the Manila Defense Force at this time. They had not been trained to fight on the ground as units, and very few had individual training as infantrymen.

Robert Ross Smith believes that the Army provisional infantry battalion made up the best of the lot, since they were mostly infantry or ground replacements stranded in Manila. However, they were not first-line men, and a big number belonged to service units.[12]

Of the Navy men, only the members of the ground defense sections of the 31st Naval Special Base Force had any kind of ground combat training.

The rest of the naval troops were aircraft maintenance men, airfield engineers, crews from ships sank in the bay, casuals, and assorted service personnel.

There were demolition squads, armed service troops, armed clerks. There were Koreans, Formosans and Japanese civilian employees who took up arms.

Naval petty officers took command of army units, naval lieutenants organized the civilians and showed them how to fight. Regular Army officers left their own troops and took in the Koreans and Formosans.

How did they fight?

"They were committed to die," Sgt. Ozzie St. George writes of the men he confronted face-to-face. "And they died, but they killed, too, and in killing, they were irrational and illogical."[13]

Sgt. St. George was in the thick of the battle. He saw how these men who were committed to die fought. He saw Japanese soldiers hurl themselves against the American tanks while carrying mines. These were five-pound, funnel-shaped chunks of explosives they held at the end of a 10-foot pole. The men slammed the funnel against the tank and the force of their lunge exploded the charge, killing themselves in the process. But the tank was disabled, and the men inside were killed too.

The principal streets were covered with standard tank and personnel mines planted singly and in doubles and in dozens. The American engineers and bomb-disposal squads easily recognized these and cleared them. But the task was hazardous and the squads were exposed constantly to crossfire from machine guns, mortars and sniper-fire.[14]

The makeshift mines and booby traps were not as easy to recognize. These were buried depth charges and boat mines over which were laid "ceramic mines" filled with picric acid. The American mine detectors did not pick up the ceramics, but 22 pounds of pressure exploded them and these explosions in turn detonated the depth charges.

The mines and booby traps were used everywhere in South Manila. They were found in homes, schools, churches, factories, shops, on disabled trucks and abandoned cars. They were found on the dead bodies of civilians and dead Japanese and American soldiers.

The Japanese buried bombs – 1/3 kg. to 250 kg. parafragmentation bombs -- nose-up and armed. Some of these had a sliver of bamboo instead of seerwire and they exploded under two pounds of pressure.

The Japanese buried 36-inch "yardstick mines" with three igniters along their length. They buried wooden boxes full of picric acid which the American mine detectors did not pick up. They caused great devastation when exploded.

The Japanese booby traps took many forms. Some were gunny sacks filled with TNT and set with push or pull igniters, powerful enough to blow-up trucks. Some were blasting caps jammed into bamboo sticks over which condoms were slipped. Some were innocent-looking figurines left on the shelves of shops, others were religious images in churches. All these caused havoc when touched.

The Japanese defense of Manila was a masterwork in military improvisation. For one thing, full use was made of existing buildings as natural defense positions.

An inventory of Japanese improvisation techniques in buildings fortified for defense listed the following: entrances were fortified with sandbags; barricades were set up in corridors and stairways; firing slits were cut through outside walls for rifles and machine guns; tunnels were dug connecting basements of various buildings, or which led outside to pillboxes and bunkers.

The Japanese constructed pillboxes and bunkers all over the city, but existing buildings constituted the first line of defense.

On the streets and intersections the Japanese set up an assortment of ingenious obstacles, a cursory listing of which included: barbed-wire entanglements; dirt or cement-filled oil drums; rails set into the pavement; ditches dug across roadways; motor vehicles overturned or lined up to block streets and intersections; and heavy machinery torn out of their mountings in factories and set up to block strategic approaches.

The Japanese mortars had areas of concentration. South Manila was laid out like a chessboard and the Japanese could zero in on any square in the entire area, every intersection, or any building. Their mortars took a heavy toll on the Americans.

Then there were the snipers. They were in the ruins of buildings, among the hillocks of rubble and debris. The snipers too, took a heavy toll.

What kind of arms did the Japanese use?

They made extensive use of automatic weapons. Robert Ross Smith notes "the great number of automatic weapons, a number all out of proportion to the troops' strength."[15]

He also notes various types of grenades the Japanese used "with great abandon." The Japanese improvised grenades ingeniously. Some were two-inch iron pipes sawed into three-inch length, sealed with a .22 cap as fuse and a five-second safety fuse.

The Manila Naval Defense Force had salvaged a great number of automatic weapons from ships sunk in Manila bay and from aircraft that had been destroyed or damaged in outlying airfields. These were adapted to infantry use. Aircraft and anti-aircraft 20-mm. and 25-mm. machine cannon, 40-mm. anti-aircraft weapons, 50-mm. to 150-mm. calibre mortars, and infantry and anti-aircraft machine guns of lesser calibre formed important parts of the great Japanese arsenal.

The Japanese relied heavily on the Imperial Navy's dual-purpose 120-mm. guns. Fifty of these were emplaced at strategic locations in the city, many of them in the Nichols Field-Fort McKinley area. The Japanese arsenal included 76.2 mm. dual-purpose guns, 75-mm. Army anti-aircraft guns adapted to ground fire, some 74-mm. Army field artillery pieces and Army 47-mm. anti-tank guns.

The Japanese employed rockets in Manila, "for the first time during the war in the Pacific," Robert Ross Smith observes. These were mainly 200-mm. Navy rockets, although they also had some 200-mm. Army rockets and 450-mm. Navy giants.

How did the Americans fight against these? They used bazookas heavily because the projectiles exploded with maximum effect against the concrete and brick walls.

"Without the bazookas," Sgt. Ozzie Sgt. George believes, "it would have taken more time and more lives."

And they used flamethrowers. With one long burst, St. George says, a flamethrower can clean out a pillbox.

The Japanese pillboxes were everywhere. Some were constructed at both ends of hallways inside the buildings and in the ruins. The bazookas would send the Japanese out of the pillboxes into adjoining rooms and halls. When the Americans burst into the hallway the Japanese would also be back in their pillboxes.

"The Japs held the advantage of position," St. George concedes.

If the Americans captured one floor and the Japanese were in the floor below, a hole would be smashed on the floor and flame-throwers used against the occupants on the lower floor. If the Japanese were trapped in the basement, TNT or dynamite would be used to demolish the ground floor. The Americans would pour gasoline over the rubble and light it with a flamethrower. The Japanese could be heard afterwards, St. George says, killing themselves with hand-grenades.

This kind of battle was the infantry's job. How they fought it is described by Sgt. Ozzie St. George: "The infantry fought hand-to-hand, and often they held one floor and the Japs the next. Sometimes they held the ground floor and the Japs held the second and the basement. The infantry learned that they could not hold a building at night unless they held all of it because the Japs knew the building and could smash holes in the ceiling and drop grenades on them, or come out of the cellar and through the tunnels leading to the pillboxes around the building until they outnumbered the infantry and could attack them."

The infantry and the cavalry-turned-infantry bore the brunt of the savage fighting. "They sent a platoon against a block," Ozzie St. George says, "and the platoon worked through the block because the streets always were covered. If the block were flattened, the infantry worked through the rubble and the ruins and the ashes, and when they could go no further they dug in and the artillery laced the city ahead of them. If the blocks were not destroyed, it took longer."

A soldier from the 1st Cavalry newly-arrived from the front dropped in at the quarters of Tressa Cates at Santo Tomás one evening. "Manila was secured?", he scoffed. "Why, I'm the only man left in my platoon!"[16]

"Most of the officers and soldiers who returned to camp said little," Tressa Cates writes in her diary, "but all were exhausted and grim-looking."

"At 11 o'clock tonight my body will be blown to bits as I have to jump into a tank," bitterly the Japanese soldier who befriended Sophy Natalie Morgin told her. "I am a poet and not a soldier by profession. I had no choice but to obey."[17]

In the last sentence the key to the behaviour of the Japanese fighters on the streets of Manila these dreadful days may be found. Here was this young man whose humanity never left him, evidently a civilian, a poet and scholar with a universal view of life, peremptorily mustered into military service.

"I began wearing this uniform only a few days ago," he told Miss Morgin. He had no choice but to obey.

When his own home on Cortada street in Ermita, just behind the A. Mabini home of his parents, was destroyed in one of the first air operations conducted by the Americans in the city of Manila in October and November 1944, Dr. Mario X. Guerrero, 27, moved his small family consisting of his wife, the former Helen Roces, and a six-month-old baby son, to his father-in-law's residence in Pasay, close to the boundary with Manila.

Later, as operations against the Rizal Stadium heightened, residents close to Vito Cruz street on the Pasay side found it prudent to move back from the battle zone. The young Guerrero family with the rest of the Ramon Roces household were welcomed at the home of Don Benigno

Toda, Sr., on Leveriza street.

Through all this time, Dr. Guerrero had lost touch with his parents on A. Mabini street. He was particularly anxious for his sister Carmen in Paco. Today the young Mario X. Guerrero, M.D., ventured out to look for his sister.

The battle line was drawn along Taft Avenue, but the parallel street, Pennsylvania, to the east, was clear. Dr. Guerrero took Pennsylvania down to California street, at the eastern terminus of which, where it touches General Luna street in Paco, the residence of the Cruz family stood. Ismael Cruz, Sr. was the son of a sister of the national hero, Jose Rizal.

Dr. Guerrero found the entire area devastated. Where habitations and business establishments had not been reduced to piles of charcoal, they were heaps of rubble and debris. Where the Ismael Cruz home stood, Dr. Mario X. Guerrero today found a hillock of debris.

Disconsolate, the young physician wound his way to the Paco Cemetery close by. The territory was in American hands. As he stood among the detritus of war, a couple of trucks full of refugees being evacuated to safe zones came up. He recognized some former neighbors in the A. Mabini-Isaac Peral area and to them he shouted inquiries about his parents.

"We did not see them," Dr. Guerrero was told. Barred from crossing Taft Avenue at this point by the ongoing operations, Dr. Guerrero walked back to Pasay by way of Pennsylvania street.

At the Hospital Español de Santiago in Makati, the Sisters of St. Paul de Chartres were reciting the Angelus in memory of their Sisters in Ermita, presumed dead. Outside, two U.S. Army trucks roared to a stop. The Sisters interrupted their prayers for the dead to bring in what they thought was a new batch of wounded from the newly-liberated zones.[18]

At the gate the American soldiers helped the passengers down the trucks. It was the St. Paul nuns from the Assumption Convent, led by Mother Bernard de Sacre Coeur, together with the Belgian and Assumption Sisters. But the Santiago Sisters could not recognize them. The arrivals were bedraggled and worn, their habits torn and frayed, many without headdresses, their faces smudged with soot and grime.

Out of the Assumption Convent compound, the nuns could not get their bearings. All familiar landmarks were gone. A thick haze hang low over the earth. The nuns clung to each other, stumbling over the rubble, circling the gaping craters, recoiling in horror from dead bodies, all the while the shells screamed overhead and kicked up more dust when they hit. At an artesian well in one intersection the nuns, their discipline never leaving them, formed two lines as one tin can was passed along from one to the other.

Through the confusion, the nuns were separated into groups. One group followed the Belgian Sisters to the property of the Belgian Fathers in Paco. Sorrow awaited them there as they came upon the dead bodies of the priests in the ruined compound.

Another group reached La Ignaciana on Herran in Santa Ana. Here the nuns found the Apostolic Delegate, Mons. Guillermo Piani, himself a refugee. He gave the nuns milk.

"It tasted like nectar," Sister Charles writes.

Now the nuns, better-composed, were reunited with the others at the Paco Catholic school. Here they celebrated their liberation with a "banquet" of boiled rice and canned pork and beans, obviously, compliments of the American forces.

Monsignor Piani had arranged with the Americans for two trucks to bring the nuns to shelter. Now the trucks arrived. The nuns piled aboard, bringing along their banquet of rice and pork and beans. This way they reached the Hospital Español de Santiago in Makati.

MONDAY, 19 FEBRUARY 1945

Past midnight the 12th Cavalry stood on Padre Faura street off Dewey Boulevard by the sea. The High Commissioner's Residence complex and the Elks Club and the Army and Navy Club beyond remained in Japanese hands.[1]

All throughout this morning the Americans threw in everything they had, including the proverbial kitchen sink, into the new Manila Police headquarters on Isaac Peral corner San Marcelino street in Ermita. They had quite an assortment. It included the 75-mm. guns of a platoon of Sherman M3 tanks, the 105-mm. SPM's and the better portion of a 105-mm. field artillery battalion.[2]

In the afternoon, Company B, 145th Infantry, battled its way into the east wing of the building. The Japanese were now concentrated in the west wing and gave back what they got, plus some more, forcing the Americans to withdraw once again.

Other troops were more successful at the Paules church and seminary in the next block. The complex fell today.

The 5th Cavalry this morning relieved the 148th Infantry at the Philippine General hospital. It remained for the 5th Cavalry to clear the Assumption Convent premises and the UP college of medicine, both along Herran street.[3]

Now the 5th Cavalry turned on Rizal Hall, the focus of resistance in the University of the Philippines campus. Centrally located on the campus and built of reinforced concrete, Rizal Hall was heavily fortified.[4]

Today, General Yokoyama renewed an order for Iwabuchi to withdraw from Manila. Iwabuchi replied that withdrawal would mean heavy losses for his command. By staying, he said, he would inflict heavy losses on the enemy.[5]

Fort McKinley fell to American hands today. Starting on the 12th February, the Fort had been under heavy attack. Through the week-long siege the Japanese held their ground. Today, all resistance ceased.

At 11 o'clock this morning, the 12th Cavalry began its northward drive on Manila's bayside boulevard. Strong opposition came from the Japanese entrenched in the United States High Commissioner's Residence and the Elks Club on the west side of the boulevard, and from the Bayview Hotel and the University Club on the east.

This morning a Cavalry patrol came upon the civilians cowering in fear in the shambles of the Elena apartments on Romero Salas and A. Mabini streets in Ermita. Among them were the Señora de Alfredo Chicote and her daughter, Maria Paz.[6]

The Americans now assembled the civilians who came out of hiding in the ruins from around the vicinity of Dewey Boulevard, to get them transported to the safe zones.

Among the men who gathered at this point were Antonio and Jose Maria Chicote. Now the assembly witnessed a deeply affecting scene this afternoon, when the brothers came upon their mother and sister.

Today, Mrs. Benita Lahoz, widow of Dr. Manuel Lahoz, lately of the San Juan de Dios hospital, sought permission from a Japanese officer to recover the body of her husband and the other dead in the Santo Domingo church ruins and give them a decent burial. The officer was Philippine-born, of a Japanese father and a Filipino mother.[7] He organized a group of 15 women from among the refugees in the ruins of the Santa Rosa college. The women recovered the bodies of the five San Juan de Dios hospital staff members and 30 others of men, women and children, and buried them in dugouts in the premises of the ruined church. When they got back to the Santa Rosa ruins, the Philippine-born Japanese officer issued to the refugees several sacks of rice, the first rations they received since they were brought to the compound.

At about 8 o'clock this evening, a squad of Japanese soldiers entered the warehouse fronting Santa Clara convent in the vicinity of Fort Santiago where 39 Spanish religious were confined. Of these, 12 were Franciscans, six Capuchins, six Recollects and 15 Augustinians. They were ordered to form ranks and march out to the street.[8]

The Spanish civilians too were ordered out of their section in the warehouse. At the head of the weary procession, marching in pairs, was Epifanio Gutierrez Muñoz. The Japanese counted 40 pairs out of the warehouse gate, or a total of 80 civilians. Then they halted the exodus. Inside the warehouse there remained 52 persons. From here on, nothing more was seen or heard of these 52.

"We were told that the building was not safe enough," Fr. Belarmino de Celis, O.S.A., writes, "and that we were to be taken to one that was even safer."

On General Luna street outside Fort Santiago, Fr. de Celis suddenly noticed that they were surrounded by a much bigger company of soldiers. Now the group was led to the bombshelter constructed in the basement of the ruins of the Palacio del Gobernador at the corner of General Luna and Aduana streets alongside Plaza McKinley, beyond which was the Manila cathedral.

On the march out of Fort Santiago, Dr. Antonio O. Gisbert was forcibly separated from his father and brother. In the dark he was jostled away from the main body of marchers and presently he found himself on the way to the church and monastery of San Agustin.[8-a]

Dr. Gisbert's father and brother were among those who were led to the caves in the ruins of the Palacio del Gobernador. He never saw them again.

The Palacio del Gobernador, also referred to as the Palacio Real, was the official residence of the Spanish governors-general. It had been the palace of the Spanish merchant Manuel Estacio de Veñegas who waxed rich from graft by capitalizing on his relationship with Governor-General Diego Fajardo (1644-1655). It was seized by the government when Veñegas was taken to account for his venalities and finally executed. His palace, the most opulently-appointed of its time, became the residence of the governor-general. It remained so until 1863 when it was destroyed by earthquake. Attempts to restore it did not prosper, until it was finally abandoned. The foundation stones of the great edifice, however, remained in place to this date. The huge blocks of granite rose four or five meters above the earth. The basement below provided excellent conditions for bomb shelters. Now the Japanese had constructed here two spacious caves, fortified with concrete and massive wooden posts.

Belarmino de Celis says that there must have been about 125 persons in the group that was herded to the caves, including the Spanish civilians.

"I was the first to enter into a very large shelter," Fr. de Celis writes,

An American contingent escorts the Japanese garrison out of the Santo Tomas internment camp. (NHI Collection)

The Battle

Having settled into the Santo Tomas camp, elements of the 1st Cavalry gird for battle. (NHI Collection)

The battle is brought to the residential and business sections of the city resulting in the demolition of thickly-populated areas. (NHI Collection)

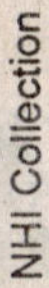

Above, troops from the 129th Infantry Regiment get ready to cross the Pasig river at the embarcation point off the Muelle de la Industria. *Below,* they scramble up the landing area below the Government Mint building.

U.S. Army Photo (MacArthur Memorial Collection)

American troops scour the ruined patios and the rubble-strewn lanes of Intramuros for the enemy. (NHI Collection)

The determination of the assault troops and the tenacity of the defenders are seen in the thoroughness of the destruction of disputed zones. (U.S. Army Photos/ MacArthur Memorial Collection)

National Archives 208-AA-293D-15

Photos taken from the north side of the Pasig river show the Walled City and the districts of Ermita and Malate on the south side going up in smoke and flames.

National Archives 208-AA-

An American GI watches Intramuros disappear in smoke from his vantagepoint in Cavite across Manila bay. (U.S. Army Photo/MacArthur Memorial Collection)

National Archives 208-AA-293D-17

The devastation north of the Pasig river is shown in this aerial photo of the Quiapo and Santa Cruz districts *(above)*. *Left*, the Binondo and Escolta areas.

The Aftermath

(NHI Collection)

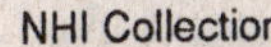

NHI Collection

National Archives 208-AA-293D-1

National Archives 208-AA-293-6

U.S. Army Photo (MacArthur Memorial Collection)

NHI Collection

Opposite page, what remained of the Legislative building after the battle. *This page,* upper photo, the Manila City Hall. Lower photo, the porch of the Central Post Office. The three edifices formed part of the arc of strongpoints on the south bank of the Pasig behind which the Japanese withdrew in their final defense of Manila.

U.S. Army Photo (MacArthur Memorial Collection)

U.S. Army Photo (MacArthur Memorial Collection)

U.S. Army Photo (MacArthur Memorial Collection)

U.S. Army Photo (MacArthur Memorial Collection)

Shown here are the ruined bridges across the Pasig and the devastation at the approaches. *Left page, upper photo,* the Jones bridge; *lower photo,* Quezon Bridge. *This page, upper photo,* the Santa Cruz bridge. *At left, this page,* is the Rizal Hall at the University of the Philippines campus on Padre Faura St. and Taft Avenue, scene of bitter hand-to-hand fighting.

National Archives 208-AA-293D-11

National Archives 208-AA-293D-13

National Archives 208-N-39452

That bomb and shell did a thorough job is shown by these photos, *left page. This page,* aerial view of the Pasig river showing all bridges down, and the devastation on both the north and south banks.

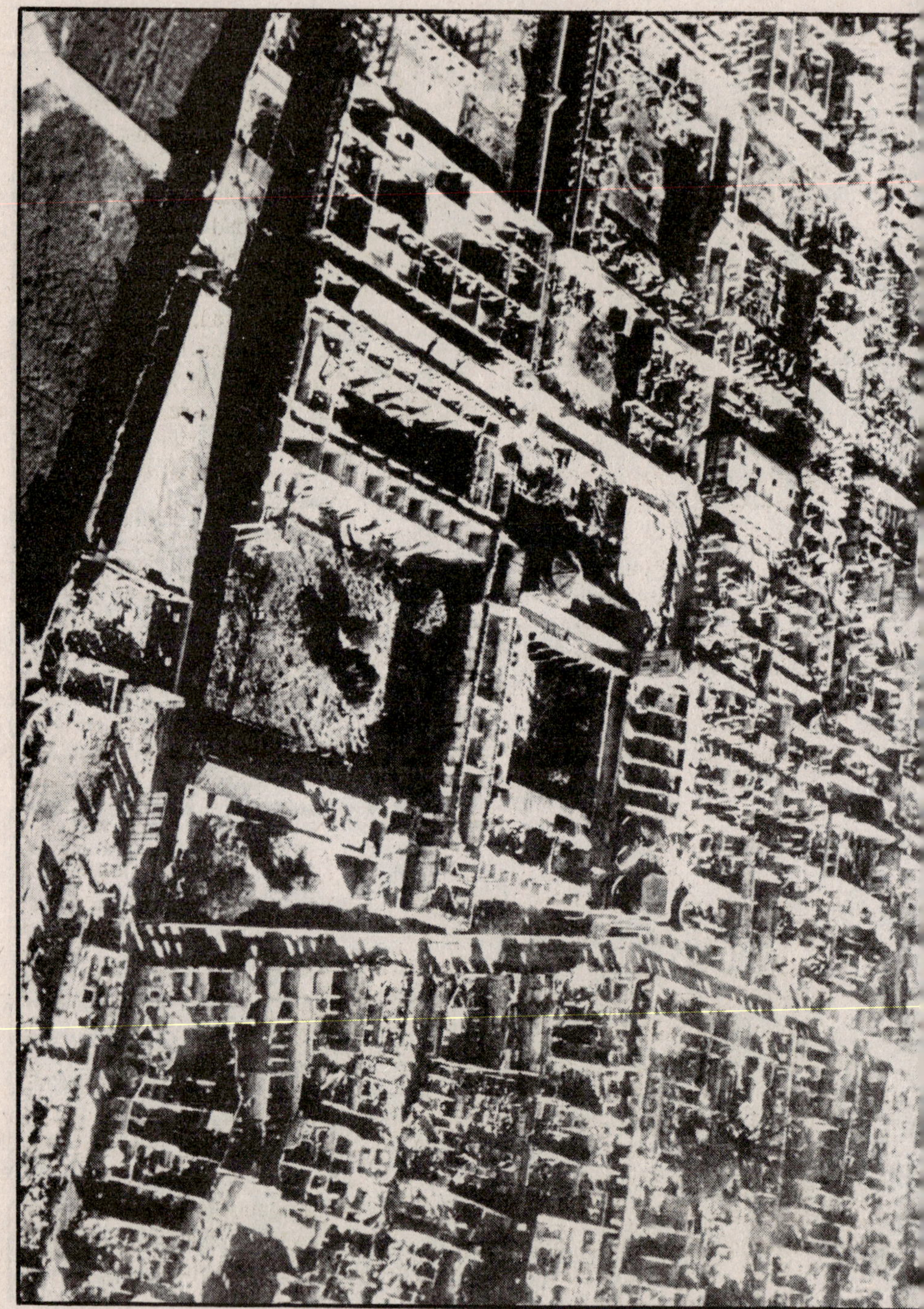

The Distinguished and Ever Loyal City of Manila, the foundation stones of which were laid in 1571, as it looked from the air after the battle of February 1945. (Acme Photo/ National Archives Collection)

"It was long and very well-made with stout timbers." There were about 80 persons in the shelter which Fr. de Celis shared.

The Spanish civilians followed the religious who were led into the underground shelters off Plaza McKinley. The first shelter was now packed to capacity. Those inside started to push back the new arrivals. To stop the jostling, the Japanese officer-in-charge drew his pistol and fired point-blank into the jammed shelter. Several fell wounded and dead.

The rest of the hostages who could not be accomodated in this cave were led to an adjoining chamber. There were 17 of them, among whom were the barkeeper Epifanio Gutierrez Muñoz and his son, Junior.

At the tail-end of this line was the Franciscan Brother Jose Maria Manjabacas, the gatekeeper of the church and monastery of San Francisco in Intramuros. He was the last to enter the second cave. Brother Jose Maria was 71, and he had had neither food nor water in the last several days. He dragged his feet, confused and bewildered at this ill-treatment.

Among the Spanish civilians who were led to the second chamber was Laurentino de Pablos, 53. When the group of 17 was inside, a Japanese soldier handed de Pablos a jute sack with the opening tightly sewn-up but from which wires ran out. De Pablos thought it might contain something to eat and he began to examine it closely, hoping to open it. He was joined by Emilio Carceller who was suspicious of the wires running out of the sack. They managed to cut the wires.

Now the Japanese returned and demanded the jute sack back. When they saw that the wires were cut they became furious. One pulled out his pistol and fired point-blank, hitting Emilio Carceller and his son, Emilio, Jr. Both died instantly.

Then the Japanese threw grenades into the shelter. When the smoke lifted, only seven of the 17 were alive, among them the keeper of the Manila Bar and the keeper of the San Francisco monastery gates.

Having been the first to enter the larger chamber, Fr. Belarmino de Celis, O.S.A., was way back inside. Inside the cave the group waited for about thirty minutes. Presently the Japanese started hurling hand-grenades into the shelter through ventilation holes. There was pandemonium in the claustrophobic cave. Those who were not killed instantly fought to the entrance. The grenade explosions went on interminably, or so it seemed to those inside. The opening was now jammed by a writhing mass of human beings. From outside the Japanese sealed the opening, rolling earthfilled barrels and huge blocks of stone against the door. Now those who escaped the hand-grenades were in danger of suffocation.

Pressed against the wall in the back, Fr. de Celis avoided being trampled by the stampede to the entrance. He was but slightly hurt by the grenade explosions although he was deafened. Desperately he made his way to the entrance and clawed through the earth by the wooden jambs. The earth gave way and finally the priest had a small hole through to the surface. He pressed his face against the hole and the precious air filtered to his lungs.

Tonight, movies were shown at the main plaza of the Santo Tomas campus for the American internees. It was a bizarre experience for A.V.H. Hartendorp. On the program was a newsreel taken months earlier of fighting in New Guinea.

"The sound effects of the moving pictures," Hartendorp writes, "were drowned out by the actual rattle of the machine guns and the crash of cannons and shells. The screen stood directly between the audience and the fires in the Walled City."

The main feature was *Rhapsody in Blue*, the film biography of George Gershwin.

"A representation of theatrical and musical life on Broadway," Hartendorp writes, "to the accompaniment of an avalance of death... Surely, no picture of the kind was ever shown under more bizarre circumstances."[9]

TUESDAY, 20 FEBRUARY 1945

Now there was but a small group that remained in the former University of Manila ROTC armory from among the male patients of the San Juan de Dios hospital who had been detained there. The rest had escaped, singly and in small bands, since they found out on the 18th when they were led here by the Japanese, that the gates were unguarded.[1]

Among those who had remained was the former seaman Conrado Tauro. At 4 o'clock this morning, Tauro joined three others and together they walked out of the former ROTC armory into the streets.

At an intersection the four were espied by a Japanese sentry who fired at them. The four, severely weakened by their illness, hunger and fright, stood still in their tracks. The Japanese ordered them back to confinement at the ruined University of Manila ROTC armory.

At dawn today, the 1st Squadron, 12th Calvary Regiment, with massive artillery support, launched the assault on the United States High Commissioner's Residence which stands on reclaimed land on the foreshore of Manila bay. At 8:15 this morning, the compound was in American hands.[2]

From here the assault carried over to the Elks Club and the Army and Navy Club and the hotels and apartment buildings on the east of Dewey Boulevard at this point.

Covered by his squad, Sgt. James W. Isham of Columbus, Georgia, rushed three pill-boxes at the Army and Navy Club grounds and silenced them with hand grenades.[3]

One single act may have cut short the Army and Navy Club battle. Pvt. Jack R. Ferguson of Seattle, Washington, sneaked into the basement and came upon a Japanese setting up a demolition charge. Ferguson put an end to the enterprise before it could prosper.[4]

Farther to the east, the Japanese strongpoints of San Marcelino were now virtually reduced, except for the strongly-defended Manila Police headquarters. The Hike shoe factory at the opposite corner of San Marcelino and Isaac Peral, with the Manila Club, the Paules church and seminary and the St. Theresa's college for girls, all on San Marcelino, had been cleared, which meant that now they were nothing more than pitiful ruins.

This morning, a new artillery and tank fire barrage was concentrated on the Manila Police headquarters building. By nightfall, the 145th Infantry Company C secured another great heap of rubble.[5]

Not far from this point, on Padre Faura street, tanks and tank destroyers laid a two-hour early-morning barrage on Rizal Hall in the University of the Philippines complex. The Japanese took refuge in the basement.[6]

At 11:30 this morning, Troop B, 5th Cavalry, entered Rizal Hall from the east, along Taft Avenue. They found the Japanese back at their defense positions.

The Americans finally secured the first floor of Rizal Hall and by 1:30 this afternoon, had made it to the second floor. At 5:00 this afternoon they were up on the top floor of the four-storey building. At 5:30 a huge detonation collapsed the central section of Rizal Hall. After a hard day's labors, Troop B, 5th Cavalry, was forced to abandon the building for the night.

The assault on the Administration building at the southwest section of the campus was assigned to Troop G, 5th Cavalry. The platoon had cleared half of the building at 5:00 this afternoon when a series of detonations in the third floor forced them to withdraw.

Inexorably the Japanese in south Manila were being pushed towards the walled city of Intramuros. The walled city was protected by an arc of strongpoints that started in the north at the Central Post Office building at the foot of Jones bridge, with the Insular Ice Plant and Cold Storage at the foot of Quezon bridge. Across the Plaza Lawton from these two structures stood the Metropolitan Theatre, and across the Mehan Gardens from this point was the Manila City Hall.

From the City Hall the arc extended to the government center on Padre Burgos Drive, formed by the Legislative building, the Finance building and the Agriculture building.

As of today, the strongpoints by the bay on the west formed by the High Commissioner's Residence and other buildings on Dewey Boulevard had been cleared.

There remained those on the east side of Intramuros.

Yesterday, the 3rd Battalion, 145th Infantry Regiment, took over from the 129th the operations against the Manila City Hall. The building was garrisonned by about 200 Japanese.

Today, the 105-mm. self propelled mounts of Cannon Company, 145th Infantry, aided by one 155-mm. howitzer, blasted an opening on the City Hall's east wing facing Arroceros street.

A platoon from the 145th Infantry covered by machine gun and riflefire quickly forced its way through the opening. Almost as quickly they were forced out.[7]

In the underground shelter infront of the cathedral the Augustinian friar Belarmino de Celis stayed glued to the tiny hole he had bored with his bare hands in the earth to the world outside. He had survived the night. Now it was morning. He was faint from hunger and thirst and fright, but he was determined to stay alive.[8]

Through the hole Fr. de Celis could sense daylight. Now a Japanese outside discovered the hole, poked a rifle through and fired repeatedly. The friar edged beyond reach. Now the hole was packed in from outside. The friar clawed at the same spot, until he struck through to daylight and precious air once more.

Inside the cave there was eerie silence, broken only by the painful moans of the dying. The dead bodies began to stink. The friar clawed some more at his hole and it grew bigger. Then he felt someone else alive near him. It was a civilian whose name he came to know only as Rocamora. Now there were the two of them alive in the cave.

There were but seven survivors in the second cave, among them the Franciscan friar Jose Maria R. Barullo. Groping around in the darkness, Fr. Barullo stumbled upon a crate which, upon examination, contained 12 bottles of rice wine and five boxes of cigars.[9]

In the darkness, amid the dead bodies, the seven men in the small cave found the tonic effect of the rice wine more bracing than they could remember, and the cigars were particularly relaxing.

Back in the premises of San Agustin, the young physician Antonio O. Gisbert was shocked to find that the church and monastery had become a virtual hospital.

"There was only Dr. Azcuna to treat the sick and wounded, and he was really a neurologist. On seeing me, he beckoned to me and stepped into the church. I went in and saw all the dead and dying lying there -- and one chubby baby playing among them. His mother was dead; somebody had picked him up and left him at San Agustin. I would have liked to claim that baby, but I was in no position to do so. I had too many wounded to see."[9-a]

Of his work in that dreadful situation, Dr. Gisbert recalls: "... it was the prostitutes I depended on as I nursed the sick and wounded. I would tell them I needed whisky or rhum to use on my patients, and they would come back with four or five bottles of 'Marca Demonio.' I'd say I needed bandages and they would bring me U.S. Army linen marked 'Sternberg Hospital,' the pre-war U.S. Army hospital in Manila. I'd say I wanted all the dead bodies cleared away and those brave women would carry out the corpses and bury them."

"There must have been hundreds of prostitutes in Intramuros at the time," Dr. Gisbert recalls. "The Japanese used to make them line up like troops."

"The real heroines at San Agustin were the prostitutes," Dr. Gisbert says, "they were the ones who helped me."

Today an American infantry patrol found the survivors of the Manila Hotel depredations at the foot of the Rizal monument at the Luneta.[10]

Scattered around the monument which is actually the tomb of Jose Rizal were the bodies of those who succumbed to their injuries, or perished from hunger, thirst and exposure. Several others were killed by Japanese snipers. Several more died when they were hit by shrapnel from the incessant American shelling.

Among the survivors were Eloisa Chicote, her aunt Encarnacion Chicote, with the baby-girl of Antonio and Camilla Chicote, six-months-old.

In the trenches near the Rizal monument were Erlinda Querubin, 25, and other women with their babies and small children, escapees from the burnt-out Alhambra apartment building to which they had been moved earlier from the Bay View Hotel.[11]

WEDNESDAY, 21 FEBRUARY 1945

Now it is past midnight. In the second cave in the basement of the ruined Palacio del Gobernador on Plaza McKinley in Intramuros the seven survivors started to roll away the stones, barrels, crates and pieces of lumber with which they had barricaded the entrance from within. They moved away the dead bodies of their comrades which they had shoved at the door to shield themselves from the Japanese who had fired at them the previous night. Now they had a hole big enough for a man to get through.[1]

At one o'clock this morning the survivors in the second cave crawled out of the hole they had made by the entrance, one-by-one, led by the Franciscan priest Jose Ma. R. Barullo. Behind him, feeling a bit of the rice wine and reeking of fine cigar, followed Epifanio Gutierrez Muñoz, his son, Junior, Laurentino de Pablos and the young brothers Eduardo and Jose Luis Carceller.

The group found its way to the ruined cathedral. Now they noted that Brother Manjabacas was not with them. They decided to wait for him.

Brother Jose Maria Manjabacas had taken his turn out of the cave and presently the aged religious was on his way to the only place he knew, the church and monastery of San Francisco of Intramuros, Manila. A line of men in single file was going up the rubble-strewn street. He followed them. They were Japanese but no one turned around as the Franciscan trailed them.[2]

In the shadows of the fledgling day made white by a brilliant moon and the shelling that did not quit, the aged Franciscan crawled on the ground, clambered over the debris and staggered from ruined-wall to ruined-wall, until he reached the great wreck that was once the church and monastery of St. Francis of Assisi of Intramuros, Manila.

At the ruined cathedral, Fr. Barullo and the others waited for Brother Jose Maria. When the elderly religious did not appear to be joining them, the group moved over to an adjacent ruin, formerly known as the Colegio de Tiples, the school for the cathedral boys' choir. Here Fr. Barullo's group waited. As the day dawned they left their shelter and dashed from cover-to-cover until they reached the ruins of the Hotel Cantabria.

To the keeper of the *Manila Bar*, Epifanio Gutierrez Muñoz, this was home.

General Yokoyama issued today a final order for Admiral Iwabuchi to withdraw from Manila. He suggested that small groups could be infiltrated through the American lines under cover of darkness, citing cases where this was done successfully in the course of the war.[3]

Iwabuchi did not reply.

The Manila Hotel was five-storeys of concrete, in the light, airy manner the Americans who constructed it conceived to be tropical-

Spanish. Thus conceived, it was highly successful in its realization. In the days before airconditioning, it had-high ceilings and wide windows, with a clean uncluttered silhouette. It billed itself as the "Aristocrat of the Orient" and many guests thought that apt. Every dignitary visiting Manila sought bed and board here. None went away unhappy. Douglas MacArthur had his home here before the outbreak of war.

For the past several days the Manila Hotel has absorbed intermittent shelling. Through the past night, the 82nd Field Artillery had lobbed hundreds of shells into the building and surrounding grounds. Across the avenue from the hotel along the northern borders of Burnham Green on the western end of the Luneta, Troop B, 1st Squadron, 12th Cavalry Regiment, had dug in to prevent Japanese in the hotel from reoccupying bunkers in the park.[4]

This morning, under artillery cover and behind a platoon of medium tanks and two 105-mm. self-propelled mounts, the 1st Squadron, 12th Cavalry, rushed the building. The fighting was fierce but by mid-afternoon, the hotel's east wing was occupied by the Americans.

Over at the Manila City Hall, self-propelled mounts and tank destroyers concentrated fire on the east wing fronting Arroceros street and enlarged the breach which was opened yesterday. Now all of Company I, 145th Infantry, smashed through the resulting breach into the building. Again the Japanese hurled them back.[5]

At the Central Post Office on Plaza Lawton, men of the 1st Battalion, 145th Infantry, also crashed into the building. Similarly, they were thrown back.[6]

Today, the Administration building at theUP campus fell to the Americans. However, Rizal Hall, by now a sorry ruin, remained in Japanese hands.[7]

At 5 o'clock this afternoon, a group of Japanese entered the erstwhile ROTC armory of the University of Manila in Intramuros and canvassed the tuberculous former patients of San Juan de Dios hospital who remained under detention. They were looking for jewelry. The tuberculars only had the clothing on their backs. The Japanese left the room. From outside, one of them hurled a hand grenade through an open window. For those inside it was but one more aggravation. Many were dead. Others were dying.[8]

This evening, as darkness fell another band of Japanese came upon the tuberculars. By the light of a torch one of them held high, the Japanese bayonetted the survivors one-by-one. Suffering from malaise caused by hunger, thirst, his illness and simply from despair, Conrado Tauro lay on the floor, quiet and still. A Japanese stopped by him and without a word stuck his bayonet into Tauro's chest. The wound was superficial, and Tauro lay in his place, feigning death.

During the night, Conrado Tauro crawled from one supine body to the other, seeking out the living. Those still alive were too weak from their wounds, and their illness, hunger and thirst had proven too much for them. Hardly any one could stand. They advised Tauro to flee for his life.

Now Tauro stepped out of the narrow hall and made it to the streets. In the distance the shadow of the cathedral loomed. He headed for the cathedral, by now a total ruin. From the cathedral he tried to return to the Santa Rosa college ruins, hoping to rejoin his San Juan de Dios group. Peering out from his hiding place he descried Japanese soldiers by the entrance to the Santa Rosa ruins. He withdrew into the rubble of an adjoining building.

In the bomb-shelter at the basement of the old Palacio del Gobernador near the cathedral, Fr. Belarmino de Celis struggled assiduously to enlarge the hole he had carved out near the entrance, all throughout this day. He had been inside since the night of the 19th. The only other survivor was the man Rocamora who was badly wounded. At this time, the cave was hellish with a multitude of decomposing bodies.[9]

Clawing and scratching with his bare hands, Fr. de Celis finally enlarged the hole enough for him to crawl out into the open. Tonight he lay among the weeds under the open sky.

The man Rocamora was fat and he could not pass through the hole.

About 300 civilians were being held by the Japanese at the ruins of the Santa Rosa college fronting Plaza Santo Tomas in Intramuros. This afternoon the hostages were herded by the Japanese in small bands to the ruined Santo Domingo church across the plaza. Here the hostages were separated into groups of ten or twelve and made to stand before firing squads.

Eleven-year-old Rosalinda Andoy stood with her family and watched her mother, her brother and her aunts fall all around her. She herself fell to the ground beside her mother. All through the night, hurting from several wounds, Rosalinda huddled close to her mother's dead body.[10]

THURSDAY, 22 FEBRUARY 1945

Day broke and the Augustinian friar Belarmino de Celis cowered among the debris at the entrance to the bomb-shelter from which he had escaped last night. As day deepened, the shelling intensified. Having escaped hand-grenades and suffocation the friar now would not risk being blown apart.[1]

He backed into the hole and returned to the cave. Great swarms of flies buzzed inside the cave. The overripe bodies had burst into mounds of maggots. The stench was not anything the priest knew. But he continued working to enlarge the hole so his portly companion could get out too.

Early this morning the final assault on the Manila Hotel began. The complex was heavily fortified.

Sgt. Henry C. Cecil of Mt. Vernon, Texas, and "C" Troops were caught in the open by heavy fire from a fortified bunker. Cecil's troops fought back and the exchange resulted in the destruction of the bunker, with 11 Japanese killed and three machine guns and two mortars captured.[2]

Pvt. Edward K. Zopp of East Rainelle, West Virginia, led his platoon into the Manila Hotel, delivering a heavy volume of fire that killed 27 defenders. A Japanese suicide squad rushed out on a banzai charge. It was met by Staff Sgt. Walter B. Lotz of North Albany, New York, and his group with demolitions and grenades. Although wounded in the fierce exchange, Sgt. Lotz's response overcame the Japanese charge.[3]

Now Cpl. Frank A. Vescere of Worcester, Massachusetts, led his squad up the grand staircase. A room-to-room hand-to-hand fight ensued, as the Japanese put up a determined resistance. From concealed positions, the defenders poured out withering light-gun fire. Cpl. Vescere and his squad replied in kind and the remaining Japanese withdrew to the basement. There they perished as the Americans pursued relentlessly.[4] As night fell, the Americans held the 1st and 2nd floor of the hotel building.

Now Douglas MacArthur went with a patrol from the 37th Division and headed for the Manila Hotel.

"I was anxious to rescue as much as I could of my home atop the Manila Hotel," he said.[5] He had been told that the penthouse was intact. He attributed this to the fact that two huge porcelain vases, gifts of the late Emperor of Japan, Hirohito's father, to his own father, General Arthur MacArthur, stood at the entrance to the penthouse apartment.

When the patrol reached the Luneta, machine gun-fire poured from the hotel itself. The patrol could not advance. As MacArthur looked, the penthouse suddenly burst into flames.

"I watched with indescribable feelings," the General would reminisce years later, "the destruction of my fine military library, my souvenirs, my personal belongings of a lifetime. It was not a pleasant moment."[6]

The Americans finally overcame the opposition. Now flanked by two sub-machine gun men, MacArthur was once again rushing up the steps of the Manila Hotel. He had left this building for Corregidor as the New Year of 1942 dawned. Now the hotel which was built in 1912 and which had billed itself as the "Aristocrat of the Orient," was a shambles. The Japanese defenders did not give in easily and had fought from floor-to-floor upwards, from landing-to-landing.

"Every landing was a fight," MacArthur said as evidence of the obstinacy of the defenders and the determination of the attackers unfolded before his eyes.[7] Of his penthouse, nothing was left. It had been used as the command post of a rearguard action. The colonel who commanded the post now lay dead, the shards of the Emperor's beautiful vases scattered around him.

"A grim shroud for his bloody bier," MacArthur commented.

Advancing slowly, fighting from house-to-house, the 37th Infantry today captured the Philippine Normal school campus and the YMCA complex in the area bounded by Ayala boulevard on the south, San Marcelino on the east, Arroceros and Taft Avenue on the west and Concepcion in the north.

The siege on the Manila City Hall gained new momentum today with a savage bombardment during which tanks, tank-destroyers, self-propelled mounts and 155-mm. howitzers laid point-blank fire on the east wing of the building, reducing it to veritable dust. All the while, 105-mm. howitzers, 4.2-inch mortars and 81-mm. mortars were directed at the roof and upper floors.

At nine o'clock this morning, Company I, 145th Infantry, rushed into the east wing breach once again. Now the Americans put to work submachine guns, bazookas, flame-throwers, demolitions and hand-grenades. The battle raged from room-to-room, corridor-to-corridor. By three o'clock this afternoon Company I had subdued the opposition.[8]

A bunch of 20 Japanese held out in a first floor room, rejecting all invitations to surrender. Knocking out holes in the ceiling, the Americans poked flame-throwers through the holes. Only then did resistance cease.

The Americans now cleared the west wing and began emplacing machine-guns aimed at Intramuros.

While Company I battled for City Hall these past several days, the 1st Battalion was engaged in a similar fight for the Central Post Office building. This was a massive structure of reinforced concrete, five-storeys high, built to withstand tropical earthquake and virtually impregnable to artillery.

The Japanese had constructed elaborate fortifications in the interior of the building. There were machine gun nests behind sandbags piled seven-feet high and ten-bags thick, strung with barbed wire. There was even a 105-mm. artillery piece up on the second floor.

The Central Post Office barred the northeastern approaches to Intramuros to which it was connected by a tunnel network. Unremitting American bombardment had reduced the garrison considerably through all this time, however, and apparently no reinforcement arrived.

Each day for the past three days while the battle for the University of the Philippines campus and City Hall raged, elements of the 1st Battalion,. 145th Infantry, pushed their way into the Post Office building. Each time they were pushed back.

Today, troops let themselves in through a second-storey window and established a secure foothold. The Japanese were finally driven to the basement where they waited for the denouement.[9]

Farther up on Taft Avenue, Troop E, 5th Cavalry, discovered caves dug through the walls of the basement of the University Hall at the University of the Philippines campus. Here the Japanese defenders held out, until the Americans poured oil and gasoline into the caves and ignited the mixture.

This evening, Troop E withdrew. When they did, the Japanese in other buildings in the UP campus reoccupied University Hall.[10]

The 240-mm. howitzers of Battery C, 544th Field Artillery, assisted by 8-inch howitzers, this morning started blasting Intramuros. The objective was to create an opening in the north wall overlooking the Pasig river and to reduce the Japanese strongpoint at the Government Mint, at the foot of Aduana street where it joins Magallanes Drive.[11]

It had been decided to launch an amphibious assault from the north bank of the Pasig against the north side of the Walled City.

Throughout this day, late into the night, batteries were brought into the north bank of the Pasig or to the east of Intramuros and placed into firing positions.

On the north bank, Battery B, 136th Field Artillery, emplaced four 155-mm. howitzers, while the 6th Field Artillery set up twelve 105-mm. howitzers. The 637th Tank Destroyer Battalion had four 76-mm. guns. Now the 76-mm. guns of a platoon of the 637th Tank Destroyer Battalion started firing point-blank from across the Pasig to blast landing points on the opposite bank.

The 148th Infantry set up 26 heavy and light machineguns in buildings north of the river to cover the amphibious assault which was to be carried out by the 129th Infantry.

On the east of Intramuros, Battery A, 136th Field Artillery, set up four 155-mm. howitzers, and Battery A, 140th Field Artillery, also had four 104-mm. howitzers. The 754th Tank Battalion had six tanks with 75-mm. tank guns, while the 637th Tank Destroyer Battalion had two platoons with eight 76-mm. guns.

In rear positions there were arrayed from various units twenty-four 4.2-inch mortars, thirty-two 105-mm. howitzers, fifteen 155-mm. howitzers, four 8-inch howitzers and two 240-mm. howitzers.

From the east, the 145th Infantry would be covered by its own machine guns, some of which were emplaced in the upper floors of the Manila City Hall.

Deep into the night, on to the early morning, the artillery of the 37th Infantry Division and the XIV Corps kept up the bombardment against the walls and into the Walled City itself.

About a thousand women and children were confined in the church and cloister of San Agustin in Intramuros, among whom were Doña Trinidad Gardiner-Mendoza, her daughter Remy, 15, and her sister Mercedes.[12]

Among the few male detainees inside San Agustin, Mrs. Mendoza could identify only the physician Jesus Azcuna and Dr. Siguenza, a lawyer and dentist, who acted as leader for the group and served as liaison with the Japanese.

All doors and windows of the cavernous 16th century edifice were shuttered tightly and it was pitch-dark inside. Shells made direct-hits on the roof of the church and shrapnel and debris rained on the people inside.

At 3:30 this afternoon, a piece of shrapnel struck 15-year-old Remy Mendoza and she died in her mother's arms. Dr. Azcuna huddled with a daughter in one corner and they died together, hit by shrapnel. Mrs. Mendoza says some 300 persons died in the confines of San Agustin this day and were hauled away in pushcarts in the evening, her daughter among them.

Combustible materials inside the church, hit by fragments of phosphorus bombs, would burst into flames. To put out these fires the women, near-1,000 strong, organized the "urine-brigade." They pooled their urine in containers and when the phosphorus bomb fragments hit, the brigade would rush up with the urine-filled containers and splash down the flames.

Trinidad Gardiner-Mendoza writes: "There was no water . . . 'Let everybody urinate,' we shouted. And we had to urinate willy-nilly all we could, to extinguish the fires that threatened our lives."

Now it was dark again and on the fourth day of his ordeal the Augustinian friar Belarmino de Celis, 37, was nearly mad with hunger and thirst. The hole he had been working on was now big enough for the stout Rocamora to pass through.[13] Near midnight, by the light of the moon and the flash of exploding bomb and shell, Fr. de Celis and Rocamora crept out of the shelter and rolling and crawling by turns across grounds made insufferable to human flesh by barbed wire and broken steel and sharp stones, the two reached the ruins of-the Bureau of Justice building on Aduana street.

Getting his bearings, Fr de Celis saw that he was near the convent of the Poor Clares. Food, he thought, and water.

The shelling was not letting-up but the priest managed to get into the foyer of the Santa Clara convent. Here he found the nuns with their bundles. They had been told by the Japanese to get ready to move to San Agustin church. They were waiting to go, how, they did not know. But it astonished them to see this priest get in without being seen by the Japanese guard. Now they begged him to go the way he came before the guard saw him. They had no food or water to give.

It had been a grim day for the nuns. A shell had zeroed in on the Santa Clara convent chapel. The nuns gathered there in frenzied prayer scattered like so many frightened chickens. Each one crawled away to nurse her injuries or to recover from shock, except for the former abbess, Mother Eufemia de la Pasion, 70, who lay dead among the rubble.

Back in the ruins of the Bureau of Justice building Fr. de Celis comforted the dying Rocamora and again went about to look for water. He found it in the tank of a water closet in the toilet. The water was near-putrid, but the friar drank his fill. Now breathing came easier and he felt new strength surge in his veins. He found a rusty tin can and filled it with the putrid water which he brought to the waiting Rocamora. He too perked up all of a sudden. Feeling better, the two crawled to the toilet to be near the water.

FRIDAY, 23 FEBRUARY 1945

The planners at the 37th Infantry Division headquarters had decided to strike first at Intramuros and take on the government center after the Walled City succumbed.[1]

Intelligence reports showed that the Japanese defenses were strongest on the southern and eastern sides of Intramuros. The vulnerable points were believed to be along the west wall, across Bonifacio Drive from the Manila Hotel. To approach Intramuros from this side, however, would require that the Port Area be cleared first.

From the north, access into Intramuros was open with only a seawall along the south bank of the Pasig providing a superficial barrier.

Against this point the planners decided to execute an amphibious assault, to be launched from the north bank of the Pasig. The 129th Infantry Regiment was chosen to carry out this assault.

A second assault, this one on the land side, was decided upon, and the planners chose the Quezon Gate on the northeastern side of the walls as the access point. The Quezon Gate fronting San Juan de Letran college was actually a breach on the walls made in 1916 to commemorate the passage of the Jones Law by the United States Congress, granting to the Filipinos autonomy over their local government. The 145th Infantry Regiment was chosen to execute this assault.

To protect the approach from the river, a huge array of artillery, tanks and tank destroyers was emplaced on the north bank.

The assault on the Quezon Gate was expected to draw heavy opposition as this section of the walls was known to be strongly defended. Moreover, it could be subjected to enfilade fire from the three buildings in the government center. Artillery would have to neutralize these buildings, and smoke screen would have to be laid between the government center and the east wall during the assault in the vicinity of the Quezon Gate.

Meanwhile, the 1st Cavalry Division would prevent exit from the Walled City on the west and southwest.

The time for the assault was set for 8:30 this morning, 23 February.

Griswold and Beightler were not willing to use infantry exclusively to assault Intramuros. Since the 17th February, Intramuros had been subjected to artillery barrages so that by today, the 23rd, hardly any single square yard of earth in the Walled City had escaped shell-marks.

Griswold and Beightler now decided to employ against Intramuros all available corps and division artillery from 240-mm. howitzers down, aside from which 75-mm. tank weapons, 76-mm. tank destroyers and infantry 81-mm. SPMs would be used for pointblank fire. Organic infantry 8-mm. and 60-mm. mortars and 4.2 inch chemical mortars were also lined up. Further, heavy and light machine guns mounted on high buildings on the north and on the east would rake the walls and the interiors of Intramuros.

"Just how civilian lives could be saved by this sort of preparation, as opposed to aerial bombardment, is unknown," Robert Ross Smith writes. "The result would be the same: Intramuros would be practically razed."

At 7:30 this morning the first salvo against Intramuros sounded. Now the great mass of artillery, tanks, tank destroyers, self-propelled mounts and mortars that had been assembled by Griswold and Beightler against the Distinguished and Ever Loyal City went to work, using both area and point fire.

The 8-mm. howitzers were used against the walls because they were extremely accurate. The 240-mm. howitzers were used against buildings because they had heavier and more powerful projectiles. These delicate points in weaponry were carefully delineated by the attackers against this city, the parameters of which were staked by Miguel Lopez de Legazpi in 1571, pushing inland from the palisaded fort of Raha Solayman which stood on the tongue of land where the Pasig river flowed into the sea.

To crack the walls, these massive slabs of moss-grown tufa quarried from Guadalupe in the south and Meycauayan in the north from as long ago as Governor Gomez Perez Dasmariñas in 1590 to as recently as Governor Pascual Enrile de Alcedo in 1835, the Americans chose the 155-mm. howitzers, using unfuzed high-explosive shells. The unfuzed shells penetrated more deeply before exploding, while the shells with delayed fuze settings exploded on impact.

When the walls were cracked, the high-explosive shells with delayed settings were put to work, to enlarge the openings.

At 8:30 the 3rd Battalion, 129th Infantry Regiment, began boarding assault boats manned by the 117th Engineers at their embarcation point at the Estero de Binondo on the north bank. The crossing was unopposed.

All through this hour the big guns boomed and keened and roared, monotonously, without feeling, without thought. Intramuros shook and heaved and crumbled. Except for a section roughly three blocks wide and four blocks long, in the middle of which was the venerable church and monastery of St. Paul, better-known as San Agustin. Why this section was spared, no explanation is given, and none is found, in any of the records.[2]

Through the rain of fire and brimstone that fell on Intramuros on this hour, the Augustinian priest Belarmino de Celis and his fat fellow-survivor Julio Rocamora, cringed in unmitigated terror in a toilet in the ruined Bureau of Justice building in Aduana street.[3]

In a niche formed by crumbled walls in the depths of the Santa Clara convent, the Franciscan chaplain Fr. Mariano Montero held the monstrance close to his chest with tembling hands. The surviving nuns crouched all around him chanting the prayers for the dying in cadences that rose and fell with the staccato of the thundering shells.

Suddenly the din lifted. It was 8:30. The fateful hour Griswold and Beightler had ordained for Intramuros was past.

During this appointed hour, 185 tons of explosives were dropped on the three-square kilometers space, or 3.083 tons of explosives every minute, or .5138 tons every second.

During the same period, 45 tons of smoke and white phosphorus shells were dumped on this space, or .75 tons per minute, or .125 tons per second.

A total of 3,700 shells rained on Intramuros during this sixty-minute period, or 61.66 shells per minute, or, 1.077 shells per second.

Between 8:35 and 8:40 the first boat carrying the 129th touched the south bank. Past the battered Mint building the 3rd Battalion dashed into Intramuros.

At 8:40 after a ten-minute respite, the sky started to fall anew. The artillery was now laying the high explosive and smoke screen along the east and west walls to allow the 145th Infantry Regiment to rush the Quezon Gate area without being observed by the Japanese in the government center buildings.

Now the 2nd Battalion, 145th Infantry Regiment, clambered across the opening south of Quezon Gate. Other troops followed, through the Quezon Gate itself and through the Parian Gate, unopposed.

At 10:30 the battalion had reached two blocks southwest and had cleared the San Juan de Letran college ruins.

Now the Japanese, regaining their wits after the hour-long pounding, emerged from cover. Now the Americans were confronted with automatic weapons and rifle-fire.

At 12 o'clock noon, the 129th's left formed by Company I with Company L in the center, reached the west wall, cutting through Aduana street from the Government Mint, and through Beaterio to Muralla by the postern gate, westward. Fort Santiago thus was effectively isolated on the landside. Now Company L turned into Fort Santiago.

At Fort Santiago, Company L found that the hour-long bombardment had done a fine job. This post-Renaissance masterwork of military architecture, whose foundation stones were laid by the third Spanish governor-general of these islands, the Knight of Santiago, Dr. Santiago de Vera, in 1585, and who named it after his patron saint, the Santiago Matamoros of Spanish legend, had been battered beyond any semblance of reality. But it was of solid material, and the workmanship was thorough. Where American bomb and shell did not make a direct-hit, the ramparts stood, the dungeons lay snug. Behind the remaining ramparts and into the dungeons the surviving Japanese took cover. And fought back.

The foot soldiers unleashed everything they had in hand-fragmentation and white phosphorous grenades, demolitions, bazookas, flame-throwers. Into the underground shelters the engineers poured oil and gasoline and ignited the mixture. The screams that issued from the burning holes were horrible to their ears.

At the Bureau of Justice building, Belarmino de Celis looked and found Julio Rocamora's condition worsened. The man could not move. The friar left his companion and sought a cozier shelter. The hours passed. The sound of battle came up to him sporadically. Then from his shelter he heard a voice that said, "Come on, come out." The accent was unfamiliar but the words were American, somehow he knew.

"My joy knew no bounds," the friar writes. "I came out as well as I was able, leaning on the walls, and the Americans picked me up."

The 145th Infantry inched southward against heavy automatic weapons and rifle-fire. The 2nd Battalion had its right on Beaterio street and was shortly in touch with the 129th. The 1st Battalion held its left along the east wall.

At 1 o'clock this afternoon, the 145th Infantry had strung a line four blocks southwest of its access point by the Quezon Gate, reaching from the east wall to Calle Beaterio.

The holocaust of February 1945 would wipe off the face of the earth the Convento de Santa Clara de Manila, founded in 1621 by Madre Jeronima.[4]

Only thrice in its long history were the gates of Santa Clara ever opened to men. The first time was during the sack of Manila by the British in 1762 when the nuns were taken by an armed escort to safety at the Guadalupe sanctuary in Makati. The second time was in the great earthquake of 1863 when a large section of the convent collapsed to earth, and the nuns had to be brought to a temporary residence. The third time was during the cholera outbreak in 1905, when a special dispensation of the archbishop of Manila allowed male doctors to enter to treat the nuns.

In this final battle for Manila, no armed escort came to take the nuns away to sanctuary. The archbishop of Manila did not issue a special dispensation in their behalf. But a Japanese captain whose name is lost to history did issue a certificate that the people inside the walls, the nuns and their chaplain, the Franciscan friar Mariano Montero, could not possibly do the Japanese any harm. This certificate in fact turned Santa Clara convent into a sanctuary itself. But the nuns could not do anything for their servants and other civilians who lived just outside the gates. These were taken away by the Japanese. They probably were in the numbers of those who perished in the dungeons of Fort Santiago.

The Japanese captain's certification effectively protected Santa Clara from the Japanese depredations. A sentry was posted at the gate and while no one could get out, none could get in either. But the captain's certificate was not protection against American bomb and shell.

Now the centuries-old walls of Santa Clara gave way. Now the numberless hits on the ancient roof told and the beams yielded and the tiles were shaken loose. Between the crumbling walls and the falling roof the nuns had nowhere to run. Five professed nuns, three lay sisters and three servants were buried under the rubble.

Mother Maria de la Eucaristia, 27, was pinned down by a fallen beam. Another nun tried to pull her out. Madre Maria urged the other nun to run and save herself.

"Do not wait a moment . . . run . . . you can't save me," Mother Maria de la Eucaristia begged the other nun who did as she was asked.

Now what remained of the moss-grown palace of Don Pedro de Chavez, Spanish conquistador of the 16th century, turned into the Santa Clara convent of Manila, was reduced to smoke and dust. In a hole in the depths of the once-inviolate walls, the chaplain Padre Mariano Montero cringed in mortal fear with the surviving Clares. Now from their hole they saw through the haze moving towards them, strange men in strange uniforms. This was salvation. Their ordeal was over. So was the romantic story began by Jeronima de la Asuncion, the venerable foundress of Santa Clara de Manila, in the 17th century."[5]

Now in the ruins of the Santo Domingo church, an American patrol came upon Rosalinda Andoy, still clinging to her mother's dead body, the only one alive in a heap of over 300 dead persons. On her 11-year-old body, Rosalinda Andoy sustained 38 wounds, including three bayonet thrusts that had penetrated from back to chest. But she survived to tell her story.[6]

Through the barrage the Japanese at San Agustin started to emplace machine-guns on the windows of the church on the General Luna street side. The women and children in the church swept over to the opposite side.

Now the refugees at San Agustin were ordered to proceed to San Juan de Letran college. But the church doors were closed. One Japanese team would open one door and another team would close it again. The refugees waited. A Japanese officer approached and asked whether the refugees wanted to go out. They replied they did, if the doors were opened. Now the officer ordered the great door on General Luna street opened. Preceded by one bearing a white flag, the refugees streamed out in a massive procession. Now they were free from the Japanese and had only to contend with the artillery barrage from the American sector.

As they moved out they began to drop one-by-one and in great swaths, from the shelling of the Americans on one side and from machine-guns of the Japanese on the other.

"We took refuge in the ruins," Father Joaquin Garcia Sanchez writes. "When we saw it was clear we came out." Smack into a group of American infantrymen on Calle Real.[7]

Through this time, civilians streamed out of the San Agustin church and the Delmonico hotel. In all, there would be an estimated 3,000 of them, mostly women and children and surviving religious, men and women.

In this company was the young physician Antonio O. Gisbert, scion of Catalan expatriates, who had been ministering to the sick and wounded at San Agustin.

Dr. Gisbert would not recall the route they took out of San Agustin. All landmarks had fallen or had been defaced, and he was lost in his own neighborhood.

"I think we turned around Cabildo and headed for Victoria," Dr. Gisbert would write. Here they found Japanese-American (Nisei) soldiers who organized the refugees for the trip to safety across the Pasig river.[7-a]

Knowing that civilians had been cleared out of San Agustin, the American tanks and SPMs now subjected the ancient edifice to new punishment.

Now Brother Jose Ma. Manjabacas, 71, faint from hunger and thirst and fatigue, decided to turn himself in to the Japanese. For two days since his escape from the cave at Plaza McKinley he had been playing hide and seek with the Japanese in the vicinity of the ruined church and monastery of San Francisco.[8]

Today, he could not take anything more. He was giving himself up. A group of uniformed men approached up the rubble-strewn smoke-shrouded street. He staggered towards them, hands in the air in the act of surrender. One of the men grinned amiably at him. They were Americans. In his half-delirious state, hardly able to keep to his feet, the Franciscan lay brother could only whisper hoarsely in Spanish. The Americans found one among them who understood the language. Brother Jose Maria's words to him were, "Brother, I am dead of hunger and thirst."

In the ruins of the severely battered Santa Rosa college the survivors among the staff of the erstwhile San Juan de Dios hospital, and their female patients, were prostrate from terror.

Sister Donatienne de Marie, Sister of St. Paul de Chartres, writes: "The shelling had become so violent that the fog of dust prevented us from seeing one another. Every moment seemed to be the last. We were all suffocating. The wounded and dead were countless. Finally, after one hour, we were given a little respite. But on opening our eyes, we found out that nothing remained to us but what we were wearing -- our bundles were buried in mud -- where the water came from we could not find out -- our reserve clothes were reduced to scraps -- not a grain of rice remained -- now we were to die of starvation."[9]

"Someone came," Sister Donatienne continues, "saying that the soldiers ordered us to leave the place for a fight was about to begin. But we, thinking that it was again a Jap trick (we had no idea that the Americans were so near . . .), we refused to move... another messenger arrived all excited saying that the Americans ordered us to leave. Then a shout of joy rang through the ruins and in a few minutes we were walking between two files of our valiant American liberators out to the road of freedom."

The Americans now used the barges which had ferried their soldiers to this side of the Pasig to haul the civilian survivors back to the other side. On the way to the barges, Sister Concepcion Gotera, Daughter of Charity, bent down to kiss the hands of the first American soldier in the line.

She writes: "Overwhelmed with gratitude, I pressed tightly and kissed the big strong hands of the first American soldier I met. He understood and gave a really assuring smile as a big brother would to a weak helpless sister."[10]

Approaching the Customs building in the Port Area, "E" Troop, 5th Cavalry, advanced cautiously, preceded by tanks. Scout for "E" Troop was Pfc. William Grabiarz of Buffalo, New York. From the Customs building a heavy fusillade poured down. The troop commander was hit and the men scattered for cover. From behind a tank Pfc. Grabiarz rushed out to the stricken troop commander and picked him up to relative safety, himself getting hit in the process. His arms rendered useless, Grabiarz tried to drag his commander beyond the enemy range. Although seriously injured himself, he provided body cover for his fallen commander, the while signalling the tank to maneuver into position between him and the enemy fire. Before the tank could do so, however, Grabiarz was riddled with concentrated fire. His commander survived.[11]

Advancing along the west wall at two o'clock this afternoon, an infantry platoon led by T/S Frank Pitcek came upon three dead bodies along the stone fence of a small building. The large building in the compound was afire and the platoon withdrew from the intense heat.

At 6:30 in the evening the platoon was back at the same spot. They found three men, ragged and worn, two of them so weakened from starvation that they could not stand. The third could manage it to his feet, and he spoke English. His name was Conrado Tauro.

Pitcek looked into the building and in one gutted hall, he counted 30 charred human remains on the floor.[12]

Through all this, outside the walls, the survivors of the Moreta house massacre languished in their shelter in the ruins of *La Casona* on San Carlos street in Ermita. They had been here since the 17th.

Today Jose Maldonado, too, gave up. On a piece of iron sheeting scorched by fire he inscribed with a piece of rubble, in Spanish: "23 February 1945. Here lie the remains of Jose Maria Maldonado, Maria Elena Lizarraga and Tirso Maldonado Lizarraga. God protect us."[13]

Presently they heard voices on the street outside, familiar voices, cheerful voices. It was a group of young people, once of this neighborhood. Among them was the youthful Jose Maria Chicote. Those who could followed the young group to safety and salvation. Those who could not waited for the stretchers.

This afternoon, the war correspondent Henry Keys, 35, crossed over to the liberated section of Intramuros with the American troops.[14]

"Come along to the St. Augustine convent if you really want to see something," a young lieutenant told Henry Keys. Keys followed the lieutenant.

"There was a statue," Keys testifies, "I forgot what statue it was, but there was a statue that had been battered and around it built up over chairs and other pieces of furniture were some crazy shelters made roughly of corrugated iron. They were about waist-high. I knelt down and the first thing I saw was a dead girl. One of her feet was crushed to a pulp and her mouth was broken and lots of blood had come from it."

From there Keys went over behind the statue into the cloisters. To his right he saw the body of a boy in a kneeling, crouching position with a bullet hole through the base of the skull.

"It was quite definitely a bullet hole," Keys says. "then I looked to the left and it took me sometime to realize what it was, but it was a pile of bodies just thrown carelessly together, more or less, I suppose, to get them out of the way and in one place. And they were covered with a fine ash and a lot of dust."

Some of those bore bayonet wounds. Others had other wounds which Keys did not recognize but which he assumed might have been caused by grenade or shell-fire. Just beyond this point, Keys saw women.

"They were just lying there like animals," say Henry Keys. "One was a woman lying back, her eyes wide and starry. She was alive but no movement. And the other was lying under a blanket and she was looking at us, no movement either."

Farther beyond, there was some rubbish and out of it Keys suddenly saw a hand move. He drew the attention of some soldiers to it.

Henry Keys now followed the lieutenant inside the convent to another hallway running behind the cloisters where there was another lieutenant kneeling beside a girl whose mouth had been battered by blows.

"I don't know what," Keys says. "It could have been a rifle butt, but it was certainly solid." The girl bore other wounds on her body and was barely breathing. The lieutenant gently patted her lips and was dropping water into her mouth.

Keys recalls that there weren't enough medics or anybody around to do anything for the people. A bit to the right of the girl was another doorway and Keys entered. It looked like a room which might have been a living room or a meeting room. It was in disarray. To the left there seemed to be a kitchen, but in this living room section was a beautiful Filipina girl lying on her back. A soldier called Keys over and said, "Look at this," and he lifted a blanket that was lying over her feet. Her feet had been cut off and the stumps tied with handkerchiefs.

"I didn't feel very good at that and I didn't look very long," Keys says. Lying almost feet to feet with this girl was a Japanese soldier.

"He was the only decent piece of humanity in the place, the only clean piece of humanity," Henry Keys observes. "He was dressed in a white singlet on the shirt and some pants. He was lying like an animal and I was told that he had been there some weeks having been brought in when he was ill and cared for by nuns."

Keys noted other women in the room, some of them bearing wounds of one kind or another. He walked back out into the corridor and the lieutenant said, "Come here, this is alive." And there crouched in the rubble was a girl, very emaciated, very thin, who could hardly be recognized as a human being, or that it lived. Only very so often, minutes, perhaps, the whole body would convulsively shudder. Swarms of flies hovered over her as they hovered over all the bodies of the wounded and dead.

"... that was practically all that I recall vividly of the St. Augustine convent," Henry Keys says, "except that when I went out the gate I saw some Chinese litter bearers and I asked them to go into the convent and get this girl with her feet cut off."

The litter bearers did that. As they passed out the gate, with the girl's head first, she lifted her hand and made a "V" sign at the soldiers. The tough Henry Keys broke down.

SATURDAY, 24 FEBRUARY 1945

Throughout this morning, the 3rd Battalion, 129th Infantry, conducted mopping-up operations at Fort Santiago. Surviving Japanese singly and in groups hid out among the ruins and continued to fight. The body count rose to 400 dead Japanese.[1]

A large contingent of Japanese withdrew into the bastion which provided a curtain to the Puerta Real on the southside of the walls on Calle Muralla, looking out to Padre Burgos Drive across the moat. The bastion had been converted in recent times into the City Aquarium.[2]

The 145th Infantry could not approach the bastion as it was well-covered from the government center by machine gun and rifle-fire. The bastion was connected to the Puerta Real, one of the entrances into the Walled City, by a covered bridge, which in earlier days was a draw-bridge over the moat. The bridge was undefended.

Now the Cannon Company's self-propelled mounts laid down a softening barrage on the City Aquarium. Whatever fish were in there had long-perished from lack of care.

This afternoon, Company C, 145th Infantry, broke into the aquarium by way of the covered bridge, using bazookas and hand-grenades. At four this afternoon, all resistance ceased. The body count showed 115 dead Japanese. This was the last organized resistance inside Intramuros.[3]

At the Port Area, the 1st Squadron, 12th Cavalry, and the 2nd Squadron, 5th Cavalry, conducted clearing operations against light opposition.

Enemy personnel in the area were Formosans, Chinese and Korean laborers, of whom 250 surrendered today. These troops were among the civilian employees of the Imperial Navy who had been pressed into battle duty. They were dispirited, poorly-trained and poorly-armed.

Among the rubble of the Hotel Cantabria, wasted by hunger and thirst and disconsolate over the irreparable loss of the achievement of his life – the *Manila Bar*, the Americans today found Epifanio Gutierrez Muñoz. The moment was grim, but in his mind, in the future, was another *Manila Bar*.[4]

Now details of the carnage perpetrated by the Japanese on civilians trapped in the Intramuros area began to unfold,

At Fort Santiago, Major Frank J. Middelberg, S-2, 129th Infantry, was tracing the source of a "strong stench of decaying flesh." He came upon a double steel door, bolted and wired shut on the outside. Assisted by some enlisted men, Middelberg had the wires cut and was able to slide the bolt and kick the door open. As the door flew open, the group was greeted by a "terrific stench (like) a blast from inside." Behind the steel doors were steel bars, and behind these were about 30 bodies in advanced state of decay. There were men and women in the group.[5]

"I could see no evidence of wounds on the bodies," Major Middelberg testified. "It appeared as if some of the occupants had been struggling to get free and collapsed against the bars of the steel cargo."[6]

The thick walls and ceilings of the dungeon had been impervious to bomb and shell. Middelberg believes that "the civilians were locked in their cell, the steel door bolted, and left to die of starvation."[7]

Through a small hole in the roof, Major Gilbert B. Ayres entered the Philippine Department building in Fort Santiago. Down crude wooden stairs which had been partially burned, Ayres and his companions, T/4 Steve W. Loska and T/5 John Jepson, proceeded along a short decline into a windowless room about 20 feet square. Here the group found about 75 bodies in an advanced state of decomposition. Ayres found it impossible to determine the race or nationality of the bodies, or the cause of death. The conditions in the room, however, gave Ayres reasons to conjecture that death for the 75 was caused by "thirst, suffocation or violence."[8]

At a corner of the walls at the intersection of Arzobispo and Santa Clara streets in Intramuros, Major Ayres with Loska and Jepson entered a small room from which a dreadful stench emanated. In the room the three found about 15 bodies, apparently all male, partly decomposed. Gun-shot or shell-fragment wounds were evident on some of the bodies. Outside the room which was strewn with clothing and personal articles, were two more bodies wrapped in blankets. All the bodies were in civilian clothes.[9]

In a small room in a large building in Fort Santiago, Col. J.D. Frederick, commanding officer of the 129th Infantry Regiment, came upon 40 to 50 bullet-riddled bodies, their hands tied together with twine. The bodies were stacked in two or three layers, and bullet holes could be seen on the bodies in the uppermost layer. Other wounds could have been inflicted by knives or bayonets. All were males, and Frederick ventured the opinion that they could have been Filipinos or Chinese.[10]

From the positions of the bodies, Frederick judged that they could have been brought into the room in batches, made to face the wall and shot, each succeeding batch falling on the bodies of the original batch.

Eight more bodies were found in another part of the building, partly covered with debris, also tied together by the hands.

The Vincentian Fathers in other houses in Manila today secured permission to cross restricted zones to see how things were in their motherhouse on San Marcelino street. They had not the least inkling as to what happened to the residents. They scoured the church and seminary ruins, they looked into adjoining lots and buildings and up and down the surrounding streets. They found not the slightest trace of their companions. No one thought of looking into the *estero*. They abandoned the search deeply agitated.[11]

During the night, the Japanese in pockets and pillboxes among the ruins continued the futile fight. Machine gun-fire punctuated the night-hours. The Japanese were dying hard. All over Intramuros and Ermita surviving Japanese, alone and in small bands, fought a running battle with the pursuing Americans. One such brief encounter tonight led to the discovery of the bodies of the Vincentian Fathers and the Chinese in the *estero* behind the Paules church and seminary on San Marcelino street.

An American infantryman caught a Japanese on the run with a bullet and chased the quarry to the spot where he saw him fall. The Japanese had fallen into the *estero* and the American soldier was horror-struck when he saw not only the body of the Japanese stuck in the murky waters but a whole army of dead bodies, or so it seemed to him then.

SUNDAY, 25 FEBRUARY 1945

"Potomac Greek," Dr. Albert Ravenholt describes the style of the buildings at the government center in Manila.[1] They derive from the courthouse architecture in North America as exemplified by government buildings in Washington, D.C. They are massive neo-classical structures that loom hugely over open spaces, imposing with their colonnaded facades and academic and remote with their allegorical friezes and statuary. From every angle each presented an impressive view.

In 1903, the United States government commissioned the eminent American architect and city planner Daniel H. Burnham to make a plan for the city of Manila. Burnham had acquired a much-deserved reputation for his designs of the city of Chicago. He contemplated a U-shaped capitol for the Philippines, in the grand manner of the Louvre in Paris, with the base along what became Taft Avenue and the tips of the U approximately along the line where the Rizal monument now stands. The base of the U-shaped building would have consisted of a set of five grandiose edifices. Only two of the five materialized. They became, respectively, the department of finance and the department of agriculture buildings in the Commonwealth government.

Along the boulevard that was to have been the venue for state processions, now named after the martyr-priest Padre Jose Burgos, Burnham planned grand structures that would have housed the city's cultural activities. Of these, only the building that would house the National Assembly materialized. It became known as the Legislative building. Completed in 1920, it was intended to be the National Library and Museum. In fact, it was patterned after the New York City Library.

Since yesterday, each of the three buildings in the government center has been under intense bombardment. The XIV Corps and the 37th Infantry Division had drawn to the government center the guns that wiped Intramuros off memory. Now here again were massed the 155-mm. howitzers, Cannon Company 105-mm. SPMs, 75-mm. tank guns, 76-mm. tank destroyer guns and 4.2-inch and 81-mm. mortars.

The Legislative building had been used for some time as headquarters of Admiral Iwabuchi's Central Force and was believed to be garrisonned by over 250 troops. The Finance building itself was believed to have been Admiral Iwabuchi's headquarters. He may have perished here.

By today, the three buildings were badly damaged from earlier bombardments. "The preparatory bombardment would lead to the severe damage, if not destruction, of all these buildings," Robert Ross Smith writes, "but again, XIV Corps really had no choice."[2]

Now the 136th Field Artillery Battalion opened pointblank fire at the government center at ranges from 150 to 800 yards. For reducing Manila's government center to nothing, Robert Ross Smith awards the artillerymen "credit of honor."[3]

Meanwhile, at Fort Santiago, the 129th Infantry continued mopping-up operations. This noon, it withdrew to avoid being hit by stray shells as the artillery bombardment on the government center proceeded.

MONDAY, 26 FEBRUARY 1945

At eight o'clock this morning, the 136th Field Artillery opened up on the three buildings in the government center at the east-end of the Luneta off Taft Avenue, in a final one-hour softening-up bombardment.

Shortly after nine o'clock, elements of the 1st Battalion, 148th Infantry, smashed into the first floor of the Legislative building, entering through the back door. The opposition was as stiff and determined as any the Americans had experienced in this battle that was being fought from building-to-building.

By one o'clock this afternoon, the 148th had control over the first floor in the north wing and the first and second floors of the central section of the Legislative building. Now the attack stalled. Progress was hardly possible, and having lost two men dead and 52 wounded, the Americans withdrew.

Over at the Agriculture building, the artillery barrage was just as cruel and punishing. When the smoke lifted, the 5th Cavalry crashed into the badly battered edifice but were driven back by enemy riflemen entrenched in the ruins of the San Luis Terrace apartments across the street. Once more the 5th attacked, and once more it was forced to withdraw.

TUESDAY, 27 FEBRUARY 1945

The bulk of the Legislative building loomed, desolate and forsaken, in the haze of dawn. Obstinately the Japanese held out. Now the Americans thought of smoking the Japanese out of the building. The attempt failed. Once again the infantry gave the signal to the artillery, and once more the assembled guns belched fire.[1]

For two hours this morning the 155-mm. howitzers and the 105-mm. self-propelled mounts fired point-blank into Daniel H. Burnham's dream translated into masonry.

When the two-hour period passed, the north wing of the Legislative building did not look like anything imaginable.

At two o'clock this afternoon, the 1st Battalion, 148th Infantry, entered the battered building again. At four they had control over the ruined first floor once more. The Japanese fought back from unlikely pockets in the rubble. By six o'clock in the evening the Americans were in the basement clearing out isolated opposition.

Having learned that interdiction fire on the Agriculture building came from apartment houses across San Luis street, the 5th Cavalry today concentrated its attention on these structures. By nightfall, the opposition in these buildings had been silenced.

At 11 o'clock this morning, solemn ceremonies were held at Malacañang to restore the seat of government to Manila. The city again became the capital of the Philippines.

"For me it was a soul-wrenching moment," Douglas MacArthur would write of this occasion. He was returning to the Filipino people as the capital of their country a city ravaged beyond measure.[2]

MacArthur described Manila at this point, thus: "As I passed through the streets with burned-out piles of rubble, the air still filled with the stench of decaying unburied dead, the tall and stately trees that had been the mark of a gracious city were nothing but ugly scrubs pointing broken fingers at the sky. Once-famous buildings were now shells. The street signs and familiar landmarks were gone. One moved by sense of direction rather than by sight."[3]

Now at the reception hall of Malacañang, unscathed by battle owing primarily to its location in what was once hinterland on the banks of the Pasig, MacArthur addressed Sergio Osmeña, the President of the Commonwealth of the Philippines, and said: "On behalf of my government, I now solemnly declare, Mr. President, the full powers and responsibilities restored to the Commonwealth, whose seat is here reestablished as provided by law. Your country, thus, is again at liberty to pursue its destiny to an honored position in the family of free nations. Your capital city, cruelly punished though it be, has regained its rightful place – citadel of democracy in the East. Your indomitable . . ."[4]

Here MacArthur's voice failed. He covered his face with his hands and wept.

"My voice broke," MacArthur would write in his *Reminiscences.* "I could not go on. To others it might have seemed my moment of victory and monumental personal acclaim, but to me it seemed only the culmination of physical and spiritual disaster."[5]

WEDNESDAY, 28 FEBRUARY 1945

On cue, at eight o'clock this morning, the 155-mm. howitzers started blasting point-blank into the first floor of the Agriculture building, aiming from positions on the north and on the west.[1]

At nine, the 75-mm. tank guns and the 76-mm. tank destroyers took over from the east and south, also blasting away point-blank. On the final minute of nine, they paused.

Promptly at ten, the 155-mm. howitzers resumed firing, again from their positions on the north and the west.

Through all this time, American troops were engaged in the Legislative and the Finance buildings. To avoid hitting them, the artillery fire on the Agriculture building was concentrated on the ground floor. So thorough was the pulverizing of this building's lower section that when the bombardment stopped, the upper section had settled drunkenly on the ground. No living creature inside could have survived the near-total disintegration of the edifice. But a few Japanese did. When the 5th Cavalry troopers poked into the rubble they were met with virulent rifle fire from the northwest and southeast corners of the smouldering ruins.

Now the troopers withdrew and a tank armed with a flame-thrower came up to subdue the southeast corner. More tanks lumbered over the debris and continued blasting point-blank from all sides.

Again the 5th Cavalry came in and put to work bazookas, flame-throwers and automatic weapons. They continued to draw fire from undeterminable positions in the great pile of debris.

All throughout this day, the Japanese in the Finance building held out. The artillery fire was remorseless. The Americans hurled all their 155-mm., 76-mm. tank destroyers and 75-mm. tank guns into every side of the building.

Today Tressa R. Cates returned to the area in Ermita where she lived when she first arrived in Manila.

"I wandered through rubble-torn streets that I could not recognize," she writes in her diary.[2] There were no landmarks, no trees, no buildings, houses or signs. She lived in this section for four years before moving to an apartment in the early spring of 1941.

"I went to the eight-storey apartment house where I had last lived and saw that it had been completely gutted from shelling, mining and bombing."

At the corner of A. Mabini and Isaac Peral street in Ermita, infront of the heaps of debris that had been once homes and business establishments, the young Jose Maria Chicote found the remains of his elder sister Adelina. He knew that it was Adelina, from one shoe that was still in one foot, from the dress that covered parts of the skeleton, and from the *bayong* nearby with what was left of the contents. Carefully, lovingly, Jose Maria and his friends gathered together the mortal remains of Adelina Chicote, so that at the proper time she would at last, get proper burial.[3]

THURSDAY, 1 MARCH 1945

Today there remained only the Finance and the Agriculture buildings unvanquished in the government center.

This morning the Americans broadcast anew over the ruined Agriculture building a message which had been broadcast on 21 February. The message said:[1]

ATTENTION ALL OFFICERS AND MEN OF THE IMPERIAL JAPANESE ARMY:

Ever since our attacks on the city of Manila you have fought bravely and you have fought well. You were ordered to engage us in the center of the city with the Walled City and this building as the core of your defense.

You were ordered to hold us away from Taft Avenue and the sea. You destroyed the bridges to hold us on the other side of the river but you failed. You were ordered to engage us to the front so that the Army could sweep down from the hills in an annihilating attack from our rear. You were promised that your Wild Eagles would blast our planes from the sky yet you see our little observation planes watching all your movements and telling our artillery where to shower you with shells. Your planes did not come on the 8th, the 11th, the 18th and on the 24th. Could your leader have lied to you to make you carry on a hopeless fight?

Your army was going to attack from Novaliches and then they were going to attack from Montalban and Mariquina. They did neither. The Army was going to silence our artillery from the north yet each hour our artillery fires with ever-increasing fury. Your comrades thought that they would find safety at Malabon, but instead met death in the rice paddies there.

Your life is yours to take or to keep as you desire, but is it true loyalty to the Emperor to throw away your life for a cause that is now hopeless?

Fate has given you these choices.

(1) You can commit suicide.

(2) You can hold out a few hours and be blown to dust.

(3) You may come to an honorable understanding with us and live to serve the new Japan when the war is over.

If you surrender (come under the protection of) to us you will not be humiliated or disgraced. Our troops will not fire for 30 minutes during the time you may come in to us.

When there was no response, the engineers poured a mixture of gasoline and oil on the debris and ignited it. When the flames died down, there was only silence stalking the ruins.

The 5th Cavalry estimated that there were 150 Japanese killed at the Agriculture building. They themselves had seven men killed and 75 wounded.

At 12:30 this afternoon, the same broadcast was aimed at the Japanese in the Finance building. When the echoes of the loudspeaker faded away, Japanese troops filed out of the ruins, one-by-one until there were twenty-two.

FRIDAY, 2 MARCH 1945

A two-hour artillery barrage that opened at eight o'clock this morning and ended at ten prepared the Finance building for a new assault by the 1st Battalion, 148th Infantry.

Shortly after the assault began, three Japanese came out of the building under a white flag. During the lull, the Japanese inside let loose with a hail of machinegun-fire. Many American infantry men joined the casualty list.

Enraged over this incident, the infantry withdrew and the artillery came in with a new barrage that lasted until one o'clock this afternoon.

By now the Finance building was but a mound of rubble. Robert Ross Smith put it picaresquely: "The portions not knocked down seemed to be standing only from sheer force of habit."[1]

At two o'clock this afternoon, the infantry came in for what turned out to be the final assault.

This is how the Americans did it.

"As building after building was captured, the technique improved until the final assault upon the Finance Building which incorporated all the techniques developed by experience up to that time. In that action 155-

mm. howitzers, tank destroyers and tanks fired against two sides of the building. Because the rest of the city was in friendly hands, the direction of fire was confined to the ground and first floor in order to prevent the danger of shells going through open windows. As the lower portions of the outer walls disintegrated the walls and the roof settled: but the concrete was so strongly reinforced that the structure bent rther than collapsed and the guns were then moved and fired at the other two walls, and the procedure continued. Just prior to the assault, tanks and M-Fs fired HE and WP into the upper stories, thereby driving the Japs into the basement, and immediately upon cessation of this fire, the infantry assault teams attacked, effected an entrance through breaches in the walls and succeeded in eliminating the last enemy garrison in about four hours."[2]

SATURDAY, 3 MARCH 1945

Day dawned and the only concern of the 148th Infantry Regiment was a pocket of resistance at the top of the ruins of the Finance building. This was easily eliminated today.

During mopping-up operations today and yesterday, 75 Japanese were killed in the Finance Building, while the 148th Infantry had one man killed and 13 wounded.

Late this afternoon, Lt. Gen. Oscar W. Griswold, commanding the XIV Corps, would report to General Walter Krueger, commanding the Sixth Army, that organized resistance in the Manila area had ceased.[1]

The battle for Manila was over.

EPILOGUE:

SOME QUESTIONS AND ANSWERS

Time has dissipated much of the rancor and bitterness caused by the events in Manila in February 1945. But time has not answered certain questions that continue to inflict anguish on the minds of many.

Questions like, why did Sanji Iwabuchi defy the orders of Yamashita and Yokoyama? Why were the outrages against the civilian population perpetrated? Were there official orders from higher authority to this purpose?

And again, why did the Americans resort to the destruction of Manila as a means to their ends? Was it any one man's, or any single group of men's decision? What value did America place on a victory that destroyed 100,000 non-combatants?

The defense of Manila by the Japanese doubtlessly was the direct and immediate cause of the carnage and destruction that befell the city. Why was Manila defended?

On the 7th December 1944 when the Americans landed at Ormoc, Yamashita gave up the battle of Leyte as lost and turned to the defense of Luzon.[1] To this end, he moved, first, to strengthen the troops and second, to unify command.[2]

To strengthen the troops, he requested the Supreme Commander of the Southern Army, Count Terauchi in Saigon, for reinforcements. During December 1944, three divisions were dispatched to the Philippines in response to this request. However, owing to attacks by the enemy by air and submarine, only 1/3 to 1/2 of the original strength actually arrived.[3]

To unify command, Yamashita requested that the 4th Area Army, the

3rd Maritime Transport Command of the Army and some 30,000 troops under the command of the Southern Army Headquarters be placed under his authority.[4]

The last of these were troops that had been stranded in Manila and environs. Some of these were in Manila for lack of transportation. Others had been rescued from sunken ships and were in or around Manila without means of proceeding to their proper units. There were also troops who had been discharged from hospitals and similarly, had no means of rejoining their units. These troops came under Yamashita's command on 1st December 1944.[5]

The 4th Area Army came under Yamashita on 1st January 1945, and between 15 January and 15 February 1945, the 3rd Maritime Transport Command passed into his authority. On 6 January 1945, Navy land units came into his command for "tactical purposes."[6]

Yamashita defined "tactical purposes" as, "For instance, command to advance or retreat. It did not include such things as personnel, punishment, billeting, supply."[7]

Yamashita explained his defense plan for Luzon thus, "Taking advantage of the mountainous terrain, my plan was to establish three strongpoints: in the north, a strongpoint at Baguio and Balete Pass; the 2nd strongpoint west of Clark Field; the 3rd strongpoint in the mountains east of Manila. These plans were to carry out a delaying action."[8]

His rationale was to divert as much American forces in Luzon so as to prevent them from attacking the Japanese homeland for as long as possible.

He said: "In my experience with the Leyte operations, I realized that the American air force and navy were exceedingly superior to ours and also the fire power of the ground forces were superior and very mobile. Therefore, I knew that I could not conduct warfare on a flat land. Therefore, I employed delaying action in the mountains."[9]

As for Manila, Yamashita had this to say: "I decided to put Manila outside the battle area. I ordered my troops out of Manila. I decided to abandon it without battle. There were three reasons for this decision. First, the population of Manila was over one million, therefore, it is impossible to feed them. The second reason is that the buildings were very inflammable. The third reason is that because it is flat, it requires tremendous strength to defend it."[10]

General Muto, his chief of staff, corroborated this position on Manila. He testified: "Manila was the principal and cultural center of the Philippines, with a population of not less than a million, and the terrain itself was of highly inflammable construction. To defend a highly inflammable city with one million inhabitants in it was considered not only impossible but disadvantageous."[11]

From the start, Yamashita was aware of opposition to his plan to abandon Manila. In his affidavit in his own defense at his trial, he said:[12]

> Although there was no open and formal opposition to my decision to turn Manila, in effect, into an open city and thereby save it from the ravages of war, I was given to understand that underneath the surface there was the opinion that Manila should be defended to the last. It is natural that there should be legitimate differences of opinion as to the pros and cons from the technical standpoint among Army men of abandoning such a strategically important commissary and supply center as Manila. This difference of opinion became more pronounced since Manila was the headquarters of major operating commands independent of and outside my direct line of authority. However, insofar as Luzon was concerned, matters relating to ground combat were not only within my jurisdiction, but my specific responsibility. I carried out my decision in spite of all adverse opinion. However, in actual practice it was inevitable that I would experience delay and procrastination in the execution of this plan, due in part, to the presence of those military men who held negative views as to the strategic wisdom of my plan. There were also those, who for some reason, were loath to abandon the cultural life of Manila, and to a greater extent many took issue because of the following: 1) the destruction of the railroads, highways and bridges by the American Air Force and guerrilla activities; 2) the lack of motor transportation in sufficient number; 3) the shortage of gasoline, and 4) the hazards of movement by day because of the Americans' air raids. To add to an already difficult problem, there was being experienced in Manila at that time, an acute shortage of foodstuff for the civilian consumption. In order to mitigate the situation, we were forced to allot a part of our heavily overburdened motor transportation facilities to this non-military end. All in all, the evacuation of Manila by the Japanese troops now progressed with much difficulty at a slower rate than I wanted.

General Muto testified, "...there was a reluctance on the part of many to leave the city of Manila and take up existence in the mountainous country, and they were not prompt about starting out of the city."[13]

To nudge the evacuation forward, nearly all of Yamashita's staff officers, including Muto, came to Manila to call personally on recalcitrant unit commanders and urge them to withdraw from the city.

As Muto put it, "...it appeared that none of them shared the idea of the imminence of the American landing which General Yamashita had and for that reason General Yamashita moved his headquarters to Ipo."[14]

This was on the night of 26 December 1944.

"I saw that some action was necessary to expedite matters," Yamashita said, "and realizing the importance of the subject, I decided to set an example and personally remove my Headquarters immediately out of Manila."[15]

Since he had decided not to defend Manila, why did not Yamashita declare Manila as an "open city" within the terms of the Geneva Convention? Although Japan was not a signatory to the Geneva Convention of 1929, it had filed an undertaking with the International Committee of the Red Cross to the effect that it will adhere to the provisions of the convention.

On 17 December, Lt. Gen. Jo Iimura, chief of staff at Terauchi's Southern Headquarters, arrived in Manila from Saigon, to try to convince Yamashita to carry out Terauchi's policy to attack the Americans at Mindoro.

Lt. Gen. Shuichi Miyazaki, chief of staff at Imperial Headquarters, arrived from Tokyo on 21 December 1944, to join the discussion and ostensibly to support Iimura.

Both Iimura and Miyazaki were instead converted to Yamashita's views. Yamashita only agreed to launch raiding parties to harass the Americans and forestall the construction of the airfields on Mindoro.

Before Miyazaki left for Tokyo, Yamashita suggested to him that Manila be declared an open city. This required the approval of the Navy, however, and Miyazaki brought up the matter with Vice Admiral Mikawa, commander of the Southwest Area Fleet. Mikawa took the position that Manila should be defended to the last, and was "violently opposed" to the idea of an open city.[16] Yamashita seems to have dropped the idea at this point.

Akira Muto makes the distinction of declaring Manila an "open city" within the terms of the Geneva Convention, and "a desire not to have fighting in the city."[17]

According to General Muto, Yamashita did not declare Manila an open city for the following reasons:[18]

First, he (Yamashita) would have had to announce it to the world, and he did not have the authority to do that.

Second, there were huge stocks of military supplies in Manila, having been the principal base of the Japanese for three years, so it was impossible to formally declare Manila as a city not to be defended, considering that there was not enough transportation to move out the supplies.

Since it was not possible to tell Tokyo to declare Manila as a city not to be defended, it was decided to evacuate Manila in a tactical manner, and having withdrawn as much of the supplies as possible, try to keep the fighting out of the city.

Muto explains this further: "While General Yamashita wished to clear the city of Japanese troops and supplies there were in the city large numbers of air force and navy troops who were not subject to his command, and that if having made an announcement, a declaration of an open city, these troops were left in the city, then despite the announcement the facts of the case would have been that the city would be defended, and he preferred to try to make the city in fact, an undefended city to the extent that he could without making any declaration to that effect."[19]

Captain Milton Sandberg summarized the non-declaration of Manila as an open city by Yamashita in these terms:[20]

"The declaration of a city as an open city has the effect in international law of making the city immune to enemy bombardment. No city is properly an open city unless it has been cleared of all military fortification and supplies.

"So long as Manila was full of war supplies, which he did not have the time, fuel or transportation to remove, and so long as the navy was basing its main operations, activities which he never had authority to curtail, he had no right to label Manila `open', and to invoke immunity from bombardment by the American forces. If he had declared Manila as an open city, then truly he would have violated the laws of war, just as the Germans did in 1944 when they declared Rome an open city, knowing that as a center of war supplies Rome had no right to immunity from bombardment. Instead, General Yamashita took the conservative course of moving to put Manila outside the area of battle without demanding any special status from the American forces for doing so."

Despite all odds, the evacuation of Manila proceeded. The order to move out was issued in the last days of December 1944 and on 10 January 1945, the Kobayashi troops started leaving for Wawa. By 25 January 1945, only about 1,800 members of the Kobayashi Detachment remained in Manila.

Before leaving for Baguio on 4 January 1945, Admiral Okoochi transferred "operational control" of the Manila Naval Defense Force to the Shimbu Group under General Yokoyama.[21]

The transfer of "operational control," in the sense of the Japanese, meant that the Army (Shimbu Group) would have control over the Navy units (Manila Naval Defense Force) to advance Army objectives within an area assigned to the Army (Luzon), if and when objectives assigned to the Navy units earlier had been attained.[22]

Operations on land on Luzon ostensibly were Army responsibility. Under Japanese armed forces practice, as Iwabuchi understood it, he was not compelled to surrender to the Army control over his Navy forces for operations on land, until after he had completed his Navy missions. He could probably have carried out his Navy orders simultaneously with his Army orders, but in his Navy mind, he was under no compulsion to function in this manner. Iwabuchi chose not to carry out Army orders, until all the directives earlier issued him by the Navy had been completed.[23]

Iwabuchi was a veteran Navy man who now found himself with two orders on hand, one from the Navy and another from the Army. As a Navy man he felt obliged to attend first to the Navy orders. As it happened, he never completed his Navy orders. Thus, he never came around to the Army orders. These were the fateful orders to withdraw from Manila.

The situation vexed Yokoyama immensely. On 4 January 1945, the day Yamashita and Okoochi left for Baguio, he learned, apparently to his surprise, that there were in Manila 16,000 Navy troops.[24] By this time, what Iwabuchi had in mind with respect to his, Iwabuchi's orders, had become clear to Yokoyama.

Before this time, Yokoyama seemed to have understood that there would be but 4,000 Naval troops in Manila, in addition to the 3,750 troops of the Noguchi Detachment and the Abe Battalion. His plans for delaying action against the enemy, the destruction of bridges and the evacuation of equipment and supplies, were based on the belief that the combined Army and Navy force of about 7,750 would be able to execute all his assigned missions. He was equipped to evacuate this number of men out of the Manila area, upon completion of his missions, on the assumption that he would have time to do so, estimating that the Americans would not arrive in the area until 20 February.[25]

Yokoyama called a series of conferences between Army and Navy representatives during the period between 8 to 13 January 1945. At these meetings the Navy representatives took the position that Manila should be defended to the last man. They believed that if the Navy withdrew from the area, they would be unable to execute their orders. They had other reasons for staying put in the city, including, 1) Manila was a natural fortress which could easily be defended while inflicting heavy losses on the enemy, and 2) they did not like the positions in the mountain country to which Yokoyama assigned them.[26]

The final decision, however, was Iwabuchi's and this was for the Navy "to carry out its primary duty of defending Naval facilities," in the words of his chief of staff.[27]

Yokoyama finally bowed to this position. He knew that Iwabuchi had prior orders from the Navy. Yokoyama could not countermand these orders.[28]

Thus Yokoyama yielded to Iwabuchi's plans for the defense of Manila and in the process, in order to unify command, placed under Iwabuchi the Army troops still in the city.

Earlier, Yokoyama had done the next best thing, being unable to get Iwabuchi out of Manila, and wrung from the latter his agreement, 1) to defend the San Juan del Monte area between the city and the advance positions of the Shimbu Group to the northeast; 2) to strengthen the defenses of Fort McKinley and to set up there an alternative headquarters in anticipation of ultimate retreat from Manila, and 3) to establish secondary wire communications between the Shimbu Group headquarters at Ipo and Fort McKinley.[29]

Late in January, Yokoyama issued orders to the Shimbu Group and to the Manila Naval Defense Force.[30]

The Shimbu Group was reminded of its primary objective of a protracted stand in the mountain area east and northeast of Manila, and was ordered to defend Manila and Fort McKinley to prevent their use by the enemy the while damaging the enemy's capacity to fight, and finally alerting the force to opportunities to counterattack from the rear.[31]

The Manila Naval Defense Force was directed to "defend already established positions and crush the enemy's fighting strength."[32]

The wording of these orders is described by Robert Ross Smith as "definitive." A question arises, however, over Yokoyama's use of the Japanese word "koshu" which ordinarily means "firm defense," but which Smith believes is weak in a Japanese order. According to Smith, the word "koshu" would indicate, not a fight to the death, but a desire to conduct limited holding action, to be followed by withdrawal.[33]

Iwabuchi's operations officers also seem to have understood that "koshu" implied that Yokoyama would order a general withdrawal once battle had been joined within city limits. The absence of the word "withdrawal" from Yokoyama's order was interpreted as deliberate so as not to impair morale.[34]

General Muto was positive of Yamashita's decision against street-fighting in Manila. "The order not to engage in street-fighting had been revealed to the commander of the Shimbu Group towards the end of December (1944)," Muto testified. "The fact that General Yamashita did not desire any street-fighting in Manila had been explained to the naval forces and they should have made preparations in accordance with those desires."[35]

Muto implies here a patent defiance on the part of the Navy against Yamashita's position. The arrangement for the Manila Naval Defense Force under Iwabuchi to come under Yamashita's command was made on 7 January 1945. Both Yokoyama and Iwabuchi, in the words of Muto, were "well aware of the necessity for withdrawing from Manila."[36]

On 9 January Admiral Iwabuchi moved his headquarters from Manila to Fort McKinley. When informed of this Yamashita was relieved. "He was relieved in his mind," Muto would testify.[37]

When subsequently Yamashita learned that Iwabuchi had returned to Manila, he said, according to Muto, "This will never do."[38]

This was on 13 February 1945. Immediately Yamashita sent an order to Yokoyama asking, "Why is all this delay? Hurry up and get the troops out of the city."[39]

"I know that Admiral Iwabuchi received the order," Muto testified.[40]

It was at this time that Yamashita learned that Yokoyama had surrendered to Iwabuchi responsibility for the defense of Manila. It stunned him to learn that there were as many as 16,000 Naval troops still in Manila. Yamashita issued a stern censure to Yokoyama with an order to counterattack against the Americans and attempt to bring the Japanese troops out of Manila.[41]

The order was indeed relayed by Yokoyama for Iwabuchi to withdraw to Fort McKinley as the first step towards evacuating the city. To this order Iwabuchi replied:

"Holding the strong point in the city is considered to be of great importance. Withdrawal of headquarters from Manila would render difficulty in the execution of operations in Manila. Moreover we did not succeed in re-establishing overland contacts with Fort McKinley. We are therefore unable to withdraw from Manila."[42]

Still, Yokoyama did launch a "rescue plan." The wireless system between Manila and the Shimbu Army headquarters in Wawa had remained open until 18 February 1945. On 14 February Col. Noguchi, responding to orders to get out, wired Yokoyama that he would attempt to break through with the remnants of the Noguchi unit on 14 February. The Shimbu Army planned to get him out, fielding 5,000 troops attacking from Caloocan, Ipo, the Quezon airfield and Antipolo.[43]

Yokoyama's rescue plan had two objectives.

1) To break up the offensive preparation being made by the Americans situated east of the Shimbu Group.

2) To rescue the Noguchi unit out of Manila.

There was no plan to retake Manila.

The rescue plan failed, as Col. Hiroshi Hashimoto said, "Because resistance of American forces confronting the Shimbu was so stiff."[44]

The fierce fighting at the Paco Railroad Station was actually the Noguchi force trying to break out when they ran into the Americans who came in from Nagtahan and Santa Ana. Two or three times the Paco Railroad Station area changed hands between 9 to 10 February. The Japanese did not make it.

From all the preceding, the onus for the carnage and destruction in Manila in February 1945 weighs heavily on Sanji Iwabuchi. He did not survive to tell his side of the story. He may have perished in the ruins of the Finance building which was known to be his last command post. As to when he met his end, and how, no one was left to tell.

Who was this man Sanji Iwabuchi?

This man would remain much a mystery, up to this writing. What is known is that he was born in Niigata Prefecture in 1893 and studied at the Naval Academy at Etajima. It is conjectured that he was a "brilliant" student and must have been "well-connected," for upon graduation he was appointed an imperial aide. From 1915 to 1942 the name disappeared from the records, and it is believed that the man may have gone into the Japanese secret service.

In the early spring of 1942, the name Sanji Iwabuchi enters the record anew as captain of the battleship *Kirishima* and the man commanded the ship in the Battle of Midway and at Guadalcanal. This ship was among those dispatched to attack Guadalcanal, but it was scuttled along with other ships in the ensuing debacle which resulted in heavy losses to the Japanese. Despite the loss of his ship in this battle, Iwabuchi was promoted to Rear Admiral, but again he disappeared from public view.

When he re-surfaced in 1945, it was as commander of Japanese naval forces in Manila.

A. Frank Reel, the counsel for Yamashita, best summed up what went on in the mind of Iwabuchi in these terms: "Before he was directed to subject himself and his men to army command, Admiral Iwabuchi had received a previous naval order to destroy the valuable harbor facilities of the finest seaport in the Orient, the dock and the naval warehouses. Faced with such a dilemma, Admiral Iwabuchi apparently did what one might expect an admiral to do under the circumstances – he stayed to carry out the directions of the Naval Ministry."[45]

Having decided to fight the Americans in Manila, the question arises as to why Iwabuchi's men resorted to atrocities against the civilian population.

Throughout the three years of the Japanese occupation of their country, the Filipinos manifested a loathing of the interloper that took many forms, from the truceless guerrilla warfare that raged all over the archipelago to the private, personal acts of defiance that individuals showed at every opportunity, ranging from expressions of ridicule to outright sabotage. This did not escape the Japanese.

The Japanese never understood why this people would prefer the friendship of the distant white power across the ocean to that of a neighbor-Asiatic.

The Japanese vision of a new order in Southeast Asia under their hegemony, something which they miserably failed to clearly define, in the first place, simply could not strike the imagination of the Filipinos. There was no affection lost between the two peoples, only mutual contempt and the irreconcilable differences between occupant and intruder, conqueror and conquered.

The day came when the Japanese gave up all pretense of trying to hold the fealty of this people, and without so declaring, categorized Filipinos as the enemy. Whether this decision was a thought half-formed in their collective mind in a fatal moment of hysteria, or a well-reasoned official policy, one can only speculate now, but the action to decimate the civilian population where this could be done arose from this decision.

Following are excerpts from a captured file of the Manila Naval Defense Force and Southwestern Area Fleet Operation Orders, dated 23 December 1944 to 14 February 1945:

"When Filipinos are to be killed, they must be gathered into one place and disposed of with the consideration that ammunition and manpower must not be used in excess. Because the disposal of dead bodies is a troublesome task they should be gathered into houses which are scheduled to be burned or demolished. They should also be thrown into the river."[46]

"All people in the battlefield with the exceptions of the Japanese military personnel, Japanese civilians and Special Construction Units will be put to death."[47]

In the final hours of the Japanese in Manila and elsewhere in the islands every Filipino male capable of bearing arms was labelled as "guerrilla." This capability was measured variously from the ages of 12 or 14 upwards.

A notebook-diary, presumed to belong to a member of the Akatsuki 16709 Force, captured in Manila had the following entries:[48]

"7 February 1945 – 150 guerrillas were disposed of tonight. I stabbed 10."

"8 February 1945 – Guarded over 1,164 guerrillas who were newly brought in today."

"9 February 1945 – Burned 1,000 guerrillas to death tonight."

"10 February 1945 – Guarded approximately 1,000 guerillas."

"13 February 1945 – Enemy tanks are lurking in the vicinity of Banzai (Santa Cruz) bridge. Our attack preparation had been completed. I am now on guard duty at guerrilla internment camp. While I was on duty approximately 10 guerrillas tried to escape. They were stabbed to death. At 1600 all guerrillas were burned to death."

Conceivably, the people referred to by this Japanese soldier were not "guerillas" in the true sense of the world. They were Filipinos, obviously males, rounded up in their communities and marked for extermination.

Early in October 1944, shortly upon assuming command, General Yamashita called a conference with his staff and the matter of guerrillas was discussed. "These armed bandits should be mopped-up," he recalled having declared at this conference.[49]

"Our principle (was) that the Philippine people were our allies and we must endeavor to gain their cooperation," Yamashita testified at his trial, "and that if only the armed bandits could be cleared out the situation would be all right."[50]

Yamashita insisted on establishing correct relations with the civilian population. "I felt that we should take measures to win the confidence of the Philippine people, and since their cooperation was necessary and since we were allied with them. And I gave such instructions at the time of my arrival."[51]

Much later, when already holding on to his defenses by his toenails, Yamashita would have occasion to reflect on his civilian relations. He told a Japanese war correspondent from the Domei News Agency named Iwamoto in an interview in his Baguio headquarters, "I think that Japan made a big mistake in the way she administered foreign populations. We lack a tradition – it's one of our national defects. And we really make no attempt to understand them."[52]

On 11 October 1944, the 14th Army Group issued an order part of which read: "In view of the special characteristics of the Philippine operations, subversive activities of the residents and attacks on our rear by airborne raiding forces must be considered. In order to avoid mistakes in conducting operations, take precautions against armed guerrillas, subjugate them quickly, and put a stop to their activities."[53]

The thinking of Yamashita on the guerrilla menace to his cause was moulded by reports he received. In his defense at his trial he recalls a report of Col. Nagahama, commanding officer of the Military Police. "The only subject in my memory at this time is his (Nagahama's) report after the Americans landed in Leyte, that the opposition of the Filipinos against the Japanese gradually became more apparent and pronounced, that there was marked increase in guerrilla activities in the vicinity of Manila."[54]

To counter this, he issued a threat: "Those who stand against the Japanese army must be regarded as the enemies. In the Philippines today, the war has come to a situation of kill or be killed. No matter who the person is, a Filipino or not, if we hesitate, we ourselves will be killed."[55]

Ultimately, the word "guerrilla" evolved into the convenient euphemism to justify for the Japanese their act of dealing death, first to all males, and eventually to all Filipinos, including women and children. The guerrilla was the enemy. All Filipinos were guerrillas. All Filipinos must be liquidated.

For a while the Japanese observed the niceties of international law where neutral nationals were concerned. Finally, in the throes of the terrible paranoia that collectively afflicted those sad, pitiful men facing inevitable defeat and the specter of death, even these niceties were dropped. Thus the massacres of nationals of neutral countries including the religious.

Although it may not have been contemplated and there was no declaration to that effect, the Japanese had in fact put in force in South Manila at this time the notorious *senko-seisaku*, the three-all principle – "kill all, burn all, destroy all."

With this policy, the Japanese had succeeded in reducing the population of North China from 44 million to 25 million in July 1941. They would succeed just as enormously in Manila, albeit in a lesser scale.[55-a]

The method was to surround a given area and destroy everything in it to make it unhabitable. According to Japanese records cited by Barbara Tuchman, a two-month "mopping-up" campaign in one district of Hopei during the Sino-Japanese war resulted in 4,500 killed, 15,000 houses burned and 17,000 persons deported to Manchuria.[55-b]

How the Japanese as individuals felt about the killing of civilians is seen in the few records that survived. The following is from the diary of Pfc. Matsuoko Itoji, 64 Infantry Regiment, 23 Division, Tominage Unit, with entries from 19 December 1944 to 29 March 1945. The last entry on 29 March reads:[56]

"Taking advantage of darkness we went to kill the natives. It was hard to kill them because they seem to be good people. Frightful cries of the children were horrible. I myself stabbed and killed several persons."

The diary of an unknown Japanese soldier presumed to be of the GIGO Force carried this undated entry for one day in November 1944 describing his participation in the execution of suspected guerrillas at the Lipa Air Depot in Lipa, Batangas:

"...I was irritated. Later, one-by-one the members of the section bayonetted the guerrillas. The first one was bayonetted by Suzuki, Yukimatsu. My turn was the second one. The moment I bayonetted the victim he cried, 'Ah,' and fell into the hole behind him. He was suffering but I felt no emotion at all."[57]

The following is from a more sensitive person, the unidentified owner of a diary-notebook found among papers captured in Lucaban (sic), Luzon, 23 May 1945, with entries from July 1944 to 22 May 1945.

"February, 1945. Everyday is spent in hunting guerrillas and natives.

I have already killed well over 100. The motive that I possessed at the time of leaving the homeland had long since disappeared. Now I am a hardened killer and my sword is always stained with blood. Although it is for my country it is brutality. May my mother forgive me."[58]

The following is an extract from a captured bound, printed and mimeographed file titled, "Police Affairs B No. 2, Incoming Reports on Public Order," dated July 1943 to 12 January 1944, issued by the 14 Army Military Police Unit, covering the July Report on Postal Censorship (mail leaving the Philippines.) The material may have been among the censored matter, excised from Japanese soldiers' mail. It read: "On 10 July, the Japanese troops gathered all the men and boys at the church and questioned those connected with the guerrilla unit. They had them drink water and hit them on the cheeks. It was pitiful, and I couldn't watch. They also shot them and speared them to death with bamboo lances. Indeed the Japanese Army does extreme things."[59]

As to whether the carnage and destruction inflicted on Manila were official orders from above, a welter of contradictions emerges.

The prosecution at the Yamashita trial, through Maj. Robert M. Kerr, had raised the issue, thus: "Time and again in these atrocities there were that same command, that same supervision, that same obvious plan. These were not wild, drunken orgies by individual soldiers on their own. Not at all."[60]

On 27 October 1945 the Liaison Committee (Tokyo) for the Japanese Army and Navy provided this information to the prosecution at the Yamashita trial.[61]

"Following the suspension of the Leyte operations, the Area Army was concentrated generally in Manila, Clark and Baguio sectors. It was being prepared for the American landings, but in January it was dispatched to meet the landing in the Lingayen sector. On this occasion, the Southern Army dispatched to the Area Army a telegram giving encouragement and also instruction embodying the following points.

"Instructions."

"a. The 14th Area Army will hold the sea and air bases firmly. If it becomes necessary to relinquish them, see that the enemy cannot use them."

Also in the same set of instructions, "In the event the Area Army is forced to give up sea, air and military bases these facilities will be completely demolished to prevent enemy use."

Further, "Manila will be defended to the utmost and in the event of loss its use to the enemy will be hampered by cutting off its water supply and other such measures."

That the document exists seems certain, but whether it was actually transmitted · to Yamashita is not certain. Yamashita denied having received it. At his trial he heatedly maintained, "I deny it; I did not receive them."[62] There is no evidence that he did.

In its transmittal letter, the Liaison Committee (Tokyo) had appended its own remarks to the document, thus: "The Southern Army and the Area Army gave no instructions of the kind you specify regarding the disposition of civilians."[63] This referred to the massacre of civilians.

At one point during his trial, Yamashita said, referring to the massacres, "Certain testimony has been given that I ordered the massacres of all Filipinos, and I wish to say that I absolutely did not order this, nor did I receive the order to do this from any superior authority, nor did I even permit such a thing, or if I had known of it would have I considered such a thing, and I will swear to heaven and earth concerning these points."[64]

In his favor was the testimony of Capt. Norman Sparnon of the Allied Translator and Interpreter Section (ATIS). Southwest Pacific Area, who said: "Nowhere in the hundred thousand odd documents captured by the U.S. was an order to destroy Manila found."[65]

On 8 March, 1945, Col. Masatoshi Fujishige, commander, Fuji Heiden (Group) which operated in Batangas and Laguna provinces from 1st January 1945, assembled officers and non-coms in his command at his Santa Clara (Santa Cruz?) headquarters and gave oral instructions, a transcription of which was among documents captured and introduced as evidence at the trial of General Yamashita. Fujishige's instructions were:[66]

"1. The object of mass training is to enable the sea raiding units to achieve impressive results in land warfare.

"2. The new duty of the group is to reverse the present battle situation on Luzon.

"3. Become a godlike warrior. Learn the art of war like a god.

"4. Be thorough in training. Do not misunderstand the meaning of affection of officers towards their men.

"5. No one must die an honorable death until he has killed 100 enemy soldiers and destroyed 10 enemy tanks.

"6. Kill American troops cruelly. Do not kill them with one stroke. Shoot guerrilla units. Kill all who oppose the Emperor, even women and children.

"7. Start thorough training immediately upon returning to your units.

Only to Item No. 6 did Col. Fujishige demur when this document was presented in court. In his testimony before the court he explained No. 6 in these terms:[67]

"First, with respect to American soldiers, I told as I did in the other paragraph, that each of them must kill 100. With respect to those guerrillas who opposed the Imperial Forces, my instructions were to suppress them with military operations. With respect to women and children, about the 1st of January, from military sources we received a warning that even women and children were carrying weapons and to be on guard for them. Therefore, and after the 1st January and or into February in my own territory there were many instances where women bearing arms inflicted considerable damage to my forces.

"When I was riding in a car, an automobile, a child threw a hand grenade at me. On another occasion a child about 15 years old came near on one occasion and I had a soldier who was nearby search him and we found a hand grenade on his person. I took the hand grenade away from this child and sent him away.

"I myself was threatened twice and my soldiers were threatened or received damage on many and numerous occasions from women and children armed. Because I had received intelligence from Shimbu units that women and children were going about armed, on this occasion I told my troops that if they were attacked by armed women and children, that of necessity, as military necessity, they must be combatted.

"I will repeat what I have just said: that if women and children attack our troops with arms it is unavoidable they be combatted in a military manner."

Lt. Cdr. Bartlett, acting as court interpreter for Fujishige on this occasion said: "For the record I would like to state that the word in the witnesses' testimony translated as 'guerrilla' can equally, although not necessarily, be translated as 'armed bandit."[68]

"Also the words translated as 'mop-up' can also be translated as 'suppress,' 'put down,' subjugate, 'punish,' or conduct a punitive expedition."[69]

In any case, there was no evidence that Fujishige issued his orders upon instruction from superiors.

The tactical considerations in the mind of Sanji Iwabuchi and his officers apart, what madness possessed these men that they would resort to bestialities unparalleled in modern times?

There was apparent system in the mass murder, such as those at Fort Santiago to which Luis Gallent, Sancho Enriquez and Juan Palada testified, and from which they survived. The massacres in Paco from which Benjamin Urrutia, Federico Davantes and Jose Cabañero survived, clearly followed a plan.

The incidents at the Pedro Campos compound, the Pax Court and the Carlos Perez-Rubio compound in Pasay, and those at the St. Paul college and the De la Salle college, appear as part of a pattern. So did the atrocities against the Spanish religious and civilians in Intramuros and San Marcelino.

The decision to make the Bayview Hotel, the Alhambra and the Miramar apartment hotels, *joro* houses was implemented with deliberate care.

For a long time the stories of babies being tossed in the air by crazed Japanese and caught at the point of a bayonet where thought apochrypal. But there are at least three recorded testimonies of witnesses to such incidents. One was the testimony of 11-year-old Rosalinda Andoy who witnessed such an incident during her ordeal in the ruins of the Santo Domingo church in Intramuros.[70] The others were sworn to by Angeles Barahona, in an incident at the St. Paul college compound and Rosario Fernandez, 25, in another incident in the premises of the residence of Dr. Herminio Velarde on Tennessee street in Malate.[71]

Also regarded as apochrypal were the stories of genital mutilation. But Francisco Lopez witnessed one such incident done on a male in the German Club compound on San Luis street in Ermita. Also, Prudencio Chicote Lalana testified to outrages committed on the bodies of three teen-age girls in the massacre in the ruins of Dr. Rafael Moreta's house on Isaac Peral street in Ermita. The girls were raped then killed with bayonet stabs. Their sex organs were ripped with bladed weapons.[72]

Many Japanese used their final days to fulfill individual curiosity, or desire, as the case may have been, of having sex with white women, i.e., Caucasians as against Orientals, i.e., Filipino or Chinese.

"They were very choosy," Elisa Beliso testified. "They wanted only mestizas."[73] She spoke of the Japanese in the San Agustin church and monastery who picked out mainly Spanish and half-breed women on whom to vent their lust.

The women hauled into the Bayview Hotel on 8 February 1945 were of many nationalities. After two days, the Japanese segregated the Filipino and Chinese women, brought some of them to an apartment hotel on Alhambra street and others to another apartment building on Roxas Boulevard, leaving only Caucasians and half-breeds in the Bayview Hotel. It is not known that the non-whites got a better deal after that, and it is extremely doubtful that the whites did.

The Americans seemed to have anticipated the quick and easy capitulation of Manila. MacArthur himself hoped he could enter Manila on 26 January 1945, his 65th birthday. He did not make it, but many of his staff believed that the delay would be brief.

On 6 February, MacArthur's headquarters issued the famous communique announcing the surrender of Manila. Congratulatory messages from all over the world poured into the GHQ SWPA. No one in the outside world knew that there had been no surrender. The press correspondents at GHQ SWPA knew, but, as William Manchester said, "The General's censors told correspondents they couldn't expose his victory communique as a lie..."[74]

MacArthur's headquarters sent out plans for a triumphal march into Manila, "a great victory parade, *a la* Champs Elysees, that the Theatre Commander in person was to lead through the city," in the words of Robert Ross Smith.[75]

The victory parade *a la* Champs Elysees never took place. "A parade was in fact impossible," Manchester gibes. "No streets would be clear of rubble, and the gutters would be running with blood."[76]

The Americans were responsible for a major part of that rubble and a goodly portion of the blood running in the gutters.

In an interview with John Deane Potter, General Krueger admitted that "much of the destruction was caused by our (American) artillery."[77]

Which raises the question, was the destruction of Manila by bomb and shell the only way to rid the city of the Japanese? What was the primary consideration of the American operations in the liberation of Manila?

The primary consideration was to save American lives. For all MacArthur's fixation on the liberation of the Philippines, the primary consideration in all military action was still and always the conservation of precious American life.

Hence the bitterness in Carmen Guerrero Nakpil's words: "The Americans had decided to risk the whole city for the sake of the few American lives in Santo Tomas, and had executed a sortie into the internment camp while the Japanese went on a rampage in the south."[78]

Though by no means the official position, Robert Ross Smith articulates what is seen in the records. He says:[79] "The artillery, mortar, tank and tank destroyer fire that had destroyed the Provisor island power plant and turned Paco Station and Concordia college into a shambles represented a striking departure from the limitations placed upon support fires during the clearing of northern Manila and the eastern suburbs. For the 37th Division, at least, cancellation of earlier limitations had become a necessity. For one thing, sufficient information had now become available from aerial observation, patrolling, and reports from civilians and guerrillas for XIV Corp's G-2 Section to conclude that the Japanese had turned almost every building from Estero de Paco to Manila bay into a veritable fortress, far stronger even than the defenses already encountered south of the Pasig.

"In addition, the operation south of the river had forced the XIV Corps and the 37th Division to the reluctant decision that all pretense at saving Manila's buildings would have to be given up -- casualties were mounting at a much too alarming rate among the infantry units. The 148th Infantry had suffered 500-odd casualties (about 200 did not require hospitalization) from 7 through 10 February. The regiment was now nearly 600 men understrength and its rifle companies averaged about 50 men understrength. Through the seizure of Provisor island the 129th Infantry had incurred 285 casualties -- 35 killed, 240 wounded and 10 missing -- and was nearly 700 men understrength. Company G had only 90 effectives; Company E was a little better off. The 148th Infantry had apparently received only five replacements since 9 January; the 129th Infantry, none."

These details of personnel losses provided the rationale for the American decision to subject Manila to carpet-shelling. Robert Ross Smith might have summed up this rationale pretty well. He writes:[80] "The losses had manifestly been too heavy for the gains achieved. If the city were to be secured without destruction of the 37th and the 1st Cavalry Division, no further effort could be made to save the buildings; everything holding up progress would be pounded, although artillery fire would not be directed against structures such as churches and hospitals that were known to contain civilians. Even this last restriction would not always be effective, for often it could not be learned until too late that a specific building held civilians. The lifting of restrictions on support fires would result in turning much of southern Manila into shambles, but there was no help for that if the city were to be secured in a reasonable length of time and with reasonable losses."

Thus, on 14 February, the 140th Field Artillery fired 2,091 rounds of high explosive 105-mm ammunition, and the 4.2-inch mortars of the 82nd Chemical Mortar Battalion poured 1,101 rounds of high explosives and 263 rounds of white phosphorus shells, into the University of the Philippines-Philippine General hospital complex on Taft Avenue.[81]

Dr. Antonio G. Sison, PGH director, who never left the premises through the battle testified that there were no Japanese inside the hospital. They were on the lawn infront of the administration building. "They were there with their guns, sometimes standing, sometimes lying with their guns pointed to the front."[82]

On 23 February, between 7:30 and 8:30 in the morning, the combined American artillery units dumped 185 tons of high explosives on Intramuros, to which the 4.2-inch mortars of the 82nd Chemical Mortar Battalion added 45 tons of smoke and high explosive shells. During the hour more than 61 shells fell on Intramuros each minute, more than three tons of explosives fell each minute. The former alone consisted of over 3,700 rounds.[83]

Aside from this, the tank guns, tank destroyer guns and field artillery howitzers of various calibers sent in 7,487 rounds of high explosive shells, 300 rounds of armor-piercing projectiles and 116 rounds of smoke and white phosphorus shells, all during those fateful 60 minutes.

No doubt the artillery did a thorough job, and the objective of keeping down American deaths was achieved. Robert Ross Smith makes the dry comment, "That the artillery had also almost razed the ancient Walled City could not be helped."[84]

No records are available of the ammunition expenditure of the infantry units consisting of 105-mm self-propelled mounts, mortars and machine guns.

General Robert S. Beightler denied Robert Ross Smith's conclusion that he, Beightler, intended to raze Intramuros and other objectives. Beightler maintained that he merely wanted to raze a small portion of the northeast corner of Intramuros. Smith argues that Beightler's contention is not supported by the records. General Griswold is of the belief that it was indeed the intention of Beightler to raze Intramuros.[85]

No one would accuse Robert S. Beightler of shying away from a confrontation with a live Japanese. His decision to lay waste the earth before sending his men where live Japanese were known to be, may in fact have arisen from genuine concern for his infantry. As it happened, the infantry sustained the highest number of personnel killed – 300 out of 1,010 – in the battle for Manila.[86]

This concern explains the apparent disregard on the part of the Americans for Filipino property, and consequently, for Filipino lives.

"The artillery pounded the city and the streets and the buildings, trading property for lives," Sgt. Ozzie St. George reported in *Yank* Magazine.[87] Of course, he meant American lives.

What was the effect of the carpet-shelling on the civilians?

This is the experience of Doña Maria Paz Zamora de Mascuñana:[88] "The explosions shook the earth and rocked the house . . . When a distant bang signals that a missile with its load of death and destruction is whistling its way towards us, everyone unconsciously holds his breath and we interrupt our prayers and ask, 'Dont't let it fall on us, Lord!'

"Finally, when another bang announces that death reached its destination far from us, there is a big audible communal exhalation of relief and we exclaim, 'Thank God, we are safe for the moment!' But until when?

"Our Father who art in heaven . . .

"These long moments of uncertainty that we have to go through between explosions wear out more stable nerves . . . no wonder then that the disoriented woman with us suffered another attack, her eyes flashing lightnings of madness . . ."

Rodolfo G. Tupas and his family were refugees in the Pediatrics Ward of the Philippine General hospital. Years and years later he would recall this experience in his young life as follows.[89] "I can hear it now -- the crushing, grinding, tearing sound of artillery shells exploding into a mass of concrete or on the hospital grounds.

"The shells were preceded by eerie whistling sounds. Every time there was a barrage, the whole ward went into fervent prayers. I can still hear it now -- the long murmur of fright!"

Years and years later, Miguel P. Avanceña would recall this experience during the shelling of the PGH: "For about a week that never seemed to end, the artillery barrages came crashing down on us unerringly, ward after ward, building after building . . . These were indeed days of terror. No sooner than a ward would be hit by a barrage of 105 mm shells than the next wing would get it. I can still hear the screams of the wounded clearly to this day, the shouting of those separated from their families calling their loved ones, the acrid sulphurous choking smoke that filled the wards as the shells exploded."[89-a]

Miguel was the son of the Honorable Ramon Avanceña, former Chief Justice of the Supreme Court of the Philippines and chairman of the Council of State in the wartime Republic. The former Chief Justice was ill and was confined at the PGH during this time, and members of this family watched over him.

The nun Concepcion Gotera, Daughter of Charity, was caught in the very heart of the great fire-offering during those fateful days of February 1945, right in the gutted Santa Rosa college of Intramuros, Here was a person schooled in the Christian virtues but nothing in her life as a nun kept her from falling into utter despair and hopelessness. Here are excerpts from her recollection of her ordeal: [90]

14 February 1945 -- "Never again shall we see days without clouds, without anguish, without worry, days when we make our oppressed hearts smile . . . Today is worse than ever . . . the cannons roar non-stop. Our hair literally stand on end."

16 February 1945 -- "We tread as though on thin air. Everything appears hazy, dark . . . very dark. Today many of the wounded from yesterday's bombardment died . . . we live from moment to moment . . . the big question is, shall we see the light of the morning?"

18 February 1945 -- "My father's face is before me . . . my beloved

father who has not disappeared from my sight these last few days . . . I weep in silence, alone with Jesus . . ."

19 February 1945 – "There is nothing to hope for, nothing to comfort us. Many of the dead remain unburied. The women are too enfeebled to dig the graves."

This is the experience of Lydia Gutierrez, then 14-years-old, as related in her diary:[91]

> Suddenly a shell fell on Wright and Remedios Sts. Then another fell and broke the wall between our house and the Amador's. We ran out into the backyard. Nong ran back to call Tony and Toots just in time, cause the next shell hit our front porch. We ran under the Bagasan's house. There were around a hundred refugees there. The next shell fell in the driveway between our houses. We ran out. The smoke and dust in the driveway reached high over our heads and choked us. We wanted to go the Hemingway's but their house was burning too. The Japanese saw us from the street and machinegunned us. We ducked and then ran back to our backyard. Nong remembered the wall they had torn down and we all jumped over to the Gonzales' house. All the refugees from the Bagasan's followed us.
>
> Under the Gonzales's house there were many, many people, most of them wounded. The shells and shrapnels and explosions fell without stopping. It was noisy with explosions, people crying of pain, despairing, praying. We held our medals tight and didn't stop praying. One shell fell and hit the Amador's house. We heard voices screaming and shouting hysterically. Then Joseling came to join us saying everyone in his house had died. Then a shell burst so near and I felt hard things hitting my face. I thought I was hit and dying. I couldn't move. None of us was hit. Then the Japs came again and they machinegunned us. We hugged the ground. Those sitting were hit. Mr. Bagasan got hit in the neck and Nong bandaged him. Baby's dress was full of blood but she said it was the man beside her who got hit and died.
>
> The houses all burned immediately whenever a shell hit. Our house, the Hemingway's, Bagasan's, Amador's were all burning now. It was getting hotter and hotter. Then the smoke came under the house as the Gonzales house caught fire too. We crawled to the next house on the left. There was a shallow hole and it was soft and sandy soil so we started digging with our hands just so we could lay flat on our stomachs. We found a mattress which we used to cover our bodies. We stuck out our heads and watched the people passing on Wright St. They were dragging their wounded. Then we saw some of the Amadors walking. We found a bottle with brown sugar and gave the children some. The heat became intense. We had to go. When we came out into the street it was very quiet, not a living body, all were dead. We could not turn right to go to Remedios and Florida as the heat from Amadors' and Montes' houses made the road like an oven. We turned left. We stumbled and walked nervously holding on to each other, afraid of stepping on parts of dead bodies. We reached Vermont and the Vasquez house but they didn't let us in because it was a Red Cross headquarters and none of us was wounded. We reached Tennessee st. and turned left. At Georgia st. we saw four Japs and they saw us. We ran fast into a building. We hid awhile but were afraid there might be Japs in the building. Then Nong peeped and they were gone. Thank God. We turned left on Georgia and came to Vermont and turned right till we reached the corner of Florida st. at last. Two blocks away was our shelter among the ruins but it was too hot to pass. But if we stood there, the Japs might see us. So

> Nong thought we'd better dash through the hot street. Irasan was burning. We saw many dead bodies. Most of them we knew. We came near the place where we had our shelter. It was very, very quiet, not a soul. There were dead bodies all over the place. When we came to our place what a mess it was. We came nearer and called Frank, nobody answered. Then we called Chars and Ini and Chito but nobody answered. We approached reluctantly. We saw Ini and Frank but we saw blood. We didn't know who was wounded. It was Chito. We did not expect it to be him. When they saw us they were so surprised. Most of us cried. They said they saw our house being hit directly and then bursting in flames and they were sure we were all dead. They told us that Chito was sitting and a shrapnel went through his leg, took out a piece of his hand and hit the other leg. When Chito heard that his friend Ding-ding died, he cried and cried.
>
> The shells never stopped one after the other and when they burst the smoke and ashes came under the tables and we were all fainting one by one. There was a man with one arm gone and he was delirious and quarreling with another man under a roof nearby. The judge was drinking and he was desperate and crying. He said his wife and all his other children died. He told us to take his daughter if he dies. Chars ran out to look for medicine and came back with a sleeping tablet from Mrs. Kalaw but the Japs almost saw her on her way back. A man just pulled her back as she was beginning to cross the street. Then the Japs came to the street and we had to stop the children from crying and had to remain very quiet. Again all the shells fell in our vicinity and debris, stones and shrapnels were falling all over. The people were screaming and crying around us. We clung to our medals and prayed and prayed. One shell fell right near us and we choked and coughed and most of us were fainting and we could see figures getting out of our shelter. Maximo went to get water, it tasted like gunpowder and smelled like the dead. We put a few drops of listerine in it and drank one sip each. The shelling never stopped the whole night.

Robert Ross Smith made what is probably the most acute synthesis of the American policy to destroy Manila to save American lives: "To the XIV Corps and the 37th Division at this stage of the battle for Manila, American lives were understandably more valuable than historic landmarks. The destruction had stemmed from the American decision to save lives in a battle against Japanese troops who had decided to sacrifice theirs as dearly as possible."[92]

Smith, nonetheless, expressed shock that while American lives were saved, Filipino lives were lost in the battle. He says, "Millions and millions of dollars worth of damage had been done and, as a final shocking note of tragedy, an estimated 100,000 Filipino civilians had lost their lives during the battle."[93]

In the Roman civil wars, A. D. 69, one of the contending generals, Antonius Primus by name, a partisan of the triumphant Vespasian, counselled his soldiers who were spoiling for plunder and carnage, in these words:

"Let us not be eager to capture than to preserve the capital. Greater will be our reward, far higher our reputation, if we secure without bloodshed the safety of the Senate and the people of Rome."[93-a]

No such sentiments were entertained by the American generals with reference to Manila in A. D. 1945.

"Aside from strategic considerations, the liberation of the Islands was important for reasons of Far Eastern politics and prestige," M. Hamlin Cannon writes. "The obligation of the United States to the subjugated Filipino people could not be lightly ignored."[93-b]

But just as important a consideration was Douglas MacArthur's raging personal feeling for revenge. In the words of Hamlin, "Furthermore, General MacArthur was imbued with a burning determination to return to the Philippine Islands and avenge the humiliating defeats suffered by the American forces in 1941 and 1942."

MacArthur's desire to return to the Philippines reached such a point of obfuscation that General George C. Marshall, the Chief of the Joint Chiefs of Staff, was prompted to caution him, "to be careful not to let personal feelings and Philippine politics" override the objective of bringing the war to an end.[93-c]

Douglas MacArthur had fought assiduously to secure priority for the liberation of the Philippines over other areas. It was a bitter struggle, fraught with plot and counter-plot, intrigue and counter-intrigue that reached up to President Roosevelt. In the end, Douglas MacArthur prevailed. Whether it was strategy that was foremost in his general's mind or revenge overflowing his egotist's heart that led him to the decision that unloosed the plagues of war on this land that he truly and unquestionably loved, one can but conjecture today.

Admiral William F. Halsey, commander of the Third Fleet, was witness to a curious exchange between Admiral Ernest King, the principal proponent of the Formosa plan, and Vice Admiral Robert B. Carney, a pro-Luzon man:[94]

King: "Do you want to make a London out of Manila?"

Carney: "No, sir, I want to make an England out of Luzon."

One of the two men was prophetic!

Had the Americans gone on to Formosa, there is strong possibility that the surrender of the Japanese forces in the Philippines after Nagasaki and Hiroshima would have been negotiated. Surely the Filipinos would have suffered too, but the chances are they would not have suffered more than they actually did.

D. Clayton James, in his two-volume *The Years of MacArthur,* suggests that "an informal deal" was entered into between MacArthur and Roosevelt at their Honolulu meeting, whereby Roosevelt would accede to MacArthur's position on the Philippine priority in exchange for reports of successes which would aid Roosevelt in the forthcoming U.S. presidential elections.

"The elections are coming up in a few days and the Philippines must be kept on the front pages back home," D. Clayton James quotes a GHQ public relations officer as having confidentially advised war correspondents who protested MacArthur's proclamation that two-thirds of Leyte had been secured, whereas, in fact, the fight was just starting.[95]

This statement and the enthusiastic communiqués that poured out lead James to surmise "that an informal deal was made at Pearl Harbor, probably without explicit verbalization, whereby MacArthur's releases would portray great battlefield successes stemming from increased Washington support, and the President's influence in behalf of the Philippines plan would be exerted on the Joint Chiefs."[96]

Did MacArthur have his way on the question of the Philippine invasion as part of a political deal?

"Both Roosevelt and MacArthur were clever schemers of the first order, so such an understanding is not implausible, even if unprovable," D. Clayton James concludes.[97]

Still, whether or not the Philippines was a pawn among or between protagonists and schemers, Douglas MacArthur bears as much responsibility as Sanji Iwabuchi does for the cruel fate that was inflicted on Manila.

By adopting the strategy of bottling up the adversary in an area with a resident population of one million, the Americans permitted the Japanese no alternative but a last-ditch, scorched-earth stand. That the Japanese behaved like the cornered rat of legend was to be expected.

Although a highly reputed military scholar, MacArthur was a Western general who may have been a bit detached from the traditional wisdom of the Orient. He may or he may not have come across, and he may or he may not have agreed with, the admonition of the great Chinese general Sun Tzu who lived 500 years B.C., and who said in his classic *The Art of War*, "When you surround an army, leave an outlet free. Do not press a desperate foe too hard."[97-a]

The illogic of barring bombing from the air and approving artillery to be used on Manila to the extent it was continue to puzzle today as when Robert Ross Smith remarked, "Just how civilian lives could be saved by this type of preparations as opposed to aerial bombardment is unknown."[98]

MacArthur's headquarters and the Sixth Army under General Krueger laid strict injunctions against the use of artillery, and more so on the use of air bombardment.

These injunctions seem to have been observed more in the breach. "Artillery support was confined to observed fire upon pinpointed targets such as Japanese gun emplacements," Robert Ross Smith writes.[99]

When actual cases where injunctions are breached are shown, however, Smith also comes up with a rationalization like, "For the 37th Division . . . cancellation of the earlier limitation had become a necessity." The injunction against the use of artillery was never officially lifted. Neither was it observed.

The intelligence service of the U.S. armed forces seems to have fallen woefully short. Robert Ross Smith noted that "Krueger was unwilling to launch an all-out drive to Manila until he had more information on the nature and extent of the potential threats to the XIV Corps' left. That no threats actually existed made no difference. Krueger was basing his plans upon his estimates of Japanese capabilities."[100]

By evening of 3 February 1945 the 1st Cavalry stood at the city gates, "and as yet the Sixth Army had little information concerning the nature of the city's defenses."[101]

Once inside the city, however, and once established on the north side, there did not seem to be too much reason to grope blindly in the dark, as it were, concerning the situation in the south side.

Why did not the Americans make extensive use of the Filipino guerrillas for intelligence work? The Filipinos knew the enemy strongholds, they could distinguish between Japanese soldiers and Filipino civilians while American artillery and small aircraft overhead could not.

The Americans did not make more use of the services of Filipino guerrillas because they did not trust them. Bertram C. Wright relates how two Filipinos who had been in the Philippine Scouts of the U.S. Army offered their services as guides to Lt. Col. Haskett L. Conner, Jr., commander of the 2nd Serial of the "Flying Column." The two Filipinos went to Conner as he approached the outskirts of the city and offered to lead him to the American objectives.

"Skeptical of the unexpected assistance at first, Colonel Conner put many questions to these men and finally had his doubts allayed," Wright tells us. "His faith was finally rewarded when they led his troops through the darkness to the front gate of Santo Tomas."[102]

How often did the Americans put faith in their Filipino allies during this period? Had this occurred often enough, such agonizing remarks as that by Rodolfo G. Tupas would probably have been made less often, too.

Tupas wrote, "For about two weeks, the PGH withstood the fiercest barrage of American artillery directed by the piper cubs overhead. Why this barrage continued for two weeks when PGH was packed with

Filipino refugees, I have not been able to understand to this day."[103]

The Americans did not trust information from the Filipino guerrillas, partly because the information they received was often belied by subsequent findings. But then, the findings of their own intelligence people often were contradicted by later information.

Robert Ross Smith points out an incident which shows how inadequate was American intelligence. The XIV Corps was ordered to capture two transmission stations of the Manila Electric Light Company, both on the south bank, one in Santa Ana and the other in Makati. They accomplished their mission in short order, but the second station turned out to be a bill-collecting office, not at all the strategic electrical facility their map-makers said it was.

"Only when the troops actually closed with principal strongpoints did they discover where the main defenses were," Smith observes.[104]

Douglas MacArthur shed bitter tears when he turned over to President Sergio Osmeña a capital city that had been virtually wiped off the face of the earth.

"It killed something inside me to see my men die," the General explained his tears in his autobiography, *Reminiscences*, obviously referring to his soldiers.[105] Indeed, 1,010 American soldiers died in the battle for Manila. But this man had led thousands and thousands of other men to battle before and had seen thousands of them die. It is not known that he ever wept in public before, the way he had at Malacañang in Manila.

In any case, MacArthur wept for the 1,010 of his men who were killed in the battle for Manila. He did not say a single word about the 100,000 Filipino civilians who perished.

"I spat on the very first American soldier I saw that unspeakable day in February 1945," Carmen Guerrero Nakpil writes. "Damn you, I thought. There's nobody here but us Filipino civilians, and you did your best to kill us."[106]

Mrs. Nakpil was scurrying down Taft Avenue on the Malate section turned into battlegrounds that "unspeakable day," a survivor of the holocaust. She was heavy with child, and in her arms she carried a sick baby girl. From behind a leafless tree an American soldier had shouted at her, "Hey, you! Wanna get yourself killed?"

"I had not eaten or slept for more than a week," Carmen Guerrero Nakpil writes. "My husband had been tortured by Japanese soldiers in my presence, and then led out to be shot. Our home had been ransacked, put to the torch, its ruins shelled again and again. I had seen the head of the aunt who taught me to read and write roll under the kitchen stove, the face of a friend who had been crawling to me on the pavement as we tried to reach the shelter under the Ermita church obliterated by a bullet, a legless cousin dragging himself out of a shallow trench in the churchyard and a young mother carrying a baby, plucking at my father's sleeve -- 'Doctor can you help me? I think I'm wounded,' and the shreds of her ribs and her lungs as she turned around.

"I had heard the screams of the girls I had grown up with as they were dragged by Japanese soldiers towards the Bayview Hotel (to be raped, as we later found out) and the mindless groans of the men, tied together by the elbows and machinegunned by stonyfaced Japanese. I had seen all the unforgettable, indescribable carnage caused by the detonation of bombs and landmines on the barricaded streets of Ermita and carpet-shelling by the Americans which went relentlessly on, long after the last Japanese sniper was a carcass on the rubble. I had nothing in all the world except the dress on my back, an unborn child in my belly and in my arms, a little daughter, burning with fever and whimpering with the fever of starvation. (Yes, the redoubtable Gemma).

"And this precious American, awaited desperately for the last three years, pinkcheeked and overfed, tall and mighty, wanted to know, his dear Americanese idioms rising over the crashing of the bullets and the shells, whether I wanted to die."

"I spat," Carmen Guerrero Nakpil writes, "but I was dry-throated and he was not aware of my scorn."

The Americans placed the number of civilians killed during the 29-day period from 3 February to 3 March 1945, arbitrarily it seems, at 100,000 in a population of one million. Admitting this figure without question, it represents the highest number of human beings killed in any siege on a city in modern times, outside of Leningrad and Nanking.

Harrison Salisbury placed the number of dead in the 900-day German siege of Leningrad at 1,100,000, out of a population of 2,500,000 at the start of the blockade. An estimated 200,000 perished in the Japanese "rape of Nanking" in 1937.[107]

Salisbury cites some figures from other sieges. In the 121-day siege of Paris from 19 September 1870 to 27 January 1871, a total of 30, 236 non-combatants perished from all causes, many from starvation, in a population of one million.

In the siege of Vicksburg during the American Civil War, 2,500 persons were killed between 18 May and 4 July 1863, in a population of 4,000 civilians and 30,000 military.

In the atomic bombing of Hiroshima, 6 August 1945, the deaths totaled 78,150, with 13,983 missing and 37,426 wounded.

How many civilians, Filipino and other nationalities, perished in the 29-day battle for Manila? The American figure of 100,000 was based on extrapolations from figures submitted by the undertakers, Mariano and Francisco del Rosario, who were commissioned to recover and dispose of dead bodies that remained in the open from the 3rd of February to the early days of March, 1945. In considering the number of bodies cited by the del Rosarios as having been disposed by their undertaker-teams by burial or cremation, it must be borne in mind that survivors had been burying their dead when they could, even at the height of the fighting. Also many bodies were left unrecovered in deep wells, ditches and drainage canals (*esteros*), that were later covered over. Many more were reduced to cinders in burning buildings, the remains later unwittingly dispersed by clean-up teams. The number 100,000 mentioned in American reports on the battle for Manila, therefore, amplified the figures cited by the del Rosarios, and made allowances for the circumstances we cite here. Still, this figure is an estimate.

There are no figures on the injured or wounded and those maimed permanently. Cases were not collected and documented properly in the chaos and disorder following the cessation of fighting in street-after-street, neighborhood-after-neighborhood. The missing must be given up for dead. The world will never know the exact figures.

The food situation in all of Manila during this period was extremely critical, to say the least. Having been liberated earlier, North Manila bounced back earlier, too. Sgt. Ozzie St. George found rice cakes and fresh clams for sale on Rizal Avenue, alongside watches, fountain pens, wooden shoes. Eggs were available for 50 centavos each (good money, no doubt) and tuba for 10 centavos a glass. In the cafes, hole-in-the-wall places among the ruins with names like *Victory, Uncle Sam's and Sloppy Joe's*, coffee was available for 20 centavos a cup with sugar, 15 centavos without. Egg sandwiches for P1.50, liquor for P1.00 a shot.[108]

But how did the civilians in South Manila eat? What food was there available through the chaos?

Apparently food could be had up to the last moments, for a price. Up to the last hour of the Japanese occupation of the city and even beyond, the "mickey mouse money" was accepted by traders. Otherwise, "good money," the pre-war Philippine peso, was the medium, apart from which, barter was the rule.

On 3 February, the day the Americans entered Manila, the Gutierrez family of Malate made these purchases at the San Andres market with "mickey mouse money": brown sugar at P800 a kilo; red beans at P400 a kilo; chicken eggs at P100 each; a bottle of peanut butter for P800; coconuts at P150 a piece; cassava flour at P500 a kilo; coconut oil at P80 a tansan bottle. Rice was P1,800 a ganta (three liters). Some sellers asked P18 "good money" for one ganta. But there was not enough to buy even when people had the money.[109]

On 4 February, the Gutierrez family bought meat at P1,500 a kilo. At the market this day there were still yellow corn, coconuts, kangkong and talinum. Not in big quantities, to be sure, but for what there was, they were available.

The people also had domestic animals, or had hoarded canned goods. On 11 February, the Gutierrez family butchered a pig. On 13 February, the Gutierrezes saw people running past their shelter. One was carrying a turkey, another was dragging a goat. In their shelter the Gutierrezes brought out a bottle of brandy and they all took a sip each. "so we'd stop fainting," 14-year-old Lydia Gutierrez said in her diary. They cooked and ate rice. Their neighbors, the Amadors, opened cans of red pimentoes, asparagus and fruit cocktail.

On 3 February, Gladys Savary in Pasay exchanged a P50-good for P4,500-mickey mouse, or an exchange rate of P1-good for P90-mickey mouse. With her mickey mouse money she bought pork at P1,000 a kilo. ."But I got some liver and carabao meat on credit," she says. In short, life went on and so did trade and commerce. She tried to get some eggs with the rest of her mickey mouse-money. "But no one wants any of that money any more."[110]

She did some bartering. One undershirt for three pieces of bananas, one cotton dress for a papaya, a sharkskin suit for a chicken.

On 8 February, "some trusting Filipino" tried to sell Madame Savary carabao meat for P10,000-mickey mouse a kilo. "We didn't buy," she huffs, outraged at the price.

On 12 February, Faustino Aguilar in San Francisco del Monte found pork at P15-good money per kilo, a large catfish for P23, prawns for P1 a piece.[111]

On the same date, in Santa Ana, Marcial P. Lichauco had the problem of feeding 113 refugees in his home at 2915 Herran street, but there was powdered milk and oatmeal for his small daughters.[112]

On 16 February, Gladys Savary sallied out "to stock up on food." Pasay was in American hands now and a semblance of order was returning. The market was burned, but people were bringing in fish, eggs and vegetables which they set up on makeshift stalls on the street near the market place. Madame brought back to the manse on Park Avenue "a bit of pork, some papayas and some native spinach."[113]

Doubtless not everyone in South Manila at this time had the resources, or resourcefulness, of the Amadors, the Gutierrezes, the Lichaucos, the Savarys. How did they survive? Many simply didn't!

The internees at the Santo Tomas camp had a Filipino food purchasing officer by the name of Luis Alcuaz. On the night the American forces seized Santo Tomas, Alcuaz had also sneaked into the camp, almost getting killed in the process when the Japanese sentry fired at him and hit his companion instead. Alcuaz feigned death and the sentry did not investigate. Alcuaz waited until the Filipino guard let him in. Alcuaz was so devoted to the Americans that he risked his life to be with them on this night when people were dropping dead on the streets.

The next day, Sunday, 4th February, a huge store of supplies Alcuaz had procured for the camp was brought in. The U.S. Army was not yet provisioning the camp, and the internees still had to use their own resources. A.V.H. Hartendorp listed the Alcuaz store as follows:[114]

Bovril, 2 oz. - 40 bot.; Coffee, Hill's Bros. – 120 lbs.; Corned beef, 12 oz. – 388 cans; Corned beef, 6 lbs. - 5 cans; Ovaltine, Choc., 1 lb. – 108 cans; Ovaltine, plain, 1 lb. – 132 cans; Lactogen,2 1/2 lbs. – 60 cans; Klim, 1 lb. – 44 cans; Milk, Rosemary, 2 1/2 lbs. – 3 cans; Milk, full cream, 4 lbs. – 3 cans; Milk, evaporated, 6 oz. – 288 cans; Milk, Bear, whole, 420 gr. – 144 cans; Milo chocolate, 1/2 lb. – 24 cans; Maggi sauce – 1 case; Margarine, 120 gr. – 144 cans; Margarine, 190 gr. – 96 cans; Margarine, 5 lbs. – 1 can; Green coffee – 306 kilos; tiki-tiki – 122 kilos; Sardines, 2 5/8 oz. – 300 cans; Dried peas, 6 oz. – 300 cans; Black bean soup, 1 lb. – 6 cans; Purse mongole, 1 lb. – 60 cans; Pineapple juice (buffet) – 144 cans; Soap, Palmolive – 100 cakes; Tea bags No. 2 – 120 pkts.; Tea Orange pekoe, 1/2 lb. – 12 pkts.; Tea Orange pekoe, 1/4 lb. – 33 pkts.; Tea, Lakawalla, 1/2 lbs. – 20 pkts; Fruit cordial, 20 oz. – 12 bot; Karo syrup, 1 1/2 lbs. – 46 cans; Quick Oats, 20 oz. – 33 cans; Sugar – 27 kilos; Cornmeal – 20 kilos; Cornflour – 12 kilos; Kidney beans – 1,239 kilos; Mongo beans – 263 kilos; Long beans – 10 cans; Purico – 2 cans; Meat, No. 2 can – 140 cans; Olive oil – 2 gallons; Cooking oil, 17 kilo cans – 6 cans.

It startles the mind that there was this much food of this kind at this time available in Manila. At least, it was available for the Americans in Santo Tomas.

When the Japanese pulled out of the Bilibid prisoner-of-war camp on 5 February, the Commandant, Capt. Nogi, left a note which said in part, "We are leaving plenty supply of food, medicine."[115]

Dr. W.H. Waterous would later relate that the "plenty supply of food" consisted of two sacks of corn and one sack of bean flour. After 5:30 in the afternoon of 5 February, however, the 37th Infantry brought rations into Bilibid.

"Our days of abject misery were at least mitigated," Dr. Waterous would write.

One domestic animal that served the purpose that may not have been originally intended for it was the dog.

On 28 January 1945, Mrs. Marcial P. Lichauco passed the Paco market and saw a man hawking some kind of "meat stew." She inquired what it was and got the answer, "Dog meat, madam . . ."

Padre Selga spoke of the man who wept unashamedly as he handed over his pet dog to other men in the confines of San Agustin to be slaughtered for food. Doubtless dogs had become premium commodity.

One dog that did survive the war was the pet bitch of Doña Maria Paz de Mascunaña, named "Lady". Through bomb and shell "Lady" had stuck close to her masters. In the climax of a suspenseful episode when the hiding place of the Mascuñanas on Padre Faura street was discovered by the Japanese and grenades rained over the place, the bitch was muzzled tightly by hand by the Mascuñana Chinese houseboy Lee Tong, to prevent it from making a sound.

Chickens did serve a premium purpose, sometimes ending in ironic climaxes. Chickens, or their unavailability to the Japanese may have caused the massacre of the Bartolome Pons family at their residence on Figueroa street in Paco (see page 200 ff.). But chickens may have saved the lives of the Mascuñana refugee party on the night of 11 February 1945 on Oregon street in Ermita (see page 271).

The professional military mind of Walter Krueger, commander of the Sixth Army, understood the sanitation needs of a city with a population of about one million. Thus his concern for the early capture of the water system of Manila.

In setting priorities for the seizure of individual installations, the Sixth Army ordered the XIV Corps to capture first the Novaliches Dam about five kilometers east of the town of Novaliches, about 30 kilometers northeast of Manila. This was effected 5 February by the 7th Cavalry Regiment.

After this came the Balara filtration plant 18 kilometers east of Manila in Diliman, which would be seized on 6 February also by the 7th Cavalry Regiment, the only element of the 1st Cavalry Division that did not fight inside the city.

Then came the San Juan reservoir on hilly terrain seven kilometers to the northeast outside Manila, which would be captured on 8th February.

Finally, the pipelines connecting these installations had to be protected, with the 7th Cavalry on patrol duty.

The unavailability of water in Manila during this period doubtless wrought untold hardships on the people. There were some 80 public artesian wells that were operational at various points in the city at this time. The value of these wells to the population is immeasurable. Gladys Savary mentions one such artesian well a block from her home on Park Avenue in Pasay. There was an artesian well in the premises of the Philippine General hospital which at this time became the only source of water for the entire compound with its refugee-population of about 7,000.

Otherwise, the people dug wells, either as communal projects for a whole neighborhood, or as a family well in the backyard. Gladys Savary had a well in her backyard. There was a well in the inner court of the De la Salle college. Benigno del Rio remembered an old well in the family compound on Taft Avenue which had not been used for a long time and in fact had been topped over. Now they uncovered the well and it yielded the water they needed.

A direct result of the violence of war was the breakdown of public order, the demoralization of the populace and the deterioration of values. Hunger, deprivation and fright caused people to discard scruples and led them to acts from which under other conditions, they probably would have desisted. This gave rise to the phenomenon of "looters," among others.

On 9 February 1945, Gladys Savary wrote in her diary:[116] "One by one, the houses around us are being torn down. Looting is the order of the day, and out go walls, roofs, pipes, bathroom fixtures, everything. There is little furniture left, but that little is going too. I can at this moment see a beautiful overstuffed armchair going down the street seemingly under its own steam . . . no, a small child, completely submerged is beneath it, carting it off . . ."

Later the same day, at 6:00 p.m. Gladys Savary adds to this entry in her diary: "I've been yelling about looting but some of our servants just showed up with cans of waterlily stems and crab flakes - from the Japanese stores ... they taste wonderful too."

When the Rizal Stadium on Vito Cruz fell, civilians rushed in close after the Americans, intent on bringing away what they could of what the Japanese garrison had left behind. This is what Benigno del Rio saw: "The people ran up Vito Cruz like mad. They carried bags, sacks and pushed small handcarts. From the stadium they emerged heavily loaded. Some carried canned goods. Others, sacks of rice or sugar. Or Japanese military boots, new and shiny, heavily studded with fat hobnails. Some carried Japanese swords or rifles."

On 25 February 1945 Benigno del Rio dropped at the burnt-out family home on Taft Avenue to look for something that may have escaped the flames. Entering the back gate, he came upon two men digging up the garden.

This exchange followed:[117]

"What are you doing?"

"We are digging up the pipes."

"Is this place yours?"

"No."

"Well..."

"Well, the house is destroyed, and the pipes will not be of any use to the owners."

"So, all right, but don't you see that what you are doing is theft and you may be jailed?"

"What we are doing is not theft. It is merely looting."

Benigno del Rio gave the pair a good dressing down and, finally, "with great dignity, the two walked away unhurriedly, muttering curses."

Two days later del Rio returned to the same spot. He found the earth all dug up and the waterpipe system in the premises all gone.

When the American investigators got to the home of Bartolome Pons at 503 Figueroa street in Paco, 15 February 1945, they found that the house had been looted clean.

Major Donald D. Forward who conducted the investigation reported, "Our minute investigation of the home showed evidence that it had been thoroughly stripped of all valuables. The remaining furniture showed good taste and wealth."[118]

Asked whether the Pons home may have been looted by the Japanese, a neighbor of the Ponses by the name of Mario Chanco, answered that "it might have been stripped by civilians after the Japanese had left."[119] The bodies of victims of the massacre perpetrated 7 February 1945, composed of five women, two men and a baby, and the family's German shepherd dog, were left undisturbed where they fell.

After Bilibid Prison was liberated, 5 February 1945, the American prisoners-of-war and civilian detainees were moved to the Ang Tibay shoe factory compound on the northern outskirts of the city, as a precautionary measure since fighting still raged in the area around Quezon Boulevard. The group spent the night of 5th February at the Ang Tibay compound and was brought back to Bilibid the following day. An American guard detachment was at Bilibid but it had been kept busy during the day fighting fires in the neighborhood.

When the American prisoners returned to Bilibid they found that the premises had been looted and their few belongings had been carted away, leaving them truly with nothing except what they had on their persons.[120]

The premises of the De la Salle college may have been looted by Filipino civilians on the night of the massacres on 12 February 1945. This is what the Redemptorist Father Francis J. Cosgrave recalled of that incident.

"On Monday night (February 12) and the following night (February 13) I could hear men in the chapel and I know that they were Tagalog because I could hear speaking and could see them moving about. Next morning when I was able to crawl down the entrance to the chapel I saw the Brothers' bags that they had already packed, open and could see that

The Victims

The 29-day battle for Manila on 3 February - 3 March 1945 took the lives of 100,000 non-combatants out of a population of one million, the highest number of civilian casualties in a conflict in modern times, after Leningrad where 1,100,000 perished from all causes out of a population of two million during the 900-days siege, and Nanking, where 200,000 died in Japanese hands in 1937. (NHI Collection)

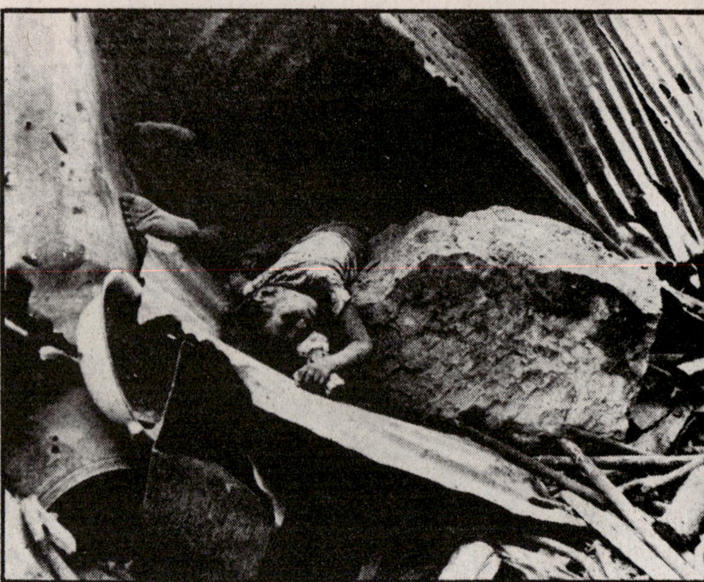

NHI Collection

The death toll of 100,000 in the battle for Manila in February 1945 was higher than that taken by the atom-bombing of Hiroshima in August the same year, which included 78,150 dead and 37,426 wounded.

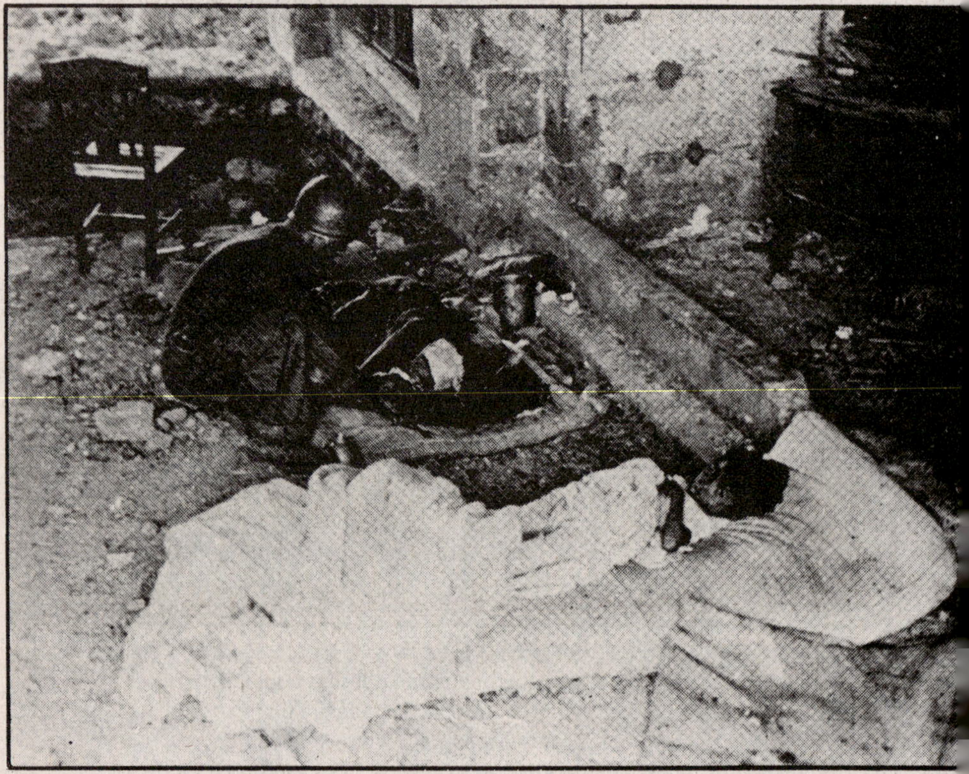

NHI Collect

The Survivors

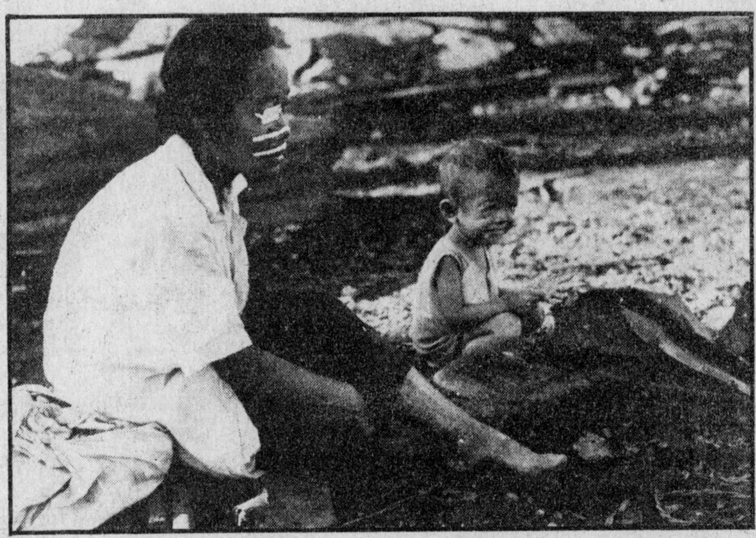

National Archives 208-N-38884

National Archives 208-N-38807

No records were kept of the wounded and permanently maimed in the battle for Manila, February 1945. Photos on this page were taken in Intramuros after the battle.

Survivors, mostly women and children, gather at the Pasig riverbank across from the ruined Government Mint building, waiting to be ferried to the opposite shore, after the battle for Intramuros. (NHI Collection)

National Archives 208-A-2935-4

Among the survivors of the battle for Intramuros were members of religious orders like the Daughters of Charity and the Sisters of St. Paul de Chartres who served as nurses at the San Juan de Dios hospital, and the Poor Clares whose only Philippine convent was in the walled city.

U.S. Army Photo (MacArthur Memorial Collection)

The barges that brought the American Infantry across the Pasig to Intramuros were used to ferry the civilian refugees to the opposite bank on the return trip. U.S. Army Photo (MacArthur Memorial Collection)

National Archives 208-N-39064

Upon establishing a beachhead on the south bank, the American forces quickly threw a pontoon bridge across the Pasig at Nagtahan. Across this bridge streamed thousands fleeing the fighting in the south side.

National Archives 208-AA-9535-6

At 11 o'clock in the morning of 27 February 1945, General Douglas MacArthur *(above)* presided over ceremonies at Malacañang, the presidential palace, to restore the capital of the Commonwealth of the Philippines to Manila and turn over the government to President Sergio Osmeña *(below).* Fighting was still raging in the south Side.

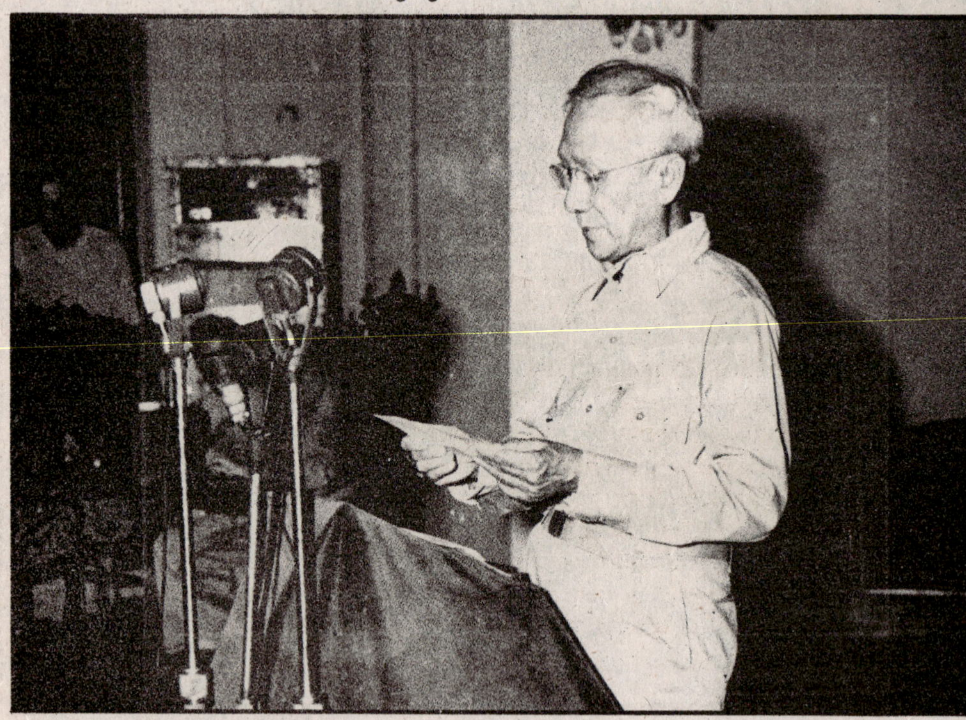

there was much missing from them, as well as from other places in the room. All my own things, including sacred vessels, were taken. The La Salle sacred vessels were also stolen."[121]

The death toll in the battle for Manila, aside from the 1,010 American dead, and the estimated 100,000 Filipino civilians killed, included 16,000 Japanese killed, of whom 12,500 were from the Manila Naval Defense Force. The other 3,500 Japanese dead were from the various Shimbu Group units. Some 4,500 men from Admiral Iwabuchi's original 17,000 were able to escape to the Shimbu lines across the Marikina river.[122]

Still, the most notable victim was the Distinguished and Ever Loyal City.

The report of Senator Millard Tydings to the United States Senate listed 613 blocks containing approximately 11,000 buildings destroyed or badly damaged. Senator Tydings, who would prove to be the conscience of America in the Manila case, and a small party visited Manila, 24 to 29 May 1945.

Tydings had been to Manila in November 1935 for the inauguration of the Commonwealth of the Philippines. Now he was appalled by what he saw. In his report to the Senate, he said: "Years of rebuilding are necessary before the former physical condition of the islands can be restored."[123]

With his party, Senator Tydings made an ocular inspection of the city. "There is some damage in all districts in Manila," he would report, "but the most valuable sections have been practically destroyed."

The Port Area and the Santa Cruz districts suffered a 90% loss; Malate and Intramuros, 93%; and Paco, Ermita and Binondo, from 68 to 85%.

The biggest losses to property outside the government were sustained by the Catholic church. Senator Tydings and his party conferred with various church officials who had designated Fr. John H. Hurley, S.J., secretary general of the Catholic Welfare Organization of the Philippines, to assemble the data on losses for the various religious orders. Using these data as basis, the total losses on all Catholic properties was estimated at $125 million (1945 values).

Ownership of church properties was vested in the different religious orders and the archbishop of Manila. There were 18 orders of men religious and 21 orders of women religious. There were also the parish properties. A considerable portion of the church losses was in Intramuros where losses were virtually total.

Tydings expressed grave concern over the high values of the contents of the buildings that were destroyed: "The libraries are valued quite highly and the question arises as to the actual value of old books, statuary which had historical value, and kindred items. The question also arises as to the actual value of churches, convents and buildings which are 300 to 400 years old."

Senator Tydings concluded that the total loss to all contents items in the city of Manila would amount to $150 million (1945 values), and that 70,000 claims would probably be filed.

The government of Sergio Osmeña, installed in that tearful ceremony at Malacañang, 27 February 1945, began to pick up the pieces. President Osmeña's report for 1945 is a testament to the resiliency of the Filipino people, their infinite capacity for survival. Here they demonstrated anew their kinship to the bamboo that thrives, feathery and green, in the Philippine landscape. In a storm it bends almost to the ground, to return to an upright position, tall and proud, when the wind has passed. Now in the wake of the disaster, the Filipino people stood upright once more.

President Osmeña's record of work accomplished during the remainder of the critical year of 1945 details an almost superhuman effort to regain balance, to restore order, to bring back to life an entire nation so mercilessly used. Here are some highlights of that report, selected vis-a-vis certain landmarks and institutions in the battle for Manila.[124]

THE BUREAU OF SCIENCE – Even while fighting in the rest of Manila was still going on, scientists and other staff members of the Bureau of Science were already salvaging its scientific collections. The bureau did not officially reopen until July 1945.

With the help of various U.S. Army units, research work was undertaken on a number of subjects, including a study of the antihelmintic properties of the sap of certain local plants, the production of printer's ink from the destructive distillation of copra meal, etc. Industrial plans for totaquina, derris, dehydration units, were also prepared.

THE WEATHER BUREAU – This bureau lost practically all its instruments and records and did not become operational again until late July 1945. By the end of the year, 30 of the 60 pre-war forecasting and meteorological stations, but only 3 of the 110 rain stations, had been reestablished.

The bureau's work was at first conducted without instruments, until December 1945, when the U.S. Army provided 100 meteorological items including anemometers, barometers, barographs, nephoscopes, theodolites, thermographs, etc., many of Japanese origin. By year's end of 1945, the bureau was releasing meteorological data to the public. Also by this time, telegraphic communication with a few stations had been restored and the first typhoon warnings were issued.

THE PHILIPPINE GENERAL HOSPITAL – Fully 50% of the physical plant of the PGH was destroyed, 80% of the equipment and 100% of the supplies and materials were lost. From the scientific point of view, the most serious loss was the destruction of 12,500 volumes of clinical histories, comprising the records of some 750,000 patients treated in the wards, and 2,250,000 patients treated in the dispensary during the 34 years of existence of the hospital.

The hospital considered itself fortunate in being able to salvage a small quantity of its radium stock. Some 60% of this element in its possession had been confiscated by the Japanese and presumably shipped to Japan. Shortly after liberation, the bigger portion of the remainder was found scattered on the floor.

The United States Army assumed control over the hospital from the time of its liberation when it was used partly as a military hospital, until 16 July 1945, when it was placed entirely in the hands of the civilian government. For a while some of the least-damaged buildings and wards were used by homeless refugees.

Through the emergency period after liberation until the end of 1945, the PGH nonetheless treated 4,875 patients in its wards and 16,834 patients in the dispensary.

THE UNIVERSITY OF THE PHILIPPINES – Unofficial salvage work by returning personnel began shortly after hostilities ended in the area in February 1945, although the formal reorganization of the university took place only in June 1945 when the board of regents met and re-elected Dr. Bienvenido M. Gonzales as president.

The university plant sustained serious damages. Nearly all buildings were untenable; the libraries, laboratories and offices were total losses.

In August 1945, the first classes were conducted at the hastily reconditioned Institute of Radium Theraphy building on Padre Faura street, by arrangement with the Philippine General hospital. The first units to function were the Colleges of Liberal Arts, Engineering, Law, Education and Medicine, including Dentistry and Pharmacy, respectively, at Padre Faura; the College of Agriculture, the School of Forestry and the Rural High School at Los Baños. The University Serum and Vaccine Laboratories at Alabang were not seriously damaged and started operations even before June 1945.

Owing to limited space, personnel and equipment, enrolment was kept down to 2,211, as against the peak pre-war enrollment of 7,743. The rehabilitation of the university plant was given priority, however, and in the second semester, more students were admitted.

THE PHILIPPINE NATIONAL LIBRARY & MUSEUM – Even while hostilities were going on, salvage teams composed of concerned individuals including one led by the American expatriate scholar Dr. H. Otley Beyer, were at work trying to retrieve what they could of library and museum properties from the smouldering ruins.

Official action to restore the Philippine National Library and the National Museum started in December 1945 when survey teams brought their findings together. What they found was catastrophic. The bulk of the holdings of the library and museum had been moved into the basement of the Legislative building in the belief that it was a stronghold, safer than the other buildings they had been stored in. The Legislative building, of course, was completely destroyed. The library holdings included 300,000 books and 25,000 assorted journals and pamphlets. The museum holdings included some 2,500 paintings, sculptures, numismatics and miscellaneous items of historical and artistic value that formed part of the national heritage.

Fortunately, some 3,000 volumes of rare Filipiniana considered among the most valuable in the library's collection, had been among those stored in the Philippine Normal school building on Ayala boulevard. The building was destroyed but the room where the books were stored was more or less whole. In the lot were the Tabacalera Collection which had been acquired by the government for P250,000 pre-war money, the famous Pardo de Tavera and Zulueta collections and the original manuscripts of Jose Rizal's novels, *Noli Me Tangere* and *El Filibusterismo*, and his poem, *Mi Ultimo Adios*, which are considered priceless.

The originals of some Rizal letters and other documents had been deposited in the Manila City Hall vault. They were not found again.

Considerable materials from the Philippine Normal school library and the Philippine School of Arts and Trades across Ayala boulevard were saved, together with records of the Philippine Language institute.

The Bureau of Science library, ranked among the greatest science libraries in the Far East with its collection of over 300,000 scientific journals, was completely destroyed, except for some 300 volumes found in an untouched office room.

The University of the Philippines library consisting of 200,000 volumes and assorted journals and publications, was totally destroyed.

The Supreme Court library which included 20,000 legal tomes was a total loss.

The Archives Division of the National Library had been transferred to a wing of the Bilibid Prisons fronting Oroquieta street on the northside. It was saved intact. The archival collection occupied 10,000 cubic feet and included 5 million items, the bulk of which consisted of the Spanish records dating to the 16th century for which the United States government had assumed responsibility under the Treaty of Paris which ended the Spanish-American War.

Apart from the archives, it was estimated that a full 50 per cent of all government records in the Manila area was destroyed or irretrievably scattered.

The collection of Dr. H. Otley Beyer, the noted anthropologist, consisting of 500,000 archaeological specimens, and his library on Philippine ethnography, had been placed in the Watson building on Aviles street near Malacañang, and was saved. Considerable material from Dr. Beyer's archaeological and manuscript collection was left in his Ermita residence, while some were at the Bureau of Science. These were all destroyed.

The bulk of the archives of the archdiocese of Manila was saved. So were the records of the Dominicans, which were transferred to the University of Santo Tomas when their church in Intramuros was destroyed by Japanese bombs in December 1941. The Augustinians had moved their archives to their motherhouse at Valladolid, Spain, providentially after the Spanish civil war and before war broke out in the Pacific. Their remaining properties at San Agustin in Intramuros were badly decimated. The records of the Franciscans and the Recollects went up in smoke, together with their respective churches and monasteries in Intramuros. The library and records of the Jesuits had been dispersed and a considerable portion was saved.

In the end, Manila would be but one more incident in an apocalyptic war that brimmed with tragedies. It would horrify and outrage the world, yes, but no more than would Warsaw, London, Dresden, Hamburg and Leningrad. The world had agonized over the cruel penalties meted on Hiroshima and Nagasaki, but over Manila the world would not recoil in greater revulsion, having known of Guernica, Nanking and Lidice. And the horrors of Auchswitz, Dachau and Treblinka were, at this time, just being revealed.

In his impassioned threnody written in 1947, the Spanish author Antonio Perez de Olaguer said, "Once more the nameless tragedy of the Philippines is here unveiled before the world, so that the whole world will know and, to honor its victims, will not forget."[125]

By exposing this nameless tragedy to generations that do not know, the present author hopes to honor the victims of February 1945, those who suffered and died on every side of the conflict, of every nationality, of every race, nameless now and now forever united in the vast brotherhood of those called – victims!

And life went on, the anger and the sorrow, the pain and the bitterness, notwithstanding.

Elpidio Quirino was elected president *pro-tempore* of the Philippine Senate upon the reconstitution of the Commonwealth government. He was elected vice president of the Commonwealth of the Philippines in May 1946, and became vice vresident of the Republic upon the declaration of Philippine independence the following July 4th.

In April 1948, Quirino succeeded Manuel Roxas as president when the latter succumbed to heart failure. Quirino was elected president in his own right in 1949, but was defeated in his bid for another term in 1953. He died in 1956.

During his term as president, Quirino approved the repatriation of Japanese prisoners who were convicted of war crimes then in detention in the Philippines and was responsible for many acts of reconciliation with the Japanese.

Elpidio Quirino's surviving daughter Victoria served as her father's official hostess when he was president. In 1951, she became the first Malacañang resident to be married in the palace. Her husband Luis Gonzales, became ambassador to Spain in 1966.

Tomas Quirino survived his injuries sustained that fateful morning on Pennsylvania street. He served with the United Nations forces in the Korean war and retired from the armed forces with the rank of major. He died in 1986.

Modesto Farolan went on to become press secretary to Manuel Roxas when the latter became president of the Philippines. Later he entered the foreign service of the new Republic and became the first Philippine consul general in Honolulu. Subsequently he left the foreign service to take up his duties anew with the *Philippines Herald*, became commissioner of tourism when this post was created in 1956, and later returned to the foreign service. As ambassador, he served in Saigon, Berne, and Jakarta. He died in 1979.

Nurse Gliceria Andaya did not fully recover from her chest wound. She became sickly all her life. Nurse Florita Loberiza resumed her career. In 1967 the two were awarded the Florence Nightingale Medal, the highest award given by the International Committee of the Red Cross for distinguished nursing work in battle conditions.

Dr. J.H. Yanzon who led the inmates of Red Cross Children's Home No. 3 on Lerma street to safety under battle conditions, became the first Filipino general manager of the Philippine Red Cross society in 1947. He died in 1983.

Marcial P. Lichauco was Manuel Roxas' law partner before the latter became President of the Philippines. In 1962, Lichauco became ambassador to the Court of St. James.

Geronima T. Pecson, the Malacañang assistant, became the first woman to be elected to the Philippine Senate. She became a member of the executive board of UNESCO and contributed enormously to the work of that body on an international scale. She continued her work for the advancement of education in her own country, and has been much-cited for her work in social service. She died in 1989.

Lydia Gutierrez took up literature studies at the University of Santo Tomas, later joined the staff of the *Sunday Times* Magazine.

Carmen Guerrero Nakpil took up journalism after the war. She became a magazine editor and a distinguished newspaper columnist. She has published several books. She served as chairman of the National Historical Commission, later became director of the Technological Resource Center. Widowed in the war by the death of Ismael Cruz, she remarried and became Mrs. Angel Nakpil. She was widowed anew in 1980.

The baby she carried in her arms through the holocaust in south Manila, named Gemma, became the first Filipino girl to win an international beauty title. Gemma Cruz became Miss International Beauty at a pageant in California in 1964, served for a time as director of the National Museum and turned to journalism herself.

The child Carmen Guerrero Cruz carried in her womb in 1945 became Ismael Guerrero Cruz, born in an emergency hospital where Mrs. Cruz was brought from South Manila. Ismael Guerrero Cruz became managing director of the Ayala Fund (International) and was chosen one of the "1980 Ten Outstanding Young Men" by the Jaycees.

A.V.H. Hartendorp, the American oldtimer in the Philippines, resumed his journalism activities after the war. He edited the American Chamber of Commerce *Journal* and the American Historical Collection *Bulletin*. He published his internment experience in *The Santo Tomas Story*, 1964; and later published *The Japanese Occupation of the Philippines*, in two volumes, 1967.

Gladys Slaugther Savary recovered her enthusiasm and elan quickly enough after the battle for liberation to set up a small French restaurant in Manila. She went back to the United States and set up a new restaurant in California. Her diary was published under the title, *Outside the Walls*, in 1954.

Tressa Cates married her fiance in June 1945 and both decided to stay in Manila. Later they returned to the States and lived in California. In 1957 she published her wartime diary as a book, titled *The Drainpipe Diary*.

Benigno del Rio married Teresa Palanca shortly after the liberation of Manila. Benigno took over the family business interests which included an interisland shipping company and a taxicab line. His wartime experiences he published in two books in Spanish, one entitled *Siete Diás en el Infierno* (Seven Days in Hell) and *Estampas de la Ocupación* (Pictures of the Occupation.)

Philip Buencamino III continued to write for the newspapers after the war. He married Zeneida Quezon, daughter of the late Commonwealth President Manuel L. Quezon, by whom he had three children. In 1950 Buencamino was killed in an ambuscade perpetrated by the Huks, together with his mother-in-law, Mrs. Aurora Aragon-Quezon, widow of the president, and his sister-in-law, Ma. Aurora Quezon.

Rodolfo G. Tupas also turned to journalism. He became editor of the *Sunday Times* Magazine, later of the *Expressweek* Magazine. A specialist on Philippine Muslim affairs, he became. the first Philippine ambassador to Libya. He died in 1983.

Julio Rocamora, the businessman whom Fr. Belarmino de Celis had abandoned in the Bureau of Justice building, survived. Father de Celis told his rescuers where to find Rocamora and he was recovered in time. Like Fr. de Celis, Julio Rocamora testified at the trial of Yamashita.

Dr. Antonio G. Sison resumed his work at the PGH. He died 5 April 1971, aged 89.

Dr. Sison's patient, the Japanese expatriate Kiyoshi Osawa, fully recovered and was repatriated to Japan in January 1946. He returned to the Philippines in September 1959 and renewed his old friendships among his former Filipino associates. In March 1976 he established the Fil-Japan Shipping and Fil-Japan Trading corporations in Manila. He is president of both. In 1978 he published an account of his experiences in the Philippines from the pre-war period through the Japanese occupation and his post-war activities.

Ramon Cojuangco who emerged from the De la Salle college massacre unhurt, was newly-married to Natividad de las Alas at the time. Cojuangco remarried and rose to great eminence in Philippine business and industry. He died in 1984.

Young Fernando Vasquez Prada grew into an advertising career. He later took up residence in California.

The wartime mayor of Greater Manila, Don Leon G. Guinto, Sr., was indicted for collaboration with the enemy after the hostilities of World War II. He benefitted from an amnesty granted everyone so indicted after the declaration of Philippine independence in 1946. The former mayor was elected governor of Quezon Province in 1955, but failed re-election in 1959. He died in 1962, aged 76.

The principal character in the great drama that was the destruction of Manila by sword and fire in 1945 would have to be Tomoyuki Yamashita. It is true that he was at least 200 kilometers away from the scene at the time, but it is around his person that the story is spun, and in the main this book is as much his story as it is the story of the city of Manila, since much of the details for it came out during the trial of the case that was officially docketed as "U.S.A. vs. Tomoyuki Yamashita."

The charge in the case of U.S.A. vs. Tomoyuki Yamashita read:

"Tomoyuki Yamashita, General, Imperial Japanese Army, between 9 October 1944 and 2 September 1945, at Manila and at other places in the Philippine Islands, while commander of the armed forces of Japan at war with the United States of America and its allies, unlawfully disregarded and failed to discharge his duty as commander to control the operations of the members of his command, permitting them to commit brutal atrocities and other high crimes against the people of the United States and its allies and dependencies, particularly the Philippines; and he, General Tomoyuki Yamashita, violated the laws of war."

The trial began at 1400 hours, 8 October 1945, and ended at 1415 hours, 7 December 1945. The trial sessions were held at the hastily rehabilitated U.S. High Commissioner's Residence on Dewey Boulevard by Manila Bay. There were 123 charges in the bill of particulars.

The Trial Commission was composed of Maj. Gen. Russel B. Reynolds, presiding officer; Maj. Gen. Clarence L. Sturdevant, law member; Maj. Gen. James A. Lester, Brig. Gen. William G. Walker, and Brig. Gen. Egbert F. Bullens, members.

The members of the prosecution were Maj. Robert M. Kerr, Inf., Prosecutor; Maj. Glicerio Opinion, Philippine Army, Special Assistant Prosecutor; and Capt. M.S. Webster, JAGD; Capt. William W. Calyer, Capt. D.C. Hill and Capt. Jack M. Pace, Assistant Prosecutors; and Lt George E. Mountz, USNR, and Lt. William S. Yard, JAGD, trial assistants.

The defense was composed of Col. Harry E. Clarke, JAGD; Lt. Col. Walter C. Hendrix, JAGD; Lt. Col. James G. Felhaus, JAGD; Maj. George F. Guy, Cav.; Capt. Adolf Frank Reel, JAGD; and Capt. Milton Sandberg, JAGD.

Two hundred and eighty-six persons testified at the trial and 423 exhibits were admitted. The trial records consisted of 4,055 pages collected into 37 volumes, mimeographed.

Found guilty of all charges, Tomoyuki Yamashita, General, Imperial Japanese Army, was sentenced to die by hanging. In the early morning hours of 23 February 1946, the sentence was carried out at Camp Eldridge, Los Baños, Laguna, south of Manila. Ironically it was one year to the day of the destruction of Intramuros that effectively put an end to the battle for Manila.

Yamashita's death poem was:

"The world I knew is now a shameful place.

"There will never come a better time for me to die."[126]

CHRONOLOGY OF EVENTS IN THE BATTLE FOR MANILA

3 FEBRUARY 1945. At daybreak the *Flying Column* crashes through Japanese defenses at Novaliches, 17 kms. northeast of Manila. The 11th Airborne reaches Imus, 23 kms. south of Manila. The Japanese torch strategic warehouses in North Harbor. The 11th Parachute Regiment drops on Tagaytay Ridge, 56 kms. south of Manila. At 6:30 in the evening, the *Flying Column* reaches the Bonifacio monument at Grace Park. At 8:40 tonight the vanguard enters the Santo Tomas internment camp. Malacañang is occupied by the Americans.

4 FEBRUARY 1945. The Japanese round-up Intramuros residents into the San Agustin church and monastery, the Manila Cathedral and Fort Santiago. Fire rages in Tondo. The 37th Infantry Division enters Manila. The Japanese set fire to Binondo area. Tonight they begin to torch Ermita.

5 FEBRUARY 1945. The 511th Parachute Infantry crosses Parañaque river on way to Manila. North Manila is apportioned between U.S. infantry and cavalry for clearing operations. Japanese at Santo Tomas are allowed to move out to rejoin comrades. Bilibid Prison is liberated.

6 FEBRUARY 1945. 11th Airborne begins siege on Nichols Airbase. MacArthur announces the "liberation of Manila." The massacre of civilians in Fort Santiago begins. Japanese order the evacuation of San Juan de Dios hospital. Staff and patients move out to Santa Rosa college ruins.

1st Cavalry Division relieved from North Manila by infantry. The nuns at Santa Teresa college on San Marcelino move out to Assumption Convent on Dakota.

The massacre of Col. Jose Guido and his three sons in Singalong this afternoon.

The massacre of civilians continues at Fort Santiago.

7 FEBRUARY 1945. General MacArthur makes triumpal entry into Manila. At 3:15 this afternoon elements of the 148th Infantry Regiment shove-off at the San Miguel Brewery on the left bank of the Pasig in the first wave of the river-crossing. Objective is the power plant on Isla de Provisor. By 8 o'clock tonight two battalions have crossed and secured a beachhead at Malacañang Park. The 511th Parachute Infantry is stalled southwest of Nichols. MacArthur visits Santo Tomas and Bilibid. The men at San Agustin church and monastery are ordered to Fort Santiago. The *convento* of San Agustin burns down this afternoon.

8 FEBRUARY 1945. The 129th Infantry crosses the Pasig into Pandacan. Assault on Isla de Provisor begins. The massacre of civilians in Fort Santiago continues. The Americans reach La Concordia college. The massacre of Col. Alejo Valdes and party in Singalong this afternoon.

9 FEBRUARY 1945. Admiral Iwabuchi moves his headquarters from Manila to Fort McKinley. The battle for Isla de Provisor rages. Elements of the 8th Cavalry Regiment cross the Pasig into Santa Ana. The battle for the Paco Railroad station opens. The first issue of Manila *Free Philippines* is distributed. The massacre of Senator Elpidio Quirino's family on Colorado street in Ermita. The massacre of civilians at the St. Paul college on Herran in Malate. The massacre of the Vincentian Fathers and Chinese civilians at the Paules church premises on San Marcelino. The women of Ermita are rounded-up into Bayview hotel this evening.

10 FEBRUARY 1945. The Americans crash into the power plant on Isla de Provisor. The Japanese hold out. Elements of the 5th Cavalry cross the Pasig into Makati. The 8th Cavalry moves down Herran and links up with the 37th Infantry on Plaza Dilao near the Paco Railroad station. Santa Ana area is liberated. The 11th Airborne overcomes opposition on the westside of Nichols. The 511th Parachutists press attack from the northwest of Nichols. All withdrawal routes from Manila are closed by American forces. The Asilo de Looban on Otis street burns down from American shelling this morning. The Spanish nationals, religious and civilians, are ordered from Fort Santiago back to San Agustin.

The massacre at the German Club on San Luis street begins today. The massacre of Vice Minister Jose Celeste and party of refugees at his residence on Pennsylvania street in Ermita this noon. The massacres at the Price compound on California street this evening. The massacre in the residence of Col. Telesforo Martinez on Colorado street. The massacres of male civilians in Paco this afternoon. The massacre of male civilians on Taft Avenue corner Padre Faura this evening. The massacres at the Red Cross headquarters on Isaac Peral, where film star Corazon Noble is wounded, also this evening.

11 FEBRUARY 1945. The massacre of Dee Cho lumber yard residents on Isaac Peral street at dawn today. Isla de Provisor falls. Paco area is liberated. Admiral Iwabuchi returns to Manila from Fort McKinley. The 511th Parachute Infantry reaches Libertad street in Pasay.

12 FEBRUARY 1945. The 5th Cavalry Regiment overruns Nielson Field in Makati, joins hands with the 511th Parachutists on Libertad street and pushes on to Dewey Boulevard. At 2:30 o'clock this afternoon the 12th Cavalry joins the 5th at the bayfront. Nichols Field defenses collapse. Elements of 5th Cavalry begin assault on Fort McKinley. The 148th Infantry reaches Pennsylvania street in Ermita. The massacres at the De la Salle college this afternoon. The massacres at the Carlos Perez -Rubio mansion on Vito Cruz street and the Pax Court on Balagtas street in Pasay.

13 FEBRUARY 1945. General Yokoyama orders Iwabuchi to return to Fort McKinley and start withdrawal of troops. The Americans begin siege on Japanese fortifications on Isaac Peral, San Marcelino and Marques de Comillas, centered on the Manila Police headquarters. Americans liberate Isaac Peral-Padre Faura area, east of Taft Avenue. From Paco, 148th Infantry reaches Taft Avenue on Remedios, links with 12th Cavalry on Harrison Boulevard to the south. The massacre at the Pedro Campos compound on Taft Avenue in Pasay. The massacre of the Venezuelan consul Alberto Delfino and refugee party on Taft Avenue. Pasay liberated. Malate liberated. The massacre of civilians at Fort Santiago continues.

14 FEBRUARY 1945. The battle for Manila Police headquarters rages. Manila Club on San Marcelino street falls. Nichols Field and Cavite Naval Base occupied by Americans. Americans bombard UP-PGH Complex.

15 FEBRUARY 1945. Yamashita in Baguio orders Yokoyama to counterattack and withdraw Japanese forces still in Manila to the hills. De la Salle college compound liberated by Americans. Siege on Rizal Stadium begins. The 3rd Battalion, 148th Infantry, reaches Dewey Boulevard. Siege of PGH from the westside begins. Battle for Manila Police headquarters continues. Japanese at Central Post Office and Manila City Hall throw back attackers.

16 FEBRUARY 1945. General Yokoyama launches counterattack across Marikina river, is repulsed. Japanese counterattack from Intramuros, are thrown back. Rizal Stadium falls. Harrison Park, Fort San Antonio Abad occupied by Americans. The battle for U.S. High Commissioner's Residence on Dewey Boulevard begins this morning. Nurses' Home in PGH compound occupied by Americans. Bureau of Science building holds out.

17 FEBRUARY 1945. The massacre of the San Juan de Dios hospital staff in Intramuros early this morning. Iwabuchi informs Yokoyama all withdrawal routes cut off. Fort McKinley stands. Santa Teresa college compound holds out. The battle for Manila Police headquarters continues. The Bureau of Science building on Taft Avenue and Herran falls. Clearing operation on UP medical college begins. This afternoon, PGH is liberated. Americans liberate Zobel compound on Dewey Boulevard. The siege of Intramuros opens. The massacre in the Moreta house on Isaac Peral street this afternoon.

18 FEBRUARY 1945. Assumption Convent premises on Dakota and Herran streets cleared today. The Spanish religious and civilians at San Agustin are ordered to Fort Santiago. Santa Teresa college compound falls. Manila Police headquarters hold out.

19 FEBRUARY 1945. The battle for the U.S. High Commissioner's residence rages, spills to Elk's Club and Army and Navy Club. Manila Police headquarters stand pat. The Paules church and seminary on San Marcelino fall. The battle for UP campus rages. Yokoyama renews orders to Iwabuchi to pull out. Iwabuchi replies he is staying put. Fort McKinley falls. The massacre of the Spanish religious and civilians in the basement of the ruined Palacio del Gobernador in Intramuros this evening.

20 FEBRUARY 1945. This morning the U.S. High Commissioner's residence falls. The Elks Club and the Army and Navy Club are occupied. The Manila Police headquarters on San Marcelino and Isaac Peral hold out. The battle for the UP campus continues. Manila City Hall and Central Post Office stand pat.

21 FEBRUARY 1945. General Yokoyama issues final order for Iwabuchi to withdraw. Iwabuchi does not reply. The battle for the Manila Hotel begins this morning. By evening the east wing is occupied by the Americans. Manila City Hall and the Central Post Office repulse all assaults. The UP Administration building on Padre Faura falls. The massacre of the Santa Rosa college refugees takes place tonight at the ruins of the Santo Domingo church.

22 FEBRUARY 1945. Manila Hotel is liberated this evening. General MacArthur inspects the ruins of his former home in the hotel's penthouse. The Philippine Normal school and the YMCA complex fall to

American hands. Manila City Hall falls at 3 o'clock this afternoon. The Central Post Office defenses collapse. University Hall in the UP campus holds out. The Americans step up the bombardment of Intramuros, prepare for amphibian and land assault in the morning.

23 FEBRUARY 1945. At 7:30 this morning the first salvo against Intramuros is sounded. Now the mass of artillery, tanks, tank destroyers, self-propelled mounts and mortars assembled by Generals Griswold and Beightler goes to work. At 8:20 the 3rd Battalion, 129th Infantry Regiment, begin boarding assault boats manned by the 117th Engineers at their embarcation point at the Estero de Binondo on the north bank of the Pasig. The crossing is unopposed. At 8:30 the hour-long artillery barrage on Intramuros stops. Between 8:35 and 8:40 the first boat carrying the 129th touches the south bank. At 8:40 the artillery begins laying the high explosive and smoke screen along the east and west walls to allow the 145th Infantry Regiment to crash through the Quezon Gate. At 12:00 noon the 129th's left flank reaches the west wall through Aduana, cutting off Fort Santiago from the landside. At 1 o'clock this afternoon the 145th reaches Calle Beaterio. San Agustin church and monastery liberated.

24 FEBRUARY 1945. Mopping-up operations at Fort Santiago. Bodies of victims of atrocities discovered. The City Aquarium, last stronghold of the Japanese in Intramuros, is overrun this afternoon. The last organized resistance in Intramuros ends. Bombardment shifts to government center.

25 FEBRUARY 1945. Now the government center, formed by the Legislative building, the Finance and the Agriculture buildings, come under full assault from the 136th Field Artillery. At noon mopping-up operations in Intramuros is suspended as 129th withdraws beyond the range of shelling on the government center.

26 FEBRUARY 1945. At 8 o'clock this morning the 136th Field Artillery resumes battering the government center. At nine o'clock the 1st Battalion, 148th Infantry, enters the Legislative building. At one o'clock the 148th controls the first floor of the north wing, and the first and second floors of the central section. Unable to press farther, the attack collapses. The Americans withdraw. At the Agriculture building the 5th Cavalry, too, is forced to withdraw.

27 FEBRUARY 1945. The Legislative building is subjected to intensive artillery bombardment for two hours this morning. At 2 o'clock the 148th Infantry crashes into the building anew. By 6 o'clock, only the basement needs to be cleared. At 11 o'clock this morning ceremonies are held at Malacañang to restore the seat of government to Manila.

28 FEBRUARY 1945. At 8 o'clock this morning the artillery assault concentrates on the Agriculture building. Resistance continues. The Finance building also comes under fierce bombardment. The Japanese fight back.

1 MARCH 1945. Resistance continues in the Agriculture and Finance buildings. The Americans broadcast a message over the ruins of the Agriculture building for the Japanese to surrender. There is no response. Now the Americans pour a mixture of gasoline and oil over the debris and light it. When the flames die down, there is only silence over the ruins. At 2:30 this afternoon the same broadcast is aimed at the Japanese in the Finance building. Twenty-two Japanese surrender.

2 MARCH 1945. At 8 o'clock this morning, the Americans launch a two-hour artillery assault on the Finance building. At 2 o'clock this afternoon, the infantry comes in for the final assault.

3 MARCH 1945. Late this afternoon, Lt. Gen. Oscar W. Griswold reports to General Walter Krueger that organized resistance in the Manila area has ceased.

NOTES

Direct sources are indicated at the start by the full name of the author and the complete title of the work as listed in the bibliography, and thereafter by the surname and the page number only, where only one work is cited. There are sources which are indicated in the notes but which are not listed in the bibliography. This means that while the source was not used for this work, it may be useful for those who wish to pursue the subject further. References to the records of the trial of Yamashita are designated *Proceedings.*

PROLOGUE: MACARTHUR OF THE PHILIPPINES

1. In his *Reminiscences,* p. 145, General MacArthur says that he made his famous "I shall return" statement upon landing at Batchelor Field, 45 miles south of Darwin. His arrival at Batchelor Field up to that moment had been kept a secret, however, and it is doubtful whether reporters were present. Charles Willoughby, in *MacArthur: 1941-1951,* says that MacArthur made his statement at Batchelor Field. Some authors like John Jacob Beck, *MacArthur and Wainwright: Sacrifice of the Philippines,* University of New Mexico, Albuquerque, 1974, believe that MacArthur made this statement at Adelaide where he changed trains on the way from Alice Springs to Melbourne. The New York *Times* issue of 21 March 1942 says on its front page that MacArthur "issued the statement at Adelaide before boarding a train for Melbourne." Quoted by Beck in *Notes.*
2. MacArthur's "I have returned" message is remarkable for his nerve in invoking the name of God in a death-dealing enterprise, but it accurately described the man that he should indeed believe himself to be an instrument of Divine Providence, not unlike the blood-stained princes who led the Great Crusades.
3. Carol Morris Petillo, *Douglas MacArthur - The Philippine Years,* p. 96.
4. Ibid., p. 241.

CHAPTER I
THE PRIZE OF THE CONQUISTADOR

1. For the life of Ferdinand Magellan, see E.G. Bourne's introduction to *The Philippine Islands,* by Blair, Emma H. and Robertson, James A., and Fray Bartolome de Argensola's *Discovery and Conquest of the Malucco and Philippine Islands* (English version), London, 1708; also in Blair and Robertson, Vol. XVI, pp. 217-317.
2. Readings in Philippine history were available to this author in Teodoro Agoncillo and Oscar Alfonso; Gregorio Zaide; Nicolas Zafra and Rafael Beltran.Basic documents are compiled in Blair, Emma H. and Robertson, James A.
3. Quoted by Rafael Beltran in *Prologue to Philippine History.*
4. Ibid.
5. Ibid.
6. Sources on Miguel Lopez de Legazpi are Nicolas de Soraluce, *Biografia del Ilustre Conquistador de Filipinas,* Tolosa, 1863, and *La Ilustracion Filipina,* Manila, June 15, 1860.
7. Juan de Salcedo is often referred to as "the last conquistador." See Carlos Quirino in *The Beginnings of Christianity in the Philippines, p. 134.*

8. For an account of the Limahong invasion, see Isabelo de los Reyes in *Expedición de Li-ma-hong contra Filipinas en 1574*, Manila, 1883, and Juan Caro y Mora, *Ataque de Limahong a Manila en 1574*, Manila 1898.
9. Material for this section was drawn from Maria Lourdes Diaz-Trechuelo and Pedro Ortiz Armenggol.
10. Zaide, *Philippine Political and Cultural History*, in two volumes.
11. For an excellent synthesis of the Dutch invasions, see Nick Joaquin, *La Naval de Manila and Other Essays*, Manila, 1964.
12. Percy Hill has a popular account of the Salcedo tragedy in *Adventures in Old Manila.*
13. The Bustamante affair is discussed in the monograph by Concepcion Pajaron Parody, *Don Fernando Manuel Bustamante y Bustillo, Gobernador de Filipinas (1717-1719)*. Escuela de Estudios Hispano-Americano, 1964.
14. An exhaustive source on the Galleon Trade is William L. Schurz, *The Manila Galleon.* New York, 1939.
15. Sources on the British occupation of the Philippines (1762-64) are found in Blair and Robertson, Vol. XLIX.
16. The church-state conflicts during the Spanish period is the subject of Zaide, Chapter XIV, *Philippine Political and Cultural History,* Vol. I, pp. 205-210.
17. John N. Schumaker, S.J., has written an excellent monograph titled *Father Jose Burgos - Priest and Nationalist,* Ateneo de Manila Press, Quezon City, 1972.
18. The following are sources on the Philippine Revolution: Emilio Aguinaldo, *Reseña Veridica*, etc.; Jose Alejandrino, *La Senda del Sacrificio*; Felipe Calderon, *Mis Memorias Sobre la revolución;* Teodoro M. Kalaw, *The Philippine Revolution;* Isabelo de los Reyes, *La Sensacional Memoria Sobre La revolucion;* Artemio Ricarte, *The Hispano-Philippine Revolution;* Manuel Sastron, *La Insurreccion en filipinas.*
19. The following are excellent biographies of the national hero of the Filipinos: Leon Ma. Guerrero, *The First Filipino;* Rafael Palma, *The Pride of the Malay Race* (English translation by Roman Ozaeta); Carlos Quirino, *The Great Malayan.*
20. For the Magdalo-Magdiwang conflict, see Zaide, *A History of the Katipunan.*

CHAPTER II
THE CHRISTIAN CITY

1. Antonio de Morga, *Sucesos de las Islas Filipinas,* Mexico. 1609. Annotated by Jose Rizal, Paris, 1890. This edition was reprinted for the Rizal Centennial, Manila, 1962.
2. Mons. Jeremiah Harty, *The Religious Situation in the Philippines.* May 1907. Quoted by Zaide, Vol. I, p. 190.
3. The source for the following account on the cathedral of Manila is Diaz-Trechuelo, Maria Lourdes. *Architectura Española en las Filipinas.* Chapter VII, pp. 185-221.
4. For an account of the life and work of the first bishop of the Philippines, see Fr. Diego de Aduarte, *Historia de la Provincia de Santo Rosario,* etc. Zaragoza, 1693.
5. Quoted in Diaz-Trechuelo, work cited, pp. 185-221.
6. Quoted in ibid.
7. Quoted in ibid.
8. Ibid.
9. The following sources provide a broad understanding of the early work of the Order of St. Augustine in the Philippines: Fr. Gaspar de San Agustin, *Conquistas de las Islas Filipinas,* Madrid, 1698, and Fr. Casimiro Diaz, a continuation of the earlier work by Fray San Agustin, Valladolid, 1890.
10. The definitive work on this subject is *The Augustinian Monastery of Intramuros* by Fr. Isacio R. Rodriguez, O.S.A. Quezon City. 1975. See also Diaz-Trechuelo. pp. 227-232.
11. There is a persistent legend about the church and monastery of San Agustin having been built by one Antonio de Herrera, variously described as the son or nephew of Juan Herrera, the builder of El Escorial outside Madrid. The legend of Antonio

de Herrera is quite exhaustively discussed by Fr. Rodriguez, pp. 17 et seq., and thereby puts the matter to rest. See also Diaz-Trechuelo, pp. 228, 231.

12. The following are excellent sources on the work of the members of the Order of the Friars Minor (O.F.M.), or Franciscans, in the Philippines: Fr. Francisco de Santa Ines, *Cronica de la Provincia de San Gregorio Magno*, etc. Manila, 1892, two volumes; Fr. Juan Francisco de San Antonio, *Cronicas*, etc. Sampaloc, 1738-44, three volumes; Fr. Felix de Huerta, *Estado geografico*, etc. Manila, 1855; Fr. Lorenzo Perez, *Labor Patriotica*, etc., Madrid, 1929.

13. The following account on the work of the Franciscans is drawn from Diaz-Trechuelo, pp. 231-232, and Ortiz Armenggol, p. 79.

14. See Diaz-Trechuelo, pp. 253-261; and Ortiz Armenggol, p. 80. See also Cacho Hermanos, *Los Misiones Catolicos en Extremo Oriente*, 1937.

15. Fr. Miguel Selga, S.J., provides sidelights on the history of the Convent of Santa Clara in Perez de Olaguer, pp. 133-139. See also Diaz-Trechuelo, pp. 261-263; and *Misiones Catolicos en Estremo Oriente.*

16. The definitive source on the early work of the Dominicans in the Philippines is Fr. Diego de Aduarte, *Historia de la Provincia de Santo Rosario*, etc. Zaragoza. 1693.

17. Quoted by Diaz-Trechuelo, op. cit. p. 239. (Translation by the author.)

18. George Miller, *Interesting Manila*, p. 69.

19. For the work of the Dominicans in education see Fr. Evergisto Bazaco. O.P. *History of Education in the Philippines*, Manila, 1939, and Encarnacion Alzona, *A History of Education in the Philippines (1565-1930)*, Manila, 1932. The following account on the UST relied much on the updated version of this institution's history found in *University of Santo Tomas, Yesterday, Today and Tomorrow*, a university folio published in 1973, edited by Fr. Fausto Gomez, O.P. The story of San Juan de Letran is drawn from Bazaco and Alzona. See also *Misiones Catolicos en Extremo Oriente.*

20. The following are basic sources on the history of the Augustinian Recollects in the Philippines: Fr. Andres de San Nicolas, *Historia General*, etc. Madrid, 1631; Fr. Gregorio Fidel Blas de la Asuncion, *Labor Evangelica*, etc. Zaragoza, 1910; Fr. Lucinio Ruiz, *Reseña Historica*, etc. 2 vols. Manila, 1925.

21. Diaz-Trechuelo, pp. 251-253; Ortiz Armenggol, p. 79.

22. Nick Joaquin, *Almanac for Manileños.*

23. The Jesuits in the Philippines are the subject of works by Fr. Pedro Chirino, *Relación*, etc., Manila, 1890; Fr. Francisco Colin, *Labor Evangelica*, etc., Barcelona, 1900-1902, annotated by Fr. Pablo Pastells, S.J.; Fr. Murillo Velarde, *Historia*, etc., Manila, 1747; Fr. Juan J. Delgado, *Historia General Sacra Profana* etc., Manila, 1892; Fr. Miguel Saderra Maso, *Misiones Jesuiticos*, etc., Manila, 1924; and Fr. Horacio V. de la Costa, *The Jesuits in the Philippines*, Cambridge, 1967.

24. See Bazaco and Alzona for the work of the Jesuits in education.

25. Miller, p. 67.

26. Joaquin, *Almanac for Manileños.*

27. Fr. Miguel Selga, S.J. in Perez de Olaguer, p. 187.

28. Source for this item on La Ignaciana is *Misiones Catolicos en Extremo Oriente.*

29. The following information on the Vincentian Fathers and the Daughters of Charity is from *Los Misiones Catolicos en Extremo Oriente.* See also Dela Goza and Cavanna, *Vincentians in the Philippines.*

30. Fr. Miguel Selga, S.J., in Perez de Olaguer, p. 190.

31. Diaz-Trechuelo, p. 241.

32. See *Los Misiones Catolicos en Extremo Oriente.*

33. Ibid.

34. Ibid. Also Fr. Miguel Selga, S.J., in Perez de Olaguer.

35. The information on the Capuchin Fathers is from *Los Misiones Catolicos*, etc.

36. Joaquin, *Almanac for Manileños.*

37. Ibid.

38. Ibid.

39. Mrs. Trinidad Gardiner-Mendoza relates that this image of Our Lady of Lourdes was transferred to the San Agustin church by a group of Intramuros residents led by one of her relatives whom she identified only as "Ricardo." See Reyes, *Terror and Redemption*, p. 56.

40. See *Los Misiones Catolicos en Extremo Oriente.*

41. Ibid. Fr. Miguel Selga compiled information on conditions among the religious orders during the Liberation period and related his findings to Perez de Olaguer in *Terror Amarillo.* "History of St. Paul College," typescript in the files of St. Paul College, made available to this author by Mother Socorro Angela Reyes, SPC, was also used for this account.

42. Ibid, Father Selga in Perez de Olaguer.

43. Ibid.

44. The sources for this narrative on the Christian Brothers and the De la Salle college are *History of De la Salle: 1911-1970,* unpublished thesis by Juanito Castillo, F.S.C., and Carlos Quirino's manuscript intended for a pictorial history of De la Salle University, unpublished as of 2 September 1985, when it was made available to the author by Bro. Andrew B. Gonzalez, F.S.C., president of De la Salle University.

44-a. The source for the story of the Congregation of the Most Holy Redeemer (Redemptorists) in the Philippines is a monograph titled *The Redemptorists in Luzon*, by Rev. Samuel J. Bonand, CSsR. The author's preface is dated 1 February 1982, San Alfonso, Rome, "being the fiftieth anniversary of the departure of the first community from Australia to Baclaran." This writer is indebted to Rev. Leo J. English, CSsR, who made this material available, together with another booklet titled *The Mother of Perpetual Help in the Philippines,* published in 1978.

45. Guerrero, in "Prologue" to *The First Filipino*, p. xxi.

46. Robert MacMicking, *Recollections of Manila and the Philippines, 1848-1850.* Filipiniana Book Guild edition. Edited and annotated by Morton J. Netzorg. Manila. 1967. p. 5.

47. *Travel Accounts of the Islands* (1832-1858), Filipiniana Book Guild, Manila, 1974, p. 230.

48. Guerrero, p. xxix.

49. A survey of Marian images venerated in the Philippines titled *Madonnas of the Philippines,* by Lutgarda A. Aviado, was published by Manlapaz Publishing Co., Quezon City, 1975. A monograph on Marian images was published by the National Marian Committee for the celebration of the centenary of the dogma of the Immaculate Conception, Manila, 1954. An earlier source on the subject is *La Virgen Maria Venerada en sus Imagenes en Filipinas,* P.R. Sanchez, S.J., Santos y Bernal, Manila, 1904.

50. Aside from Diaz-Trechuelo and Ortiz Armenggol, other contemporary sources on the building of Intramuros are Alexander E.W. Salt and H.O.S. Heistand, "Manila Walls and their Fortifications," American Chamber of Commerce Journal, February 1934, reprinted in *Focus on Manila*; Jose P. Apostol, "Notes on Manila," *The Journal of History,* March-June 1964; Miguel A. Bernad, S.J., "The Walled City of Manila and Its Gates," in *Intramuros: Our Heritage In Stone*, published by the Intramuros Restoration Committee, undated. A broad understanding of Intramuros is provided by *Intramuros and Beyond,* a compilation published by Letran College in 1974. Also a set of monographs published by the National Historical Commission in connection with the 4th centennial of Manila which includes, *Pre-Spanish Manila* by Jesus T. Peralta and Lucila A. Salazar; *The Western Community of Manila* by Miguel A. Bernad, S.J., and *The Colonization of the Philippines and the Beginnings of the Spanish City of Manila,* by Nicholas Zafra.

George Miller in *Interesting Manila,* first issued in 1912, provides many insights from the American point of view.

51. See the above-listed sources for information on Fort Santiago. Also Carlos da Silva, "Plans, Policies & Problems of Restoration" in *Intramuros: Our Heritage in Stone;* Encarnacion Alzona, *Rizal in Fort Santiago*, Pasay City, 1960.
52. A recent monograph which updated the origin and development of Bagumbayan is *Rizal Park*, published by Travel & Trade, Manila, 1971.
53. On 16 November 1602, the general of the Augustinians, Don Fulvius de Ascoli in Rome issued a decree partitioning the Philippines into two Augustinian provinces. One province retained the name *Santissimo Nombre de Jesus* and the other whose members became known as Discalced (barefoot) Augustinians or Recollects, was given the name *San Nicolas de Tolentino*.
54. A backgrounder on the Madonna of Ermita is provided by Padre Sanchez, *La Virgen Maria Venerada en sus Imagenes en Filipinas*, Santos y Bernal, Manila, 1904. The parish of Ermita on the occasion of its fiesta publishes a commemorative program which contains a minute history of the church and the image venerated here. The author has examined those of 1963 and 1967, the last of which interprets Nuestra Señora de Guia as "Our Lady of the Way."
55. Buzeta and Bravo, Vol. II, pp. 202-206.
56. For a detailed account of this monument, see Alexander E.W. Salt and H.O.S. Heistand, "Monuments and Inscriptions of Manila," and "The Streets of Manila and Their Origins," *Focus on Manila*, edited by Mauro Garcia and C.O. Resurreccion, published by the Philippine Historical Association, Manila, 1971, for the 4th centennial of the founding of Manila.
57. Buzeta and bravo, Vol., II. p. 385.
58. On Pandacan's reputation as a town of artists, see Nick Joaquin (Quijano de Manila), *Almanac for Manileños*.
59. Buzeta and Bravo, Vol. II, p. 27 (Annex).
60. Ibid., Vol. I, p. 291.
61. Ibid., Vol. II, p. 457.
62. Ibid., Vol. I, pp. 386-387.
63. Ibid., Vol. I, p. 560.
64. Ocampo, Galo B. *Malacañang: House of the People*. Unpublished manuscript.
65. Buzeta and Bravo, Vol. II, p. 324.
66. See Nick Joaquin (Quijano de Manila). *Almanac for Manileños*.
67. Buzeta and Bravo. Vol. II, p. 421.
68. Nick Joaquin (Quijano de Manila) reminisces about the Gardenia district in "Fun by Night," *Philippines Free Press*, 3 September 1966.
69. *University of Santo Tomas: Yesterday, Today and Tomorrow*, a UST folio edited by Fr. Fausto Gomez, O.P. Manila. 1973.
70. The authoritative source on the Santo Tomas Internment Camp is A.V.H. Hartendorp. *The Santo Tomas Story*, McGraw-Hill Book Company, New York. 1964.

CHAPTER III
THE PREY OF THE INTERLOPER

1. See Agoncillo, p. 89.
2. Ibid.
3. Ibid.
4. Ibid. p. 93.
5. George Dewey. *Autobiography of George Dewey*. New York. Charles Scribner's Sons. 1913. p. 195.
6. Ibid. p. 22.
7. Agoncillo, p. 125.
8. Readings on this subject are found in Austin Craig, *The Filipinos' Fight for*

Freedom, Manila, Oriental Commercial Co. 1933; Manuel Sastron, *La Insurreccion en las Filipinas y Guerra hispano-americano en el archipelago*, Madrid 1901; Karl Irving Faust, *Campaigning in the Philippines*, San Francisco, 1899; R.A. Alger, *The Spanish-American War*, New York and London, Harper and Brothers, 1961; (the author was U.S. Secretary of War from 5 March 1897 to 1 August 1899); James A. Leroy, *The Americans in the Philippines*, Boston & N.Y., Houghton Co., 1914, 2 vols.; Alden March, *The History & Conquest of the Philippines* and *Our Other Island Possessions*, Philadelphia, 1899; Charles B. Elliot. *The Philippines to the End of the Military Regime*, Indianapolis, Bobbs-Merrill Co., 1916.

9. Apolinario Mabini wrote his memoirs entitled, *The Rise and Fall of the Philippine Revolution*.
10. See Kalaw, *The Philippine Revolution*.
11. Addressing a group of Protestant clergymen who called on him at the White House, 21 November 1899, McKinley said, "The truth is, I didn't want the Philippines and when they came to us as a gift from the gods, I did not know what to do with them . . . When next I realized that the Philippines had dropped into our lap, I confess that I did not know what to do with them . . . I went down on my knees and prayed Almighty God for light and guidance more than one night." Quoted by Zaide, pp. 227-228.
12. Zaide, p. 212 et seq.
13. The full text of Aguinaldo's manifesto is in Teodoro M. Kalaw, *The Philippine Revolution*. Manila. Manila Bookstore Company. 1925. pp. 280-282.
14. See the *Report of the Schurman Commission*, Senate Document, 56th Congress, 1st Session, No. 138. Also Jacob Gould Schurman, *Philippine Affairs: A Retrospect and Outlook*, New York. 1902.
15. For the early years of the American occupation of the Philippines, see Elihu Root, *The Military and Colonial Policy of the United States. Address and Reports*. New York. 1970 edition. Also Charles Burke Elliot, *The Philippines to the End of the Commission Government*. New York, 1968 edition; Dean Worcester, *The Philippines Past and Present*. New York. 1921; W. Cameron Forbes, *The Philippine Islands* (two volumes). Boston. 1928; and Leon Wolff, *Little Brown Brother*. New York. 1961 edition. Two recent works by American scholars shed new light on certain personages and events during this period. They are, *Benevolent Assimilation: The American Conquest of the Philippines, 1899-1903*, by Creighton Miller Stuart, Yale University Press, 1982, and *The Philippines and the United States, 1899-1922*, by Peter W. Stanley, Harvard University Press, 1974.
16. U.S. *Congressional Record*, 66th Congress, 3rd session, Vol. 60. Part I, p. 26.
17. See William Cameron Forbes. *The Philippine Islands*. Vol. II, Appendix XXXII.
18. Elliot. *The Philippines to the End of the Commission Government*.
19. This man William D. McKinnon damned himself in history by giving testimony justifying atrocities committed by the U.S. military against the Filipino civilian population, at a time when these atrocities had assumed genocide proportions. Named bishop of Manila despite protests filed by the revolutionary Republic of the Philippines with the Pope in Rome, this man would also justify the desecration of Philippine churches, monasteries and convents by American soldiers.
20. Encarnacion Alzona. *A History of Education in the Philippines*.
21. Gilbert S. Perez. *Bulletin* of the American Memorial Collection. Vol. I, No. 5, September 1973, p. 15.
22. Elliot, op. cit. p. 246.
23. Zaide, p. 264.
24. Ibid. p. 77.
25. Lt. Col. James Parker in an article titled "Some Random Notes on Fighting in the Philippines," *Journal of the Military Service Institution in the U.S.*, Vol. 27, No. 108. November 1900. Quoted by Netzorg in footnote to MacMicking, p. 11.
26. U.S. *Senate Document* No. 331, Part 2, 1st Session, 57th Congress. Quoted by Netzorg in footnote to MacMicking, p. 11.

27. "66 Years of Service," a commemorative monograph published by Meralco on the inauguration of its new administration building in Pasig, Rizal, March 1969.

28. For a survey of the development of air travel in the Philippines, see Enrique B. Santos, *Trails in Philippine Skies - A History of Aviation in the Philippines from 1909 to 1944*. Manila. 1981.

29. See *History of Journalism in the Philippines* by Jesus Valenzuela. Manila. 1933.

30. Gleeck, *American Institutions in the Philippines*, p. 303.

31. A good backgrounder for this era is the work of Joseph Ralston Hayden, *The Philippines: A Study in National Development*. New York. 1945.

32. For an exhaustive account of this period in the life of the American general, see Petillo, *Douglas MacArthur, The Philippine Years*.

33. The following are first-hand accounts of the Japanese occupation of the Philippines: Teodoro M. Agoncillo, *The Fateful Years* (two volumes); A.V.H. Hartendorp, *The Japanese Occupation of the Philippines* (two volumes); Manuel E. Buenafe, *Wartime Philippines;* Armando J. Malay, *Occupied Philippines*; Eliseo Quirino, *A Day to Remember*.

34. The text of the famous announcement of the fall of Bataan over the Voice of Freedom on Corregidor was written by Salvador P. Lopez and broadcast by announcer Norman Reyes.

35. The full text of Jorge B. Vargas' speech is reproduced in *Occupied Philippines* by Armando J. Malay, p. 191.

36. Geronima T. Pecson to author. Mrs. Pecson was present on this occassion. The Tagalog words mean "we are on the other side," but they are also a play on Kalibapi.

37. For some aspects of guerilla activity in the Philippines see Uldarico S. Baclagon, *Philippine Campaigns*. Manila. 1952; Russell Volckmann, *We Remained*. New York. 1954; Yay Panlilio, *The Crucible*. New York. 1950.

38. Baclagon, p. 243.

CHAPTER IV
MANILA WAITS

1. The definitive work on the naval engagements is *History of United States Naval Operations in World War II*, in particular Vol. XII, *Leyte, June 1944-January 1945*, and Vol. XIII, *The Liberation of the Philippines: Luzon, Mindanao, the Visayas*, by Samuel Eliot Morison. The definitive source for the land battles is *Triumph in the Philippines. The War in the Pacific. The United States Army in Word War II*, by Robert Ross Smith. The present work would not have been possible without recourse to Morison and Smith, and the author is forever indebted to both.

2. Arthur Swinson, *Four Samurai: A Quartet of Japanese Commanders in the Second World War*, p. 194.

3. Ibid., p. 194.

4. Ibid., p. 195.

5. Ibid., p. 207.

6. Smith, pp. 237 et seq. Also Swinson, pp. 207 et seq., and Stanley A. Frankel, *The 37th Division in World War II*, pp. 248-250.

7. Lt. Gen. Tomoyuki Yamashita told his counsel, Col. Harry E. Clarke in Manila in October 1945: "On the evening of January 3, I left Ipo and arrived at Fort McKinley on the outskirts of Manila and held my conference with Lt. Gen. Yokoyama. I left Fort McKinley on the early morning of the 4th and arrived in Baguio that evening." Reproduced in Kenworthy, p. 78. Swinson says on p. 207, "On the 2nd January, Yamashita moved still farther north, to Baguio, which lies inland from Lingayen gulf, 7,400 feet up in the mountains and set up his command post for the Shobu Group."

8. Smith, p. 212.
9. Ibid.
10. Bertram C. Wright, *The 1st Cavalry Division in World War II*, p. 120.
11. Smith, footnote in *Triumph*, p. 230.
12. Ibid. Brig. Gen. William C. Dunckel told Eichelberger, "When you were pushing on Manila so rapidly, I visited 6th Army Headquarters and found them greatly agitated over the fact that you would be in Manila before they were." Dunckel commanded the ground units that occupied Southwest Mindoro, designated Western Visayas Task Force, 19th Regimental Combat Team of the 24th Division, and the 503rd Parachute Regimental Combat Team. See also D. Clayton James, *The Years of MacArthur*, p. 634.
13. See Edward M. Flanagan, Jr., *The Angels: History of the 11th Airborne Division*, for a detailed account of the Nasugbu landings and the battle for Tagaytay Ridge, p. 67 et seq.
14. The disposition of the Japanese defense force is described in Smith, p. 237 et seq. Also in Frankel, p. 248 et seq.
15. The narrative on Mayor Leon Guinto, Sr., was pieced together from interviews with his daughter, Mrs. Virtudes Guinto-Gallegos, and from accounts related in a monograph titled *Highlights in the Life of Leon G. Guinto, Sr.*, by Ruperto G. Cristobal, published in 1974, a copy of which was made available to the author by Mrs. Gallegos. Mrs. Gallegos was with the Guinto family at their residence in Singalong through all the events related in this work. Mrs. Gallegos was a journalist and worked with the *Manila Chronicle* until that publication was proscribed in 1972 following the imposition of martial law by Ferdinand Marcos. Later, she did publicity work for the Ministry of Tourism.
16. Frankel, p. 249.

CHAPTER V
THE ORDEAL BY SWORD AND FIRE
SATURDAY, 3 FEBRUARY 1945

1. Wright, p. 125.
2. Flanagan, Jr., p. 75.
3. A.V.H. Hartendorp, *The Japanese Occupation*, etc., p. 543. See footnote on Fr. Paul de Guzman's account of events in Tondo.
4. A.V.H. Hartendorp, *The Santo Tomas Story*, p. 405.
5. The account of the Tondo fire is related by Fr. Paul de Guzman, S.J., in Hartendorp, *The Japanese Occupation*, etc., pp. 543-544.
6. Smith, p. 224.
7. The wartime story of the Vincentian Fathers is related by Rolando S. Dela Goza, C.M., and Jesus Ma. Cavanna, C.M., in *Vincentians in the Philippines*, Chapter Thirteen, p. 349 et. seq. See also Fr. Miguel Selga, S.J., in Antonio Perez de Olaguer, *El Terror Amarillo en las Filipinas*, p. 190 et seq.
8. Kiyoshi Osawa, *A Japanese in the Philippines.*
9. Tressa R. Cates, *The Drainpipe Diary*, p. 245.
10. Wright, p. 128 et seq.
11. Manuel G. Buenafe, *Wartime Philippines*, p. 254.
12. Gladys Savary, *Outside the Walls*, p. 160. Gladys Savary shared a house at the corner of Fernando Rein and Park Avenue in Pasay that belonged to the Belgian Consul, M. Verlinden, who was interned at the University of Santo Tomas camp. Madame Savary's housemates were the Swedish Consul Helge A Janson and his wife, Dorothy, who had lived in the Philippines since 1935.
13. Lydia C. Gutierrez, "The Longest Wait," *Sunday Times Magazine*, 23, April 1967, p. 54.

14. Cates, p. 245.
15. Federic H. Stevens, *Santo Tomas Internment Camp*, p. 362.
16. Benigno del Rio, *Estampas de la Ocupacion*, p. 281.
17. Natalie Crouter, *Forbidden Diary*, pp. 464-468. Mrs. Crouter and her family were American civilian internees at Bilibid prisons.
18. Stevens, p. 362.
19. The story of the Assumption Sisters is told by Fr. Miguel Selga, S.J., in Perez de Olaguer, pp. 213 et seq.
20. Cates, p. 246.
21. Hartendorp, *The Japanese Occupation*, p. 524.
22. Ibid.
23. Cates, p. 246.
24. Stevens, p. 364.
25. Ibid.
26. Geronima T. Pecson to author. Mrs. Pecson had had an extensive career as educator and social worker when World War II broke out in the Philippines in December 1941. She was in Zamboanga at this time where her husband, Judge Potenciano Pecson, had his court and where she taught at the Zamboanga Normal school. From Zamboanga Mrs. Pecson returned to Manila in 1942 at the behest of Brig. Gen. Manuel A. Roxas. She would serve as unofficial liaison between the civilian government that the Japanese instituted upon occupying the country, and which was first headed by Jorge B. Vargas and later by Jose P. Laurel, and the dependents of Filipino military personnel who needed health and welfare assistance. Through Mrs. Pecson, money, equipment and supplies for the dependents of the military, many of whom were in the resistance movement, and for many other needy persons, were channelled. She held office in Malacañang and had quarters there too. She was variously referred to as "Malacañang Housekeeper," "Social Secretary," "Private Secretary to the President," etc., but in fact she had no official designation. Mrs. Pecson continued her work to the end of the Japanese occupation.
27. Mrs. Geronima T. Pecson's account is contained in her speech delivered at the annual convention of the Philippine Department, American Auxiliary, 20 May 1978, Cebu City.
28. The account of Dr. J.H. Yanzon's work is in the files of the Philippine National Red Cross. This incident is also related in *The Conscience of the Nation* by Alfonso J. Aluit, p. 356.
29. Stevens, pp. 365 et seq.

SUNDAY, 4 FEBRUARY 1945

1. The story of Fukuchi Fukomoto is in *Free Philippines*, issue of 26 February 1945, p. 1.
2. The narratives of Mrs. Trinidad Gardiner-Mendoza and Mrs. Isabel B. de Santa Isabel are in Jose G. Reyes, *Terror and Redemption*, pp. 53 et seq.
3. Fr. de Guzman's story is in Hartendorp, *The Japanese Occupation*, etc. p. 543.
4. The account of the capture of the Santo Tomas internment camp is in Smith, p. 251. See also Hartendorp, *The Japanese Occupation*, etc., p. 524; Stevens, p. 365; Cates, p. 246; and Wright, p. 125.
5. Flanagan, p. 79 et seq.
6. Gutierrez, "The Longest Wait."
7. Angel Dionzon, Exhibit No. 1114 (Statement, 3 October 1945), and Yu Cheng Kho, Exhibit No. 1116 (Statement, 18 October 1945), in *Proceedings* of the Yamashita trial.
8. The story of Modesto Farolan is told in his deposition included in T*he Sack of Manila*, p. 28 et seq.

9. Sister Charles, SPC, "Memoirs of a French Sister, etc.", unpublished manuscript in the files of the St. Paul College of Manila.
10. Smith, p. 252.
11. Crouter, p. 470.
12. See W.H. Waterous in the *Bulletin* of the American Historical Collection, Vol. II, No. 1, January 1974, pp. 47 et seq. Dr. Waterous dates the events narrated here as 5 February 1945. See also Smith, p. 254 and Crouter, pp. 472-474.
13. This narrative of events at the De la Salle college was pieced together from accounts related by Fr. Francis J. Cosgrave, CSsR, in *Proceedings,* Vol. III, pp. 263 et seq., and in *Report of the Resident Commissioner,* p. 17; by Fr. Miguel Selga, S.J., in Perez de Olaguer, pp. 206-209, and by Gonzalez and Reyes in *These Hallowed Halls, passim.*
14. Marcial P. Lichauco, *Dear Mother Putnam,* p. 205.
15. Hartendorp, *The Japanese Occupation,* etc., p. 529.
16. Rodolfo G. Tupas, "Sanctuary in an Outraged Manila," p. 10, *Sunday Times Magazine,* 23 April 1967.
17. See Smith, p. 254. Smith dates the battle around Bilibid as 4 February 1945. Smith and Crouter say that on 5 February the internees were moved out to the Ang Tibay shoe factory compound in Grace Park to the north of Manila, and were brought back to Bilibid the following day, 6 February. Dr. W.H. Waterous dates these events 5 February 1945.

MONDAY, 5 FEBRUARY 1945

1. Flanagan, p. 79 et seq.
2. Smith, p. 265 et seq.
3. Nemesio Francisco's experiences are related by Jose P. Santos in Manila *New Day,* 3 March 1945, and reproduced by Pedro G. Gimenez, *Under the Shadow of the Kempei,* pp. 333-336.
4. Hartendorp, *The Japanese Occupation,* p. 529 et seq.
5. The story of Lt. Robert Viale is related in Frankel, p. 256. For this rare example of self-immolation, Lt. Viale was awarded the Congressional Medal of Honor posthumously.
6. Fr. Paul de Guzman's account is in Hartendorp, *The Japanese Occupation,* pp. 543-544.
7. The testimonies of Michael Goldenberg and Ramsingh Mayasingh are in the *Proceedings* of the Yamashita trial, marked Exhibit No. 1122 (Statement, 17 October 1945), and Exhibit No. 1119 (Statement, 8 October 1945), respectively.
8. Sancho Enriquez and Juan Palada, *Proceedings,* Vol. X, pp. 1193-1203 and pp. 1206-1211, respectively.
9. Rosalinda Andoy, Vol. X, pp. 1161 et seq., *Proceedings.*
10. Luis Gallent, Vol. X, pp. 1182-1192, *Proceedings.*
11. This account concerning the La Concordia college is related by Fr. Miguel Selga, S.J., in Perez de Olaguer, pp. 22 et seq. Also mentioned in Hartendorp, *The Japanese Occupation,* p. 554.
12. Hartendorp, *The Japanese Occupation,* pp. 543-544.
13. Crouter, pp. 472-475.
14. Smith, p. 255.
15. Ibid.
16. Ibid.
17. Sister Charles, SPC, "Memoirs of a French Sister, etc."

TUESDAY, 6 FEBRUARY 1945

1. Flanagan, p. 81 et seq.

2. Fr. Paul de Guzman in Hartendorp, *The Japanese Occupation* etc. pp. 543-544.
2-a. The *Free Philippines* of Friday, 9 February 1945, relates an incident where the Tondo parish priest, Monsignor Jose Jovellanos, led a crowd of 300 from the church through the burning streets and exploding shells, the Blessed Sacrament in his hands and the famous image of the Holy Child Jesus enshrined in the Tondo church, on the shoulders of a bunch of Tondo residents, in a mad dash to safety.
2-b. See "Jovellanos of Tondo" by Quijano de Manila, originally published in the Philippines *Free Press*, included in *Doveglion and Other Cameos*, by Quijano de Manila, Manila, 1977.
3. Francisco Lopez, *Proceedings*, Vol. VII, p. 667 et seq.
4. The text of General MacArthur's announcement of the liberation of Manila is reproduced in Carlos P. Romulo, *I See the Philippines Rise*, p. 22.
5. Savary, p. 166.
6. Sister Charles, SPC, "Memoirs of a French Sister . . ."
7. The account of Col. Jose Guido and his family is related by his widow, Mrs. Justa G. Guido, in *Proceedings*, Vol. III, pp. 202-213.
8. The story of the Franciscans is told by Fr. Miguel Selga, S.J., in Perez de Olaguer, p. 198 et seq. and Brother Jose Ma. Manjabacas, O.F.M., in his deposition at the Yamashita trial found in *Proceedings*, Vol. XI, pp. 1320-1326.
9. Epifanio Gutierrez Muñoz in Perez de Olaguer, p. 105 et seq.
10. Sister Caridad Ocampo, Daughter of Charity, *Proceedings*, Vol. XI, pp. 1274-1286.
11. Luis Gallent, *Proceedings*, Vol. X, pp. 1182-1192.
12. Rosalinda Andoy, *Proceedings*, Vol. X, pp. 1161 et seq.
13. Sancho Enriquez and Juan Palada, *Proceedings*, Vol. X, pp. 1193-1203; pp. 1206-1211.
14. Carolina Coruna, *Proceedings*, also deposition included in *The Sack of Manila*, p. 21.
15. Dr. Antonio G. Sison, *Proceedings*, Vol. VI, pp. 570-581.
16. Tupas, "Sanctuary."
17. Lichauco, p. 206.
18. Savary, pp. 164 et seq.
19. Tupas, "Sanctuary."
20. The account of Remedios Rodriguez and her family is related by her surviving daughter Helena Rodriguez in *Proceedings*, Vol. VII, pp. 690-702.
21. The incidents involving the San Juan de Dios hospital staff are related in *Proceedings* by Mrs. Benita Lahoz, Vol. X, pp. 1131-1150, and Sister Nelly de Jesus Virata, Ibid., pp. 1151 et seq; Sister Donatienne de Marie, Exhibit D-3; Sister Teresa Vilatela, Exhibit D-4, and Sister Concepcion Gotera, Exhibit D-5.
22. The chaplain was the secular priest Fr. Pio Sawal. He was taken away by the Japanese from the Santa Rosa college ruins on 19 February 1945 together with the male patients and never returned. This author could not find particulars as to the manner of his death.
23. The quotations from Sister Concepcion Gotera, DC, used in this narrative are in her *Diary*.
24. The account of the Assumption Sisters at the Madrigal compound on General Luna street in Paco is found in Perez de Olaguer, p. 215.
25. See Gonzalez and Reyes, *These Hallowed Halls*, etc., p. 15.

WEDNESDAY, 7 FEBRUARY 1945

1. The account of MacArthur's entry into Manila is told in Wright, *The 1st Cavalry Division*, p. 134; Douglas MacArthur, *Reminiscences*, p. 285; Manchester, *American Caesar*, p. 413.
2. Smith, pp. 256 et seq.

3. The account of the crossing on the Pasig is related in Smith, pp. 258 et seq.; and Frankel, p. 269 et seq.
4. MacArthur, *Reminiscences*, p. 269.
5. Crouter, pp. 477-479.
6. Hartendorp, *The Japanese Occupation* etc., pp. 545-546.
7. Ibid., p. 554.
8. Morgin, "Manila's Liberation."
9. The incidents at the De la Salle college are related in Gonzalez and Reyes, *passim;* by Fr. Miguel Selga, SJ, in Perez de Olaguer, pp. 206-209, and by Fr. Francis J. Cosgrave, CSsR, in his testimony found in *Proceedings* and in his deposition included in *Report of the Resident Commissioner*, p. 17.
10. This narrative on the religious at San Agustin is pieced together from the accounts of Fr. Miguel Selga, SJ, in Perez de Olaguer, pp. 97-105, and of Bro. Jose Maria Manjabacas, OFM, in *Proceedings*, Vol. XI, pp. 1320-1327; Fr. Belarmino de Celis, OSA, Vol. XI, pp. 1247-1249; Fr. Joaquin Garcia Sanchez, OFM, Exhibit C-10; Fr. Manuel Diez Canseco, OSA, in *Proceedings* and in their respective depositions in *Report*, pp. 22 et seq.
11. Epifanio Gutierrez Muñoz in Perez de Olaguer, p. 105 et seq.
11-a. See "Fatal February" by Nick Joaquin in *Small Beer*, Philippine *Daily Inquirer*, 12 March 1988.
12. The fire at San Agustin and at the Santa Isabel college is described by Sister Caridad Ocampo, DC, in *Proceedings*, Vol. XI, pp. 1274-1286.
13. Sister Charles, SPC, "Memoirs of a French Sister . . ."
14. Certain details of the massacre of the Don Bartolome Pons household are related by Basilio Umagap in *Proceedings*, Vol. IV, pp. 428 et seq., and by Mario Chanco to American investigators, included in *Report of the Resident Commissioner*, pp. 101-102.
15. del Rio, pp. 277 et seq.
16. The testimony of Antonio J. Beltran, an executive of Botica Boie, is in *Proceedings*, Vol. III, pp. 253-258.
17. The account of Col. Alejo Valdes is related by his widow, Mrs. Angela Lopez Valdes, and his brother, General Basilio J. Valdes, in *Proceedings*, Vol. III, pp. 222-240.
18. The story of Alberto P. Delfino and his party is related by Beatriz Teodora Amigo, the family help, in *Proceedings*, Exhibit No. 772, (Statement, 27 June 1945).
19. The story of the Alfredo Chicote Beltran family is told by surviving son Prudencio Chicote Lalana in his testimony at the Yamashita trial, found in *Proceedings*, Vol. VII, pp. 259 et seq. Don Alfredo Chicote is the same person who, with fellow-businessman Don Enrique de la Riva, acquired the Sulucan estate from the Franciscan Sisters of the Santa Clara Convent and developed it into the modern Sampaloc district of Manila. See p. 107 of this book Some of the streets of that district to this day bear the names of his children - Prudencio, Alfredo, Josefina, Carola, Eloisa, Pilina, Adelina, Paquita, Concepcion, Antonio, etc. Of the 24 persons in the Alfredo Chicote Beltran family gathered this day at *La Casona* in Ermita, 14 perished in the incidents related here.
20. Mario X. Guerrero, M.D., to author in an interview, 6 October 1984.
21. The story of the Lizarraga family is related by Jose Manuel Maldonado and his wife, Maria Elena Lizarraga de Maldonado, in their respective testimonies and depositions at the Yamashita trial, found in *Proceedings*, Vol. VII, pp. 737-751, and in Perez de Olaguer, pp. 28 et seq.
22. Sancho Enriquez, *Proceedings*, Vol. X, pp. 1193-1203.

THURSDAY, 8 FEBRUARY 1945

1. The battle accounts related here are in Smith, pp. 258-263; and Frankel, pp. 271 et seq.
2. Perez de Olaguer, p. 195.
3. Testimonies of Mrs. Benita Lahoz and Sister Nelly de Jesus Virata in *Proceedings*. The six foreigners who were taken away were identified as Ms. Ada Aplin, British; Leo Gump, American; Kenneth Huebsch, American; Edgar Christiansen, Danish; Rev. Fr. Cornelius van Roessel of the Missionaries of the Sacred Heart, Dutch, and William Mitchell, American.
4. Luis Gallent, *Proceedings*, Vol. X, pp. 1182-1192. Bill of Particulars No. 52 in the charge sheet against Yamashita states that there were 4,000 detainees in Fort Santiago during the period from 10 to 23 February 1945.
5. Sancho Enriquez, *Proceedings*.
6. Maria Paz Zamora de Mascuñana, "Nuestro Ultimo Cinco Dias," in *Bulletin* of the Philippine Historical Association, June 1958.
7. Perez de Olaguer, pp. 222-224.
8. The incidents at the German Club are related by Helena Rodriguez and Francisco Lopez in *Proceedings*. Bill of Particulars No. 98 in the Charge Sheet against Yamashita said that there were 500 persons at the German Club on San Luis street on 10 February 1945.
9. Morgin, "Manila's Liberation."
10. There seems to be a discrepancy as to the date when the men at the San Agustin church and monastery were ordered out to Fort Santiago. The deposition of Fr. Belarmino de Celis, O.S.A., dated 9 March 1945 and included in the *Report of the Resident Commissioner*, pp. 22-26, states:

    "On February 8th, all the men were taken to Fort Santiago . . . We were imprisoned there for three days . . . Feb. 8, 9, 10 . . . On the 10th in the afternoon we were returned to San Agustin."

    In his deposition also dated 9 March 1945 and also included in *Report*, Fr. Manuel Diez Canseco, O.S.A., says: "On February 8th, we were all taken in Fort Santiago, two days later we were returned to San Agustin."

    The deposition of Fr. Joaquin Garcia Sanchez 9 March 1945, included in *Report*, pp. 29-32, states: "The following morning, the 7th, at about 8:00 or 9:00 in the morning, orders were given that all males should go downstairs . . . we were being taken to Fort Santiago . . . On the third day, they took us out of there... they were taking us to San Agustin . . ."

    Epifanio Gutierrez, in *El Terror Amarillo*, pp. 107 et seq., says: "Al dia siguiento, dia-7 . . . las autoridades Japoneses dan un orden . . . y sean trasladados, pese a los peligrosos materiales que ello entrana a Fort Santiago . . . Al tercer dia - 10 Febrero, como el Estado Mayor comprende que no los puede atenden, a trueva en ellos, a San Agustin."

    The incidents at the San Agustin church and monastery are related by Fr. Belarmino de Celis, OSA, in *Proceedings*, and in a deposition included in *Report of the Resident Commissioner*, p. 22. Bill of Particulars No. 61 in the Charge Sheet against Yamashita said that there were 6,000 civilian refugees at San Agustin from 6 to 22 February 1945.
11. Angela Lopez Valdes, *Proceedings*.
12. Virtudes Guinto-Gallegos to author.
13. Antonio J. Beltran, *Proceedings*.
14. Eulogio Malibiran, *Proceedings*, Vol. VI, pp. 616 et seq.

FRIDAY, 9 FEBRUARY 1945

1. Smith, p. 271; Frankel, p. 273.
2. Eulogio Malibiran, *Proceedings*.
3. The story of Pfc. Joseph J. Cichetti is related in Frankel, pp. 273-274. For this act Cichetti was awarded the Congressional Medal of Honor posthumously.
4. Smith, pp. 261-263; Frankel, pp. 272-273.
5. The story of Pfcs. John N. Reese and Cleto Rodriguez is in Frankel, p. 274. For this action, Pfcs. Reese and Rodriguez were awarded the Congressional Medal of Honor, the former posthumously.
6. The flyer has the headline, "MacArthur Frees Manila." The main story begins with the sentence, "MacArthur has liberated Manila." It is published by P.W.B., G.H.Q., O.W.I. Unit, which had taken over the facilities of the PSP Press at 920 Lepanto St., Sampaloc, Manila, where the guerrilla newspaper, *The Liberator*, official organ of the President Quezon's Own Guerrillas (PQOG), II Corps, was printed.
7. Morgin, "Manila's Liberation."
8. Modesto Farolan, his deposition in *The Sack of Manila*, pp. 28-29.
9. Perez de Olaguer, pp. 214-218.
10. The story of General Charles E. Nathorst and his party is related by his nurse Asuncion R. Marbas in *Proceedings*, Vol. VII, pp. 796 et seq.
11. The story of Adelina Chicote is related by her surviving brother Prudencio in Perez de Olaguer, pp. 46 et seq. A neighbor, not identified in Prudencio's account, witnessed the incident through a crack in a window overlooking the street.
12. Gutierrez, "The Longest Wait."
13. Lichauco, p. 208.
14. The account of the work of Teresa S. Nava is in the files of the Philippine National Red Cross. It is also related in Aluit, p. 353. For her devotion to duty in this action Miss Nava was awarded the Silver Medal of the American Red Cross after the war.
15. Estelita G. Juco, interview with author, 15 February 1984.
16. Mascuñana, "Nuestro Ultimo Cinco Dias."
17. The incidents involving the Honorable Elpidio Quirino and his family and the Mendoza and Syquia families, respectively, were related to the author by surviving family member Tomas Quirino y Syquia in an interview, 10 October 1985. Sol H. Gwekoh in his biography of President Quirino, *The Barrio Schoolteacher Who Became President*, gives a brief account of the incidents on Colorado street in pp. 51-53. But in no way does Gwekoh's account tally with that narrated by Tomas Quirino. Gwekoh says that the Quirino family's laundrywoman, Andrea Jacla, 27, whom Tomas Quirino remembers as "Andang," and Leticia Santamaria, 12, a student at the Philippine Normal School training department, gave eyewitness accounts of this incident at the trial of Lt. Gen. Shizuo Yokoyama. This author was not able to locate the records of the Yokoyama trial at the Philippine Supreme Court Library, even after an exhaustive search assisted by the library staff. Otherwise, most of the records of the trials of Japanese military officials indicted as war criminals in Manila are found at the Supreme Court Library.

    Mrs. Alicia Syquia Quirino suffered machine gun wounds in the back of the head. Norma Quirino, 18, did not sustain any injury, and Tomas Quirino believes that she may have died of heart failure. The forehead of little Fe Angela was badly bruised and Tomas Quirino is led to believe that she may have fallen to the pavement when her mother was hit. The baby may have been rendered unconscious by the fall and after she regained consciousness, a Japanese may have come by and bayonetted her to death. The baby had bayonet wounds on one side of the body.
18. Armando Quirino, 20, nicknamed "Dody," had ran up Colorado street that morning of 9 February 1945 and came upon the dead bodies of his mother and sisters. Unable

to cross California street to his grandmother's home, either because of the American shelling or the interdiction by the Japanese machine gun emplacement at the corner of California and Pennsylvania streets, he ran back to the vicinity of his own home which was now ablaze.

Confused and bewildered, dodging the Japanese teams and the American shelling at the same time, the young Dody Quirino seemed to have run along with other people and reached San Gregorio street in Paco, almost a kilometer east from Colorado. But he later returned to his own neighborhood and joined friends in their hiding places.

Armando gave this information about himself to Ralph Bennett, a friend who lived on Pennsylvania street. It was Ralph who gave this information about Armando to the Quirino family after the war.

It is almost certain that Armando and Ralph Bennett, an American mestizo, were among those rounded up from this vicinity on the night of 10 February 1945 and herded to the corner of Padre Faura and Taft Avenue, where they were machine-gunned by the Japanese. Armando and Ralph fell to the ground in this incident but were not hurt. When the Japanese had gone, they made their escape. Ralph related the incident of being lined up with others and shot, but he did not specify the place. From this point, the two were together all the time. On or about 12 February 1945, the two were huddled with others on a staircase in a house in their neighborhood. Armando sat two steps below Ralph on the staircase. During one artillery barrage, the young Armando Quirino was struck dead by a piece of shrapnel in the back of the head. Ralph Bennett suffered a leg wound in the same incident.

This information was given to the author by Tomas Quirino, 10 October 1985.

19. The incidents at the YMCA of Manila on Oregon street are related by Antonio de Mayo in *Proceedings*, Exhibit No. 342 (Statement, 18 August 1945).
20. Mrs. James Woo, Sr. (a.k.a. Chua So Ping), *Proceedings*, Exhibit No. 342 (Statement, 31 July 1945).
21. Mrs. Maria Rosenzwaig, *Proceedings*, Exhibit No. 342, (Statement, 12 July 1945).
22. Carolina Coruna, *Proceedings*, and her deposition in *The Sack of Manila*, p. 21, and in *Report of the Resident Commissioner*, pp. 68-72.
23. This narrative on the incidents at the St. Paul college of Manila on Herran street was pieced together from the testimonies of Sister Anna de Jesus, SPC; Winifred Colma, Angeles Barahona, Luisa Barahona and Dr. Luis Vasquez, found in *Proceedings*, Vol. IV, pp. 442-485, and that of Rosario Fernandez, Exhibit No. 495 (Statement, 4 July 1945). Bill of Particulars No. 32 in the Yamashita trial stated that 370 persons were killed by bayonetting, machine gun and rifle fire at the St. Paul college compound and immediate vicinity in the incidents on 9 February 1945.
24. Sister Charles, SPC, "Memoirs of a French Sister . . ."
25. Ibid.
26. Eulogio Malibiran, *Proceedings*, Vol. VI, pp. 616 et seq.
27. Eduardo de los Reyes, *Proceedings*, Vol. VI, pp. 622-627.
28. Savary, p. 172.
29. Cates, pp. 252-253.
30. Hartendorp, *The Japanese Occupation*, etc., p. 540.
31. Modesto Farolan, deposition included in *The Sack of Manila*, pp. 28-29, and *Report of the Resident Commissioner*, pp. 41-42.
32. Co Ching, *Proceedings*, Vol. IV, pp. 405-413; see also Fr. Miguel Selga's narrative in Perez de Olaguer, pp. 189-193.
33. The Vincentians killed in the San Marcelino church massacre were Rev. Fr. Jose Tejada, provincial superior; Rev. Fr. Jose Fernandez, parish priest; Rev. Frs. Jose Aguirreche, Adolfo Sato, Luis Egeda, Julio Ruiz; Brothers Antolin Marcos, Gregorio Indurain, Valentin Santidrian, Alejandro Garcia. The list of dead religious

was compiled by the Archdiocese of Manila and marked "Exhibit C-9" in the Yamashita trial.

34. See Gonzalez and Reyes, pp. 16-17.
35. Helen Kremleff, *Proceedings.*
36. The incidents at Plaza Fergusson and the Bayview Hotel are related in *Proceedings,* Vol. V, pp. 500-515; pp. 516-et seq., pp. 524 et seq. The names of the witnesses cited in this narrative were deliberately omitted here. The charge in Bill of Particulars No. 34 is for "cruelly mistreating and abusing approximately 400 women" at the Bayview Hotel.

SATURDAY, 10 FEBRUARY 1945

1. Prudencio Chicote Lalana in Perez de Olaguer, p. 46.
2. Maria Elena Lizarraga de Maldonado in Perez de Olaguer, p. 31.
3. The incidents on Leveriza street in Pasay are related by Fortunato Baredo, Eduardo de los Reyes and Fred Canillas in *Proceedings,* Vol. VI, pp. 622-640.
4. Smith, pp. 261-263.
5. Ibid., p. 265.
6. Ibid., pp. 265-266; Wright, pp. 136 et seq.
7. Modesto Farolan, deposition in *The Sack of Manila.*
8. Gutierrez, "The Longest Wait."
9. The story of Jose G. Villanueva is in Jose G. Reyes, *Terrorism and Redemption,* pp. 40-45.
10. Estelita G. Juco to author.
11. Related by Fr. Miguel Selga, SJ, in Perez de Olaguer, p. 195.
12. Fr. Belarmino de Celis, OSA, deposition included in *Report of the Resident Commissioner,* pp. 22-26.
13. Lichauco, p. 208.
14. The incidents at the German Club on San Luis street in Ermita are related by Francisco Lopez, Helena Rodriguez and Asuncion R. Marbas, respectively, in *Proceedings.* Mr. Ohauss was not the German Club Manager.
15. Gonzalez and Reyes, *passim.*
16. Tomas Quirino to author.
17. Carolina Coruna in *Report of the Resident Commissioner,* p. 68.
18. This incident is related by Faustino Aguilar in *Nang Magdaan ang Daluyong.*
19. The incidents at the Price mansion on California street are related by Jose Carcereny Barta and Dr. Joaquin Marañon in *Proceedings,* Vol. VII, pp. 645-655; 661-664. Bill of Particulars No. 99 in the charge sheet against General Yamashita said that there were "more than 100" persons in the Price compound at 525 Colorado street on this day.
20. Mascuñana, "Nuestro Ultimo Cinco Dias."
21. The fate of the Jose Goicochea family is related by Prudencio Chicote Lalana in Perez de Olaguer, pp. 46 et seq.
22. Dolores Iturralde to author.
23. A narrative of events in diary form covering the period from the 3rd to the 17th February 1945 appears on p. 2 of the 22 February 1945 issue of *Free Philippines.* There is no byline. The narrator is obviously male and head of a family and is referred to here as the "Unknown Diarist."
24. Morgin, "Manila's Liberation."
25. Co Ching, *Proceedings,* Vol. IV, pp. 405-413.
26. Benjamin Urrutia, *Proceedings,* Vol. VIII, pp. 822-826.
27. Federico Davantes, *Proceedings,* Vol. VIII, pp. 804-811.
28. Jose Cabañero, *Proceedings,* Vol. VIII, pp. 796-802.
29. A witness here deliberately unnamed related this incident in *Proceedings.*

30. Mascuñana, "Nuestro Ultimo Cinco Dias."
31. The incidents at the YMCA building and the massacre at the corner of Taft Avenue and Padre Faura street in Ermita are related by Antonio de Mayo, Maria Rosenzwaig, Mrs. James Woo, Sr. (a.k.a. Chua So Ping), Delfin de la Paz, Jr., Alfredo Lagmay, Priscilo Mendiola and Chua Kok Hun in *Proceedings.* Bill of Particulars No. 28 states that 39 persons were killed in the incident at the corner of Taft Avenue and Padre Faura street.
32. The incidents at Red Cross headquarters on Isaac Peral street are related by Patrocinio Abad, a.k.a. Corazon Noble, Juan P. Juan, Gliceria Andaya, John K. Lewy and Florita Loberiza in *Proceedings,* Vol. II, pp. 106-183, and by Modesto Farolan in his deposition filed at the Yamashita trial. Bill of Particulars No. 30 said that "more than 53" persons were killed in the Red Cross headquarters massacre.
33. John K. Lewy identified the German Jews with him in the women's toilet as Mr. and Mrs. Kohnke and their daughter Irene to whom Lewy was engaged, Mr. and Mrs. Koos, Mr. and Mrs. Goetz, Mrs. Karfer and her Filipina servantmaid, for a total of ten persons. A little Filipino girl had crept into the toilet but was spared. *Proceedings,* Vol. II, pp. 161-167.

SUNDAY, 11 FEBRUARY 1945

1. Modesto Farolan, his deposition in *The Sack of Manila,* pp. 28-29.
2. Ang Be, *Proceedings,* Vol. VII, pp. 713 et seq.
3. So Peng, *Proceedings,* Vol. VII, pp. 720 et seq.
4. So Luan, *Proceedings,* Exhibit No. 736 (Statement, 6 September 1945). A friend later told So Luan of having encountered Ang Be and So Peng in the emergency hospital to which the two and other survivors had been brought. So Luan visited them at the hospital and this way learned of the cruel fate meted on his comrades.
5. Mascuñana, "Nuestro Ultimo Cinco Dias . . ."
6. Frankel, p. 276.
7. For this act, Lt. Donald C. Zimmer was awarded the Distinguished Service Cross.
8. Perez de Olaguer, p. 217.
9. Savary, pp. 174-176.
10. Constantine Strashnikow, deposition included in *Report of the Resident Commissioner,* etc., p. 107.
11. Estelita Juco to author.
12. Aluit, p. 353.
13. Tupas, "Sanctuary . . ."
14. Smith, p. 272.
15. Del Rio, p. 290.
16. Gutierrez, "The Longest Wait."
17. The incidents at the De la Salle college are related by Gonzalez and Reyes in *These Hallowed Halls, passim,* and by Fr. Francis J. Cosgrave, CSsR, in *Proceedings.*
18. The battle reports are from Smith, Chapter XV, *passim;* Frankel, Chapter 36, *passim;* Flanagan, Chapter 9, *passim;* and Wright, pp. 135 et seq.
19. Morgin, "Manila's Liberation."
20. Helena Rodriguez, *Proceedings,* Vol. VII, pp. 690-702.
21. Luis Gallent, *Proceedings,* Vol. X, pp. 1182-1192.
22. The incidents involving Chicote family members are related in Perez de Olaguer, p. 48. Those involving the Guerrero family were related to the author by Mario X. Guerrero, M.D., in an interview, 6 October 1984.
23. Raymond Joseph Toomey, *Proceedings,* Exhibit No. 2755, (Statement, 14 Sept. 1945).
24. Tomas Quirino to author.

25. Helena Rodriguez, *Proceedings,* Vol. VII, pp. 690-702.
26. Mascuñana, "Nuestro Ultimo Cinco Dias."
27. Perez de Olaguer, pp. 22 et seq.; Hartendorp, p. 554.
28. del Rio, p. 291.

MONDAY, 12 FEBRUARY 1945

1. Del Rio, p. 291. Tomas del Rio was a Spaniard who came to the Philippines as a soldier in 1896. He was president of the Compañia Cooperativa de Caramay and general manager of the Rio y Olabarrieta, shipowners, lumber dealers, merchants and consignees.
2. Mascuñana, "Nuestro Ultimo Cinco Dias . . ."
3. The battle reports are in Smith, Chapter IV, *passim;* Wright, pp. 135 et seq.; and Flanagan, Chapter 9, *passim.*
4. Smith, p. 273.
5. Dr. Antonio G. Sison, *Proceedings*, Vol. VI. pp. 570-581.
6. Smith, p. 286.
7. Osawa, *A Japanese in the Philippines.*
8. Carmen Locsin, *Proceedings,* Exhibit No. 390.
9. Erlinda Querubin, Zenaida G.R. Lyons, Nadia Nestrenko, and Lourdes Pedro, *Proceedings,* Exhibit No. 564.
10. The incidents concerning the Quirino, Syquia and Mendoza families were related to the author by Tomas Quirino y Syquia in an interview, 10 October 1985.

10-a. Gregorio Mendoza, 18, may have thought himself abandoned in the midst of that barrage, and fearful of getting hit, he crawled back to the narrow passageway in the building on Pennsylvania street, where his aunt and uncle, Margarita and Hector Syquia, and the Mendoza family *mayordoma* (identified only as "Teriang" by Tomas Quirino), lay dead. He may have died as he lay alongside them.

When, after the fighting, recovery parties from the Quirino-Mendoza-Syquia families and their friends came around to this building, only the concrete staircase remained, rising surrealistically into the air.

The recovery parties went to all the places where the clan left its dead and retrieved what they could of human remains at the approximate spots where the dead had lain. These were later deposited in a common grave at the Manila South Cemetery. This information was given the author by Tomas Quirino.

11. This narrative on the incidents at the De la Salle college was pieced together from the testimonies of Fr. Francis J. Cosgrave, CSsR; Bro. Anthony (Anton Heitmann) FSC; Rosario Carlos and Servillano Aquino, found in *Proceedings,* Vol. III, pp. 263 et seq., and from that of Teofilo Candari, Exhibit No. 297 (Statement, 7 June 1945). Fr. Miguel Selga, SJ, relates his own findings in Perez de Olaguer, pp. 206-209. Fr. Cosgrave also filed an affidavit included in *Report of the Resident Commissioner,* p. 17.

Invaluable to the purposes of this work was the monograph by Andrew Gonzalez, FSC, and Alejandro T. Reyes titled *These Hallowed Halls - The Events of February 1945 at De la Salle College,* published by De la Salle University 1982. The authors of this monograph cite as a vital source for their work a document titled "An Account of the Massacres in De la Salle College During February 1945," which was compiled by Bro. Bertin Raymund Barry, FSC, shortly after the incidents. This account is in typescript, a copy of which is found at the Philippine District Archives of the FSC Provincialate in Greenhills, San Juan, Metro-Manila. Brother Barry was an American national who was confined for tuberculosis at the Philippine General hospital at the time of the massacre. Because of this illness, he was not interned at Los Baños like the other American Christian Brothers. Bro. Barry went to De la Salle college right after the liberation of the PGH and had opportunity to record the incidents as related to him by persons involved. Bill of Particulars No. 17 in the charge sheet against General Yamashita states that 41 persons were killed in the incidents at De la Salle college.

12. The story of the massacre at the Carlos Perez-Rubio compound is based on the testimonies of Jose Balboa and Florencio Homol, respectively, found in *Proceedings*, Vol. VII, pp. 774 et seq. Bill of Particulars No. 41 said that "more than 29" civilians were shot or burned to death in this incident.
    Virtually the entire Perez-Rubio clan was wiped out, including the father and mother, two sons and one daughter. Only one son, Miguel, survived. Two sisters of Don Carlos Perez-Rubio also perished in this incident.
13. Walter R. Frankel and Hans Luerse, *Proceedings*, Vol. VI, pp. 584-594; pp. 600-602. Also Dr. Frankel's deposition included in *Report of the Resident Commissioner*, pp. 82-85. Bill of Particulars No. 59 at the Yamashita trial said 15 persons were killed in the Pax Court incident.
14. Jose G. Villanueva in Reyes, pp. 40-45.
15. Modesto Farolan, *The Sack of Manila.*
16. Beatriz Teodora Amigo, *Proceedings*, Exhibit No. 772, (Statement, 27 June 1945).
17. Jose G. Villanueva in Reyes, pp. 40-45.
18. Mascuñana, "Nuestro Ultimo Cinco Dias . . ."

TUESDAY, 13 FEBRUARY 1945

1. Smith, p. 272.
2. Mascuñana, "Nuestro Ultimo Cinco Dias . . ."
3. Modesto Farolan, his deposition in *Report of the Resident Commissioner*, pp. 41-42.
4. Florita Loberiza, *Proceedings*, Vol. II. pp. 132-142.
5. Jose G. Villanueva, related in Reyes, pp. 40-45.
6. Smith, p. 286.
7. The account of the incidents at the De la Salle college is based on the testimonies of Bro. Anthony (Anton Heitmann), FSC; Fr. Francis J. Cosgrave, CSsR; and Servillano Aquino, found in *Proceedings* of the Yamashita trial. Fr. Miguel Selga, SJ, related his findings in Perez de Olaguer, pp. 206-209. See also Gonzalez and Reyes, *These Hallowed Halls, passim.*
8. Maria Campos Lopez, *Proceedings*, Vol. IV, pp. 367-372.
9. Carmen Locsin, *Proceedings*, Exhibit No. 390 (Statement).
10. Bill of Particulars No. 31 in the charge sheet against General Yamashita stated that "more than 100 Filipino and French civilians" were killed in the Campos compound at 1462 Taft Avenue in this incident.
11. Luis Gallent, *Proceedings*, Vol. X, pp. 1182-1192.
12. Umberto de Poli *Proceedings* Vol. VII, pp. 765-780.
13. Gutierrez, "The Longest Wait."
14. del Rio, p. 293.
15. Dr. Walter Frankel, *Proceedings*, and his deposition included in *Report of the Resident Commissioner*, pp. 82-85.
16. Dr. Aristeo Ubaldo Rizal's story is related in Faustino Aguilar, *Nang Magdaan ang Daluyong*, pp. 444-445.
17. Tomas Quirino to author.
18. Felipe Buencamino III, *Free Philippines*, Tuesday, 20 February 1945; Vol. I, No. 6, p. 2.
19. Elpidio Quirino, speech delivered at the 1st National Convention, Philippine National Red Cross, 18 April 1947, quoted by Aluit in *The Conscience of the Nation*, p. 259.
20. Geronima T. Pecson to author.

21. Remedios hospital served as a convalescent home for ailing Americans who were allowed out of the Santo Tomas internment camp for treatment. The serious cases were sent to the Philippine General hospital. The elderly and the incapacitated were sent to the Hospicio de San Jose which was ran by the Vincentian Fathers and the Daughters of Charity on the Isla de Convalescencia on the Pasig, until the *hospicio* residents were moved to La Concordia college on Herran street in Paco in early 1945. The College of the Holy Ghost on Mendiola street near Malacañang Palace was used as a nursery for the internees' children below two years old.
22. All the five Irish Columbans of the Malate parish church perished. Fr. John Lallor was ascertained to have been killed by American shrapnel while ministering to patients at the Remedios hospital. How the other four met death was never established for sure. One version says that the four - Fr. Patrick Kelly, the parish priest; Fr. John Henaghan, the provincial; and Frs. Peter Fallon and Joseph Monaghan were trapped inside the parish house together with many civilians when it burned down. Another version says that the four priests were among a number of civilians who were hauled over by the Japanese to nearby Mitchell apartment building and shot and bayonetted to death. Father Selga says in Perez de Olaguer that some people recognized their voices shouting for help during this incident. However, Bill of Particulars No. 38 charged that Frs. Fallon, Monaghan, Kelly and Henaghan were killed by the Japanese near the Syquia apartment building on A. Mabini street in Malate on 7 February 1945.
23. The circumstances of the death of Maria Y. Orosa are related by her niece Rosalinda L. Orosa in an article included in the compilation, *Maria Y. Orosa: Her Life and Work*, Helen O. del Rosario, compiler and editor.
24. Erlinda Querubin, *Proceedings*, Exhibit No. 564, (Statement, 30 June 1945).
25. Sister Teresa Vilatela, DC, and Sister Concepcion Gotera, DC, *Proceedings.*
26. Luis Gallent, *Proceedings.*
27. Morgin, "Manila's Liberation."

WEDNESDAY, 14 FEBRUARY 1945

1. The battle accounts are drawn from Smith, p. 282, and Frankel, p. 278.
2. The ordeal of the Chicote family is related by Prudencio Chicote Lalana in his testimony at the Yamashita trial found in *Proceedings* and in Perez de Olaguer, pp. 57 et seq.
3. Nadia Nestrenko, *Proceedings*, Exhibit No. 564 (Statement, 17 July 1945).
4. Carmen Locsin, *Proceedings*, Exhibit No. 390 (Statement, 29 August 1945).
5. The battle accounts are in Smith, p. 268, and Flanagan, pp. 88-89.
6. Francisco Lopez, *Proceedings*, Vol. VII, pp. 667 et seq.
7. For this display of exemplary heroism, Pfc. Stanley F. Perkins was awarded the Distinguished Service Cross posthumously.
8. Smith, pp. 286-287.
9. Tupas, "Sanctuary."
10. *Free Philippines*, Thursday, 22 February 1945, p. 2.
11. This is related by Prudencio Chicote Lalana in Perez de Olaguer, p. 58.
12. The De la Salle college account is related by Fr. Francis J. Cosgrave, CSsR, and Servillano Aquino in *Proceedings.* See also Gonzalez and Reyes, *These Hallowed Halls.*
13. Five-year-old Fernando Vasquez-Prada was calm and dry-eyed when finally rescued, 15 February 1945. When asked why he did not cry, he answered, "Why should I cry when Mamita is now in heaven. She told me so. She told me not to cry because she is happy." See Perez de Olaguer, p. 128.
14. *Free Philippines*, Thursday, 15 February, 1945, Vol. I, No. 4.
15. Padre Selga in Perez de Olaguer.

THURSDAY, 15 FEBRUARY 1945

1. The incidents concerning the San Carlos street group are related by Prudencio Chicote Lalana and the spouses Jose Maldonado in Perez de Olaguer, p. 28 et seq.
2. Smith, p. 272.
3. Ibid., p. 277-279.
4. Fr. Francis J. Cosgrave, *Proceedings*.
5. Smith, p. 278; Frankel, pp. 278-279.
6. Ibid., p. 287; Ibid., p. 279.
7. Tupas, "Sanctuary."
8. Smith, p. 282.
9. Prudencio Chicote Lalana in Perez de Olaguer, p. 58.
10. The story of the young Japanese Salesian is told by Fr. Miguel Selga, S.J., in Perez de Olaguer, p. 231. The name of the Japanese Salesian is not given by Fr. Selga.
11. Sister Concepcion Gotera, Daughter of Charity, in her *Diary*. It seems that when she was interviewed by American investigators, Sister Gotera was shy and hardly coherent. She was asked to write down her experiences instead, and her remarkable "diary" was the result.
12. Fr. Miguel Selga, S.J., in Perez de Olaguer, says that the nun killed in this incident was named "Sister Felicitas." Sister Concepcion, in the typescript of her diary the author examined, spells the name as "Sister Solisitas." It is possible that the name in the typescript of Sister Concepcion was misspelled. Sister Nelly de Jesus Virata also identified the nun as "Sister Felicitas" in her testimony at the Yamashita trial. Mother Socorro Angela Reyes, SPC, confirmed to this author that the nun's name was Sister Felicitas.
13. Ibid.

FRIDAY, 16 FEBRUARY 1945

1. Smith, p. 272.
2. Ibid., p. 278; Wright, p. 138.
3. Wright, pp. 138-139.
4. Smith, p. 294.
5. This is related by Jose Maldonado in Perez de Olaguer, p. 33.
6. The text of the surrender message is reproduced from *Proceedings,* admitted as "Exhibit A-2."
7. Smith, p. 282.
8. Ibid., p. 287.
9. Tupas, "Sanctuary."
10. Smith, p. 287.

SATURDAY, 17 FEBRUARY 1945

1. Mrs. Benita Lahoz and Sister Nelly de Jesus Virata, *Proceedings,* Vol. X, pp. 1131-1151.
2. Rosa Calalang, *Proceedings,* Vol. X, pp. 1169 et seq.
3. Smith, p. 272.
4. Ibid., p. 275.
5. For this act, Pfc. Manuel Perez Jr. was awarded the Congressional Medal of Honor. One week later, he was killed in another engagement. Flanagan, *The Angels,* pp. 89-91.
6. Smith, p. 282.
7. Frankel, 281.

8. The incidents concerning the Juco family were related to the author by Estelita G. Juco, 15 February 1984.

Estelita Juco did not remember how long she lay on the floor in that San Lazaro hospital corridor. It may have been three days. During this time she received but minimum attention from the hugely undermanned emergency staff. Hundreds and probably thousands were in similar straits as Estelita's in that building alone. Estelita believed that her life might have been saved by a Boy Scout who came along where she lay one day. She told the Boy Scout to look for the physician Dr. Antonio Hernandez, a family friend, who lived on Yakal street not far from Rizal Avenue where San Lazaro hospital stands.

Shortly, Dr. Hernandez was at Estelita's bedside. He brought her to the attention of the hospital authorities and personally ministered to her.

Estelita Juco did not recall at what point she was separated from her brother, the eight-year-old Teddy. The boy might have died from his grievous stomach wound, and taken away for disposal as an unidentified casualty, as so many others may have been in that catastrophic situation. The Juco family never was able to ascertain the circumstances of Teddy's death.

Estelita Juco recovered the use of her left arm, although she would be in pain from her injuries for the rest of her life. She learned to write with her left hand and resumed schooling when she was well enough. She overcame her handicaps and rose to considerable eminence as writer, teacher and civic leader in the post-war years.

She became a living demonstration of reconciliation with the Japanese when peace was restored, as well as an example that physical handicaps could be overcome.

She died 12 July 1989, while serving as appointed member of the Congress of the Philippines representing women and the handicapped, much beloved and admired.

9. Tupas, "Sanctuary."

10. Osawa, op. cit.

11. Dr. Antonio G. Sison, *Free Philippines*, Thursday, 22 February 1945, p. 2.

12. F. Theo Rogers, *Free Philippines*, Friday, 23 February 1945, p. 1.

13. Tupas, "Sanctuary."

14. Aluit, pp. 353-356.

15. The figure of 7,000 is given by A.V.H. Hartendorp, *The Japanese Occupation*, etc., p. 558. Stanley Frankel in *The 37th Infantry Division* says that "an estimated seven thousand civilians" was rescued in the area, p. 282.

16. Sister Charles, SPC, in "Memoirs of a French Sister . . ."

Shortly after the fighting ended, the nuns from the Congregation of St. Paul de Chartres went over to the St. Paul college on Herran street to inspect the damage. Among the debris they found the body of Fr. Elias H. Gonzalez in an advanced state of decomposition, still in his religious robes and his hands tied behind his back. The other chaplain, Fr. Pedro Martinez, survived everything. He lived to a ripe old age, dying in Manila on 9 August 1984, almost 100 years old.

17. Osawa, op. cit.

18. Morgin, "Manila's Liberation."

19. Smith, p. 294.

20. The story of the massacre at the Moreta house on Isaac Peral street in Ermita is told in *Proceedings* by Prudencio Chicote Lalana, Vol. VII, pp. 759 et seq., Jose Maldonado, Vol. VII, pp. 737-746, and his wife Maria Elena Lizarraga de Maldonado. See also *Proceedings*, Vol. VII, pp. 747-751; Perez de Olaguer, p. 28 et seq. A boy, Joaquin Gonzalez, 11, escaped unscathed.

SUNDAY, 18 FEBRUARY 1945

1. Mrs. Benita Lahoz, *Proceedings*, Vol. X, pp. 1131-1150.
2. Sister Donatienne de Marie, *Proceedings* and her deposition.
3. Conrado Tauro, *Proceedings*, Exhibit D-2.
4. Charge Sheet Bill of Particulars No. 91 said that there were 2000 civilian detainees at the Manila Hotel during the period from 25 January to 17 February. The figure in this story is from the account of Eloisa Chicote, *Proceedings*, Vol. V, pp. 552-557.
5. The San Carlos street account is by Prudencio Chicote Lalana and the Maldonados in Perez de Olaguer, p. 28 et seq.
6. Sister Charles, SPC, "Memoirs of a French Sister . . ."
7. Fr. Manuel Diez Canseco, O.S.A., his deposition at the Yamashita trial, also included in *Report of the Resident Commissioner*, p. 28.
8. Fr. Joaquin Garcia Sanchez, O.F.M. his deposition at the Yamashita trial, also included in *Report of the Resident Commissioner*, p. 29.
9. Epifanio Gutierrez Muñoz in Perez de Olaguer, p. 105.
10. Smith, p. 283.
11. Ibid.
12. Ibid., Chapter XIII, passim.
13. Ozzie St. George, "Two-Faced City." YANK FAREAST, 22 April 1945.
14. The description of the Japanese defenses in the battle for Manila is based on *Japanese Defense of Cities As Exemplified by the Battle for Manila, A Report by XIV Corps*, published by A.C. of S., G-2 Headquarters, Sixth Army, 1 July 1945. See also Smith, Chapter XIII, "The Defenders and the Defenses," pp. 237 et seq. and Ozzie St. George, "Two-Faced City."
15. Smith, p. 247.
16. Cates, p. 253.
17. Morgin, "Manila's Liberation."
18. Sister Charles, SPC, "Memoirs of a French Sister . . ."

MONDAY, 19 FEBRUARY 1945

1. Smith, p. 279.
2. Ibid., p. 283.
3. Ibid., p. 287.
4. Ibid., p. 288.
5. Ibid., p. 273.
6. Prudencio Chicote Lalana in Perez de Olaguer, p. 58.
7. Mrs. Benita Lahoz, *Proceedings*. The name of the Philippine-born Japanese officer was Major Okagawa.
8. This narrative concerning the Spanish religious and civilians is based on the testimonies of Fr. Belarmino de Celis, O.S.A.; Brother Jose Maria Manjabacas, O.F.M.; and Laurentino de Pablos in *Proceedings*. Thirty six religious perished in this incident, distributed as follows: Augustinians- eight priests, six lay brothers; Franciscans -- seven priests, three lay brothers; Recolets - four priests, two lay brothers; Capuchins - three priests, three lay brothers.

8-a. See "Fatal February" by Nick Joaquin, op. cit.

9. Hartendorp, *The Japanese Occupation*, etc. p. 560.

TUESDAY, 20 FEBRUARY 1945

1. Conrado Tauro, *Proceedings*, Exhibit D-2.
2. Smith, p. 279.

3. Wright, p. 139.
4. Ibid.
5. Smith, p. 283.
6. Ibid., p. 288.
7. Ibid., p. 284.
8. Fr. Belarmino de Celis, O.S.A., *Proceedings,* Vol. X, pp. 1247-1269; also his deposition included in *Report,* pp. 22-26.
9. Fr. Jose Ma. R. Barullo, O.F.M., *Proceedings,* Exhibit C-5.
9-a. See "Fatal February" by Nick Joaquin, op. cit.
10. Eloisa Chicote, *Proceedings,* Vol. V, pp. 522-557.
11. Erlinda Querubin, *Proceedings*, Exhibit No. 564 (Statement, 30 June 1945).

WEDNESDAY, 21 FEBRUARY 1945

1. Fr. Jose Ma. R. Barullo, O.F.M. *Proceedings.*
2. Bro. Jose Ma. Manjabacas, O.F.M., *Proceedings.*
3. Smith, p. 273.
4. Ibid., p. 280.
5. Ibid., p. 284.
6. Ibid., p. 285.
7. Ibid., p. 288.

Conrado Tauro, *Proceedings,* Exhibit D-2.

Fr. Belarmino de Celis, O.S.A. *Proceedings,* his testimony in Vol. X, pp. 1247-1269; his statements in Exhibits C-2, C-2a & C-2-1, and his deposition in *Report,* p. 22.

10. Rosalinda Andoy, *Proceedings.*

THURSDAY, 22 FEBRUARY 1945

1. Fr. Belarmino de Celis, O.S.A., *Proceedings.*
2. Wright, p. 128.
3. Ibid.
4. Ibid.
5. MacArthur, *Reminiscences,* p. 285.
6. Ibid.
7. Ibid.
8. Smith, p. 285.
9. Ibid.
10. Ibid., p. 289.
11. Ibid., p. 295 et seq. See also Glenn Steckel, "Role of Field Artillery in the Siege of Intramuros, Manila, P.I.," paper submitted to The Armored School, Fort Knox, Kentucky, U.S.A., 7 May 1948.
12. The account of Mrs. Trinidad Gardiner-Mendoza is in Reyes, p. 53.
13. Fr. Belarmino de Celis, O.S.A., *Proceedings.* Julio Rocamora was a Spanish expatriate from Limpias, Santander, Spain. He became a Filipino citizen in 1937. He operated a sawmill, a coconut plantation and a cattle ranch in Davao in Mindanao.

FRIDAY, 23 FEBRUARY 1945

1. This narrative on the assault of Intramuros is based on Smith, Chapter XVI, p. 291 et seq.; Frankel, p. 288 et seq.; Wright, p. 140; and Glenn A. Steckel, "The Role of

the Artillery in the Siege of Intramuros."

2. Smith, p. 295.
3. Fr. Belarmino de Celis, O.S.A., *Proceedings,* and his deposition.
4. The experiences of the Santa Clara residents are related by Fr. Mariano Montero, O.F.M., Chaplain of the community, in his deposition included in *Report of the Resident Commissioner,* p. 26, and by Fr. Miguel Selga, S.J., in Perez de Olaguer, p. 134 et seq.
5. The Clairist Sisters who perished in the Santa Clara convent in Intramuros were Mother Eufemia de la Pasion, ex-Abbess; Sisters Agapita de San Joaquin, Dolores de las Mercedes, Maxima de Santa Clara, Rosa de Santa Teresita, Maria de la Eucaristia, Ines de la Cruz, and lay servants Porfiria Tuoso and Esperanza Bioso. Sister Rita de San Jose was rescued but later died of her injuries. Reyes, p. 33.
6. Rosalinda Andoy, *Proceedings;* also Kenworthy, p. 62.
7. Fr. Joaquin Garcia Sanchez, O.F.M., *Proceedings,* Exhibit C-10, and his deposition in *Report.*

7-a. See "Fatal February" by Nick Joaquin, op. cit.

8. Fr. Jose Ma. Manjabacas, O.F.M., *Proceedings.*
9. Sister Donatienne de Marie, Sister of St. Paul de Chartres, *Proceedings.*
10. Sister Concepcion Gotera, Daughter of Charity, *Proceedings.*
11. The story of Pfc. William Grabiarz is related in Wright, p. 140. For his sacrifice, Pfc. William Grabiarz was awarded the Congressional Medal of Honor posthumously, the second man in the 1st Cavalry Division to receive this medal in World War II.
12. T/S Frank Pitcek, deposition included in *Report,* pp. 56-57.
13. Jose Maldonado in Perez de Olaguer, p. 39.
14. Henry Keys, *Proceedings,* Vol. XI, pp. 1333-1340.

SATURDAY, 24 FEBRUARY 1945

1. Smith, p. 300.
2. Ibid.
3. Ibid.
4. Perez de Olaguer, p. 109.
5. Frank J. Middelberg, affidavit reproduced in *Report,* pp. 52-53.
6. Ibid.
7. Ibid.
8. Gilbert B. Ayres, affidavit reproduced in *Report* pp. 52-53.
9. Ibid., p. 61.
10. J.D. Frederick, affidavit reproduced in *Report,* pp. 50-51.
11. Fr. Miguel Selga, S.J., in Perez de Olaguer, pp. 192-193.

SUNDAY, 25 FEBRUARY 1945

1. Albert Ravenbolt, *The Philippines - A Young Republic on the Move.* D. Van Nostrand Co. Inc. New Jersey. 1962. p. 149.
2. Smith, p. 303.
3. Ibid., p. 306.

MONDAY, 26 FEBRUARY 1945

1. The following narrative is pieced together from material in Wright, *The First Cavalry Division,* p. 139; Frankel *The 37th Infantry Division,* pp. 393-395; and Smith, *Triumph in the Philippines,* pp. 301-306.

TUESDAY, 27 FEBRUARY 1945

1. See Wright, Frankel and Smith.
2. MacArthur, *Reminiscences*, p. 290.
3. Ibid.
4. Ibid.
5. Ibid.

WEDNESDAY, 28 FEBRUARY 1945

1. Smith, p. 305.
2. Cates, *Drainpipe Diary*.
3. Perez de Olaguer, p. 50.

THURSDAY, 1 MARCH 1945

1. Text found in Smith, op. cit.

FRIDAY, 2 MARCH 1945

1. Smith, p. 306.
2. Ibid.

SATURDAY, 3 MARCH 1945

1. Smith, p. 306.

EPILOGUE: SOME QUESTIONS & ANSWERS

1. Tomoyuki Yamashita, testimony in *Proceedings*, Vol. XXVIII, p. 3524. His deposition is reproduced in Kenworthy, p. 73. See also Reel, p. 20; Swinson, p. 200.
2. Ibid., pp. 3524-3525. Also in Kenworthy, p. 73 and Reel, p. 21.
3. Ibid., p. 3525.
4. Lt. Gen. Akira Muto, *Proceedings*, Vol. XXII, pp. 3008-3010.
5. Ibid.
6. Yamashita, *Proceedings*, Vol. XXVIII, p. 3526.
7. Ibid.
8. Ibid., pp. 3526-3527.
9. Ibid., p. 3527.
10. Ibid., quoted by Smith, p. 240.
11. Muto, *Proceedings*, Vol. XXII, p. 3013.
12. Yamashita deposition in *Proceedings;* reproduced in Kenworthy, p. 76.
13. Muto, *Proceedings*, Vol. XXII, p. 3014.
14. Ibid.
15. Yamashita, *Proceedings*; reproduced in Kenworthy, p. 77.
16. Swinson, p. 204.
17. Muto, *Proceedings*, Vol. XXIV, p. 3096.
18. Ibid., p. 3097.
19. Ibid., p. 3098.
20. Capt. Milton Sandberg, *Proceedings*, Vol. XXXIII, p. 3914.
21. Vice Admiral Denshichi Okoochi, *Proceedings*, Vol. XVIII, p. 2538.
22. See Smith, pp. 241 et seq.
23. Ibid.

24. Lt. Gen. Shizuo Yokoyama, *Proceedings*, Vol. XIX, pp. 2662 et seq. See also Smith, p. 242 et seq.
25. Ibid.
26. Ibid.
27. Ibid.
28. Ibid.
29. Ibid.
30. Ibid.
31. Ibid.
32. Ibid.
33. Smith, p. 244.
34. Ibid.
35. Muto, *Proceedings*, Vol. XXII, p. 3062.
36. Ibid.
37. Ibid., p. 3066.
38. Ibid.
39. Ibid.
40. Ibid.
41. Smith, p. 272.
42. Swinson, p. 211.
43. Smith, p. 272.
44. Hiroshi Hashimoto, *Proceedings*, Vol. XXIV, p. 3112.
45. Reel, p. 24.
46. XIV Corps ATIS Advanced Echelon, Translation No. 00084, Item 7, Exhibit No. 393.
47. Ibid., Exhibit No. 394.
48. ATIS Document No. 603720, ATIS *Bulletin* 529. Item 4.
49. Yamashita, *Proceedings*, Vol. XXIX, p. 3578.
50. Ibid.
51. Ibid., Vol. XXIX, pp. 3604-3605.
52. Swinson, p. 213.
53. *Proceedings*, Vol. XXII, p. 3036.
54. Yamashita, *Proceedings*.
55. Quoted in Agoncillo, *The Fateful Years*, p. 848.

55-a. The "three-all" principle is described in *Peasant Nationalism and Communist Power* by Chalmers Johnson, Stanford University Press, Palo Alto 1962, pp. 57-59. See also Stuart R. Schram, *Mao Tse Tung*. Penguin Books. London 1966. p. 219.

55-b. Barbara Tuchman, *Stilwell and the American Experience in China, 1911-45*, p. 216.

56. ATIS Document No. 605074, ATIS *Bulletin* No. 2018, p. 4.
57. ATIS Document No. 18892, ATIS *Bulletin* No. 2065, p. 2.
58. ATIS Document No. 605849, ATIS *Bulletin* No. 2071, p. 17.
59. ATIS Document No. 17487, ATIS *Bulletin* No. 1862, p. 1.
60. Robert M. Kerr, *Proceedings*, Vol. XXX, p. 3998.
61. *Proceedings*, Vol. XXX, pp. 3626-3627.
62. Yamashita, *Proceedings*, Vol. XXX, p. 3627.
63. *Proceedings*, Vol. XXX, pp. 3626-3627.
64. Yamashita, *Proceedings*, Vol. XXX, pp. 3656-3657.
65. Capt. Norman Sparnon, *Proceedings*, Vol. XXIII, p. 2894.
66. Col. Masatoshi Fujishige, *Proceedings*, Vol. XX, pp. 2810-2838.
67. Ibid.
68. Lt. Cdr. Bartlett, *Proceedings*, Vol. XXII, p. 3062.
69. Ibid.
70. Rosalinda Andoy, *Proceedings*, Vol. X, pp. 1161 et seq.

71. Rosario Fernandez, *Proceedings,* Exhibit No. 495; Angeles Barahona, Vol. IV, pp. 481-485.
72. Prudencio Chicote Lalana, *Proceedings*, Vol. VII, pp. 759 et seq.
73. Elisa Beliso, *Proceedings*, Exhibit No. 1358 (Statement, 3 October 1945.)
74. Manchester, p. 413.
75. The plan for the triumphal march "a la Champs Elysees" was dated 2 February 1945 and was officially titled "Plan for Entry of the Commander-in-Chief and Official Party into the City of Manila." The march would have come down Rizal Avenue from the Bonifacio Monument at Grace Park, through Santa Cruz bridge down on Taft Avenue, right to Vito Cruz Street in Malate and right to Dewey Boulevard, around Burnham Green into Padre Burgos Drive, winding up at the Legislative Building where the ceremonies were to have been held. The plan read in part:
"After arrival of the Commander-in-Chief at the Legislative Building and as the Commander-in-Chief approaches the speaker's stand, four ruffles and four flourishes will be sounded followed by "The General." Upon completion of the honors the Commander-in-Chief makes an address.
"After the Commander-in-Chief has completed his address and the applause has subsided . . ."
A photocopy of the mimeographed instructions was secured from the Jefferson Cultural Center, 395 Buendia Ave. Ext., Makati, Metro-Manila.
76. Manchester, p. 413.
77. John Deane Potter in *Life and Death of a Japanese General.*
78. Carmen Guerrero Nakpil, "Consensus of One", Sunday *Times Magazine*, 23 April 1967.
79. Smith, pp. 263-264.
80. Ibid., p. 264.
81. Ibid., p. 286.
82. Dr. Antonio G. Sison, *Proceedings,* Vol. VI, pp. 570-571.
83. Smith, pp. 295-296.
84. Ibid., p. 301.
85. Ibid., Footnote, p. 293.
86. Ibid., Table V, p. 307.
87. St. George, "Two-Faced City."
88. Mascuñana, "Nuestro Ultimo Cinco Dias . . ."
89. Tupas, "Sanctuary."
89-a. See "Days of Terror -- Nights of Fear," by Miguel P. Avanceña. Manila *Bulletin,* 27 February 1987.
90. Sister Concepcion Gotera's "Diary."
91. Gutierrez, "The Longest Wait."
92. Smith, p. 301.
93. Ibid., p. 307.
93-a. Tacitus, *The Annals.* New York. New Library Series. Random House p. 574.
93-b. M. Hamlin Cannon. *Leyte: The Return to the Philippines. United States Army in World War II.* Office of the Chief of Military History. Department of the Army. Washington, D.C. p. 2.
93-c. Ibid., p. 4.
94. William F. Halsey, *Admiral Halsey's Story,* pp. 194-199. Also quoted by Cannon, op. cit., p. 5, and by Smith, p. 10.
95. D. Clayton James, *The Years of MacArthur,* Vol. II, p. 534. Also Carol Petillo. *Douglas MacArthur, The Philippine Years,* Footnote in Chapter 6, p. 280.
96. Ibid.
97. Ibid.
97-a. Quoted by Stuart Schram in *Mao Tze-tung - Political Leaders of the 20th Century.*

Penguin Books Edition. Great Britain. 1966. p. 244.

98. Smith, p. 294.
99. Ibid., p. 213.
100. Ibid.
101. Ibid.
102. Wright, p. 128.
103. Tupas, "Sanctuary."
104. Smith, p. 251.
105. MacArthur, *Reminiscences,* p. 291.
106. Nakpil, "Consensus of One."
107. Harrison Salisbury, *900 Days, The Siege of Leningrad.* (Avon books pocketbook edition). pp. 590-594.
108. St. George, "Two-Faced City."
109. Gutierrez, "The Longest Wait."
110. Savary, p. 162.
111. Aguilar, p. 109.
112. Lichauco, p. 211.
113. Savary, p. 180.
114. Hartendorp, *The Japanese Occupation,* etc. p. 539.
115. Waterous, "Bilibid Prison."
116. Savary, p. 170.
117. del Rio, p. 324.
118. Maj. Donald D. Forward, Affidavit dated 15 February 1945, included in *Report of the Resident Commissioner,* pp. 101-102.
119. Ibid.
120. Waterous, "Bilibid Prison."
121. Fr. Francis J. Cosgrave, CSsR, deposition dated 6 March 1945, included in *Report,* pp. 1718.
122. Smith, pp. 306-307.
123. Report of Senator Millard Tydings on "War Damage in the Philippines" to accompany S. 1610 Providing for the Rehabilitation of the Philippine Islands, 20 November 1945.
124. The Annual Report for 1945 of Philippine Commonwealth President Sergio Osmeña to the President of the United States was drafted by A.V.H. Hartendorp, then acting technical assistant to President Osmeña. The draft was based on the reports of the department secretaries and heads of various government offices and corporations. It is doubtful, however, whether this report was ever officially transmitted to President Harry S Truman. A copy of the draft was in the possession of Hartendorp who, as editor of the *Bulletin* of the American Historical Collection, had it published in a serial that appeared in the issues from Vol. I, No. 3 to Vol. II No. 4, inclusive, of that publication.
125. Perez de Olaguer, *Terror Amarillo*, etc.
126. John Deane Potter, *Life and Death of a Japanese General.*

BIBLIOGRAPHY

Part One of this work relied on the standard sources on Philippine history basically as contained in Blair, Emma H. and Robertson, James A., *The Philippine Islands, 1483-1898,* the Manila 1973 Edition by Cacho Hermanos in nineteen volumes. The following were also useful:

AGONCILLO, TEODORO A. *Malolos: The Crisis of the Republic.* University of the Philippines. Quezon City. 1960.

BELTRAN, RAFAEL. *Prologue to Philippine History.* Translated from the Spanish by Ramon Echevarria. Serialized in *Solidarity,* July-September 1966; Oct.-Dec. 1966.

BERNAD, S. J. MIGUEL A. *The Christianization of the Philippines: Problems and Perspectives.* The Filipiniana Book Guild. Manila. 1972.

CACHO HERMANOS (Publishers). *Misiones Catolicos en Extremo Oriente.* Manila. 1937.

COSTA, S. J. HORACIO V. DE LA. *The Jesuits in the Philippines. 1581-1768.* Harvard University Press. Cambridge. 1967.

DIAZ-TRECHUELO, MARIA LOURDES. *Architectura Española en Filipinas (1565-1800).* Escuela de Estudios Hispanos-Americanos. Sevilla. 1959.

ELLIOT, CHARLES BURKE. *The Philippines to the End of the Commission Government.* Greenwood Press. New York. 1968.

GLEECK, LEWIS E., JR. *The Manila Americans (1901-1964).* Carmelo and Bauermann, Inc. Manila. 1977.

______________. *American Institutions in the Philippines.* (*1898-1941*). Historical Conservation Society. Manila. 1976.

HARTENDORP, A.V.H. *History of Industry and Trade of the Philippines.* (A revision and expansion of the author's previously published *Short History of Industry and Trade of the Philippines, 1953*). American Chamber of Commerce of the Philippines, Inc. Manila. 1958.

JOCANO, F. LANDA. *The Philippines at the Spanish Contact.* MC Enterprises, Inc. Quezon City. 1975.

LETRAN COLLEGE (Publisher). *Intramuros and Beyond.* (Compilation). Manila. 1974.

ORTIZ ARMENGGOL, PEDRO. *Intramuros de Manila. De 1571 Hasta su Destruccion en 1945.* Ediciones Cultura Hispanica. Manila. 1958.

ROOT, ELIHU. *The Military and Colonial Policy of the United States. Addresses and Reports.* AMS Press. New York. 1970.

THE QUADRICENTENNIAL COMMISSION (Compilation). *The Beginnings of Christianity in the Philippines.* Manila. 1965.

WERNSTEDT, FREDERICK L. & SPENCER, JOSEPH E. *The Philippine Island World. A Physical, Cultural and Regional Geography.* University of California Press. Berkeley & Los Angeles. 1967.

ZAFRA, NICOLAS, *Philippine History Through Selected Sources.* Alemar-Phoenix Publishing House. Quezon City. 1967.

ZAIDE, GREGORIO F. *Philippine Political & Cultural History. Volumes I & II.* Philippine Education Co. Manila. 1957.

ZAMORA, O.S.A. FR. ELADIO *Las Corporaciones Religiosas en Filipinas.* Imprenta y Libreria Religiosa de Andres Martin. Valladolid. 1901.

The following sources were used for Part Two of this work, aside from the enormous documentation in the proceedings of the case of *U.S.A. vs. Tomoyuki Yamashita,* bound in 37 volumes, mimeographed.

AGONCILLO, TEODORO A. *The Fateful Years: Japan's Adventure in the Philippines. 1941-1945.* Vols. I & II. R. P. Garcia Publishing Co. Quezon City. 1965.

AGUILAR, FAUSTINO. *Nang Magdaan Ang Daluyong.* Printed by PSP Press Publications. Manila. No date.

ALUIT, ALFONSO J. *The Conscience of the Nation. A History of the Red Cross in the Philippines.* Manila. 1963.

BARKER, H. J. *Yamashita.* Ballantine Books. New York. 1973.

BERGAMINI, DAVIS. *Japan's Imperial Conspiracy.* Pocket Books. New York. 1972.

BERNIA, JUAN. *Viaje a Nueva Castilla.* Instituto de Cultura Hispanica. Madrid. 1947.

BERNSTEIN, DAVID.*Philippine Story*. Farrar, Strauss. New York. 1947.

BONNET, GABRIEL. *Les Campagnes de Philippines et Enseignments.* Editions Berger-Levrault. Paris. 1948.

BUENAFE, MANUEL B. *Wartime Philippines.* Philippine Education Foundation, Inc. Manila. 1950.

CANNON, M. HAMLIN. *Leyte: The Return to the Philippines. The United States Army in World War II.* Office of the Chief of Military History. Department of the Army. Washington, D. C. 1954.

CATES, TRESSA R. *The Drainpipe Diary.* Vantage Press. New York. 1954.

CROUTER, NATALIE. *Forbidden Diary. A Record of Wartime Internment.* Edited and with an Introduction by Lynn Z. Bloom. Burt Franklin & Company. New York. 1980.

DELA GOZA, ROLANDO, C.M., and JESUS MA. CAVANNA, C.M. *Vincentians in the Philippines.* Congregacion de la Mision en Filipinas, Inc. Manila. 1985.

EICHELBERGER, ROBERT L. (With Milton Mackaye). *Our Jungle Road to Tokyo.* Viking Press. New York. 1950.

FAHEY, JAMES J. *Pacific War Diary, 1942-1945.* Houghton Mifflin Company. Boston. 1963.

FLANAGAN, EDWARD M., JR. *The Angels: History of the 11th Airborne Division.* Infantry Journal Press. Washington. 1947.

FRANKEL, STANLEY A. *The 37th Division in World War II.* Infantry Journal Press. Washington. 1948.

FRIEND, THEODORE. *Between Two Empires: The Ordeal of the Philippines, 1929-1946.* New Haven. Yale University Press. 1965.

GARCIA, MAURO. (Ed.) *Documents on the Japanese Occupation of the Philippines.* Manila.

GIMENEZ, PEDRO M. *Under the Shadow of the Kempei.* A. Narvaez Publishing House. Manila. 1946.

GONZALEZ, ANDREW, FSC, & ALEJANDRO T. REYES. *These Hallowed Halls. The Events of February 1945 at De la Salle College.* De la Salle University. Manila. 1982.

GUNTHER, JOHN. *The Riddle of MacArthur: Japan, Korea, The Far East.* Harper. New York. 1951.

GWEKOH, SOL H. *Elpidio Quirino. The Barrio Schoolteacher Who Became President.* Philippine Education Foundation, Inc. Manila. 1949.

HALSEY, WILLIAM F. *Admiral Halsey's Story.* New York. 1947.

HARTENDORP, A. V. H. *The Santo Tomas Story.* McGraw-Hill Book Company. New York. 1964.

The Japanese Occupation of the Philippines. Vols. I & II. Bookmark.

Manila, 1967.
JAMES, D. CLAYTON. *The Years of MacArthur. Vols. I & II* Houghton Mifflin Co. Boston. 1970-1975.
KATO, MASUO. *The Lost War. A Japanese Reporter's Inside Story.* Alfred Knopf. 1946.
KENNEY, GEN. GEORGE C. *General Kenney Reports. A Personal History of the Pacific War.* New York. 1969.
KENWORTHY, AUBREY SAINT. *The Tiger of Malaya. The Inside Story of the Japanese Atrocities.* Exposition Press. New York. 1953.
KRUEGER, GEN. WALTER. *From Down Under to Nippon. The Story of the Sixth Army in World War II.* Combat Forces Press. Washington, D.C. 1953.
KYO, MATSUMURA. *Sunset in Manila.* Maru Shobo. 1956.
LICHAUCO, MARCIAL P. *Dear Mother Putnam. A Diary of the War in the Philippines.* No imprint. Undated.
MACARTHUR, GEN. DOUGLAS. *Reminiscences.* MacGraw Book Company. New York. 1964.
A Soldier Speaks. Public Papers and Speeches of General of the Army Douglas MacArthur. Praeger Press. New York. 1965.
MADVAL. *Las Estrellas Vencen El Sol.* National Printing Co.Manila. 1946.
MALAY, ARMANDO J. *Occupied Philippines.* Filipiniana Book Guild. Manila. 1967.
MANCHESTER, WILLIAM G. *American Caesar.* Little, Brown & Co. Boston. 1978.
MANUEL, E. ARSENIO. *Dictionary of Philippine Biography. Vol. II.* Filipiniana Publications. Quezon City. 1970.
MARSHALL, GEN. GEORGE C. *Biennial Report of the Chief of Staff of the United States Army, July 1, 1943 to June 30, to the Secretary of War.* Infantry Journal Press. Washington, D.C. 1946.
MAYER, SYDNEY. *MacArthur.* Ballantine Books. New York. 1971.
MELNIK, STEVE. *Philippine Diary/1939-1945. With a Foreword by Carlos P. Romulo.* Van Nostrand Reinhold Co. 1969.
MILLER, FRANCIS TREVELYAN. *General MacArthur: Soldier-Statesman.* The John Winston Company. Philadelphia P Toronto. 1951.
The Complete History of World War II. Armed Services Memorial Edition. 1945.
MONAGHAN, S.J., FORBES. *Under the Red Sun: A Letter From Manila.* McMullen. New York. 1946.
MORISON, SAMUEL ELIOT. *History of United States Naval Operations in World War II; Vol. XII, Leyte, June 1944-January 1945; Vol. XIII, The Liberation of the Philippines: Luzon, Mindanao, the*

Visayas. Atlantic-Little, Brown & Co. Boston. 1959.

OSAWA, KIYOSHI. *A Japanese in the Philippines*. Shinkosha. Tokyo. 1978.

OSMEÑA, SERGIO. *Ten Months of President Osmeña's Administration. A Review of Work Done Under Unprecedented Difficulties.* Philippines. 1946.

PEREZ DE OLAGUER, ANTONIO. *El Terror Amarillo en Filipinas.* Editorial Juventud, S.A. Barcelona. 1947.

POTTER, JOHN DEANE. *Life and Death of a Japanese General.* New American Library. New York. 1962.

REEL, A. FRANK.*The Case of General Yamashita.* University of Chicago Press. 1949.

REYES, JOSE G. *Terrorismo y Redención: casos concretos de atrocidades cometidos por los Japoneses en Filipinas.* Manila. 1947. (*Terrorism and Redemption: Japanese Atrocities in the Philippines.* The English translation by Jose Garcia Insua. Manila. 1945.)

RIO, BENIGNO DEL. *Estampas de la Occupación. Fragmentos de mi diario de guerra y liberación.* Manila. 1953.

ROMULO, CARLOS P. *I See The Philippines Rise*. Doubleday & Co. New York. 1946.

ROSARIO, HELEN O. DEL. (Compiler & Editor). *Maria Y. Orosa, Her Life and Work.* Printed by R. P. Garcia Publishing Co. Quezon City. 1970.

SAVARY, GLADYS. *Outside the Walls.* Vantage Press. New York. 1954.

SMITH, ROBERT ROSS. *Triumph In the Philippines. The War In the Pacific. The United States Army in World War II.* Office of the Chief of Military History, Department of the Army. Washington, D.C. 1963.

STEINBERG, DAVID JOEL. *Philippine Collaboration in World War II.* Ann Arbor. University of Michigan Press. 1967.

STEVENS, FREDERIC H. *Santo Tomas Internment Camp.* Limited Private Edition. Stafford House, Inc. 1946.

STRATTON, SAMUEL S. *Tiger of Malaya.* U.S. Naval Institute Proceedings, February 1945.

SWINSON, ARTHUR. *Four Samurai: A Quartet of Japanese Commanders in the Second World War.* Hutchinson. London. 1968.

TACITUS. *Complete Works of Tacitus.* Modern Library Series. Random House. New York. 1942.

TAKUSHIRO HATTORI. *A Complete History of the Pacific War.* Nasu Shobo. 1953.

TUCHMAN, BARBARA. *Stilwell and the American Experience in China, 1911-45*. Macmillan Publishing Co., Inc. New York, 1970.

WRIGHT, Maj. BERTRAM C. *The 1st Cavalry Division in World War II.* Toppan Printing Co. Ltd. Tokyo. 1947

YOSHIRO AKIYAMA. *The Philippines: Attack and Defense.* Mainichi Press. Tokyo. 1956.

ARTICLES IN MAGAZINES, NEWSPAPERS AND OTHER PUBLICATIONS

"Two-Faced City," by Ozzie St. George in YANK FAREAST, 27 April 1945.

"Nuestro Ultimo Cinco Dias Bajo el Yugo Nipon," by Maria Paz Zamora de Mascuñana in the *Historical Bulletin* of the Philippine Historical Association, Manila, June 1958.

"The Longest Wait: Liberation Diary," by Lydia C. Gutierrez in *World War II in the Philippines, The Sunday Times Magazine,* Manila, 23 April 1967.

"Benevolence," from CONSENSUS OF ONE, by Carmen Guerrero Nakpil in *World War II in the Philippines, The Sunday Times Magazine,* Manila, 23 April 1967.

"Sanctuary In An Outraged Manila," by Rodolfo G. Tupas in *World War II in the Philippines, The Sunday Times Magazine,* Manila, 23 April 1967.

"Bilibid," by Dr. W.H. Waterous in the *Bulletin* of the American Memorial Collection, Vol. II, No. 1, Manila, January 1974.

"On This the Fourth Anniversary of Manila's Liberation," by Sophie Natalie Morgin in *The Nation Weekly,* Manila, 29 January 1949.

FREE PHILIPPINES. Published by the Office of War Information. Issues from February 5 to April 30, 1945.

Report on the Destruction of Manila and Japanese Atrocities. February 1945. Released by the Office of the Resident Commissioner of the Philippines to the United States. Washington, D.C. 1945.

The Sack of Manila. Published by the United States Senate Committee on Military Affairs. Washington, D.C. 1945. Illustrated with pictures.

"Days of Terror - Nights of Fear," by Miguel P. Avanceña in *Manila Bulletin,* 27 February 1987.

"Fatal February," from SMALL BEER by Nick Joaquin, Philippine *Daily Inquirer,* 12 March 1988.

Japanese Defense of Cities As Exemplified by the Battle for Manila, A Report by XIV Corps. Published by A. C. of S., G-2 Headquarters, Sixth Army. 1 July 1945.

UNPUBLISHED SOURCES

"The Diary of Sister Concepcion Gotera, Daughter of Charity." Typescript copy in the MacArthur Memorial, MacArthur Square, Norfolk, Virginia, U.S.A.

"The Role of Field Artillery in the Siege on Intramuros, Manila, P.I.", by Glenn A. Steckel, Captain, Cavalry. Paper submitted to The Armored School, Fort Knox, Kentucky, U.S.A., 7 May 1948. Typescript copy in the American Historical Collection & Library, U.S. Embassy, Manila.

"Memoirs of a French Sister On the Three Years Passed Under Japanese Domination." This forms part of "History of St. Paul College" (typescript), which was made available for the purposes of this work by Mother Socorro Angela Reyes, formerly Superior of the Congregation of St. Paul de Chartres in Manila, and Directress of St. Paul College of Manila. The "French Sister" was Sister Charles, SPC, who was actually Swiss, and head of St. Paul College's music department.

History of De la Salle: 1911-1970. Unpublished graduate thesis by Juanito Castillo, F. S. C. Typescript at De La Salle University, Manila.

INDEX

X

Y

Z

THE AUTHOR

ALFONSO JESUS ALUIT is well-known as the author of the Galleon travel guidebook series, although his work in historiography has also been noted. The American bibliographer and Filipinist Morton J. Netzorg has described his book, *The Conscience of the Nation: A History of the Red Cross in the Philippines,* as "a most respectable piece of writing that displays a care and scrupulousness quite foreign to most of what has purported to be historical writing about the modern Philippines."

Journalist, editor and publisher, and university lecturer, Alfonso J. Aluit studied journalism at the Far Eastern University, Manila and undertook special studies at Standford University, California, U.S.A.; at the International Center for Advanced Tourism Studies, Turin, Italy; and at the International Red Cross Study Center, Geneva, Switzerland.